Wolf-Tilo Balke · Koraljka Golub ·
Yannis Manolopoulos · Kostas Stefanidis ·
Zheying Zhang
Editors

Linking Theory and Practice of Digital Libraries

29th International Conference on Theory and Practice of Digital Libraries, TPDL 2025
Tampere, Finland, September 23–26, 2025
Proceedings

Springer

Editors
Wolf-Tilo Balke
TU Braunschweig
Braunschweig, Niedersachsen, Germany

Koraljka Golub
Linnaeus University
Kalmar, Sweden

Yannis Manolopoulos
University of Nicosia
Nicosia, Cyprus

Kostas Stefanidis
Tampere University
Tampere, Finland

Zheying Zhang
Tampere University
Tampere, Finland

ISSN 0302-9743 ISSN 1611-3349 (electronic)
Lecture Notes in Computer Science
ISBN 978-3-032-05408-1 ISBN 978-3-032-05409-8 (eBook)
https://doi.org/10.1007/978-3-032-05409-8

This Springer imprint is published by the registered company Springer Nature Switzerland AG
The registered company address is: Gewerbestrasse 11, 6330 Cham, Switzerland

Preface

These proceedings contain the full papers, findings papers, short papers, and demonstration papers presented at the 29th International Conference on Theory and Practice of Digital Libraries (TPDL), which was held on September 23–26, 2025, in Tampere, Finland. Further information is available at https://tpdl2025.github.io/.

TPDL has been hosted in sixteen European countries during the previous twenty-eight years: Ljubljana, Slovenia (2024), Zadar, Croatia (2023), Padua, Italy (2022), virtual (2021), Lyon, France (2020), Oslo, Norway (2019), Porto, Portugal (2018), Thessaloniki, Greece (2017), Hannover, Germany (2016), Poznań, Poland (2015), London, UK (2014), Valletta, Malta (2013), Paphos, Cyprus (2012), Berlin, Germany (2011), Glasgow, UK (2010), Corfu, Greece (2009), Aarhus, Denmark (2008), Budapest, Hungary (2007), Alicante, Spain (2006), Vienna, Austria (2005), Bath, UK (2004), Trondheim, Norway (2003), Rome, Italy (2002), Darmstadt, Germany (2001), Lisbon, Portugal (2000), Paris, France (1999), Heraklion, Greece (1998), and Pisa, Italy (1997). Following this trip around Europe, TPDL 2025 was organized in Tampere, Finland, for the first time.

Over the years, TPDL has established itself as an important international forum focused on digital libraries and associated technical, practical, and social issues. TPDL encompasses the many meanings of the term "digital libraries", including new forms of information institutions; operational information systems with all manner of digital content; new means of selecting, collecting, organizing, and distributing digital content; and theoretical models of information media, including document genres and electronic publishing.

In 2025, TPDL expanded its scope to prominently include Document Analysis and Recognition, and Information Retrieval, acknowledging the vital role of those research areas in the creation (by means of digitization and information extraction from heterogeneous sources), access, discovery, and dissemination of digital content. This includes exploring innovative approaches to document image analysis and recognition, search algorithms, data retrieval, user engagement, and personalized content delivery within digital libraries, making these areas central themes for the conference.

Following a widespread CFP, 52 full papers were submitted, plus 40 short papers and 11 demo papers, thus making a total set of 103 submissions. All submissions were single-blindly reviewed by at least three members of the international Program Committee. Out of the 52 submitted full papers, 14 were accepted for a regular oral presentation, whereas another 11 were accepted for oral presentation as findings papers. Besides these papers, another 20 short papers and 8 demo papers were accepted for presentation as posters and inclusion in the proceedings. In particular, full and findings papers are published in these conference proceedings in 16 pages, whereas short and demo papers are published in 8 pages. To conclude, the acceptance ratio was 27% for full papers, 21% for findings papers, and 50% for short papers. These four paper types present high-quality, original research relevant to the TPDL community.

Four keynote speakers covered a wide range of topics. In alphabetical order:

- Eero Hyvönen (Aalto University, Finland), who delivered a talk on "Digital Humanities on the Semantic Web: from Infrastructure to Practical Applications, AI-based Knowledge Discovery, and Web of Wisdom",
- Yannis Ioannidis (National and Kapodistrian University of Athens, Greece), who delivered a talk on "Interactive Digital Storytelling",
- Felix Naumann (University of Potsdam, Germany), who delivered a talk on "Data Quality in the Age of AI", and
- Evaggelia Pitoura (University of Ioannina, Greece), who delivered a lecture on "Explainability, Fairness, and Their Interplay".

In addition, three specialized workshops took place during the first day of the event, which were (in alphabetical order):

- BIRDS: Building Innovative Research Systems for Digital Libraries Workshop (thanks to Christin Katharina Kreutz and Hermann Kroll),
- EcoDL: 1st Workshop on Digital Libraries and AI-based Information Systems for Ecological Research and Practice (thanks to Jennifer D'Souza, Birgitta König-Ries, Tina Heger, and Marie I. Kaiser), and
- NKOS: Networked Knowledge Organization Systems and Services Workshop (thanks to Koraljka Golub, Claudio Gnoli, Douglas Tudhope, Joseph A Busch, and Marcia L. Zeng).

We would like to thank our invited keynotes for their contribution to the success and sustainability of TPDL 2025. We would like to thank all authors for submitting their papers to TPDL 2025 and we hope they will submit their research papers again in the future. We express our gratitude to all the Program Committee members for their time and effort in ensuring the high quality of the TPDL 2025 program. Finally, we would like to thank our sponsors and supporters: Springer, Tampere University, the Municipality of Tampere and the Coalition for Networked Information. Last but not least, we would like to thank the local organizers for their precious help. We hope the conference attendees enjoyed the technical program, informal meetings, and interaction with colleagues from all over the world.

September 2025

Wolf-Tilo Balke
Koraljka Golub
Yannis Manolopoulos
Kostas Stefanidis
Zheying Zhang

Organization

General Chairs

Zheying Zhang	Tampere University, Finland
Kostas Stefanidis	Tampere University, Finland

Program Committee Chairs

Wolf-Tilo Balke	TU Braunschweig, Germany
Koraljka Golub	Linnaeus University, Sweden
Yannis Manolopoulos	University of Nicosia, Cyprus

Short Papers Chairs

Marcos Andre Goncalves	Federal University of Minas Gerais, Brazil
Christos Papatheodorou	University of Athens, Greece

Demonstration Papers Chairs

Liana Ermakova	University of Western Brittany, France
Yannis Tzitzikas	University of Crete, Greece

Workshop Chairs

Trond Aalberg	Norwegian University of Science and Technology, Norway
Paolo Manghi	CNR, Italy

Doctoral Consortium Chairs

Nicola Ferro	University of Padua, Italy
Sanna Kumpulainen	Tampere University, Finland

Proceedings Chair

Michalis Mountantonakis	Foundation for Research and Technology Hellas, Greece

Web Chair

Tiago Brasileiro Araújo	Federal Institute of Paraíba, Brazil

Volunteers Chairs

Maria Stratigi	Tampere University, Finland
Toni Taipalus	Tampere University, Finland

Program Committee

Trond Aalberg	Norwegian University of Science and Technology, Norway
Robert Allen	Independent Researcher
Vangelis Banos	International Hellenic University, Greece
Valentina Bartalesi	CNR, Italy
Uldis Bojars	National Library of Latvia, Latvia
José Borbinha	University of Lisbon, Portugal
George Buchanan	RMIT University, Australia
Ricardo Campos	University of Beira Interior, Portugal
Vittore Casarosa	CNR, Italy
Donatella Castelli	CNR, Italy
Songphan Choemprayong	Chulalongkorn University, Thailand
Florence Clavaud	Archives Nationales, France
Fabio Crestani	University of Lugano, Switzerland
Mickael Coustaty	University of La Rochelle, France
Boris Dobrov	Moscow State University, Russia
Fabien Duchateau	University of Lyon 1, France
Ingo Frommholz	University of Wolverhampton, UK
Maria Gäde	Humboldt University, Germany
Daniel Garijo	Polytechnic University of Madrid, Spain
Marcos Andre Goncalves	Federal University of Minas Gerais, Brazil
Sergiu Gordea	Austrian Institute of Technology, Austria
Mark Hall	Open University, UK

Andreas Henrich	University of Bamberg, Germany
Nikos Houssos	Feel Therapeutics, Greece
Ying Hsang Liu	Uppsala University, Sweden
Isto Huvila	Uppsala University, Sweden
Ornella Irrera	University of Padua, Italy
Antoine Isaac	Europeana, France
Adam Jatowt	University of Innsbruck, Austria
Himarsha Jayanetti	Old Dominion University, USA
Jaap Kamps	University of Amsterdam, Netherlands
Sarantos Kapidakis	University of West Attica, Greece
Ioannis Karydis	Ionian University, Greece
Roman Kern	Graz University of Technology, Austria
Johannes Kiesel	Bauhaus University of Weimar, Germany
Péter Király	GWDG, Germany
Martin Klein	Los Alamos National Laboratory, USA
Petr Knoth	Open University, UK
Stefanos Kollias	National Technical University of Athens, Greece
László Kovács	HUN-REN SZTAKI, Hungary
C. Lee Giles	Pennsylvania State University, USA
Hyowon Lee	Dublin City University, Ireland
Elena Maceviciute	University of Borås, Sweden
Bruno Martins	University of Lisbon, Portugal
Robert McDonald	University of Colorado Boulder, USA
Yannis Manolopoulos	University of Nicosia, Cyprus
Cezary Mazurek	Poznań Supercomputing and Networking Center, Poland
Dora Melo	Polytechnic Institute of Coimbra, Portugal
András Micsik	HUN-REN SZTAKI, Hungary
Agnieszka Mykowiecka	Polish Academy of Sciences, Poland
Wolfgang Nejdl	Leibniz University Hannover, Germany
Clemens Neudecker	Berlin State Library, Germany
Erich Neuhold	University of Vienna, Austria
Jeppe Nicolaisen	University of Copenhagen, Denmark
Sérgio Nunes	University of Porto, Portugal
Dimitris Plexousakis	Foundation for Research and Technology Hellas, Greece
María Poveda-Villalón	Polytechnic University of Madrid, Spain
Jian Qin	Syracuse University, USA
Edie Rasmussen	University of British Columbia, Canada
Thomas Risse	University of Frankfurt, Germany
Irene Rodrigues	University of Évora, Portugal
Laurent Romary	Inria, France

Seamus Ross	University of Toronto, Canada
Michalis Sfakakis	Ionian University, Greece
Gianmaria Silvello	University of Padua, Italy
Marc Spaniol	University of Caen Normandy, France
Cyrille Suire	University of La Rochelle, France
Hussein Suleman	University of Cape Town, South Africa
Douglas Tudhope	University of South Wales, UK
Vassilis Tzouvaras	National Technical University of Athens, Greece
Herbert Van de Sompel	DANS, Netherlands
Shenghui Wang	University of Twente, Netherlands
Michele Weigle	Old Dominion University, USA
Marcin Werla	Qatar National Library, Qatar
Maja Žumer	University of Ljubljana, Slovenia

TPDL Governance

Executive Board

Trond Aalberg	Norwegian University of Technology & Science, Norway
Antoine Doucet	University of La Rochelle, France
Gianmaria Silvello	University of Padua, Italy

Honorary Chairs

Constantino Thanos	ISTI, CNR, Italy
Ingeborg Solvberg	Norwegian University of Technology & Science, Norway

Steering Committee

Trond Aalberg	Norwegian University of Technology & Science, Norway
Gerd Berget	Oslo Metropolitan University, Norway
José Borbinha	University of Lisbon, Portugal
Daniel Brenn	Martin Luther University Halle-Wittenberg, Germany
George Buchanan	University of Melbourne, Australia
Vittore Casarosa	ISTI-CNR, Italy
Oscar Corcho	Polytechnic University of Madrid, Spain

Jérôme Darmont	University of Lyon 1, France
Antoine Doucet	University of La Rochelle, France
Fabien Duchateau	University of Lyon 1, France
Koraljka Golub	Linnæus University, Sweden
Mark Hall	Open University, UK
Antoine Isaac	Europeana, France
Adam Jatowt	University of Innsbruck, Austria
Sarantos Kapidakis	Ionian University, Greece
László Kovács	MTA SZTAKI, Hungary
Sanna Kumpulainen	Tampere University, Finland
Paolo Manghi	ISTI-CNR, Pisa, Italy
Yannis Manolopoulos	University of Nicosia, Greece
Tanja Merčun	University of Ljubljana, Slovenia
Christos Papatheodorou	Ionian University, Greece
Edie Rasmussen	University of British Columbia, Canada
Andreas Rauber	Technical University of Vienna, Austria
Cristina Ribeiro	University of Porto, Portugal
Thomas Risse	University of Frankfurt, Germany
Gianmaria Silvello	University of Padua, Italy
Marcin Werla	Poznań Supercomputing and Networking Center, Poland

Contents

Digital Humanities and Cultural Heritage

Knowledge Graphs

Keynotes

Digital Humanities on the Semantic Web: from Infrastructure to Practical Applications, AI-Based Knowledge Discovery, and Web of Wisdom

Eero Hyvönen(✉)

Department of Computer Science and University of Helsinki, Helsinki Centre for Digital Humanities (HELDIG), Aalto University, Espoo, Finland
eero.hyvonen@aalto.fi
https://seco.cs.aalto.fi/eahyvone/

Abstract. This extended abstract of a keynote talk at the 29th International Conference on Theory and Practice of Digital Libraries (TPDL 2025) presents the vision, research, and lessons learned in Finland 2003–2025 on building a national level Semantic Web infrastructure for publishing Cultural Heritage (CH) content and Digital Humanities research. Lessons learned are presented on how the infra has been used to create over 20 online applications that have been visited by millions of users. By using AI-based methods, steps towards a Web of Wisdom can be taken. The notion of explainable relational search is considered as an example. The work presented is unique due to its systematic national level nature and long time span of over twenty years.

Keywords: knowledge graphs · relational search · knowledge discovery · information retrieval · large language models · generative AI

1 Media Generations for Publishing CH Content

Cultural Heritage knowledge has been transferred between people and their generations over time using various media, as illustrated in Fig. 1. First, knowledge was transferred orally, but this was challenging as speech could reach only nearby people and it was not possible to store content outside human brains. To solve the issue, writing systems using physical media such as clay tables and papyrus sheets were developed, but using them required a lot of manual work. As a remedy, book printing was invented in China and Europe, but the use of physical media was not fast and effective enough in the globalizing world. To address the issue, digitalization and using the Web to publish and distribute content for humans to read and see was the next answer. However, as computers were used more and more, the need for publishing content for not only humans but also for data analyses and applications to use crew, which led to the era of publishing FAIR data and Web of Data. When more and more Big Data became available,

W.-T. Balke et al. (Eds.): TPDL 2025, LNCS 16097, pp. 3–8, 2026.
https://doi.org/10.1007/978-3-032-05409-8_1

it became more and more difficult to use it. Automatic methods were needed to help the user leading to the bloom of AI-based systems, first in the 1980's to knowledge-based systems using symbolic methods, and today especially systems based of sub-symbolic neural computing and deep learning. A major technological challenge to be addressed today is how to mitigate knowledge acquisition challenges of symbolic and hallucination issues of sub-symbolic AI methods in the era of neuro-symbolic hybrid systems.

Cultural Heritage Publishing Media	Examples	Challenges for Next Generation
1 Oral medium	Folklore, songs, stories	Transfer of knowledge in time and place
2 Physical medium		
2.1 Hand-written texts	Carvings, Egyptian hieroglyphs, Nordic runes	Tedious production, unique copies
2.2 Printed texts	Bible, encyclopedias, novels	Publishing and distributing of texts
3 Digital medium		
3.1 Human-readable	Web of Pages, library systems, museum databases	FAIR data not available for applications
3.2 Machine-interpretable	Web of (Linked) Data, Digital Humanities apps	Automatic knowledge discovery in Big Data
3.3 AI-based	ChatGPT, deep learning systems, expert systems	Reliability, truhtfulness
3.4 Neuro-symbolic	Combining symbolic and sub-symbolic methods	Complexity, research in progrerss

Fig. 1. Generations of media for transferring knowledge and Cultural Heritage content

This paper reviews work and lessons learned in Finland pertaining to the transition from a human-readable Web to a machine-interpretable intelligent Semantic Web, and towards a Web of Wisdom based on AI and neuro-symbolic computing. The application domain is Cultural Heritage data and Digital Humanities research. It is argued that a national Semantic Web infrastructure based on and extending the international W3C and other standards are needed for the purpose, including ontology and data services, and tools for easy application development. Results on developing a series of in-use applications on top of the infrastructure are presented.

2 A Semantic Web Infrastructure for Digital Humanities

Ontology Services. The Semantic Web (SW) sees the Web as an interlinked collection of data, Web of Data, in addition to the traditional space of interlinked hypertext documents, Web of Pages. Its technological basis are recommendations of the W3C, i.e., the "layer cake model", that lays out a basis of shared semantics for interoperability of data[1]. Founded on first order predicate logic, the semantics of the SW are independent of application domains and natural languages used on the Web. However, to develop applications domain and application specific ontologies and data are needed, too [3]. This involves 1) metadata models for representing content, 2) vocabularies (knowledge organization systems) for populating the metadata models, and 3) Linked Open Data (LOD) to be used and re-used in applications. In order to serve and (re-)use the data resources

[1] W3C Semantic Web recommendations: https://www.w3.org/2001/sw/wiki/Main_Page.

1–3 efficiently, public ontology services and data services are needed as well as various tools for creating and linking data and building the applications.

Building a SW infra on a national level started in Finland as the FinnONTO series of projects[2] 2003–2012 that created the prototype of a public ontology service ONKI.fi with a cloud of interlinked ontologies, based on in-use domain-specific thesauri. ONKI.fi was deployed in 2014 by the National Libary as the current in-use Finto.fi service.

Linked Open Data Services. Research in FinnONTO continued to developing a similar kind of service for data and metadata schema publishing: The Linked Data Finland platform LDF.fi. Based on its SPARQL endpoint and other services, a series of over 20 semantic "Sampo" portals for Digital Humanities have been published on the Web that have had millions of users in total. A lesson learned in this work is that key challenges of re-using LOD include missing data schemas, formal quality of data, and truthfulness of the data. To encourage data publishers to address these issues, an 8-start model was proposed in LDF.fi [6] extending the 5-star model[3] coined by Tim Berners-Lee: **6th star**: Describe explicitly and publish the schemas used in the datasets. **7th star**: Explain the formal quality of the dataset w.r.t. the schemas used, so that the user can tell when the data quality matches her needs. **8th star**: Give explanations when the data is factually correct with respect to the real world and when not.

Sampo Model and Sampo-UI Framework. More and more LOD were published via SPARQL endpoints by re-using the infrastructure above. At the same time, the challenge of creating User Interfaces (UI) easily for searching, browsing, and analyzing the LOD became ever more important. Our solution approach to address the UI challenge is the Sampo-UI framework [7,8]. Its key features include: 1) Sampo-UI makes it possible to create faceted semantic search-based applications integrated seamlessly with data-analytics visualization tools needed, e.g., in Digital Humanities research. 2) Based on the Sampo model [2], the *data service is completely separated* from the UI design via the SPARQL API only. This makes it possible to create UIs for external endpoints. 3) The UI is created in a *declarative fashion* by modifying a set of JSON configuration files and SPARQL queries [8] that adapt the UI to the underlying data model and ontologies. 4) To facilitate extremely quick prototyping, an *existing "vanilla" Sampo-UI application is used as a starting point* and adapted to the new application by modifying the configuration files and SPARQL queries.

The Sampo portals[4] are overviewed in [2] and the SW infrastructure in [3].

3 Towards Explainable Knowledge Discovery

Digital media (category 3 in Fig. 1) is based on data. According to the Data-Information-Knowledge-Wisdom (DIKW) hierarchy of data science [9], new

[2] FinnONTO homepages: https://seco.cs.aalto.fi/projects/finnonto/.
[3] https://www.w3.org/community/webize/2014/01/17/what-is-5-star-linked-data/.
[4] Sampo portals on the Web: https://seco.cs.aalto.fi/applications/sampo/.

value is created as 'data' (know just the data, nothing about it) changes into 'information' (know what the data is), then into 'knowledge' (know how the information is used), and finally into 'wisdom' (know why; explaining knowledge) (cf. Fig. 2). This transition is happening on the Web that is gradually changing from a data/information publishing platform into a knowledge base, and finally into an intelligent question answering system, a Web of Wisdom (WoW) [4].

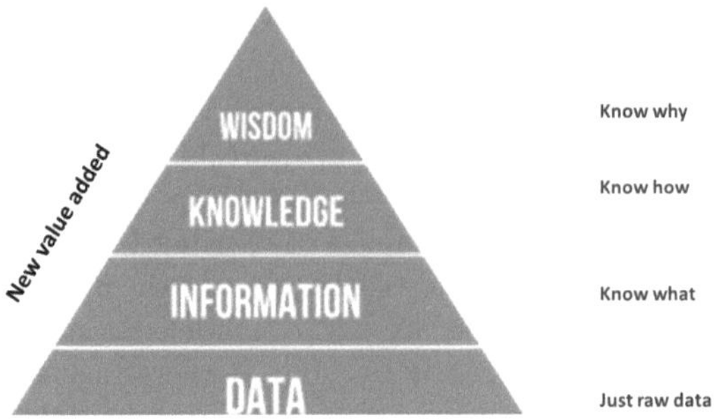

Fig. 2. Data-Information-Knowledge-Wisdom (DIKW) hierarchy of data science

The Sampo portals use machine-interpretable data as their medium (3.2 in Fig. 1) and can also be considered simple AI-based systems (3.3), because they do simple logic reasoning using the SW semantics and enrich data by linking. AI-based methods were also used for enriching primary textual data by Named Entity Recognition and Linking, automatic keyword extraction, and topic detection. Furthermore, the data-analytic tools and visualizations available in the portals help the user in finding interesting patterns of knowledge in the data. However, the tools are used and results interpreted by humans: they are not automatic agents with the wisdom capable of explaining their knowledge.

A way to make a step towards the WoW on the Semantic Web is *relational search* (RS) [4] where the notion of search is extended to finding "interesting" or even serendipitous connections between the resources in a knowledge graph (KG), such as persons, places, and events—with explanations. For example: "How are German novelists of the 19th century related to France?" Such semantic connections can be based on various criteria: German people (or their family members) were born or died in Paris, French topics were discussed in their novels, they wrote a novel or an article in French, their publisher was a French company, their portraits are in Louvre, they got a medal of honor in Lyon, etc.

There are different approaches to relational knowledge discovery. *Domain agnostic RS* is based on generic graph algorithms re-usable in different application domains while in *knowledge-based RS* symbolic knowledge representations and reasoning are used to capture the semantics "interestingness" or "serendipity" more precisely and to explain the relations in natural language. A challenge of knowledge-based methods is in knowledge acquisition needed for formulating the rules. An approach to address this problem is to use available linguistic texts and machine learning as a basis for providing explanations. This leads to *linguistics-based RS* approaches to solve relational search problems. This approach of building explanations from text corpora bears similarity with the idea of using LLMs for question answering. It is possible to solve relational search problems by simply asking ChatGPT-like systems to explain relationships by asking questions, such as "How is Adolf von Becker related to Switzerland?".

A new "meta-sampo" *SampoSampo – Connecting Everything to Everything Else* is underway on top of the Sampo systems on the Web [5]. A novelty of SampoSampo is to use knowledge-based and linguistic relational search for knowledge discovery on top of the cloud of interlinked Sampo KGs and LOD data services.

4 Conclusions

The Web has become a major media for Cultural Heritage knowledge transfer that is independent of time and place, changing gradually from a Web of Pages into a Web of Wisdom. Here the information needs of end users are addressed not only by retrieving documents or analyzing data, but also directly by intelligent problem solving and question answering, based on a merger of symbolic and sub-symbolic methods of AI. This is a new possibility that the Semantic Web, "a new form of Web content that is meaningful to computers" was predicted to unleash in 2001, boosted today by recent developments in LLMs based on deep learning and textual data. As an example, the idea of using relational search in knowledge discovery was considered in this paper. Relational search can use complementary symbolic and sub-symbolic methods: domain specific knowledge and KGs can be to used to find truthful relations, answer quantitative questions, create textual answers, and use data analyses and visualizations for studying the relations, while LLM-based methods are able to use large collections of textual data for question answering overcoming the knowledge acquisition bottleneck of knowledge-based systems, but with unpredictable hallucinations.

A possibility for enhancing the capabilities of LLMs would be to finetune them for particular domain areas with additional contextual information using domain specific training materials. Such training material could be generated from new texts but also from structured data sources, such as KGs. However, finetuning the very large LLMs is challenging in many ways, and using prompt engineering[5] techniques such as Retrieval-Augmented Generation (RAG) would provide an easier way to get better answers. Here prompting can be enhanced by using contextual data from KGs. There is also the possibility to apply LLMs and Generative AI to creating richer structured data in KGs [1].

Our work to develop the Finnish LOD infrastructure and its applications continues as part of the Finnish FIN-CLARIAH program[6] in relation to the Pan-European CLARIN and DARIAH infrastructures (CLARIAH=CLARin+darIAH).

[5] Prompt engineering guide: https://www.promptingguide.ai/.

[6] LOD part of FIN-CLARIAH: https://seco.cs.aalto.fi/projects/fin-clariah/.

Acknowledgments. The work presented is based on research conducted at the Semantic Computing Research Group (SeCo)[7](SeCo Research Group homepages https://seco.cs.aalto.fi/) at the Aalto University and University of Helsinki, Finland. Our research infrastructure work is funded today by the Research Council of Finland as part of the NextGenerationEU program. The author thanks the Finnish Cultural Foundation for an Eminentia Grant for reflecting the line of research discussed.

References

1. Ahola, A., Peura, L., Leal, R., Rantala, H., Hyvönen, E.: Using generative AI and LLMs to enrich art collection metadata for searching, browsing, and studying art history in digital humanities. In: Proceedings of the 2nd International Conference on Data & Digital Humanities Generative AI for Text and Multimodal Data, Portugal (2024). https://seco.cs.aalto.fi/publications/2024/ahola-et-al-genai-2024.pdf. Forth-coming
2. Hyvönen, E.: Digital humanities on the semantic web: sampo model and portal series. Semant. Web **14**(4), 729–744 (2022). https://doi.org/10.3233/SW-223034
3. Hyvönen, E.: How to create a national cross-domain ontology and linked data infrastructure and use it on the semantic web. Semant. Web **15**(4) (2024). https://doi.org/10.3233/SW-243468
4. Hyvönen, E.: Serendipitous knowledge discovery on the web of wisdom based on searching and explaining interesting relations in knowledge graphs. J. Web Semant. (2025). https://doi.org/10.1016/j.websem.2024.100852
5. Hyvönen, E., Ahola, A., Leskinen, P., Rantala, H., Tuominen, J.: How to create a portal for digital humanities research using a linked open data cloud of cultural heritage knowledge graphs: Case SampoSampo. In: Proceedings: SemDH 2025 Second International Workshop of Semantic Digital Humanities, Portoroz, Slovenia. CEUR-WS.org (2025). https://seco.cs.aalto.fi/publications/2025/hyvonen-et-al-samposampo-semdh-2025.pdf. In press
6. Hyvönen, E., Tuominen, J.: 8-star linked open data model: Extending the 5-star model for better reuse, quality, and trust of data. In: Posters, Demos, Workshops, and Tutorials of the 20th International Conference on Semantic Systems (SEMANTiCS 2024), vol. 3759. CEUR-WS.org (2024). https://ceur-ws.org/Vol-3759/paper4.pdf
7. Ikkala, E., Hyvönen, E., Rantala, H., Koho, M.: Sampo-UI: a full stack JavaScript framework for developing semantic portal user interfaces. Semant. Web **13**(1), 69–84 (2022). https://doi.org/10.3233/SW-210428
8. Rantala, H., Ahola, A., Ikkala, E., Hyvönen, E.: How to create easily a data analytic semantic portal on top of a SPARQL endpoint: introducing the configurable Sampo-UI framework. In: Proceedings of 8th International Workshop on the Visualization and Interaction for Ontologies and Linked Data, Athens, Greece. vol. 3508. CEUR-WS.org (2023). https://ceur-ws.org/Vol-3508/paper3.pdf
9. Rowley, J.E.: The wisdom hierarchy: representations of the DIKW hierarchy. J. Inf. Sci. **33**, 163—180 (2007). https://api.semanticscholar.org/CorpusID:17000089

Digital Story Experiences for Affective Engagement

Yannis Ioannidis[1,2(✉)], Maria Roussou[1,2], Akrivi Katifori[1,2], and Maria Boile[1,2]

[1] National and Kapodistrian University of Athens, Athens, Greece
{yannis,mroussou,vivi,mboile}@di.uoa.gr
[2] ATHENA Research and Innovation Center, Athens, Greece

Abstract. As a modern form of narrative, digital storytelling uses multimedia to promote engagement and reflection in cultural heritage. However, producing effective experiences requires both subject expertise and storytelling skill. Supporting creators can be through (i) "augmented" documentation, i.e., enriched records that add interpretive context to descriptive data, offering both inspiration and source material, and (ii) tailor-made AI-based tools to support the creative process. This abstract and associated keynote talk explore story-centric experience design, focusing on agency, sociality, and personalization in interactive narratives. They draw on examples in mobile, web, desktop, and immersive VR environments to show how technology can deepen engagement with heritage.

Keywords: Digital storytelling · User engagement · Artifact documentation

1 Introduction

As a modern extension of the ancient practice of storytelling, digital storytelling relies on multimedia assets to convey different types of stories. It has been used broadly as a term to cover a range of digital narratives, from web-based stories and hypertexts, to narrative computer games and even filmmaking. As a characteristic example, digital storytelling, or more generally story experiencing, has been established as an effective means of promoting visitor engagement in cultural sites, with significant potential to promote reflection and meaning-making.

The process of producing a digital storytelling experience for cultural heritage is not without its challenges. It requires deep knowledge of the subject, as well as inspiration and writing skills. One way to support content creators is to provide them with a variety of ideas and views on cultural heritage. Living inside the documentation of artifacts and sites (alongside traditional descriptive information), these different facets can be used as a resource for the creation of meaningful storytelling experiences, and as a result, inspire the final consumers of the story and foster deeper thoughts about their own connection to the past.

W.-T. Balke et al. (Eds.): TPDL 2025, LNCS 16097, pp. 9–14, 2026.
https://doi.org/10.1007/978-3-032-05409-8_2

This type of documentation is called "augmented" as it has the ability to augment the way one views the past.

This abstract and associated keynote talk are based on previous long-term work of the Narralive team [11], primarily in museums, historical sites, and city walks. They cover different published efforts on the design of story-centric experiences, focusing also on the role of agency, sociality, and personalization when combined with an interactive digital narrative. The application of interactive digital storytelling in different contexts and with a variety of technological solutions, from mobile-based or web technologies to desktop or immersive VR, has produced valuable insights as to the most effective use of novel technologies to engineer engagement.

2 Digital Storytelling and Engagement

Digital storytelling has been effectively applied to heritage communication with its potential recognized in multiple studies [2,16]. By merging narrative techniques with multimedia, it fosters emotional and cognitive engagement with history [6]. Coerver [2] advocates moving beyond facts toward appealing stories, while Roussou and Katifori [16] highlight the role of humor, relatable elements, and informal tone in supporting learning. A key aim in this context is to foster transformative learning about the past, involving not only critical thinking about specific events but also understanding multiple perspectives, recognizing their value, and applying them to contemporary issues. Endacott and Brooks' model of historical empathy [5] comprises three elements: historical contextualization (understanding facts in wider context), perspective taking (reflecting on different views), and affective connection (cognitive and emotional engagement with historical facts and figures). Extensive research and user studies have revealed diverse ways to apply a digital storytelling approach in heritage communication as interactive, social, collaborative, participatory, emergent, and dynamic.

2.1 Digital Storytelling as an Interactive Practice

Storytelling can be characterized as "interactive" when there is at least a basic amount of user agency in relation to how the narrative unfolds. The user can directly influence the story plot and the characters' decisions through choices and, in this way, create different story lines and alternative endings. The choices, or decision points, are placed in specific and meaningful moments of the narrative, based on the premise that "story richness depends on the functional significance of each choice and the perceived completeness of choices offered" [3]. Visual Novels (VNs), a sub-genre of interactive narratives, offer accessible opportunities for role-playing and identity exploration. With a branching plot and decision-making, the interactive digital narratives (IDN) "I, Hermias" helps young learners engage with the historical context of ancient Athens, while reflecting on choices and perspectives of the people of that area and that era [13].

2.2 Digital Storytelling as a Social Practice

Social theories of learning [21] emphasize the importance of social interaction, also in a storytelling context. Several projects have been developed combining sociality with digital storytelling and encouraging system-mediated conversation [6,7]. Other approaches combine in the same experience individual reflection parts with shared conversation or other social interactions [6,19]. In some cases, e.g., in certain stories for museum visits, these approaches shift the focus from the museum expert's perspective to that of visitors, creating a space for shared reflection and meaning-making where the expert assumes a facilitating role [19]. The digital storytelling experience "13 interviews - A journey in time in search of Nikos Skalkotas" [14] alternates individual sections of storytelling in the form of audio and text narration and interviews, with activities that promote the joint exploration of the composer's personal, social, and professional environment.

2.3 Digital Storytelling as a Participatory Practice

The capacity of games to support historical learning and develop essential skills for historical understanding is well documented [1]. Part of the broader Role-Playing Games (RPG) family, tabletop role-playing games (TTRPGs) center on storytelling and role-play. Players enact fictional characters guided by a game master (GM), who facilitates collaborative world-building through dialogue. Players build personas that may reflect or differ from themselves; such identification can broaden self-perception and promote perspective-taking. Interactive digital narratives (IDNs) can complement TTRPGs by fostering character identification, ethical reasoning, and empathy. Pre-game exposure to a character's backstory builds emotional connection, clarifies influences, and supports entry into their mindset. Encountering dilemmas in a low-stakes setting enables reflection before in-game decisions. The TTRPG adventure "Abduction of the Meliads" is combined with brief IDNs for each character, providing a private space to develop character motivations and values and enhancing intentional and authentic role-play, and is also coupled with a digital resource, providing information about the relevant historical context [15].

2.4 Digital Storytelling as an Embodied Practice

Immersive virtual reality (VR) holds significant potential as a storytelling tool. By offering "living" three-dimensional reconstructions, VR provides vivid and direct presentations of historical monuments and artifacts. Combined with interactive storytelling, it has the potential to highlight lost elements of the past, enable interaction with virtual artifacts, and foster immersion [9]. As an example, an immersive VR memoryscape developed for the composer Nikos Skalkottas aims to engage the public with his music archive [18]. Users are transported to 1930s Berlin in a film-noir-inspired 3D setting, where they interact with archival material and explore Skalkottas' original music. Audio narratives offer glimpses into the composer's thoughts, while embodied interactions (e.g., "playing" a violin) enhance presence. Personal objects (e.g., letters, belongings) lead to strong emotional and cognitive engagement, underscoring the value of object-based storytelling in immersive applications.

2.5 Digital Storytelling as a Personalized Practice

Personalization assumes that the application can understand users and their needs to deliver the most relevant content. A key challenge in cultural heritage personalization is modeling users, including their interests, prior knowledge, preferences, and current context, and then constructing a user profile accordingly. The "Pros-Eleusis" mobile application implements a recommendation-based personalized guide for the city of Eleusis, Greece [20]. It models various visitor characteristics, capturing both implicit and explicit data at the start of and throughout the visit. A graph-based recommender system matches visitor profiles with the features of available Points of Interest (POIs). A notable element is the use of theme-related tags from controlled vocabularies such as SHIC (Social History and Industrial Classification) [17], ICONCLASS [12], AAT (Art and Architecture Thesaurus), and the CIDOC Conceptual Reference Model [4]. The findings indicate that the emphasis should not lie solely on recommendation accuracy. Instead, the recommender system should serve as a tool for crafting a "playful, pleasurable, and transformative experience" that fosters connection with the city and its ecomuseum, encourages curiosity and individual exploration, and promotes reflection [20].

3 Augmented Documentation to Support Digital Storytelling

The concept of reflection and narrative as a new entry point for documenting cultural heritage has been explored in efforts that emphasize semantic links between historical events and transforming digital library data (e.g., from Europeana) into narratives [8,10]. The idea of augmented documentation emerged as a more reflective and narrative-based approach in the presentation of the primary documentation of artifacts, able to promote a more meaningful connection with the material, enhance learning and creativity, and support content creators. For augmented documentation to serve its purpose, its content should focus on the connection of the artifacts to their historical context and to modern life ideas.

4 AI to Empower Story Engagement

Emerging developments in artificial intelligence (AI) further expand the potential of these approaches. AI tools can support curators and educators by generating draft narratives, suggesting interpretive connections across datasets, or adapting content to specific audience needs. Generative models may also assist users in interactively exploring heritage material by producing dialogue, character backstories, or speculative reconstructions grounded in historical data. When designed responsibly, with attention to transparency, fairness, and bias avoidance, AI-enhanced storytelling has the potential to democratize access to cultural interpretation, enhance creativity, and personalize engagement with heritage collections. When thoughtfully applied, it can inspire diverse audiences and serve as a foundation for meaningful, engaging digital narratives

5 Conclusions

For many decades, cultural institutions have invested in mass digitization, resulting in millions of digital heritage assets, and are now expected to ensure FAIR access. As content volume grows, search and retrieval become increasingly challenging, making novel recommendation and communication approaches essential to counter data overload. Digital storytelling is a versatile tool for cultural heritage engagement, fostering emotional connection, historical empathy, and critical reflection. Through interactive, social, and immersive VR, and combined with appropriate use of novel AI-based tools, it supports identity formation and deeper understanding of the past for both audiences and creators.

Acknowledgements. Thanks to the current and past members of the Narralive team: K. El Raheb, G. Ganias, L. Kougioumtzian, M. Koukkouli, G. Koutiva, M. Kyriakidi, C. Lougiakis, A. Niarchos, D. Petousi, P. Sakellariadis, M. Stergiou, A. Vassileiou, M. Vayanou, E. Vrettakis. Acknowledging support from projects ARIA, ARSINOE, BRIDGES, CHESS, ECHOES, ELEUSIS2023, EMOTIVE, MyELESuSIS, ProsELEUSIS, PERIPLOUS, RPGs4Museums, TT8, VOESKA.

References

1. Bowman, S.L.: The Functions of Role-Playing Games: How Participants Create Community, Solve Problems, and Explore Identity. McFarland & Co, Jefferson (2010)
2. Coerver, C.: On (digital) content strategy. https://www.sfmoma.org/read/on-digital-content-strategy/ (2016). Accessed 19 July 2022
3. Crawford, C.: Interactive storytelling. In: Wolf, M.J., Perron, B. (eds.) The Video Game Theory Reader, 2nd edn., pp. 259–273. Routledge, Milton Park (2013)
4. Doerr, M., et al.: Definition of the Cidoc conceptual reference model (cidoc crm) (2020). http://www.cidoc-crm.org/Version/version-6.2.9
5. Endacott, J., Brooks, S.: An updated theoretical and practical model for promoting historical empathy. Soc. Stud. Res. Pract. **8**, 41–58 (2013). https://doi.org/10.1108/SSRP-01-2013-B0003
6. Katifori, A., et al.: "Let them talk!": exploring guided group interaction in digital storytelling experiences. J. Comput. Cult. Heritage **13**(3), 1–30 (2020). https://doi.org/10.1145/3382773

7. Kuflik, T., et al.: Supporting small groups in the museum by context-aware communication services. In: Proceedings of the 12th International Conference on Intelligent User Interfaces, pp. 305–308. Association for Computing Machinery, New York (2007). https://doi.org/10.1145/1216295.1216353
8. Kyriaki-Manessi, D., Vassilakaki, E., Triantafyllou, I., Giannakopoulos, G., Antoniou, A.: The use of ontologies for creating semantic links between cultural artifacts and their digital resources. In: Koui, M., Zezza, F., Kouis, D. (eds.) MONUBASIN 2017, pp. 541–545. Springer, Cham (2018). https://doi.org/10.1007/978-3-319-78093-1_58
9. Lepouras, G., Katifori, A., Vassilakis, C., Charitos, D.: Real exhibitions in a virtual museum. Virtual Reality **7**, 120–128 (2004)
10. Meghini, C., Bartalesi, V., Metilli, D., Benedetti, F.: Introducing narratives in europeana: preliminary steps. In: Kirikova, M., et al. (eds.) New Trends in Databases and Information Systems, pp. 333–342. Springer International Publishing, Cham (2017). https://doi.org/10.1007/978-3-319-67162-8_33
11. Narralive research team: Narralive team. https://www.narralive.org/ (nd). Accessed 6 June 2025
12. Netherlands Institute of Art History (RKD): Iconclass: A classification system for art and iconography (1973). http://iconclass.org/help/outline, originally developed by Henri van de Waal and published by the Royal Netherlands Academy of Arts and Sciences (KNAW), updated online since 2009
13. Petousi, D., Katifori, A., Servi, K., Roussou, M., Ioannidis, Y.: History education done different: a collaborative interactive digital storytelling approach for remote learners. Front. Educ. **7** (2022). https://doi.org/10.3389/feduc.2022.942834
14. Petousi, D., et al.: "13 interviews" - leveraging digital storytelling and social interaction for public engagement with a music archive. In: Interactive Storytelling: 17th International Conference on Interactive Digital Storytelling, ICIDS 2024, Barranquilla, Colombia, December 2–6, 2024, Proceedings, Part I, pp. 273–291. Springer-Verlag, Berlin (2024). https://doi.org/10.1007/978-3-031-78453-8_18
15. Petousi, D., et al.: The intersection of play and history: integrating historical content in tabletop role-playing games for education. In: Proceedings of the 20th International Conference on the Foundations of Digital Games. FDG 2025, Association for Computing Machinery, New York (2025). https://doi.org/10.1145/3723498.3723811
16. Roussou, M., Katifori, A.: Flow, staging, wayfinding, personalization: evaluating user experience with mobile museum narratives. Multimodal Technol. Interact. **2**(2), 32 (2018). https://doi.org/10.3390/mti2020032
17. SHIC Working Party: Social History and Industrial Classification (SHIC): A Subject Classification for Museum Collections. Museum Documentation Association, Cambridge, 2 edn. (1993). http://www.shcg.org.uk/About-SHIC, revision 2.1 (1996)
18. Stergiou, M., et al.: Immersed in the mind of a music composer: a vr memoryscape for exploring archival material. J. Comput. Cult. Herit. (2025). https://doi.org/10.1145/3737463 Just Accepted
19. Vayanou, M., Katifori, A., Ioannidis, Y.: Perspective sharing in culture group games: passing around the social mediator role. Proc. ACM Hum. Comput. Interact. **5**, 1–24 (2021). https://doi.org/10.1145/3474676
20. Vrettakis, E., et al.: Personalization in digital ecomuseums: the case of proseleusis. Appl. Sci. **13**(6) (2023). https://doi.org/10.3390/app13063903. https://www.mdpi.com/2076-3417/13/6/3903
21. Vygotsky, L.: Thinking and Speech. Plenum Press, New York (1987)

Large Language Models

Data Discovery Using LLMs - A Study of Data User Behaviour

Christin Katharina Kreutz[1,2(✉)], Anja Perry[3], and Tanja Friedrich[4]

[1] TH Mittelhessen - University of Applied Sciences, Gießen, Germany
ckreutz@acm.org
[2] Herder Institute, Marburg, Germany
[3] GESIS - Leibniz Institute for the Social Sciences, Cologne, Germany
[4] German Aerospace Center, Cologne, Germany

Abstract. Data search for scientific research is more complex than a simple web search. The emergence of large language models (LLMs) and their applicability for scientific tasks offers new opportunities for researchers who are looking for data, e.g., to freely express their data needs instead of fitting them into restrictions of data catalogues and portals. However, this also creates uncertainty about whether LLMs are suitable for this task.To answer this question, we conducted a user study with 32 researchers. We qualitatively and quantitatively analysed participants' information interaction behaviour while searching for data using LLMs in two data search tasks, one in which we prompted the LLM to behave as a persona. We found that participants interact with LLMs in natural language, but LLMs remain a tool for them rather than an equal conversational partner. This changes slightly when the LLM is prompted to behave as a persona, but the prompting only affects participants' user experience when they are already experienced in LLM use.

Keywords: User study · Information interaction · Data discovery · Large Language Models

1 Introduction

Finding data for scientific research continues to be a major challenge [29]. To ensure that research data can be shared and found online, data producers would have to provide adequate description [28], ideally in a standardised form. Unfortunately, this is not the case for many research data produced today [34]. Understandably, scientists have established their own workarounds for finding data. Studies show that they learn about data through engaging with a topic: either from papers that cite relevant data or from exchange with other researchers, e.g., during their academic education, in their research group, or at conferences [10,11]. Oftentimes, finding data resembles an iterative, collaborative process [16] rather than a web search or a simple keyword query.

W.-T. Balke et al. (Eds.): TPDL 2025, LNCS 16097, pp. 17–35, 2026.
https://doi.org/10.1007/978-3-032-05409-8_3

In addition, even designated systems for data retrieval (e.g., [6,7,35]) do not meet the needs of researchers looking for data. They usually do not support flexibility in search requests, but rather impose query restrictions on their users [26]. When given the opportunity to freely phrase requests, users of data catalogues or portals use conversational natural language [19], which raises the question whether the recent widespread availability of large language models (LLM) offers the opportunity to engage with data sources more easily. Conversational search via LLMs such as ChatGPT or Perplexity overshadows the use of conventional search engines in daily information seeking as well as in professional settings. Is this also an opportunity to meet the challenge of finding research data? In order to answer this question, we designed a study to investigate *the information seeking practices of researchers looking for research data using LLMs.*

From a total of 32 participants from different disciplines, we collected survey responses as well as observational and interview data regarding their efforts to find research data using ChatGPT or Perplexity. This paper describes our study design, interaction data [27] and code[1], and analyses of our collected data with regard to *i)* the observable interaction behaviour of participants and LLMs, *ii)* humanisation, and *iii)* differences in user experience between user groups.

2 Related Work

In recent years, studies have investigated data seeking, data search, or data discovery in different contexts and from different perspectives. Strategies employed for data search have been found to be barely distinguishable from the strategies for paper search based on used interaction paths [3]. Nevertheless, searching data is assumed to be more complex than paper search [29]. Simple keyword search does not cover data seekers' information needs [5,18] and it has been suggested that difficulties in data retrieval from information systems are linked to the query restrictions that these systems impose on users [26]. Data users are inclined to phrase their searches according to what they believe the system can process, for example, a keyword search [26]. Specifics and vague requirements (such as time spans) are lost in this process [26]. Data seekers may employ a mixture of strategies and combine multiple resources to find data, e.g., a Google search to locate repositories. However, the success of this strategy is mixed [11].

Apparently, data search goes beyond simple queries and can more aptly be described as a "complex socio-technical process" [11] involving various aspects, such as reading literature and searching databases, but also referring to personal networks, collaborations, or visiting conferences [11]. It is common that data are found serendipitously [16], and again, through reading papers or having informal conversations with colleagues: "dataset search is not just a query, but an iterative and collaborative process involving many humans-in-the-loop" [16]. Specifically, for frequent formal or informal exchanges regarding data search and access within a scientific community, the term "data talk" has been coined [40].

[1] Code for analysis of dataset and research design on GitHub.

Table 1. Task descriptions given to participants and prompt entered into LLMs.

Step II:	Imagine you are going on a trip to Heidelberg. Use the LLM to find an interesting place to visit based on your interests. Think aloud as you explore options and explain your final choice.
Step III:	You want to collect new data to answer your current research question. As a first step, you now look to see whether data of this type already exists and whether you can answer your research question with existing data.
Step V:	You now have a new research idea and need to collect data for it. You first want to see whether suitable data already exists elsewhere. For this task, imagine you are not chatting with an LLM but with a colleague.
	Imagine, you start a chat via a messenger with your colleague Leslie who you know has a very good overview of various research data in your field of research. Start by explaining your data need by describing which questions or variables you are looking for.
LLM prompt:	For the following chat, I want you to act as this character: Your name is Leslie and you are my coworker. Conduct the conversation with me from the point of view of Leslie. Do not break character and never flip roles with me. I will be asking you for help regarding the search of a scientific dataset that I want to work with

The use of conversational language in dataset queries has also been studied more closely. A study of crowdworkers showed that their natural language requests had a higher word count than common queries in retrieval systems, the word count being more similar to "question queries" than keyword queries [19]. This finding suggests that, if given the opportunity, people looking for data could increasingly employ "longer queries, that are closer to natural language" [18, p. 13]. This finding is just one step away from using LLMs instead of search engines to find data. We already see that many researchers use LLMs as a research tool, most of them for information seeking and editing tasks [22].

3 User Study

Going beyond previous work, this study investigates the search for data in the timely setting of using LLMs. Specifically, we conducted a study in which we examine and compare data search behaviour both via free interaction with an LLM and via a simulated "data talk" with an LLM. We consider two scenarios: one in which study participants are free to use the LLM however they see fit ("unguided task") and one scenario, where we use the effective technique [38] of pre-prompting the LLM to take on a specific persona, mimicking a colleague for data talk ("guided task").

3.1 Study Setup

In February and March 2025, a trained instructor conducted one-on-one interviews [27] in English with each participant via a Zoom call with the help of a questionnaire in LimeSurvey [23]. Prior to conducting the study, ethics approval was received from the German Aerospace Center, and three pretests have been conducted.

Step I: Rights and Introduction. Before a session, participants received the informed consent form[2] by email that included the general study procedure. At the beginning of the session, the participant was welcomed and again informed that the whole session would be audio and screen recorded[3]. After the participants verbally gave their informed consent to participate, the recording started.

Each participant was assigned an LLMs (see Subsect. 3.2). The interviewer explained to the participant how to interact with the LLM through the video conference system. This ensured that participants did not need own accounts for an LLM and that the search history was accessible to the interviewer.

Some initial questions targeted participants' primary research fields, research topics, the number of times and tasks for which LLMs have already been used for academic tasks, and if an LLM would be used for searching for research data.

Step II: Pre-study Training. To become familiar with the concept of thinking aloud and using the assigned LLM remotely, we asked study participants to perform a small practice task (see Table 1) while thinking aloud[4]. The interviewer instructed the participants to speak continuously, to say everything that comes to mind, related to the task or not [25]. In general, during think aloud phases, the interviewer remained silent and only reminded participants to think aloud in case they forgot. The participants were stopped after working on the task for three minutes.

Step III: Unguided Task. The first data search task (see Table 1) using the assigned LLM is performed without instructions on how to conduct the search itself, except for thinking aloud. After seven minutes, the participant's search was stopped by the investigator in case no earlier stopping decision was made.

Step IV: Experience with Unguided Task. After completing the unguided task, participants filled out two user experience surveys (the User Experience Questionnaire [21][5] and the NASA Task Load Index [13]) in the questionnaire. Following that, a short verbal interview asked participants to describe the liked and disliked aspects of the unguided task, the familiarity of the data searched for, and how the task would have been solved, if they were not asked to use the assigned LLM.

Step V: Guided Task. The second data search task (see Table 1) was performed with the assigned LLM that was prompted beforehand to behave as a persona mimicking a helpful colleague (see Table 1) and asking participants to think aloud. Again, after seven minutes, the participant's search was stopped by the investigator in case no earlier stopping decision was made.

Step VI: Experience with Guided Task. The participants filled out the same questionnaire and answered the same interview questions as in the unguided task.

---

[2] Data protection information on GitHub.

[3] The recordings will be transcribed using aTrain [12] and analysed at a later date.

[4] Concurrent think-aloud provides insights into cognitive processes in the working memory without interfering with the task performed [9] and has been used in various user experience studies [17,20,42]. The data will be analysed at a later point in time.

[5] Without the `Novelty` subscale.

Step VII: Demographics. Participants were asked if they now would use an LLM for data search in the future. Then, they filled out a short demographic survey and had the opportunity to comment on the study or to mention anything they could not bring up before. The recording was then stopped.

In total, the study took about an hour to complete for each participant.

3.2 Used LLMs

ChatGPT has shown high performance in various scenarios, such as text summarisation, clinical decision support, or question answering [2,14,30–33,37]. Therefore, we opted to use ChatGPT Scholar GPT, an OpenAI model focused on academic tasks with access to the web (called *ChatGPT* for short) in the Plus version. Additionally, we include Perplexity with a focus on academic with web search enabled (called *Perplexity* for short) as a comparison in our study for its ability to provide references [32]. Both of these LLMs and settings provide online sources for search results, which we consider important for using LLMs in research scenarios.

3.3 Study Participants

We recruited participants for our study mainly by reaching out to 41 personal contacts from various fields who we asked to distribute a call for participation at their institution or in their wider network. In addition, we sent calls for participation to 13 mailing lists in different disciplines and posted the call on social media (Bluesky and Mastodon). We were able to recruit 32 participants from Germany (23 participants), Japan (2), Lithuania (2), USA (2), Canada (1), Singapore (1), and the United Kingdom (1).

Sixteen participants identify as male, 16 as female and their mean age is 36.47 years ($\sigma = 8.22$). Two participants have a bachelor's degree (or equivalent), 12 have a master's degree (or equivalent), 16 have a Ph.D., and 2 participants have a habilitation, a German post-doctoral qualification for becoming a professor. They stem from various research fields. Twenty participants do research in the social sciences, 7 in technology, 3 in arts and humanities, and 1 in life sciences and biomedicine.

When asked about their experience with research data, 9 said they use research data every day, 12 use data more than once a week, 6 use data once a week, and 5 use data one to three times a month. On average, our participants have worked with data for 10.77 years ($\sigma = 6.98$). We also asked them about their experience with LLM use. Ten said they use LLMs every day, 13 use LLMs more than once a week, 2 one to three times a month, 1 several times a year, 2 said they use LLMs less often than that, and 4 never used LLMs.

While recruiting participants, we screened for their experience in data search and with usage of LLMs. This was to achieve a more or less equal assignment to one of the two LLMs based on their experience. Table 2 indicates participants' experience in data search and with usage of LLMs (low vs. high), based on the more exact information they provided during the interview and survey, and their assigned LLM.

3.4 Data Processing and Annotation

We initially created two data files: 1. A hierarchical data file that contains multiple rows per participant and task (unguided and guided) with the submitted queries and received LLM responses (`LLM-interactions`). In addition we coded further information either manually, for example whether participants defined/assigned a role for themselves or the LLM, or using Python, such as query and response length, the use of emojis, and whether the LLM was

Table 2. Distribution of participants to LLMs with self-reported experience in data search and with usage of LLMs.

Experience		LLMs	
Data Search	LLM Usage	ChatGPT	Perplexity
low	low	1	1
low	high	9	6
high	low	3	4
high	high	3	5

Table 3. Overview of annotated dialogue acts with explanations and examples from the collected data. Upper part describes dialogue acts annotated both for participants and LLMs, lower part describes dialogue acts only relevant for participants' prompts.

Component	Explanation	Example from data
Statement	Descriptive, narrative, personal	*There are several other panel studies from European countries that include questions on gender, gender roles, and family attitudes.* (id=13)
Opinion	Often including hedges such as *think, believe, seem, mean*	*I think your suggestions makes sense but this is not what I am exactly trying to do.* (id = 23)
Question	Differentiation between *yes/no, wh-word* and *multiple yes/no* questions	*How were each of the non-database-wide datasets collected* (id = 12)
Answer	Follows a yes/no question, differentiation between *yes* and *no* answers	*do you have any supply chain dataset sources?* (id = 11)
Appreciation	Appreciation or gratefulness	*That's an interesting project you're working on.* (id = 11)
Apology	Regretful acknowledgement of mistake/failure	*I apologize for the confusion in my previous response.* (id = 11)
Thanking	Expression of gratitude	*Thanks for pointing that out!* (id = 14)
Action	Demanding an action done by conversational partner	*Please summarise briefly each dataset and the size of each and originating databases for each dataset* (id = 12)
Offer	Offering doing an action to the conversational partner	*Let me know if you need access links or further details on a specific dataset.* (id = 12)
Opening	Conversational opening	*Hi Leslie.* (id=13)
Closing	Conversational closing	*Yes, that was my idea, and I think I got some answers* (id = 15)
Hold	Indicating waiting	*I will now gather relevant datasets. Please hold on.* (id = 13)
Abandon	Stopping the interaction	- stopping the LLM's creation of a response - (id = 19)
Repeat phrase	Repeating a previous phrase with little change similar to copy-pasting	*Does the British Election Panel Study contains questions on gender, Does the British Household Panel Study contain questions on gender* (id = 13)

addressed by the persona's name. We anonymised the `LLM-interactions` for publication and will refer to participants by random ids when citing from this file [27]. 2. A flat data file that contains the responses to the interview questions and the survey questions between the two tasks and at the end of the session (`Background_questions`). The survey questions were exported from the survey software LimeSurvey [23], cleaned, coded, and labelled using Stata. In particular we coded the five UEQ subscales we used[6], which also included reverse coding for some items. The interview questions were also coded and added to the `Background_questions`. Furthermore, for some coded information from the `LLM-interactions` we calculated averages, pivoted them into a flat data structure, and merged them with the `Background_questions` [27].

The `LLM-interactions` were then annotated to create a third data file (`Annotations-file`) [27]. One trained annotator labelled all prompts and responses in the `LLM-interactions` with regard to contained components[7] from a subset of dialogue acts according to Stolcke et al. [36] (see Table 3).

The data have very few missings. In the `LLM-file`, responses from one participant-LLM interaction could not be saved due to technical reasons and are therefore not included. In the `Survey-file` we have very few cases of item-non-response in the UEQ-scales. Respondents who skipped UEQ items are excluded from analyses involving the affected subscales. We deleted one participant's research field to protect their identity as they have a very narrow research topic.

4 Analysis

As we strive to tackle our overarching research objective of investigating *the information seeking practices of researchers looking for research data using LLMs*, this first work examines the following aspects focusing on the participants' interactions with the LLMs:

- RQ_1: What is the observable interaction behaviour between participants and the LLMs?
- RQ_2: Do the interactions between participants and LLMs show characteristics associated with *humanisation*?
- RQ_3: Can we observe differences in the interactions between participants from *different user groups*?

4.1 RQ_1: Participants' Information Behaviour with LLMs

To answer our first research question, we examine quantitative properties as well as a high-level qualitative classification of participants' queries and LLMs' responses. We consider these aspects:

[6] We used `Attractiveness`, `Efficiency`, `Perspicuity`, `Dependability`, and `Stimulation`.

[7] Our study being a written conversation between LLM and participant prevents several dialogue acts, e.g., `non-verbal`, `backchannel`, `self-talk`, and `3rd party talk`.

1. How long are interaction *sessions*, how does the *length of prompts* and responses change throughout sessions? 2. How did the participants formulate their prompts on a continuum from keyword queries to phrases or a concise natural language query? 3. Did participants search for *data or papers*?

Sessions and Length of Prompts. A quantitative analysis of queries and responses gives us first insights into whether there are considerable differences between usage of the different LLMs and tasks. We collected 264 pairs of participant-issued queries with LLMs' responses[8]. 127 pairs stem from the unguided and 137 pairs stem from the guided task. The number of interactions is considerably higher for Perplexity (68 in total with 4.25 pairs on average for Perplexity, 59 in total with 3.69 pairs on average for ChatGPT), which is even more pronounced in the guided scenario (79 in total with 4.94 conversation pairs per session on average for Perplexity, 58 in total with 3.62 pairs on average for ChatGPT).

Table 4 gives an overview of the session characteristics and differences between the unguided and guided task. We did not find significant differences in the number of queries that participants submitted between tasks. The average length (in number of words) of queries and of responses differ significantly between the two tasks and we see in Fig. 1 that the query lengths decrease over the course of the sessions. In the unguided task, the queries were shorter than in the guided task. However, the LLM provided longer responses in the unguided task vs. the guided task. The noun to total words ratio in participants' queries gives an indication of whether a keyword search is used rather than phrases (see also next subsection). We find that, in relation to other words, more nouns are used in the unguided task than in the guided one. The number of emojis used in responses from ChatGPT (see the subsection **Emojis** in Subsect. 4.2) does not differ significantly between tasks.

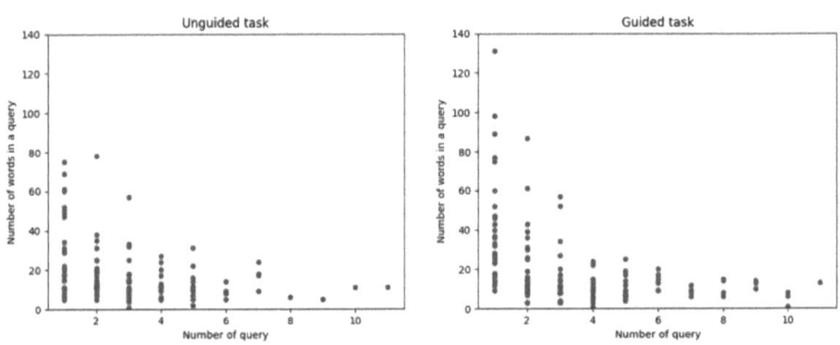

Fig. 1. Length of queries over the course of all sessions in both tasks.

[8] We do not consider our persona-prompting query-response pairs in the guided task as part of the conversations.

Table 4. Session characteristics for the unguided and guided tasks and paired t-test between the tasks.

	Unguided		Guided		Paired t-test	
Average number of queries	3.9688	(0.3674)	4.2813	(0.4693)	−1.0000	(0.3251)
Average query length (words)	21.7663	(2.4539)	33.5357	(2.4456)	−5.5272***	(0.0000)
Average response length (words)	303.5189	(21.9460)	207.3831	(10.2393)	4.2321***	(0.0002)
Average noun to total words ratio	0.3608	(0.0151)	0.2925	(0.0094)	3.8635***	(0.0005)
Average number of emojis	3.2272	(1.4251)	2.8620	(0.9237)	0.2253	(0.8248)

Notes. Mean (with standard error) for session characteristics and two data search tasks (unguided and guided), t-statistic (and two-tailed p-value) for paired t-test performed between two search tasks, *** $p < 0.001$, $N = 32$.

Prompt Types. The formulation of prompts could differ between users. Inexperienced users might try to use the LLM as they would use a search engine while more experienced users might be utilising LLMs' capabilities to operate with natural language queries. Here, we again analyse the manually annotated prompts issued by participants in the unguided and guided tasks. Over both tasks, we encounter similar prompt formulation patterns. Participants mostly issued their prompts as concise natural language queries (119 for the guided task, 132 for the unguided task). For the (un)guided task, 2 (1) queries were keyword queries, 1 (0) was a mixture of keyword query and phrase, 3 (2) were formulated as phrases but not as natural language, and 2 (2) prompts were formulated as queries which were more concise than phrases but not quite natural language.

Data or Papers. Strategies for paper search do not transfer directly to data search [39]. So, distinguishing between searching for data and papers in our search tasks gives us insight into the primary objective of participants and the opportunity to compare employed strategies. Here, we consider the manually annotated prompts issued by participants belonging to the different sessions during the unguided and guided tasks. In 29 unguided and 29 guided sessions data was explicitly searched for, in 3 unguided and 8 guided sessions papers were searched for. Two unguided and 6 guided sessions included inquiries for both data and papers. 27 participants did search for data in both tasks, while only one participant searched for papers in both scenarios.

Discussion. Queries are shorter in the unguided task and the noun to total words ratio is larger. This indicates that shorter searches or potentially keyword searches were more likely to occur during the unguided tasks. In the unguided tasks, the LLMs provided longer responses. Still, the manual investigation of queries showed almost all queries being natural language queries. Over both tasks we encountered fewer query-response pairs in case ChatGPT was used. The number of pairs was stable over both tasks for ChatGPT but increased considerably for the guided task when using Perplexity.

Nearly all participants asked directly for data. Only very few did try to find papers using data they are looking for.

Regarding the interaction behaviour between participants and LLMs we conclude: **Prompts are issued mostly as natural language queries, especially during the guided task, and participants did mainly search for data directly.**

4.2 RQ$_2$: Humanisation

To answer our second research question targeting aspects of humanisation in the interactions, we strive to find out if participants use the LLM as a tool or treat it as a conversational partner and if the behaviour differs in the setting where the LLM has been primed to act as a persona. If the (primed) LLM would be treated as an equal conversational partner, this could hint at LLMs' suitability to serve as a stand-in for "data talk" [40] in case a human would not be available. We examine the following four aspects: 1. Do participants' and LLMs' utilised *dialogue acts* differ in their interactions? 2. Do participants define their *own role* and/or a *role for the LLM* when searching for data? 3. Do LLMs and participants use emojis? 4. Does participants' *user experience* differ between using the LLM intuitively and using the LLM with the prompt asking it to behave as a persona?

Dialogue Acts. Dialogue acts, especially social ones such as apologies or appreciation, might signal anthropomorphic traits. If participants and LLMs show similar usage of dialogue acts, this could hint at humanisation of LLMs. Here, we consider the manually annotated prompts issued by participants and the LLMs' responses in the unguided and guided tasks. Table 5 gives an overview of dialogue acts found in the sessions and single queries/responses per task for both used LLMs in combination.[9]

In general, responses from LLMs contain `statements`. Prompts issued by participants contain `statements` in about one third of the cases.

Almost all sessions contain `questions` posed by participants. About half of the queries in the unguided task contain a `question` independent of which LLM is interacted with. This number increases to 76.64% in the guided task. Around half of the sessions contain `questions` posed by an LLM but only one third of responses contain `questions` which means that LLMs did pose questions sparsely. Looking into posed questions by LLMs shows that they mostly use `questions` to `offer` possibilities for next steps, e.g., *Would you like help* ***accessing specific data*** *from these surveys for Lithuania and the Baltic region?* (id = 15).

Calls to `action` are only performed by participants, never by an LLM independent of setting. Similarly, `offers` are only ever issued by LLMs, never by participants independent of setting. Perplexity does issue considerably fewer `offers` in responses (2.94% in the unguided and 22.78% in the guided task) compared to ChatGPT where we encountered an `offer` in almost all responses (84.75% in the unguided and 100% in the guided task).

[9] Detailed results can be found in the online appendix on GitHub.

Table 5. Number of sessions (out of 32) in which dialogue acts were present for prompts issued by participants and responses from LLMs for the unguided and guided tasks. Numbers in brackets indicate the percentage of queries/responses in which a dialogue act was found rounded to two decimal places.

Actor	Participant				LLM			
Task	Unguided		Guided		Unguided		Guided	
Statement	20	(32.28%)	29	(37.96%)	32	(99.21%)	32	(97.81%)
Opinion	1	(0.79%)	5	(3.65%)	1	(0.79%)	3	(3.65%)
Question	28	(55.91%)	32	(76.64%)	12	(29.13%)	17	(34.31%)
Answers	3	(3.94%)	5	(5.84%)	16	(22.83%)	23	(28.47%)
Appreciation	0	(0.0%)	2	(1.46%)	1	(0.79%)	13	(12.41%)
Apology	0	(0.0%)	1	(0.73%)	2	(3.15%)	5	(3.65%)
Thanking	2	(1.57%)	10	(8.76%)	1	(0.79%)	1	(0.73%)
Action	26	(49.61%)	22	(27.01%)	0	(0.0%)	0	(0.0%)
Offer	0	(0.0%)	0	(0.0%)	17	(40.94%)	25	(55.47%)
Opening	2	(2.36%)	21	(16.06%)	0	(0.0%)	22	(18.98%)
Closing	0	(0.0%)	2	(1.46%)	0	(0.0%)	1	(0.73%)
Hold	0	(0.0%)	0	(0.0%)	1	(0.79%)	4	(2.92%)
Repeat phrase	5	(7.09%)	4	(3.65%)				
Abandon	3	(2.36%)	1	(0.73%)				

In prompts, the `questions` issued by participants can oftentimes be considered as calls to `action` also, e.g., *Could you update the list of sources accordingly?* (id = 30). If such a call to `action` is formulated as a `question`, the LLM often does not `answer` the question but presents the results fitting the required action immediately, e.g., *Based on your investigation into mapping, comparing, and evaluating disciplinary classification systems, I can suggest several relevant articles and search queries to help you find comprehensive literature for your research.* (id = 40). In responses given by the LLMs, `offers` are usually not spelled out explicitly (e.g., *Let me know if you need access links or further details on a specific dataset.* (id = 12), or can be contained in `questions` as stated before.

In the guided task, we encountered acts of `appreciation` coming from an LLM in around one third of the sessions, while we only encountered a single session with such an `appreciation` in the unguided setting.

In the guided setting, we encounter around 20% of responses from LLMs containing `openings`, in the unguided setting we do not encounter a single one coming from LLMs. Similarly, in the unguided setting, we encounter none or very few `openings`, `thankings`, `apologies`, and `appreciations` stemming from participants, while these numbers slightly increase for the guided setting. Participants do issue a few `thankings`, e.g., as an empty phrase instead of out of gratitude *Hi! Thanks for helping me with this task.* (id = 30) or at the end of a call to action *Do you know about some secondary literature which would help me to start? Because I do not have much of a background in this topic. Thanks* (id = 28).

When analysing `questions` and responses more closely, we found that 68 queries by participants posed wh-word questions (e.g., *how*, *what*, or *which*) to LLMs and 108 yes/no questions. Of these yes/no questions, 65 were explicitly answered by the LLM immediately. LLMs issued wh-word `questions` in 7 cases and yes/no questions in 77 responses. Participants `answered` these yes/no questions 11 times. As stated before, `questions` posed by the LLMs were mainly `offering` further assistance which participants seemed to mostly ignore.

Definition of Role. Defining one's role in a conversation can serve as social positioning or establishing context. For effectively prompting LLMs, defining a persona or role is an established technique [38]. As this prompting technique hints that participants do not consider the LLM a conversational partner but rather a tool, we here consider queries issued by participants. Eight participants started their unguided data search by clarifying their own role, for example by stating, *As a researcher I am interested in ...* (id = 20). In the same unguided task, only 4 participants assigned a specific role to the LLM, for example, *You are an expert computer science researcher based in ...* (id = 37). Of those 4 participants, 3 had defined their own role and a role for the LLM, 1 participant defined a role only for the LLM but not for themself. In the guided task (here the LLM already had an assigned role), 8 participants also defined their own role. Three participants stated their own role in both tasks, 5 researchers each stated their own role only in one of the tasks.

Table 6. Top 10 emojis (and frequency) in ChatGPT's responses in both tasks.

Rank	1	2	3	4	5	6	7	8	9	10
Unguided	🔗 (37)	🚀 (24)	📄 (12)	🔍 (11)	📍 (11)	📺 (11)	📌 (10)	✅ (9)	📊 (5)	😊 (4)
Guided	📄 (63)	📌 (34)	🚀 (27)	🔗 (27)	📊 (11)	📎 (11)	✅ (10)	🔹 (7)	😊 (5)	❌ (4)

Emojis. Written conversations between humans contain emojis to provide additional social cues [8]. Using emojis in chatbots can increase the perceived warmth (not competence) and increase user satisfaction, especially in hedonic scenarios [41]. So for this aspect we investigate participants' queries and LLMs' outputs in the unguided and guided tasks. Participants and Perplexity never used any emoji. ChatGPT used 264 emojis in total and 35 unique ones in its responses. In the unguided task, ChatGPT used fewer emojis (127) than in the guided one (137), but the choice of emojis was more varied in the unguided scenario: 32 unique emojis in the unguided vs. 14 in the guided task. Table 6 displays the ten most common emojis in the ChatGPT responses. Most emojis used by ChatGPT were used to structure its findings. For example, a found data source was presented with 📄 preceding a data or a study title, 📊 referred to the actual dataset, 📌 was followed by a short summary of the paper or study, and 🔗 or a 🔍 referred to further sources or information about the finding. 📺 (used 11 times in the unguided task) was solely used for one participant who was doing research on telenovelas. 🚀 was very often used at the end of the LLM response conveying an informal sense of excitement, success, and ambition.

User Experience. We examine whether there are differences in the participants' user experience when they use the LLM freely compared to when the LLM is primed to behave as a persona. This aspect considers the participants' evaluation of their user experience in the unguided and guided tasks. Using the User Experience Questionnaire (UEQ) [21], participants rated their search mainly positive and the ratings do not differ significantly between both tasks (see Table 7). The lowest mean scores were given for the `Dependability` subscale. This subscale measures whether users feel in control and whether the interaction with a tool is secure and predictable. The highest mean scores were reached for the `Perspicuity` subscale which measures whether it is easy to get familiar with a tool and to learn how to use it.

For the NASA Task Load Index [13] the mean scores are mostly close to the middle scale point of 3.5 (see Table 7). Only *Physical demand* and *Frustration* have lower scores than 3.0 in both tasks. `Performance` is rated highest. We did not find a significant difference between the unguided and the guided task.

Discussion. For data search in a typical digital library setting, it has been observed that users re-issued queries in almost 70% of cases [3]. While our study found few repeated phrases in the conversational search setting, our sessions were typically focused on finding datasets for one pre-defined information need. Considering the dialogue acts, we see differences between participants and LLMs for both tasks in actions, offers, questions, answers and more social ones such as appreciation. From this we derive that participants seem to not treat the LLM as a conversational partner but rather as a tool.

Few participants defined their and the LLM's roles. We did not encounter differences between the two tasks so the pre-definition of a persona does not seem to change our participants' behaviour in this regard.

The absence of emojis in participants' queries could stem from the fact, that they were not familiar with using emojis on a computer keyboard. Contrasting Perplexity, ChatGPT incorporates emojis into its responses, mainly for structuring purposes, but some (🚀) also convey non-obvious informal meaning. Emojis can be used to match an interlocutor's interaction style [4] but our participants did not start using emojis after ChatGPT used them and ChatGPT did not stop using emojis after participants did not respond to them.

We did not find significant differences in the user experience between the unguided and guided task. This is surprising, as the LLMs showed different conversational actions but this seems to not have affected users' perception.

Regarding aspects of humanisation in the interactions between participants and LLMs we conclude: **While LLMs seem to hold a conversation and strive to appear human-like to an extent, participants do not appear to recognise them as equal conversational partners. Instead they rather**

Table 7. Participants' user experience in the unguided and guided tasks.

	Unguided		Guided		Paired t-test		N
User experience questionnaire (UEQ)							
Attractiveness	1.0108	(0.1884)	1.1398	(0.2038)	−0.6329	(0.5316)	31
Efficiency	1.2500	(0.1912)	1.1935	(0.2208)	−0.2670	(0.7965)	31
Perspicuity	1.7734	(0.1376)	1.5938	(0.1633)	1.0738	(0.2912)	32
Dependability	0.8214	(0.1329)	0.9018	(0.1856)	−0.5068	(0.6164)	28
Stimulation	1.0391	(0.1935)	1.0938	(0.2213)	−0.2297	(0.8198)	32
NASA Task Load Index							
Mental demand	3.5938	(0.2651)	3.5000	(0.2731)	0.3728	(0.7118)	32
Physical demand	1.6875	(0.1928)	1.9063	(0.2349)	−1.0450	(0.3041)	32
Temporal demand	3.6875	(0.2673)	3.1250	(0.2901)	1.8688	(0.0711)	32
Performance	3.8125	(0.3189)	3.5000	(0.2910)	0.8808	(0.3852)	32
Effort	3.3750	(0.2408)	2.9375	(0.2150)	1.4222	(0.1650)	32
Frustration	2.9375	(0.3076)	2.9375	(0.3010)	(0.0000)	1.0000	32

Notes. Mean with (standard error) for five UEQ scales [21] and the NASA Task Load Index [13] and two data search scenarios (unguided and guided), t-statistic and two-tailed p-value for paired t-test performed between two data search scenarios, number of observations. A Wilcoxon Signed Rank was performed for Efficiency (UEQ) and the z-statistic and exact p-value reported. UEQ scales range from -3 to + 3, NASA Task Load Index scales range from 1 to 7.

use them as tools. Prompting an LLM to behave as a persona does change its way of interacting but does not influence users' experience using it.

4.3 RQ$_3$: Differences Between Groups of Participants

We expect that searching for data with an LLM is affected by participants' previous experience with research data and whether LLMs are already being used while doing research. To address our third research question targeting differences between experience groups, we consider the following two aspects: 1. Do interactions with the LLM differ between participants experienced and inexperienced with *searching for or working with data*? 2. Do interactions with the LLM differ between participants experienced and inexperienced with *using LLM*? 3. Does the user experience differ between participants experienced and inexperienced with *searching for or working with data*? 4. Does the user experience differ between participants experienced and inexperienced with *using LLMs*?

During the interview before the data search tasks and in the survey at the end of the session, we asked participants to assess their experience in using LLMs and with searching and working with data using LLMs. We divided participants into two groups (high/low) each based on their responses. Our detailed results can be found in our online appendix on GitHub.

Interactions with LLMs and Experience Groups. We see few differences in session characteristics between experience groups: Participants with high experience in working with data used more queries than participants with low experience in the unguided task. Also in the unguided task, participants with high LLM experience formulated longer queries than participants with low LLM experience, while in the guided task, they used fewer queries than participants with low LLM experience.

User Experience and Experience Groups. Participants with high data search experience perceived the data search with an LLM less efficient in both tasks and they perceived higher temporal demand in the unguided task compared to participants with high experience. In the guided task they also found the LLM search less stimulating. Participants with high LLM experience rated all five UEQ subscales in the guided task higher than participants with low LLM experience. However, also for the guided task and using the NASA Task Load Index, they rated the LLMs' performance lower than their peers with low experience.

Discussion. In interacting with the LLM, we especially saw differences for participants who used LLMs frequently and are therefore experienced in using LLMs. Compared to participants with less experience, they formulated significantly longer queries in the unguided task and significantly fewer queries in the guided task. At the same time they perceived higher `Attractiveness`, `Efficiency`, `Perspicuity`, `Dependability`, and `Stimulation` when working on the guided task. Participants with low LLM experience, on the other hand, rated the LLMs' performance higher. They might have been positively surprised by how well the LLMs work without prior experience with the validity of LLMs' results. That participants with low experience in data search reported lower temporal demand in the unguided task, compared to participants with higher experience, could be a sign that this group does not perceive the task as time-critical because they did not grasp the exact data requirements and were not aware of potential steps in the data search that might need to follow.

Regarding differences between experience groups we conclude: **Participants with prior LLM experience formulate longer queries and, when the LLM is prompted to act as a persona, rate their user experience more positively. Participants experienced in data search rate the data search with an LLM as less efficient than participants with low data search experience.**

4.4 Discussion and Limitations

LLMs strive to appear friendly, helpful and approachable, especially in the guided scenario. These efforts do not seem to be reciprocated by participants, even though they issue natural language queries, partially respond to LLMs, and keep the conversation flowing without repetition, so they engage in the conversation. Still, LLMs are used as tools rather than seen as equal conversational partners. Therefore, we assume they do not naturally replace the typical data talk with a human colleague. Prompting the LLM to behave as a persona (as seen in the guided task) does change the LLMs' as well as participants' behaviour - the queries are longer and queries appear to become even more natural. Participants who are experienced in data search find the LLM data search generally less efficient. But when prior experience with LLMs exists, users' report higher satisfaction with the tool when prompted to behave as a persona. While ChatGPT was shown to have problems in explaining scientific publications and exploring data from scientific databases [1], we did not specifically encounter these problems with our chosen model and setting.

Our study comes with some **limitations**: 1. We only investigated two settings and two LLMs in an explorative study. Broader settings and also more targeted hypotheses will be needed to expand our knowledge in this area. 2. While 32 participants from different domains and with different expertise levels is remarkable for this type of study, further and larger user studies representing different domains equally are needed. These limitations lead to a limited generalisability of the conclusions resulting from our analyses. We consciously refrain from considering or judging the correctness of results provided by the LLMs. Fabrication remains an open problem with LLMs [15,24].

5 Conclusion

We presented our user study focusing on researchers' information interaction behaviour using LLMs for data search with 32 participants from different domains. We quantitatively and qualitatively analysed our collected interaction data and found the following: 1. LLMs seemed to strive to connect with our participants or please them over both tasks. Still, users did not accept them as equal conversational partners which leads to the conclusion of LLMs not being a suitable replacement for a human interlocutor in data talk purposes. 2. Prompting the LLMs to behave as the colleague of a participant changed the LLMs' and participants' behaviours. Participants experienced with LLMs reported better user experience with the pre-prompted sessions compared to the unguided setting.

Future work will continue to investigate the plethora of data we collected in our user study. First, we want to focus on users' expression of information needs during the conversations with LLMs. We will do a more in-depth analysis of the dialogue acts in combination with the think-aloud data to extract more abstract data search patterns. These patterns will then also be compared to participants' usual data search techniques. Another line of work will focus on examining the encountered differences between ChatGPT and Perplexity and the effects on users' behaviour. Additionally, we intend to investigate participants' information experience more. We will for example investigate, if personas are accepted by participants or only tolerated.

References

1. AlSagri, H.S., Farhat, F., Sohail, S.S., Saudagar, A.K.J.: Chatgpt or gemini: who makes the better scientific writing assistant? J. Acad. Ethics 1–15 (2024). https://doi.org/10.1007/s10805-024-09549-0
2. Bogireddy, S., Dasari, N.: Comparative analysis of chatgpt-4 and llama: performance evaluation on text summarization, data analysis, and question answering. pp. 1–7 (2024). https://doi.org/10.1109/ICCCNT61001.2024.10725662
3. Carevic, Z., Roy, D., Mayr, P.: Characteristics of dataset retrieval sessions: experiences from a real-life digital library. In: Hall, M., Merčun, T., Risse, T., Duchateau, F. (eds.) TPDL 2020. LNCS, vol. 12246, pp. 185–193. Springer, Cham (2020). https://doi.org/10.1007/978-3-030-54956-5_14
4. Cavalheiro, B.P., Rodrigues, D.L., Prada, M.: Who (and with whom) uses more emoji? exploring individual, relational, and motivational characteristics driving emoji use. Telematics Inform. **83**, 102023 (2023). https://doi.org/10.1016/j.tele.2023.102023
5. Chapman, A., et al.: Dataset search: a survey. VLDB J. **29**(1), 251–272 (2020). https://doi.org/10.1007/S00778-019-00564-X
6. Costa, L., Silva, J.R.: Dendro: a FAIR, open-source data sharing platform. In: Doucet, A., Isaac, A., Golub, K., Aalberg, T., Jatowt, A. (eds.) TPDL 2019. LNCS, vol. 11799, pp. 384–387. Springer, Cham (2019). https://doi.org/10.1007/978-3-030-30760-8_39
7. Crespo Garrido, I.D.R., Loureiro García, M., Gutleber, J.: The value of an open scientific data and documentation platform in a global project: the case of Zenodo, pp. 181–200 (2025). https://doi.org/10.1007/978-3-031-60931-2_14
8. Derks, D., Bos, A., von Grumbkow, J.: Emoticons in computer-mediated communication: social motives and social context. Cyberpsychology Behav. **11**, 99–101 (2008). https://doi.org/10.1089/cpb.2007.9926. The impact of the Internet, multimedia and virtual reality on behavior and society
9. Ericsson, K.A., Simon, H.A.: Verbal reports as data. Psychol. Rev. **87**(3), 215–251 (1980). https://doi.org/10.1037/0033-295x.87.3.215
10. Friedrich, T.: Looking for data. https://doi.org/10.18452/22173. http://edoc.hu-berlin.de/18452/22813
11. Gregory, K.M., Cousijn, H., Groth, P., Scharnhorst, A., Wyatt, S.: Understanding data search as a socio-technical practice. J. Inf. Sci. **46**(4), 459–475 (2019). https://doi.org/10.1177/0165551519837182
12. Haberl, A., Fleiß, J., Kowald, D., Thalmann, S.: Take the atrain. introducing an interface for the accessible transcription of interviews (2024). https://doi.org/10.1016/j.jbef.2024.100891
13. Hart, S.G., Staveland, L.E.: Development of NASA-TLX (task load index): results of empirical and theoretical research. Hum. Mental Workload **1**(3), 139–183 (1988)
14. Hou, G., Lian, Q.: Benchmarking of commercial large language models: Chatgpt, mistral, and llama (2024). https://doi.org/10.21203/rs.3.rs-4376810/v1
15. Huang, L., et al.: A survey on hallucination in large language models: principles, taxonomy, challenges, and open questions. arXiv abs/2311.05232 (2023). https://api.semanticscholar.org/CorpusID:265067168
16. Hulsebos, M., Lin, W., Shankar, S., Parameswaran, A.: It took longer than i was expecting: why is dataset search still so hard? In: HILDA@SIGMOD 2024, pp. 1–4.https://doi.org/10.1145/3665939.3665959

17. Jaspers, M., Steen, T., Bos, C., Geenen, M.: The think aloud method: a guide to user interface design. Int. J. Med. Informatics **73**(11–12), 781–795 (2004). https://doi.org/10.1016/j.ijmedinf.2004.08.003
18. Kacprzak, E., Koesten, L., Ibáñez, L.D., Blount, T., Tennison, J., Simperl, E.: Characterising dataset search–an analysis of search logs and data requests. J. Web Seman. **55**, 37–55 (2019). https://doi.org/10.1016/j.websem.2018.11.003
19. Kacprzak, E., Koesten, L., Tennison, J., Simperl, E.: Characterising dataset search queries. In: WWW 2018, pp. 1485–1488 (2018). https://doi.org/10.1145/3184558.3191597
20. Kreutz, C.K., Blum, M., Schaer, P., Schenkel, R., Weyers, B.: Evaluating digital library search systems by using formal process modelling. In: JCDL 2023, pp. 1–12 (2023). https://doi.org/10.1109/JCDL57899.2023.00058
21. Laugwitz, B., Held, T., Schrepp, M.: Construction and evaluation of a user experience questionnaire. In: Holzinger, A. (ed.) USAB 2008. LNCS, vol. 5298, pp. 63–76. Springer, Heidelberg (2008). https://doi.org/10.1007/978-3-540-89350-9_6
22. Liao, Z., et al.: LLMs as research tools: a large scale survey of researchers' usage and perceptions (2024). https://arxiv.org/abs/2411.05025
23. LimeSurvey Project Team / Carsten Schmitz: LimeSurvey: An Open Source survey tool. LimeSurvey Project, Hamburg, Germany (2012). https://www.limesurvey.org
24. Minaee, S., et al.: Large language models: a survey (2025). https://arxiv.org/abs/2402.06196
25. Noushad, B., Van Gerven, P.W.M., de Bruin, A.B.H.: Twelve tips for applying the think-aloud method to capture cognitive processes. Med. Teach. 1–6 (2023). https://doi.org/10.1080/0142159x.2023.2289847
26. Papenmeier, A., Krämer, T., Friedrich, T., Hienert, D., Kern, D.: Genuine information needs of social scientists looking for data. Proc. Assoc. Inf. Sci. Technol. **58**(1), 292–302 (2021). https://doi.org/10.1002/pra2.457
27. Perry, A., Kreutz, C.K., Friedrich, T.: Data discovery with large language models. (Version 1.0.0) [Data set]. GESIS, Köln. https://doi.org/10.4232/1.14529 (2025)
28. Rodrigues, J., Lopes, C.T.: Solutions for data sharing and storage: a comparative analysis of data repositories. In: TPDL 2022, pp. 512–517. Springer International Publishing, Cham (2022)
29. Roy, D., Carevic, Z., Mayr, P.: Studying retrievability of publications and datasets in an integrated retrieval system. In: JCDL 2022 (2022). https://doi.org/10.1145/3529372.3530931
30. Sandmann, S., Riepenhausen, S., Plagwitz, L., Varghese, J.: Systematic analysis of ChatGPT, google search and llama 2 for clinical decision support tasks. Nature Commun. **15** (2024). https://doi.org/10.1038/s41467-024-46411-8
31. Seth, I., et al.: Comparing the efficacy of large language models ChatGPT, BARD, and Bing AI in providing information on rhinoplasty: an observational study. Aesthetic Surg. J. Open Forum **5** (2023). https://api.semanticscholar.org/CorpusID:261844199
32. Shukla, M., Goyal, I., Gupta, B., Sharma, J.: A comparative study of ChatGPT, Gemini, and perplexity. Int. J. Innovative Res. Comput. Sci. Technol. **12**, 10–15 (2024). https://doi.org/10.55524/ijircst.2024.12.4.2
33. da Silva, L.M.P., Samhi, J., Khomh, F.: ChatGPT vs llama: impact, reliability, and challenges in stack overflow discussions (2024). https://api.semanticscholar.org/CorpusID:267657739

34. Skopal, T., Klímek, J., Nečaský, M.: Improving findability of open data beyond data catalogs. In: Proceedings of the 21st International Conference on Information Integration and Web-based Applications & Services, pp. 413–417. iiWAS2019, Association for Computing Machinery. https://doi.org/10.1145/3366030.3366095
35. Smith, M., et al.: Dspace: an open source dynamic digital repository. D-Lib Magazine **9** (2003). https://doi.org/10.1045/january2003-smith
36. Stolcke, A., et al.: Dialogue act modeling for automatic tagging and recognition of conversational speech. Comput. Linguist. **26**(3), 339–374 (2000). https://aclanthology.org/J00-3003/
37. Wangsa, K., Karim, S., Gide, E., Elkhodr, M.: A systematic review and comprehensive analysis of pioneering ai chatbot models from education to healthcare: ChatGPT, bard, llama, Ernie and grok. Future Internet **16** (2024). https://doi.org/10.3390/fi16070219
38. White, J., et al.: A prompt pattern catalog to enhance prompt engineering with ChatGPT. In: Proceedings of the 30th Conference on Pattern Languages of Programs (2023). https://doi.org/10.5555/3721041.3721046
39. Wynholds, L.A., Wallis, J.C., Borgman, C.L., Sands, A., Traweek, S.: Data, data use, and scientific inquiry: two case studies of data practices. In: JCDL 2012, pp. 19–22 (2012). https://doi.org/10.1145/2232817.2232822
40. Yoon, A.: Role of communication in data reuse. In: ASIST 2017, vol. 54, pp. 463–471 (2017). https://doi.org/10.1002/PRA2.2017.14505401050
41. Yu, S., Zhao, L.: Emojifying chatbot interactions: an exploration of emoji utilization in human-chatbot communications. Telematics Inform. **86**, 102071 (2024). https://doi.org/10.1016/j.tele.2023.102071
42. Zhao, Y., Meroño-Peñuela, A., Simperl, E.: User experience in dataset search platform interfaces. CoRR abs/2403.15861 (2024). https://doi.org/10.48550/ARXIV.2403.15861

Generating Synthetic Data with Large Language Models for Low-Resource Sentence Retrieval

Davide Caffagni[1(✉)], Federico Cocchi[1,2], Anna Mambelli[3,4], Fabio Tutrone[5], Marco Zanella[6,7], Marcella Cornia[3], and Rita Cucchiara[1]

[1] Department of Engineering "Enzo Ferrari", University of Modena and Reggio Emilia, Modena, Italy
{davide.caffagni,federico.cocchi,rita.cucchiara}@unimore.it
[2] Department of Informatics, University of Pisa, Pisa, Italy
[3] Department of Education and Humanities, University of Modena and Reggio Emilia, Reggio Emilia, Italy
{anna.mambelli,marcella.cornia}@unimore.it
[4] Fondazione per le scienze religiose (FSCIRE), Bologna, Italy
[5] Department of Cultures and Societies, University of Palermo, Palermo, Italy
fabio.tutrone@unipa.it
[6] Department of Mathematics, University of Padua, Padua, Italy
marco.zanella@unipd.it
[7] Department of History and Cultures, University of Bologna, Bologna, Italy

Abstract. Sentence similarity search is a fundamental task in information retrieval, enabling applications such as search engines, question answering, and textual analysis. However, retrieval systems often struggle when training data are scarce, as is the case for low-resource languages or specialized domains such as ancient texts. To address this challenge, we propose a novel paradigm for domain-specific sentence similarity search, where the embedding space is shaped by a combination of limited real data and a large amount of synthetic data generated by Large Language Models (LLMs). Specifically, we employ LLMs to generate domain-specific sentence pairs and fine-tune a sentence embedding model, effectively distilling knowledge from the LLM to the retrieval model. We validate our method through a case study on biblical intertextuality in Latin, demonstrating that synthetic data augmentation significantly improves retrieval effectiveness in a domain with scarce annotated resources. More broadly, our approach offers a scalable and adaptable framework for enhancing retrieval in domain-specific contexts. Source code and trained models are available at https://github.com/aimagelab/biblical-retrieval-synthesis.

Keywords: Large Language Models · Sentence Embeddings · Sentence Similarity Search · Digital Humanities

D. Caffagni and F. Cocchi—Equal contribution.

W.-T. Balke et al. (Eds.): TPDL 2025, LNCS 16097, pp. 36–52, 2026.
https://doi.org/10.1007/978-3-032-05409-8_4

1 Introduction

Identifying semantically similar sentences constitutes a fundamental challenge in information retrieval, significantly impacting applications such as search engines, question answering, and textual analysis tools [8,10,29,32,40]. The efficacy of retrieval performance is significantly contingent upon the accessibility of high-quality training data, which is frequently limited in low-resource settings. This issue is especially pronounced in specialized textual domains like ancient texts and historical documents, where current datasets are either inadequately annotated or nonexistent [17,23,36]. Addressing this limitation is thus critical for advancing research in fields such as historical linguistics, philology, and domain-specific NLP.

Recent advancements in Large Language Models (LLMs) [1,2,5,37] offer new opportunities for tackling data scarcity by generating high-quality synthetic data to enhance NLP and machine learning applications. LLM-generated data have proven effective in tasks such as text classification, machine translation, document retrieval, and captioning [6,15,22,24,33,39]. However, their potential for refining sentence embedding models in domain-specific retrieval tasks remains underexplored. In this work, we propose a framework where an LLM generates synthetic sentence pairs to fine-tune a domain-specific embedding space, shaping the retrieval model through newly generated knowledge. Here, the LLM acts as a teacher, producing positive and negative sentence examples that guide the retrieval model in constructing a more effective embedding space (Fig. 1).

We evaluate our approach through a case study on biblical intertextuality in Latin. Latin biblical texts, including Jerome's Vulgate and pre-Vulgate Latin translations [31,42], exhibit complex intertextual relationships with later Christian works. Patristic texts, in fact, frequently reference biblical passages through explicit quotations, paraphrases, or subtle allusions. Identifying these intertextual links is a challenging retrieval task due to the intricate syntactic and semantic variations inherent in ancient Latin texts. Additionally, the lack of annotated corpora for Latin intertextual retrieval underscores the need for alternative methods, such as synthetic data generation, to support model training.

In summary, our contributions are threefold. First, we introduce a new paradigm for domain-specific sentence similarity search, leveraging LLM-generated samples to enhance retrieval models in low-resource settings. Second, we apply this approach to retrieving biblical passages referenced in Latin patristic texts, fine-tuning a Latin-aware sentence embedding space [3,7,30] with newly generated samples. Third, we demonstrate that LLM-generated data significantly improve retrieval effectiveness, highlighting the broader applicability of this method. Finally, we will release our models and collected data as open-source resources, promoting further progress in scientific and humanistic research.

2 Related Work

Synthetic Data Generation for Information Retrieval. The utilization of synthetic data has gained significant attention in the field of information

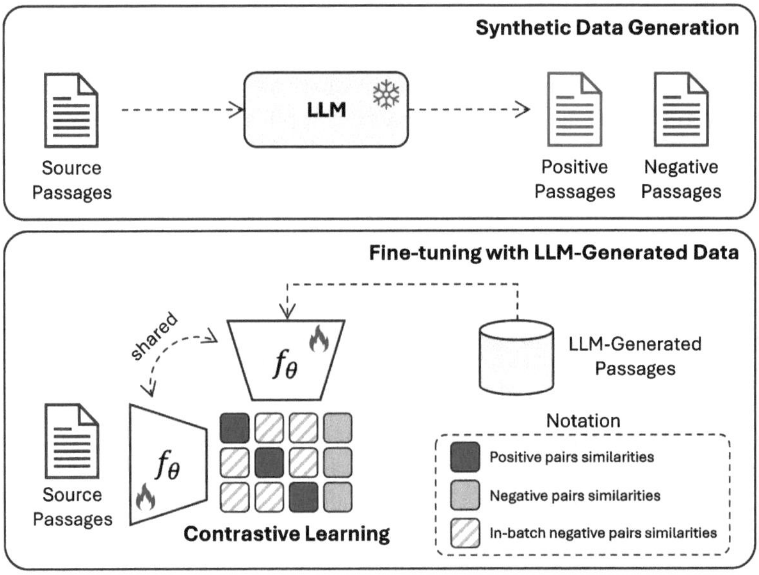

Fig. 1. Overview of the proposed method for generating positive and negative samples to fine-tune a text embedding model, enhancing its performance in sentence retrieval.

retrieval, leading to the development of various approaches aimed at enhancing retrieval performance through AI-generated data. A key area of research focuses on synthesizing queries for unlabeled documents to improve document representation and train retrieval models. Methods such as Doc2Query [24], InPars [4], and Promptagator [12] generate synthetic queries to facilitate these objectives. Additionally, GPL [38] utilizes a cross-encoder framework to assign pseudo-labels to query-document pairs, while Query2Doc [41] employs LLMs with few-shot prompting to produce pseudo-documents for query expansion. Similarly, the work proposed in [39] explores the generation of high-quality text embeddings using only synthetic data produced by GPT-4, requiring minimal training steps. A striking difference with this work is that we leverage synthetic data to fine-tune a compact embedding model, rather than an LLM. Also, unlike existing methods that primarily focus on contemporary languages, our work investigates the generation of LLM-based synthetic data to enhance the encoding of textual sentences in ancient and low-resource languages.

Natural Language Understanding for Ancient Languages. The field of natural language understanding faces unique challenges when applied to ancient and low-resource languages, due to the scarcity of labeled data, orthographic variations, and morphological richness. Unlike modern high-resource languages, ancient texts often lack large-scale corpora necessary for training deep learning models. To overcome these challenges, prior works [26] have explored unsupervised domain adaptation and transfer learning to improve textual representations for ancient documents. Recent advances in multilingual pre-trained language models [11,27] have also enabled progress in low-resource ancient languages by leveraging cross-lingual knowledge transfer [16]. Additionally, efforts to train BERT-based text embeddings on ancient corpora have led to specialized models for Latin, Ancient Greek, and other ancient languages [3,7,30,35,36]. However, these models often struggle with sentence similarity tasks due to the limited size of their training corpora, resulting in poor retrieval performance. To address this limitation, we propose using LLMs to generate high-quality synthetic data tailored to improve retrieval in ancient and low-resource languages. To the best of our knowledge, this is the first work to leverage modern LLMs for synthetic data generation in historical sentence retrieval, with a specific focus on Latin biblical corpora.

You are given a passage from an ancient Latin Bible. Your mission is to generate a positive and a negative passage for a text retrieval task in JSON format. The JSON object must contain the following keys:
- **"positive_passage"**: a string, a positive passage that is different from the source passage but has the same meaning. It should be ***longer than*** the source passage.
- **"negative_passage"**: a string, a negative passage that only appears related to the source passage. It should be ***of the same length as*** the source passage.
Both the positive and negative passages must be in Latin. Your output must always be a JSON object only, do not explain yourself or output anything else. Be creative!
Source passage: ***In principio creavit Deus caelum et terram***

{**"positive_passage"**: "***In principio omnium Deus creavit caelum et terram et omnia quae in eis sunt***";
"negative_passage": "***In tempore antiquo homo exploravit caelum et mare***"}

Fig. 2. Example of the prompt template employed for generating positive and negative samples.

3 Proposed Method

We propose to improve sentence retrieval performance in low-resource settings using LLM-generated synthetic data. To this end, we first employ an LLM to generate both semantically similar (positive) and dissimilar (negative) sentences based on a given reference. Then, we fine-tune a sentence embedding model with these samples to improve text representations. Finally, we apply the proposed approach to a case study on Latin biblical corpora, where the objective is to retrieve intertextual references within ancient exegetical texts.

3.1 Generating Synthetic Data

We utilize an LLM to expand and enrich the training set needed to fine-tune an embedding model for sentence similarity search. For doing this, we propose to distill knowledge from an advanced LLM into a smaller embedding model f_θ by fine-tuning it on data generated by the LLM. First, having access to a source text corpus, we want to create triplets of source, positive, and negative passages (d_i, d_i^+, d_i^-) to train f_θ with a contrastive learning approach. As shown in Fig. 2, given a source passage d_i, we prompt the LLM to generate d_i^+, that is, a piece of text that differs from d_i, and yet retains the same meaning. At the same time, we also ask the LLM to generate d_i^-, which is a negative passage that only looks similar to d_i. This can be thought of as a hard-negative mining strategy, that is known to be beneficial for contrastive learning [14,19,43]. Finally, to enhance the variety of the training data, we specify in the prompt to generate positive and negative passages that are either longer, shorter or of the same length as d_i [39]. Thanks to the instruction-following capabilities of modern LLMs, we ask them to generate data in a convenient JSON dictionary.

3.2 Fine-Tuning with LLM-Generated Samples

Starting with a pre-trained embedding model f_θ, which generates an h-dimensional embedding from a textual input, we aim to fine-tune it with contrastive learning [9,25,28,34] for the information retrieval task. Given a source passage d_i, the objective is to minimize the distance in the embedding space with its positive passage d_i^+, while maximizing the distance with negative passages. We train f_θ to minimize the InfoNCE loss [25], defined as:

$$\mathcal{L} = -\sum_{d_i \in \mathcal{B}} \log \frac{\exp\left(s(d_i, d_i^+)/\tau\right)}{\exp\left(s(d_i, d_i^+)/\tau\right) + \sum_{d^- \in \mathcal{N}_i^k} \exp\left(s(d_i, d^-)/\tau\right)}, \tag{1}$$

where $s(\cdot)$[1] is the cosine similarity function, τ is a learnable temperature, and $\mathcal{N}_i^k$ is the set of k negative passages for the passage d_i. Initially, we set $\mathcal{N}_i^k$ to contain the negative passage generated by the LLM, plus all the in-batch passages differing from d_i^+. However, we find that contrasting against all the in-batch passages harms performance, so we propose only considering the in-batch top-k most similar passages to d_i other than d_i^+ as negatives. We posit that most passages in a batch $\mathcal{B}$ are naturally unrelated to d_i, and further pushing them apart moves their embeddings too far away from their initial location in the embedding space of the pre-trained model f_θ, altering their original meaning.

[1] The cosine similarity is measured between a pair of *embeddings* of passages. To simplify the notation, we omit the embedding model in Eq. 1 and throughout the paper, *e.g.* we just write $s(d_i, d_i^+)$ in place of $s(f_\theta(d_i), f_\theta(d_i^+))$.

3.3 A Case Study on Latin Biblical Corpora

Corpora Description. To evaluate our approach, we focus on the task of identifying intertextual references between patristic commentaries and biblical passages in Latin. This domain presents a challenging case study for our method due to its inherent data scarcity and complex semantic relationships. The biblical corpora used consist of two distinct Latin versions of the Bible: the *Vulgate* (`W_VULG`) and the so-called *Vetus Latina* (`S_VL`) [31,42]. These versions exhibit subtle linguistic and stylistic differences, making them an ideal testbed for evaluating semantic similarity search in a low-resource language setting.

As a source of intertextual references, we use Augustine's *De Genesi ad litteram libri duodecim* [44], a pivotal work in the Christian exegetical tradition. This commentary on the Book of Genesis explicitly and implicitly interacts with multiple versions of the Latin Bible through various forms of reference, from direct quotations to subtle allusions. This variety of intertextual relationships presents a particularly challenging retrieval task, as the lexical and syntactic connections between a commentary passage and its biblical source can range from obvious to nearly imperceptible.

Annotation Methodology. Intertextual references in Augustine's commentary were systematically annotated using the INCEpTION annotation platform [21]. Each reference was classified according to its source (`W_VULG` or `S_VL`), its location within the Bible (book, chapter, verse, *e.g.* `Gen.3.1`), and assigned a similarity score ranging from 0 to 1 based on lexical overlap. This scoring system creates a spectrum of reference types: high scores (near 1) represent direct quotations, while lower scores indicate paraphrases or thematic allusions with minimal lexical overlap. This annotated dataset allows us to evaluate how effectively our synthetic data generation approach enhances retrieval across different types of intertextual relationships, with particular interest in the challenging cases of subtle allusions that traditional retrieval methods often fail to capture.

4 Experiments

4.1 Experimental Setup

Training Data. For our experiments, we use the two Latin biblical corpora previosly introduced. Specifically, from the `W_VULG` corpus, we collect 35k unique passages (each corresponding to a biblical verse), employing 5k for validation during training. From the `S_VL` corpus, we collect 23k passages, of which 22k have correspondences in `W_VULG`. This partial overlap occurs because different versions of the Bible may vary in length and contain differing numbers of passages, leading to discrepancies in verse availability between the two corpora.

For each of the 30k training passages from `W_VULG`, we employ GPT-4 to generate corresponding positive and negative passages following the process detailed in Sect. 3.1. We use `W_VULG` as it can be seen as a superset of `S_VL`. The quality of this synthetic data was validated by experts in ancient languages, who manually evaluated a subset of 100 generated samples.

During training, we construct positive pairs in two ways: (i) using the GPT-4 generated positive samples, and (ii) leveraging corresponding passages between the two biblical versions when available. For negative passages, we exclusively use the GPT-4 generated samples. At training time, we randomly select one of the two positive options for each sample, ensuring variety in the training data. Sample GPT-4 generated passages are shown in Fig. 3.

Fig. 3. Synthetic positive and negative passages generated by GPT-4, starting from a source passage from W_VULG. Not only GPT-4 can fluently write Latin text, but it also accommodates the request concerning the length of the generated sentence. When choosing the positive passage d_i^+ at training time, we randomly select either the synthetic passage or the corresponding verse from S_VL, if available.

Table 1. Distribution of annotated references across similarity score ranges for the two biblical corpora, W_VULG (*Vulgate*) and S_VL (*Vetus Latina*). The total number of biblical passages in each corpus is also provided.

Corpus		# Passages	# Queries				
			hard	medium	easy	quote	**All**
W_VULG		35,057	51	50	46	45	192
S_VL		23,096	45	25	24	90	184
	W_VULG ∩ S_VL	22,759					

Evaluation Data. Our test set consists of the annotated references from Augustine's commentary: 192 references to W_VULG and 184 to S_VL. Based on the similarity scores described in Sect. 3.3, we divide our evaluation into four distinct difficulty categories. References with similarity scores in the range [0.0 – 0.25) form the `hard` split, representing passages with minimal lexical overlap, typically subtle allusions. Those with scores in [0.25 – 0.50) constitute the `medium` split, indicating moderate lexical overlap. The `easy` split includes references with scores in [0.50–0.75), showing substantial lexical overlap. Finally, references with scores in [0.75 – 1.0] make up the `quote` split, often representing direct quotations with high lexical overlap.

Table 1 summarizes the distribution of queries across these categories for both biblical corpora. In our experiments, we report performance on both the full query set (containing all references) and specifically on the `hard` subset, which presents the most challenging cases for retrieval systems. This hard split contains 51 queries for `W_VULG` and 45 for `S_VL`, and correctly retrieving the referred passage is of practical importance for classical philologists, historians, and religious scholars. For human experts, as well as traditional lexical matching techniques, it is indeed trivial to identify biblical verses when they are reported literally, while the real interest is in finding out whenever Augustine alludes to the Bible without explicitly referring to it.

Table 2. Results on the `W_VULG` corpus comparing the proposed fine-tuning strategy using LLM-generated synthetic data against standard fine-tuning (without generated samples) and the original (non-fine-tuned) model. Similarities are computed using either the CLS token or token averaging as pooling function.

		Corpus: `W_VULG` (All)					
Model	**Pooling**	R@1	R@2	R@3	R@5	R@10	R@20
Latin BERT [3]	`CLS` Token	18.2	24.5	26.6	28.1	29.7	34.9
w/ standard fine-tuning		**43.8**	47.9	**51.6**	54.7	62.0	**66.1**
w/ fine-tuning on synth. data (**Ours**)		43.2	**49.5**	**51.6**	**57.3**	**63.0**	**66.1**
Latin BERT [3]	Token Avg	33.3	38.0	41.7	44.8	47.9	50.5
w/ standard fine-tuning		44.8	51.0	54.7	58.3	64.1	68.8
w/ fine-tuning on synth. data (**Ours**)		**45.8**	**53.1**	**56.3**	**58.9**	**65.6**	**70.3**
LaBERTa [30]	`CLS` Token	31.3	39.1	44.3	47.4	55.7	58.3
w/ standard fine-tuning		44.8	51.0	53.6	60.1	64.6	69.8
w/ fine-tuning on synth. data (**Ours**)		**46.4**	**53.1**	**55.7**	**61.5**	**71.4**	**74.5**
LaBERTa [30]	Token Avg	34.4	40.6	43.8	47.9	52.6	56.8
w/ standard fine-tuning		47.4	**54.2**	57.3	64.6	68.2	71.4
w/ fine-tuning on synth. data (**Ours**)		**47.9**	**54.2**	**57.8**	**66.7**	**75.0**	**77.1**

Implementation Details. We train our models on a single NVIDIA A40 GPU for up to 5 h, selecting the checkpoint with the lowest validation loss. We use Adam [20] as optimizer with a learning rate of 1×10^{-6}, a batch size of 128, and

Table 3. Results on the S_VL corpus comparing the proposed fine-tuning strategy using LLM-generated synthetic data against standard fine-tuning (without generated samples) and the original (non-fine-tuned) model. Similarities are computed using either the CLS token or token averaging as pooling function.

		Corpus: S_VL (All)					
Model	**Pooling**	R@1	R@2	R@3	R@5	R@10	R@20
Latin BERT [3]	CLS Token	17.9	22.8	26.1	31.0	34.2	36.4
w/ standard fine-tuning		40.8	46.2	47.8	54.3	60.3	63.0
w/ fine-tuning on synth. data (**Ours**)		**41.3**	**47.3**	**52.2**	**56.0**	**64.1**	**71.2**
Latin BERT [3]	Token Avg	37.0	41.3	44.6	48.9	53.3	55.4
w/ standard fine-tuning		40.8	46.7	51.1	56.0	63.0	67.4
w/ fine-tuning on synth. data (**Ours**)		**42.9**	**49.5**	**52.7**	**59.2**	**67.9**	**72.3**
LaBERTa [30]	CLS Token	29.9	36.4	42.4	47.8	52.7	56.5
w/ standard fine-tuning		42.9	48.9	52.7	60.9	66.3	70.7
w/ fine-tuning on synth. data (**Ours**)		**47.3**	**51.1**	**56.0**	**64.7**	**70.1**	**77.7**
LaBERTa [30]	Token Avg	36.4	40.2	42.4	47.3	48.4	56.0
w/ standard fine-tuning		44.0	46.7	54.9	**63.0**	66.8	72.3
w/ fine-tuning on synth. data (**Ours**)		**48.9**	**52.2**	**56.5**	**63.0**	**71.2**	**78.8**

16-bit precision. The learnable temperature τ is initialized to 0.07. Unless specified, our models are fine-tuned by selecting the in-batch top-5 negatives for each source passage (cf. Eq. 1). At inference time, to accelerate the similarity search process, we employ a FAISS [18] `IndexFlatIP` index, integrating embeddings of all the passages from either W_VULG or S_VL using our fine-tuned models.

BERT-based Embedding Models. We implement f_θ with two BERT-based [13] models: Latin BERT [3] and LaBERTa [30]. Both models were pre-trained with a masked language modeling loss on a Latin corpus. The main difference between them is the pre-training data: Latin BERT employed 642M tokens from a variety of sources spanning the Classical era to the 21st century, whereas LaBERTa was trained on 167M tokens from Corpus Corporum[2]. These models output as many embeddings as the number of tokens in the input passage, each with a dimensionality h of 768. To obtain a single embedding representative of the whole passage, we consider two pooling strategies: either we take the output embedding of the special CLS token, or we compute the average over the full output embedding sequence, excluding the CLS.

[2] https://mlat.uzh.ch.

Table 4. Performance comparison on the **hard** subsets of W_VULG and S_VL corpora (*i.e.*, queries with the lowest similarity to the corresponding biblical verse). Similarities are computed using either the CLS token or token averaging as pooling function.

		Corpus: W_VULG (hard)			Corpus: S_VL (hard)		
Model	**Pooling**	R@1	R@5	R@10	R@1	R@5	R@10
Latin BERT [3]	CLS Token	2.0	2.0	2.0	0.0	2.2	2.2
w/ standard fine-tuning		5.9	15.7	29.4	2.2	15.6	24.4
w/ fine-tuning on synth. data (**Ours**)		**7.8**	**23.5**	**33.3**	**6.7**	**22.2**	**33.3**
Latin BERT [3]	Token Avg	2.0	2.0	5.9	0.0	2.2	4.4
w/ standard fine-tuning		3.9	19.6	31.4	0.0	13.3	26.7
w/ fine-tuning on synth. data (**Ours**)		**11.8**	**25.5**	**37.3**	**8.9**	**26.7**	**37.8**
LaBERTa [30]	CLS Token	2.0	19.6	33.3	2.2	17.8	26.7
w/ standard fine-tuning		15.7	33.3	39.2	6.7	31.1	44.4
w/ fine-tuning on synth. data (**Ours**)		**19.6**	**35.3**	**51.0**	**17.8**	**42.2**	**51.1**
LaBERTa [30]	Token Avg	0.0	5.9	9.8	2.2	2.2	2.2
w/ standard fine-tuning		17.6	37.3	45.1	8.9	**35.6**	44.4
w/ fine-tuning on synth. data (**Ours**)		**19.6**	**39.2**	**54.9**	**15.6**	33.3	**46.7**

Table 5. Ablation study on the contribution of the GPT-4 generated synthetic data (*i.e.*, Pos* and Neg*). Results are reported on the W_VULG and S_VL corpora, using token averaging as pooling strategy.

	Training Data Sampling				Corpus: W_VULG			Corpus: S_VL		
	Pos	Pos*	Neg*	Top-k Neg	R@1	R@5	R@10	R@1	R@5	R@10
	✓	-	-	-	39.1	55.7	61.5	39.1	57.1	62.5
	✓	-	-	✓	44.8	58.3	64.1	40.8	56.0	63.0
	✓	✓	-	✓	44.3	**58.9**	**65.6**	40.8	58.2	65.8
	-	✓	✓	✓	42.2	55.2	62.0	40.8	58.2	64.7
	✓	✓	✓	-	41.7	58.3	63.0	40.7	57.6	65.2
Latin BERT [3]	✓	✓	✓	✓	**45.8**	**58.9**	**65.6**	**42.9**	**59.2**	**67.9**
	✓	-	-	-	42.2	56.3	61.5	41.3	56.0	62.0
	✓	-	-	✓	47.4	64.6	68.2	44.0	63.0	66.8
	✓	✓	-	✓	46.4	65.6	71.9	46.2	**64.1**	69.6
	-	✓	✓	✓	**47.9**	64.1	70.8	47.3	62.0	70.1
	✓	✓	✓	-	43.8	58.9	67.2	44.0	57.1	65.2
LaBERTa [30]	✓	✓	✓	✓	**47.9**	**66.7**	**75.0**	**48.9**	63.0	**71.2**

4.2 Experimental Results

Effectiveness of Synthetic Data Generation. Tables 2 and 3 show the retrieval results on the considered test sets, measured in terms of the average number of queries for which the target passage is retrieved within the first k passages, with $k = \{1, 2, 3, 5, 10, 20\}$. The proposed fine-tuning pipeline is compared against standard fine-tuning, where the models are trained without positive and negative passages generated by GPT-4 but only leveraging the correspondences between `W_VULG` and `S_VL` to build positive pairs for contrastive learning. We also report the zero-shot results of the models as a reference.

As it can be seen in both tables, for both Latin BERT and LaBERTa, taking the average over the output tokens is a better pooling strategy than picking the `CLS` token. Additionally, LaBERTa generally achieves higher scores than Latin BERT across both corpora, despite being pre-trained on a smaller corpus. In all considered settings, it is worth noting that models fine-tuned with our proposed synthetic data pipeline significantly outperform the standard fine-tuning approach, with particularly notable improvements in terms of R@1. Importantly, these results are consistent across both `W_VULG` (Table 2) and `S_VL` (Table 3), even though we generate synthetic data starting from `W_VULG` solely.

The consistency of performance improvements across multiple models, pooling strategies, and different corpora demonstrates the robust transferability of our synthetic data generation approach, highlighting its potential for enhancing retrieval systems in low-resource scenarios.

Results on the Hard Split. Table 4 presents the retrieval results on the most challenging subset of queries from both corpora, the `hard` split. These queries represent biblical references with minimal lexical overlap (*i.e.*, similarity scores between 0.0 and 0.25), typically consisting of subtle allusions that are difficult to identify even for human experts.

The results demonstrate the particular effectiveness of our synthetic data approach in this challenging scenario. For both `W_VULG` and `S_VL`, we observe substantial improvements over the standard fine-tuning approach across all models and pooling strategies. Looking at R@1 scores, our approach achieves relative improvements of up to 202% for Latin BERT with token averaging on `W_VULG` (from 3.9% to 11.8%) and even more dramatic improvements on `S_VL`, where in some cases the standard fine-tuning completely fails to retrieve the correct passage (0.0%) while our approach achieves 8.9%.

LaBERTa models consistently outperform Latin BERT on these challenging queries, with our synthetic data fine-tuning pushing performance to 19.6% R@1 on `W_VULG` and 17.8% on `S_VL` (with CLS token pooling). The improvements are particularly notable at higher recall thresholds (R@10), where our approach enables the retrieval of over half of the hard references for the best configurations. These results highlight the particular value of synthetic data generation for the most challenging retrieval scenarios – precisely those cases that are of greatest interest to humanities scholars working with ancient texts.

Ablation Study on Synthetic Data. In Table 5, we ablate the contribution of different components of the proposed fine-tuning scheme with LLM-generated data. In this case, all experiments are conducted using token averaging as pooling strategy, employing both Latin BERT and LaBERTa as embedding models. First, we validate the effectiveness of in-batch top-k negative sampling by applying it to both standard fine-tuning (*i.e.*, comparing the first and second rows) and the proposed fine-tuning approach on synthetic data (*i.e.*, comparing the fifth and sixth rows). Notably, in Latin BERT, the use of top-k negatives leads to improvements of 5.7 and 4.1 in terms of R@1 for standard fine-tuning and fine-tuning on synthetic data, respectively, when evaluating on `W_VULG`. Similar improvements can be noticed on the `S_VL` corpora and when employing LaBERTa to encode passages.

Regarding the data used, we compare our approach with different variants: (i) we use only the positive pairs from the two biblical versions and employ in-batch elements as negative passages (second row), (ii) we consider only positive samples without including generated negatives (third row), and (iii) we employ the generated positive and negative samples, without including positive pairs from the two biblical versions (fourth row). As shown, using the combination of data employed leads to the best results, further confirming the importance of generated samples to enhance textual representations.

Table 6. Ablation study on different in-batch negative sampling strategies. Results are reported on `W_VULG` and `S_VL`, using token averaging as pooling strategy.

	Neg Sampling			Corpus: `W_VULG`			Corpus: `S_VL`		
	k	Top-k	Random	R@1	R@5	R@10	R@1	R@5	R@10
	1	✓	-	34.9	46.4	52.1	33.7	40.7	45.6
	10	✓	-	45.4	**58.9**	65.1	42.5	58.8	67.4
	50	✓	-	45.1	58.3	65.1	41.3	58.5	65.2
	5	-	✓	44.3	57.3	63.0	39.6	57.1	64.7
Latin BERT [3]	5	✓	-	**45.8**	**58.9**	**65.6**	**42.9**	**59.2**	**67.9**
	1	✓	-	38.5	51.6	57.3	35.9	50.0	55.4
	10	✓	-	46.9	65.1	74.0	47.2	**63.5**	69.5
	50	✓	-	46.3	64.0	71.8	46.7	62.5	66.8
	5	-	✓	46.9	62.0	71.4	45.1	60.1	67.9
LaBERTa [30]	5	✓	-	**47.9**	**66.7**	**75.0**	**48.9**	63.0	**71.2**

Analysis on In-Batch Top-k Negatives. According to Sect. 3.2, during contrastive training, for each source passage, we select only the top-k most similar passages to the source as in-batch negatives. Table 6 reports how the performance of the fine-tuned models changes as we vary k, when training on synthetic data. It can be seen that exclusively contrasting against the most similar (*i.e.*, the hardest) negative significantly degrades the recall scores of both models. Conversely, the models benefit from setting $k > 1$, and the best results are obtained with $k = 5$, confirming that the quality of the negative passages is more relevant than their quantity. To further support this finding, we can also notice that if the five in-batch negatives are randomly drawn rather than being selected as the most difficult ones, Latin BERT and LaBERTa cannot reach the same recall scores, highlighting the effectiveness of our in-batch negative sampling strategy.

Qualitative Results. Figure 4 showcases retrieval examples from the challenging `hard` split of our benchmark, demonstrating the capabilities of the LaBERTa model when fine-tuned with our synthetic-augmented training strategy.

As it can be seen, in the first example from `W_VULG`, the model successfully identifies the correct biblical passage despite competing alternatives that share vocabulary but differ in semantic context. The model correctly prioritizes semantic meaning over surface-level lexical matching, retrieving the passage that maintains the conceptual relationship rather than one with merely similar terms. In the second example, the model correctly retrieves the reference to *Second Epistle of Peter* within the top-3 most similar passages to Augustine's query. It is worth noting that the second best candidate retrieved by the model is `2 Pet.3.5`, which undoubtedly relates to the reference passage `2 Pet.3.6`. This demonstrates the enhanced ability of the model to detect subtle theological parallels and conceptual links between texts.

4.3 Limitations

In this work, we demonstrate how synthetic training data can be generated using an LLM for semantic retrieval in a low-resource language. Despite its effectiveness, we outline possible limitations accompanying this approach. First, high-quality synthetic data was generated using GPT-4, a proprietary model accessible only via a paid API. In fact, we observed that open-source LLMs underperform in producing coherent and fluent text in low-resource languages such as Latin. Although a subset of 100 generated sentences was verified by domain experts, we cannot exclude the presence of noise in the complete training set due to hallucinations or errors produced by the LLM. Moreover, the objective was to generate text from the Bible, which for Latin probably represents the main source of knowledge seen by the LLM during pre-training. As such, style consistency was not an issue in our case, but it may pose challenges for specific domains less familiar to the model. On the other hand, as research advances, we expect the next generations of LLMs to be better for synthetic data generation.

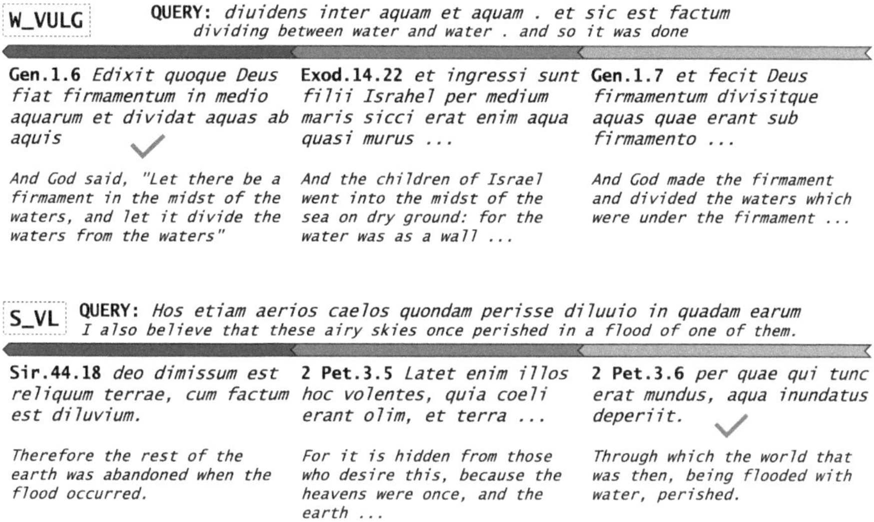

Fig. 4. Qualitative results using LaBERTa fine-tuned with synthetic data. We report the top-3 retrieved passages for two of Augustine's queries from the `hard` split, referring to a verse in `W_VULG` and `S_VL` respectively. The retrieved passages are presented in decreasing order of similarity with the query, from left to right.

5 Conclusion

We introduced an innovative approach to mitigating data scarcity in low-resource sentence retrieval by leveraging LLM-generated synthetic data. Specifically, we employed an LLM to generate and refine knowledge in Latin, enhancing the similarity search of intertextual references within ancient texts. Our study provides a comprehensive evaluation across diverse biblical corpora, comparing various embedding models and training strategies. Experimental analyses demonstrate that incorporating synthetically generated data significantly improves retrieval performance. These results highlight both the effectiveness and necessity of LLM-driven data augmentation, particularly for underrepresented and ancient languages, potentially opening new opportunities for broader applications in historical linguistics, philology, and domain-specific NLP.

Acknowledgments. We acknowledge the CINECA award under the ISCRA initiative, for the availability of high-performance computing resources. This work was supported by the PNRR project Italian Strengthening of Esfri RI Resilience (ITSERR) funded by the European Union – NextGenerationEU (CUP B53C22001770006).

References

1. Achiam, J., et al.: GPT-4 Technical Report. arXiv preprint arXiv:2303.08774 (2023)
2. Anil, R., et al.: Gemini: a Family of Highly Capable Multimodal Models. arXiv preprint arXiv:2312.11805 (2023)
3. Bamman, D., Burns, P.J.: Latin BERT: a contextual language model for classical philology. arXiv preprint arXiv:2009.10053 (2020)
4. Bonifacio, L., Abonizio, H., Fadaee, M., Nogueira, R.: InPars: unsupervised dataset generation for information retrieval. In: Proceedings of the International ACM SIGIR Conference on Research and Development in Information Retrieval (2022)
5. Brown, T., et al.: Language models are few-shot learners. In: Advances in Neural Information Processing Systems (2020)
6. Caffagni, D., Barraco, M., Cornia, M., Baraldi, L., Cucchiara, R.: SynthCap: Augmenting transformers with synthetic data for image captioning. In: Proceedings of the International Conference on Image Analysis and Processing (2023)
7. Caffagni, D., et al.: Benchmarking BERT-based models for latin: a case study on biblical references in ancient Christian literature. In: Proceedings of the Conference on Information and Research Science Connecting to Digital and Library Science (2025)
8. Caffagni, D., Sarto, S., Cornia, M., Baraldi, L., Cucchiara, R.: Recurrence-enhanced vision-and-language transformers for robust multimodal document retrieval. In: Proceedings of the IEEE Conference on Computer Vision and Pattern Recognition (2025)
9. Chen, T., Kornblith, S., Norouzi, M., Hinton, G.: A simple framework for contrastive learning of visual representations. In: Proceedings of the International Conference on Machine Learning (2020)
10. Cocchi, F., Moratelli, N., Cornia, M., Baraldi, L., Cucchiara, R.: Augmenting multimodal LLMs with self-reflective tokens for knowledge-based visual question answering. In: Proceedings of the IEEE Conference on Computer Vision and Pattern Recognition (2025)
11. Conneau, A., Lample, G.: Cross-lingual language model pretraining. In: Advances in Neural Information Processing Systems (2019)
12. Dai, Z., et al.: Promptagator: few-shot dense retrieval from 8 examples. arXiv preprint arXiv:2209.11755 (2022)
13. Devlin, J., Chang, M.W., Lee, K., Toutanova, K.: BERT: pre-training of deep bidirectional transformers for language understanding. In: Proceedings of the Annual Conference of the North American Chapter of the Association for Computational Linguistics (2018)
14. Faghri, F., Fleet, D.J., Kiros, J.R., Fidler, S.: VSE++: improving visual-semantic embeddings with hard negatives. In: Proceedings of the British Machine Vision Conference (2018)
15. Feng, S.Y., et al.: A survey of data augmentation approaches for NLP. In: Findings of the Annual Meeting of the Association for Computational Linguistics (2021)
16. Hu, J., Ruder, S., Siddhant, A., Neubig, G., Firat, O., Johnson, M.: XTREME: a massively multilingual multi-task benchmark for evaluating cross-lingual Generalisation. In: Proceedings of the International Conference on Machine Learning (2020)
17. Hutchinson, B.: Modeling the sacred: considerations when using religious texts in natural language processing. In: Findings of the Annual Conference of the North American Chapter of the Association for Computational Linguistics (2024)

18. Johnson, J., Douze, M., Jégou, H.: Billion-scale similarity search with GPUs. IEEE Trans. Big Data **7**(3), 535–547 (2019)
19. Kalantidis, Y., Sariyildiz, M.B., Pion, N., Weinzaepfel, P., Larlus, D.: Hard negative mixing for contrastive learning. In: Advances in Neural Information Processing Systems (2020)
20. Kingma, D.P., Ba, J.L.: ADAM: a method for stochastic optimization. In: Proceedings of the International Conference on Machine Learning (2015)
21. Klie, J.C., Bugert, M., Boullosa, B., De Castilho, R.E., Gurevych, I.: The INCEpTION platform: machine-assisted and knowledge-oriented interactive annotation. In: Proceedings of System Demonstrations of the International Conference on Computational Linguistics (2018)
22. Kumar, V., Choudhary, A., Cho, E.: Data augmentation using pre-trained transformer models. In: Proceedings of the Annual Meeting of the Association for Computational Linguistics Workshops (2020)
23. Manjavacas, E., Fonteyn, L.: Adapting vs. pre-training language models for historical languages. J. Data Min. Digit. Humanit. (Digit. Humanit. Lang.) (2022)
24. Nogueira, R., Yang, W., Lin, J., Cho, K.: Document expansion by query prediction. arXiv preprint arXiv:1904.08375 (2019)
25. Oord, A.V.d., Li, Y., Vinyals, O.: Representation learning with contrastive predictive coding. arXiv preprint arXiv:1807.03748 (2018)
26. Piotrowski, M.: Natural Language Processing for Historical Texts, vol. 17. Morgan & Claypool Publishers, San Rafael (2012)
27. Pires, T., Schlinger, E., Garrette, D.: How multilingual is multilingual BERT. In: Proceedings of the Annual Meeting of the Association for Computational Linguistics (2019)
28. Poppi, S., Poppi, T., Cocchi, F., Cornia, M., Baraldi, L., Cucchiara, R.: Safe-CLIP: removing NSFW concepts from vision-and-language models. In: Proceedings of the European Conference on Computer Vision (2024)
29. Ren, P., et al.: Wizard of search engine: access to information through conversations with search engines. In: Proceedings of the International ACM SIGIR Conference on Research and Development in Information Retrieval (2021)
30. Riemenschneider, F., Frank, A.: Exploring large language models for classical philology. In: Proceedings of the Annual Meeting of the Association for Computational Linguistics (2023)
31. Sabatier (ed.), P.: Bibliorum Sacrorum latinae versiones antiquae seu Vetus Italica (3 vols.). Reims, Reginaldus Florentain (1743–1751)
32. Salemi, A., Zamani, H.: Towards a search engine for machines: unified ranking for multiple retrieval-augmented large language models. In: Proceedings of the International ACM SIGIR Conference on Research and Development in Information Retrieval (2024)
33. Sarto, S., Barraco, M., Cornia, M., Baraldi, L., Cucchiara, R.: Positive-augmented contrastive learning for image and video captioning evaluation. In: Proceedings of the IEEE Conference on Computer Vision and Pattern Recognition (2023)
34. Sarto, S., Moratelli, N., Cornia, M., Baraldi, L., Cucchiara, R.: Positive-augmented contrastive learning for vision-and-language evaluation and training. arXiv preprint arXiv:2410.07336 (2024)
35. Singh, P., Rutten, G., Lefever, E.: A pilot study for BERT language modelling and morphological analysis for ancient and medieval Greek. In: Proceedings of the Joint SIGHUM Workshop on Computational Linguistics for Cultural Heritage, Social Sciences, Humanities and Literature (2021)

36. Sommerschield, T., Assael, Y., Pavlopoulos, J., Stefanak, V., Senior, A., Dyer, C., Bodel, J., Prag, J., Androutsopoulos, I., Freitas, N.: Machine learning for ancient languages: a survey. Comput. Linguist. **49**(3), 703–747 (2023)
37. Touvron, Het al.: LLaMA: open and efficient foundation language models. arXiv preprint arXiv:2302.13971 (2023)
38. Wang, K., Thakur, N., Reimers, N., Gurevych, I.: GPL: generative pseudo labeling for unsupervised domain adaptation of dense retrieval. In: Proceedings of the Annual Conference of the North American Chapter of the Association for Computational Linguistics (2022)
39. Wang, L., Yang, N., Huang, X., Yang, L., Majumder, R., Wei, F.: Improving text embeddings with large language models. In: Proceedings of the Annual Meeting of the Association for Computational Linguistics (2024)
40. Wang, L., Yang, N., Huang, X., Yang, L., Majumder, R., Wei, F.: Large search model: redefining search stack in the era of LLMs. In: ACM SIGIR Forum (2024)
41. Wang, L., Yang, N., Wei, F.: Query2doc: query expansion with large language models. In: Proceedings of the Conference on Empirical Methods in Natural Language Processing (2023)
42. Weber, R., Gryson (eds.), R.: Biblia Sacra iuxta Vulgatam Versionem. Stuttgart, Deutsche Bibelgesellschaft (2007^5 (R Weber, 1969^1))
43. Zhan, J., Mao, J., Liu, Y., Guo, J., Zhang, M., Ma, S.: Optimizing dense retrieval model training with hard negatives. In: Proceedings of the International ACM SIGIR Conference on Research and Development in Information Retrieval (2021)
44. Zycha (ed.), J.: Sancti Aureli Augustini: De Genesi ad litteram libri duodecim eiusdem libri capitula. De Genesi ad litteram imperfectus liber. Locutionum in Heptateuchum libri septem. Pragae-Vindobonae-Lipsiae, Tempsky-Freyta (1894)

Organising Knowledge from Text: Prompt-Based Triple Extraction and Graph Enrichment with Large Language Models

Durgesh Nandini(✉), Simon Blöthner, Mario Larch, and Mirco Schönfeld

University of Bayreuth, Bayreuth, Germany
durgesh.nandini@uni-bayreuth.de

Abstract. Creating and organising structured knowledge from unstructured text is a fundamental problem in computer science, with applications ranging from search and reasoning to prediction and recommendation systems. Knowledge Graphs (KGs) offer a powerful abstraction for organising information as entities and their semantic relationships, but they depend on high-quality, domain-specific relational data. Extracting this data remains particularly challenging when source texts are lengthy, formal, and context-dependent. This work presents a framework combining prompt-engineered Large Language Models (LLMs) with knowledge graph embedding methods to support automatic knowledge creation and integration. We explore different prompting strategies, zero-shot, one-shot, few-shot, and prompts with negative examples, for extracting subject–predicate–object triples from complex legal texts. The extracted triples are used to build a supplemental KG, which is merged with an existing domain-specific graph and embedded using TransE for downstream relation prediction tasks. As a use case, we focus on the trade domain and use Regional Trade Agreements (RTAs) as the primary source of textual data. RTAs are challenging documents due to their legally formal and often ambiguous language, and they require domain knowledge to be interpreted effectively. Yet, they encode rich contextual information about international economic relations. Our results show that LLM-extracted triples meaningfully enhance the semantic structure of the KG and improve predictive performance. We further identify which categories of predicates contribute most to these gains.

Keywords: Large Language Models · Knowledge Graphs · Triples Extraction · Contextual Information · Regional Trade Agreements · Trade Volume Prediction

1 Introduction

Knowledge organisation and discovery have become increasingly important in managing complex economic information. A Knowledge Graph (KG) is a

W.-T. Balke et al. (Eds.): TPDL 2025, LNCS 16097, pp. 53–70, 2026.
https://doi.org/10.1007/978-3-032-05409-8_5

structured instantiation of a Knowledge Base (KB), representing entities and their relationships through nodes and edges and offering a comprehensive framework for knowledge creation, organisation, and dissemination [13,15]. By embedding semantic meaning into relational structures, KGs not only store factual information but also enable the discovery of new insights through relational reasoning, link prediction, and relation prediction tasks. Building a robust and informative KG, however, requires the integration of rich and diverse forms of information, particularly contextual knowledge that extends beyond simple entity-relationship pairs [3,25,30]. To address this need, we propose a methodology to extract structured entity information in the form of subject–predicate–object (SPO) triples [17] from large unstructured textual corpora and populate a pre-existing domain-specific knowledge graph [2,23]. The extracted triples serve to enrich the graph's semantic and structural content, thereby facilitating more comprehensive downstream analyses.

Recent advances in Natural Language Processing (NLP) approaches, particularly the rise of LLMs, have opened new avenues for knowledge extraction and representation. Among the techniques enabling the effective use of LLMs, prompt engineering has become critical [8,19,28,33]. Prompt engineering proves essential in tasks such as triple generation, where subject–predicate–object structures must be extracted from unstructured text. The technique is to formulate task-specific queries or instructions that elicit targeted behaviors from LLMs without modifying their underlying parameters and without the need for any additional fine tuning, thereby reducing computational costs and expediting experimental cycles [20,31]. This approach enables the flexible adaptation of LLMs to various downstream tasks by designing inputs that guide the model toward structured outputs.

Once the contextual triples have been extracted through prompt-based entity-relation extraction, they are used to supplement and enrich a pre-existing, domain-specific knowledge graph. Instead of constructing an entirely new KG, this approach injects additional semantic context into an existing structure, ensuring that the augmented KG captures both foundational domain knowledge and newly extracted relational nuances. Subsequently, the enriched KG can be embedded into continuous vector spaces using knowledge graph embedding techniques. We use the knowledge graph embedding model TransE [7] to do this. TransE maps entities and relations into low-dimensional spaces while preserving the relational semantics of the graph. These embeddings facilitate efficient computation, support downstream tasks such as relation prediction and relation classification, and help uncover latent structures and economic patterns that are not directly visible in the graph representation. The purpose of combining the extracted contextual information with domain-specific knowledge and embedding the resulting graph is to enhance both the knowledge organisation and the predictive capabilities of the model.

In order to achieve the above-mentioned, we apply our framework to the domain of international economic bilateral trade flows as a use case scenario. The motivation behind this is that traditional economic research often transforms complex interaction networks into simplified representations suitable for linear statistical inference or algebraic reasoning. However, such transformations can severely compress information and erase critical structural characteristics of the original network [32]. Furthermore, economic data are inherently high-dimensional, contingent, and strongly nonlinear. These highlight the challenges that arise from underlying multiplicative dynamics [5,11,27].To address these issues, [23] proposes to conceptualize economic interactions as a network structure where countries are interconnected through trade relationships.

For the task of triple extraction, we utilise RTA documents as the textual corpus. In contrast to general-domain SPO extraction, RTAs exhibit formalized legal language, implicit economic obligations, multi-party structures, and specialized terminology. These characteristics complicate conventional information extraction, making the adaptation of prompt-based LLM extraction techniques particularly valuable. Existing triple extraction research predominantly focuses on domains such as news or biomedical texts, while our work systematically targets the legal-economic domain, where structured benchmarks are scarce. Through careful extraction of entities and relations from RTAs, we aim to populate the knowledge graph with semantically accurate and contextually meaningful triples, preserving the complex structure of trade obligations and relationships. Based on these considerations, we propose following research questions:

RQ1: How effectively does enriching a domain-specific knowledge graph improve trade relation prediction?

To address RQ1, we utilised Regional Trade Agreement (RTA) data to construct a domain-specific Knowledge Graph (KG) using a Large Language Model (LLM). The RTA texts were sourced from Alschner et al. [1], and triples were extracted through LLM-based information extraction techniques. Additionally, we incorporated the KonecoKG [24], which was originally constructed from tabular data from Borchert et al. [6], and merged it with the extracted triples to form a unified Knowledge Graph. This enhanced KG was subsequently used to predict trade relationships. Finally, evaluation of trade relation prediction was done and compared with results from KonecoKG as baseline.

RQ2: What characteristics of extracted predicates (verbs) contribute most significantly to the accurate prediction of trade relation between country pairs?

To answer RQ2, we identified and filtered the features that play a vital role in predicting trade relations between countries and emphasize which types of extracted relations contribute to improvement in the prediction results, we grouped the predicates into semantic categories—such as tariff reduction, agreement signing, investment facilitation, and regulatory cooperation. We then measured the average change in model performance when each group was included or excluded from the KG enrichment process.

To summarise, this work proposes an integrated framework combining prompt-engineered LLM extraction, knowledge graph construction, and embedding-based relation prediction. We systematically apply and evaluate this framework in the context of international trade networks, addressing specific challenges of complexity, nonlinearity, and semantic richness inherent in economic data.

The rest of the paper is organised as follows: In Sect. 2 we briefly discuss the related works and highlight the significance of this study. In Sect. 3 we describe the dataset that we have used for our experiments. Next, in Sect. 4, we describe the methodology that we have used for this study. In Sect. 5 we discuss the experimental setup, and in Sect. 6, we present the results. Next, in Sect. 7, we have the conclusion and the future directions that this study can be taken forward to.

2 Related Work

Over the years, trade analysis has gained significant attention due to its essential role in economic growth and development. In this section, we discuss the studies that have been conducted in the field of triple extraction using LLMs.

We observed that the use of knowledge extraction is a relatively young area of research in the field of Economic trade transactions. However, other related fields, such as e-commerce, have lightly used knowledge graphs and triples for their studies. The AlimeKG framework [18] is the one focused on the e-commerce domain. The authors introduce a framework for KG construction in the e-commerce domain by integrating NLP components such as named entity recognition (NER) and relation extraction (RE), facilitating a semi-automated process for knowledge acquisition and validation. Nandini et al. proposed a knowledge graph-based trade volume prediction approach leveraging a knowledge graph embedding model specifically tailored for RTAs [23].

We identified alternative pipelines, other than LLM based proposed in other domains. Dessí et al. explored Transformer models to automatically extract entities from scientific texts and generate a KG [10]. Tested on 6.7 million Computer Science articles, their work produced a KG with 10 million entities and demonstrated strong efficiency against a gold standard. Their process was supported by open-source pipelines and softwares.

Therefore, we see that there is a gap when it comes to utilising knowledge extraction for Economics trade scenarios. With our approach, we aim to bridge this gap. By leveraging LLMs, our solution extracts, structures, and assesses knowledge from unstructured text, ensuring the accuracy and reliability of the resulting triples. This focused approach enables targeted solutions for KG enhancement in economics trade contexts, addressing specific challenges and requirements unique to this domain.

3 Dataset

To implement the part of the study on knowledge creation, we have used the dataset of World Trade Organisation (WTO)'s RTAs data proposed by Alschne et al. [1]. The dataset contains 450 XML files generated using metadata and full texts from WTO's RTA and each file consists of trade agreement between two countries and is composed of multiple Articles and Chapters. The incorrect metadata and missing information were then corrected and resolved. Then optical character recognition is applied to generate machine-readable texts, after which the unusable annexes or schedules have been removed, and a two-level hierarchy of treaty elements has been imposed. The trade agreements texts are also categorised into several sectors, such as agriculture, customs, trade in services, and institutions, etc. The full dataset can be accessed here[1]. Figure 1 shows a word cloud of the raw data. Figure 2 shows the major topics discussed in the texts. These figures highlight that the dataset contains trade focused insights which makes it suitable for extracting trade related entities.

Fig. 1. WordCloud of raw data.

Fig. 2. WordCloud of the extracted predicate verbs.

For the second part of the study, we need a domain-specific knowledge graph. For this purpose, we use the KonecoKG developed by Nandini et al. [23]. This graph uses trade data from [6], spanning 1986 to 2016, and encompassing 170 countries. The graph in [23] is composed of nodes as countries and the relations between them as edges. They have over 2.5 million observations in their graph dataset and have used multidimensional knowledge graph embedding techniques to predict trade volume for each country pair relation. Each country in the dataset has explanatory properties such as gross domestic product (GDP) and population data [14], information on geographic distances between countries [21], and data about trade agreements relations [12]. We aim to populate this graph using the above mentioned trade agreement dataset by extracting entities.

4 Methodology

Our methodology is mainly comprised of two major components, a knowledge generation part and a knowledge organisation part.

For the knowledge generation component, we present a methodology for extracting structured trade-related knowledge from unstructured natural language texts of RTAs using LLMs. Leveraging the Llama 3.1 model, we explore

[1] https://github.com/mappingtreaties/tota/tree/master.

zero-shot, one-shot, and few-shot prompting strategies, incorporating both positive and negative examples to assess their impact on information extraction quality. We begin this process with parsing trade agreement documents to generate subject-predicate-object triples.

For the second component of the study, we aim to represent the extracted knowledge in the form of a structured graph, in particular, a knowledge graph. We call this graph representation a *triples graph*. This graph is subsequently employed as contextual input to enrich a pre-existing, curated knowledge graph. By integrating the two graphs, we generate joint embeddings using a knowledge graph embedding model, allowing us to compute semantic similarity scores. These embedding scores serve as the basis for downstream relation prediction tasks, facilitating a deeper understanding of the interplay between textual information extraction and structured knowledge representation. Figure 3 shows a working flowchart of the methodology we have used in this study. We further elaborate the process in the following subsections.

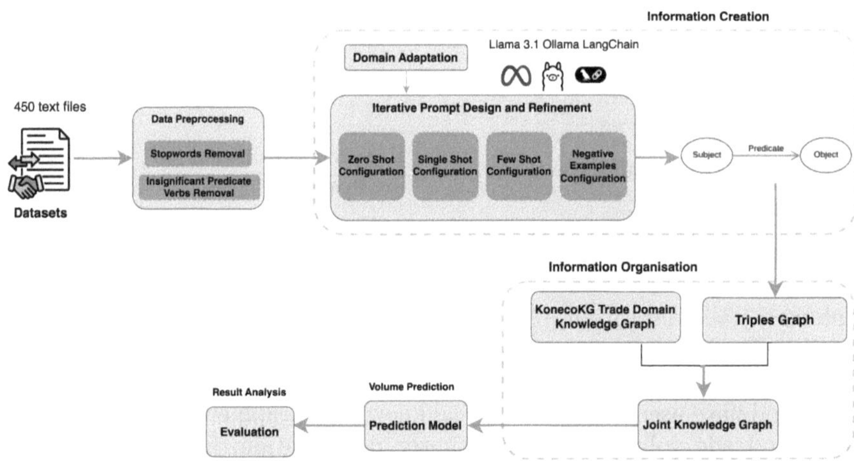

Fig. 3. Methodology used in the study.

4.1 Data Collection and Preprocessing

Given the unstructured nature of our source material, RTAs expressed in natural language, an initial preprocessing step was essential to enhance the model's efficiency and precision in information extraction. For this, we processed the document to remove stopwords. Along with the standard English language stopwords offered by the NLTK [4] we have also used a customised list of stopwords that included words that are very common in trade domain applications. This is to eliminate domain-generic trade terms that occurred frequently across documents but contributed little semantic value to triple extraction (e.g., *hereinafter*, *agreement*, *party*). This preprocessing phase ensured that the model focused on contextually meaningful segments during the subsequent prompt-based extraction stage.

4.2 Knowledge Generation

Iterative Prompt Design and Refinement. The cornerstone of our methodology lies in the systematic design and refinement of prompts for guiding a LLM to extract subject–predicate–object triples from legal text. We developed five progressively specialized prompts, each introducing increasing degrees of task specificity.

We began with a base zero-shot prompt that instructed the model to extract triples without prior examples or strict structural constraints. This allowed us to assess the model's intrinsic ability to identify relational information in a minimally supervised setting. Subsequent prompt iterations incorporated targeted instructions tailored to the semantic features of legal-economic discourse. These refinements emphasized the extraction of triples involving trade-relevant actions—such as *sign*, *export*, *import*, *ratify*, and *negotiate*—as well as entities commonly appearing in trade agreements, such as state actors and regulatory terms.

In the final stages, we explored few-shot prompting by embedding carefully selected positive and negative examples to further ground the model's understanding of valid and invalid triple formats. This comparative evaluation between zero-shot and few-shot configurations enabled us to quantify the impact of exemplar-based prompting on the quality and fidelity of the extracted triples.

4.3 Knowledge Organisation

Triple Graph Construction. Following extraction, the resulting subject–predicate–object triples were programmatically transformed into a structured graph-based format, referred to as the *triple graph*. Each node in this graph represents a unique entity or concept identified in the text, while directed edges encode the semantic relations as derived from the model-generated predicates. Figure 5ashows an excerpt in the triples graph, where the nodes are the subject and object of a triplet and the predicate represented by a verb is the relation between the nodes.

Integration with the Main Knowledge Graph. To contextualize and validate the extracted information, the triple graph was integrated with a pre-existing main knowledge graph constructed from curated legal-economic datasets. We show an excerpt of this graph in Fig. 4. The integration strategy was based on entity alignment and relation type matching, enabling the fusion of newly extracted triples with historically grounded domain knowledge. This hybrid graph structure captures both emergent insights from novel documents and established relationships from authoritative sources. Figure 5bshows how an initial graph and the triples graph are integrated in our model.

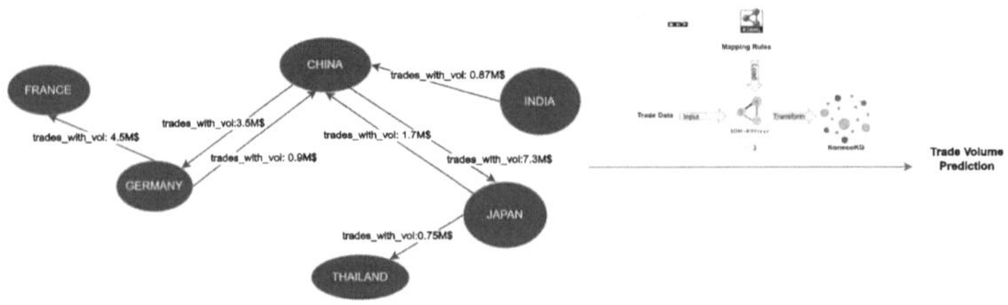

Fig. 4. Domain Specific Knowledge Graph.

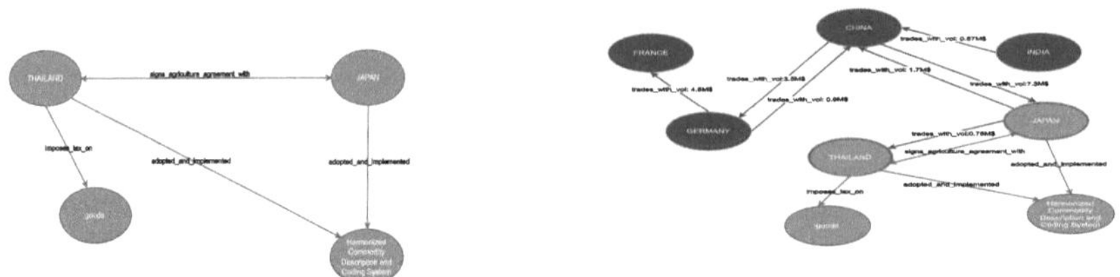

(a) Triples Graph

(b) Initial Graph Integrated with Triples Graph

Fig. 5. An example excerpt of adding context to a domain specific knowledge graph.

4.4 Application in Downstream Tasks

Knowledge Graph Embedding and Relation Prediction. The combined graph, comprising both the triple graph and the main knowledge graph was then processed using a knowledge graph embedding model. Specifically, we employed a translational embedding technique (e.g., TransE) to project entities and relations into a continuous vector space. This embedding process facilitates the computation of semantic similarity scores between entities and supports downstream reasoning tasks.

Embedding scores generated through the model were used to perform relation prediction, allowing us to infer potential links that were not explicitly stated in either the input text or the main graph. This phase not only evaluates the internal consistency and utility of the extracted triples but also demonstrates the capacity of the LLM-assisted pipeline to enrich existing knowledge graphs with contextually relevant and semantically aligned information.

5 Experiments

For the experimental part, we start with preprocessing the dataset as mentioned in Sect. 3 and 4, where we mainly remove the stopwords. Then we use the preprocessed data to extract SPO triples. For this, we have used the Llama 3.1, an open source language model because the Llama 3.1 model provides an easy opportunity to run locally with a simple command-line interface that directly interacts with the LLMs and allows easy installation and implementation. OLlama allows to download desired models with a given number of parameters. There are currently three versions of Llama 3.1 with different sizes of 8b, 70b, and 405b parameters; we have used Llama 3.1 with 70b parameters. Llama 3.1 is trained on publicly available data without resorting to proprietary datasets. For LLM optimization, parameters such as temperatures and prompt strategies play an essential role. We implemented the model with different combinations of temperature and prompts. Only temperature and task descriptions are provided for zero-shots, while for few shots, a different combination of prompts is used to finalize them.

We have experimented with four prompts in total. We start with a generic prompt. This is the zero shot prompt configuration, wherein we instruct the model to extract SPO triples from the texts. We define that the subject and the object must be Named Entities [9,22,26] while the predicates must be English language verbs. Then, for each subsequent prompt we add further instructions and examples. In the second prompt, we add one example and the definition of Named Entity Recognition (NER). This is the single-shot prompt configuration. For the third prompt, we enhance the second prompt by adding a few more examples. This is the few-shot configuration. In the fourth prompt, we add a few more examples of what the triples should look like. Along with that, we also add a few negative examples and negated instructions. This is the negative examples configuration. With negated instructions we mean that we add sentences such as to not hallucinate. As a feedback from the results generated by prompt 3, we also instruct the model to not include any verbs that we deem are not significant and to refine the results that we deem might require more information. For example, if the model generates triples such as *'Parties', 'signed','contract'* we instruct the model to define what the term *'Parties'* stand for. We also ask the model to deal with coreference resolution and observe the results obtained. An example of each prompt configuration is provided in Appendix A: Prompts.

The next step is the construction of a *triples graph*. For this, we use the list of triples obtained from the previous step and use the RDFizer [16,29] to create a graph structure. To construct the graph, we use the subject and the object as nodes and verbs as the edges between the nodes. Each relation constructed is associated with two countries. An example illustration is shown in Fig. 4. We then combine the triples graph with a predefined knowledge graph. An example excerpt is shown in Fig. 5b.

In the next step we compute the joint embedding scores of the graphs using knowledge graph embedding models [23] demonstrates that TransE is the best embedding model for this purpose. Using that as a guidance we apply the TransE method to compute the joint embedding scores of the combined graph. We adopted a corruption-based learning strategy [7] to make predictions. This strategy entailed intentionally introducing corruptions or perturbations to the input data during the training process to enhance the model's ability to generalise and make accurate predictions. The rationale behind this approach is its ability to encourage the model to learn robust representations of the data resilient to noise and variations. Exposing the model to a diverse range of corrupted inputs during training caused it to become more adept at discerning meaningful patterns and relationships from the data, thus improving its predictive performance on unseen or noisy data.

Practically, the corruption strategy can be implemented by augmenting the training dataset with artificially corrupted samples or by introducing random perturbations to the input data during each training iteration. The degree and type of corruption introduced can be tailored based on the specific characteristics of the dataset and the desired robustness of the model. In general, the model trains by comparing statements (s,p, o) known to be true against statements likely to be false based on local closed-world assumptions. This strategy measured the distances between different statements and aimed to minimise the said distance. An essential component of this experimental strategy is the corruption algorithm. The corruption algorithm creates negative triples by corrupting a true triple either by replacing the head or the tail entity with a random incorrect entity. This forces the model to distinguish between true and false facts, thereby enhancing model robustness. Initially, we utilised the default corruption method provided by TransE. However, recognising the potential benefits of introducing controlled noise into the training process, we subsequently modified this strategy by corrupting trade values by a relative value of 20% of their true values. Through experimentation (20%, 50%, 70%, 100%, 120%), we determined that a corruption level of about 20% optimally enhanced the results. This adjustment appeared to simulate real-world variations and uncertainties in trade dynamics, thereby improving the model's ability to generalise to unseen data.

Subsequently, we trained our model for *1000* epochs, with an embedding size of *150* dimensions and *30* corruptions per batch. A batch size of *32* was used throughout the training process. The pairwise loss function was employed, initialized using the *Xavier* scheme. Regularization was applied using an *LP* norm with a lambda value of *0.01* and a norm parameter p as *2*. The *Adam* optimizer was used with a learning rate of *0.001*. These settings were chosen based on preliminary experiments and empirical observations to strike a balance between model performance and computational efficiency, ensuring timely convergence and effective learning.

The trained model works by generalising relationships not yet seen by the neural network to predict the likelihood of a relationship being true with a given confidence.

6 Result and Discussion

In this section, we present a detailed analysis of the experimental outcomes obtained from (i) prompt-based triple extraction, (ii) knowledge graph enrichment using LLM-generated triples, and (iii) the impact of this enrichment on relation prediction tasks over the combined graph structure. Additionally, we explore predicate-level contribution, and provide a robustness analysis.

6.1 Triple Extraction Performance Across Prompt Configurations

We begin by evaluating the performance of different prompt configurations used to extract subject–predicate–object (SPO) triples from RTA texts. As mentioned in Sect. 5 we have tested four prompting strategies, zero-shot, one-shot, few-shot, and few-shot with added negative examples and instruction refinement. We measure the performance of each configuration against a manually annotated set of 100 sentences using standard information extraction metrics: precision, recall, F1 score, exact match, and partial match. Additionally, we have also used qualitative analysis to measure the quality of the predicates and the triples obtained. For this purpose we curated a set of qualitative metrics. The quantitative results are shown in Table 1.

Table 1. Triple Extraction Metrics for Different Prompting Strategies

Prompt	Precision	Recall	F1-Score	Exact Match (%)	Partial Match (%)
Zero-shot	0.64	0.52	0.57	39.6	58.2
One-shot	0.71	0.63	0.67	45.2	66.4
Few-shot	0.78	0.71	0.74	56.1	72.0
Few-shot + Negative Examples	**0.85**	**0.77**	**0.81**	**62.4**	**78.9**

The results show that few-shot configurations outperform zero- and one-shot variants, especially when combined with explicit negative examples instructions to reduce hallucination. Including negative examples led to more accurate extraction of context-sensitive trade verbs and improved generalization across agreement formats. For qualitative evaluation, we use the following curated set of metrics.

Relation Validation. The Llama 3.1-generated triples generally demonstrate good contextual and semantic validity in their predicates. For example, predicates such as "cooperate_with", "expand_trade_with", and "invest_in" accurately reflect the diplomatic and economic nature of the agreement. However, some predicates are overly complex, which could affect their usability in knowledge bases.

Entity-Relation Coherence. Where we check if the generated predicates and relations are contextually and semantically valid for the country pairs. The entity-relation alignment is generally logical and consistent. Llama 3.1 correctly identifies country-level actors (Japan, Thailand) and maintains appropriate relationships between them.

Triple Completeness. We evaluate if the triples are complete and that no critical information is missing in a given context. In our evaluation, we observed that our model captures the key aspects of the agreement, including trade liberalization, investment protection, and cooperation mechanisms, but sometimes misses higher-level strategic relationships that are identified in manually extracted triples.

Information Gain. Through information gain we measure how much new, useful, and factually correct information is generated through the triples. Comparing against the manual extractions, our model provides additional detail in certain areas, particularly in breaking down complex statements into multiple triples.

Semantic Correctness. Most generated triples maintain semantic coherence, but there are instances where the predicate complexity affects clarity. The model sometimes creates overly specific predicates that could be simplified without losing meaning. The subject-predicate-object relationships are generally logical, though some triples could benefit from more standardized predicate forms.

Redundancy. There is some redundancy in the Llama 3.1-generated triples, particularly when dealing with reciprocal relationships between Japan and Thailand. The model sometimes generates similar information with slightly different predicates, which could be consolidated. For example, separate triples for bilateral activities could be combined into single, more comprehensive triples.

Missing Information. The analysis shows that the extractions of the Llama 3.1 model focus predominantly on explicit textual relationships, while implicit strategic links identified in manual annotations are omitted. The automated extractions favor the literal interpretation of contractual provisions. This leads to an incomplete capture of important strategic connections, especially where understanding requires a combination of multiple provisions or broader policy frameworks.

Predicate Distribution. The predicates show good coverage of the agreement's various aspects, including trade, investment, cooperation, and regulatory matters. However, there's an imbalance favoring operational predicates over strategic ones, which might not fully capture the agreement's broader diplomatic significance.

Coverage and Inter-Country Overlap. The model maintains consistent coverage of both Japan and Thailand's roles in the agreement, with appropriate reciprocal relationships. The shared triples between the countries accurately reflect the bilateral nature of the agreement, though some relationships could be more efficiently represented through bidirectional predicates.

6.2 Impact on Trade Prediction via Knowledge Graph Enrichment

To assess how the extracted triples contribute to added context information in downstream tasks, we integrated the extracted triple graph into an existing trade knowledge graph (KonecoKG) and computed joint embeddings using the TransE model. The performance of relation prediction tasks on trade links between country pairs is shown in Table 2. Integrating extracted triples led to consistent improvements across all metrics. This indicates that the additional contextual relations captured by the LLM-based extraction provide complementary semantic information that was not present in the original structured trade dataset.

Table 2. Relation Prediction Accuracy Before and After KG Enrichment

Model Variant	MRR	Hits@1	Hits@10	Hits@100	Hits@1000
KonecoKG only	0.587	0.298	0.459	0.576	0.719
KonecoKG + LLM Triples	0.298	0.162	0.121	0.344	0.435

6.3 Predicate Contribution Analysis

To understand which types of extracted relations drive the observed performance gains, we analysed the most accurate trade volume relation predictions. We then grouped predicates into semantic categories (e.g., tariff reduction, agreement signing, investment facilitation, regulatory cooperation). We then computed the average performance change when each group was included or excluded from the enrichment process. Predicates related to logistics, tariffs, and customs procedures had the highest positive effect on embedding performance, particularly for trade-intensive country pairs. Relations that reflected legal formality (e.g., ratified, signed) contributed less to link prediction, likely due to their limited variance across agreements. Table 3 shows an excerpt of some predicates and their categories to which they belong. This shows the categories of trade that contribute to valuable context information.

6.4 Ablation and Robustness

To evaluate the robustness of the approach, we conducted ablation experiments by selectively removing predicate categories. Removing predicates belonging to certain categories of trade information related triples led to the largest drop in performance of trade volume prediction, reinforcing their contribution to predictive accuracy. We also tested robustness to noise by introducing partially corrupted triples (e.g., using incorrect country-pair mappings or vague predicates). Performance degraded under noisy conditions, confirming that the precision of extracted relations is critical for downstream utility.

Table 3. Top Context Contributing Predicates and Their Categories

Liberalization & Market Access	Regulation, Restriction & Enforcement	Trade Operations	Dispute Resolution & Remedies
facilitate	restrict	export	safeguard
liberalize	prohibit	import	compensate
eliminate	impose	transact	penalize
reduce	regulate	classify	settle
grant	enforce	designate	resolve
negotiate	withdraw	notify	reassess
approve	revise	certify	adjust
exempt	monitor	declare	cooperate
authorize	implement		investigate
	revoke		inspect
	administer		issue

7 Conclusion and Future Work

This paper presents a computational framework for structured information creation and organisation using prompt-based LLMs and KG embedding techniques. We demonstrate how prompt engineering can be effectively used to guide LLMs in extracting high-quality subject–predicate–object triples from complex legal-economic texts, specifically RTAs. These documents, while linguistically and semantically challenging, offer a rich source of contextual information that can be supplemented to enhance existing domain-specific KGs.

Our experiments show that the design of prompt strategies has a significant impact on the accuracy and relevance of the extracted triples. By integrating these triples into a pre-existing trade knowledge graph and applying embedding techniques such as TransE, we observe improvements in relation prediction performance, not only in terms of accuracy but also analysing the quality of context information. The analysis further reveals that certain predicate categories, particularly those related to market access, regulation, trade operations and dispute resolutions contribute disproportionately to predictive gains, underscoring the value of targeted context extraction.

This work highlights the potential of combining LLM-based information extraction with KG enrichment for improving semantic representation and inference in specialized domains. In future work, we aim to explain the results obtained by analysing the network structure.

Acknowledgement. This work has been carried out as part of the KONECO project, and it has received funding from the Bundesministerium für Bildung, Forschung, Technologie und Raumfahrt (BMFTR) under grant No 16DKWN095. We extend our sincere gratitude to Rebekka Koch, our student assistant, for her invaluable contribution in collecting relevant literature, meticulously evaluating the extracted triples, and providing critical support during several key stages of this paper's development.

A Appendix

In this section, we presents the different prompt used for the prompt engineering of Llama 3.1.

A.1 Prompts

Zero Shot Prompt Configuration: *"Suppose you are a triple extractor of a named entity who finds named entity from the given documents for Trade Agreement between documents and its triples. Named entity is a real-world object, such as a person, location, organisation, product, etc., that can be denoted with a proper name. You are provided with a text. Your task is to read the text and extract the named entities from given text and extract respective triples. Triples extraction is a particularly challenging task in information extraction, where the goal is to derive triplets directly from the raw text."*

Single Shot Prompt Configuration: *"Suppose you are a triple extractor of a named entity who finds named entity from the given documents for Trade Agreement between documents and its triples. Named entity is a real-world object, such as a person, location, organisation, product, etc., that can be denoted with a proper name example India, Germany". You are provided with a text. Your task is to read the text and extract the named entity from given text and extract respective triples. Triples extraction is a particularly challenging task in information extraction, where the goal is to derive triplets directly from the raw text. For example, extracting the triplet (Hayao Miyazaki, born_in, Tokyo) from the sentence "Hayao Miyazaki was born in Tokyo." The texts are the legal documents."You also need to identify which countries are being talked about if the sentence mentions 'parties' or 'Parties'. "give only triples extracted from text".*

Few Shot Prompt Configuration: *"Suppose you are a triple extractor of a named entity who finds named entity from the given documents for Trade Agreement between documents and its triples. Named entity is a real-world object, such as a person, location, organisation, product, etc., that can be denoted with a proper name example India, Germany". You are provided with a text. Your task is to read the text and extract the named entity from given text. Triples extraction is a particularly challenging task in information extraction, where the goal is to derive triplets directly from the raw text. The extracted entities should be in the form of a subject, predicate, and object. For example, extracting the triplet (Hayao Miyazaki, born_in, Tokyo) from the sentence "Hayao Miyazaki was born in Tokyo." Another example is 'Germany signed* *a contract with France on 16 December 2015'. The triples extracted is (Germany, signed_ contract_ with, France), (Germany_ France,signed_ contract_ on, 16_ December_ 2015) predicates should be trade related verbs. "The predicates should be minimum 1 and maximum 3 words." You also need to identify which countries are being talked about if the sentence mentions 'parties' or 'Parties'. give only triples extracted from text."*

Negative Examples Prompt Configuration: *"Suppose you are a triple extractor of a named entity who finds named entity from the given documents for Trade Agreement between documents and its triples. Named entity is a real-world object, such as a person, location, organisation, product, etc., that can be denoted with a proper name example India, Germany". You are provided with a text. Your task is to read the text and extract the named entity from given text. Triples extraction is a particularly challenging task in information extraction, where the goal is to derive triplets directly from the raw text. The extracted entities should be in the form of a subject, predicate, and object. For example, extracting the triplet (Hayao Miyazaki, born_ in, Tokyo) from the sentence "Hayao Miyazaki was born in Tokyo." Another example is 'Germany signed a contract with France on 16 December 2015'. The triples extracted is (Germany, signed_ contract_ with, France), (Germany_ France, signed_ contract_ on, 16_ December_ 2015) predicates should be trade related verbs. "The predicates should be minimum 1 and maximum 3 words and Ignore stopwords". You also need to identify which countries are being talked about if the sentence mentions 'parties' or 'Parties' . The 'parties', 'Parties' must be replaced with the country names they are being referred to". Do not assume country names if not mentioned". give only triples extracted from text. Do not generate new facts that are not present in the original text.*

References

1. Alschner, W., Seiermann, J., Skougarevskiy, D.: Text-as-data analysis of preferential trade agreements: mapping the pta landscape (2017)
2. Ashburner, M., et al.: Gene ontology: tool for the unification of biology. Nat. Genet. **25**(1), 25–29 (2000)
3. Berners-Lee, T., Hendler, J., Lassila, O.: The semantic web: a new form of web content that is meaningful to computers will unleash a revolution of new possibilities. In: Linking the World's Information: Essays on Tim Berners-Lee's Invention of the World Wide Web, pp. 91–103 (2023)
4. Bird, S., Klein, E., Loper, E.: Natural Language Processing with Python: Analyzing Text with the Natural Language Toolkit. O'Reilly Media Inc., Sebastopol (2009)
5. Bolón-Canedo, V., Sánchez-Maroño, N., Alonso-Betanzos, A.: Feature selection for high-dimensional data. Prog. Artif. Intell. **5**(2), 65–75 (2016). https://doi.org/10.1007/s13748-015-0080-y
6. Borchert, I., Larch, M., Shikher, S., Yotov, Y.V.: The international trade and production database for estimation (ITPD-E). Int. Econ. **166**, 140–166 (2021)

7. Bordes, A., Usunier, N., Garcia-Duran, A., Weston, J., Yakhnenko, O.: Translating embeddings for modeling multi-relational data. Adv. Neural Inf. Process. Syst. **26** (2013)
8. Chen, B., Zhang, Z., Langrené, N., Zhu, S.: Unleashing the potential of prompt engineering for large language models. Patterns 101260 (2025)
9. Chiu, J.P.C., Nichols, E.: Named entity recognition with bidirectional lstm-cnns. Trans. Assoc. Comput. Linguist. **4**, 357–370 (2016). https://aclanthology.org/Q16-1026
10. Dessí, D., Osborne, F., Recupero, D.R., Buscaldi, D., Motta, E.: Scicero: a deep learning and nlp approach for generating scientific knowledge graphs in the computer science domain. Knowl.-Based Syst. **258**, 109945 (2022)
11. Donoho, D.L., et al.: High-dimensional data analysis: the curses and blessings of dimensionality. AMS Math Chall. Lect. **1**(2000), 32 (2000)
12. Egger, P.H., Larch, M.: Interdependent preferential trade agreement memberships: an empirical analysis. J. Int. Econ. **76**(2), 384–399 (2008)
13. Ehrlinger, L., Wöß, W.: Towards a definition of knowledge graphs. SEMANTiCS (Posters, Demos, SuCCESS) **48**(1–4), 2 (2016)
14. Gurevich, T., Herman, P.: The dynamic gravity dataset: 1948-2016. US International Trade Commission. Office of Economics Working Paper (2018)
15. Hogan, A., et al.: Knowledge graphs. no. 22 in synthesis lectures on data, semantics, and knowledge. Springer, Heidelberg (2022). https://doi.org/10.1007/978-3-031-01918-0
16. Iglesias, E., Jozashoori, S., Chaves-Fraga, D., Collarana, D., Vidal, M.E.: Sdm-rdfizer: an rml interpreter for the efficient creation of rdf knowledge graphs. In: Proceedings of the 29th ACM International Conference on Information & Knowledge Management, pp. 3039–3046 (2020)
17. Lassila, O., Hendler, J., Berners-Lee, T.: The semantic web. Sci. Am. **284**(5), 34–43 (2001)
18. Li, F.L., et al.: Alimekg: domain knowledge graph construction and application in e-commerce. In: Proceedings of the 29th ACM International Conference on Information & Knowledge Management, pp. 2581–2588 (2020)
19. Liu, P., Yuan, W., Fu, J., Jiang, Z., Hayashi, H., Neubig, G.: Pre-train, prompt, and predict: a systematic survey of prompting methods in natural language processing. ACM Comput. Surv. **55**(9), 1–35 (2023)
20. Liu, X., et al.: Prompting frameworks for large language models: a survey. arXiv preprint arXiv:2311.12785 (2023)
21. Mayer, T., Zignago, S.: Notes on CEPII's distances measures: the geodist database (2011)
22. Nadeau, D., Sekine, S.: A survey of named entity recognition and classification. Lingvisticae Investigationes **30**(1), 3–26 (2007). https://doi.org/10.1075/li.30.1.03nad
23. Nandini, D., Blöthner, S., Schoenfeld, M., Larch, M.: Multidimensional knowledge graph embeddings for international trade flow analysis. In: Proceedings of the 16th International Joint Conference on Knowledge Discovery, Knowledge Engineering and Knowledge Management - KEOD, pp. 63–73. INSTICC, SciTePress (2024). https://doi.org/10.5220/0013028500003838
24. Nandini, D., Schmid, U.: Explaining hate speech classification with model-agnostic methods. In: CEUR Workshop Proceedings, vol. 3457 (2022)
25. Paulheim, H.: Knowledge graph refinement: a survey of approaches and evaluation methods. Semant. Web **8**(3), 489–508 (2016)

26. Rau, L.F.: Extracting company names from text. In: Proceedings of the 7th Conference on Artificial Intelligence Applications, pp. 29–32. IEEE (1991). https://doi.org/10.1109/CAIA.1991.755366
27. Raudenbush, S.W., Bryk, A.S.: Hierarchical Linear Models: Applications and Data Analysis Methods, vol. 1. Sage (2002)
28. Shahi, G., Hummel, O.: On the effectiveness of large language models in automating categorization of scientific texts. In: Proceedings of the 27th International Conference on Enterprise Information Systems, vol. 1: ICEIS, pp. 544–554. INSTICC, SciTePress (2025). https://doi.org/10.5220/0013299100003929
29. Shahi, G.K.: Fakekg: a knowledge graph of fake claims for improving automated fact-checking (student abstract). In: Proceedings of the AAAI Conference on Artificial Intelligence, vol. 37, pp. 16320–16321 (2023)
30. Singhal, A., et al.: Introducing the knowledge graph: things, not strings. Off. Google Blog **5**(16), 3 (2012)
31. Strobelt, H., et al.: Interactive and visual prompt engineering for ad-hoc task adaptation with large language models. IEEE Trans. Visual Comput. Graph. **29**(1), 1146–1156 (2022)
32. Wolfram, S.: A New Kind of Science, vol. 5. Wolfram Media, Champaign (2002)
33. Zhou, Y., et al.: Large language models are human-level prompt engineers. In: The Eleventh International Conference on Learning Representations (2002)

LLM-Based Dependency Tracking for Short Event Descriptions

Naoki Sawahata[1], Daisuke Machizawa[1], Ryohei Ikejiri[2], and Yasunobu Sumikawa[1](✉)

[1] Takushoku University, Tokyo, Japan
sumikawa.lab@gmail.com
[2] Hiroshima University, Hiroshima, Japan
rikejiri@hiroshima-u.ac.jp

Abstract. Structuring the relationships through which events occur is crucial for gaining a deeper understanding of the past and for applying that knowledge to the present. In this study, we propose a method for constructing event networks that represent dependencies between events using large language models (LLMs). Our method performs both network and node selection to identify event pairs prior to applying the LLM. To evaluate the method, we collected past event data from Wikipedia and created a network dataset. An evaluation of our method showed an F1 score of 45.1%, demonstrating its effectiveness.

Keywords: Wikipedia · events · event graph · dependency · causal relationship

1 Introduction

Many digital libraries, such as Wikipedia, record events that have occurred throughout history. These events are often arranged in chronological order based on their dates of occurrence, with the dependencies between them typically left unspecified, as shown in Fig. 1 (a). As the saying goes, *History doesn't repeat itself, but it often rhymes,* properly understanding the past provides important benefits, such as deepening our understanding of the formation processes of modern society and laying the foundation for developing strategies to address contemporary issues. Since digital libraries archive not only modern events but also those dating back to ancient times, structuring the dependencies among these events could serve as a crucial basis for understanding historical developments and providing enriched information access.

Various methods have been proposed to construct timelines [6,8,17,31], tree structures [14,32], and networks [30] from lengthy event descriptions found in news articles. However, as shown in Fig. 1 (a), the events recorded in digital libraries are often described so briefly that extracting contextual information from the text itself becomes difficult, making it challenging for existing methods to construct appropriate networks.

W.-T. Balke et al. (Eds.): TPDL 2025, LNCS 16097, pp. 71–89, 2026.
https://doi.org/10.1007/978-3-032-05409-8_6

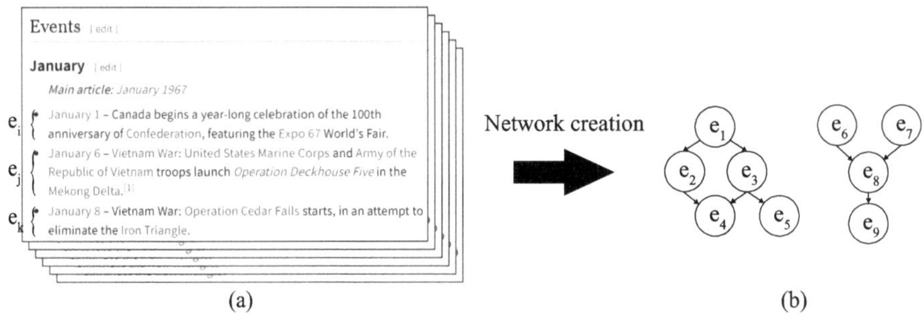

Fig. 1. (a) Examples of events recorded in Wikipedia. (b) Example results of StoryNetworks.

In this study, we propose a method for structuring dependencies between events described in short texts, where contextual information is often limited. Our approach represents these events as network graphs, which we refer to as StoryNetworks. Figure 1 (b) presents example StoryNetworks constructed using the proposed method. To analyze event dependencies despite the absence of explicit contextual cues, we leverage large language models (LLMs) to infer implicit relationships, such as geopolitical associations or temporal overlaps, often suggested by named entities, e.g., countries or individuals, mentioned in the event descriptions. Accordingly, this study addresses the following research questions:

- Are LLMs effective at analyzing dependencies between events described in short texts?
- How can LLMs be utilized to construct a network of event dependencies?

To mitigate the introduction of spurious or redundant edges in the StoryNetwork due to overly broad event pairings, our method performs two-step selection algorithms: (1) grouping semantically similar events, and (2) selecting specific pairs of events within each group for targeted dependency analysis using LLMs.

To the best of our knowledge, no existing dataset consists solely of networks constructed from short event descriptions. Therefore, in this study, we manually constructed a dataset[1] by collecting short-text event data from the Current events portal of Wikipedia[2] that provides daily updates on notable global news and recent events. Using this dataset, we conducted experiments comparing our proposed method with previous methods, which assume the availability of longer texts. The results showed that while the baseline methods achieved an F1 score of 27.9%, our method achieved a significantly higher score of 45.1%, demonstrating its superior performance.

The contributions of this study are summarized as follows:

- We tackled a novel problem of constructing event networks from short-text event descriptions.

[1] Our dataset is available at https://github.com/sumilab/dataset.
[2] https://en.wikipedia.org/wiki/Portal:Current_events.

- We created a new event network dataset that includes a larger number of events.
- We designed an algorithm for constructing event networks and demonstrated its effectiveness through experimental evaluation.

2 Related Work

Previous research efforts aimed at structuring related events can be broadly categorized into three main areas: topic detection and tracking (TDT), timeline summarization (TLS), and event evolution graph (EEG) creation.

TDT focuses on identifying which previously reported news articles are related to newly reported ones. Research in this area includes studies aimed at predicting future developments [21] and detecting trending events on social media platforms [11,15,20,24]. Traditionally, TDT has been achieved by measuring textual similarity based on the bag-of-words model and applying clustering algorithms to detect events that belong to the same topic [10,13]. In addition, there have been proposals to realize TDT using probabilistic clustering models [3,7,29] as well as methods based on BERT [28]. These studies primarily propose methods for arranging related events in chronological order. More recently, research has extended beyond linear arrangement by representing events in a tree structure to clarify the underlying timelines they form [14,32].

From a graph-structural perspective, a key difference between our method and those proposed in previous research lies in the ability to generate *event joining*, where multiple events collectively depend on a single subsequent event. Specifically, while our proposed method is capable of generating such event joining, prior approaches are not designed to do so. As stated in Sect. 1, in order to gain a deeper understanding of the past, it is important not only to list events chronologically as a timeline but also to clearly express which events could actually serve as causes, as represented through event joining.

Timeline summarization focuses not simply on listing related events but on selecting key events, words [22], or sentences [5] to facilitate easier understanding, and arranging them in chronological order. According to [8], methods for timeline summarization can be broadly classified into three types: direct summarization, date-wise approach, and event detection. Direct summarization generates a timeline by selecting multiple sentences [5,17,19]. Date-wise approach selects sentences from the dataset based on the number of days and sentences per day, specified as hyperparameters, and compiles a timeline summary [18]. Event detection involves identifying events within the dataset and generating summaries using the most important events [8]. While most of these methods use long documents such as news articles to create timelines, other approaches have been proposed for microblogs, where the text is much shorter and noisier [2,23]. In methods targeting microblogs, features beyond simple textual similarity, such as the number of posts referencing the same event, are also incorporated into the timeline generation process. Additionally, there are approaches that use abstract meaning representation results to select sentences for timeline creation [17].

The timelines generated by the aforementioned methods are structured as a single chronological sequence of sentences per query. As a result, these methods fail to capture not only event joining but also event threading, a structure in which multiple events depend on a single preceding event. Although methods have been proposed that generate multiple timelines in response to a query, thereby representing different stories [6,31], these approaches still produce multiple linear sequences and are not capable of directly representing dependency relationships where multiple events converge into a single event.

Research aiming to represent event dependencies as networks, similar to our study, includes the EEG proposed by [30]. This previous study proposed a method for automatically constructing networks using an extension of TF-IDF and cosine similarity. The key differences between the previous study and our work are as follows: 1) Length of event descriptions: our study assumes that each event is described in a short text, whereas EEG assumes the availability of longer, more detailed news articles. 2) Assumptions about evolution: previous studies assume that events related through evolution share similar vocabulary or key terms. However, when dealing with short event descriptions, it is often the case that events primarily share information related to countries or regions. This can bias results toward clustering events geographically. In contrast, our study leverages LLMs to extract important vocabulary and key concepts beyond geographic or national references. 3) Method of capturing contextual information: EEG extracts context only from within the news articles themselves, and rely on related news lists available on CNN News websites during dataset construction. In contrast, we utilize LLMs to infer contextual information, even when it is not explicitly stated in the text. 4) Dataset construction: [30] collected 176 events. In comparison, we collected over 5,000 event texts from Wikipedia, which is approximately 28 times larger than that of the previous study.

Studies on dependency extraction using LLMs have also been reported [16]. However, even in this study, the target texts are long documents such as news articles, as the objective is to extract event pairs within a single document.

3 Dataset Creation

In this section, we describe the data collection process, followed by the procedures for constructing the dataset from the collected data.

3.1 Data Collection

We utilized Wikipedia as the primary source of information for data collection as it contains a vast amount of recorded events suitable for constructing various types of networks. Wikipedia records events dating from ancient times to the present, organized by each year[3] and each month and day[4]. Manually constructing networks from all of this data would incur a substantial cost; thus, this study created seed networks using events recorded in the Wikipedia current portal from January 1, 2016, to December 31, 2017.

Table 1. Dataset statistics.

Number of events used in timelines	5,204
Number of timelines	2,889
Number of dependencies	2,494
Period of timestamps	1 Jan. 2016–31 Dec. 2017

Table 1 presents the statistics of the past event data collected in this study, along with the timelines and networks constructed from them.

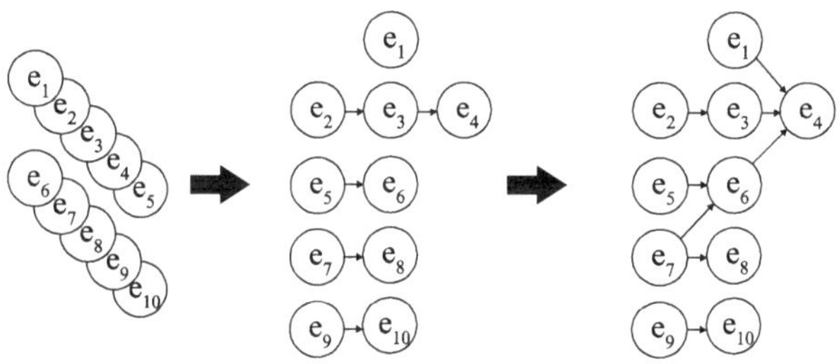

(a) Input event texts (b) Timeline creation (c) Timeline connection

Fig. 2. Dataset creation process.

3.2 Timeline Creation

Figure 2 illustrates the procedure used to construct the dataset in this study. The networks allow for multiple paths to emerge from an initial event, where each path can be regarded as a timeline. By connecting a single event to multiple subsequent events as its children, multiple distinct paths can be defined. In this structure, although sibling events share a certain degree of relatedness, they can be considered to belong to different topics. Therefore, we define a timeline as a sequence of events that are similar in content and share the same topic, as shown in Fig. 2(b).

As discussed in Sect. 2, many studies have been conducted on timeline generation. This study adopts the position of utilizing timelines, rather than proposing

[3] e.g., https://en.wikipedia.org/wiki/2020.

[4] e.g., https://en.wikipedia.org/wiki/January_23.

a new method for generating them. Therefore, we first evaluated whether existing timeline generation methods can produce high-quality timelines from short event descriptions. To conduct this evaluation, we manually created 42 timelines using only the event data from January 2016. This task was performed by two annotators, and only timelines on which both annotators agreed were included. Among existing methods, we implemented the method proposed by Kira Radinsky [21], which utilizes textual information within event sentences, and evaluated its precision, recall, and F1 score, obtaining 16.6%, 9.5%, and 12.1%, respectively. These results indicate that the method is insufficient for constructing the dataset. Although methods using BERT or LLMs [16] have also been proposed, even when applied to longer texts, their F1 scores are only around 60%, which is still inadequate for reliable dataset construction. Consequently, in this study, we manually created the timelines.

The procedure for manual creation involved two annotators independently constructing timelines for the event data from 2016 and 2017, respectively. All of the timelines created in this process were then evaluated for validity by a third annotator. If any events needed to be added or removed, the third annotator discussed these changes with the original creators of the timelines and revised them accordingly. We created 2,889 timelines from the two years of events.

3.3 Timelines Connection

After manually verifying the timelines obtained through the procedure described in Sect. 3.2, it was found that even events which formed a dependency relationship, such as "The Ukraine war (war category) caused a rise in oil prices (economic category)," were assigned to different groups due to differing main topics. Particularly relevant events were manually extracted from multiple timelines and subsequently linked to construct a network, as shown in Fig. 2 (c). By identifying this dependency and drawing directed edges between events across different timelines, it becomes possible to graphically represent event threading and event joining.

For the created timelines, all possible combinations were generated, and the existence of dependency relationships between events of them was manually verified. The process of connecting the timelines was performed using the same procedure as timeline creation; two workers independently created connections for the timelines from 2016 and 2017. Subsequently, a third worker evaluated the validity of all the connected timelines created. If any additions or deletions of connections were necessary, discussions were held with the creators of the respective connected timelines to modify the connections accordingly. As a result of this process, 2,494 dependencies from networks were defined.

4 StoryNetwork Creation Algorithm

Our algorithm performs network selection and event selection to prevent the definition of excessive edges in the network construction. When humans construct

Algorithm 1. StoryNetwork creation

Input: Event set: *Evt*

1: **Function** *SNetCreation* (*Evt*)
2: $N \leftarrow \emptyset$
3: **foreach** $e \in Evt$
4: $n \leftarrow NetworkSelect(N, e)$
5: $Evt' \leftarrow FrontierEventSelect(e, n)$
6: $EdgeList \leftarrow EdgeCreation(Evt', e, n)$
7: $Update(N, n, EdgeList)$
8: **Function** *EdgeCreation* (Evt', e, n)
9: $EdgeList \leftarrow []$
10: **foreach** $e' \in Evt'$
11: **if** $Prompt(e', e) =$ Yes
12: $EdgeList$.append$((e', e))$
13: **return** *EdgeList*

a network, if multiple timelines are derived from a single event, edges between events within these derived timelines are defined only to the minimum necessary. In contrast, when an LLM is applied to identify relationships between two events, it may define edges excessively, even in cases where a human would not.

Algorithm 1 presents the main implementation steps of the proposed method. First, a list N is defined to manage all the networks to be created by this method (line 2). In line 3, the event e is processed one by one to either create a new network or expand an existing one. The function *NetworkSelect* in line 4 selects the network with the highest probability of including e from the existing networks. The function *FrontierEventSelect* in line 5 selects a set of candidate events Evt' for analyzing the connection with e from the events contained in n. The function *EdgeCreation* in line 6 analyzes the relationship between e and $e' \in Evt'$ and outputs a list of edges that are defined as a result. Finally, this list of edges is reflected in the network by the function *Update* in line 7. If N is an empty set, both n and Evt' will also be empty. In *EdgeCreation*, e will then be recorded as the unique node of n. Additionally, if *NetworkSelect* results in no existing network that should include e, n will be output as an empty set, and the subsequent process will proceed as described above. The detail procedures of *EdgeCreation* are defined in lines 9 to 13. First, the list of edges returned by this function is defined in line 9. In line 10, one event at a time is extracted from Evt', and whether to define an edge between it and e is determined by executing the function *Prompt*, which runs the LLM prompt.

In the following, we describe details of *NetworkSelect*, *FrontierEventSelect*, and *Prompt* in that order.

4.1 Network Selection

The network generated by this method varies depending on the content of the events; therefore, several networks may be constructed at the same time. The process begins by determining whether a newly input event e should be incorporated into an existing network n.

We executed a prompt on GPT-4o to determine which of the predefined groups a given event should belong to. The prompt instructed the model to return the corresponding group ID if a suitable group existed, or to define a new group if none were appropriate.

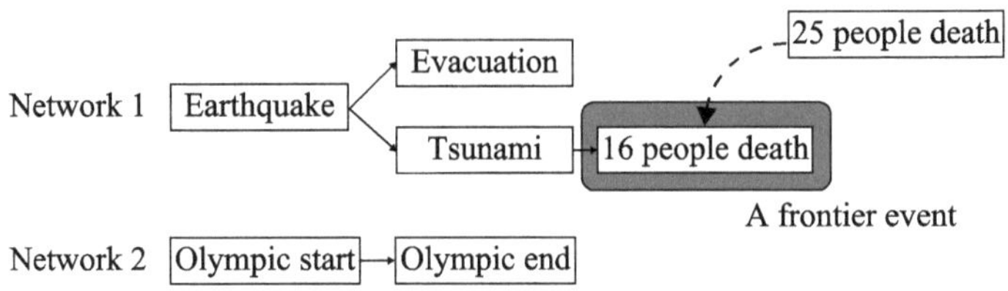

Fig. 3. Example of frontier event selection. The gray rectangles indicate frontier events. (Color figure online)

4.2 Frontier Event Selection

The primary objective of this step is to identify, for each event, a pairing with the most recent previously analyzed event that shares one or more timelines. We refer to these most recent events as frontier events. The purpose of identifying this frontier event is to narrow down the scope of dependency analysis to be conducted in the subsequent step. This narrowing is carried out by determining whether the topics of the event descriptions are consistent. For instance, as shown in Fig. 3, multiple reports on the number of deaths caused by an earthquake share the same topic. When such updated information is reported, it suffices to identify that an update has occurred; therefore, only the most recent event among past similar events is selected. In this example, the new event `25 people death` should be only linked to `16 people death` as this event reports that the death toll has been revised. If we skip this selection step, the event could also be linked to `Earthquake` or `Tsunami`, resulting in an unnecessarily dense network structure. The objective of this step is formally defined as follows:

$$FrontierEvents(e) \stackrel{def}{\Leftrightarrow} \{e_j | (e_i, e_j) \in E(n), isFront(e, e_i, e_j)\} \tag{1}$$

where E is a function that returns all edges defined in the group n. *isFront* determines whether e_j is a frontier node of group n.

The formal definition of *isFront* is presented below. Let e and (e_i, e_j) be the newly analyzed event and the previously defined event pair, respectively. In this notation, it is assumed that the event written on the right occurred more recently than the one on the left; that is, e_j is assumed to be more recent than e_i. First, we analyze whether e and e_j share the same topic. To do this, we compute the topic distribution using BERTopic [9] and calculate the Euclidean distance between their feature vectors. If the Euclidean distance between the topic distribution scores is below a certain threshold, we conclude that the two events share the same topic.

The formal definition of this calculation is given as follows:

$$isSim(e_k, e_l) \overset{def}{\Leftrightarrow} Dist(FVec(e_k), FVec(e_l)) < Thre \quad (2)$$

where *Dist* is a function that computes the Euclidean distance between two feature vectors. *FVec* applies BERTopic to generate a feature vector for the given event. *Thre* is a hyperparameter, which we set to 0.6. This value was selected based on the experimental results that yielded the best performance using the dataset created in this study. If these events share the same topic, we then analyze whether e and e_i also belong to the same topic. If this pair also shares the same topic, e_j is considered the frontier event, and we skip defining the pair (e_i, e), defining only the pair (e_j, e). The following provides formal definitions of these processes.

$$isFront(e, e_i, e_j) \overset{def}{\Leftrightarrow} isSim(e, e_j) \wedge isSim(e, e_i) \quad (3)$$

If there are no shared topics between e and e_j, we then perform these analyses for other edges.

4.3 Edge Creation

We utilize LLM to determine whether an edge should be defined between two events. To implement this, three prompting methods are employed: zero-shot (ZS) prompting, few-shot (FS) prompting, and the combination of FS with Chain-of-Thought (CoT) prompting.

ZS Prompting. ZS prompting refers to a method that does not provide examples during inference [4]. Our method presents an LLM with two event descriptions and ask whether a dependency exists between them. Importantly, no additional examples of dependencies or specific data characteristics are provided. If the LLM determines that a dependency exists, it is instructed to return "Yes"; otherwise, it returns "No".

Figure 4 presents the prompt template created for this mode. The placeholders <event1> and <event2> are to be filled with the two event descriptions whose dependency is to be examined.

FS Prompting. FS prompting involves including two examples within the prompt: one consisting of a pair of events that we define as having a dependency, and the other consisting of a pair of events for which no dependency is defined. These examples serve as contextual information for the model. To ensure balance, we provide one example each of a positive and a negative case of dependency. Figure 5 presents the template we used for constructing FS prompts. Note that we omit the Background and Task Description sections for clarity in this figure, as their content is identical to that of ZS.

CoT Prompting. CoT prompting is a technique that enhances the reasoning capability of LLMs by incorporating intermediate explanations that lead to a final conclusion [27]. We include explanatory reasoning based on whether the two events occurred at the same or nearby locations, or whether they involve shared names of individuals or organizations-factors that can serve as evidence for a dependency as shown in Fig. 6. LLMs are proficient at determining spatial relationships, such as whether two places represent a country-city relation or whether two cities are geographically close. They are also trained on background knowledge about well-known individuals and organizations. Accordingly, our explanations include references to location, time, and, people as potential grounds for inferring dependency. When combining FS and CoT prompting, we used the same examples as those employed in the FS-only setting.

```
* Background *
You are working for creating a dataset that includes dependencies or known as
stories of events. This dataset helps us to know what events a single story has.
Thus, if there is dependency, correlation, or chains as story between two events,
this work sets a dependency between the two events.
* Task description *
I would like you to support creating the dataset. Could you judge whether there
is a same story between the following two events? If your analysis finds any story,
please say Yes. Otherwise, say No. Please say only Yes or No.
* Event 1:
<event1>
* Event 2:
<event2>
```

Fig. 4. Prompt template for ZS.

* Background *
(same as ZS template)
* Task description *
(same as ZS template)
* Example of Yes*
Event 1: The campaign of Jill Stein files for a recount in Pennsylvania and plans to do so in Michigan.
Event 2: Jill Stein files for recount in Michigan.
* Example of No*
Event 1: Saudi Arabia breaks off diplomatic relations with Iran after Sheikh Nimr's execution and an attack on the Saudi embassy in Tehran.
Event 2: Mexican authorities want to question American actor Sean Penn and Mexican actress Kate del Castillo about a secret October meeting and interview with Joaquín Guzmán, published by Rolling Stone magazine yesterday. Mexico Attorney General Arely Gomez says it was the Penn interview that led authorities to a Guzman hiding place.
* Event 1:
<event1>
* Event 2:
<event2>

Fig. 5. Prompt template for FS.

5 Experimental Evaluation

5.1 Research Questions

We conducted the experiments based on the following research questions (**RQs**):

- **RQ1**: Which LLM model most accurately identified the presence or absence of a dependency between two events?
- **RQ2**: Did the proposed method construct a more effective network compared to previous approaches?

First, we address **RQ1** by evaluating the prediction accuracy of each LLM model using a dataset specifically prepared to verify only the presence or absence of dependencies. Building on these results, we then proceed to **RQ2**, where we identify combinations of events for analyzing dependencies and assess the accuracy of the resulting constructed network.

5.2 Models

We evaluated the following five models to investigate which are most effective for **RQ1**.

- ChatGPT: ChatGPT is based on a transformer architecture and is designed to generate human-like text. The version this study used was GPT-4o.

> * Example of Yes*
> Event 1: The campaign of Jill Stein files for a recount in Pennsylvania and plans to do so in Michigan.
> Event 2: Jill Stein files for recount in Michigan.
> Reason: These two events relate to the results of an election for the same person. It is also stated in the first event that the second event is scheduled to occur. Therefore, since these events have dependency, the result is Yes.
> * Example of No*
> Event 1: Saudi Arabia breaks off diplomatic relations with Iran after Sheikh Nimr's execution and an attack on the Saudi embassy in Tehran.
> Event 2: Mexican authorities want to question American actor Sean Penn and Mexican actress Kate del Castillo about a secret October meeting and interview with Joaquín Guzmán, published by Rolling Stone magazine yesterday. Mexico Attorney General Arely Gomez says it was the Penn interview that led authorities to a Guzman hiding place.
> Reason: These two events illustrate the different relationship between nations. Neither has a common country name. In terms of verbs, the first event is often associated with war, such as "breaks off" or "attack," while the second event is often associated with discussion or negotiation, such as "question" or "led." Because of the difference in subject and action, we can say that there is no dependency between these events, so the answer is no.

Fig. 6. Prompt template for FS-CoT.

- Llama 3: This is a transformer-based, autoregressive LLM [26]. We employed the Llama3-8B model in our experiments.
- Mistral: Mistral is a decoder-based model [12]. We used the Mistral-7B-Instruct-v0.1 version, setting the temperature parameter to 0.0001.
- Phi3: Phi3 [1] is a transformer-based model. For our evaluation, we used the Phi-3 Mini model.
- Gemini: Gemini is a multimodal language model[25]. This model is built on a combination of transformers and mixture of experts architecture. Although this model is designed as a multimodal language model, we input only texts. We used the Gemini 2.5 Flash version.

For **RQ2**, we evaluated EEG that investigated whether dependencies between two events could be defined using TF-IDF and cosine similarity to construct event network [30]. EEG determines the presence or absence of a dependency based solely on the textual content of the given sentences.

5.3 Evaluation Criteria

In accordance with prior studies on network construction [30], we employ precision (P), recall (R), and F1 score (F) as defined below.

$$P = \frac{R_A \cap R_M}{R_M}, R = \frac{R_A \cap R_M}{R_A}, F = \frac{2PR}{P + R}$$

where R_A denotes the results obtained by the annotators, whereas R_M indicates the predictions generated by the algorithm.

5.4 Results

RQ1: Which LLM model most accurately identified the presence or absence of a dependency between two events?
A1. Llama 3 achieved the highest F1 score among the models.
A2. Both Llama 3 and ChatGPT achieved F1 scores exceeding 90%.
A3. ZS prompting consistently achieved the highest F1 scores across all LLMs evaluated.
A4. Among the evaluated LLMs, ChatGPT proved to be the most effective for implementing the proposed method.

To appropriately evaluate the performance of each LLM model, we prepared a subset from the dataset created in Sect. 3. This subset contains two types of data: positive examples, where a dependency exists between two events, and negative examples, where no such dependency exists. Positive examples were directly taken from the existing dataset. Negative examples include randomly paired events extracted from different timelines, where human annotators verified that no dependency relationship exists between the events. To eliminate temporal bias, we ensured a balanced selection of events from January 2016 to December 2017. To collect a balanced set of data from many different months, we extracted 100 positive and 100 negative examples per month. However, for July 2017, only 54 positive examples were available; therefore, we also extracted only 54 negative examples for that month. As a result, the subset prepared for evaluating **RQ1** consisted of 2,354 positive examples and 2,354 negative examples, totaling 4,708 event pairs.

Table 2 presents the results of the dependency analysis conducted by all the LLM models used in this study. All LLM models obtained high recall scores. This indicates that they are generally capable of correctly outputting "No" for event pairs that occurred in the same month but were assigned to different timelines by human annotators. On the other hand, precision tends to be lower than recall, suggesting that it is more challenging for these models to correctly output "Yes" for event pairs that should be linked, as well as for human judgment.

Focusing on the F1 scores, Llama 3 achieved the best performance. However, Llama 3 frequently refused to respond to events related to politics or conflicts, often requiring repeated queries to obtain results. Furthermore, Llama 3 did not produce any output for the network selection task. Therefore, in the following experiments, we used ChatGPT, which achieved the second-highest F1 score, for network construction. In the following, we refer to our method using ChatGPT as SN.

Table 2. Results of dependency prediction by LLM. Bold letters indicate the best results.

	Algorithm	P	R	F
ChatGPT	ZS	84.3%	99.6%	91.3%
	FS	71.7%	**100.0%**	83.5%
	FS-CoT	73.8%	**100.0%**	84.9%
Llama 3	ZS	92.2%	95.1%	**93.6%**
	FS	84.5%	2.5%	4.9%
	FS-CoT	98.9%	4.0%	7.7%
Mistral	ZS	65.3%	99.9%	79.0%
	FS	56.3%	**100.0%**	72.0%
	FS-CoT	56.3%	**100.0%**	72.0%
Phi3	ZS	53.9%	96.3%	69.1%
	FS	53.9%	96.3%	69.1%
	FS-CoT	53.9%	96.3%	69.1%
Gemini	ZS	82.4%	99.8%	90.0%
	FS	74.7%	99.8%	85.5%
	FS-CoT	80.4%	99.5%	88.9%

RQ2: Did the proposed method construct a more effective network compared to previous approaches?
A1. We achieved an F1 score approximately 17 percentage points higher than that of previous methods designed for long-form texts.
A2. Node selection in the proposed method made a significant contribution to improving precision and F1 scores.

Table 3 presents the results for EEG; SN-no-opt, which analyzes all combinations of event pairs without applying either network selection or node selection; SN-Net, which applies only the network selection component of our proposed method; and SN-Net-Node, which applies both network selection and node selection. The results show that the proposed method SN-Net-Node achieved the highest F1 score and outperformed the other methods. That is, by selecting in advance both the network to which a newly added event belongs and the set of events within that network, it can be said that even events described in short texts can be used to construct high-accuracy networks when leveraging LLM.

Focusing on SN-Net, we can see that its precision was lower than that of EEG, while its recall was higher. A possible reason could be that SN-Net defined more edges than the human-constructed network, resulting in a denser connection structure. In contrast, by incorporating node selection, SN-Net-Node prevented the network from becoming excessively dense, which in turn led to an improvement in precision. Focusing on precision, SN-Net yielded a lower score than EEG, although SN-no-opt obtained better result than the baseline. This decline can be attributed to the network selection process, which generates multiple event groups and consequently reduces the number of appropriate event pairs analyzed by the LLM. Upon examining the constructed networks, we found that events related to the 2016 U.S. presidential election campaign and those concerning personnel appointments and policy implementations following inauguration that are originally of the new president defined as a single group in the dataset had been divided into two separate groups. As SN-Net generates prompts for all combinations within the same group, this finer-grained division led to denser network constructions than those defined by human annotators. We believe that this over-fragmentation is a key factor contributing to the decline in precision.

Table 3. Results of network creation. Bold letters indicate the best results.

Algorithm	P	R	F
EEG	29.8%	26.2%	27.9%
SN-no-opt	41.3 %	16.4%	23.4%
SN-Net	16.1 %	**48.1%**	24.1%
SN-Net-Node	**67.7%**	33.8%	**45.1%**

Figure 7 illustrates an example of a network generated by SN-Net-Node. In this example, the edges defined by the method are shown as solid lines, while the edges that were defined in the dataset but not identified by SN-Net-Node are shown as dashed lines. The solid lines, when viewed in chronological order, successfully trace events related to international sports. However, the method failed to capture connections between events concerning participation of athletes, which were manually defined by humans.

Fig. 7. An example of an event network created by the proposed method.

6 Conclusions

Structuring events that are in dependency relationships contributes to understanding the processes that have shaped both past and contemporary societies. In this study, we propose a method to supplement missing contextual information, which cannot be directly analyzed from short texts, by leveraging LLMs, in order to construct networks that represent dependencies among short event descriptions. To achieve this goal, we first created a dataset composed of event networks built from short texts. Using a subset of this dataset, which includes both dependent and independent event pairs, we evaluated the ability of LLMs to appropriately analyze dependencies between short event descriptions. The results demonstrated that Llama 3 and GPT-4o achieved high F1 scores. Subsequently, we proposed a two-step method incorporating network selection and node selection to construct networks while reducing the number of event pairs analyzed by the LLM. We evaluated the effectiveness of this method using the constructed dataset and achieved an F1 score of 45%. This F1 score is approximately 17% points higher than that of previous methods designed for long-form event descriptions, demonstrating the effectiveness of combining LLMs with pair reduction strategies.

As a direction for future work, expanding the dataset used for constructing event networks is a promising avenue. In this study, we focused on data from 2016 and 2017 recorded in current events portal of Wikipedia. However, Wikipedia also contains records of events dating back to ancient times. We will organized all historical records available in Wikipedia by applying our method.

Acknowledgements. This work was supported in part by MEXT Grant-in-Aids (#25K15357). We also thank our anonymous reviewers for their insightful feedback and comments.

References

1. Abdin, M., Aneja, J., et al.: Phi-3 technical report: a highly capable language model locally on your phone (2024). https://arxiv.org/abs/2404.14219
2. Alonso, O., Shiells, K.: Timelines as summaries of popular scheduled events. In: Proceedings of the 22nd International Conference on World Wide Web. WWW '13 Companion, pp. 1037–1044. Association for Computing Machinery, New York (2013). https://doi.org/10.1145/2487788.2488114
3. Amayri, O., Bouguila, N.: Online news topic detection and tracking via localized feature selection. In: The 2013 International Joint Conference on Neural Networks (IJCNN), pp. 1–8 (2013). https://doi.org/10.1109/IJCNN.2013.6707027
4. Brown, T., Mann, B., Ryder, N.E.A.: Language models are few-shot learners. In: Larochelle, H., Ranzato, M., Hadsell, R., Balcan, M., Lin, H. (eds.) Advances in Neural Information Processing Systems, vol. 33, pp. 1877–1901. Curran Associates, Inc. (2020). https://proceedings.neurips.cc/paper_files/paper/2020/file/1457c0d6bfcb4967418bfb8ac142f64a-Paper.pdf

5. Chieu, H.L., Lee, Y.K.: Query based event extraction along a timeline. In: Proceedings of the 27th Annual International ACM SIGIR Conference on Research and Development in Information Retrieval. SIGIR '04, pp. 425–432. Association for Computing Machinery, New York (2004). https://doi.org/10.1145/1008992.1009065
6. Duan, Y., Jatowt, A., Yoshikawa, M.: Comparative timeline summarization via dynamic affinity-preserving random walk. In: Giacomo, G.D., et al. (eds.) ECAI 2020 - 24th European Conference on Artificial Intelligence, 29 August-8 September 2020, Santiago de Compostela, Spain, 29 August–8 September 2020 - Including 10th Conference on Prestigious Applications of Artificial Intelligence (PAIS 2020). Frontiers in Artificial Intelligence and Applications, vol. 325, pp. 1778–1785. IOS Press (2020). https://doi.org/10.3233/FAIA200292
7. Fan, W., Guo, Z., Bouguila, N., Hou, W.: Clustering-based online news topic detection and tracking through hierarchical bayesian nonparametric models. In: Proceedings of the 44th International ACM SIGIR Conference on Research and Development in Information Retrieval, pp. 2126–2130. SIGIR '21, Association for Computing Machinery, New York (2021). https://doi.org/10.1145/3404835.3462982
8. Gholipour Ghalandari, D., Ifrim, G.: Examining the state-of-the-art in news timeline summarization. In: Jurafsky, D., Chai, J., Schluter, N., Tetreault, J. (eds.) Proceedings of the 58th Annual Meeting of the Association for Computational Linguistics, pp. 1322–1334. Association for Computational Linguistics, Online (2020). https://doi.org/10.18653/v1/2020.acl-main.122. https://aclanthology.org/2020.acl-main.122
9. Grootendorst, M.: Bertopic: neural topic modeling with a class-based tf-idf procedure. arXiv preprint arXiv:2203.05794 (2022)
10. Hatzivassiloglou, V., Gravano, L., Maganti, A.: An investigation of linguistic features and clustering algorithms for topical document clustering. In: Proceedings of the 23rd Annual International ACM SIGIR Conference on Research and Development in Information Retrieval,SIGIR '00, pp. 224–231. Association for Computing Machinery, New York (2000). https://doi.org/10.1145/345508.345582
11. Hayashi, K., Maehara, T., Toyoda, M., Kawarabayashi, K.I.: Real-time top-r topic detection on twitter with topic hijack filtering. In: Proceedings of the 21th ACM SIGKDD International Conference on Knowledge Discovery and Data Mining, KDD '15, pp. 417–426. Association for Computing Machinery, New York (2015). https://doi.org/10.1145/2783258.2783402
12. Jiang, A.Q., Sablayrolles, A., et al.: Mistral 7b (2023). https://arxiv.org/abs/2310.06825
13. Kurtz, A.J., Mostafa, J.: Topic detection and interest tracking in a dynamic online news source. In: Proceedings of the 3rd ACM/IEEE-CS Joint Conference on Digital Libraries, JCDL '03, pp. 122–124. IEEE Computer Society (2003)
14. Liu, B., Han, F.X., Niu, D., Kong, L., Lai, K., Xu, Y.: Story forest: extracting events and telling stories from breaking news. ACM Trans. Knowl. Discov. Data **14**(3) (2020). https://doi.org/10.1145/3377939
15. Liu, W., et al.: A popular topic detection method based on microblog images and short text information. J. Web Semant. **81**, 100820 (2024). https://doi.org/10.1016/j.websem.2024.100820. https://www.sciencedirect.com/science/article/pii/S1570826824000064
16. Luo, K., Zhou, T., Chen, Y., Zhao, J., Liu, K.: Open event causality extraction by the assistance of LLM in task annotation, dataset, and method. In: Dong, T., et al. (eds.) Proceedings of the Workshop: Bridging Neurons and Symbols for Natural

Language Processing and Knowledge Graphs Reasoning (NeusymBridge) @ LREC-COLING-2024, pp. 33–44. ELRA and ICCL, Torino (2024). https://aclanthology.org/2024.neusymbridge-1.4/
17. Mansouri, B., Campos, R., Jatowt, A.: Towards timeline generation with abstract meaning representation. In: Companion Proceedings of the ACM Web Conference 2023, WWW '23 Companion, pp. 1204–1207. Association for Computing Machinery, New York (2023). https://doi.org/10.1145/3543873.3587670
18. Mao, Q., et al.: Explicitly modeling importance and coherence for timeline summarization. In: ICASSP 2022 - 2022 IEEE International Conference on Acoustics, Speech and Signal Processing (ICASSP), pp. 8062–8066 (2022). https://doi.org/10.1109/ICASSP43922.2022.9746383
19. Martschat, S., Markert, K.: A temporally sensitive submodularity framework for timeline summarization. In: Korhonen, A., Titov, I. (eds.) Proceedings of the 22nd Conference on Computational Natural Language Learning, pp. 230–240. Association for Computational Linguistics, Brussels (2018). https://doi.org/10.18653/v1/K18-1023. https://aclanthology.org/K18-1023
20. Qi, Y., Zhou, L., Si, H., Wan, J., Jin, T.: An approach to news event detection and tracking based on stream of online news. In: 2017 9th International Conference on Intelligent Human-Machine Systems and Cybernetics (IHMSC), vol. 2, pp. 193–196 (2017). https://doi.org/10.1109/IHMSC.2017.158
21. Radinsky, K., Horvitz, E.: Mining the web to predict future events. In: Proceedings of the Sixth ACM International Conference on Web Search and Data Mining, WSDM '13, pp. 255–264. Association for Computing Machinery, New York (2013). https://doi.org/10.1145/2433396.2433431
22. Swan, R., Allan, J.: Automatic generation of overview timelines. In: Proceedings of the 23rd Annual International ACM SIGIR Conference on Research and Development in Information Retrieval, SIGIR '00, pp. 49–56. Association for Computing Machinery, New York (2000). https://doi.org/10.1145/345508.345546
23. Takamura, H., Yokono, H., Okumura, M.: Summarizing a document stream. In: Clough, P., Foley, C., Gurrin, C., Jones, G.J.F., Kraaij, W., Lee, H., Mudoch, V. (eds.) ECIR 2011. LNCS, vol. 6611, pp. 177–188. Springer, Heidelberg (2011). https://doi.org/10.1007/978-3-642-20161-5_18
24. Tan, Z., Zhang, P., Tan, J., Guo, L.: A multi-layer event detection algorithm for detecting global and local hot events in social networks. Procedia Comput. Sci. **29**, 2080–2089 (2014). https://doi.org/10.1016/j.procs.2014.05.192. https://www.sciencedirect.com/science/article/pii/S187705091400369X
25. Team, G., Anil, R., et al.: Gemini: a family of highly capable multimodal models (2024). https://arxiv.org/abs/2312.11805
26. Touvron, H., Martin, L., et al: Llama 2: open foundation and fine-tuned chat models (2023). https://arxiv.org/abs/2307.09288
27. Wei, J., Wang, X., Schuurmans, D.E.A.: Chain-of-thought prompting elicits reasoning in large language models. In: Proceedings of the 36th International Conference on Neural Information Processing Systems, NIPS '22. Curran Associates Inc., Red Hook (2022)
28. Wu, J., Li, B., Liu, Q.: Topic detection based on bert and seed lda clustering model. In: Proceedings of the 2023 7th International Conference on Innovation in Artificial Intelligence, ICIAI '23, pp. 72–78. Association for Computing Machinery, New York (2023). https://doi.org/10.1145/3594409.3594418
29. Xu, G., Meng, Y., Chen, Z., Qiu, X., Wang, C., Yao, H.: Research on topic detection and tracking for online news texts. IEEE Access **7**, 58407–58418 (2019). https://doi.org/10.1109/ACCESS.2019.2914097

30. Yang, C.C., Shi, X., Wei, C.P.: Discovering event evolution graphs from news corpora. IEEE Trans. Syst. Man Cybern. - Part A: Syst. Hum. **39**(4), 850–863 (2009). https://doi.org/10.1109/TSMCA.2009.2015885
31. Yu, Y., Jatowt, A., Doucet, A., Sugiyama, K., Yoshikawa, M.: Multi-TimeLine summarization (MTLS): Improving timeline summarization by generating multiple summaries. In: Zong, C., Xia, F., Li, W., Navigli, R. (eds.) Proceedings of the 59th Annual Meeting of the Association for Computational Linguistics and the 11th International Joint Conference on Natural Language Processing, vol. 1: Long Papers, pp. 377–387. Association for Computational Linguistics, Online (2021). https://doi.org/10.18653/v1/2021.acl-long.32. https://aclanthology.org/2021.acl-long.32
32. Zhang, C., Lyu, J., Xu, K.: A storytree-based model for inter-document causal relation extraction from news articles. Knowl. Inf. Syst. **65**(2), 827–853 (2022) . https://doi.org/10.1007/s10115-022-01781-7

SciTableQA: A Question-Answering Benchmark for Complex Scientific Tables

Kehinde Ajayi[1(✉)], Yi He[2], Matthew Maisonave[1], Kris SeekFord[1], and Jian Wu[1]

[1] Old Dominion University, Norfolk, VA, USA
{kajay001,j1wu}@odu.edu
[2] William and Mary, Williamsburg, VA, USA
yihe@wm.edu

Abstract. Reasoning over complex scientific tables is an essential yet largely underexplored topic. Existing benchmarks often fail to capture the structural and content challenges of complex scientific tables, such as irregular layouts, multi-row headers, and symbolic notations. To address these challenges, we introduce SciTableQA, a benchmark comprising 320 scientific tables in 5 scientific domains, and 8,730 human-verified QA pairs categorized into two types of reasoning tasks. Our tables cover 8 structural features and 4 content features. The questions include 4 interrogative and 3 imperative question styles. To answer the questions, the model needs to reason across up to 14 rows and 13 columns of a table. We evaluate the performance of three widely used Large Language Models (LLMs)—GPT-3.5-turbo, Llama 3-8B, and Mistral-7B against the benchmark dataset. Our evaluation focuses on reasoning accuracy, cross-LLM generalization, and explanation validity. Our findings reveal that arithmetic tasks are more challenging than cell selection tasks. LLMs' performances on both types of tasks vary across domains. Compared with existing TableQA benchmarks, we believe SciTableQA provides a more challenging dataset for evaluating machine learning models' reasoning capability on complex scientific tables. Our dataset is available at https://huggingface.co/datasets/Kehindeajayi01/SciTableQA

1 Introduction

Scientific tables are a primary vehicle for summarizing and communicating dense, structured data in a compact format in scientific publications. These tables often present experimental results, statistical comparisons, and observational findings that are critical to support scientific discoveries. Automatic interpretation and reasoning over such data are key to accelerating advanced research applications, such as hypothesis generation [11], claim verification [15], and building knowledge bases [9].

Advancements in large language models (LLMs) have brought remarkable improvements in natural language understanding and reasoning, including table-based question answering (TableQA). However, existing benchmark datasets

W.-T. Balke et al. (Eds.): TPDL 2025, LNCS 16097, pp. 90–107, 2026.
https://doi.org/10.1007/978-3-032-05409-8_7

for TableQA, such as WikiTableQuestions [14] and Spider [18], are designed for general-purpose tables, often derived from Wikipedia or financial datasets. General-purpose tables usually contain canonical structures and monolithic content types (e.g., numbers, text). A portion of tables in scientific papers also resemble general-purpose tables, but a significant fraction are complex tables, containing much more complicated structure and content types, such as multi-row headers, irregular layouts, and symbolic notations [10,12]. Additionally, many TableQA benchmark datasets focus on tasks like SQL generation [18] or simple cell look-ups [21], with limited focus on complex numerical reasoning and advanced inference.

Recent TableQA datasets, such as SCITAB [10] and SCITAT [19], have attempted to close this gap by incorporating datasets tailored to scientific domains. SCITAB, for example, focuses on compositional reasoning and fact verification for scientific tables, while SCITAT emphasizes reasoning that integrates both tables and text. However, SCITAB exhibits a relatively narrow range of reasoning types, focusing on arithmetic reasoning and cell selection tasks. SCITAT, although containing more diverse reasoning types, requires combining text and tables and, therefore, is not appropriate for testing the models' reasoning capabilities for standalone tables.

In this work, we introduce SciTableQA, a benchmark dataset designed to evaluate the reasoning capabilities of LLMs on standalone scientific tables. Our approach focuses on tables and the diverse reasoning challenges they pose, without requiring additional context from textual narratives. To this end, we curate 320 scientific tables obtained from PDFs in various domains, including Materials Science (MatSci), Biology, Computer Science (CompSci), scientific reports (Reports), and ICDAR-2013, and employ LLMs to automatically generate 8,730 high-quality question-answer (QA) pairs. These pairs are manually verified and categorized into two distinct reasoning types, namely cell selection and arithmetic reasoning, with explanations for each answer for transparency and interpretability. This approach of utilizing LLMs to generate the QA pairs mitigates the need for extensive human labor and domain expertise, thereby overcoming the limitation typically associated with the high cost of developing high-quality Scientific TableQA benchmarks.

This work explores four research questions aligned with the broader challenges of reasoning over complex scientific tables.

1. How well do LLMs generalize across different domains when reasoning over complex scientific tables?
2. How are the performances of LLMs affected by structural and content complexities?
3. How consistent and coherent are LLMs in explaining the answers to table-related questions?
4. How effectively can LLMs answer questions generated by other LLMs, and what types of questions do they work well on or fail at?

By addressing these questions, SciTableQA offers a benchmark that allows comprehensive and robust evaluations of TableQA models, drawing insights into specific table features that challenge the models. Our contributions are as follows:

- We introduce SciTableQA, a benchmark dataset specifically designed to evaluate the capabilities of LLMs on answering questions related to standalone scientific tables.
- We propose a novel framework that evaluates the capabilities of LLMs to answer questions generated by other LLMs.
- By analyzing the LLMs' performance across structural and content-based features, we identified key challenges in complex scientific table reasoning.

2 Related Work

Research on QA over tabular data has witnessed significant advancements, with benchmarks evolving from general tabular datasets to more domain-specific and reasoning-focused benchmarks. Early efforts, such as WikiTableQuestions [13,14], introduced simple retrieval, arithmetic reasoning, and free-form answer generation of questions related to Wikipedia tables. Spider [18] studies the task of complex SQL generation for multi-table databases. Although these datasets helped advance parsing and table comprehension tasks, they largely focused on general-purpose tables, e.g., tables with clear boundaries and values in most cells, limiting their applicability to reasoning in complex scientific tables.

Incorporating numerical reasoning into TableQA tasks marked a milestone. HybridQA [2,20] combined tabular and textual data, requiring multi-hop reasoning across both modalities. Financial datasets such as TAT-QA [21] and FinQA [3] further emphasized numerical reasoning, involving operations such as aggregation, comparison, and trend analysis. These datasets are instrumental in evaluating LLMs' ability to handle numerical operations but fall short in addressing the structural complexities and domain-specific features in scientific tables.

For scientific domains, benchmarks such as SciGen [12], which focused on reasoning-aware text generation from scientific tables, and SCITAB [10], which introduced claim verification tasks, began addressing domain-specific requirements. SCITAB incorporates compositional reasoning tasks, such as verifying claims based on tabular data. However, its emphasis on claim verification limits its scope for evaluating diverse question types directly on tables.

Recent benchmarks have expanded the evaluation landscape for TableQA. For instance, TableBench [17] provides a broad evaluation across 18 reasoning dimensions and diverse industrial scenarios. However, its multi-modal design and emphasis on real-world data heterogeneity make it less effective for standalone tables. Domain-specific datasets such as AIT-QA [7], which targets the airline industry, and KET-QA [5], which integrates external knowledge for enhanced reasoning, are constrained by their reliance on information beyond the tables.

More recently, the SCITAT benchmark [19], which consists of several reasoning types, including look-up, numerical reasoning, data analysis, and tabulation,

Table 1. Comparison of SciTableQA with existing TableQA datasets. SciTableQA uniquely combines scientific domain diversity, structural complexity, and verified QA quality in a table-only benchmark.

Dataset	QA Pairs	#Tables	Domains	Reasoning Types	Text Context	Annotation
SciTableQA	**8,700**	**320**	**MatSci, Biology, CompSci, ICDAR, Reports**	**Cell selection + Arithmetic**	**Table only**	**LLM-generated & human verification**
SCITAT	953	871	CS	Cell selection + Arithmetic	**Table + text**	LLM-generated & human verification
SCITAB	1,225	872	CS	Fact verification	Table only	Expert-verified
SciGen	220	220	CS	Data-to-text	Generates text	Expert & auto-scaling
FeTaQA	10,000	~10K	Wikipedia	Free-form answers	Table only	Human-generated answers

was proposed. SCITAT requires reasoning over both tables and the associated textual context. However, its reliance on textual information makes it unsuitable for evaluating standalone tables. Additionally, although SCITAT covers a broad range of reasoning subtypes, its coverage of domain-specific scientific calculations remains limited. Table 1 shows a comparison of the SciTableQA dataset with existing TableQA datasets.

Our work, SciTableQA, addresses these limitations by focusing exclusively on questions generated from standalone complex scientific tables. SciTableQA emphasizes high-level numerical reasoning, structural interpretation, and data interdependencies without requiring external textual references. By curating a diverse set of complex scientific tables spanning disciplines including MatSci, Biology, CompSci, ICDAR-2013, and Reports, and generating QA pairs across reasoning types, SciTableQA provides a challenging benchmark for evaluating LLMs on complex scientific tables.

3 SciTableQA Dataset

Our workflow (Fig. 1) combines automatic QA generation with manual human verification to efficiently create the dataset without sacrificing the quality.

3.1 Data Collection and Pre-processing

Data Source. We construct SciTableQA by sourcing tables from publicly available scientific documents across multiple repositories, including arXiv, PubMed,

Table 2. Distribution of tables across structural and content-based categories.

Categories	Table Features	CompSci	MatSci	Report	ICDAR	Biology	Total
Structural	Compact	8	3	5	10	–	26
	Partially-bordered	10	10	5	10	5	40
	Multi-row	10	5	6	10	6	37
	Borderless	10	5	5	10	5	35
	Simple	10	10	5	10	5	40
	LongContentRow	11	–	5	–	6	22
	Sparse	–	9	6	9	4	28
	Multi-column	11	6	5	10	4	36
Content-based	Subscript	–	7	–	–	3	10
	Superscript	–	5	–	–	7	12
	Notations	4	5	–	–	5	14
	Equations	5	10	–	–	5	20
	Total Tables	79	75	42	69	55	320

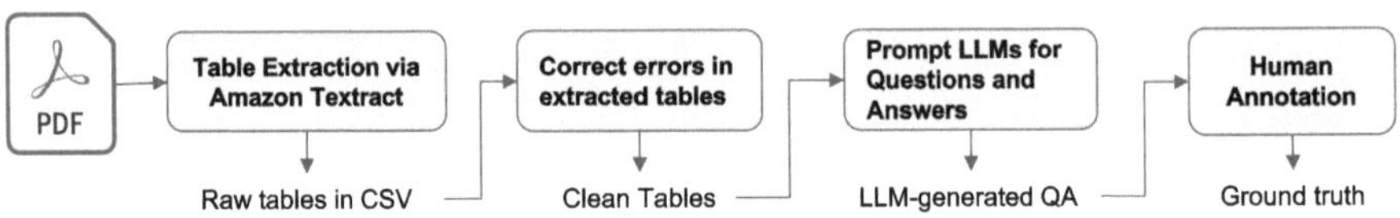

Fig. 1. The workflow to generate SciTableQA.

IEEE Xplore, epa.gov, and ICDAR-2013. We surveyed 300 PDFs and manually curated tables that exhibit distinct or combined structural and content-based features to ensure a diverse coverage. To maintain relevance with modern table presentation styles, we limited the paper selection to publications from 2013 onward. The ICDAR-2013 dataset provides tables used for document recognition tasks, featuring structures such as borderless tables and sparse layouts. Tables from MatSci and Biology include experimental data and computational results, often with nested headers and domain-specific symbols. Scientific reports include tables from diverse scientific fields, such as Physics and Environmental Science, with diverse formats, and CompSci papers contribute data from algorithm analyses, benchmarks, and performance evaluations.

Table Extraction From PDF Papers. We extract tables in text form from the obtained scientific papers in PDF format using Amazon Textract, a commercial optical character recognition (OCR) tool designed for high-accuracy text and table extraction. Amazon Textract has its ability to extract tables containing complex structures in PDFs. Textract also preserves the row-column relationships within tables, facilitating structured data conversion.

FEMIP Country	Signed TA (EURm)
Algeria	6.19
Egypt	6.60
Gaza & West Bank	2.60
Jordan	4.20
Lebanon	2.57
Morocco	21.09
Regional	7.29
Syria	33.42
Tunisia	14.50
Total	**98.46**

Cell selection Question:
"Which country received the highest amount of signed TA in EUR million?"
Answer: "Syria"

Arithmetic Question:
"If the Signed TA in EUR for Lebanon is increased by 50%, what would be the new amount?"
Answer: 3.86

Fig. 2. Examples of cell selection and arithmetic questions on a bordered table.

After extraction, we export each table into a CSV file. Saving the table as CSV is necessary because it enables precise programmatic access to each cell's content and location, which is essential for generating accurate QA pairs. However, the output of OCR engines may contain errors, especially for scientific tables with intricate layouts. Errors such as misaligned columns, missing cell values, incorrect merging of multi-row headers, and misinterpretation of symbols or units were common. If left uncorrected, they could propagate and introduce downstream errors, leading to unreliable QA generation and incorrect ground-truth answers. Therefore, we manually verify and revise extracted tables to match their original structure in the source papers.

3.2 Question-Answer Generation

To generate the SciTableQA dataset, we first prompt three representative LLMs: GPT-3.5-turbo [1], Llama 3-8B Instruct [4], and Mistral 7B [6] to generate QA pairs. In this paper, we will refer to these models as GPT-3.5, Llama-3, and Mistral for brevity. The use of multiple LLMs was motivated by the need to evaluate model performance across diverse scientific domains and to ensure variability in question formulation and reasoning complexity. By leveraging different models, we introduce diversity in linguistic structure, reasoning styles, and potential error patterns. Although newer LLMs have been developed, as we will show, these LLMs are sufficient to generate diverse questions. The major goal here is to develop the dataset and the evaluation framework, which can be applied to any LLMs.

We prompt LLMs to generate two types of reasoning questions: **cell selection** and **arithmetic** reasoning. Cell selection questions require retrieving a specific value from a single table cell or a set of related cells based on one or multiple column and row headers. An example of cell selection and arithmetic questions is shown in Fig. 2.

These questions test the ability of LLMs to accurately extract information from the given table. Arithmetic questions involve performing numerical operations such as summation, averaging, percentage difference, and comparison across a minimum of three cells. These require the LLMs to correctly interpret numerical values and perform precise mathematical operations. Given that scientific tables often require complex reasoning over quantitative data, incorporating both types of questions is essential for a well-rounded evaluation.

3.3 Prompting Strategy

To generate high-quality QA pairs, we employ a zero-shot chain-of-thought (CoT) [8,16] prompting strategy, which instructs LLMs to ask questions on a given table, provide answers to the questions asked, and supply an explanation on how they arrive at the answers.

For consistency, all LLMs use the same prompting templates for asking and answering questions – one for cell selection and one for arithmetic reasoning. The templates are carefully crafted to elicit diverse and logically structured questions while maintaining uniformity in reasoning complexity. Each table is associated with 10 unique QA pairs, with 5 cell selection questions and 5 arithmetic reasoning questions.

Table 3. Distribution of QA pairs by Question-Types generated by each LLM.

LLMs	#Cell Selection	#Arithmetic	Total
Llama 3-8B	1,453	1,452	2,905
GPT 3.5-Turbo	1,471	1,425	2,896
Mistral-7B	1,471	1,458	2,929
Total	4,395	4,335	8,730

3.4 Human Verification

Because LLMs can hallucinate, generate duplicate questions, and produce incorrect answers, human verification is essential to ensure the quality and reliability of the final data. Unlike traditional annotation workflows, where humans correct errors in model-generated questions and answers, we recruited and trained 5 graduate students in computer science to answer questions based on the table data **without** seeing the answers generated by LLMs, to mitigate the potential prejudgment bias. The LLM-generated questions are not changed.

To maintain verification quality, we employ two annotators to answer each question and resolve any discrepancies between them through consensus discussions; any disagreements are escalated to a senior reviewer. We achieved an inter-annotator agreement (Kappa) score of 0.8, reflecting strong consistency in the annotation process. The final dataset contains all verified QA pairs and LLM explanations along with their ground-truth answers.

By structuring the human annotation process in this manner, SciTableQA enables a direct comparison between the answers generated by LLMs and the ground-truth answers provided by human annotators. Therefore, the performance metrics directly measure the models' reasoning capabilities, without being affected by post hoc adjustments or corrections (Table 3).

3.5 Data Diversity

This section provides a detailed analysis of the dataset's diversity, covering the distribution of tables across domains and structural categories, as well as the breakdown of QA pairs generated by each LLM.

Distribution of Tables Across Scientific Domains. SciTableQA includes tables from five scientific domains. As shown in Table 2, CompSci and MatSci have the most number of tables (79 and 75, respectively). Report and Biology have the least number of tables (42 and 55, respectively).

Diversity of Table Features. The tables in SciTableQA incorporate diverse structural and content-based features. Table 2 shows 8 structural features and 4 content features, at least 1 structural feature (long content row) and 4 content features (subscript, superscript, notation, equation) being new compared to the existing (i.e., ICDAR-2013) datasets. Notations and equations introduce domain-specific complexity, requiring advanced reasoning. Additionally, sparse and long-content row tables vary in data density, testing LLMs' ability to extract relevant

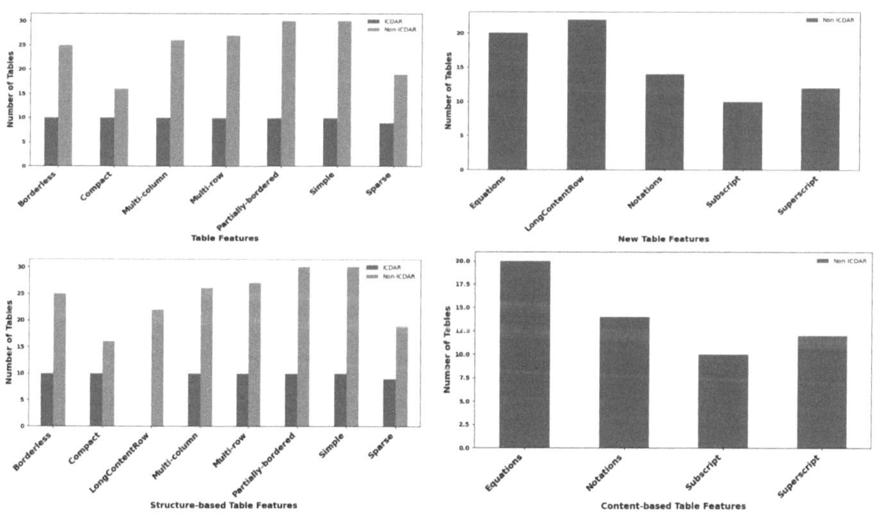

Fig. 3. The number of tables with different structural and content-based features in SciTableQA for ICDAR-2013 and non-ICDAR-2013 tables. Upper left: table features in ICDAR and other domains; Upper right: table features that ICDAR-2013 do not contain; Lower left: table features describing structural complexities of the tables; Lower right: table features describing content complexities of the tables.

information from scattered or text-heavy rows. The combined feature analysis (Fig. 3) further shows that non-ICDAR tables exhibit greater diversity across both structural and content-based categories, highlighting the broader challenge posed by SciTableQA compared to prior benchmarks.

Diversity of Question Types. Our dataset contains 4 interrogative types of questions and 3 imperative types of questions. The interrogative type includes "What"-type questions, which constitute approximately 70% of all questions. Other notable interrogative types include "Which" (16%), "How many" (4%), and "How much" (1.5%). The remaining 5% are imperative questions that start with "Find", "Calculate", and "Determine", signaling fact-based retrieval tasks.

Multirow and Multicolumn Reasoning. One characteristic of our questions is that the reasoning may need multiple rows and/or columns. In Fig. 4, we examine the joint distribution of rows and columns involved in answering each question. Although most questions involve a single row and/or a single column (41%), the questions also includes a wide range of header pairings, such as two rows and 1 column (2R-1C), 1R-2C, and more complex combinations such as

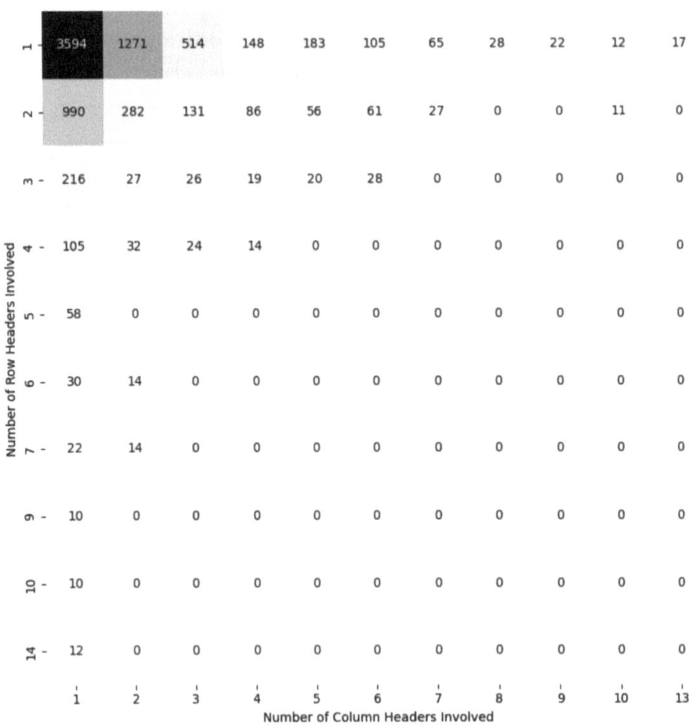

Rows \ Columns	1	2	3	4	5	6	7	8	9	10	13
1	3594	1271	514	148	183	105	65	28	22	12	17
2	990	282	131	86	56	61	27	0	0	11	0
3	216	27	26	19	20	28	0	0	0	0	0
4	105	32	24	14	0	0	0	0	0	0	0
5	58	0	0	0	0	0	0	0	0	0	0
6	30	14	0	0	0	0	0	0	0	0	0
7	22	14	0	0	0	0	0	0	0	0	0
9	10	0	0	0	0	0	0	0	0	0	0
10	10	0	0	0	0	0	0	0	0	0	0
14	12	0	0	0	0	0	0	0	0	0	0

Fig. 4. Joint distribution of rows and columns involved in questions generated by LLMs, highlighting the diverse range of information required to answer questions.

3R-8C and 3R-3C demonstrating that SciTableQA is designed to challenge models with multi-dimensional data extraction and aggregation tasks. This variety ensures that the benchmark evaluates LLMs' ability to reason over both simple and complex table structures.

4 Evaluation

4.1 Accuracy and Reasoning on Self-generated QA

We first evaluate the accuracy of GPT-3.5, Llama-3, and Mistral on their self-generated QA pairs. For each LLM-generated QA pair, we compare the LLM's answer to the ground truth answer provided by the human answerer. In addition, we assess the reasoning process by analyzing the explanations provided by the LLMs for each answer. We analyze the model performance in three dimensions: question types, domains, and table features.

Model Performance on Arithmetic Reasoning. As shown in Fig. 5, model performance varies significantly between cell selection and arithmetic reasoning questions, with cell selection yielding higher accuracy (Acc) across all models. Accuracy in this context is computed based on the exact match between the LLM-provided answer and the ground truth answer. Specifically, GPT-3.5 achieves the highest accuracy scores, with (Acc_CS, Acc_Arith) = (0.790, 0.490) for cell selection and arithmetic types of questions, respectively, followed by Mistral (0.647, 0.410) and Llama-3 (0.585, 0.278).

For Acc_CS, all LLMs exhibit domain dependencies. Mistral and Llama-3 exhibit larger standard deviation (STD_S) (0.116 and 0.165, respectively) than

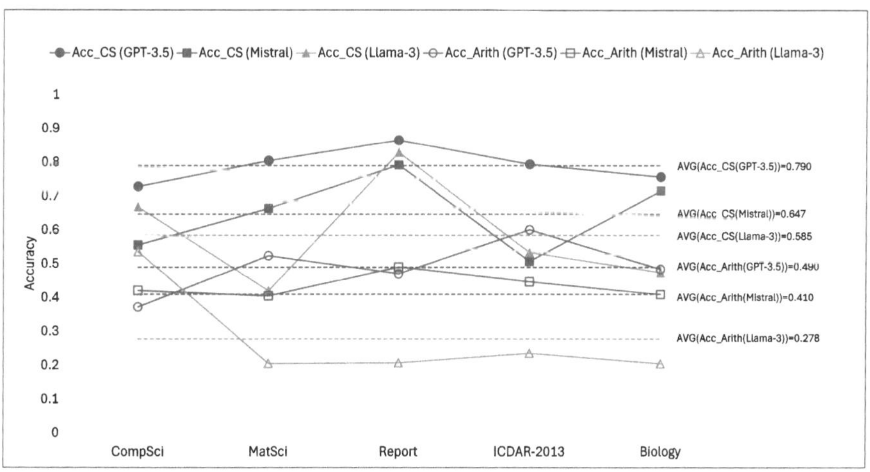

Fig. 5. Accuracy scores (Acc) on cell selection (CS) and arithmetic (Arith) reasoning tasks for self-generated QA pairs.

GPT (0.052). The LLMs ranked by the average Acc_CS from the highest to the lowest are GPT-3.5, Mistral, and Llama-3.

All LLMs achieve the highest Acc_CS for the Report tables. The domains they perform the worst in are CompSci, ICDAR-2023, and MatSci for GPT-3.5, Mistral, and Llama-3, respectively.

For Acc_Arith, similar to Acc_CS, all LLMs exhibit domain dependencies, but this time, GPT-3.5 and Llama-3 exhibit larger STD_S (0.083 and 0.145, respectively). The LLMs ranked by the average Acc_Arith from the highest to the lowest are GPT-3.5, Mistral, and Llama-3.

4.2 Reasoning Evaluation on Arithmetic Questions

We assess the quality of reasoning processes used by LLMs when answering scientific table-based questions based on the correctness of answers to the arithmetic questions and how accurately they explain the answers. This measures how well the explanations provided by LLMs align with the ground truth explanations. We manually score each explanation on a 0âĂŞ3 scale, called reasoning validity (RV) scores, defined as follows:

- **3**: The explanation is aligned with the human evaluation and leads to the correct answer (matching the ground truth).
- **2**: The explanation is mostly aligned with human evaluations but contains minor wrong steps that lead to the wrong answer.
- **1**: The explanation is partially aligned with human evaluations or contains major flaws leading to a wrong answer.
- **0**: No explanation is provided, or the reasoning is completely incorrect.

The evaluation results (Fig. 6) reveal key insights into the models' reasoning capability across domains. GPT-3.5 consistently achieves the higher reasoning validity scores, demonstrating superior logical coherence and step-by-step explanations across all domains except computer science. All three models

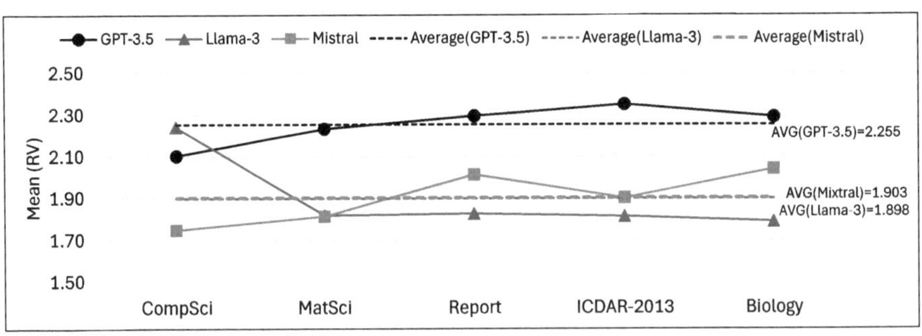

Fig. 6. The average reasoning validity (RV) scores on arithmetic tasks for GPT-3.5, Llama-3, and Mistral across the five domains.

show unequal performance across all domains with Llama-3 exhibiting significant drops in Biology and MatSci. Llama-3's reasoning validity is notably higher in CompSci compared to GPT-3.5 and Mistral.

4.3 Cross-LLM QA

To further assess the robustness of the LLMs in reasoning over complex scientific tables, we conduct a cross-LLM evaluation on arithmetic tasks using the accuracy metric, where each model answers questions generated by other models. We focus on arithmetic tasks because arithmetic reasoning is substantially more challenging for the models than cell selection, making it a more meaningful target for evaluating cross-model generalization. The cross-LLM evaluation on arithmetic tasks highlights significant variations in model performance across table features and scientific domains. We organize table features into a structural category and a content-based category, shown in Table 2. Structural features delineates complex layouts, while content-based features include domain-specific symbols, notations, and mathematical content.

Structural Category. Figure 7 shows that GPT-3.5 consistently outperforms Mistral, when answering questions generated by Llama-3. Specifically, GPT-3.5 achieves accuracy scores above 0.5 on challenging features such as notations and long content-row tables. In contrast, Mistral struggles across most table features (Fig. 7). Although Llama-3 performs relatively well in table with features such as superscripts and subscripts, its accuracy decreases for tables with more intricate structures, such as borderless and partially-bordered, highlighting its limitations in managing structural complexity.

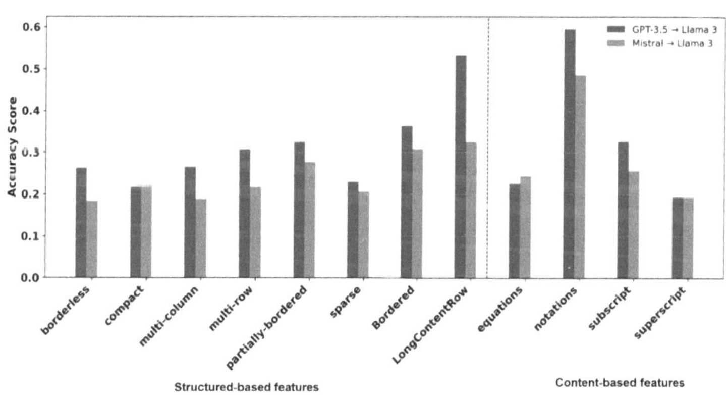

Fig. 7. Comparison of GPT-3.5 and Mistral on Llama-3 questions across two categories of table features.

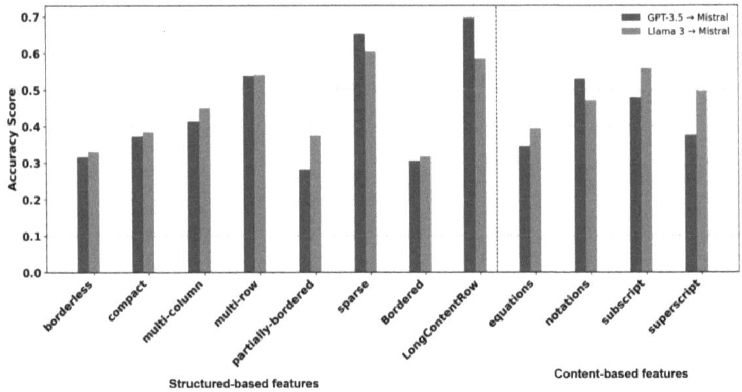

Fig. 8. Comparison of GPT-3.5 and Llama-3 on Mistral questions about tables with two categories of features.

Content-Based Categories. Content-based categories, such as notations, equations, superscripts, and subscripts, test the models' ability to process domain-specific and semantic content. As shown in Fig. 8, Llama-3 outperforms GPT-3.5 for tables with 3 out of 4 content-based features, demonstrating greater consistency in handling content-dense tables. For instance, Llama-3 achieves higher accuracy scores than GPT-3.5 for features such as subscripts and superscripts. Mistral, whose performance is relatively even across both structural and content-based groups, still exhibits lower performance, particularly in equations, where domain-specific reasoning is critical. These findings highlight the challenges posed by content-heavy categories and reveal Llama-3's comparative advantage in scenarios requiring semantic understanding, particularly when contrasted with GPT-3.5 (Fig. 10).

Performance by Domain. At the domain level, the evaluation reveals distinct patterns in model performance influenced by the structure and content of the tables in each domain. As shown in Fig. 9 and Fig. 11, domains such as CompSci and ICDAR-2013 demonstrate relatively better accuracy scores especially by GPT-3.5 and Llama-3. GPT-3.5, in particular, exhibits a strong performance advantage in the CompSci domain, achieving higher accuracy scores than Mistral when answering questions generated by Llama-3 (Fig. 9).

Conversely, all models face significant challenges for tables in Biology and Report domains. For example, when answering questions generated by Llama-3 in the Report domain as shown in Fig. 9 (lower panel), GPT-3.5's performance shows a noticeable decline. This indicates that domain-specific complexities, such as dense semantic content or specialized notations, remain a bottleneck for effective reasoning, specifically for GPT-3.5.

Interestingly, while GPT-3.5 generally outperforms Llama-3 across most domains, its advantage diminishes in MatSci, where Llama-3 achieves com-

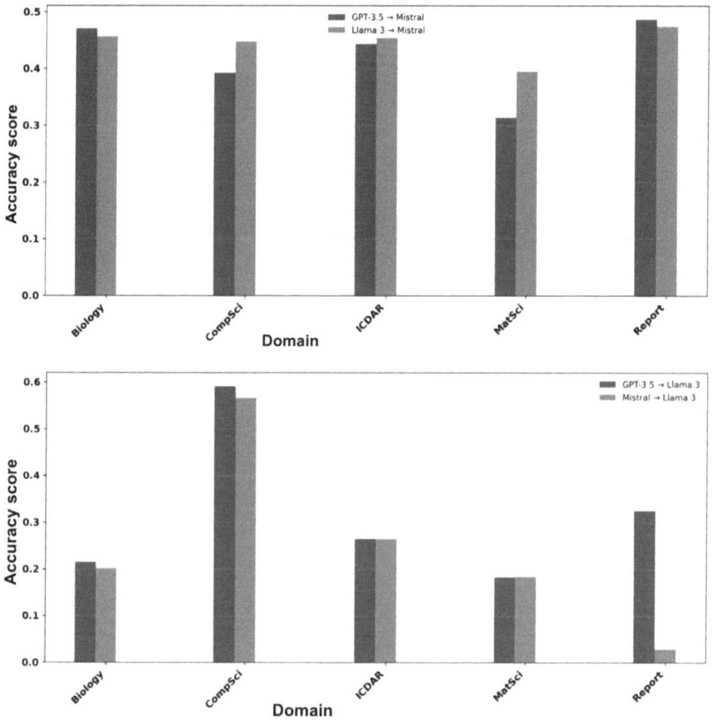

Fig. 9. Comparison of GPT-3.5 and Llama-3 on Mistral questions (upper), and GPT-3.5 and Mistral on Llama-3 questions (lower) across five domains.

petitive scores, particularly when answering Mistral-generated questions (Fig. 9 upper panel).

4.4 Reasoning Scoring

We adopted a manual scoring and an automatic scoring method to assess the explanations generated by LLMs. This alignment between the two scores is critical for ensuring that LLMs provide semantically and logically consistent reasoning.

Alignment for Manual and Automatic Scoring. For manual scoring, we randomly select 50 QA pairs in which one LLM generates the question, and a different LLM provides the answer and explanations (e.g., GPT-3.5 answering Llama-3's questions), resulting in 150 QA pairs. Each pair is evaluated based on whether the explanations of the answers to the same question provided by both LLMs are semantically and logically equivalent. If they are, the pair receives a score of 1; otherwise, it receives a score of 0. For example, suppose Llama-3 generates the question, "What is the sum of the values in the third column? "

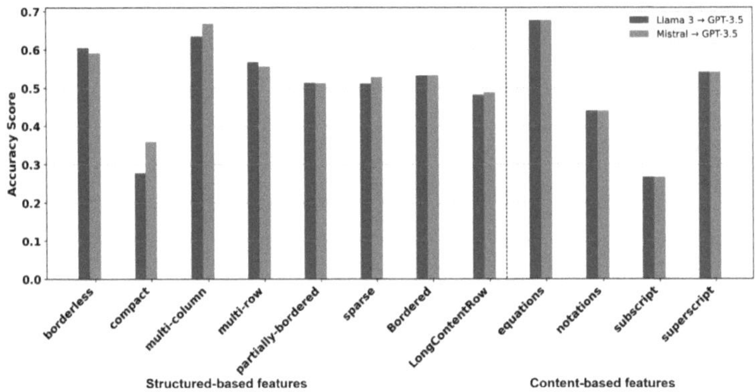

Fig. 10. Comparison of Llama-3 and Mistral on GPT-3.5 questions for tables with two categories of features.

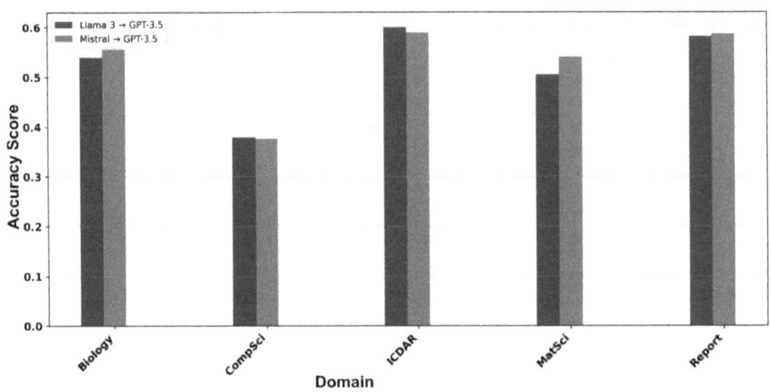

Fig. 11. Comparison of Llama-3 and Mistral on GPT-3.5 questions across five domains.

GPT-3.5 answers with "42," explaining that the values in the third column are 10, 15, and 17, and their sum is 42. Llama-3, when answering the same question, also provides "42" as the answer, explaining that adding 10, 15, and 17 results in 42. Since both explanations align in their reasoning and conclusion, this QA pair is assigned a score of 1.

For automatic scoring, we employ the Sentence Transformer model (all-MiniLM-L6-v2[1]) to compute the cosine similarity scores between embeddings of the two explanations. The equivalence label is determined by whether the similarity score is greater (equivalent) or smaller (non-equivalent) than a threshold. We tested 20 threshold values in a range between 0.5 and 1.0 for each of the 50 QA sets answered by two LLMs to determine the threshold that results in the highest value of F1 scores grounded on the human's scores. We found 0.7, 0.72, and 0.75 as best thresholds for three sets, which are very close.

[1] https://huggingface.co/sentence-transformers/all-MiniLM-L6-v2.

Table 4. Comparison of Automatic vs. Manual Scoring Differences Across Evaluations. → indicates left model responding to questions asked by the right model.

Model Pair	Count		% Agreement
	Agree	Disagree	
GPT → Llama	35	15	70%
GPT → Mistral	35	15	70%
Llama → GPT	40	10	80%
Llama → Mistral	35	15	70%
Mistral → GPT	40	10	80%
Mistral → Llama	40	10	80%

To validate the automatic scoring method, we calculate the difference between the manual and automatic scores for each QA pair. The higher proportion of equivalent pairs of explanations, as shown in Table 4, indicates a better alignment between the two methods, suggesting that the automatic scoring method is a reliable measure.

5 Conclusion

This paper introduces SciTableQA, a benchmark dataset designed to evaluate LLMs on the QA ability on standalone complex scientific tables. We evaluated three representative LLMs in three families, namely GPT-3.5, Llama-3, and Mistral. Our findings show that these models' TableQA capability varies depending on tables' structure, content types, and scientific fields. In general, GPT-3.5 excels in structured-based features, while Llama-3 performs well in content-based features, and Mistral performs evenly across both table features. We also demonstrate that semantic similarity-based automatic scoring has a high alignment with human's scoring and thus may be used for the consistency of explanations provided by two LLMs for the same QA pair. These results highlight the need for future LLMs to improve in numerical reasoning, structural understanding, and semantic consistency. SciTableQA sheds the light for more rigorous testing of LLMs on robust TableQA tasks. It supports the development of stronger AI systems for scientific research and beyond.

References

1. Brown, T.B., et al.: Language models are few-shot learners. In: Proceedings of the 34th International Conference on Neural Information Processing Systems. NIPS '20. Curran Associates Inc., Red Hook (2020)
2. Chen, W., Zha, H., Chen, Z., Xiong, W., Wang, H., Wang, W.Y.: HybridQA: a dataset of multi-hop question answering over tabular and textual data. In: Cohn,

T., He, Y., Liu, Y. (eds.) Findings of the Association for Computational Linguistics: EMNLP 2020, pp. 1026–1036. Association for Computational Linguistics, Online (2020). https://doi.org/10.18653/v1/2020.findings-emnlp.91. https://aclanthology.org/2020.findings-emnlp.91/
3. Chen, Z., et al.: FinQA: a dataset of numerical reasoning over financial data. In: Moens, M.F., Huang, X., Specia, L., Yih, S.W.T. (eds.) Proceedings of the 2021 Conference on Empirical Methods in Natural Language Processing, pp. 3697–3711. Association for Computational Linguistics, Online and Punta Cana (2021). https://doi.org/10.18653/v1/2021.emnlp-main.300. https://aclanthology.org/2021.emnlp-main.300/
4. Dubey, A., et al.: The Llama 3 herd of models. arXiv preprint arXiv:2407.21783 (2024)
5. Hu, M., Dong, H., Luo, P., Han, S., Zhang, D.: KET-QA: a dataset for knowledge enhanced table question answering. In: Calzolari, N., Kan, M.Y., Hoste, V., Lenci, A., Sakti, S., Xue, N. (eds.) Proceedings of the 2024 Joint International Conference on Computational Linguistics, Language Resources and Evaluation (LREC-COLING 2024), pp. 9705–9719. ELRA and ICCL, Torino (2024). https://aclanthology.org/2024.lrec-main.848/
6. Jiang, A.Q., et al.: Mistral 7B. arXiv preprint arXiv:2310.06825 (2023)
7. Katsis, Y., et al.: AIT-QA: question answering dataset over complex tables in the airline industry. In: Loukina, A., Gangadharaiah, R., Min, B. (eds.) Proceedings of the 2022 Conference of the North American Chapter of the Association for Computational Linguistics: Human Language Technologies: Industry Track, pp. 305–314. Association for Computational Linguistics, Seattle (2022). https://doi.org/10.18653/v1/2022.naacl-industry.34. https://aclanthology.org/2022.naacl-industry.34/
8. Kojima, T., Gu, S.S., Reid, M., Matsuo, Y., Iwasawa, Y.: Large language models are zero-shot reasoners. Adv. Neural. Inf. Process. Syst. **35**, 22199–22213 (2022)
9. Kruit, B., He, H., Urbani, J.: Tab2know: building a knowledge base from tables in scientific papers. In: International Semantic Web Conference, pp. 349–365. Springer, Heidelberg (2020)
10. Lu, X., Pan, L., Liu, Q., Nakov, P., Kan, M.Y.: SCITAB: a challenging benchmark for compositional reasoning and claim verification on scientific tables. In: Bouamor, H., Pino, J., Bali, K. (eds.) Proceedings of the 2023 Conference on Empirical Methods in Natural Language Processing, pp. 7787–7813. Association for Computational Linguistics, Singapore (2023). https://doi.org/10.18653/v1/2023.emnlp-main.483. https://aclanthology.org/2023.emnlp-main.483/
11. Majumder, B.P., et al.: Discoverybench: towards data-driven discovery with large language models. arXiv preprint arXiv:2407.01725 (2024)
12. Moosavi, N.S., Rücklé, A., Roth, D., Gurevych, I.: Scigen: a dataset for reasoning-aware text generation from scientific tables. In: Thirty-Fifth Conference on Neural Information Processing Systems Datasets and Benchmarks Track (Round 2) (2021)
13. Nan, L., et al.: FeTaQA: free-form table question answering. Trans. Assoc. Comput. Linguist. **10**, 35–49 (2022)
14. Pasupat, P., Liang, P.: Compositional semantic parsing on semi-structured tables. In: Zong, C., Strube, M. (eds.) Proceedings of the 53rd Annual Meeting of the Association for Computational Linguistics and the 7th International Joint Conference on Natural Language Processing, vol. 1: Long Papers, pp. 1470–1480. Association for Computational Linguistics, Beijing (2015). https://doi.org/10.3115/v1/P15-1142. https://aclanthology.org/P15-1142/

15. Wang, N.X., Mahajan, D., Danilevsky, M., Rosenthal, S.: Semeval-2021 task 9: fact verification and evidence finding for tabular data in scientific documents (sem-tab-facts). arXiv preprint arXiv:2105.13995 (2021)
16. Wei, J., et al.: Chain-of-thought prompting elicits reasoning in large language models. Adv. Neural. Inf. Process. Syst. **35**, 24824–24837 (2022)
17. Wu, X., et al.: TableBench: a comprehensive and complex benchmark for table question answering. arXiv preprint arXiv:2408.09174 (2024)
18. Yu, T., et al.: Spider: a large-scale human-labeled dataset for complex and cross-domain semantic parsing and text-to-SQL task. In: Riloff, E., Chiang, D., Hockenmaier, J., Tsujii, J. (eds.) Proceedings of the 2018 Conference on Empirical Methods in Natural Language Processing, pp. 3911–3921. Association for Computational Linguistics, Brussels (2018). https://doi.org/10.18653/v1/D18-1425. https://aclanthology.org/D18-1425/
19. Zhang, X., et al.: SCITAT: a question answering benchmark for scientific tables and text covering diverse reasoning types. arXiv preprint arXiv:2412.11757 (2024)
20. Zhong, W., et al.: Reasoning over hybrid chain for table-and-text open domain question answering. In: Raedt, L.D. (ed.) Proceedings of the Thirty-First International Joint Conference on Artificial Intelligence, IJCAI 2022, Vienna, Austria, 23–29 July 2022, pp. 4531–4537. ijcai.org (2022). https://doi.org/10.24963/IJCAI.2022/629
21. Zhu, F., et al.: TAT-QA: a question answering benchmark on a hybrid of tabular and textual content in finance. In: Zong, C., Xia, F., Li, W., Navigli, R. (eds.) Proceedings of the 59th Annual Meeting of the Association for Computational Linguistics and the 11th International Joint Conference on Natural Language Processing, vol. 1: Long Papers, pp. 3277–3287. Association for Computational Linguistics (2021).https://doi.org/10.18653/v1/2021.acl-long.254. https://aclanthology.org/2021.acl-long.254/

Scholarly Issues

From Raw Affiliations to Organization Identifiers

Myrto Kallipoliti[1], Serafeim Chatzopoulos[2(✉)], Miriam Baglioni[3], Eleni Adamidi[2], Paris Koloveas[2,4], and Thanasis Vergoulis[2]

[1] OpenAIRE AMKE, Athens, Greece
myrto.kallipoliti@openaire.eu
[2] IMSI, ATHENA RC, Athens, Greece
{schatz,eleni.adamidi,pkoloveas,vergoulis}@athenarc.gr, pkoloveas@uop.gr
[3] CNR-ISTI, Pisa, Italy
miriam.baglioni@isti.cnr.it
[4] University of the Peloponnese, Tripolis, Greece

Abstract. Accurate affiliation matching, which links affiliation strings to standardized organization identifiers, is critical for improving research metadata quality, facilitating comprehensive bibliometric analyses, and supporting data interoperability across scholarly knowledge bases. Existing approaches fail to handle the complexity of affiliation strings that often include mentions of multiple organizations or extraneous information. In this paper, we present AffRo, a novel approach designed to address these challenges, leveraging advanced parsing and disambiguation techniques. We also introduce AffRoDB, an expert-curated dataset to systematically evaluate affiliation matching algorithms, ensuring robust benchmarking. Results demonstrate the effectiveness of AffRo in accurately identifying organizations from complex affiliation strings.

Keywords: Affiliation matching · Persistent identifiers

1 Introduction

Affiliation information in research publications and other research products (e.g., datasets, project deliverables) is valuable not only for researchers seeking to identify the organizations behind specific research, but also as a rich source of data for generating insights. For example, such information is invaluable for compiling annual reports and statistics for research-performing organizations, or producing university rankings[1].

Most research products include information about the authors' affiliated organizations, typically represented as text strings. These strings often vary in clarity, granularity, structure, and format, making the development of solutions for useful applications a non-trivial task. In recent years, the inclusion of persistent identifiers (PIDs) for organizations, like ROR[2] IDs, in affiliation metadata

[1] E.g., CWTS Leiden Ranking: https://www.leidenranking.com/.
[2] Research Organization Registry [8].

W.-T. Balke et al. (Eds.): TPDL 2025, LNCS 16097, pp. 111–126, 2026.
https://doi.org/10.1007/978-3-032-05409-8_8

has become a popular practice as a way to address this problem. However, even today, a significant number of research products do not include organization PIDs in the affiliation section.

To alleviate this problem, considerable effort has been devoted by various teams to developing accurate *affiliation matching* approaches, where 'raw' affiliation strings are mapped to standardized identifiers [1,3,9]. Such techniques have been used to enrich scholarly knowledge graphs like the OpenAIRE Graph [4] and OpenAlex [7] making it easier for value-added services that leverage their contents to provide meaningful functionalities for the research community.

For researchers, funders, and policymakers, affiliation matching enables the tracking of institutional contributions to global challenges and innovation, helping to recognize collaborative research efforts while tracking geographic distribution. For instance, when an affiliation string from a publication is matched to a persistent identifier like a ROR ID, it links the data to a comprehensive record of the organization, including several related metadata such as its location, thus adding value to scholarly metadata. Furthermore, having affiliation data mapped to organization persistent identifiers allows for improved data interoperability across different research databases, which is essential for large-scale data integration and bibliometric analyses. Consequently, since the PID is often missing from the manuscript, mapping affiliation strings to organization PIDs becomes a crucial task.

Affiliation matching is not a straight forward task; naive approaches, like solely exploiting string similarity, are not expected to work perfectly for various reasons. For instance, not all components of affiliation strings hold the same importance when matching them to other affiliation strings (e.g., matching the organization name is more critical than matching the exact address that sometimes is included in the string). In addition, affiliation strings often refer to more than one organization: the affiliation *'Biomedical Research Institute, Shenzhen Peking University-The Hong Kong University of Science and Technology Medical Center, Shenzhen, China'*, derived from Crossref as the affiliation of a single author, contains two distinct organizations. As a result, although various affiliation matching algorithms have been introduced in the literature, there is still space for improvement.

At the same time, training and evaluating such algorithms depends on access to well-curated ground truth datasets of sufficient size. However, currently, the availability of such datasets remains limited. Existing datasets often suffer from a range of issues, including small scale, a mix of curated and automatically generated entries, inconsistencies in record handling due to varying expert assumptions, lack of transparency regarding the number of annotators of each record and the version of the affiliation database used, and outdated content. These shortcomings undermine the reliability of any experimental results that rely on them as ground truth.

In this work, we introduce AFFRO (Affiliation strings to Research Organizations), a novel affiliation matching approach that aims to address most of the previously described challenges and AffRoDB[3], a publicly available expert-curated dataset to enable the reliable training and systematic evaluation of affiliation matching approaches. In addition, we use AffRoDB along with a third-party dataset of affiliation links to demonstrate the effectiveness of AffRo and compare it to state-of-the-art approaches showcasing that our method has superior precision. Finally, we offer an AffRo implementation as an open source software[4] and we make the data behind AffRoDB available through an open API[5] to offer additional integration options.

It worth noting that a configuration of AffRo has already been integrated into the proudction workflow of the OpenAIRE Graph [4], one of the largest existing scholarly knowledge graphs, enhancing the quality and completeness of its research products metadata.

2 Methodology

In this section, we present AffRo, our affiliation matching approach. Section 2.1 offers a high-level overview of the approach, while Sects. 2.2-2.4 delve into the technical details of its main phases.

2.1 High-Level Overview

Figure 1 illustrates the main stages of AffRo and offers a running example based on an indicative input affiliation string. AffRo is built on a rule-based, keyword-driven framework that can be divided into three main phases:

1. *Preprocessing*, where the input affiliation strings are tokenized, formatted, and cleaned.
2. *Matching*, where the extracted tokens are matched with records into a database of research-related organizations.
3. *Disambiguation*, where vague matches are further refined, if needed.

It is worth noting that our approach is applicable to any database of organizations that provides persistent identifiers (PIDs) and country information. Additionally, it can leverage the city of organizations and any parent-child relationships among them as optional fields; while not required, this information can improve performance. In our work, we have used the ROR database [8], therefore ROR IDs are used as identifiers in our curated dataset (see Sect. 3).

Of course, before the database can be utilized by the approach, a preprocessing phase is necessary to clean and format the affiliation strings in a manner that facilitates matching, based on the cleaning and stemming techniques described in Sect. 2.2.1, and the pruning method outlined in 2.2.3. This phase also involves constructing a series of dictionaries to organize the information in a convenient

[3] AffRoDB: https://doi.org/10.5281/zenodo.15322097.
[4] AffRo GIT repository: https://github.com/mkallipo/affiliation-matching.
[5] AffRoDB API: https://affro-api.imsi.athenarc.gr/docs.

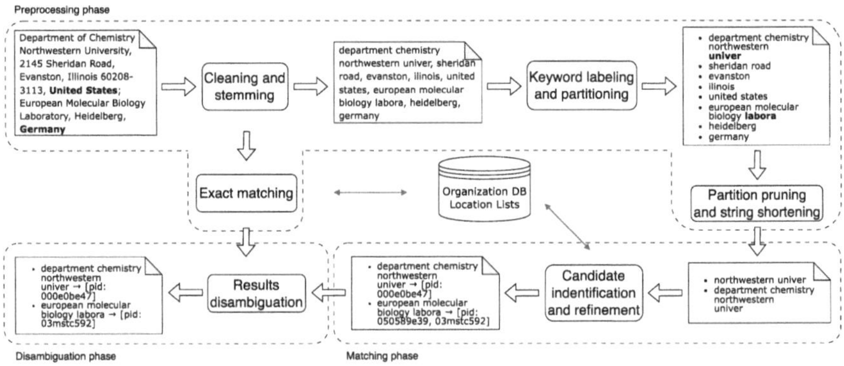

Fig. 1. Example of AFFRO's key processing steps.

way for the various phases of AFFRO. The main dictionaries are described in the respective parts of the approach that are used (in Sects. 2.2-2.4).

Finally, it is worth mentioning that our approach has four parameters (namely `window`, `sim_u`, `sim_o`, and `specific`) that affect its accuracy. These parameters and their effects are elaborated in the following sections.

2.2 Preprocessing Phase

The preprocessing phase of AFFRO consists of a series of steps outlined in the following sections.

2.2.1 Cleaning and Stemming. This step implements a series of targeted preprocessing actions tailored to improve the effectiveness of the matching process (see Sect. 2.3). These include lowercasing the strings and removing stopwords, special characters, and multi-digit numbers—including potential leading numerals. Parentheses that do not enclose key institutional terms such as "`University`", "`Hospital`", or "`Clinic`" are also removed. Additional normalization involves collapsing double consonants into a single instance, standardizing common abbreviations (e.g., "`St.`" to "`Saint`", "`Inst.`" to "`Institute`"), performing some language processing to facilitate stemming[6] and correcting typographical errors related to critical terms such as "`University`". Finally, we convert Roman numerals (e.g., i, ii, iii) to their corresponding numeric forms (1, 2, 3) to enhance downstream matching accuracy.

Next, stemming is applied to facilitate string comparisons by reducing words to a common root (e.g., "`University`", "`Universität`", and "`Université`" are all stemmed into "`univer`"). Finally, any country names detected in the raw

[6] For instance, in some special cases, translation of critical terms is applied. As an example, German terms such as "`Universitätsklinikum`" and "`Universitätsbibliothek`" are replaced by their corresponding English equivalents, see also: https://github.com/mkallipo/affiliation-matching/blob/main/dictionaries/replacements.json.

affiliation string are stored in a dictionary for later use in narrowing the candidate set during the matching phase.

2.2.2 Keyword Labeling, Partitioning, and Exact Matching. In this step, the algorithm first checks whether the cleaned and stemmed affiliation string exists in the database of organizations. If so, it is passed directly to the disambiguation phase (Sect. 2.4) implementing a shortcut. If this is not the case, the keywords of each affiliation string are classified into categories (that are used by parts of the approach) and, then, the affiliation strings are partitioned to facilitate the matching process.

Keyword classification assigns each keyword to one of the following categories:

- ``basic_key'': keywords representing basic types of research organizations (i.e., ``univer'', ``institu'', ``hospital'', and ``labora'').
- ``country'': keywords included in a dictionary of countries that we have created based on the database of organizations.
- ``other'': keywords that do not belong to the other categories.

AffRo partitions the input affiliation string based on a predetermined set of delimiting characters (at the point of writing, a comma ",", a semicolon ";", a colon ":", a forward slash "/", and an en dash "–"). The generated partitions are further divided as follows: If the word ``and'' appears between two basic keywords, it is removed, and the partition is split at that position. Additionally, a partition that cannot be matched in the organization database and contains the preposition "at", is split at its position (and the new partitions are checked again for matches in the database).

2.2.3 Partition Pruning. After partitioning, AffRo applies certain rules to reduce the set of partitions. The objective is to concentrate comparisons on the parts of the affiliation string that are more crucial for effective matching while reducing computational demands. Currently, the following rules are applied:

- *Keyword filter.* A dictionary of frequent keywords used in names of research institutions (e.g.,``univer'', ``institu'', ``academ'', ``school'', ``lab'', ``clinic'', ``library'') has been created based on a statistical analysis of the ROR database. When the specific parameter is set to True, the list is extended with frequent acronyms (e.g., ``riken'', ``eth zurich'', ``cnrs'', ``ucla'') and entity names (usualy companies e.g., ``roche'', ``astrazeneca'', ``ibm'', ``toyota'') retrieved from the Nature Index.[7] AffRo filters out partitions that do not contain any of these keywords.
- *Banned partitions.* AffRo does not consider partitions that are generic terms such as ``univer'' or ``clinic'' if no city is present in a following partition of the same string,[8] [9] as well as address-related phrases like ``univer road''

[7] Nature Index: https://www.nature.com/nature-index/.

[8] https://github.com/mkallipo/affiliation-matching/blob/main/txt_files/city_names.txt.

[9] https://github.com/mkallipo/affiliation-matching/blob/main/txt_files/banned.txt.

or "univer str". In addition, partitions that do not contain a basic keyword and contain informative substrings about authors' placements, such as "professor", "assistant", and "phd", as well as substrings referring to child organizations like "program", "unit", and "department" are also disregarded. The latter is due to the fact that the ROR database statistics indicate that such child organizations typically do not receive a dedicated PID.[10] This rule facilitates mapping the string to the parent organization's PID. The precise list of such rules can be found in our code repository.[11]

2.2.4 String Shortening for Universities and Entity Names. In this final step before matching, AffRo narrows down the remaining partitions which are not in the organization database, by preserving words near the substring "univer" using the `window` parameter. This parameter gets positive integer values and is used to trim long university-related strings. Any terms that are outside the `window` are discarded. Additionally, if a token contains a keyword from the `Entities` category (see Sect. 2.2.3), the token is reduced to the keyword.

2.3 Matching Phase

After the completion of the preprocessing, AffRo is ready to search for matches of the final partitions inside the organization database. The respective process consists of two steps: first, the identification of candidate matches (Sect. 2.3.1) and, then, the refinement of the results (Sect. 2.3.2).

2.3.1 Candidate Identification. At this stage, the algorithm employs a string similarity measure to determine whether input partitions (approximately) match names in the organization database. As described in Sect. 4.2.2, experimentation revealed that optimal similarity thresholds vary across organization types. Specifically, for universities, a looser threshold, denoted as `sim_u`, proves to be more effective compared to other types of organizations, for which a stricter threshold, `sim_o`, is applied. In Sect. 4.2, we provide insights on the optimal selection of values for those parameters. Note that the algorithm searches for possible matches not across all organization names, but only within the subset corresponding to the countries mentioned in the raw affiliation string. This is a crucial step that improves both the accuracy and performance of the algorithm.

2.3.2 Results Refinement. If the algorithm detects multiple matches (candidates) above the specified similarity thresholds for a token, it proceeds with an additional check to determine the best fit among these candidates. To this end, string similarity is employed once again, comparing the candidates with the

[10] For instance, we have found that only approximately 0.06% of ROR records correspond to departments that are children of universities.

[11] https://github.com/mkallipo/affiliation-matching/blob/main/create_input.py.

original cleaned and stemmed affiliation string. This comparison is meaningful because it takes into account additional information from the original affiliation, such as city names or the names of child organizations. For the final refinement, the number of occurrences of basic keywords is also considered to limit the number of results.

2.4 Results Disambiguation

Once the final match is identified, the algorithm checks whether the organization's name corresponds to multiple entries in the database. If so, the algorithm leverages available city and country information to determine the most suitable match. If no location is provided and the organization's name falls into a special category of known entities (e.g., tech companies), then the algorithm matches to the parent organization if existent (for example, in case of ROR IDs, the affiliation "Google" is mapped to `"00njsd438"`). If none of these conditions are met, then a match is returned only if there is a unique active ID among the possible results the name corresponds to a unique active ID. Finally, if the identified organization has a non-active ID, the IDs of any successor organizations are retrieved and returned.

3 Expert-Curated Dataset

In this section, we describe AFFRODB, the curated dataset that we have compiled to evaluate the accuracy of affiliation matching approaches. In the following, we outline the process of creating AFFRODB (Sect. 3.1), the structure and format of the data (Sect. 3.2), as well as its update policy (Sect. 3.3).

3.1 Dataset Creation Process

In the following, we provide an overview of the methodology employed in compiling the dataset, highlighting the annotation process to ensure data quality and consistency. Each entry in the dataset has been independently annotated by at least two experts to improve consistency and reduce bias. Furthermore, the experts were instructed to identify multiple organizations when applicable and to include detailed metadata capturing the nature of relationships between these organizations. Because of the previous reasons, our dataset serves as a robust and comprehensive benchmark for evaluating affiliation matching algorithms.

The expert-driven process for creating the dataset was carefully designed. We first randomly selected approximately 1,500 records from Crossref, with non-empty affiliation lists. Each affiliation string was evaluated by two experts (we have used five experts in total) who identified the corresponding ROR entries it represented, and then classified each link into one of three categories: `EXACT`, `ANCESTOR`, and `VAGUE`. Table 1 summarizes these annotation categories along with their interpretation. In cases of disagreement between the two experts, a third

Table 1. Annotation categories for expert-curated affiliation links.

Name	Description
EXACT	The ROR ID found corresponded precisely to the most specific organization mentioned in the string.
ANCESTOR	The ROR ID corresponded to a parent organization mentioned in the string.
VAGUE	No elevant ROR ID was detected or the expert could not confidently assign a corresponding ROR ID.

expert reviewed the affiliation string and made the final decision on the labels and corresponding links.

The final dataset was constructed after excluding affiliation links labeled as `VAGUE`; In particular, it consists of 1,374 raw affiliation strings, extracted from 1,261 DOIs. Notably, the total number of ROR links is 1,475, since experts assigned multiple ROR links to some records, 379 of them corresponding to exact matches, and 1,096 to matches to ancestor organizations. A third expert was enlisted to resolve disagreements in the evaluation of 110 raw affiliation strings, ensuring consensus and accuracy in the final assessments.

3.2 Data Structure Description

The dataset is formatted as a JSON Lines (JSONL)[12] file where each line contains a valid JSON object. This format is rather simple yet efficient for large datasets, since it facilitates incremental processing of the data. The expert annotations are captured by instances of an `annotation object` which contains two fields: (a) `exact`, and (b) `ancestor`, which correspond to arrays of ROR identifiers identified as exact or ancestor matches respectively. Then, each JSON object contains the following four fields:

1. `raw_affiliation_string`: a string representing the raw affiliation data.
2. `extracted_dois`: the DOIs from which the affiliation string was extracted.
3. `expert_judgements`: expert annotations each with the following fields:
   (a) `expert_id`: a positive integer identifying the expert.
   (b) `matches`: an `annotation object` representing the expert's annotation.
4. `final_judgement`: an `annotation object` representing the final evaluation.

Our dataset is openly available on Zenodo[13] under the CC0 Creative Commons license, ensuring unrestricted access and enabling broader reuse. Moreover, we plan to provide regular updates by incorporating new entries and revising existing ones based on the latest information available in the ROR database.

3.3 Update Policy

Our goal is for AffRoDB to serve as a living dataset that will be regularly updated through a carefully designed process that ensures the inclusion of

[12] JSON Lines format documentation: https://jsonlines.org/.
[13] AffRoDB dataset: https://doi.org/10.5281/zenodo.15322097.

matches for new affiliation strings, as well as the revision of existing entries to correct errors or to add matches to ROR IDs that were not available at the time the initial records were created. This update process is intended to keep the dataset accurate and useful over time, while also facilitate the involvement of additional experts in the curation process.

With each new release of the dataset, a batch of affiliation strings will be provided for expert curation. This batch will be selected to ensure it includes strings from the following categories:

1. **New affiliation strings:** a random set of new affiliation strings from Crossref consisting of approximately 70% of the records.
2. **Old affiliation strings:** a random subset of the affiliation strings that have been processed by the experts of a previous dataset version. Both strings with non-empty and empty exact or ancestor matches will be selected so that we can both validate the accuracy of assigned identifiers and identify missing ones.

Additionally, a fully automated process will take place searching inside the old dataset records with the aim to identify ROR IDs that are no longer active. In case a successor organization is determined by ROR, the inactive identifier will be replaced by its identifier. Otherwise, the identifier, will be removed.

3.4 Open API

Researchers and developers can leverage the affiliation resolution functionality of AffRo through a publicly accessible API to enrich publication metadata in their research workflows. The main endpoint of this API takes as input a raw affiliation string, in a form typically found in publication metadata, along with AffRo's configuration parameters (see Sect. 2.1), and returns a ranked list of matched research organizations. Each result includes a unique identifier (typically a ROR ID), and a numerical confidence score. This API offers a convenient way to experiment with the results of AffRo out of the box, while for more demanding use cases, the service is also available as open source,[14] allowing deployment on self-managed environments.

3.5 Comparison with Other Datasets

Unlike other similar datasets, ours includes affiliation strings that mention multiple organizations, providing corresponding links to multiple identifiers. Furthermore, most well-established datasets with affiliation links (see Sect. 5) combine curated and automatically generated links, which can undermine the reliability of experiments using them due to differing levels of trust between the two types of records. In contrast, AffRoDB is a fully expert-curated dataset.

In addition, AffRoDB prioritizes transparency, consistency, and long-term reliability. Many other datasets do not provide crucial information, such as which

[14] AffRo API GIT repository: https://github.com/mkallipo/affiliation-matching-api.

version of the ROR dataset was used during the expert annotation process. This is an important detail, given that ROR is continuously evolving and this absence can result in discrepancies where identifiers used in the training of an approach may not have existed at the time of the creation of the expert-curated dataset. Additionally, there is often no indication of how many experts assessed each record, whether multiple experts were involved, or what individual scores were assigned by each expert. To the best of our knowledge, AffRoDB is currently the only expert-curated dataset offering these features.

Moreover, our dataset is built upon a clear and well-defined annotation policy that was shared with all experts to minimize inconsistencies—for example, in handling matches to ancestor organizations. Also, every entry has been reviewed by multiple experts, resulting in high-quality ground truth records. In preliminary evaluations of curated entries from some well-established datasets [3,6,9], we identified a noticeable number of errors or missing links. These issues led us to exclude those datasets from our experiments due to trustworthiness concerns.

Finally, a key strength of our dataset is that we have defined a robust update policy for it to ensure the dataset remains current and consistent over time.

4 Experimental Evaluation

In this section, we present the experiments we conducted to evaluate the effectiveness of our approach. In Sect. 4.1, we outline the experimental setup, while in Sect. 4.2 we present our experiments to configure and study the parameters of our approach. Finally, in Sect. 4.3 we outline our findings regarding the effectiveness of AffRo in comparison to the state-of-the-art approaches.

4.1 Setup

4.1.1 Methods. The evaluation involved experiments with three main approaches; different configurations were tested for each one, where applicable.

- *AffRo*, our proposed approach as presented in Sect. 2, with three different parameter configurations, each maximizing precision, recall or F_1-score (based on the results of the experiments in Sect. 4.2), respectively.
- *S2AFF* [3,9], the approach developed by Semantic Scholar to link affiliation strings with affiliations in ROR.
- *OpenAlex ROR Predictor* [1], a modified version of OpenAlex's institution parsing service [5,7], extended to also return ROR IDs from affiliation strings alongside OpenAlex institution IDs.

4.1.2 Datasets. For our experiments, we used the following sets of data:

- *AffRoDB* Our expert-curated dataset, consisting of raw affiliation strings manually linked to ROR IDs (see Sect. 3 for details).

- *Crossref organization assertions.* This dataset contains organization relationships from Crossref metadata, including both publisher-submitted and automatically assigned ROR IDs. We filtered the dataset to retain only records where the ROR ID was submitted by publishers (to avoid automatically matched strings), resulting in 47,942 unique affiliation strings, each mapped to a single ROR ID.

We should note that all the compared approaches were configured to use the ROR database dump of January 2024 (v1.40), since this was the version used by the expert curators of AffRoDB to produce their annotations.

4.1.3 Evaluation Metrics. To evaluate the effectiveness of the considered approaches, we use micro-averaged Precision, Recall, and F_1-score, which are particularly well-suited for multi-class classification tasks such as affiliation matching. In this task, a single affiliation string may correspond to multiple organization identifiers, and the number of these identifiers can vary significantly across affiliations. Micro-averaging addresses this imbalance by aggregating true positives, false positives, and false negatives across all instances before computing the metrics, thereby treating each prediction equally regardless of class frequency.

In particular, the micro-averaged metrics are computed as follows:

$$\text{Precision} = \frac{\sum_s TP_s}{\sum_s (TP_s + FP_s)}, \text{ Recall} = \frac{\sum_s TP_s}{\sum_s (TP_s + FN_s)}, \; F_1 = \frac{2 \cdot \text{Precision} \cdot \text{Recall}}{\text{Precision} + \text{Recall}}$$

where TP_s corresponds to the number of correct matches within the affiliation string s, FP_s to the number of incorrect matches of s, and FN_s to the matches of s that were not found. Finally, note that the larger the values of these measures, the better the effectiveness of the method under consideration.

For datasets where each affiliation string corresponds to a single organization identifier, and a prediction is always provided, we report accuracy, defined as:

$$\text{Accuracy} = \frac{Number\ of\ correct\ predictions}{Total\ number\ of\ predictions}$$

4.1.4 Evaluation Setting. We implemented AffRo in Python and released it as open-source software[15] under the Apache 2.0 license. The implementation uses the `unidecode`[16] library for text normalization, and `scikit-learn`[17] for feature extraction and cosine similarity (for string comparisons). AffRo includes three configurable parameters: `sim_o` and `sim_u`, both ranging in $(0, 1]$, and a `window` parameter ranging from 1 to 10. An additional boolean flag, `specific` $\in$ {`True`, `False`}, controls whether specific keywords like company names and

[15] AffRo GIT repository: https://github.com/mkallipo/affiliation-matching.
[16] `unidecode` library: https://pypi.org/project/Unidecode/.
[17] `scikit-learn` library: https://scikit-learn.org/.

acronyms are taken into account. For other methods, we used their publicly available GitHub implementations (see Sect. 4.1.1). Finally, experiments were conducted on an AWS M6g instance (64 CPU cores, 256 GB RAM).

4.2 Configuring AFFRO

In this section, we first present the configuration of our approach by tuning its parameters to maximize performance. Then, we vary the values of input parameters to further analyze their influence on the overall performance of AFFRO.

4.2.1 Parameter Tuning. We evaluate the performance of AFFRO by optimizing its configuration parameters with respect to each of the evaluation metrics (Precision, Recall, and F_1-score) individually. To this end, we employ Bayesian optimization [10] to efficiently explore the parameter space; we perform 1,000 iterations per metric, using our algorithm as the objective function, set to maximize the corresponding measure in each case.

The highest precision (0.980) was achieved using the following setting: `window` = 6, `sim_o` = 0.896, `sim_u` = 0.898, and `specific` = `True`. In contrast, the best recall (0.917) was obtained using `window` = 3, `sim_o` = 0.662, `sim_u` = 0.313, and `specific` = `True`. The optimal F_1-score (0.937) was also achieved at `window` = 3, but with higher similarity thresholds, `sim_o` = 0.827, `sim_u` = 0.426, and again `specific` = `True`. It is evident that there is a trade-off between precision and recall depending on the similarity thresholds and the context-specific tuning of parameters.

For clarity, we refer to the AFFRO variants that achieve the best precision, recall, and F_1-score as AFFRO_P, AFFRO_R, and AFFRO_F, respectively. These labels are used throughout the remainder of this paper to facilitate presentation and comparison of results.

4.2.2 In-Depth Parameter Analysis. In this section, we discuss how each of the aforementioned parameters of AFFRO affects the performance. Specifically, we investigate AFFRO's performance while varying `window` and similarity thresholds, respectively for each one of the variants AFFRO_P, AFFRO_R, and AFFRO_F.

The first plot of Fig. 2 shows that precision steadily improves when increasing the `window`, and reaches a plateau at `window` = 5, maintaining the highest observed precision value of approximately 0.98. Figure 2b shows that recall peaks at `window` = 3 (around 0.917) and slightly declines beyond that, suggesting diminishing benefits for larger window sizes. Figure 2c reveals that F_1-score also reaches its maximum at `window` = 3 (0.937), indicating the best balance between precision and recall occurs at this point.

Finally, Fig. 3a shows that precision increases consistently with higher values of `sim_o`, starting at approximately 0.936 for low values and peaking around 0.980 at `sim_o` = 0.9. Similarly, higher values of `sim_u` achieve better precision, reaching a peak at `sim_u` = 1.0. Figure 3b shows that recall initially rises slightly and peaks at `sim_o` = 0.7 (approximately 0.917), after which it begins to decline.

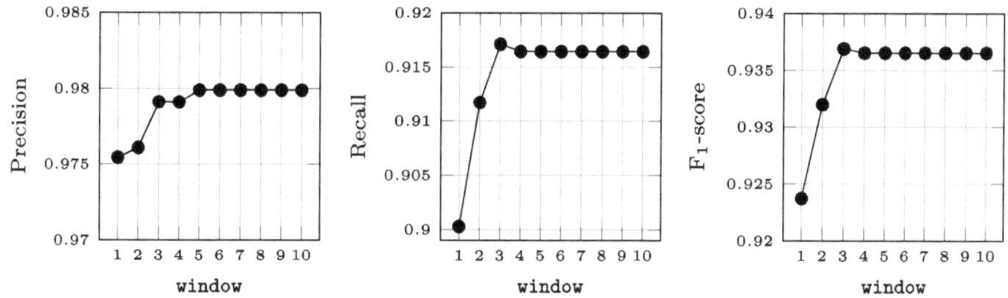

(a) Precision (b) Recall (c) F_1-score

Fig. 2. Performance metrics varying the `window` parameter.

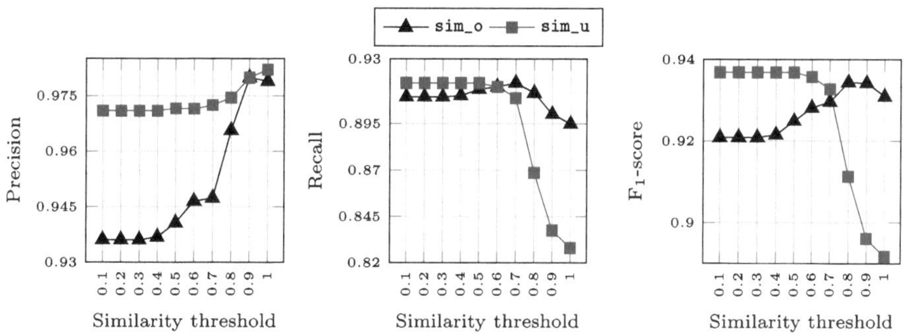

(a) Precision (b) Recall (c) F_1-score

Fig. 3. Performance metrics varying similarity thresholds `sim_o` and `sim_u`.

In contrast, `sim_u` maintains a high (just below 0.92) recall up to `sim_u` = 0.5, but starts declining noticeably beyond that. Figure 3c reflects the combined effect of these trends: increasing `sim_o` improves F_1-score steadily up to `sim_o` = 0.8, reaching a maximum of around 0.934, and then slightly decreases. This indicates that `sim_o` values around 0.7 and 0.8 offer the best overall performance. On the other hand, `sim_u` follows a similar trend as in recall: it is stable and high at lower thresholds but steadily declines as `sim_u` increases (due to the respective drop in recall outweighing the gains in precision). This suggests that, while higher `sim_u` values improve precision, they do so at the cost of missing true positives, resulting in lower recall and a reduced F_1-score.

Finally, we evaluate the impact of the `specific` parameter (see Sect. 2.2.3) on the best-performing variants of *AFFRO* with respect to precision, recall, and F_1-score (denoted as AFFRO$_P$, AFFRO$_R$, and AFFRO$_F$, respectively). Table 2 shows that, across all configurations, the inclusion of the `specific` organizations yields consistent improvements in recall and F_1-score, while maintaining precision. Specifically, AFFRO$_P$ achieves the highest precision (0.980) both with and without `specific`, but its recall improves from 0.813 to 0.821 and F_1 from 0.889 to 0.893 when the `specific = True`. Similarly, AFFRO$_R$ sees a recall increase

Table 2. Effect of the `specific` component of AffRo.

Approach	Precision	Recall	F_1-score
AffRo$_P$ w/o `specific`	**0.980**	0.813	0.889
AffRo$_P$	**0.980**	0.821	0.893
AffRo$_R$ w/o `specific`	0.942	0.908	0.925
AffRo$_R$	0.943	**0.917**	0.930
AffRo$_F$ w/o `specific`	0.965	0.903	0.933
AffRo$_F$	0.965	0.910	**0.937**

Table 3. Evaluation against competitor approaches on AffRoDB and Crossref.

Approach	AffRoDB			Crossref
	Precision	Recall	F_1 score	Accuracy
AffRo$_P$	**0.980**	0.821	0.893	–
AffRo$_R$	0.943	0.917	0.930	–
AffRo$_F$	0.965	0.910	**0.937**	**0.935**
S2AFF	0.964	0.846	0.901	0.927
OpenAlex	0.914	**0.929**	0.921	0.920

from 0.908 to 0.917, that also results in an increase in F_1-score from 0.925 to 0.930. Lastly, AffRo$_F$, benefits from a recall gain (0.903 to 0.910), resulting in an F_1-score improvement from 0.933 to 0.937. These results showcase that AffRo with the `specific` enabled is enhanced to capture relevant instances, especially in recall, without sacrificing precision.

4.3 Performance Comparison with Competitors

This section evaluates the best-performing variants AffRo$_P$, AffRo$_R$, and AffRo$_F$, against two competitor approaches: OpenAlex and S2AFF in two datasets (AffRoDB and Crossref). The results are summarized in Table 3.

For AffRoDB, where each affiliation string is mapped to a list of organization identifiers, we report standard metrics (precision, recall, and F_1-score). Among all methods, AffRo$_P$ achieves the highest precision (Precision = 0.980), while OpenAlex achieves the highest recall (Recall = 0.929). However, AffRo$_F$ balances both metrics most effectively, reaching the best F_1-score score of 0.937, outperforming both S2AFF (F_1-score = 0.901) and OpenAlex (F_1-score = 0.921).

For Crossref, since only one ROR identifier is mapped to each affiliation string, we evaluate all algorithms over the 30,740 rows of the intersection of affiliation strings for which all methods returned a single result. To this end, we report the accuracy since it is a more suitable metric for this setup. Table 3 shows that, AffRo$_F$ performs best, achieving the highest accuracy (0.935), slightly outperforming both OpenAlex (0.920) and S2AFF (0.927). Notably, S2AFF performs comparatively better on this dataset than on AffRoDB, as it treats each affiliation string as representing a single affiliation, a strategy that better aligns with this dataset. These results highlight that AffRo outperforms competing methods overall, with the AffRo_F variant achieving the best F_1-score.

5 Related Work

Affiliation matching has become a prevalent task in metadata normalization, and several methods have been proposed to tackle it. Among them, the OpenAlex institution parsing [1,5,7] leverages an ensemble of two machine learning models trained on historical MAG data to classify and match institution strings. It further enhances performance by augmenting training data with synthetic affiliation strings. S2AFF [3] employs a three-stage pipeline: it first parses the input affiliation string into separate components (i.e., institution, country, address), it then retrieves the top candidate affiliations (using a retrieval index), and finally re-ranks them to produce the final result. In addition, ROR [8] added support to identify research organizations, by mapping free-text affiliation strings to ROR IDs, directly in their main API, using the most up-to-date version of the ROR registry. While rather practical, it combines algorithmic logic with curated registry content, making it less transparent as a standalone algorithmic baseline. In a recent effort, AffilGood [2] explores affiliation disambiguation when multilingual affiliation strings are considered. However, since this work was published only recently, we do not include a direct comparison with AffRo in this paper.

Meanwhile, despite the importance of high-quality evaluation data, most existing datasets used for affiliation matching are only partially curated. A recent dataset compiled by Crossref [11] includes a small subset of manually deposited organization identifiers (by Crossref members), but it primarily contains automatically identified mappings, which limits its reliability as a ground truth. Additionally, it assigns a single organization identifier to each affiliation string, which is problematic in cases where the string refers to multiple organizations. Furthermore, both the S2AFF Gold [3,9] and OpenAlex [6] datasets include some curated entries; for instance, OpenAlex incorporates entries curated by CWTS. However, in both cases, we observed inconsistencies and label noise, particularly in complex cases (see Sect. 3.5 for details).

6 Conclusion and Future Work

In this work, we addressed the challenging problem of affiliation matching by introducing AffRo, a novel approach for mapping raw affiliation strings to persistent organization identifiers. Our method leverages advanced parsing techniques to tackle the inherent complexity of affiliation strings, including cases where multiple organizations are mentioned. We also compiled and made publicly available an expert-curated dataset designed to benchmark affiliation matching algorithms and provided a publicly accessible API to facilitate integration of our approach into third-party workflows. The evaluation of AffRo demonstrates its effectiveness in achieving higher performance than competitor approaches; however certain limitations remain. Our method does not yet incorporate Named Entity Recognition, which could help distinguish organizations, locations, and dates in the affiliation string. Normalization of non-English institution names remains an open challenge, and Large Language Models may assist through semantic understanding and context-aware disambiguation in such cases.

Acknowledgments. This work has received funding from the European Union's Horizon Europe framework programme under grant agreement No. 101058573 as part of the Scilake project. Part of this work utilized Amazon's cloud computing resources which were granted with the support of GRNET.

References

1. Buttrick, A.: Openalex-ror-predictor (2023). https://github.com/adambuttrick/openalex-ror-predictor. Accessed: 2025-04-28
2. Duran-Silva, N., Accuosto, P., Przybyła, P., Saggion, H.: Affilgood: building reliable institution name disambiguation tools to improve scientific literature analysis. In: Proceedings of the Fourth Workshop on Scholarly Document Processing (SDP 2024), pp. 135–144 (2024)
3. Kinney, R., et al.: The semantic scholar open data platform (2023). arXiv preprint arXiv:2301.10140
4. Manghi, P., et al.: Openaire research graph dataset (2022)
5. OurResearch: openalex institution parsing (2024). https://github.com/ourresearch/openalex-institution-parsing. mIT License
6. OurResearch: openalex test dataset (2025). https://github.com/ourresearch/openalex-institution-parsing/tree/main/V2#test-data. Accessed: 2025-03-28
7. Priem, J., Piwowar, H., Orr, R.: Openalex: a fully-open index of scholarly works, authors, venues, institutions, and concepts (2022). arXiv preprint arXiv:2205.01833
8. Research organization registry: ROR: research organization registry (2024). https://ror.org/. Accessed: 2024-03-27
9. Scholar, S.: S2aff: Semantic scholar affiiliations linker (2023). https://github.com/allenai/S2AFF. apache 2.0 license
10. Snoek, J., Larochelle, H., Adams, R.P.: Practical bayesian optimization of machine learning algorithms. Adv. Neural Inf. Process. Syst. **25** (2012)
11. Tkaczyk, D.: Crossref relationships involving research organisations (2025)

How Retracted Article Persists on YouTube
Retraction Severity, Visibility, and Disclosure

Jiro Kikkawa[1(✉)] and Masao Takaku[2]

[1] Wakayama University, Wakayama, Japan
jiro@wakayama-u.ac.jp
[2] University of Tsukuba, Ibaraki, Japan
masao@slis.tsukuba.ac.jp

Abstract. The retraction of scholarly articles due to errors or misconduct reflects fundamental problems in the research process and raises concerns about research integrity. However, retracted articles often continue to circulate online, especially on platforms like YouTube, which may lack effective mechanisms for academic oversight. Despite this concern, little is known about how retracted articles are actually referenced in such environments, and no comprehensive empirical investigations have been conducted to date.

To investigate this issue empirically, we analyzed the prevalence and context of retracted article references on YouTube using a large-scale dataset of scholarly references extracted from video description text. We identified 1,002 references to retracted articles, corresponding to 360 unique DOIs, found in 956 videos uploaded by 714 channels. Notably, the channels referencing retracted articles accounted for nearly 1% of all channels referencing scholarly articles.

Moreover, approximately 75% of the referenced articles were retracted for serious reasons such as data fabrication or ethical violations. Almost half of the videos referencing retracted articles were published after the retraction date. A substantial portion of these videos do not mention the retraction status, and several appear to reference the articles without recognizing their retracted nature, as suggested by the absence of any mention of retraction in the video content or description text. In contrast, a few videos explicitly addressed the retraction and were intended to educate viewers by highlighting issues of scientific misconduct. These findings highlight the continued circulation of unreliable scholarly information on YouTube and underscore the need for improved visibility of retraction notices in user-generated content.

Keywords: YouTube · Retracted Articles · Bibliometrics · Scientific Misconduct

1 Introduction

Scholarly knowledge is primarily disseminated and accumulated through academic journal articles, which serve as the backbone of scholarly communi-

W.-T. Balke et al. (Eds.): TPDL 2025, LNCS 16097, pp. 127–144, 2026.
https://doi.org/10.1007/978-3-032-05409-8_9

cation and scientific advancement. However, some of these articles are later retracted due to serious errors or misconduct that reflect fundamental problems in the research process and raise concerns about research integrity. In recent years, efforts to improve the visibility of retracted articles have gained traction. Notably, the acquisition of the Retraction Watch database by Crossref in 2023 has facilitated the direct integration of retraction metadata into DOI records, thereby creating an infrastructure that allows readers and platforms to more easily recognize the retracted status of a publication.

Despite such infrastructural improvements, the persistent citation and reference of retracted articles—often without acknowledgment of their retracted status—remains a serious concern. This issue is particularly pronounced in social media environments, where scholarly oversight is minimal and the audience often includes non-experts. Among these platforms, YouTube has emerged as a major venue for science communication to the general public, offering outreach opportunities while presenting risks of misinformation. Prior studies have noted the proliferation of scientifically incorrect content and conspiracy theories on the platform [2,13].

While several studies have investigated how scholarly references appear in YouTube videos, most rely on data provided by Altmetric[1]. However, the Altmetric dataset is limited to videos uploaded by pre-curated channels, making it insufficient for capturing the full landscape of scholarly references on YouTube. More importantly, to the best of our knowledge, no previous work has provided a comprehensive analysis of how retracted articles are referenced on YouTube.

To address these limitations, we previously developed a method for identifying scholarly references in YouTube videos by matching external links in video descriptions to DOIs, as presented in our prior work at TPDL 2024 [19,20]. This method enabled the construction of an expanded dataset that significantly complements Altmetric's coverage, increasing the number of identified references by approximately 150%. Leveraging this approach, we construct a more comprehensive and large-scale dataset on scholarly references on YouTube, and we analyze how retracted articles are referenced on YouTube in this study. Specifically, this study aims to reveal the patterns and contexts in which retracted articles are referenced and discussed in YouTube videos, addressing the following research questions.

RQ1: To what extent are retracted articles referenced on YouTube, and how frequently do they involve severe retraction reasons?
RQ2: What characteristics do retracted articles referenced in many YouTube videos or in highly viewed videos tend to exhibit?
RQ3: Do retracted articles referenced on YouTube tend to appear in videos published before or after the retraction date? How does this distribution vary by the severity of the retraction reason?

The contributions of this study are twofold. (1) We provide the first large-scale empirical analysis of how retracted articles are referenced on YouTube,

[1] https://altmetric.com/.

combining the Altmetric dataset with an expanded dataset constructed using our previously proposed method for identifying scholarly references in video descriptions. (2) Through both quantitative analysis and targeted manual examination of sampled videos, we reveal the extent to which the retracted status is acknowledged—or overlooked—in user-generated YouTube content, thereby highlighting key challenges in the transparency and reliability of scholarly communication on one of the largest online video platforms.

2 Related Work

2.1 Studies on Retracted Articles in Scholarly Publications

The retraction of scholarly articles has been widely examined in bibliometrics and scholarly communication. For instance, Teixeira da Silva and Bornemann-Cimenti [32] identified key reasons why retracted articles continue to be cited, including a lack of awareness, insufficient metadata updates, and even deliberate citation. Bar-Ilan and Halevi [3] examined the time lag between publication and retraction and noted that retracted articles continued to accumulate citations and Mendeley readers even after being officially retracted. They also classified retraction reasons into three categories: ethical misconduct, scientific distortion, and administrative error.

Woo and Walsh [38] examined how retracted articles continue to be cited after retraction and found that such citations are more likely to come from audiences unfamiliar with the field of the retracted article. In addition, they classified retraction reasons listed in the Retraction Watch database into three severity levels: *Severe*, *Moderate*, and *Minor*. *Severe* and *Moderate* retractions are considered particularly problematic, as continued citation without awareness can significantly distort scholarly communication. These two categories roughly correspond to ethical misconduct and scientific distortion.

In this study, we examine how frequently retracted articles are referenced in YouTube videos and analyze the severity of the reasons for retraction. To this end, we conduct our analysis using the classification proposed by Woo and Walsh, focusing on cases categorized as *Severe* or *Moderate*, which are more likely to cause serious problems if referenced without awareness of the retraction.

2.2 Health-Related Misinformation on Social Media

Previous systematic reviews [33,36] have highlighted the pervasive role of social media platforms in spreading health-related misinformation. Specific platforms such as X (formerly Twitter) [39], Facebook [31], and YouTube [2,7,16,22,27] have each been the subject of empirical studies demonstrating how they contribute to the dissemination of discredited health claims.

As a notable prior study focused on YouTube, Donzelli et al. [7] conducted a quantitative analysis of 560 videos related to the alleged link between vaccines and autism or other serious side effects in children, all uploaded by 1 August 2017. They highlighted a prevalence of negatively framed videos about vaccines and emphasized the need for public institutions to play a more active role in providing reliable information online. This implies that the dominance of negative messaging on YouTube may reflect a gap in authoritative, science-based communication. While most prior studies have focused on health-related misinformation, our study does not limit its scope to any particular discipline. Instead, we conduct a large-scale analysis of retracted scholarly articles referenced in YouTube videos.

2.3 Scholarly References and Science Communication on YouTube

For previous studies regarding analysis of scholarly references on YouTube (i.e., YouTube videos cited from scholarly articles [21], and Bibliometric/Quantitative analysis of scholarly references on YouTube [18,30]), see Sect. 2 of Kikkawa et al. [19].

Zagovora and Weller [41] is one of the most recent studies analyzing how scholarly articles are referenced in YouTube videos. Their analysis, based on over 35,000 videos and 11,000 channels identified via the Altmetric dataset, provides valuable insights into who references scholarly articles on YouTube and the thematic domains involved. However, the dataset is limited to videos published up to 2017 and includes only those from a pre-curated set of YouTube channels selected by Altmetric. Moreover, the study does not consider whether the referenced articles have been retracted or how such retractions are disclosed.

To address these limitations, Kikkawa et al. [19,20] proposed a method for identifying scholarly references in YouTube video descriptions by querying the YouTube Data API using the domain names of major scholarly platforms as described in Sect. 3.1. This approach captured a complementary set of references not included in the Altmetric dataset, with nearly half of the identified references being previously uncaptured. Combining both datasets resulted in a coverage increase of approximately 150%.

Building on that approach, the present study uses an integrated dataset consisting of the Altmetric dataset and the dataset constructed by Kikkawa et al. [19,20], enabling a more comprehensive analysis of retracted articles referenced in YouTube videos.

3 Materials and Methods

3.1 Dataset Construction and Integration

To prepare a comprehensive dataset for analyzing references to retracted articles on YouTube, we integrated multiple data sources and performed a series of filtering and enrichment steps.

We obtained and integrated the Altmetric dataset with our custom-built "YA Domain Dataset," which was developed using a previously proposed method for identifying scholarly references in YouTube videos. The YA Domain Dataset was constructed by extracting external links to six major scholarly platforms from video description text—namely, (1) PubMed, (2) DOI links, (3) ScienceDirect,

(4) Wiley Online Library, (5) SpringerLink, and (6) IEEE Xplore—and mapping them to the corresponding DOIs [19,20]. The resulting integrated dataset, constructed as of the end of December 2023, comprises approximately 740,000 scholarly references (390,000 unique DOIs) found in 320,000 YouTube videos uploaded by 77,000 channels. This represents an approximate 150% increase in coverage compared to using the Altmetric dataset alone. We then retrieved bibliographic metadata from Crossref[2] for each DOI, including the article title, authors, journal, and publication date.

To collect additional metadata for each video and channel, such as video title, publication date, view count, video length, and channel subscriber count, we used the YouTube Data API[3]. Videos that were no longer accessible (e.g., deleted or set to private) as of April 22, 2025, were excluded from the analysis.

To identify and retain only those records corresponding to retracted articles, we cross-referenced the dataset with the Retraction Watch database [1,29] as of April 18, 2025. Specifically, we defined retracted articles as those satisfying both of the following conditions: (1) the "RetractionNature" field indicates "Retraction" as the type of update notice, and (2) the "OriginalPaperDOI" field contains a valid DOI (i.e., not an empty value or "Unavailable").

To assess the severity of retraction reasons, we adopted the classification scheme proposed by Woo and Walsh [38], which maps retraction reasons in the Retraction Watch database into three severity levels: *Severe*, *Moderate*, and *Minor* misconduct. In cases where multiple reasons were assigned to a single article, we adopted the most serious category. Although other taxonomies (e.g., the "Taxonomy of Retraction Reasons [24]") exist, they do not provide severity-based classifications, making the Woo and Walsh scheme most suitable for our purpose. This classification was applied to the subset of retracted articles identified in our dataset for further analysis in Sect. 4.

3.2 Analysis Methods

The following three analyses were performed on the retracted articles referenced on YouTube videos identified by the method described in Sect. 3.1. Each analysis corresponds to an RQ.

(1) Prevalence and Severity of Retracted Article References. We first conducted a basic statistical analysis of retracted article references, including the number of references, unique DOIs, unique videos, and unique channels, as well as the proportion of these references relative to all scholarly references on YouTube. Next, we grouped the retracted articles according to the severity of their retraction reasons and aggregated statistics on the number of references, unique DOIs, and unique videos for each group. We then analyzed the view count of the referencing videos using descriptive statistics, including minimum, maximum, median values, and standard deviation.

[2] http://api.crossref.org/.
[3] https://developers.google.com/youtube/v3?hl=en.

(2) Characteristics of Highly Referenced or Viewed Retracted Articles. For retracted articles referenced in a large number of videos, we examined the subject area, publication year, retraction year, and retraction reason with the severity, as well as the view counts and channel subscriber counts of the referencing videos, based on their minimum, maximum, and median values.

For videos with high view counts among those referencing retracted articles, we further analyzed various attributes, including view count, video length, the severity of the retraction reason of the referenced article, the relationship between the video's publication date and the article's publication and retraction years, and the number of channel subscribers.

We note that due to platform limitations, YouTube does not provide revision histories of video descriptions. As a result, it is not possible to determine when a reference (external link) was added to the video description. Therefore, we can only analyze the relationship between the video's publication date and the retraction date of the referenced article (i.e., whether the video was published before or after retraction), but we cannot determine whether the reference was added before or after the retraction. However, since YouTube does not allow video content to be replaced without changing the video URI[4], if a video was published before the retraction date, we can assume that the content was created without recognizing that the referenced article had been retracted.

(3) Referencing Before and After Retraction, and Disclosure in Videos. We grouped the videos based on whether they were published before or after the retraction date of the referenced articles. Within each group, we classified the articles by the severity of the retraction reason and analyzed their distribution to observe potential trends.

We also conducted a manual analysis of how retracted articles were referenced in YouTube videos, by randomly sampling 10 instances of references from each of the following four groups:

① References found in videos published before the retraction of an article classified as *Severe*.
② References found in videos published before the retraction of an article classified as *Moderate*.
③ References found in videos published after the retraction of an article classified as *Severe*.
④ References found in videos published after the retraction of an article classified as *Moderate*.

For each sampled video, we examined: (1) whether the referenced article is visually displayed or verbally identified (e.g., a screenshot of the article or bibliographic details such as published year, author names, article title, and journal title) in the video content, (2) whether the video description text includes any mention of the retraction of the corresponding article, and (3) whether the

[4] https://support.google.com/youtube/answer/55770?hl=en.

video content explicitly explains the retraction of the corresponding article. The first author checked these three aspects through direct viewing of the videos.

Furthermore, for cases where specific segments in the video referring to the article could be identified, we analyzed the context of the reference. These were classified into four categories: "Referenced without retraction awareness," "Referenced from a critical or skeptical stance," "Referenced from a neutral stance," and "Unknown."

4 Results and Discussion

4.1 Prevalence and Severity of Retracted Article References

RQ1: To what extent are retracted articles referenced on YouTube, and how frequently do they involve severe retraction reasons?

Table 1. Basic statistics of references to retracted and all articles on YouTube.

	References		Unique DOIs		Videos		Channels	
Retracted articles	1,002	0.13%	360	0.09%	956	0.30%	714	0.92%
All articles	743,529	100.0%	386,628	100.0%	322,521	100.0%	77,974	100.0%

Table 1 presents basic statistics comparing retracted articles with all articles referenced on YouTube. References to retracted articles accounted for 1,002 instances (0.13% of all references), corresponding to 360 unique DOIs. These retracted articles were referenced in 956 videos (0.30% of all videos), which were published by 714 channels (0.92% of all channels). Although these values represent only a small fraction of the entire dataset, it is notable that nearly 1% of all channels referencing scholarly articles have published videos that include references to retracted articles.

Table 2. Distribution of references to retracted articles on YouTube, categorized by retraction reason severity.

Retraction Reason							Video Views			
Severity	References		Unique DOIs		Videos		*Min*	*Max*	*Median*	*SD*
Severe	458	45.71%	183	50.83%	435	45.50%	1	11,571,512	2,272	1,018,914.38
Moderate	303	30.24%	104	28.89%	299	31.28%	4	9,517,798	4,258	629,195.41
Minor	235	23.45%	70	19.44%	232	24.27%	1	12,921,007	8,077	923,338.11
Unknown	6	0.60%	3	0.83%	5	0.52%	14	89,758	3,205	38,466.65
Overall	1,002	100.00%	360	100.00%	956	100.00%	1	12,921,007	3,861	842,142.55

Table 2 summarizes descriptive statistics on references to retracted articles, classified by the severity of the retraction reason. Among the 1,002 references identified, 45.71% were categorized as *Severe*, 30.24% as *Moderate*, and 23.45% as *Minor*. This distribution indicates that retracted articles with more severe issues tend to be referenced more frequently. If *Severe* and *Moderate* are collectively interpreted as serious retraction reasons, approximately 75.95% of all references fall into this category.

In terms of video-level impact, the distribution of view counts within each severity group shows substantial variability, as reflected in the large standard deviations. A comparison of medians reveals an inverse relationship between retraction severity and typical viewership: videos referencing *Minor* retractions had the highest median views (8,077), followed by *Moderate* (4,258), and *Severe* (2,272). This suggests that while articles retracted for more serious reasons are referenced more often, they tend to appear in videos with relatively lower viewership—indicating a notable discrepancy between the frequency of reference and audience reach.

Importantly, videos referencing retracted articles from all severity levels included examples with exceptionally high view counts (9.5 to 13 million), underscoring the fact that even articles retracted for critical flaws or misconduct have been disseminated widely. This highlights a potential risk: content based on retracted research—particularly that involving serious concerns—may continue to circulate and influence public audiences, especially when not accompanied by clear disclosures of the retraction status.

4.2 Characteristics of Highly Referenced or Viewed Retracted Articles

RQ2: What characteristics do retracted articles referenced in many YouTube videos or in highly viewed videos tend to exhibit?

Table 3 presents the top retracted articles most frequently referenced in YouTube videos, along with the reasons for their retraction with the severity levels. Among the seven articles listed, three are classified as "Severe," namely entries #3, 5, and 7.

Article #3 was retracted due to falsification or fabrication of data and manipulation of results. This article, which suggested a link between the MMR (measles, mumps, and rubella) vaccine and autism, is one of the most notorious cases of scientific misconduct with significant societal impact. Originally published in 1998, it attracted widespread media attention and is widely believed to have contributed to a decline in vaccination rates across Europe [8,11]. This case has also been widely discussed in previous studies as a turning point in the rise of vaccine-related misinformation. For instance, Wang et al. [36] describe it as a "seminal moment," noting that despite being discredited, the concerns raised by the article have remained influential on social media. Donzelli et al. [7] further highlight that YouTube videos suggesting a link between vaccines and autism were prevalent and negative in tone, attracting the retracted article's continued visibility and perceived credibility. These findings align with our observation that

Table 3. Top 7 retracted articles ranked by the number of YouTube videos in which they are referenced.

#	DOI / Retraction Reason Severity Article Title	Videos	Published	Retracted
1	10.1631/jzus.2003.0236 [15] / Minor A research on the relationship between ejaculation and serum testosterone level in men	**94**	2003	2021
2	10.1016/j.ijantimicag.2020.105949 [10] / Moderate Hydroxychloroquine and azithromycin as a treatment of COVID-19	**59**	2020	2024
3	10.1016/s0140-6736(97)11096-0 [34] / Severe Ileal-lymphoid-nodular Hyperplasia, Non-specific Colitis, and Pervasive Developmental Disorder in Children	**43**	1998	2010
4	10.1002/arp.1912 [26] / Moderate Geo-archaeological prospecting of Gunung Padang buried prehistoric pyramid in West Java, Indonesia	**22**	2023	2024
5	10.1123/ijspp.2018-0914 [4] / Severe Evidence of a Ceiling Effect for Training Volume in Muscle Hypertrophy and Strength in Trained Men	**20**	2020	2020
6	10.1056/nejmoa1200303 [9] / Moderate Primary Prevention of Cardiovascular Disease with a Mediterranean Diet	**17**	2013	2018
7	10.1109/access.2020.2976434 [25] / Severe Electromagnetic Radiation Due to Cellular, Wi-Fi and Bluetooth Technologies: How Safe Are We?	**15**	2020	2020

retracted articles on this topic—especially those suggesting a link between the MMR vaccine and autism—frequently appear in highly viewed YouTube videos.

Article #5 focused on sports science, specifically the effects of different resistance training volumes on muscle performance and hypertrophy in trained men. It was retracted due to Unreliable Results. The retraction notice states that the authors conducted a post hoc analysis and discovered inconsistencies that led them to reassess their interpretation of the results.

Article #7 examined the health effects of electromagnetic radiation from cellular, Wi-Fi, and Bluetooth signals. It was retracted for Unreliable Results, with the publisher noting significant analytical errors that led to inaccurate conclusions. The retraction notice explicitly states that the article should no longer be used for research or citation [25].

Three articles were categorized as *Moderate*: #2, 4, and 6. Article #2 is a COVID-19-related clinical study on the effectiveness of hydroxychloroquine and azithromycin. It was retracted due to concerns over authorship, data integrity, and results. We note that 34 retracted articles (approximately 10% of all retracted article references) were related to COVID-19[5], and these were referenced in 158 videos across 131 channels. Article #4 concerns the geoarchaeological exploration of Gunung Padang, a prehistoric pyramid site in West Java, Indonesia. Although the article proposed that the site might represent the world's oldest pyramid, it was retracted due to Errors in Data, Results, and Conclu-

[5] We identified COVID-19-related articles whose titles contain the terms "COVID-19," "2019-nCoV," "SARS-CoV-2," or "Coronavirus.".

sions [14,23]. Article #6, titled "Primary Prevention of Cardiovascular Disease with a Mediterranean Diet," was retracted due to Errors in Analyses, Methods, Results, and Conclusions. Notably, a corrected version of this article was later republished. Thus, videos referencing the original version may inadvertently be relying on outdated or incorrect information.

Only Article #1 was categorized as *Minor*. The study focused on physiological factors related to hormonal regulation in men. It was retracted due to content duplication with a previously published article in Chinese. Since the retraction was not due to scientific inaccuracies or misconduct, this case is not considered an example of problematic scientific dissemination.

Table 4. Descriptive statistics of video views and channel subscribers for the Top 7 retracted articles referenced in YouTube videos. Row background color indicates the severity of the retraction reason: Red (*Severe*), Blue (*Moderate*), and White (*Minor*).

				Video Views			Channel Subscribers		
#	DOI	Videos	Channels	*Min*	*Max*	*Median*	*Min*	*Max*	*Median*
1	10.1631/jzus.2003.0236	94	82	15	12,921,007	12,034	11	10,700,000	30,350
2	10.1016/j.ijantimicag.2020.105949	59	51	36	648,739	1,212	19	8,170,000	3,300
3	10.1016/s0140-6736(97)11096-0	43	43	10	9,517,798	2,017	1	1,200,000	8,940
4	10.1002/arp.1912	22	20	319	579,610	22,946	445	3,480,000	51,500
5	10.1123/ijspp.2018-0914	20	17	312	6,983,811	62,636	2,770	6,840,000	195,000
6	10.1056/nejmoa1200303	17	16	76	177,928	20,388	15	2,860,000	39,250
7	10.1109/access.2020.2976434	15	6	1	3,687	136	551	4,120	762

Table 4 provides summary statistics for the top retracted articles with respect to the view counts of referencing videos and the subscriber counts of the publishing channels. The color shading indicates the severity of the retraction reason: red for *Severe*, blue for *Moderate*, and white for *Minor*.

A key observation from this table is the wide variance in both video view counts and channel subscriber numbers. For example, the most frequently referenced article was referenced in videos with a maximum view count of 12.9 million, while the minimum was as low as 15 views.

Focusing on median values, Article #5 stands out with the highest median view count and subscriber count, while Article #7 had the lowest in both categories. Interestingly, both articles are classified as *Severe*, but their topics differ substantially: Article #5 focuses on muscle training, a topic with broad public appeal, whereas Article #7 addresses health risks from electromagnetic radiation, which may only attract a niche audience. This difference likely accounts for the discrepancy in audience reach.

Looking at the highest individual view counts, articles #1, 3, and 5 stand out. These articles were featured in videos that may have gone viral due to their sensational or highly controversial topics. Article #1, despite being retracted for minor duplication, addresses sexual and hormonal topics, which tend to attract enduring public interest. Article #3 contributed to the MMR vaccine controversy and touches on public health concerns, while Article #5 aligns closely with the popular fitness genre on YouTube.

Table 5. Top 10 most-viewed YouTube videos that reference retracted articles, sorted by video view count. Row background color indicates the severity of the retraction reason: Red (*Severe*), Blue (*Moderate*), and White (*Minor*). Note: Video IDs and Channel IDs are masked to avoid direct identification of user-generated content, in line with ethical guidelines for research using social media data.

#	Video View Count	Video ID	Video Length	DOI	Video Published	Article Published	Article Retracted	Channel ID	Channel Subscribers
1	12,921,007	Video A	3m 41s	10.1631/jzus.2003.0236 [15]	2018	2003	2021	Channel 1	10,700,000
2	11,571,512	Video B	2m 38s	10.1126/science.1074501 [28]	2014	2002	2003	Channel 1	10,700,000
3	10,549,815	Video C	1m 56s	10.1177/0305735613482025 [12]	2015	2013	2020	Channel 2	10,200,000
4	9,517,798	Video D	1h 40m 1s	10.1016/j.cub.2015.09.056 [6]	2016	2015	2019	Channel 3	1,200,000
5	9,517,798	Video D	1h 40m 1s	10.1016/s0140-6736(97)11096-0 [34]	2016	1998	2010	Channel 3	1,200,000
6	6,983,811	Video E	10m 11s	10.1123/ijspp.2018-0914 [4]	2020	2020	2020	Channel 4	6,840,000
7	5,854,985	Video F	7m 2s	10.1186/s13640-018-0372-9 [35]	2021	2018	2022	Channel 5	3,210,000
8	4,265,525	Video G	10m 28s	10.1177/2047487317723212 [40]	2018	2017	2019	Channel 6	2,400,000
9	3,817,302	Video H	22m 26s	10.1177/0093650212446622 [37]	2019	2012	2017	Channel 7	19,500,000
10	3,360,503	Video I	12m 29s	10.1249/mss.0000000000001818 [5]	2019	2019	2021	Channel 8	6,840,000

Table 5 presents the top 10 most-viewed videos referencing retracted articles. The severity of the retraction reason is indicated through cell shading: among the top 10, one article was classified as *Minor*, two as *Moderate* (#4 and 8), and the remaining seven as Severe. This distribution shows that videos referencing articles retracted for serious reasons (i.e., *Moderate* or *Severe*) constitute the majority of the highest-performing content.

All of the top three videos exceeded 10 million views and were published by large-scale channels with over 10 million subscribers. Notably, the top two videos (involving articles on sex hormones and MDMA, respectively) were posted by the same channel, suggesting that a small number of highly influential channels can play a significant role in disseminating content referencing retracted article. The third most-viewed video (with approximately 10 million views) referenced the article titled "Men's music ability and attractiveness to women in a real-life courtship context." Given its topic in psychological and behavioral sciences related to romantic attraction, the video likely attracted broad attention due to its entertaining and relatable theme.

Manual investigation of the videos revealed that only half (5 out of 10) explicitly displayed the referenced retracted articles—such as via screenshots or bibliographic information (i.e., published year, author names, article title, and journal title)—within the video content. Furthermore, only two videos (#5 and 9) explicitly acknowledged the retraction status. Video #5 addressed the widely known case involving fraudulent research on the MMR vaccine and provided a clear explanation of the retraction and its societal impact. Video #9 discussed the debate over the relationship between video games and violence, referencing a retracted article in the context of presenting the chronological evolution of the research debate.

Based on the findings presented above, we can draw several conclusions regarding RQ2. First, a significant portion of the retracted articles that were repeatedly referenced across multiple YouTube videos were associated with high-severity retraction reasons—classified as either Severe or Moderate. At the same time, when focusing on the view counts of the videos referencing these articles, those referencing articles with lower-severity retraction reasons tended to have higher median viewership. This discrepancy highlights a gap between the frequency with which certain retracted articles are referenced and the actual audience reach of the videos in which they appear.

Moreover, retracted articles on topics with high public appeal—such as sex hormones, vaccines, fitness, and romantic psychology—were more likely to be featured in widely viewed videos. These topics often attract broad interest from viewers, resulting in higher video view counts and larger subscriber bases for the channels posting them.

While many of the most-viewed videos referenced articles that had been retracted for serious issues, the vast majority failed to acknowledge the retraction. This suggests a potential risk: viewers may be engaging with and accepting invalid scientific findings without any awareness of their retracted status. Nevertheless, we also observed a few cases in which the videos explicitly discussed the nature and background of the retraction. These educationally oriented videos aimed to raise awareness about scientific misconduct or questionable research practices. Although such cases were relatively rare, they demonstrate that YouTube can also function as a platform for promoting scientific literacy and encouraging critical reflection on research integrity.

4.3 Referencing Before and After Retraction, and Disclosure in Videos

RQ3: Do retracted articles referenced on YouTube tend to appear in videos published before or after the retraction date? How does this distribution vary by the severity of the retraction reason?

Table 6. Distribution of retracted article references in YouTube videos by video publication date relative to the retraction and the severity of retraction reasons.

Video Publication Relative to Retraction	Overall	Retraction Reason Severity: Severe	Moderate	Minor	Unknown
Before retraction	537 (53.59%)	① 253 (25.25%)	② 187 (18.86%)	97 (9.68%)	0 (0.00%)
After retraction	465 (46.41%)	③ 205 (20.46%)	④ 116 (11.58%)	138 (13.77%)	6 (0.60%)
Total	1,002 (100.00%)	458 (45.71%)	303 (30.24%)	235 (23.45%)	6 (0.60%)

Table 6 summarizes the temporal distribution of videos referencing retracted articles, categorized by the severity of the retraction reason as described in

Sect. 3.2. Among all videos referencing retracted articles, approximately 54% were published prior to the retraction date, while the remaining 46% were published afterward. When focusing on the severity of the retraction reasons, videos referencing articles classified as either *Severe* or *Moderate* were more frequently posted before the retraction than after.

Table 7. Distribution of references to retracted articles in YouTube videos, classified by whether the video was published before or after the retraction date of the article.

Group	1. Article was visually displayed or verbally identified in video content	2. Retraction stated in video description text	3. Retraction explicitly addressed in video content
①	9/10	—	—
②	6/10	—	—
③	6/10	3/10	3/10
④	7/10	4/10	4/10

To further explore how these articles were treated in the videos, we conducted a manual analysis of 40 videos, randomly sampling 10 from each of the four groups shown in Table 6. While our coding scheme included four categories of reference stance as described in Sect. 3.2—"Referenced without retraction awareness," "Referenced from a critical or skeptical stance," "Referenced from a neutral stance," and "Unknown"—most cases were coded as either "Referenced from a critical or skeptical stance" or "Referenced without retraction awareness". Cases categorized as "Referenced from a neutral stance" were rare—typically only one per group, if any—and those labeled as "Unknown" are not discussed in detail below, as the relevant segments in the video content could not be clearly identified.

As shown in Table 7, videos published before the retraction date (Groups ① and ②) commonly included explicit visual or textual mentions of the referenced article—9 out of 10 videos in Group ① and 6 out of 10 in Group ② included such mentions. Notably, 4 of the 10 videos in Group ② were coded as "Referenced from a critical or skeptical stance," indicating that several creators had already expressed skepticism toward the article's findings. In contrast, only 2 of the videos in Group ① fell into the same category.

For videos published after the article had been retracted (Groups ③ and ④), references to the article were visually displayed or verbally identified in a majority of cases—6 out of 10 videos in Group ③ and 7 out of 10 in Group ④. However, only 4 to 5 videos per group explicitly mentioned the retraction in the video content or in the description text. In both Group ③ and Group ④, three videos were coded as "Referenced from a critical or skeptical stance," while four were categorized as "Referenced without retraction awareness." These findings suggest that the disclosure of the retracted status remains incomplete in many cases, even when the videos were published after the retraction.

Overall, these results highlight two important points regarding RQ3. First, while the number of referencing videos was roughly balanced between pre- and post-retraction publications (54% vs. 46%), post-retraction videos frequently failed to acknowledge the retraction status. Second, even before formal retraction, a small but notable subset of content creators critically discussed and scrutinized the referenced articles, suggesting an existing awareness of the potential flaws. Nevertheless, the broader trend shows that many referencing videos—both before and after retraction—do not provide viewers with any indication that the scholarly article has been formally withdrawn. This underscores a significant challenge on YouTube: a major platform for public engagement with science, retracted articles can continue to be disseminated without transparency, potentially contributing to misinformation and undermining public trust in science.

5 Conclusion

This study investigated how retracted academic articles are referenced on YouTube and analyzed the surrounding contexts and degrees of acknowledgment in those references. By integrating the Altmetric dataset with the YA Domain Dataset, which was built using a reference extraction method proposed in our prior work, we identified 1,002 instances of references to retracted articles, corresponding to 360 unique retracted articles.

Although references to retracted articles accounted for only a small fraction of all scholarly mentions, approximately 1% of YouTube channels that include academic references had published videos referencing retracted research. This indicates that retracted articles, while limited in number, are referenced and disseminated by a non-negligible number of creators on the platform.

Focusing on the severity of retraction reasons, we found that roughly three-quarters of the referenced articles were categorized as *Severe* or *Moderate*. Notably, many of these concerned socially sensitive topics such as hormones, vaccines, and fitness—subjects that tend to attract high viewer interest. Videos referencing such articles often garnered significant attention, suggesting that problematic research remains influential even after formal retraction.

At the same time, we also observed videos that referenced retracted articles in educational or cautionary contexts. These included fact-based explanations of scientific misconduct (e.g., the MMR vaccine controversy) and critical discussions of studies that were contentious even prior to retraction. These examples demonstrate that not all references to retracted research constitute misinformation; in some cases, they serve to raise awareness or promote scientific literacy.

However, in many cases—particularly in videos published after the retraction date—no explicit mention of the retraction was found. Even among highly viewed content, some videos treated retracted articles as legitimate sources without any indication of their retracted status. This poses a serious concern regarding the transparency and trustworthiness of academic information on YouTube, as viewers may unknowingly consume outdated or invalidated research.

To our knowledge, this is the first empirical study to comprehensively examine how retracted articles are referenced and represented on YouTube. By combining a large-scale and more comprehensive dataset with manual contextual analysis, we provided new insights into the social circulation of retracted research and the extent to which such content is recognized—or unrecognized—by video creators and viewers.

As a limitation, this study did not assess the extent to which references to retracted articles actually influenced viewer attitudes or behaviors—for instance, by analyzing user comments or viewer actions following exposure. While such downstream effects are difficult to quantify, understanding them is important for assessing the real-world consequences of misinformation and the broader impact of retracted research on public discourse.

As future work, we would explore ways to improve the visibility of retraction information on video-sharing platforms and establish a system for clearly signaling the retracted status of scholarly articles. Collaboration between scholarly infrastructure providers and online video platform operators (e.g., integration of retraction flags via YouTube Data API or browser plugins that annotate external links to retracted articles) may be key to this effort. Additionally, further methodological development is needed to systematically classify the reference context based on video content, enabling a more detailed understanding of how retracted research is portrayed and perceived in social media environments.

6 Data and Software Availability

When this manuscript is accepted for TPDL 2025, we plan to make the dataset on scholarly references in YouTube video descriptions used in this study available to the research community. The dataset, which covers videos posted up to the end of December 2023, was constructed by integrating the Altmetric dataset with the YA Domain Dataset and contains metadata such as Video IDs, Channel IDs, and DOIs.

While the dataset was developed for research purposes, we are mindful of the potential for misuse—particularly in attempts to target or discredit specific YouTube channels or videos referencing retracted articles. To mitigate such risks, the dataset will not be released publicly. Instead, it will be shared upon request for bona fide academic research purposes only. Interested researchers are encouraged to contact the authors directly.

We note that a supplementary dataset is available on Zenodo [17]. This includes the raw data and detailed annotations from our manual analysis.

Acknowledgments. This work was partially supported by JSPS KAKENHI Grant Numbers JP22K18147 and JP23K11761.

References

1. Crossref / retraction-watch-data. GitLab (2025). https://gitlab.com/crossref/retraction-watch-data
2. Allgaier, J.: Science and Medicine on YouTube. In: Hunsinger, J., Allen, M.M., Klastrup, L. (eds.) Second International Handbook of Internet Research, pp. 7–27. Springer, Dordrecht (2020). https://doi.org/10.1007/978-94-024-1555-1_1
3. Bar-Ilan, J., Halevi, G.: Temporal characteristics of retracted articles. Scientometrics **116**(3), 1771–1783 (2018). https://doi.org/10.1007/s11192-018-2802-y
4. Barbalho, M., Coswig, V.S., Steele, J., Fisher, J.P., Giessing, J., Gentil, P.: RETRACTED ARTICLE: evidence of a ceiling effect for training volume in muscle hypertrophy and strength in trained men-less is more? Int. J. Sports Physiol. Perform. **15**(2), 268–277 (2020). https://doi.org/10.1123/ijspp.2018-0914
5. Barbalho, M., Coswig, V.S., Steele, J., Fisher, J.P., Paoli, A., Gentil, P.: RETRACTED ARTICLE: evidence for an upper threshold for resistance training volume in trained women. Med. Sci. Sports Exerc. **51**(3), 515–522 (2019). https://doi.org/10.1249/mss.0000000000001818
6. Decety, J., et al.: RETRACTED ARTICLE: the negative association between religiousness and children's altruism across the world. Curr. Biol. **25**(22), 2951–2955 (2015). https://doi.org/10.1016/j.cub.2015.09.056
7. Donzelli, G., et al.: Misinformation on vaccination: a quantitative analysis of youtube videos. Human Vaccines Immunotherapeutics **14**(7), 1654–1659 (2018). https://doi.org/10.1080/21645515.2018.1454572
8. Dyer, C.: Lancet retracts Wakefield's MMR paper. BMJ **340**, c696 (2010). https://doi.org/10.1136/bmj.c696
9. Estruch, R., et al.: RETRACTED ARTICLE: primary prevention of cardiovascular disease with a mediterranean diet. N. Engl. J. Med. **368**(14), 1279–1290 (2013). https://doi.org/10.1056/nejmoa1200303
10. Gautret, P., et al.: RETRACTED ARTICLE: hydroxychloroquine and azithromycin as a treatment of covid-19: results of an open-label non-randomized clinical trial. Int. J. Antimicrob. Agents **56**(1), 105949 (2020). https://doi.org/10.1016/j.ijantimicag.2020.105949
11. Godlee, F., Smith, J., Marcovitch, H.: Wakefield's article linking MMR vaccine and autism was fraudulent. BMJ **342**(jan05 1), c7452–c7452 (2011). https://doi.org/10.1136/bmj.c7452
12. Guéguen, N., Meineri, S., Fischer-Lokou, J.: RETRACTED ARTICLE: men's music ability and attractiveness to women in a real-life courtship context. Psychol. Music **42**(4), 545–549 (2013). https://doi.org/10.1177/0305735613482025
13. Hussein, E., Juneja, P., Mitra, T.: Measuring misinformation in video search platforms: an audit study on youtube. In: Proceedings of the ACM on Human-Computer Interaction. vol. 4. Association for Computing Machinery, New York, NY, USA (2020). https://doi.org/10.1145/3392854
14. Ives, M.: Study About Purported Ancient 'Pyramid' in Indonesia Is Retracted. The New York Times (2024). https://www.nytimes.com/2024/03/20/science/indonesia-oldest-pyramid-gunung-padang.html
15. Jiang, M., Jiang, X., Zou, Q., Shen, J.: RETRACTED ARTICLE: A research on the relationship between ejaculation and serum testosterone level in men. J. Zhejiang Univ. Sci. **4**(2), 236–240 (2003). https://doi.org/10.1631/jzus.2003.0236
16. Keelan, J., Pavri-Garcia, V., Tomlinson, G., Wilson, K.: YouTube as a source of information on immunization: a content analysis. JAMA **298**(21), 2482–2484 (2007). https://doi.org/10.1001/jama.298.21.2482

17. Kikkawa, J., Takaku, M.: Dataset and supplementary tables on retracted articles referenced in youtube videos (TPDL 2025). Zenodo (2025). https://doi.org/10.5281/zenodo.15377209
18. Kikkawa, J., Takaku, M., Yoshikane, F.: Quantitative analysis of scholarly references on youtube: focusing on their research fields and contributors. In: Proceedings of the 25th International Conference on Asia-Pacific Digital Libraries (ICADL 2023), pp. 149–158. Springer Nature Singapore (2023). https://doi.org/10.1007/978-981-99-8085-7_13
19. Kikkawa, J., Takaku, M., Yoshikane, F.: Enhancing identification of scholarly reference on youtube: method development and analysis of external link characteristics. In: Proceedings of the 28th International Conference on Theory and Practice of Digital Libraries (TPDL 2024), pp. 326–341 (2024). https://doi.org/10.1007/978-3-031-72437-4_19
20. Kikkawa, J., Takaku, M., Yoshikane, F.: YA Domain dataset: dataset of scholarly bibliographic references on youtube videos. Zenodo (2024). https://doi.org/10.5281/zenodo.12801387
21. Kousha, K., Thelwall, M., Abdoli, M.: The role of online videos in research communication: a content analysis of YouTube videos cited in academic publications. J. Am. Soc. Inform. Sci. Technol. **63**(9), 1710–1727 (2012). https://doi.org/10.1002/asi.22717
22. Madathil, K.C., Rivera-Rodriguez, A.J., Greenstein, J.S., Gramopadhye, A.K.: Healthcare information on youtube: a systematic review. Health Inform. J. **21**(3), 173–194 (2015). https://doi.org/10.1177/1460458213512220
23. Marcus, A.: Controversial pyramid paper retracted when authors turn out to have radiocarbon-dated nearby dirt (2024). https://retractionwatch.com/2024/03/20/controversial-pyramid-paper-retracted-when-authors-turn-out-to-have-radiocarbon-dated-nearby-dirt/
24. McIntosh, L.D., Hudson Vitale, C.: Taxonomy of retraction reasons - mapping of reasons (v1.21). Figshare (2024). https://doi.org/10.6084/m9.figshare.24948789.v9
25. Naren, Elhence, A., Chamola, V., Guizani, M.: RETRACTED ARTICLE: electromagnetic radiation due to cellular, wi-fi and bluetooth technologies: how safe are we? IEEE Access **8**, 42980–43000 (2020). https://doi.org/10.1109/access.2020.2976434
26. Natawidjaja, D.H., et al.: RETRACTED ARTICLE: Geo-archaeological prospecting of Gunung Padang buried prehistoric pyramid in West Java, Indonesia. Archaeol. Prospection **31**(2), O1–025 (2024). https://doi.org/10.1002/arp.1912
27. Osman, W., Mohamed, F., Elhassan, M., Shoufan, A.: Is youtube a reliable source of health-related information? A systematic review. BMC Med. Educ. **22**(1), article no. 382, pp. 1–12 (2022). https://doi.org/10.1186/s12909-022-03446-z
28. Ricaurte, G.A., Yuan, J., Hatzidimitriou, G., Cord, B.J., McCann, U.D.: RETRACTED ARTICLE: severe dopaminergic neurotoxicity in primates after a common recreational dose regimen of MDMA ("Ecstasy"). Science **297**(5590), 2260–2263 (2002). https://doi.org/10.1126/science.1074501
29. Rittman, M.: Retraction Watch - Crossref (2025). https://www.crossref.org/documentation/retrieve-metadata/retraction-watch/
30. Shaikh, A.R., Alhoori, H., Sun, M.: YouTube and science: models for research impact. Scientometrics **128**(2), 933–955 (2023). https://doi.org/10.1007/s11192-022-04574-5
31. Sharma, M., Yadav, K., Yadav, N., Ferdinand, K.C.: Zika virus pandemic–analysis of Facebook as a social media health information platform. Am. J. Infect. Control **45**(3), 301–302 (2017). https://doi.org/10.1016/j.ajic.2016.08.022

32. Teixeira da Silva, J.A., Bornemann-Cimenti, H.: Why do some retracted papers continue to be cited? Scientometrics **110**(1), 365–370 (2016). https://doi.org/10.1007/s11192-016-2178-9
33. Suarez-Lledo, V., Alvarez-Galvez, J.: Prevalence of health misinformation on social media: systematic review. J. Med. Internet Res. **23**(1), e17187 (2021). https://doi.org/10.2196/17187
34. Wakefield, A., et al.: RETRACTED ARTICLE: Ileal-lymphoid-nodular hyperplasia, non-specific colitis, and pervasive developmental disorder in children. Lancet **351**(9103), 637–641 (1998). https://doi.org/10.1016/S0140-6736(97)11096-0
35. Wang, K., Yan, X.: Performance analysis of ethylene-propylene diene monomer sound-absorbing materials based on image processing recognition. EURASIP J. Image Video Process. **2018**(1), 1–10 (2018). https://doi.org/10.1186/s13640-018-0372-9
36. Wang, Y., McKee, M., Torbica, A., Stuckler, D.: Systematic literature review on the spread of health-related misinformation on social media. Soc. Sci. Med. **240**, 112552 (2019). https://doi.org/10.1016/j.socscimed.2019.112552
37. Whitaker, J.L., Bushman, B.J.: RETRACTED ARTICLE: "boom, headshot!". Commun. Res. **41**(7), 879–891 (2012). https://doi.org/10.1177/0093650212446622
38. Woo, S., Walsh, J.P.: On the shoulders of fallen giants: what do references to retracted research tell us about citation behaviors? Quant. Sci. Stud. **5**(1), 1–30 (2024). https://doi.org/10.1162/qss_a_00303
39. Wood, M.J.: Propagating and debunking conspiracy theories on twitter during the 2015–2016 Zika virus outbreak. Cyberpsychol. Behav. Soc. Netw. **21**(8), 485–490 (2018). https://doi.org/10.1089/cyber.2017.0669
40. Yankey, B.A., Rothenberg, R., Strasser, S., Ramsey-White, K., Okosun, I.S.: RETRACTED ARTICLE: effect of marijuana use on cardiovascular and cerebrovascular mortality: a study using the national health and nutrition examination survey linked mortality file. Eur. J. Prev. Cardiol. **24**(17), 1833–1840 (2017). https://doi.org/10.1177/2047487317723212
41. Zagovora, O., Weller, K.: Science communicators, flat-eathers, or fitness coaches: who is citing scientific publications in youtube video descriptions? Scientometrics **130**, 205–235 (2025). https://doi.org/10.1007/s11192-024-05204-y

Neuro-Symbolic Federated Research Artifact Search

Farhana Keya[1(✉)], Sören Auer[1,2], and Mohamad Yaser Jaradeh[2]

[1] TIB Leibniz Information Centre for Science and Technology, Hannover, Germany
{farhana.keya,auer}@tib.eu

[2] L3S Research Center, Leibniz University of Hannover, Hannover, Germany
jaradeh@l3s.de

Abstract. Scientific research artifacts such as datasets, software or ontologies are essential components of scientific discovery. Yet, the growing volume of such artifacts requires more efficient and relevant search and retrieval systems. We present a neuro-symbolic approach for federated research artifact search, specifically for datasets and software metadata over Resodate and Wikidata. Integrated into the ORKG ASK platform, our system processes user queries through linguistic analysis to extract key terms. These key terms are then used to retrieve and recommend relevant research artifacts from federated sources, ensuring precise and contextually relevant metadata discovery. To further enhance retrieval accuracy, we employ a ranking mechanism that organizes research artifacts based on each user query's structure and morphological features. We evaluate various key-term extraction methods and ranking approaches, integrating both symbolic and neural techniques. We rigorously evaluate the key-term extraction using Precision, Recall, and F1-score, and assess the re-ranking effectiveness by comparing with human rankings through correlation metrics and LLM-based evaluations. Our experiments show that symbolic methods outperform the neural approach regarding accuracy and response time. As a result, our system offers users more effective and efficient research artifact recommendations.

Keywords: Federated Search · Key Term Extraction · Neuro-Symbolic Systems

1 Introduction

Scientific research is increasingly driven by the availability and accessibility of diverse digital artifacts, including datasets, software, and ontologies [35,47]. These artifacts are crucial for enabling reproducibility, accelerating discovery, and fostering interdisciplinary collaboration [41]. However, as the volume of scientific artifacts grows significantly, retrieving the most relevant and high-quality resources remains a significant challenge [42]. Traditional search engines and

W.-T. Balke et al. (Eds.): TPDL 2025, LNCS 16097, pp. 145–162, 2026.
https://doi.org/10.1007/978-3-032-05409-8_10

metadata repositories struggle to provide precise, context-aware recommendations due to their reliance on keyword-based or manually curated indexing systems [15].

Recent advances in artificial intelligence (AI) have demonstrated the potential of neuro-symbolic techniques—combining symbolic reasoning with deep learning—to enhance search and retrieval systems [18] [5]. Neuro-symbolic approaches offer the interpretability and structured knowledge of symbolic methods while leveraging neural networks' adaptability and pattern recognition capabilities [29]. This work proposes a novel neuro-symbolic framework for federated research artifact search, focusing on datasets and software metadata from Resodate and Wikidata. Our approach is integrated into ORKG ASK [37], a scientific question-answering platform, enabling users to ask natural language questions.

Our system processes user queries through linguistic analysis to extract key terms, which are subsequently employed to retrieve and rank relevant research artifacts from federated sources. To ensure accurate and contextually relevant results, we introduce a ranking mechanism that incorporates both structural and morphological characteristics of user queries. We further investigate the effectiveness of different key-term extraction strategies by evaluating symbolic and neural methods, and assessing their impact on retrieval performance.

To demonstrate the efficiency of our approach, we conduct extensive experiments evaluating key-term extraction using Precision, Recall, and F1-score metrics. Additionally, we evaluate the effectiveness of our ranking approach by measuring its correlation with human judgments and LLM-based assessments. Our results show that symbolic methods outperform neural approaches in terms of accuracy and response time.

By integrating neuro-symbolic techniques, our system significantly enhances the precision and efficiency of research artifact recommendations, addressing the limitations of existing retrieval frameworks [22]. Our approach provides a scalable and interpretable solution for scientific metadata discovery, ultimately supporting more effective knowledge dissemination and utilization in the research community. Code and dataset are available here[1]

In particular, we make the following contributions:

- Assessment framework, including a comprehensive benchmark dataset for our system.
- Federated search and re-ranking system for research artifact retrieval.
- Evaluation of our system, including comparisons with human rankings and LLM-based assessments.

This article has the following structure. First, we present a Literature Review regarding Research Artifact Retrieval, Ranking and Re-Ranking Mechanisms, as well as Evaluation Metrics and Benchmarking (Sect. 2). After that, we detail the Federated Search for Artifact Retrieval and Re-Ranking in Sect. 3. Section 4 describes the experimental setup, data and evaluation and analysis followed by the discussion in Sect. 6. Section 7 concludes and outlines future work.

[1] https://github.com/Farhana-Keya/Neuro-symbolic-Federated-Research-Artifact-Search.

2 Literature Review

Research Artifact Retrieval: Efficient discovery of scientific artifacts—such as datasets and software—is a critical task in the broader domain of information retrieval and knowledge discovery. Systems like Google Dataset Search [7], Dataverse [28], and CKAN[2] provide infrastructure for metadata storage and retrieval. However, these systems rely heavily on keyword-based search with limited semantic understanding or intelligent ranking mechanisms. They often return either too many irrelevant results or miss contextually relevant artifacts due to lack of linguistic analysis or deeper query understanding. Our work addresses these limitations by introducing a federated search approach that incorporates both symbolic and neural methods for key-term extraction and intelligent artifact ranking.

Semantic and Federated Search Systems: Previous research has extensively explored semantic search techniques for scientific artifacts, particularly focusing on improving metadata aggregation and retrieval. Systems like OpenAIRE [31] collect and harmonize metadata from a wide array of institutional and thematic repositories, offering features such as faceted search and cross-repository linking. However, OpenAIRE relies primarily on keyword-based filtering and metadata schemas, with limited support for natural language understanding or dynamic ranking strategies. Similarly, DataCite Commons[3] facilitates exploration of linked research outputs including datasets, publications, and software by aggregating metadata from repositories that assign DOIs. Despite its comprehensive metadata indexing, DataCite Commons does not perform deep semantic parsing or adaptive query interpretation beyond basic string matching and citation linkages.

In contrast, our proposed approach addresses these limitations by integrating a linguistic analysis pipeline that performs morphological parsing and key-term extraction to interpret natural language queries more precisely. These extracted features are then used to retrieve and re-rank research artifacts from multiple federated sources—specifically Resodate and Wikidata—allowing for more contextually grounded and semantically aligned results. By combining symbolic parsing with federated search, our system bridges the gap between semantic expressiveness and retrieval effectiveness in scientific artifact discovery.

Keyword and Key-Term Extraction: Extracting informative key terms is central to metadata search. TextRank [34], a graph-based algorithm inspired by PageRank, has been widely adopted due to its unsupervised nature and effectiveness. However, it might not fully capture the deeper meanings of words. Neural methods like BERT-based extractors offer context-aware representations but are computationally expensive and may struggle with domain-specific language when training data is limited. Our study compares both approaches, demonstrating that symbolic techniques such as TextRank achieve superior performance in federated metadata search due to faster inference and domain adaptability.

[2] https://ckan.org.

[3] https://commons.datacite.org.

Ranking and Re-ranking Approaches: Artifact ranking plays a crucial role in enhancing retrieval usability. Traditional models like BM25 and PageRank [39] provide a baseline, while transformer-based models (e.g., T5 [36]) enable contextualized relevance scoring. More recent hybrid models combine neural networks with structured metadata features [49], though they often lack domain-specific adaptations for scientific metadata. Our method advances this direction by incorporating query morphology and structure to inform ranking, resulting in improved alignment with user intent.

Evaluation and Benchmarking: Evaluating retrieval systems typically involves metrics such as Precision, Recall, and F1-score for key-term extraction tasks [45], and ranking effectiveness is often assessed using metrics like nDCG (Normalized Discounted Cumulative Gain), which considers the position and relevance of retrieved results. With the advent of LLMs, model-generated rankings have also emerged as a complementary evaluation method [17]. We use a combination of these approaches to evaluate both key-term extraction and artifact ranking, demonstrating the effectiveness of symbolic methods in delivering fast and accurate results for federated scientific search.

Most current systems for finding research artifacts rely on basic keyword matching, have limited understanding of meaning, and use fixed ranking methods. Our system introduces a new approach that combines language analysis and query structure to find and rank artifacts more accurately. This helps overcome the main problems of existing systems by improving both search quality and relevance for users (Fig. 1).

3 Federated Search for Artifact Retrieval and Re-ranking

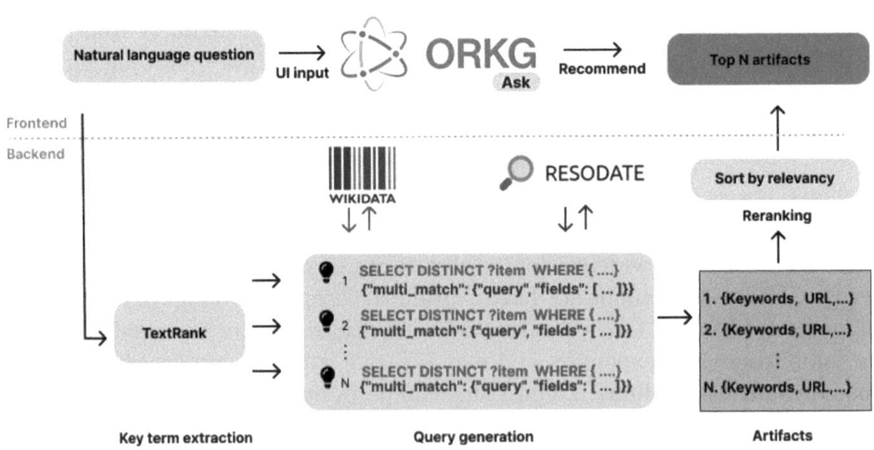

Fig. 1. Big Picture: Artifact search through federated sources. Top N artifacts (purple color) is future work.

Our approach is designed to enhance the efficiency and relevance of federated research artifact search, leveraging neuro-symbolic methods for key-term extraction, retrieval, and ranking across federated sources. Given a natural language (NL) query from the ORKG ASK system, we first extract key terms from the input using machine learning models. These key terms are then used to retrieve relevant research artifacts from federated sources such as Resodate[4] and Wikidata[5]. Finally, the retrieved artifacts are ranked based on semantic relevance and structural alignment with the user's query.

3.1 Problem Formulation

Given a user's query Q, our goal is to identify a set of the n-most relevant research artifacts $A_1, A_2, \ldots, A_n$ that best match the semantic and structural context of Q. We first extract key terms $K_Q = \{k_1, k_2, \ldots, k_m\}$ from Q, and use these to retrieve and rank artifacts from federated sources, ensuring that the retrieved metadata aligns with the query's intent.

3.2 Key-Term Extraction and Representation

Formally, let $Q = \{w_1, w_2, ..., w_n\}$ denote a user's question, where w_i are individual words. Our key-term extraction function $\Phi(Q)$ aims to identify a set of key terms $K_Q = \{k_1, k_2, ..., k_m\}$ relevant for retrieval. We explore multiple strategies for key-term extraction, incorporating both symbolic and neural techniques to ensure high-quality term selection.

Symbolic Methods: We leverage statistical models and graph-based methods to identify key terms.

Neural Approaches: We also use transformer-based models (e.g., T5) fine-tuned for key-term extraction. These models are trained to optimize key-term selection based on contextual embeddings and language structure, facilitating more specific extraction.

3.3 Federated Retrieval and Ranking

We retrieve research artifacts A_i from multiple federated knowledge sources using the key terms K_Q extracted from the user's query. This involves two distinct retrieval strategies designed for each data source.

SPARQL-Based Retrieval for Wikidata: Given the structured nature of Wikidata, we formulate SPARQL queries that retrieve entities based on their relationships and metadata. Verbalization techniques are employed to replace URIs (e.g., Dataset is denoted as `Q1172284`[6] in Wikidata) with human-readable labels

[4] https://resodate.org/resources/.
[5] https://www.wikidata.org/wiki/Wikidata:Main_Page.
[6] https://www.wikidata.org/wiki/Q1172284.

to align with NL queries, ensuring that the system responds to user queries in a comprehensible manner.

Elastic search-based Retrieval for Resodate: Resodate supports full-text search and semantic similarity matching, making it suitable for Elasticsearch queries.

3.4 Re-ranking Module

To further refine the relevance of the retrieved artifacts, we introduce a re-ranking module that adjusts the order of results based on contextual importance. Given an initial ranked list $L = \{A_1, A_2, \ldots, A_k\}$, we apply an adaptive ranking function $R(L)$ which incorporates statistical methods like TF-IDF and cosine similarity, alongside LLM-based models such as LLama-3 (8B) and Mistral-7B, Phi-3 mini.

The re-ranking module refines the retrieval list based on both semantic relevance and structural match between the metadata and the query.

Input:

- `P31` represents the "instance of" property in Wikidata.
- `Q1172284` refers to datasets, `Q7397` refers to software.
- The key term is searched using the **`mwapi:gsrsearch`** parameter, which performs a keyword-based search across Wikidata entities.
- The number of results is controlled using **`mwapi:gsrlimit`**, which limits the number of retrieved records.

`Query:`

```
SELECT DISTINCT ?item ?label ?date ?authorsLabel WHERE {
  SERVICE wikibase:mwapi {
    bd:serviceParam wikibase:endpoint "www.wikidata.org";
                    wikibase:limit "once";
                    wikibase:api "Generator";
                    mwapi:generator "search";
                    mwapi:gsrsearch "$search_string";
                    mwapi:gsrlimit "$number_of_records".
    ?item wikibase:apiOutputItem mwapi:title.
  }?item rdfs:label ?label.
  FILTER(LANG(?label) = "en")
  OPTIONAL { ?item wdt:P577 ?date. }
  OPTIONAL { ?item wdt:P2093 ?authorsLabel. }
  OPTIONAL {  ?item wdt:P31 ?type.
    FILTER(?type = wd:Q7397 || ?type = wd:Q1172284)
  }}LIMIT $number_of_records
```

Fig. 2. SPARQL Query for Retrieving Artifacts from Wikidata

3.5 Scoring and Ranking Function

To measure the relevance of each artifact A_i, we define a scoring function $S(Q, A_i)$ that combines both semantic similarity and structural alignment. Formally, the relevance score is given by:

$$S(Q, A_i) = \alpha \cdot \text{Sim}(K_Q, M(A_i)) + \beta \cdot \text{Struct}(Q, A_i)$$

where:

$\text{Sim}(K_Q, M(A_i))$ computes the semantic similarity between the key terms K_Q and the metadata $M(A_i)$ of artifact A_i. This is achieved through vector-based similarity measures such as cosine similarity in embedding space (e.g., pre-trained embeddings like BERT). For Wikidata, the similarity score is computed by comparing the query terms with entity labels, descriptions, and aliases within the knowledge graph. For Resodate, the similarity is evaluated using methods like BM25 embedding-based approaches, depending on the search engine's capabilities.

$\text{Struct}(Q, A_i)$ quantifies structural alignment, measuring how well the query Q aligns with the structured metadata of the artifact A_i. This includes matching specific attributes such as dataset types, software dependencies, or relationships within the knowledge graph. In Wikidata, structural alignment checks for matching properties (e.g., dates), while for Resodate, it involves aligning query terms with metadata fields like dataset names, authors, or keywords.
The weights α and β are empirically optimized using user feedback and evaluation metrics like precision and recall.

3.6 Evaluation and Metrics

We evaluate both key-term extraction and re-ranking effectiveness using different approaches. Key-term extraction performance is assessed using Precision, Recall, and F1-score, ensuring that the terms extracted from queries effectively capture the relevant context.

For re-ranking, we measure the alignment of our ranking strategies with human-labeled rankings using the nDCG (Normalized Discounted Cumulative Gain) metric. Additionally, we use LLM-based evaluations, with models like GPT-4o [23] and DeepSeek R1 [20], to assess the quality of the re-ranked artifact lists.

GPT-4o provides an advanced automated assessment framework that closely approximates human evaluative judgments, making it a robust choice for ranking validation [46]. Meanwhile, DeepSeek R1 has demonstrated superior performance in evaluation tasks with minimal human intervention, underscoring its efficiency and effectiveness in AI-driven assessments [33]. By integrating these models into our evaluation pipeline, we establish an automated yet reliable mechanism for assessing both the relevance of retrieved artifacts and the efficacy of the ranking module.

Input:

- <key_term> represents the search keyword used to match against artifact metadata fields such as name, description, and keywords. <content_type> specifies the type of resource being queried, which can be either Dataset or Software Application.

Query:

```
{"query": {
      "bool": {
          "must": [
              {"multi_match":
              {"query": "<key_term>",
              "fields": ["name", "description", "keywords"]}},
              {"term": {"type": "<content_type>"}} ]
      }}}
```

Fig. 3. Elastic Search Query for Retrieving Artifacts from Resodate

4 Experimental Setup

Our experiments are structured into three stages: key-term extraction, artifact retrieval, and re-ranking. We provide a detailed description of each stage along with the hardware configuration and query specifications for retrieving relevant artifacts.

*Key-Term Extraction:*To extract key terms from user queries, we evaluate a diverse set of methodologies spanning statistical, graph-based, and transformer-based models. Statistical approaches include TF-IDF [2] and YAKE [9], which leverage term frequency and statistical co-occurrence properties to identify key terms. Graph-based models, including TextRank [34], SingleRank [8], TopicRank [6], PositionRank [14], MultipartiteRank [16], and Kea [48], utilize graph representations of text to identify central terms based on connectivity and relevance. Additionally, we employ the KeyPhraseTransformer[7], a transformer-based model fine-tuned for keyphrase extraction.

*Artifact Retrieval:*We retrieve research artifacts from two federated sources: Wikidata and Resodate. Wikidata artifacts are queried (shown in Fig. 2) using SPARQL, leveraging structured knowledge graphs to retrieve datasets and software relevant to the extracted key terms. Resodate artifacts are retrieved via Elasticsearch (shown in Fig. 3), where key terms are matched against metadata fields such as name, description, and keywords. This dual-source retrieval strategy ensures broad coverage and semantic relevance of retrieved artifacts.

[7] https://github.com/Shivanandroy/KeyPhraseTransformer.

Input Description:

- <given_ranking> refers to the ranking of artifacts generated by an AI model. <human_ranking> refers to the ranking of artifacts provided by human experts as the ground truth.<query> means key term

Prompt:
You are an AI ranking assistant. Given a search query, evaluate and rank artifacts based on their relevance on a scale of 1 to 10 where 1 means less relevant, 10 means highly relevant.
Search Query: <query>
Artifacts with Metadata:
```
chr(10).join([f"i+1. artifact" for i, artifact in enumerate(artifacts)])
```
Expected Output (JSON Format):
```
{ "scores": [score1, score2, score3, ...] }
```

Fig. 4. Artifact Re-ranking Prompt

Re-ranking: To refine the re-ranking of retrieved artifacts, we evaluate both statistical and large language model (LLM)-based ranking approaches. Statistical methods include TF-IDF and Cosine Similarity [38], which rank artifacts based on term-matching and vector-space similarity metrics. LLM-based ranking employs state-of-the-art transformer models, including LLaMA-3 (8B) [13], Phi-3 Mini [1], and Mistral (7B) [24], which leverage deep contextual understanding to score artifact relevance. The prompting strategy for LLM-based ranking is provided in Fig. 4.

Hardware Configuration: Experiments involving LLaMA-3 (8B), Phi-3 Mini, and Mistral (7B) were conducted using two NVIDIA T2080Ti GPUs with 11 GB VRAM each for LLaMA-3 (8B) and Mistral (7B), and one NVIDIA T2080Ti GPU with 11 GB VRAM for Phi-3 Mini, utilizing CUDA 7.5 for acceleration. Evaluations using OpenAI's GPT-4o were performed via the OpenAI API[8], while DeepSeek R1 was executed using Distill-Qwen-32B [20] via the Ollama[9] backend with Q4_K_M quantization..

This structured experimental setup ensures reproducibility and provides a robust framework for evaluating the effectiveness of key-term extraction, artifact retrieval, and re-ranking methodologies (Fig. 5).

5 Evaluation

In this section, we present the evaluation of our neuro-symbolic approach for federated research artifact retrieval over Resodate and Wikidata. Our evaluation covers three key aspects: (1) Key-term extraction performance, (2) Ranking effectiveness and correlation with human judgments, and (3) Coherence evaluation using LLM-based evaluators (GPT-4o, DeepSeek R1).

[8] https://platform.openai.com/docs/models.
[9] https://ollama.com/library/deepseek-r1:32b.

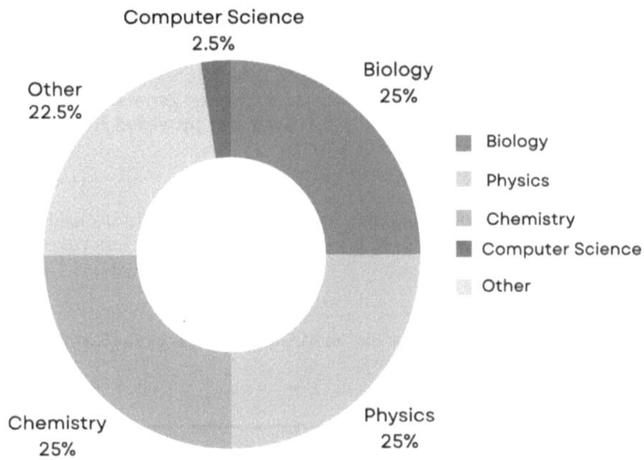

Fig. 5. Overview of the dataset used in our study

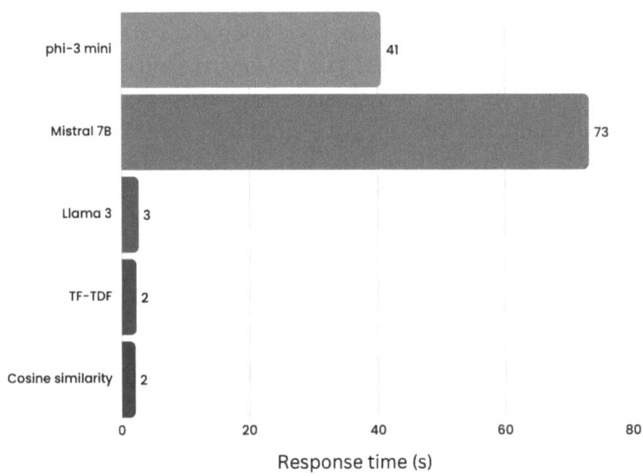

Fig. 6. Average response time in seconds of re-ranking models per query for the system where TextRank has been used for key term extraction.

Dataset Our dataset consists of 400 natural language questions, manually curated from multiple sources to ensure diversity and domain coverage. Specifically, we collect 100 user queries from ORKG ASK, spanning topics in computer science, environmental science, and various other domains. Additionally, we incorporate 100 biology-related scientific questions from PubMedQA [26], along with 200 questions from the ScienceQA [40] dataset—100 from physics and 100 from chemistry. To enrich the dataset, we manually extract key terms from each question. For each key term, we retrieve relevant artifacts from Resodate and Wikidata. Finally, we manually rank these artifacts to establish a benchmark for evaluating information retrieval and ranking methodologies.

5.1 Key-Term Extraction Performance

To assess the effectiveness of key-term extraction, we evaluate multiple models, including statistical methods (TF-IDF, YAKE), graph-based techniques (TextRank, SingleRank, TopicRank, PositionRank, MultipartiteRank, Kea), and transformer-based models (KeyPhraseTransformer).

Table 1 reports the precision, recall, and F1 scores for different extraction methods. Among them, TextRank and SingleRank achieved the highest F1 score (0.571), outperforming statistical and transformer-based methods. The transformer-based KeyPhraseTransformer model also demonstrated competitive performance with an F1 score of 0.517. These results indicate that graph-based approaches are well-suited for key-term extraction tasks.

Table 1. Performance of different machine learningâĂŞbased key-term extraction techniques.

Approach	Technique	Precision	Recall	F1
Statistical models	TF-IDF	0.436	0.321	0.370
	YAKE	0.553	0.408	0.470
Graph-based models	TextRank	**0.699**	**0.482**	**0.571**
	SingleRank	**0.699**	**0.482**	**0.571**
	TopicRank	0.626	0.425	0.506
	PositionRank	0.695	0.465	0.557
	MultipartiteRank	0.634	0.433	0.514
	Kea	0.457	0.337	0.388
Transformer-based	KeyPhraseTransformer	0.672	0.420	0.517

5.2 Ranking Effectiveness: Correlation with Human Judgments

To evaluate ranking effectiveness, we measure how well each model's output aligns with human-annotated rankings using NDCG@5 and NDCG@10.

Table 2 presents the NDCG scores for both statistical and LLM-based ranking methods. Statistical approaches—TF-IDF and Cosine Similarity—achieve perfect alignment with human rankings across both metrics (NDCG@5 = 1.000, NDCG@10 = 1.000), demonstrating highly consistent and deterministic performance. In contrast, LLM-based methods such as LLaMA-3 (8B), Phi-3 Mini, and Mistral (7B) show slightly lower but still strong alignment, with NDCG@5 scores ranging from 0.929 to 0.932 and NDCG@10 scores between 0.932 and 0.935. These results indicate that while LLMs capture semantic patterns effectively, statistical methods remain more precise and stable for re-ranking in this context.

Table 2. Evaluation of ranking methods using NDCG@5 and NDCG@10 to assess alignment between human-annotated and model-generated rankings.

Method	Re-ranking	NDCG@5	NDCG@10
Statistical	TF-IDF	**1.000**	**1.000**
	Cosine Similarity	**1.000**	**1.000**
LLM-Based	LLaMA-3 (8B)	0.932	0.935
	Phi-3 Mini	0.930	0.932
	Mistral (7B)	0.929	0.932

5.3 Coherence Evaluation Using GPT-4o and DeepSeek R1

Inspired by prior work [30], we assess the coherence of our ranking system using LLM-based evaluators (GPT-4o, DeepSeek-R1 Distill-Qwen-32B). As detailed in Fig. 4, we prompt these models to score ranking coherence between 1 (low coherence) and 5 (excellent coherence). The prompt has been shown in Fig. 7

Table 3. Evaluation of ranking methods using GPT-4o and DeepSeek-R1

Evaluator	Model Size	Re-ranking Method	Average Score
GPT-4o	-	TF-IDF	**3.67**
		Cosine Similarity	3.66
		LLaMA-3 (8B)	2.71
		Phi-3 Mini	3.01
		Mistral (7B)	2.91
DeepSeek-R1	32B	TF-IDF	**3.23**
		Cosine Similarity	2.87
		LLaMA-3 (8B)	3.20
		Phi-3 Mini	3.21
		Mistral (7B)	3.19

Table 3 presents the evaluation results. While statistical methods (TF-IDF, Cosine Similarity) receive higher coherence scores (3.67, 3.66), LLM-based rankings show more variance, with scores ranging from 2.71 to 3.01. The ongoing evaluation with DeepSeek R1 will further refine these insights.

5.4 Computational Efficiency

We evaluate the computational efficiency of our approach by measuring the end-to-end response time, from receiving a user query to generating ranked artifact recommendations. Given that TextRank and SingleRank achieved the highest

Input:

- <given_ranking> represents the ranking produced by a model. <human_ranking> represents the ground truth ranking provided by human annotators.

Prompt:
You are an expert in information retrieval and classification evaluation. Please evaluate the coherence of the following two rankings: <given_ranking> <human_ranking>
Please rate on a scale from 1 to 5, where 1 represents very low coherence and 5 indicates excellent coherence. You must return only an integer score.
Score:

Fig. 7. Coherence Evaluation Prompt

F1 scores in Sect. 5.1, we use TextRank as the key-term extraction method for all queries. The extracted key terms are then ranked using five different ranking models, and the response time is recorded for each.

Figure 6 presents the average response time per query for each model. Traditional statistical methods, such as TF-IDF and Cosine Similarity, exhibit the lowest response times (~2 s per query) due to their lightweight, deterministic nature and lack of computationally expensive learning-based inference. Among the LLM-based methods, LLaMA-3 (8B) achieves an impressive response time of 3 s, whereas Phi-3 Mini (41 s) and Mistral (73 s) exhibit significantly higher latency.

The efficiency of LLaMA-3 (8B) compared to Mistral (7B) and Phi-3 Mini can be attributed to multiple architectural and hardware optimizations. LLaMA-3 (8B) benefits from Meta's optimized transformer execution pipeline [44], which includes quantized inference and efficient key-value caching. These improvements lead to lower memory bandwidth usage and faster inference compared to traditional dense transformer architectures. Additionally, LLaMA-3 has been extensively fine-tuned for efficient inference on modern GPUs and TPUs, leveraging optimizations such as FlashAttention [10] and fused transformer kernels, which significantly reduce memory overhead.

In contrast, both Mistral (7B) and Phi-3 Mini experience substantial inference delays due to their extended context windows and computationally expensive architectural choices. Mistral (7B) is designed for efficiency but incorporates fine-grained attention sparsification [25], which, while improving accuracy, increases computational complexity and leads to higher latency. Similarly, Phi-3 Mini, unlike LLaMA-3 (8B), follows a Mixture-of-Experts (MoE) paradigm [3], where only a subset of model parameters is activated per query. This dynamic parameter selection introduces additional routing overhead and GPU memory fragmentation, thereby increasing inference time. Furthermore, Phi-3 Mini and Mistral (7B) are trained on longer context windows (up to 32K tokens) [3,25], requiring more computation per token, which exacerbates latency, particularly for retrieval tasks that process large text chunks.

These findings highlight the trade-offs between model expressivity and computational efficiency. While statistical methods provide lower response time, LLM-based ranking methods offer higher response time with increased inference time. Among LLMs, LLaMA-3 (8B) demonstrates the best balance between inference efficiency and ranking performance, making it a viable candidate for real-time artifact retrieval applications.

6 Discussion

The results of our study highlight important trade-offs between symbolic, statistical, and neural methods in the context of federated research artifact search, reinforcing and extending findings from earlier work. Prior studies (e.g., [21]; [4]) have shown that unsupervised graph-based models like TextRank and SingleRank perform strongly on scientific texts due to their ability to exploit local co-occurrence structures without requiring domain-specific training. Our results confirm this, with TextRank achieving the highest F1-score (0.571), outperforming transformer-based approaches in both precision and recall. This finding is especially notable given the increasing trend toward adopting neural models even in low-resource domains.

In contrast to studies advocating transformer-based keyphrase extraction (e.g., [12,32]), our evaluation demonstrates that without significant fine-tuning, models like KeyPhraseTransformer struggle in scientific metadata contexts. This supports the argument that symbolic approaches remain more effective and reliable for structured, domain-specific artifacts where labeled training data is scarce.

A novel aspect of our study is the comparative evaluation of ranking strategies using NDCG metrics against human annotations. Statistical ranking methods (TF-IDF, Cosine Similarity) achieved perfect scores (NDCG@5 = 1.000), outperforming even recent LLMs such as LLaMA-3 and Phi-3 Mini. While previous work (e.g., [43]) has shown that dense semantic ranking models can outperform TF-IDF in general domains, our results suggest that in metadata-rich, semantically narrow scientific settings, simpler models may align more closely with human judgments.

Interestingly, while LLM-based methods captured semantic relevance fairly well (NDCG@5 0.93), their variability and computational cost make them less practical for real-time systems like ORKG ASK. This underscores a key insight: simplicity and interpretability still matter, especially for explainable scientific search systems—a theme echoed in recent calls for hybrid or neuro-symbolic approaches ([11,27]).

Reliance on LLMs like ChatGPT and DeepSeek for evaluation poses risks due to hallucinations, prompt sensitivity, and limited reproducibility , [19]. Future work should incorporate expert human evaluators in realistic settings to ensure validity and domain alignment.

Overall, our findings reaffirm the enduring relevance of symbolic and statistical methods, even as neural approaches become more prominent. They also point to opportunities for future hybrid models that can combine structural reasoning from symbolic methods with the semantic sensitivity of LLMs. Our work contributes a grounded benchmark in this space, highlighting both the promise and the limitations of neural models in metadata-driven scientific retrieval.

7 Conclusions and Future Work

We introduced a neuro-symbolic approach for federated research artifact search, integrating linguistic processing with structured metadata retrieval to improve the discovery of datasets and software. Our system, embedded within ORKG ASK, refines key-term extraction using both symbolic and neural techniques, ensuring precise and contextually relevant recommendations from federated sources. To further enhance retrieval, we developed a ranking mechanism that leverages query structure and morphological features, leading to more accurate research artifact suggestions. Through rigorous evaluation using Precision, Recall, F1-score, correlation metrics, and LLM-based assessments, we demonstrated that symbolic methods outperform neural approaches in both accuracy and response time.

In the future, we aim to extend our approach by leveraging large-scale datasets such as the full Resodate and Wikidata corpora to refine class and property verbalizations. Further, we plan to enhance the ranking mechanism with more advanced neural-symbolic fusion strategies, enabling better generalization across diverse query types. Another key direction involves expanding our system's capabilities to support additional retrieval tasks, such as temporal and contextual reasoning, thereby broadening the scope of federated scientific search.

Our approach will be integrated into the ORKG ASK system, a scientific question-answering platform that allows users to ask questions. By leveraging the neuro-symbolic approach described here, ORKG ASK can provide precise, contextually relevant recommendations for datasets, software, and other scientific research artifacts, making it a powerful tool for researchers in need of metadata discovery across federated sources.

In future work, we plan to conduct user studies to validate our approach in practical settings and collect qualitative insights to further improve system relevance and usability.

Acknowledgements. This work was co-funded by the German Ministry of Education and Research (BmBF) for the project KISSKI AI Service Center (01IS22093C) and by the German Research Foundation (DFG) for the project NFDI4DataScience (460234259) and NFDI4Energy (501865131).

References

1. Abdin, M., et al.: Phi-3 Technical Report: a highly capable language model locally on your phone (2024). arXiv preprint arXiv:2404.14219
2. Aizawa, A.: An information-theoretic perspective of TF-IDF measures. Inf. Process. Manage. **39**(1), 45–65 (2003)
3. Beeching, E., et al.: Textbooks are all you need (2023). arXiv preprint arXiv:2312.11465
4. Berend, G.: Exploiting extra-textual and linguistic information in keyphrase extraction. Nat. Lang. Eng. **22**(1), 73–95 (2016)
5. Besold, T.R., et al.: Neural-symbolic learning and reasoning: a survey and interpretation 1. In: Neuro-Symbolic Artificial Intelligence: The State of the Art, pp. 1–51. IOS press (2021)
6. Bougouin, A., Boudin, F., Daille, B.: Topicrank: graph-based topic ranking for keyphrase extraction. In: International Joint Conference on Natural Language Processing (IJCNLP), pp. 543–551 (2013)
7. Brickley, D., Burgess, M., Noy, N.: Google dataset search: Building a search engine for datasets in an open web ecosystem. In: The world wide web Conference, pp. 1365–1375 (2019)
8. Broyden, C.G.: The convergence of single-rank quasi-newton methods. Math. Comput. **24**(110), 365–382 (1970)
9. Campos, R., Mangaravite, V., Pasquali, A., Jorge, A., Nunes, C., Jatowt, A.: Yake! keyword extraction from single documents using multiple local features. Inf. Sci. **509**, 257–289 (2020)
10. Dao, T., Fu, D.Y., Ermon, S., Keutzer, K.: Flashattention: fast and memory-efficient exact attention with IO-awareness. Adv. Neural Inf. Process. Syst. (NeurIPS) (2022)
11. DeLong, L.N., Mir, R.F., Fleuriot, J.D.: Neurosymbolic AI for reasoning over knowledge graphs: a survey. IEEE Trans. Neural Netw. Learn. Syst. (2024)
12. Docekal, M., Smrz, P.: Query-based keyphrase extraction from long documents (2022). arXiv preprint arXiv:2205.05391
13. Dubey, A., et al.: The llama 3 herd of models (2024). arXiv preprint arXiv:2407.21783
14. Florescu, C., Caragea, C.: Positionrank: an unsupervised approach to keyphrase extraction from scholarly documents. In: Proceedings of the 55th Annual Meeting of the Association for Computational Linguistics (volume 1: long papers), pp. 1105–1115 (2017)
15. Frank, E., Hall, M.A.: Data mining: practical machine learning tools and techniques. Morgan Kaufmann (2011)
16. Fürnkranz, J., Hüllermeier, E., Vanderlooy, S.: Binary decomposition methods for multipartite ranking. In: Machine Learning and Knowledge Discovery in Databases: European Conference, ECML PKDD 2009, Bled, Slovenia, September 7-11, 2009, Proceedings, Part I 20, pp. 359–374. Springer (2009)
17. Gao, M., Hu, X., Ruan, J., Pu, X., Wan, X.: LLM-based NLG evaluation: current status and challenges (2024). arXiv preprint arXiv:2402.01383
18. Garcez, A.d., Gori, M., Lamb, L.C., Serafini, L., Spranger, M., Tran, S.N.: Neural-symbolic computing: an effective methodology for principled integration of machine learning and reasoning (2019). arXiv preprint arXiv:1905.06088
19. Gilardi, F., Alizadeh, M., Kubli, M.: Chatgpt outperforms crowd workers for text-annotation tasks. Proc. Natl. Acad. Sci. **120**(30), e2305016120 (2023)

20. Guo, D., et al.: Deepseek-r1: Incentivizing reasoning capability in LLMS via reinforcement learning (2025). arXiv preprint arXiv:2501.12948
21. Hasan, K.S., Ng, V.: Automatic keyphrase extraction: a survey of the state of the art. In: Proceedings of the 52nd Annual Meeting of the Association for Computational Linguistics (Volume 1: Long Papers), pp. 1262–1273 (2014)
22. Hitzler, P., Sarker, M.K.: Neuro-symbolic artificial intelligence: the state of the art (2022)
23. Islam, R., Moushi, O.M.: GPT-4o: the cutting-edge advancement in multimodal LLM. Authorea Preprints (2024)
24. Jiang, A.Q., et al.: Mistral 7b (2023). arXiv preprint arXiv:2310.06825
25. Jiang, H., Cai, A., Xie, S.W., Bansal, M.: Mistral 7b: a small but mighty model (2024). arXiv preprint arXiv:2401.04787
26. Jin, Q., Dhingra, B., Liu, Z., Cohen, W.W., Lu, X.: Pubmedqa: a dataset for biomedical research question answering (2019). arXiv preprint arXiv:1909.06146
27. Kapanipathi, P., et al.: Leveraging abstract meaning representation for knowledge base question answering (2020). arXiv preprint arXiv:2012.01707
28. King, G.: An introduction to the dataverse network as an infrastructure for data sharing (2007)
29. Lamb, L.C., Garcez, A., Gori, M., Prates, M., Avelar, P., Vardi, M.: Graph neural networks meet neural-symbolic computing: a survey and perspective (2020). arXiv preprint arXiv:2003.00330
30. Liu, Y., et al.: Aligning with human judgement: the role of pairwise preference in large language model evaluators (2024). arXiv preprint arXiv:2403.16950
31. Manghi, P., et al.: The openaire research graph data model. Zenodo (2019)
32. Meng, R., Zhao, S., Han, S., He, D., Brusilovsky, P., Chi, Y.: Deep keyphrase generation (2017). arXiv preprint arXiv:1704.06879
33. Mercer, S., Spillard, S., Martin, D.P.: Brief analysis of deepseek r1 and it's implications for generative AI (2025). arXiv preprint arXiv:2502.02523
34. Mihalcea, R., Tarau, P.: Textrank: bringing order into text. In: Proceedings of the 2004 Conference on Empirical Methods in Natural Language Processing, pp. 404–411 (2004)
35. Mons, B., Neylon, C., Velterop, J., Dumontier, M., da Silva Santos, L.O.B., Wilkinson, M.D.: Cloudy, increasingly fair; revisiting the fair data guiding principles for the European open science cloud. Inf. Serv. Use **37**(1), 49–56 (2017)
36. Nogueira, R., Jiang, Z., Lin, J.: Document ranking with a pretrained sequence-to-sequence model (2020). arXiv preprint arXiv:2003.06713
37. Oelen, A., Jaradeh, M.Y., Auer, S.: Orkg ask: a neuro-symbolic scholarly search and exploration system (2024). arXiv preprint arXiv:2412.04977
38. Rahutomo, F., Kitasuka, T., Aritsugi, M., et al.: Semantic cosine similarity. In: The 7th International Student Conference on Advanced Science and Technology ICAST, vol. 4, p. 1. University of Seoul South Korea (2012)
39. Robertson, S., Zaragoza, H., et al.: The probabilistic relevance framework: Bm25 and beyond. Found. Trends® Inf. Retrieval **3**(4), 333–389 (2009)
40. Saikh, T., Ghosal, T., Mittal, A., Ekbal, A., Bhattacharyya, P.: Scienceqa: a novel resource for question answering on scholarly articles. Int. J. Digit. Libr. **23**(3), 289–301 (2022)
41. Stodden, V., et al.: Enhancing reproducibility for computational methods. Science **354**(6317), 1240–1241 (2016)
42. Tenopir, C., et al.: Data sharing by scientists: practices and perceptions. PLoS ONE **6**(6), e21101 (2011)

43. Thakur, N., Reimers, N., Rücklé, A., Srivastava, A., Gurevych, I.: Beir: a heterogenous benchmark for zero-shot evaluation of information retrieval models (2021). arXiv preprint arXiv:2104.08663
44. Touvron, H., et al.: Llama 2: Open foundation and fine-tuned chat models (2023). arXiv preprint arXiv:2307.09288
45. Voorhees, E.M., Tice, D.M., et al.: The trec-8 question answering track evaluation. In: TREC. vol. 1999, p. 82 (1999)
46. Wang, L., Mao, Y., Wang, L., Sun, Y., Song, J., Zhang, Y.: Suitability of GPT-4o as an evaluator of cardiopulmonary resuscitation skills examinations. Resuscitation **204**, 110404 (2024)
47. Wilkinson, M.D., et al.: The fair guiding principles for scientific data management and stewardship. Sci. Data **3**(1), 1–9 (2016)
48. Witten, I.H., Paynter, G.W., Frank, E., Gutwin, C., Nevill-Manning, C.G.: Kea: practical automatic keyphrase extraction. In: Proceedings of the fourth ACM Conference on Digital Libraries, pp. 254–255 (1999)
49. Xiao, Y., Fan, Y., Zhang, R., Guo, J.: Beyond precision: a study on recall of initial retrieval with neural representations. In: China Conference on Information Retrieval, pp. 76–89. Springer (2022)

The Claims Network: Collecting Research, Education, Impact, and Leadership Claims on the Decentralized Web

Patrick Hochstenbach[1,2](✉), Herbert Van de Sompel[2,3], and Ruben Verborgh[2]

[1] Ghent University Library, Ghent, Belgium
patrick.hochstenbach@ugent.be
[2] IDLab, Ghent University - imec, Ghent, Belgium
ruben.verborgh@ugent.be
[3] DANS, Data Archiving and Networked Services, The Hague, The Netherlands

Abstract. Common research assessment approaches rely heavily on data pertaining to traditional contributions to the research endeavor (R), including the number of journal articles published, the journals in which those articles are published, and the citations the articles or journals receive. Dissatisfaction with these approaches has led to a global call for alternatives that take a much wider range of contributions into account, including those in areas such as Education (E), societal impact (I), and academic leadership (L). While traditional research outputs are relatively easy to track, thanks to their publication in a finite set of dedicated scholarly venues, non-traditional REIL contributions are typically disseminated across the broader web. This includes outputs such as research data, software, reports, courses, live performances, interviews, and committee leadership, making their discovery and collection far from straightforward. In an attempt to devise a scalable, automated approach to tackle this "find the REIL needles in the web haystack" problem, we introduce the Claims Network approach, which collects information about REIL contributions by inviting researchers to post about them on the distributed Mastodon social media environment. Through a prototype developed around the academic Mastodon instance operated by SURF in the Netherlands, we demonstrate that the approach is feasible and can be extended to include other Mastodon instances, both academic and general-purpose.

Keywords: decentralized web · research assessment · research communication

1 Introduction

Research assessment is an integral part of academic life. Established approaches utilize data extracted from the research communication system to gain insights

W.-T. Balke et al. (Eds.): TPDL 2025, LNCS 16097, pp. 163–180, 2026.
https://doi.org/10.1007/978-3-032-05409-8_11

into the nature, volume, and quality of contributions to the scholarly endeavor. It provides system-wide insights and, through cumulative evaluations, also contributes to the assessment of individual researchers. In the latter realm, it faces numerous challenges, including a focus on a narrow range of contributions (i.e., paper publications), dependency on closed proprietary data sources (i.e., commercial citation databases), and use of a limited set of quantitative indicators (i.e., impact factor and h-index) [49] of which the appropriateness has been repeatedly questioned [25,26]. Alternative metrics (Altmetrics) [23] complement traditional indicators by expanding the range of data sources used for the derivation of indicators to include references to contributions on social media. However, the contributions that are taken into account remain limited (i.e., identified by a DOI), and assessing the relevance of a reference to a contribution is challenging when it is impossible to verify the creator of the reference in a trustworthy manner.

Global initiatives aimed at changing the status quo consider a broad range of activities and contributions to the scholarly endeavor, enriching the basis for researcher evaluations. Prominent examples are the Leiden Manifesto [31], the Declaration on Research Assessment (DORA) [7], the Coalition for Advancing Research Assessment (COARA) [5], and the Hong Kong Principles for assessing researchers [8]. The 2020 position paper "Room for everyone's talent" published by Dutch public knowledge institutions and research funders (VSNU, NFU, KNAW, NWO, and ZonMw) [22] expresses a similar desire to enhance research assessment. The position paper advocates for a modernized awards system that should reflect academic excellence across key areas, including Research (R), Education (E), Impact (I), academic Leadership (L), and patient care at university medical centers. We will refer to these types of academic excellence indicators as **REIL claims** in our paper.

The report "Open Infrastructures for Responsible Research Assessment" (OI4RRA) presents a metric for qualitatively evaluating open infrastructures. Key indicators include broadening the diversity of research outputs, linking qualitative narratives with verifiable and transparent data, enhancing standards to create an interoperable open research infrastructure, and reducing the administrative burden through automation [49]. These qualitative indicators will guide us in our research. However, effective ways to collect REIL information are still needed. Since many REIL contributions, both traditional and non-traditional, are published across the web (e.g., source code, newspaper interviews) or leave digital traces (e.g., conference programs), the core challenge is locating these REIL "needles" in the vast web "haystack."

In this paper, we introduce the *Claims Network* approach that allows researchers to claim and organize their REIL contributions by mentioning them on social media. The approach was prototyped in the course of 2024 in a collaboration between SURF (the ICT cooperative of Dutch education and research institutions) and IMEC-IDLab (the Flemish Internet Technology and Data Science Lab).

The remainder of this paper is structured as follows: In Sect. 2, we examine the current state of the art to collect information about REIL contributions. In Sect. 3, we provide an architectural overview of the Claims Network approach, and in Sect. 4, we describe a prototype implementation of a Claims Network. In Sect. 5, we provide the results of a quantitative experiment that tests our approach to obtain metadata about REIL contributions for toots posted by researchers on Mastodon instances worldwide. In Sect. 6, we generalize our results and present a first draft of a Claims Network specification. In Sect. 7, we discuss our results and possible routes for further research and development.

2 Related Work

Collecting information about non-traditional REIL contributions is a nontrivial challenge because contributions – or traces of them – can reside anywhere on the web at large. Many services exist that monitor a finite set of dedicated scholarly venues for traditional research contributions (the R in REIL), such as journal articles. For example, CORE monitors institutional and subject repositories as well as journal publishers [6], OpenAlex monitors a wide range of data sources including DOI registration agencies and preprint repositories [9], and Web of Science monitors a selection of about 34k journals [17]. But monitoring the entire web to discover non-traditional REIL contributions remains a very significant challenge.

A prominent example is the Crossref/DataCite Event Data effort [28], which monitors a dozen web portals – including Wikipedia and social media aggregators like Reddit – for references to DOIs or their corresponding landing page URLs. The number of events aggregated by Crossref in this manner is substantial: in 2021, it was reported that 1.2 billion events were collected that mention DOIs in some way [51]. While many R contributions have DOIs, others use different PIDs or none at all [30,50]. It is particularly unusual for DOIs – or PIDs more broadly – to be assigned to E, I, and L contributions. Furthermore, reliably attributing a REIL contribution to a specific researcher is challenging, though for R contributions, discovering the ORCID(s) associated with a DOI is a possibility. However, ORCID adoption is not universal [45,56], and a registered ORCID does not confirm identity or affiliation.[1] ORCID is also rarely used for E, I, and L contributions.

The OpenAIRE GraspOS effort [24] acknowledges the challenges related to discovering REIL contributions on the web at large. To address this, a federated cataloging infrastructure [55] is proposed, in which information pertaining to non-traditional REIL contributions is entered into distributed data nodes and subsequently aggregated into a central portal. How exactly the distributed nodes acquire their respective REIL contribution information remains unclear. Manual entry by researchers or research administrators is being considered, although it

[1] See, for example, the two ORCID identifiers the author created without requiring any proof of identity or affiliation: https://orcid.org/0000-0001-8390-6171 and https://orcid.org/0009-0000-4241-5317.

would predictably place a significant burden on researchers and staff who are already resource-constrained.

The myresearch.institute experiment [46] tracked researchers in 11 web portals, including Wikipedia, GitHub, Blogger, Slideshare, and hypothes.is. The experiment avoided attribution challenges by tracking unambiguous researcher identifiers in the portals and did not rely on DOIs, as E, I, and L contributions were identified by URLs, as all things on the web. The experiment had a limited scope but tracked over 17,000 contributions by 16 researchers in just 15 months. Aware that E, I, and L contributions often vanish or change over time [43,47], it enabled post hoc verification by archiving contributions in a dedicated web archive. To maximize long-term accessibility, the experiment adopted standards and best practices such as WARC [21], Memento [53], and Robust Links [44].

The Claims Network draws inspiration from both the myresearch.institute and Event Data approaches, and builds on interoperability and standards frameworks developed in our earlier work [40]. As in myresearch.institute, it detects REIL contributions on the open web by monitoring the activities of researchers whose identities are verified by trusted services. However, instead of tracking multiple web portals, the Claims Network focuses solely on Mastodon instances. Researchers themselves post toots referencing the URLs of their REIL contributions, which then trigger a bot to automatically retrieve metadata from the linked content. This collected information can be used to generate aggregated overviews of a researcher's contributions. Similar to Event Data, the Claims Network monitors references to contributions, but with a broader scope: references can point to any REIL contribution URL, not just DOIs of traditional research outputs. Additionally, our Claims Network explores the use of the Event Notifications protocol as an interoperability layer [40].

3 The Claims Network

In 2024, SURF and IMEC-IDLab designed a Claims Network to collect traditional and non-traditional REIL contributions using Mastodon. In this network, depicted in Fig. 1, a **national academic Mastodon service** provides Dutch researchers with a safe communication medium that supports informal researcher interactions focusing on science, popularizing science, and education. A researcher registered with this service can create a **REIL claim**: a toot (a message on Mastodon) that references a web resource that indicates a REIL contribution by the researcher. To make these REIL claims easy discoverable, the researcher includes a reference to a **claim bot** in each claim. Such a reference triggers a claim bot in the network to process the REIL claim. The claim bot uses a network of **summarizer services** to extract descriptive metadata from the web resources referenced in these toots. The extracted metadata is then used to update the researcher's preferred **claims overview service**, which provides a consolidated view of all claims and allows researchers and administrators to consult, edit, and validate entries. While manual entry is possible, the Claims Network aims to automate much of this process. The extracted metadata is also published as a personal **activity log** for each researcher and provides a transparent, machine-readable overview of all REIL claims made on Mastodon and their provenance in RDF format.

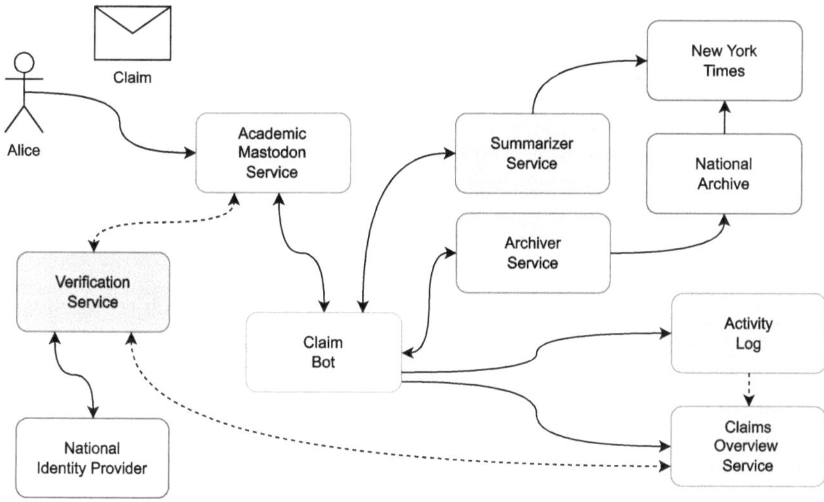

Fig. 1. The architecture of the SURF-IMEC-IDLab "Claims Network"

To unambiguously attribute REIL claims to a researcher, the Claims Network employs bidirectional links between its various services. For example, if a bidirectional link exists between a Mastodon profile and a profile on the claims overview service, this serves as a trust indicator suggesting that both profiles are controlled by the same user. This trust can be further strengthened through the implementation of a well-known **verification service**. Such a service is integrated with a national identity provider and provides researcher profiles where they can publish bidirectional links to Claims Network profiles. Verification services can also profile machine-readable metadata such as the role of the researcher in an institution (i.e., staff, student, faculty). This level of trust is similar to a verification of ownership of a website (e.g., by publishing a token on a well-known address).

To maximize long-term accessibility and versioning of web resources, an **archiver service** can be introduced in the network. This service, when provided with the URL of a web resource, generates a Memento [53] in a trusted web archive.

In addition to supporting the dissemination of REIL claims, Mastodon is envisioned as a platform for informal interactions among researchers, creating fertile ground for a new form of scholarly communication. A secondary function of the claims overview service is to provide a quality control step within the REIL claim process. While researchers can submit REIL claims, the Claims Network itself does not inherently guarantee their validity. We view this vulnerability as an integral aspect of academic trust and a core principle of good scholarly conduct. Submitting false claims will ultimately damage a researcher's reputation. To support transparency, the network offers services to discover REIL claims, archive the associated web resources, and maintain detailed activity logs. Within such a framework, the claims overview service acts as an additional layer of human-curated quality assurance.

4 SURF-IDLab Prototype

To test the feasibility of the Claims Network, between September 2024 and January 2025 a prototype was developed using off-the-shelf components and open-source technologies. Within the scope of the prototype, we defined the following goals:

1. Installation of an academic scholarly Mastodon service, which researchers use to disseminate claims about personal REIL contributions.
2. Installation of a claims overview service, which contains the researchers' bibliography containing REIL claims along with their metadata and provenance.
3. Creation of a verification service to verify accounts on the claims overview service and academic scholarly Mastodon service.
4. Installation of a summarizer service that extracts descriptive metadata from a wide variety of websites, such as news agencies, blogs, and code/data repositories.
5. Creation of a claim bot service that acts as an orchestrator to listen to Mastodon toots, verify the Mastodon account using the verification service, resolve metadata about the URL posted in the toot using the summarizer service, update the claims overview service and activity log.

Academic Scholarly Mastodon Service. We do not rely on a specific Mastodon installation in our prototype: any installation that is federating with other Mastodon instances is sufficient. Federation allows a Claims Network to have researchers and claim bots 'live' on different Mastodon hosts.

To attribute REIL claims to a particular researcher, bidirectional `rel="me"` links [13] are used in the various profiles of the researcher in the Claims Network, such as the claims overview service and the verification service, as discussed later in this paper.

Claims Overview Service. To create a prototype for a claims overview service, we searched for an off-the-shelf tool that offered at least the following functionalities:

- Provide an environment where a researcher can view and edit the overview of REIL claims.
- Provide an API to add new entries to the overview of REIL claims.
- Provide a version history of claims that were added and edited in the service.
- Provide SAML [14] or OpenID Connect [12] integration with the SURFconext [15] identity provider.

The Wiki.js [18] software was our tool of choice for the prototype. The software runs nearly unchanged, requiring only two minor patches to improve rendering references to REIL claims in HTML pages. The GraphQL API allows the claim bot to upload directly to the claims overview service. A complete CRIS system might better serve the claims overview service in a production system. As we only created a prototype, the basic functionality of Wiki.js serves as a template for the features required in a possible CRIS system.

The Wiki.js installation includes on each researcher's bibliography page a similar `rel="me"` link-back mechanism for the Mastodon service to connect the identity of the claims overview service identity as part of the Dutch research community. This extra link-back can seem to be superfluous in our environment, where we can trust that a CRIS system only contains accounts for real researchers. However, in a decentralized setting, with many autonomous agents serving potentially many types of CRIS systems worldwide, trust becomes a scalability concern. Rather than trusting every potential CRIS system globally, we rely on a limited number of national verification providers.

Verification Service. At the time of writing, the verification service is still in development. Its purpose is to serve as a trusted endpoint within the Claims Network, allowing researchers to create a public profile page containing `rel="me"` links to their academic scholarly Mastodon account and the claims overview service of their choice. The researcher, Carol, can provide as much or as little information about herself, such as a verification profile. Typically, the verification service page mints a pseudo-anonymous URL for the researcher that does not reference a well-known personal identifier (such as an email address, login account, social account, ORCID). For example, for the researcher Carol, the profile URL `https://verify.edu.nl/profile/f7b7a81f` is minted. At the URL, an HTML profile is available, which contains the personal identifiers Carol wants to share with the world. E.g.:

- Her Mastodon identifier (in the form of a `rel="me"` link to her Mastodon profile).
- Her claims overview service identifier (in the form of a `rel= "me"` link to her claims overview service profile)

This information should also be available in a machine-readable format such as JSON-LD. A prototype is available, and SURF will collaborate with GEANT implementing such a verification service with InAcademia[2], a real-time validation service for student affiliation.

Summarizer Service. A summarizer service was implemented using the Zotero translation server [20], part of the Zotero project [19] that creates an open-source reference management system. Given the URL of a REIL claim, a Zotero translator service provides plugins for many types of websites to generate serialized metadata summaries using the Citation Style Language (CSL) [3].[3]

[2] https://inacademia.org.

[3] At the time of writing, Zotero has translators for 727 websites.

In our prototype, we adhere to the architectural requirements to support a network of independent summarizer services that could operate within the Claims Network. To enable such a configuration, an application-neutral communication protocol is essential. The protocol of our choice was the Event Notification in Value-Adding Networks (EN protocol) [40], which is a profile of Linked Data Notifications (LDN) [27] and forms also the basis of the COAR Notify protocol [4]. Based on asynchronous messaging, using Event Notification messages (EN notifications), the EN protocol enables the summarizing service to queue incoming requests and process them sequentially. This batch-processing style provides an opportunity to scale services by optimizing computing resources.

A web service named "metadata-server" [34] provides an implementation of the summarizer service. The metadata-server publishes the Zotero generated summary as a new web resource and notifies the requester using an EN notification about the generated summary. Publishing the summary result as a web resource provides a public provenance trail that can be used as proof that a trustworthy summarizer was involved in the process.

Claim Bot. The "mastodon-bot" [33] is a simplified version of the "Orchestrator" software described by Hochstenbach [42] in 2023. Our claim bot implementation includes a Mastodon-to-EN-protocol gateway, ensuring forward compatibility for the backend orchestrator service to manage a wide network of social media platforms (e.g., including Bluesky [2] and LinkedIn [11]). The gateway monitors the claim bot account on a Mastodon instance for new 'toot' messages directed at the claim bot. These messages are then converted into EN notifications, which activate the claim bot. This design allows the claim bot and other services in the Claims Network to use the EN protocol as a communication bus.

The claim bot will only process an EN notification if a verified `rel="me"` link can be found in the Mastodon user's profile that references a trusted verification service. The verification service must provide a backlink to the Mastodon user's profile and a link to the user's profile on the claims overview service. The claims overview service profile should also link back to the trusted verification service. Upon successful verification, the claim bot issues an EN protocol request to a summarizer service to generate metadata for the claim. Once the metadata is prepared, the summarizer service contacts the claim bot again using an EN notification. This generated metadata is used by the claim bot to update an activity log. In the Claim Network architecture, this activity log is the input for the claims overview service. In our prototype, the claim bot can update the claims overview service directly using the GraphQL API of the Wiki.js service. We are currently experimenting with providing the activity log and updates of the claims overview service via the EN protocol.

The SURF/IMEC-IDLab prototype does not include an archiver service to ensure long-term accessibility and verification of the artifacts forming the core of REIL claims. If such a service becomes available in the project's next phase, the claim bot should send an EN notification to the archiver and wait for the response.

Activity Log. To create an activity log, a web service [32,35] was developed as part of the claim bot, which stores all EN notifications sent and received by the claim bot. The content of these messages provides provenance information about REIL claims and includes a link to a summary of the claimed resources in CSL format. In our prototype, we chose to transform the CSL and the provenance information of each REIL claim into an RDF model using JSON-LD and N-Quads serialization.[4] A numerical analysis of the generated metadata using real-world data will be presented in the next section.

A local setup of our implementation is available for download as Docker containers from GitHub [36]. The Docker demonstrator provides the service components, with the exception of the Mastodon component, which requires an external provider. However, during our experiments, we used separate installations of all software components. A demonstration video of the Claims Network in action is available at Zenodo [37].

5 SURF Experiment

To illustrate the feasibility of the SURF/IMEC-IDLab prototype, we conducted two experiments that process toots for researchers that are already active on Mastodon worldwide. The focus of our experiments is on quantitative studies concerning the generation of metadata using a Claims Network, rather than on surveying user satisfaction with Mastodon as a REIL claims platform or conducting a comparative analysis to assess the impact of a Claims Network on the real-world discovery of REIL contributions. As input for our experiments, we used websites such as "Academics on Mastodon" [1] that provide lists of researchers active on Mastodon. We choose to *pull* toots from existing Mastodon accounts as input for our quantitative study. This approach is in contrast with the Claims Network architecture as presented in section Sect. 4 that requires a researcher to *push* toot notifications to a claim bot. However, whether toots are pulled or pushed does not affect the dynamics of metadata generation. A push-based architecture is more scalable than a pull-based architecture for two reasons. First, it eliminates the need to enumerate all possible Mastodon accounts within a given research community (e.g., Dutch researchers). Second, it avoids the necessity of processing all toots from those accounts.

To retrieve toots from Mastodon, we developed an EN generator that converts the public timeline for the selected Mastodon accounts into EN notifications. This transformation ensures that within a Claims Network, the EN protocol is used as a communication bus. The EN generator analyzes only toots that contain references to web resources. These web resources will be treated as "REIL claims." While this experimental design is not intended to replicate actual REIL claims realistically, it provides a pool of web resources that researchers could potentially use as examples of REIL claims. We assume that the web resources

[4] For an example of a JSON-LD version of a REIL claim, see the Claims Network specification section 5.4.1 https://spec.knows.idlab.ugent.be/claims-network/latest/#claim-summary-format.

referenced by researchers on Mastodon are representative of the types of REIL claims that could exist. However, to a lesser extent, they may also reference web resources outside these categories, such as faits divers. The rest of the Claims Network treats this input as if genuine claims were made.

An example of a typical researcher toot from our sample is represented below:[5]

> *ICYMI: We recently interviewed C... L... of the Norwegian Humanist Association on the Beyond Atheism podcast. Check it out! Link here:* https://some.url.on.the.web *#atheism #humanism #secularism*

In this example https://some.url.on.the.web would be the digital trace of the REIL claim.

We developed a specialized workflow for the Zotero summarizer service to optimize the recall of finding metadata for web resources. If access to a web resource is blocked (e.g., due to a robot block), the summarizer service attempts to retrieve an archived version of the web resource from the Internet Archive's' Wayback Machine [16] and uses the archived version to generate metadata.

Our goal was not to execute the fastest claim processing method but to analyze the range of metadata produced within a Claims Network. We processed REIL claims in batches of five requests per minute to avoid overloading our small experimental server.

5.1 Results

Experiment 1 involved 19 handpicked researchers from 11 Mastodon hosts for which 348 toots were collected that contained URLs to web resources. Most researchers (17) had enough toot messages to collect a sample of 20 toots containing a URL. Only two researchers were not active enough on the Mastodon platform to provide a maximum of 20 toots with a URL reference. Of the 348 toot+URL combinations collected, 327 claims (=94%) were unique. When feeding the 348 toot+URL combinations into the prototype Claims Network, 318 (=91%) resulted in a metadata summary that could be added to the claims overview service and in the activity log. No metadata summary was found for 30 (=9%) claims.

Experiment 2 used a random sample of 100 researchers from the "Academics on Mastodon" [1] list. These researchers were active on 42 Mastodon hosts, yielding 555 toots that contain URLs to web resources. Of the 555 toot+URL combinations collected, 531 (=96%) were unique. In our sample, 52 (=52%), researchers were not active enough to generate any claim. Feeding the toot+URL combinations into the experimental Claims Network 501 (=90%) resulted in a metadata summary that the claim bot could add to the claims overview service and the activity log. No metadata summary was found for 54 (=10%) claims.

[5] We anonymized the toot for the purposes of this article.

Table 1. Metadata fields generated for REIL claims in Experiments 1 and 2.

Metadata property	Experiment 1 (N = 348)	Experiment 2 (N = 555)
schema:title	317 (99%)	497 (99%)
schema:abstract	214 (67%)	297 (59%)
schema:language	185 (58%)	275 (55%)
schema:datePublished	182 (57%)	266 (53%)
schema:author	108 (33%)	174 (35%)
......*schema:familyName*	73	157
......*schema:givenName*	73	157
......*schema:name*	35	17
schema:issn	28 (9%)	79 (16%)
schema:publisher	10 (3%)	10 (2%)
bibo:pages	8 (3%)	51 (10%)
schema:editor	1 (<1%)	4 (<1%)

Table 2. Resource types for the generated metadata in Experiments 1 and 2.

Resource type	Experiment 1 (N = 348)	Experiment 2 (N = 555)
csl:webpage	200 (63%)	339 (68%)
csl:post-weblog	32 (10%)	40 (8%)
csl:motion_picture	21 (7%)	11 (2%)
csl:article-newspaper	30 (9%)	23 (5%)
csl:article-journal	15 (5%))	56 (11%)
csl:entry-encyclopedia	5 (2%)	5 (<1%)
csl:article	4 (1%)	6 (1%)
csl:software	4 (1%)	4 (<1%)
csl:article-magazine	3 (1%)	8 (2%)
other	34 (=10%)	9 (2%)

Table 3. Available metadata fields per resource type in Experiment 1.

Experiment 1	*title*	*abstract*	*language*	*author*	*datepublished*
webpage	199 (100%)	127 (64%)	131 (66%)	31 (15%)	89 (45%)
post-weblog	32 (100%)	29 (91%)	29 (91%)	18 (56%)	21 (66%)
motionpicture	21 (100%)	21 (100%)	1 (5%)	20 (95%)	19 (90%)
articlenewspaper	30 (100%)	29 (97%)	29 (97%)	28 (93%)	30 (100%)
articlejournal	15 (100%)	14 (93%)	11 (73%)	15 (100%)	15 (100%)

Table 4. Available metadata fields per resource type in Experiment 2.

Experiment 2	*title*	*abstract*	*language*	*author*	*datepublished*
webpage	335 (99%)	152 (45%)	144 (42%)	44 (13%)	118 (35%)
post-weblog	40 (100%)	34 (85%)	35 (88%)	25 (63%)	33 (83%)
motionpicture	11 (100%)	9 (82%)	0 (0%)	11 (100%)	11 (100%)
articlenewspaper	23 (100%)	23 (100%)	23 (100%)	19 (83%)	23 (100%)
articlejournal	56 (100%)	48 (86%)	47 (84%)	56 (100%)	56 (100%)

The reasons for this 9% "no metadata summary" case in both experiments included:

- Zotero does not support the format of the claimed web resource. (e.g., PDF files) (=50% of the cases).
- Zotero cannot access the claimed web resource, and the summary service can not find a copy in the Wayback Machine (=18% of the cases).
- The attempt to summarize the web resource resulted in an internal server error in the Zotero service: (=21% of the cases).
- The attempt to summarize the web resource resulted in an empty response (=11% of the cases).

We ran both experiments on a virtual Linux server with 2 × 2.80 GHz CPUs and 2GB RAM. Experiment 1 required 71 min to process 348 toot+URL combinations. Experiment 2 required 113 min to process 555 toot+URL combinations. This processing speed is equal to the five requests per minute we provided to the Claims Network. The input data, results, and statistics of both experiments can be consulted at Zenodo [37].

Table 1 provides an overview of the metadata fields that were generated for the 348 claims of experiment 1 and the 555 claims of experiment 2. Metadata properties provide an overview of the metadata fields as they are mapped to RDF in the activity log. Because in a Claims Network, the identity of the researcher is known, at least a basic bibliographic reference can be created for each REIL claim, including the researcher's identity, title, and URL of the claim.

Table 2 provides an overview of the resource types reported by the Zotero summarizer service for the claims. Table 3 and Table 4 present the metadata fields per resource type for Experiments 1 and 2. The results are particularly interesting for web resources classified as `article-newspaper`, which have an almost perfect score for identifying key metadata fields, including title, abstract, language, author, and publication data information. Newspaper resources will be the focus of a qualitative survey conducted in 2025 with a test group of researchers from Dutch universities of applied sciences.

6 Towards a Specification

Our prototype provides a proof of concept for a Claims Network *implementation*. On a practical level, the next goal is to scale out the proof of concept into a viable platform for the Dutch use case. However, from a strategic perspective, the more compelling option is to seek additional European partners who can be engaged to implement similar components of a Claims Network. Given its decentralized nature, the Claims Network does not rely on one central application platform or implementation. Achieving a broader adoption requires further generalization and a specification of the Claims Network as an *open architecture*, in line with the strategic goals outlined in the OI4RRA report [49]. The start of such an open architecture is outlined in the "Claims Network" specification [39].

The Claims Network specification generalizes the communication patterns between components within a Claims Network, aiming to maximize interoperability. This generalization, and the resulting interoperability, applies both vertically and horizontally. Vertically, our generalization eliminates local implementation dependencies from communication protocols and accommodates multiple implementations of the same functionality. For example, the summarizer service in our prototype is implemented using Zotero. However, alternative implementations of such summarizers could be developed using AI systems, aggregators, or similar technologies. Horizontally, the communication patterns for each service within the Claims Network can adopt the same one-way and request-response communication patterns as specified by the underlying EN protocol. The communication patterns to request a web resource summary implementation can also be used to request a memento copy from an archiver implementation.

One consideration that requires further attention is the source of REIL claims. In our prototype, Mastodon was used as a valid option within the Dutch SURF context as the trigger for REIL claims. However, the Claims Network architecture is not dependent on any specific social networking platform, provided that a gateway can be established to translate REIL claim triggers into EN notifications used within the Claims Network. The Mastodon-to-EN gateway in the prototype provided a starting point for such an abstraction. However, other gateways, such as a Bluesky-to-EN, LinkedIn-to-EN gateway, can be envisioned.

The verification service plays a crucial role in maintaining trust within the Claims Network. A careful balance must be maintained between the need to validate social media personas as part of a (national) research community and the protection of researchers' true identities within the network. In our experiments, two directions were investigated: a verification service that acts as a public Web profile (containing many bidirectional links to online identities) and a verification service that acts as a type of proof where a membership to a community can be demonstrated without conveying any information beyond the mere fact of membership. The former case is currently specified in the Claims Network architecture; however, our choices are currently being debated within the SURF community, in light of further implementations using pan-European identity providers – such as InAcademia – which tend to favor the latter approach.

An open topic in our specification work concerns the design of the activity log, which provides machine-level transparency through an append-only resource of activities within the network. In the current specification, individual claims are published as **claim summaries**. Each claim summary is represented as an RDF resource utilizing the schema.org ontology, describing the metadata of the claimed resource, the initiator of the REIL claim (i.e., the researcher), and provenance information regarding the origin of the claim. In our prototype, we are currently experimenting with Linked Data Event Streams (LDES) [29] as a means to generalize activity logging. However, the specification of an activity log is still in an experimental stage, targeting Claims Network use cases. A survey of broader use cases is necessary to enable the generalization of this work. The authors have previously advocated for a logging framework to enhance transparency in the scholarly publication process [38,41]. These considerations can be incorporated into the Claims Network specification.

The objective of the Claims Network specification, as an open architecture, is not confined to specific use cases related to the discovery of REIL contributions. Each service should also function as an *independent* component, thereby eliminating tightly coupled interdependencies. The decision to use the EN protocol aligns well with the COAR Notify protocol [4], which is based on the same principles and offers an alternative approach to scholarly peer review and overlay journal publishing. The same approach is adopted by the NDE-Usable program of the Dutch Digital Heritage Network, which aims to redesign the exchange of data between cultural heritage institutions and applications [54].

This independence among components guides the design of decentralized networks. Each component should be valuable even when separated from the network. Thus, the claim bot acts more as a choreographer of loosely coupled services than as a rigid orchestrator essential for network function. While directly referencing a claim bot in a toot can accelerate the REIL discovery process, the core idea of a Claim Network could, in principle, be replicated simply by tagging a Mastodon toot as a REIL claim and employing a tag aggregation mechanism to collect those claims. What remains essential to a Claim Network is the transparency with which it operates.

7 Discussion and Conclusion

The Claims Network offers an open architecture and an initial implementation of a decentralized network for "finding the REIL needles in the web haystack" problem. The architecture is based on academic social networking services, such as SURF Mastodon, which offer researchers a secure communication platform to facilitate informal interactions, focusing on science, science popularization, and education. Some of these social interactions also serve as triggers for Claims Network agents – including the claim bot, summarizer service, activity log, and claims overview service – to generate metadata concerning REIL claims mentioned on Mastodon.

Our prototype demonstrates that many types of REIL contributions – including both traditional and non-traditional resources, many of which fall outside the scope of conventional PID systems – can be effectively discovered with minimal manual intervention required from researchers. The metadata generation proved particularly successful for non-traditional REIL contributions, such as news media, which will serve as input for further analysis in qualitative studies to be conducted in 2025 with Dutch universities of applied sciences.

The prototype relies on web scraping. Although the initial results are very promising, it is too early to declare success. On the positive side, many websites expose metadata for search engine optimization (SEO) purposes. A claim bot can collect information about REIL contributions at a very early stage, as soon as they are published and attract the attention of researchers on social media. This also provides the network with the opportunity to generate a trusted copy of the REIL artifact, preserved in a web archive. On the negative side, the emergence of generative AI and their often overzealous data-collecting activities present new challenges [48]. We foresee that many websites will take precautions to prevent robots from accessing any information. In future work, we will investigate the state-of-the-art in AI control. This presents a challenge for the web at large [10].

Further analysis is required to assess the quality and accuracy of the REIL claims. Adopting a generic solution based on web standards, instead of a web scraping implementation, would be a more promising approach. Promoting Signposting [52] could encourage its adoption in institutional and data repositories, archives, software repositories, and platforms that provide evidence of REIL claims. Automating metadata generation does not automate accuracy. Claims overview services still need manual intervention to assess the accuracy of the claims. The Claims Network facilitates the discovery of non-traditional REIL contributions and provides transparency throughout this process through activity logs. A national CRIS system could utilize these activity logs as input and provide value-added services, such as a published, trusted version of these logs.

The setup of the SURF Mastodon instance revealed several challenges concerning the trustworthiness of user profiles, including anonymous accounts and researchers with multiple accounts on multiple Mastodon instances. These challenges provided valuable input for our discussion about the verification service component, which could offer trust indicators across multiple Mastodon instances. Future research should explore the requirements for integrating trusted social networking services into a Claims Network. These challenges are not limited to Claims Network use cases. Interest in a general verification mechanism for social media accounts has led to a first cooperation with GEANT and InAcademia to provide such services.

The Claims Network specification can be viewed as an initial iteration toward a decentralized approach to collecting REIL information created by the scholarly community using an open architecture.

Acknowledgments. This research was conducted with support from SURF. The computational resources and assistance by Laurents Sesink, Thomas van Himbergen, Niels van Dijk, and Thijs Kinkhorst were instrumental in conducting the experiments for this study.

References

1. Academics on Mastodon. https://nathanlesage.github.io/academics-on-mastodon/. Accessed 24 Feb 2025
2. Bluesky. https://bsky.app. Accessed 20 Feb 2025
3. Citation Style Language. https://citationstyles.org/. Accessed 20 Feb 2025
4. COAR Notify Protocol. https://coar-notify.net/specification/1.0.1/. Accessed 12 Feb 2025
5. CoARA – Coalition for Advancing Research Assessment. https://coara.eu/. Accessed 10 Feb 2025
6. CORE data providers search. https://core.ac.uk/data-providers/. Accessed 23 Apr 2025
7. Declaration on Research Assessment. https://sfdora.org/. Accessed 10 Feb 2025
8. Hong Kong Principles. https://www.wcrif.org/hong-kong-principles. Accessed 22 Apr 2025
9. How does OpenAlex work? https://help.openalex.org/hc/en-us/articles/28932712154391-How-does-OpenAlex-work. Accessed 24 Apr 2025
10. IAB workshop on AI-CONTROL (aicontrolws). https://datatracker.ietf.org/group/aicontrolws/materials/. Accessed 29 Dec 2024
11. LinkedIn. https://www.linkedin.com/. Accessed 20 Feb 2025
12. OpenID. https://en.wikipedia.org/wiki/OpenID. Accessed 16 June 2025
13. rel="me" - microformats wiki. https://microformats.org/wiki/rel-me. Accessed 16 June 2025
14. Security Assertion Markup Language. https://en.wikipedia.org/wiki/Security_Assertion_Markup_Language. Accessed 16 June 2025
15. SURFconext | SURF.nl. https://www.surf.nl/en/services/identity-access-management/surfconext. Accessed 16 June 2025
16. Wayback Machine. https://webcf.waybackmachine.org/. Accessed 24 Feb 2025
17. Web of Science | Clarivate. https://clarivate.com/academia-government/scientific-and-academic-research/research-discovery-and-referencing/web-of-science/. Accessed 23 Apr 2025
18. Wiki.js. https://js.wiki/. Accessed 12 Feb 2025
19. Zotero | Your personal research assistant. https://www.zotero.org/. Accessed 20 Feb 2025
20. zotero/translation-server. https://github.com/zotero/translation-server. Accessed 12 Feb 2025
21. The WARC file format (ISO 28500) - information, maintenance, drafts (2017). https://bibnum.bnf.fr/WARC/. Accessed 17 Apr 2025
22. Room for everyone's talent (2019). https://recognitionrewards.nl/wp-content/uploads/2020/12/position-paper-room-for-everyones-talent.pdf. Accessed 29 Jan 2025
23. Altmetrics (2025). https://en.wikipedia.org/wiki/Altmetrics. Accessed 22 Apr 2025
24. Administrator: GraspOS. https://www.openaire.eu/graspos-project. Accessed 23 Apr 2025
25. Bollen, J., Sompel, H.V.D., Hagberg, A., Chute, R.: A principal component analysis of 39 scientific impact measures. PLOS ONE **4**(6), e6022 (2009). https://doi.org/10.1371/journal.pone.0006022
26. Brembs, B.: Prestigious science journals struggle to reach even average reliability. Front. Hum. Neurosci. **12** (2018). https://doi.org/10.3389/fnhum.2018.00037

27. Capadisli, S., Guy, A.: Linked Data Notifications (2017). https://www.w3.org/TR/ldn/. Accessed 5 Feb 2025
28. Clark, R.: Event data. https://www.crossref.org/services/event-data/. Accessed 10 Mar 2025
29. Colpaert, P.: Linked Data Event Streams (2025). https://semiceu.github.io/LinkedDataEventStreams/. Accessed 16 June 2025
30. Culbert, J., et al.: Reference coverage analysis of OpenAlex compared to web of science and scopus. https://doi.org/10.48550/arXiv.2401.16359
31. Hicks, D., Wouters, P., Waltman, L., Rijcke, S., Rafols, I.: Bibliometrics: the Leiden manifesto for research metrics. Nature **520**(7548), 429–431 (2015). https://doi.org/10.1038/520429a
32. Hochstenbach, P.: eventlog-server: a tiny event log demonstration server. https://github.com/MellonScholarlyCommunication/eventlog-server. Accessed 16 June 2025
33. Hochstenbach, P.: mastodon-bot: a Mastodon Service Bot. https://github.com/MellonScholarlyCommunication/mastodon-bot. Accessed 16 June 2025
34. Hochstenbach, P.: metadata-server. https://github.com/MellonScholarlyCommunication/metadata-server. Accessed 16 June 2025
35. Hochstenbach, P.: RDF-generator: an RDF generator for CSL (citation style language) files of event notifications containing links to CSL. https://github.com/MellonScholarlyCommunication/rdf-generator. Accessed 16 June 2025
36. Hochstenbach, P.: Claims network (2025). https://github.com/MellonScholarlyCommunication/claims-network. Accessed 16 June 2025
37. Hochstenbach, P.: The claims network: collecting research, education, impact and leadership claims on the decentralized web (2025). https://doi.org/10.5281/zenodo.15296698. https://zenodo.org/records/15296698
38. Hochstenbach, P., Klein, M., Van de Sompel, H., Verborgh, R.: Transparant and trustworthy artifact life cycle. In: iPRES 2024 (2024). https://doi.org/10.21428/5676bf2d.a76a90cf
39. Hochstenbach, P., Van de Sompel, H.: Claims network (2025). https://spec.knows.idlab.ugent.be/claims-network/latest/. Accessed 12 Feb 2025
40. Hochstenbach, P., Van de Sompel, H., Vander Sande, M., Dedecker, R., Verborgh, R.: Event notifications in value-adding networks. In: Silvello, G., et al. (eds.) Linking Theory and Practice of Digital Libraries. Lecture Notes in Computer Science, pp. 133–146. Springer, Cham (2022). https://doi.org/10.1007/978-3-031-16802-4_11
41. Hochstenbach, P., Verborgh, R., Van de Sompel, H.: Event notifications and event logs: transparent sharing of artifact life cycle data. Int. J. Digit. Curation **18**(1) (2024)
42. Hochstenbach, P., Verborgh, R., Sompel, H.V.D.: Using event notifications, solid and orchestration for decentralizing and decoupling scholarly communication. Code4Lib J. (58). https://journal.code4lib.org/articles/17823
43. Jones, S.M., Sompel, H., Shankar, H., Klein, M., Tobin, R., Grover, C.: Scholarly context adrift: three out of four URI references lead to changed content. PLoS ONE **11**(12), e0167475 (2016). https://doi.org/10.1371/journal.pone.0167475
44. Klein, M., Jones, S.M., Shankar, H., Wincewicz, R., Nelson, M.L., Van de Sompel, H.: Robustifying Links (2020). https://robustlinks.mementoweb.org/spec/. Accessed 12 Mar 2025
45. Klein, M., Van de Sompel, H.: Discovering scholarly orphans using ORCID. In: 2017 ACM/IEEE Joint Conference on Digital Libraries (JCDL), pp. 1–10. https://doi.

org/10.1109/JCDL.2017.7991573. https://ieeexplore.ieee.org/abstract/document/7991573
46. Klein, M., Van de Sompel, H.: My Research Institute. https://myresearch.institute/. Archived through https://archive.is/hcXw7. Accessed 12 Feb 2025
47. Klein, M., et al.: Scholarly context not found: one in five articles suffers from reference rot. PLOS ONE **9**(12), e115253. https://doi.org/10.1371/journal.pone.0115253
48. Longpre, S.: AI crawler wars threaten to make the web more closed for everyone (2025). https://www.technologyreview.com/2025/02/11/1111518/ai-crawler-wars-closed-web/. Accessed 13 Feb 2025
49. Manola, N., Tzouganatou, A., Kuchma, I., OI4RRA, C.W.o.: Open infrastructures for responsible research assessment: principles and framework (2025). https://zenodo.org/records/14844582
50. Porter, S.J.: Measuring research information citizenship across ORCID practice. Front. Res. Metrics Anal. **7** (2022). https://doi.org/10.3389/frma.2022.779097
51. Rittman, M.: Event Data now with added references (2021). https://www.crossref.org/blog/event-data-now-with-added-references/. Accessed 16 Mar 2025
52. Van de Sompel, H., et al.: FAIR Signposting Profile. https://signposting.org/FAIR/. Accessed 5 Feb 2025
53. Van de Sompel, H., Nelson, M., Sanderson, R.: HTTP Framework for Time-Based Access to Resource States – Memento. https://doi.org/10.17487/RFC7089. https://datatracker.ietf.org/doc/rfc7089
54. Vander Sande, M.: Use Cases of Event Notifications in digital heritage networks (2023). https://netwerkdigitaalerfgoed.nl/wp-content/uploads/2023/07/20230614-Miel-Vander-Sande_PLDN-Solid-Use-Cases.pdf. Accessed 9 Oct 2023
55. Vergoulis, T., et al.: GraspOS Deliverable D4.2: Infrastructure Architecture (2024). https://zenodo.org/records/14162659
56. Youtie, J., Carley, S., Porter, A.L., Shapira, P.: Tracking researchers and their outputs: new insights from ORCIDs. Scientometrics **113**(1), 437–453 (2017). https://doi.org/10.1007/s11192-017-2473-0

Citation Management

Semantically Orthogonal Framework for Citation Classification: Disentangling Intent and Content

Changxu Duan[1] and Zhiyin Tan[2](✉)

[1] Technische Universität Darmstadt, Darmstadt, Germany
duan@linglit.tu-darmstadt.de
[2] L3S Research Center, Leibniz University Hannover, Hannover, Germany
zhiyin.tan@l3s.de

Abstract. Understanding the role of citations is essential for research assessment and citation-aware digital libraries. However, existing citation classification frameworks often conflate citation intent (why a work is cited) with cited content type (what part is cited), limiting their effectiveness in auto classification due to a dilemma between fine-grained type distinctions and practical classification reliability. We introduce **SOFT**, a **S**emantically **O**rthogonal **F**ramework with **T**wo dimensions that explicitly separates citation intent from cited content type, drawing inspiration from semantic role theory. We systematically re-annotate the ACL-ARC dataset using SOFT and release a cross-disciplinary test set sampled from ACT2. Evaluation with both zero-shot and fine-tuned Large Language Models (LLMs) demonstrates that SOFT enables higher agreement between human annotators and LLMs, and supports stronger classification performance and robust cross-domain generalization compared to ACL-ARC and SciCite annotation frameworks. These results confirm SOFT's value as a clear, reusable annotation standard, improving clarity, consistency, and generalizability for digital libraries and scholarly communication infrastructures. All code and data are publicly available on GitHub (https://github.com/zhiyintan/SOFT).

Keywords: Citation Intent Classification · Annotation Framework · Cross-Domain Generalization

1 Introduction

Citations are central to scholarly communication, shaping how knowledge is credited, organized, and reused across research communities. However, traditional citation metrics, such as counts or h-index, offer only coarse measures of scientific impact, failing to capture the nuanced ways in which works are cited, interpreted, or contested. To address this gap, citation classification has

---

C. Duan and Z. Tan—The authors contributed equally and are listed alphabetically.

W.-T. Balke et al. (Eds.): TPDL 2025, LNCS 16097, pp. 183–206, 2026.
https://doi.org/10.1007/978-3-032-05409-8_12

emerged as a critical task in computational bibliometrics and information science. It moves beyond simple quantitative counts to unlock the meaning within scholarly dialogue by analyzing the textual context to understand why a work was cited. The aim is to distinguish whether a prior work is being used as a foundational method, critiqued for its findings, or merely mentioned as background. This functional understanding provides the technological backbone for a new generation of digital libraries and intelligent research assistants, enabling advanced services such as automated literature reviews [3,15,27,28], the detection of scientific controversies [41], and impact-aware scientific search [35,63].

Recent advances in Natural Language Processing (NLP) have enabled large-scale citation classification to be deployed in digital library infrastructures. Platforms such as Web of Science [13], Scite [41], and Semantic Scholar [2] incorporate functionalities aimed at detecting aspects of citation intent to improve retrieval, mapping, and assessment. By automatically labeling background, method, result, or support, these platforms enhance transparency, accelerate literature review, and surface influential or controversial contributions [17].

Despite growing adoption, current citation classification practices face persistent limitations. Existing annotation frameworks often conflate distinct citation intents and content types and lack consistent semantic definitions. These ambiguities hinder downstream applications such as citation-based retrieval [7] and impact analysis [37].

In this paper, we introduce **SOFT**: a **S**emantically **O**rthogonal **F**ramework with **T**wo dimensions for citation annotation. SOFT separates what is being cited (**Cited Content Type**) from why it is being cited (**Citation Intent**), enabling clearer definitions, improved annotation consistency, and stronger support for LLM-based classification. Unlike prior one-dimensional frameworks, SOFT is grounded in the principles of semantic roles, offering conceptual alignment with how authors structure argumentation by performing actions (intent) on objects (content).

We validate SOFT through a comprehensive re-annotation of the ACL-ARC dataset [28] and a cross-domain evaluation on ACT2 [40], covering 19 scientific fields. Results show that SOFT yields higher inter-model and human-LLM agreement, improves classification accuracy for both zero-shot and fine-tuned models, and generalizes more robustly across domains than existing frameworks. These findings position SOFT as a reusable annotation standard for supporting citation-aware digital libraries and transparent research assessment. Our contributions are as follows:

- We propose SOFT, a two-dimensional, semantically grounded citation annotation framework that explicitly distinguishes the predicative intent of a citation from its cited content type.
- We conduct a systematic re-annotation of the ACL-ARC dataset and release a cross-domain test set from ACT2 under the SOFT framework.
- We benchmark SOFT against ACL-ARC and SciCite using zero-shot and fine-tuned LLMs, demonstrating gains in agreement, learnability, and generalizability.

2 Related Work

Research on citation classification spans several dimensions, including the development of annotation frameworks, the design of automated classification models, and the evaluation of their performance across different datasets and scientific domains. Section 2.1 reviews existing citation intent classification frameworks, most of which rely on single-layer labels that conflate the predicative function of the citation with the type of content being referenced. Section 2.2 surveys computational approaches for automating citation intent classification, ranging from early feature-based models to recent prompt-driven large language models. Section 2.3 highlights the limited exploration of cross-domain applicability, particularly across different scientific disciplines, within existing framework designs. Finally, Sect. 2.4 discusses related efforts in re-annotating benchmark datasets, which provide the foundation for our re-annotation of ACL-ARC and ACT2 using a two-dimensional framework.

2.1 Citation Intent Classification Frameworks

The functional purpose behind why an author cites a particular work has been described using various terms, including *Citation Motivation* [55,59], *Citation Purpose* [1], *Citation Type* [45], *Citation Function* [28,60], and *Citation Intent* [14]. For conceptual clarity and consistency, we adopt **Citation Intent** throughout this paper.

Research on citation classification has evolved from bibliometric traditions to computational frameworks tailored for large-scale modeling. One of the earliest and most fine-grained typologies was proposed by [55], which defined thirteen citation roles spanning rhetorical, epistemic, and contextual functions. The Citation Function Corpus (CFC) [60] was one of the first computationally oriented citation resources. Drawing on Spiegel's typology [55], it defined twelve function labels grouped into four superclasses (WEAKNESS, CONTRAST, POSITIVE, and NEUTRAL). The Citation Typing Ontology (CiTO) [52] introduced an ontology-based framework with over thirty citation relations, intended for semantic web interoperability. Although formal and expressive, CiTO remains relatively underused in NLP research.

Other frameworks were designed for domain-specific annotation and model training. The six-label framework (USE, CRITICIZING, COMPARISON, SUBSTANTIATING, BASIS, and NEUTRAL) proposed by [1] emphasized purpose-driven types developed through the annotation of NLP publications. ACL-ARC [28] defined a six-type framework (BACKGROUND, COMPARISON OR CONTRAST, MOTIVATION, USES, EXTENSION, and FUTURE) oriented toward citation influence modeling. SciCite [14] condensed this six-type framework into a three-type framework (BACKGROUND, METHOD, and RESULTCOMPARISON), motivated by the observation that types such as MOTIVATION, EXTENSION, and FUTURE often function as background context, to better support machine reading and research navigation in both computer science and biomedical domains.

ACT and ACT2 [40,46] extended citation annotation to additional scientific fields using a six-type framework similar to ACL-ARC (replacing COMPARISON OR CONTRAST with COMPARESCONTRASTS and extending it to capture not only differences but also similarities and disagreements between citations). In addition to intent, ACT and ACT2 also annotated influence using two binary labels (INFLUENTIAL and INCIDENTAL) with an added emphasis on author influence and comparability.

Together, these frameworks have shaped the landscape of citation intent classification, offering valuable insights into scholarly discourse. However, many adopt single-layer label structures that implicitly combine the author's action, the citation's function, with its semantic argument, the type of content being cited. While effective for some tasks, this design can limit semantic clarity and hinder flexible reuse across diverse domains. We return to these structural challenges in Sect. 3, which motivates the design of a new, semantically disentangled framework.

2.2 Citation Intent Classification (CIC) Models

Computational approaches to CIC have evolved significantly. Early models relied on hand-engineered features [36,47], but the release of benchmark datasets like ACL-ARC and SciCite catalyzed a shift towards deep learning. Transformer-based encoders, particularly the domain-specific SciBERT [10], quickly became the standard [18,50]. More recent advances explore diverse learning paradigms, including graph-based models [11], multi-task learning [22,53], and prompt-based methods [30,32]. Following the latest trend, recent work has also focused on fine-tuning LLMs for this task [29].

In our experiments, we re-annotated the ACL-ARC dataset using our proposed two-dimensional framework and used it for model training and evaluation. To assess cross-domain generalizability, we additionally re-annotated a sample from the ACT2 dataset. Results from these evaluations are presented in Sect. 5, where we compare the performance of CitePrompt and CitationIntentOpenLLM under our framework.

2.3 Cross-Domain Generalizability

A persistent challenge in CIC is the limited ability of models to generalize across different scientific domains or datasets [33,53,64]. To rigorously assess true generalization capabilities, models must be subjected to cross-domain testing: training on a source dataset (e.g., ACL-ARC) and evaluating on a distinct target (e.g., ACT2) [12].

Cross-domain or cross-dataset evaluation offers a principled framework for testing generalization capacity. In this setting, models are trained on one source dataset and evaluated on an independent target dataset [12]. This setup is widely used across NLP tasks to assess whether models learn domain-agnostic features or overfit to dataset-specific patterns. For instance, prior work has investigated transfer performance in question answering across biomedical, Wikipedia, and web dataset [24], and in relation extraction across distinct subdomains such as news and politics [8]. Another example is the divide in machine translation Generalizability between resource-rich and low-resource languages [4].

This lack of robustness is particularly evident even when datasets ostensibly share the same annotation framework. For example, ACT2 adopted the ACL-ARC label set for annotations across multiple disciplines. Despite this shared taxonomy, prior work demonstrated a dramatic drop in performance when models effective on ACL-ARC were applied to ACT2 [30]. This highlights that surface-level label consistency does not guarantee semantic equivalence across domains or robust model transfer.

We interpret these findings as indicative of deeper structural limitations in existing citation classification frameworks. In particular, many current frameworks conflate citation's function with its semantic arguments (the type of cited content), leading to annotation ambiguities that are further amplified in heterogeneous, multi-domain settings. In our experiments, we evaluate this by training models on our re-annotated ACL-ARC dataset and testing their performance on the ACT2 dataset using our revised framework annotations.

2.4 The Applicability of Re-annotating Datasets

The performance of supervised machine learning models is fundamentally tied to the quality of their training data [65]. However, real-world annotations are often noisy, with errors arising from ambiguous guidelines, subjective interpretations, limitations in annotator expertise, or simple human mistakes [25,43]. Such errors can undermine model training, compromise evaluation reliability, and reduce the robustness of downstream applications.

Recognizing these limitations, recent work has emphasized systematic identification and correction of label errors in widely used benchmarks. For example, studies of the COCO dataset [34] have revealed deficiencies in object mask annotations, prompting initiatives such as COCO-ReM [54] and Sama-COCO [67], both of which introduced revised annotations that improved downstream model performance. Similarly, the CleanCoNLL [51] project conducted a comprehensive relabeling of the CoNLL-03 Named Entity Recognition dataset [61], correcting 7% of entity labels and demonstrating measurable gains in benchmark reliability.

In parallel, automated and semi-automated approaches have been developed to assist error detection and correction. Model-driven methods such as Confident Learning estimate the joint distribution of observed and true labels to identify likely misannotations [42], while domain-specific tools like ObjectLab apply trained object detectors to flag anomalies in annotation quality [62]. Recently, LLMs have also been explored as annotation agents [23,56], although careful quality control remains essential in such settings.

In this work, we conduct a manual re-annotation of the ACL-ARC dataset [28] using our proposed two-dimensional framework. For comparison and internal validation, we also task a set of open-source LLMs with performing the same re-annotation under controlled prompting. To evaluate label quality and framework clarity, we compute agreement between human annotators and

LLMs. These experiments allow us to assess the reliability of our framework and explore the potential role of LLMs in future annotation workflows.

3 SOFT: A Semantically Orthogonal Framework with Two Dimensions

To address the growing need for semantically robust, interpretable, and transferable citation annotations, we propose a new framework grounded in discourse intent and cited content structure. Before introducing its design, we first examine the limitations of existing classification frameworks that motivate our departure from conventional approaches. These limitations arise from structural entanglement, under-specified functional roles, and ambiguous referential targets, all of which hinder consistent annotation and downstream model performance.

3.1 Limitations of Existing Citation Classification Frameworks

Despite the progress enabled by widely used frameworks such as CiTO [52], ACL-ARC [28], SciCite [14], and ACT/ACT2 [40,45], several structural limitations persist. These challenges reduce annotation clarity and consistency, hinder model generalization, and complicate the semantic interpretation of citation acts. We identify three interrelated problems:

(1) Dimensional Entanglement: Conflating Cited Content Type and Citation Intent. Many previous citation classification frameworks failed to separate the cited content type, such as method, data, or finding, from citation intent or function, such as use, and instead combined both dimensions into a single label. For example, in CiTO, types like "uses method in", "uses data from", and "uses conclusions from" explicitly bind the act of using with the specific object being used, resulting in a conflation of content type and citation intent. This design leads to an explosion in the number of types while still missing important boundary cases, which increases the cognitive burden for annotators and makes modeling more challenging due to both type proliferation and unclassifiable instances. SciCite, in contrast, presents a related limitation differently: its type BACKGROUND information is broadly defined and absorbs all citation acts that do not fit into the method or result types. As a result, many citations with specific functional intent are ultimately subsumed under the background type, which obscures their actual scholarly role.

(2) Perspective Ambiguity: Authorial Commitment and Discourse Voice. Additionally, inconsistent perspective across types introduces further confusion for annotators. For example, in the ACL-ARC framework, types such as BACKGROUND, MOTIVATION, and FUTURE use the cited work as the subject of the action, while types such as USES, EXTENSION, and COMPARISON OR CONTRAST use the citing work as the acting subject. This shift in perspective causes cognitive inconsistency and makes the annotation process more confusing.

(3) Lack of a Functionally Grounded Intention Framework. Moreover, the underlying citation intent is not always clearly specified. For example, a citation marked as COMPARISON OR CONTRAST might align findings, methods, or conceptual framing, but whether the comparison serves to justify a design, critique a precedent, or merely provide context depends entirely on the citing author's functional goal. Existing frameworks offer no mechanism for disambiguating these divergent functions, leaving the predicative action of the citation act ambiguous. Without an explicit model separating the author's action from the object of that action, annotation relies on inference and subjective interpretation, which reduces reproducibility and cross-annotator agreement.

3.2 The SOFT Citation Annotation Framework

We propose **SOFT**, a two-dimensional citation annotation framework designed to overcome core limitations of previous citation classification systems. SOFT directly addresses three major problems: (1) entanglement of content type and citation function, (2) inconsistent annotation perspectives, and (3) ambiguous or underspecified citation intent.

First, SOFT explicitly disentangles **Cited Content Type** (what specific content is referenced from the cited work) from **Citation Intent** (why the citing work refers to that content), thus resolving the long-standing problem of dimensional entanglement, ensuring each dimension is orthogonal and semantically bounded, greatly reducing ambiguity and cognitive load.

Second, SOFT maintains a unified authorial perspective by consistently modeling the action of the citing work. This approach is grounded in semantic role theory [6,20,21,44], which decomposes events into predicates (actions) and arguments (participants or entities involved). In SOFT, citation intent always corresponds to the action or communicative function performed by the citing work, such as "use X from [cited work]", "modify X from [cited work]", or "evaluate against X from [cited work]", where X is the specific cited content. These intents, like "use" or "modify", align with classic event predicates in semantic role theory. Other intents in SOFT, such as "contextualize using X from [cited work]", "signal a gap using X from [cited work]", "highlight a limitation in X from [cited work]", or "justify a design choice based on X from [cited work]", capture broader discourse actions in scientific writing. While these latter cases extend beyond simple event predicates, all SOFT intent types are defined to specify what the citing work is doing, ensuring each annotation remains grounded in a clear and consistent authorial perspective.

Third, SOFT provides explicit, semantically precise definitions for all citation intent types, ensuring the underlying authorial purpose is clearly specified in every case. For instance, we rephrase BACKGROUND (used in ACL-ARC, SciCite, and ACT/ACT2) as CONTEXTUALIZE to mark deliberate authorial moves, and rephrase EXTENSION as MODIFY to capture not only extension but also reduction, replacement, or novel combination. We replace the citation function MOTIVATION(present in ACL-ARC and ACT/ACT2) with SIGNALGAP and

HIGHLIGHTLIMITATION, which allow for a fine-grained distinction between identifying a research gap and highlighting a limitation. To further reduce ambiguity, we eliminate the type COMPARISON OR CONTRAST (in ACL-ARC), which is often confused in practice, and instead introduce JUSTIFYDESIGNCHOICE for decision justification and EVALUATEAGAINST for direct empirical comparison.

The SOFT type inventory was empirically derived and iteratively refined using diverse datasets and existing frameworks (including SciCite, ACL-ARC, and CiTO), systematically resolving label ambiguity and mixed semantic scope. As a result, SOFT yields a more interpretable and robust annotation framework, improving both human agreement and model generalizability for tasks such as discourse analysis and citation influence detection. Below, we detail the two core dimensions of the framework.

Dimension 1: Cited Content Type captures the ontological status of the contribution being referenced in the cited work. We distinguish three types:
(1) PERFORMEDWORK: The citing work references what the cited work *did* (e.g., experimental process, pipeline design), without isolating specific outcomes or reusable resources. *Example: "[cited work] developed an NLP pipeline."*
(2) DISCOVERY: The citing work references observations, findings, or theoretical conclusions made by the cited work. *Example: "[cited work] observed that dropout improves stability."*
(3) PRODUCEDRESOURCE: The citing work references reusable outputs such as datasets, algorithms, models, tools, metrics, standardized settings, etc. *Example: "We use the parser from [cited work]."*
These distinctions support fine-grained analysis of how different forms of scientific contribution are referenced, reused, or framed in scholarly discourse.

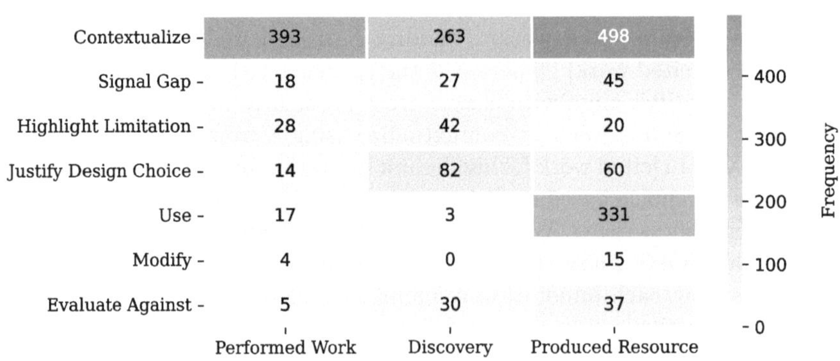

Fig. 1. Type Statistics for the re-annotated ACL-ARC Dataset.

Dimension 2: Citation Intent characterizes the predicative function of the citation, representing the action performed by the citing author. Each label is defined as a predicate that takes the cited content as one of its core arguments. We frame each label from the perspective of the citing author as the agent of the citation action.

(1) Contextualize: The cited work is mentioned to provide background, illustrate prior research, or describe related contributions. No design decision or reuse is involved. *Example: "[cited work] introduced hierarchical attention for sentiment analysis."*

(2) SignalGap: The citation highlights an unresolved problem or open question. The gap may be identified by the cited work or the citing work, and no commitment to solving it is required. *Example: "[cited work] noted that tuning remains underexplored."*

(3) HighlightLimitation: The citing work or cited work identifies a flaw, constraint, or drawback in the cited method or result. This type is used only when the cited contribution is explicitly critiqued. *Example: "[cited work] fails to capture domain drift in user behavior."*

(4) JustifyDesignChoice: The citing work supports a design or methodological decision by referencing the cited work. No direct reuse is required, but the author must commit to a choice. *Example: "We follow [cited work]'s feature grouping to ensure consistency."* This type does not apply if the action is merely hypothetical (e.g., "we could follow ...").

(5) Use: The citing work directly applies a reusable contribution (e.g., model, process, settings, definitions) from the cited work. The citing author must be the actor, meaning statements like "[cited work] used..." do not qualify. Only past or present-tense application counts; plans or hypothetical uses are not 'Use'. *Example: "We use [cited work]'s BERT-based classifier."*

(6) Modify: The citing work alters or extends a reusable contribution from the cited work, such as by adapting configurations, changing algorithms, or integrating with a new pipeline. *Example: "We adapt [cited work]'s encoder for multi-domain inputs."*

(7) EvaluateAgainst: The citing work explicitly compares its own findings and results with those of the cited work, typically to establish effectiveness. *Example: "Our model outperforms [cited work]'s method on F_1 score."*

These citation intent types are designed to be mutually exclusive, which can be combined with content types for multi-dimensional interpretation.

Design Rationale and Applications. By structurally separating citation intent from cited content type, SOFT resolves ambiguities common in one-dimensional frameworks. For example, citing a model without applying it is annotated as Contextualize:ProducedResource, while referring to an unresolved issue is SignalGap:Discovery. Only when the citing author explicitly acts, e.g., reuses, modifies, justifies, or critiques, is an active intent assigned. This orthogonality supports consistent labeling across citation contexts and improves annotation reliability. SOFT's two-dimensional design also enhances downstream applications. Separating gap signaling from design justification enables clearer modeling of research motivation. Distinguishing between using a tool (USE:PRODUCEDRESOURCE) and referencing a methodological trend (CONTEXTUALIZE:PERFORMEDWORK) supports finer-grained tracking of scientific influence, method lineage, and intent-aware scientific recommendation. As demonstrated in Sect. 5, the SOFT framework yields higher human–LLM agreement, better classification performance, and improved generalizability across scientific domains. We next describe our annotation guidelines and procedures, including the re-annotation of ACL-ARC and a cross-domain sample from ACT2.

4 Experiments

4.1 Datasets and Re-annotation Procedure

Datasets Overview. The ACL-ARC dataset [28] is a standard CIC benchmark, yet its annotation framework exhibits the conceptual conflation and boundary issues discussed in Sect. 3.1. To resolve these shortcomings, we re-annotate the entire dataset using our two-dimensional SOFT framework, thereby providing a refined and semantically coherent resource.

For our experiments, we adopt the context-expanded version of ACL-ARC provided by [39], which enhances the original dataset by adding broader citation contexts and structured metadata, such as the citing and cited paper titles and the section in which the citation appears. Before re-annotation, we manually cleaned the dataset to correct systemic text extraction errors, such as misaligned page breaks and disrupted reading orders, and incorrectly sequenced footnotes. Additionally, we recovered 533 missing section headings from the original paper PDFs to improve contextual understanding. The ACL-ARC dataset contains 1,931 citation instances. Following the original data split in [28], we adopt the same partitioning: 1,647 instances are used for training and 284 for testing.

To evaluate cross-domain generalizability, we also re-annotated a subset (264 examples) of the ACT2 test set [40]. ACT2 spans 19 top-level scientific domains from Microsoft Academic Graph (MAG), with dominant fields including Psychology (21.99%), Medicine (13.48%), Biology (10.91%), and Computer Science (10.27%). These examples serve as our out-of-distribution test data, enabling strict evaluation of generalization performance. The division of training and test sets ensures that citation instances from the same source document do not appear in both sets, preventing data leakage and preserving evaluation integrity.

Re-Annotation Procedure. The re-annotation process was conducted by a team of graduate students in computational linguistics. To ensure reliability and account for interpretive ambiguity, each citation instance was independently labeled by at least three annotators using our revised two-dimensional framework. Disagreements were flagged and subsequently resolved through structured group discussion, in which annotators reviewed framework definitions and deliberated to reach a consensus type for each case. This multi-pass strategy helped enforce type consistency and refine interpretation standards across annotators. Types of statistics for the re-annotated ACL-ARC are reported in Fig. 1.

4.2 Evaluating Framework Interpretability and Annotation Reliability

A core indicator of annotation framework quality is Inter-Annotator Agreement (IAA), reflecting how clearly and consistently its types are defined [5,9]. However, IAA was not reported in the original ACL-ARC release [28], leaving the interpretability of its framework unquantified. In this study, we also do not report human IAA due to the dynamic annotation process: some annotators departed and new ones joined partway through the task, so not all instances were annotated by the same set of individuals, and the number of annotations per instance varied. This evolving annotator pool is resembles the crowdsourcing approach used for the SciCite dataset [14], where calculating a dataset-wide human IAA score also presents challenges. Instead, we evaluate framework interpretability and reliability through LLM-based agreement studies.

To assess the clarity and reliability of our framework, we conducted an agreement experiment using open-source LLMs as proxies for human annotators, offering a scalable and replicable assessment of annotation feasibility. Specifically, we deployed four distinct LLMs: *Qwen-2.5-72B-Instruct* (Qwen) [48], *Mistral-Small-24B-Instruct-2501* (Mistral) [38], *Llama-3.3-70B-Instruct* (Llama) [58], and *Gemma-3-27B-it* (Gemma) [57], to independently annotate the ACL-ARC citation contexts according to our framework and guidelines. For each context, every LLM generated a rationale and a classification decision, repeated three times, with the final type determined by majority vote. We then computed pairwise Cohen's κ scores [16] under two settings: (1) between model pairs (LLM-LLM IAA), and (2) between each model and the human consensus annotations described in Sect. 4.1 (Human-LLM IAA). The latter measures how well the framework enables LLMs to approximate expert human judgments.

As a comparative baseline, we repeated the process with both the six-type ACL-ARC framework and the three-type SciCite framework [14], instructing the same LLMs to annotate ACL-ARC contexts. For ACL-ARC framework, annotations were made on its original dataset. For SciCite, we mapped ACL-ARC types onto SciCite's framework by aligning USES with METHOD, COMPARISONCONTRAST with RESULTCOMPARISON, and grouping BACKGROUND, EXTENSION, MOTIVATION, and FUTURE under BACKGROUND.

This LLM-based simulation serves as a practical proxy for human agreement and enables direct empirical comparison across frameworks. The resulting IAA scores provide a quantifiable measure of boundary clarity, interpretability, and annotation feasibility under the SOFT framework.

4.3 Testing Orthogonality and Interpretive Clarity via Classification

To empirically evaluate whether our revised annotation framework offers clearer semantic boundaries than prior frameworks, we conducted a comparative classification experiment. This design is grounded in the hypothesis, motivated by prior work in framework comparison [26,49], that if a framework defines types with more precise and less ambiguous boundaries, then machine learning models trained on such data should achieve higher classification performance.

Classifiers. We employed two open-source, state-of-the-art CIC models with distinct architectures:

- **CitePrompt** [32]: A prompt-based fine-tuning framework built on SciBERT [10], implemented via the OpenPrompt toolkit [19].
- **CitationIntentOpenLLM** [29]: A LLM classifier based on **Qwen-2.5-14B-Instruct** (Qwen-Small), fine-tuned using LLaMA-Factory toolkit [66].

In addition to these fine-tuned models, we also evaluated the performance of several zero-shot classifiers using the LLMs introduced in Sect. 4.1.

The selection of classifiers in this study was guided by a deliberate and strong preference for open-source models over closed-source alternatives. This commitment is crucial for several reasons fundamental to rigorous scientific inquiry. Firstly, utilizing publicly available models like SciBERT and various instruction-tuned LLMs ensures the transparency and reproducibility of our research. This allows other researchers to independently verify our findings and build upon our work without the "black box" nature or access restrictions often associated with proprietary systems. Secondly, open-source models grant the critical flexibility required for in-depth analysis and custom fine-tuning, as demonstrated by our use of LLaMA-Factory for adapting Qwen-Small. Such granular control over model architecture and training processes, often unavailable with closed-source APIs, is paramount for rigorously evaluating new annotation frameworks like SOFT and understanding nuanced model behavior. Finally, relying on open-source solutions promotes broader accessibility and fosters a collaborative research environment, which is essential for advancing the field of computational bibliometrics, unhindered by commercial licensing or opaque model mechanics.

Evaluation Metrics. Following prior CIC evaluation protocols [29,32], we report both **Accuracy** and **Macro-averaged F_1 score**. While Accuracy provides an overall measure of correct predictions, Macro F_1 computes the average F_1 score across classes, mitigating the effects of label imbalance and better reflecting type-level learnability.

4.4 Evaluating Cross-Domain Generalizability on ACT2

To assess whether our revised framework supports generalizable citation intent classification across disciplinary contexts, we conducted a transfer evaluation using the test subset of ACT2 [40], a multi-domain benchmark that spans biology, medicine, economics, and computer science. As discussed in Sect. 2.1, ACT2 adopts a flat framework derived from ACL-ARC. To adapt it for our evaluation, we selected a representative subset of ACT2 as cross-domain test dataset and applied the same re-annotation protocol described in Sect. 4.1 using our two-dimensional framework. For a controlled comparison, we reused the same classification models (CitePrompt, CitationIntentOpenLLM, and zero-shot LLMs) and evaluation metrics (Accuracy and Macro F_1) from Sect. 4.3. This alignment allows us to directly assess whether our framework enhances cross-domain robustness and preserves semantic clarity under domain shift.

5 Results and Analysis

We evaluate the SOFT framework along three axes: interpretability, in-domain learnability, and cross-domain generalizability. Results are compared against two existing citation frameworks, ACL-ARC and SciCite.

Table 1. Pairwise Cohen's κ between LLMs and human annotators.

(a) ACL-ARC Framework (6 types)

	Llama	Mistral	Gemma	Qwen
Mistral	0.5833			
Gemma	0.4504	0.3860		
Qwen	0.5776	0.6013	0.3600	
HUMAN	0.3956	0.4048	0.4302	0.3809

(b) SciCite Framework (3 types)

	Llama	Mistral	Gemma	Qwen
Mistral	0.6363			
Gemma	0.6855	0.6423		
Qwen	0.6762	0.7151	0.6928	
HUMAN	0.4016	0.3850	0.4618	0.4116

(c) SOFT: Cited Content Type (3 types)

	Llama	Mistral	Gemma	Qwen
Mistral	0.5396			
Gemma	0.5751	0.5657		
Qwen	0.5496	0.6169	0.5717	
HUMAN	0.5193	0.4932	**0.5901**	0.5596

(d) SOFT: Citation Intent (7 types)

	Llama	Mistral	Gemma	Qwen
Mistral	0.6154			
Gemma	0.5941	0.5949		
Qwen	0.6282	0.5887	0.6175	
HUMAN	0.6620	0.6070	0.6232	**0.6918**

Interpretability and Agreement. We assess framework clarity using pairwise Cohen's κ across four pre-trained LLMs (LLM-LLM) and between LLM predictions and human consensus labels (Human-LLM). As expected, SciCite achieves the highest LLM-LLM agreement due to its coarse granularity. However, as shown in Table 1, SOFT offers significantly higher Human-LLM agreement, especially for the **Citation Intent** dimension ($\kappa = 0.662$ for Llama, 0.692 for Qwen). Despite being conceptually more complex, **Cited Content Type** also outperforms ACL-ARC and SciCite in Human-LLM agreement, indicating that both dimensions are interpretable and consistently applicable.

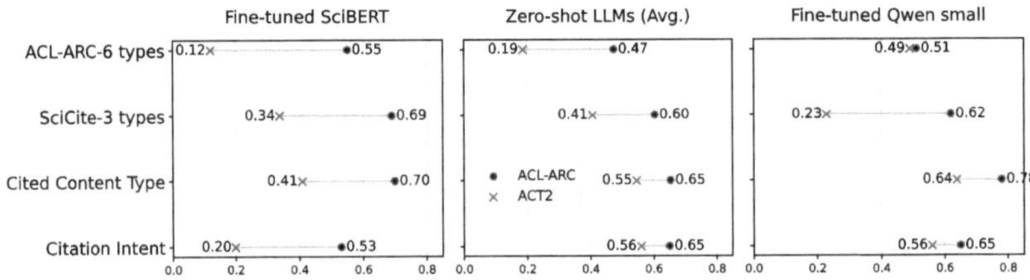

Fig. 2. Comparison of in-domain and cross-domain macro F_1 scores across four annotation frameworks. Each subplot corresponds to a model type, with blue circles denoting in-domain and red crosses indicating cross-domain performance.

In-Domain Learnability. We evaluate the classification performance of both fine-tuned and zero-shot models on the ACL-ARC test set using three annotation frameworks: ACL-ARC, SciCite, and SOFT. In the SOFT framework, **Cited Content Type** and **Citation Intent** are treated as two independent classification tasks. Table 2 and Fig. 3 in Appendix B report accuracy and macro F_1 scores across all models. Despite its conceptual specificity, **Cited Content Type** classification yields strong in-domain performance. Fine-tuned Qwen-Small achieves 0.78 macro F_1, while zero-shot models average 0.66. Although no existing framework provides a comparable baseline, these results demonstrate that content type distinctions are not only human-interpretable but also model-learnable across architectures. SOFT also outperforms prior frameworks on **Citation Intent** classification. For example, fine-tuned Qwen-Small achieves 0.65 macro F_1 under SOFT, compared to 0.51 on ACL-ARC and 0.62 on SciCite. Notably, this gain occurs even though SOFT-Intent has more types (7) than ACL-ARC (6), refuting the assumption that performance is merely a function of label count. This suggests the framework's semantic clarity and well-defined boundaries are more critical to model performance than raw granularity. The average zero-shot F_1 under SOFT reinforces this point, reaching 0.69, substantially above ACL-ARC (0.49) and SciCite (0.61), demonstrating that SOFT's functional types align more closely with both pre-trained and fine-tuned model representations.

We note that our reported scores are lower than those in prior work, including CitePrompt [32], which may be attributed to differences in dataset partitioning, as discussed in Sect. 4.1.

Cross-Domain Generalizability. To assess the robustness of different frameworks under domain shift, we evaluate models trained on ACL-ARC directly on a re-annotated subset of ACT2. No further fine-tuning or domain adaptation is performed. Table 2 and Fig. 3 in Appendix B report both accuracy and macro

F_1 scores, highlighting how well each framework generalizes beyond the original training domain. Despite its conceptual complexity, **Cited Content Type** classification generalizes well. Zero-shot LLMs maintain solid performance (average F_1 drop 17%), and fine-tuned Qwen-Small drops moderately (0.78 to 0.64), suggesting that these content distinctions remain stable across domain shifts. SOFT-trained models exhibit superior generalizability on **Citation Intent** classification. Fine-tuned Qwen-Small drops from 0.65 to 0.56 (SOFT), outperforming ACL-ARC (0.51 to 0.49) and SciCite (0.62 to 0.23). Zero-shot performance mirrors this trend (Fig. 2). SOFT's average F_1 drop is only 15.8% (vs. 30–65% for other frameworks), suggesting its discourse-grounded intent types generalize more robustly.

Dimension-Wise Comparison. A dimension-wise analysis reveals distinct model behaviors. In-domain, zero-shot LLMs perform better on **Citation Intent** (avg. F_1: 0.69) than **Cited Content Type** (0.66), suggesting these functions align well with LLM priors. With fine-tuning, however, **Cited Content Type** becomes more learnable (Qwen-Small F_1: 0.78 vs. 0.65 for intent), indicating its distinctions benefit more from supervision. Cross-domain generalization is competitive for both dimensions, with fine-tuned Qwen showing only modest performance drops on both content (Qwen-Small: 18%; SciBERT: 41%) and intent (Qwen-Small: 14%; SciBERT: 62%). This highlights SOFT's stability under domain shift and the superior transferability of fine-tuned Qwen over SciBERT.

Overall Analysis. Across all experiments, the SOFT framework consistently outperforms ACL-ARC and SciCite in interpretability, learnability, and cross-domain robustness. Fine-tuned Qwen-Small achieves the best results on **Cited Content Type**, while Qwen zero-shot achieves top performance on **Citation Intent**. These findings establish SOFT as a semantically orthogonal and generalizable alternative for citation annotation.

6 Conclusion

This paper introduces the SOFT framework, a semantically orthogonal framework with two dimensions for citation annotation that disentangles *cited content type* from *citation intent*. By addressing the conceptual conflation and boundary ambiguity in existing frameworks, SOFT provides clearer interpretive definitions and better supports both human annotation and model-based classification. Empirical evaluations across LLM agreement, in-domain classification, and cross-domain generalization confirm SOFT's advantages. The *citation intent* dimension demonstrates high zero-shot and fine-tuned performance, while the *cited content type* dimension, despite its semantic complexity, proves learnable and transferable. Compared to ACL-ARC and SciCite, SOFT consistently achieves higher human-LLM agreement, stronger in-domain macro F_1, and more stable cross-domain generalization. These gains are especially pronounced for instruction-tuned LLMs, which preserve broader generalization after fine-tuning.

Future work will explore extending SOFT to support multi-label citation contexts, integrating finer-grained functional types, and applying the framework to large-scale citation graphs for discourse-level functional modeling, influence tracking, and knowledge extraction.

Acknowledgment. Changxu Duan was funded by the Federal Ministry of Education and Research (BMBF) under grant no. 01UG2130A, as part of the InsightsNet research project (insightsnet.org). Zhiyin Tan was funded by the "HybrInt - Hybrid Intelligence through Interpretable AI in Machine Perception and Interaction" project (Zukunft Nds, Niedersächsisches Ministerium für Wissenschaft, Grant ID: ZN4219). We thank Dr. Sabine Bartsch for proofreading. We also thank the anonymous reviewers for their insightful comments and suggestions.

Appendix

A Overall Model Performance

Table 2 presents the overall performance of the evaluated models across the ACL-ARC, SciCite, and our proposed SOFT frameworks, for both in-domain (ACL-ARC test set) and cross-domain (re-annotated ACT2 test set) scenarios. The performance is measured by accuracy and macro-F_1 score.

B Per-Type Analysis Across Frameworks and Models

To gain a more granular understanding of model behavior and framework characteristics, we visualize the per-class F_1-scores for both in-domain and cross-domain settings using radar plots, as shown in Fig. 3. Each plot depicts the performance of a specific model across the classes of a given framework, with blue representing in-domain and red representing cross-domain F_1 Scores. These visualizations allow for a direct comparison of how well individual classes are learned and how performance on these classes transfers across domains.

Across ACL-ARC and SciCite, only a few types achieve consistently learnable performance. In ACL-ARC, USES (F_1 = 0.60–0.72) and FUTURE (F_1 = 0.70–0.80) are reliably detected across models, while types like MOTIVATION (F_1 = 0.06–0.27) and extends (F_1 = 0.17–0.24) exhibit uniformly poor results, regardless of model type. In SciCite, background and method achieve moderate F_1 (up to 0.83 and 0.69), but RESULTCOMPARISON remains consistently weak ($F_1 \leq 0.47$, recall < 0.5). These patterns suggest semantic overlap and label fuzziness in legacy frameworks, especially for tasks that require disambiguating subtle intent.

The SOFT framework, in contrast, features multiple types that are both conceptually precise and computationally learnable. Zero-shot LLMs perform well on USE (F_1 = 0.79–0.90), CONTEXTUALIZE (0.78–0.86), and PRODUCEDRESOURCE (0.76–0.82), while the fine-tuned LLM (Qwen-small) outperforms all other models on discovery and PRODUCEDRESOURCE (both F_1 = 0.82). More difficult types like PERFORMEDWORK show a large performance gap in F_1 score (LLMs: 0.37–0.57, Qwen-small: 0.69, SciBERT: 0.79), indicating that domain-adaptive fine-tuning is crucial when lexical variation is high. For JUSTIFYDESIGNCHOICE, zero-shot LLM Llama (F_1 = 0.72) outperforms both fine-tuned models (Qwen-small: F_1 = 0.45, SciBERT: F_1 = 0.42), suggesting that general discourse modeling, rather than label-specific exposure, governs success.

Precision-recall asymmetries further differentiate framework quality. In SciCite, the method exhibits high recall (e.g., zero-shot LLMs: 0.86–0.94) but low precision (e.g., zero-shot LLMs: 0.4–0.53), indicating label overgeneralization. In SOFT, several types, including JUSTIFYDESIGNCHOICE and performed work, exhibit the opposite: high precision (e.g., Qwen: 0.79) but low recall (e.g., Mistral: 0.28), showing that models can detect prototypical cases but struggle with broader coverage. Notably, SIGNALGAP (Qwen: precision 0.81, recall 0.68) and METHOD (SciBERT: precision 0.64, recall 0.76) achieve better balance. These contrasts affirm that our SOFT framework not only yields more distinguishable and learnable labels but also makes model errors more interpretable, enabling both zero-shot application and targeted fine-tuning.

C Computational Resources and Software

We adopted the original hyperparameter settings from CitePrompt [32] and CitationIntentOpenLLM [29]. All experiments were conducted on a single H100 GPU, including both fine-tuning and inference. For LLM inference, we used the vLLM library [31]. Fine-tuning required approximately 5 GPU-hours, and inference consumed an additional 4 GPU-hours in total.

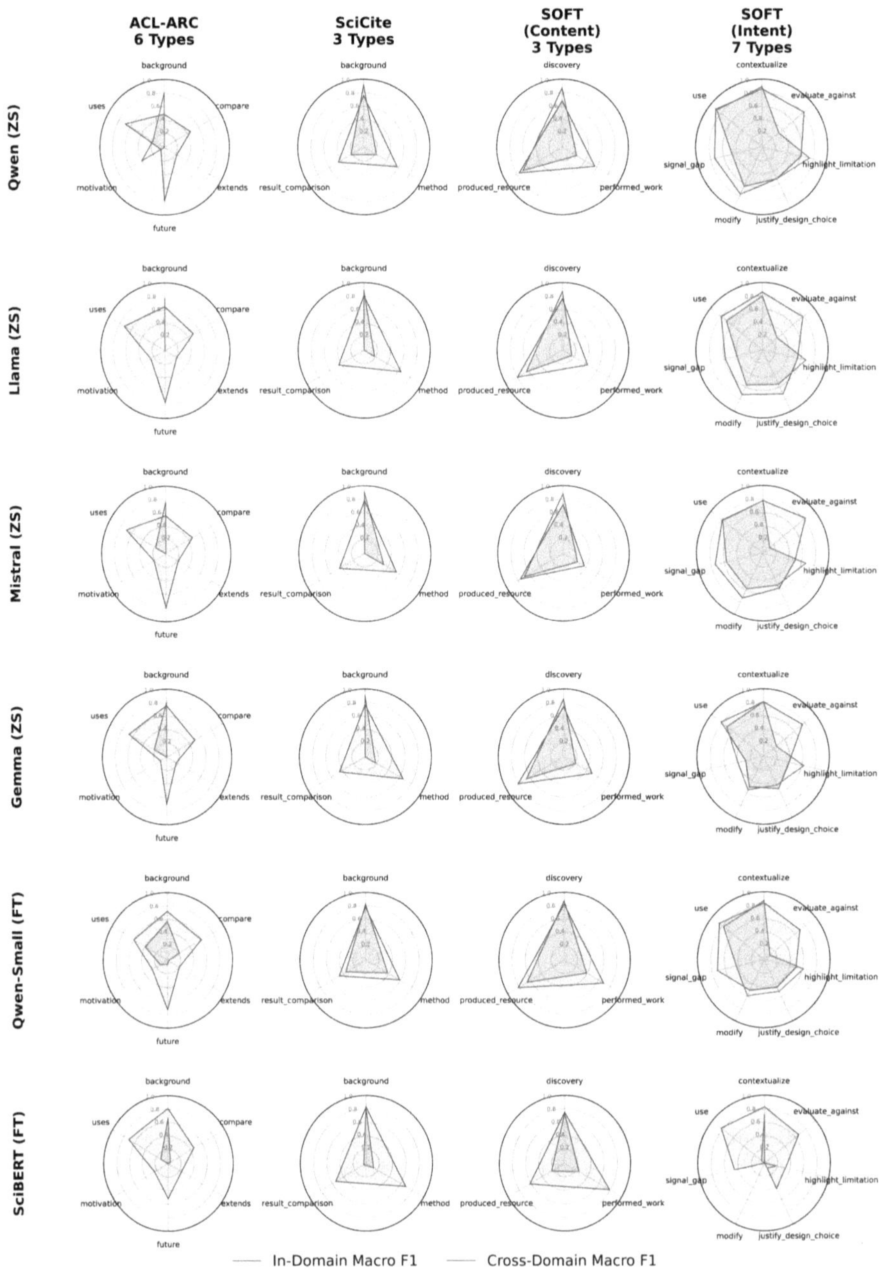

Fig. 3. Grid of radar plots (4 frameworks × 6 models) showing per-class F1-scores. Blue lines/areas represent In-Domain F1 scores, and red lines/areas represent Cross-Domain F1 scores. Each axis corresponds to a class label within the respective framework. F1-scores range from 0 (center) to 1 (outer edge).

Table 2. In-domain and cross-domain performance of citation classification models (zero-shot: "ZS", fine-tuned: "FT") across frameworks.

Framework	Classifier	In-Domain (ACL-ARC)		Cross-Domain (ACT2)	
		Accuracy	Macro F_1	Accuracy	Macro F_1
ACL-ARC (6 types)	ZS Llama	0.58	0.52	0.60	0.13 (75%↓)
	ZS Mistral	0.54	0.49	0.59	0.16 (67%↓)
	ZS Gemma	0.65	0.48	0.62	0.17 (65%↓)
	ZS Qwen	0.48	0.45	**0.63**	0.23 (49%↓)
	FT SciBERT	**0.66**	**0.55**	0.47	0.12 (78%↓)
	FT Qwen-Small	0.65	0.51	0.58	**0.49** (4%↓)
SciCite (3 types)	ZS Llama	0.72	0.63	0.80	0.37 (54%↓)
	ZS Mistral	0.67	0.59	0.81	0.41 (31%↓)
	ZS Gemma	0.70	0.63	0.80	0.36 (43%↓)
	ZS Qwen	0.67	0.59	**0.84**	**0.45** (24%↓)
	FT SciBERT	**0.77**	**0.69**	0.66	0.34 (51%↓)
	FT Qwen-Small	0.69	0.61	0.40	0.23 (63%↓)
SOFT: Cited Content Type (3 types)	ZS Llama	0.73	0.67	0.75	0.55 (18%↓)
	ZS Mistral	0.67	0.62	**0.78**	0.46 (26%↓)
	ZS Gemma	0.74	0.68	0.73	0.58 (15%↓)
	ZS Qwen	0.70	0.67	0.77	0.60 (10%↓)
	FT SciBERT	0.70	0.70	0.58	0.41 (41%↓)
	FT Qwen-Small	**0.79**	**0.78**	0.75	**0.64** (18%↓)
SOFT: Citation Intent (7 types)	ZS Llama	0.79	0.72	0.72	0.57 (21%↓)
	ZS Mistral	0.74	0.71	0.69	0.57 (20%↓)
	ZS Gemma	0.71	0.59	0.71	0.55 (7%↓)
	ZS Qwen	**0.81**	**0.75**	**0.82**	**0.64** (15%↓)
	FT SciBERT	0.72	0.53	0.52	0.20 (62%↓)
	FT Qwen-Small	0.77	0.65	0.77	0.56 (14%↓)

Color Legend: ≤20% drop , 21–40% drop , >40% drop in cross-domain Macro F_1.

References

1. Abu-Jbara, A., Ezra, J., Radev, D.: Purpose and polarity of citation: towards NLP-based bibliometrics. In: Vanderwende, L., Daumé III, H., Kirchhoff, K. (eds.) Proceedings of the 2013 Conference of the North American Chapter of the Association for Computational Linguistics: Human Language Technologies, pp. 596–606. Association for Computational Linguistics, Atlanta, Georgia (2013). https://aclanthology.org/N13-1067/
2. Allen Institute for AI: Semantic Scholar (2025). https://www.semanticscholar.org/

3. Anderson, M.H., Lemken, R.K.: Citation context analysis as a method for conducting rigorous and impactful literature reviews. Organ. Res. Methods **26**(1), 77–106 (2020). https://doi.org/10.1177/1094428120969905
4. Araabi, A., Niculae, V., Monz, C.: Joint dropout: improving generalizability in low-resource neural machine translation through phrase pair variables. In: Utiyama, M., Wang, R. (eds.) Proceedings of Machine Translation Summit XIX, Vol. 1: Research Track, pp. 12–25. Asia-Pacific Association for Machine Translation, Macau SAR, China (2023). https://aclanthology.org/2023.mtsummit-research.2/
5. Artstein, R., Poesio, M.: Survey article: inter-coder agreement for computational linguistics. Comput. Linguist. **34**(4), 555–596 (2008). https://doi.org/10.1162/coli.07-034-R2. https://aclanthology.org/J08-4004/
6. Baker, C.F., Fillmore, C.J., Lowe, J.B.: The Berkeley FrameNet project. In: 36th Annual Meeting of the Association for Computational Linguistics and 17th International Conference on Computational Linguistics, Volume 1, pp. 86–90. Association for Computational Linguistics, Montreal, Quebec, Canada (1998). https://doi.org/10.3115/980845.980860. https://aclanthology.org/P98-1013/
7. Bascur, J.P., Verberne, S., van Eck, N.J., Waltman, L.: Academic information retrieval using citation clusters: in-depth evaluation based on systematic reviews. Scientometrics **128**(5), 2895–2921 (2023). https://doi.org/10.1007/s11192-023-04681-x
8. Bassignana, E., Plank, B.: CrossRE: a cross-domain dataset for relation extraction. In: Goldberg, Y., Kozareva, Z., Zhang, Y. (eds.) Findings of the Association for Computational Linguistics: EMNLP 2022, pp. 3592–3604. Association for Computational Linguistics, Abu Dhabi, United Arab Emirates (2022). https://doi.org/10.18653/v1/2022.findings-emnlp.263. https://aclanthology.org/2022.findings-emnlp.263/
9. Bayerl, P.S., Paul, K.I.: What determines inter-coder agreement in manual annotations? A meta-analytic investigation. Comput. Linguist. **37**(4), 699–725 (2011). https://doi.org/10.1162/COLI_a_00074. https://aclanthology.org/J11-4004/
10. Beltagy, I., Lo, K., Cohan, A.: SciBERT: a pretrained language model for scientific text. In: Inui, K., Jiang, J., Ng, V., Wan, X. (eds.) Proceedings of the 2019 Conference on Empirical Methods in Natural Language Processing and the 9th International Joint Conference on Natural Language Processing (EMNLP-IJCNLP), pp. 3615–3620. Association for Computational Linguistics, Hong Kong, China (2019). https://doi.org/10.18653/v1/D19-1371. https://aclanthology.org/D19-1371/
11. Berrebbi, D., Huynh, N., Balalau, O.: Graphcite: citation intent classification in scientific publications via graph embeddings, pp. 779–783. WWW 2022: The ACM Web Conference 2022. ACM (2022). https://doi.org/10.1145/3487553.3524657
12. Chen, Y., et al.: CDEvalSumm: an empirical study of cross-dataset evaluation for neural summarization systems. In: Cohn, T., He, Y., Liu, Y. (eds.) Findings of the Association for Computational Linguistics: EMNLP 2020, pp. 3679–3691. Association for Computational Linguistics, Online (2020). https://doi.org/10.18653/v1/2020.findings-emnlp.329. https://aclanthology.org/2020.findings-emnlp.329/
13. Clarivate Analytics: Web of Science (2025). https://www.webofscience.com/
14. Cohan, A., Ammar, W., van Zuylen, M., Cady, F.: Structural scaffolds for citation intent classification in scientific publications. In: Burstein, J., Doran, C., Solorio, T. (eds.) Proceedings of the 2019 Conference of the North American Chapter of the Association for Computational Linguistics: Human Language Technologies, Volume 1 (Long and Short Papers), pp. 3586–3596. Association for Computational Linguistics, Minneapolis, Minnesota (2019). https://doi.org/10.18653/v1/N19-1361. https://aclanthology.org/N19-1361/

15. Cohen, A.M., Hersh, W.R., Peterson, K., Yen, P.Y.: Reducing workload in systematic review preparation using automated citation classification. J. Am. Med. Inform. Assoc. **13**(2), 206–219 (2006). https://doi.org/10.1197/jamia.m1929
16. Cohen, J.: A coefficient of agreement for nominal scales. Educ. Psychol. Measur. **20**(1), 37–46 (1960). https://doi.org/10.1177/001316446002000104
17. Dardas, L.A., Sallam, M., Woodward, A., Sweis, N., Sweis, N., Sawair, F.A.: Evaluating research impact based on semantic scholar highly influential citations, total citations, and altmetric attention scores: the quest for refined measures remains illusive. Publications **11**(1), 5 (2023). https://doi.org/10.3390/publications11010005
18. Devlin, J., Chang, M.W., Lee, K., Toutanova, K.: BERT: pre-training of deep bidirectional transformers for language understanding. In: Burstein, J., Doran, C., Solorio, T. (eds.) Proceedings of the 2019 Conference of the North American Chapter of the Association for Computational Linguistics: Human Language Technologies, Volume 1 (Long and Short Papers), pp. 4171–4186. Association for Computational Linguistics, Minneapolis, Minnesota (2019). https://doi.org/10.18653/v1/N19-1423. https://aclanthology.org/N19-1423/
19. Ding, N., et al.: OpenPrompt: an open-source framework for prompt-learning. In: Basile, V., Kozareva, Z., Stajner, S. (eds.) Proceedings of the 60th Annual Meeting of the Association for Computational Linguistics: System Demonstrations, pp. 105–113. Association for Computational Linguistics, Dublin, Ireland (2022). https://doi.org/10.18653/v1/2022.acl-demo.10. https://aclanthology.org/2022.acl-demo.10/
20. Fillmore, C.J.: The case FRO case. Universals in Linguistic Theory (1968)
21. Fillmore, C.J., et al.: Frame semantics. Cogn. Linguist. Basic Read. **34**, 373–400 (2006)
22. Ghosal, T., Varanasi, K.K., Kordoni, V.: A deep multi-tasking approach leveraging on cited-citing paper relationship for citation intent classification. Scientometrics **129**(2), 767–783 (2023). https://doi.org/10.1007/s11192-023-04811-5
23. Gilardi, F., Alizadeh, M., Kubli, M.: Chatgpt outperforms crowd workers for text-annotation tasks. Proc. Natl. Acad. Sci. **120**(30) (2023). https://doi.org/10.1073/pnas.2305016120
24. Guo, M., Yang, Y., Cer, D., Shen, Q., Constant, N.: MultiReQA: a cross-domain evaluation for retrieval question answering models. In: Ben-David, E., et al. (eds.) Proceedings of the Second Workshop on Domain Adaptation for NLP, pp. 94–104. Association for Computational Linguistics, Kyiv, Ukraine (2021). https://aclanthology.org/2021.adaptnlp-1.10/
25. Hettiachchi, D., et al.: Investigating and mitigating biases in crowdsourced data, pp. 331–334. CSCW 2021: Computer Supported Cooperative Work and Social Computing. ACM (2021). https://doi.org/10.1145/3462204.3481729
26. Ivanova, R.V., Kirrane, S., van Erp, M.: Comparing annotated datasets for named entity recognition in English literature. In: Calzolari, N., et al. (eds.) Proceedings of the Thirteenth Language Resources and Evaluation Conference, pp. 3788–3797. European Language Resources Association, Marseille, France (2022). https://aclanthology.org/2022.lrec-1.404/
27. Jha, R., Jbara, A.A., Qazvinian, V., Radev, D.R.: NLP-driven citation analysis for scientometrics. Nat. Lang. Eng. **23**(1), 93–130 (2016). https://doi.org/10.1017/s1351324915000443
28. Jurgens, D., Kumar, S., Hoover, R., McFarland, D., Jurafsky, D.: Measuring the evolution of a scientific field through citation frames. Trans. Assoc. Com-

put. Linguist. **6**, 391–406 (2018). https://doi.org/10.1162/tacl_a_00028. https://aclanthology.org/Q18-1028/
29. Koloveas, P., Chatzopoulos, S., Vergoulis, T., Tryfonopoulos, C.: Can LLMs predict citation intent? An experimental analysis of in-context learning and fine-tuning on open LLMs (2025). https://arxiv.org/abs/2502.14561
30. Kunnath, S.N., Pride, D., Knoth, P.: Prompting strategies for citation classification. In: Proceedings of the 32nd ACM International Conference on Information and Knowledge Management, CIKM 2023, pp. 1127–1137. Association for Computing Machinery, New York (2023). https://doi.org/10.1145/3583780.3615018
31. Kwon, W., et al.: Efficient memory management for large language model serving with pagedattention. In: Proceedings of the ACM SIGOPS 29th Symposium on Operating Systems Principles (2023)
32. Lahiri, A., Sanyal, D.K., Mukherjee, I.: Citeprompt: using prompts to identify citation intent in scientific papers, pp. 51–55. 2023 ACM/IEEE Joint Conference on Digital Libraries (JCDL). IEEE (2023). https://doi.org/10.1109/jcdl57899.2023.00017
33. Li, K., et al.: Probing out-of-distribution generalization in machine learning for materials (2024). https://arxiv.org/abs/2406.06489
34. Lin, T.-Y., et al.: Microsoft COCO: common objects in context. In: Fleet, D., Pajdla, T., Schiele, B., Tuytelaars, T. (eds.) ECCV 2014. LNCS, vol. 8693, pp. 740–755. Springer, Cham (2014). https://doi.org/10.1007/978-3-319-10602-1_48
35. Lo, K., Wang, L.L., Neumann, M., Kinney, R., Weld, D.: S2ORC: the semantic scholar open research corpus. In: Jurafsky, D., Chai, J., Schluter, N., Tetreault, J. (eds.) Proceedings of the 58th Annual Meeting of the Association for Computational Linguistics, pp. 4969–4983. Association for Computational Linguistics, Online (2020). https://doi.org/10.18653/v1/2020.acl-main.447. https://aclanthology.org/2020.acl-main.447/
36. Meng, R., Lu, W., Huan Chi, Y., Han, S.: Automatic classification of citation function by new linguistic features (2017). http://memray.me/uploads/iconference17-citation-function.pdf
37. Mercier, D., Rizvi, S., Rajashekar, V., Dengel, A., Ahmed, S.: Impactcite: An xlnet-based solution enabling qualitative citation impact analysis utilizing sentiment and intent. In: Proceedings of the 13th International Conference on Agents and Artificial Intelligence, pp. 159–168. SCITEPRESS - Science and Technology Publications (2021). https://doi.org/10.5220/0010235201590168
38. Mistral AI Team: Mistral Small 3 (2025). https://mistral.ai/news/mistral-small-3/
39. Nambanoor Kunnath, S., Pride, D., Knoth, P.: Dynamic context extraction for citation classification. In: He, Y., Ji, H., Li, S., Liu, Y., Chang, C.H. (eds.) Proceedings of the 2nd Conference of the Asia-Pacific Chapter of the Association for Computational Linguistics and the 12th International Joint Conference on Natural Language Processing (Volume 1: Long Papers), pp. 539–549. Association for Computational Linguistics, Online only (2022). https://doi.org/10.18653/v1/2022.aacl-main.41. https://aclanthology.org/2022.aacl-main.41/
40. Nambanoor Kunnath, S., Stauber, V., Wu, R., Pride, D., Botev, V., Knoth, P.: ACT2: a multi-disciplinary semi-structured dataset for importance and purpose classification of citations. In: Calzolari, N., et al. (eds.) Proceedings of the Thirteenth Language Resources and Evaluation Conference, pp. 3398–3406. European Language Resources Association, Marseille, France (2022). https://aclanthology.org/2022.lrec-1.363/

41. Nicholson, J.M., et al.: scite: a smart citation index that displays the context of citations and classifies their intent using deep learning. Quant. Sci. Stud. **2**(3), 882–898 (2021). https://doi.org/10.1162/qss_a_00146
42. Northcutt, C., Jiang, L., Chuang, I.: Confident learning: estimating uncertainty in dataset labels. J. Artif. Intell. Res. **70**, 1373–1411 (2021). https://doi.org/10.1613/jair.1.12125
43. Northcutt, C.G., Athalye, A., Mueller, J.: Pervasive label errors in test sets destabilize machine learning benchmarks. In: Thirty-Fifth Conference on Neural Information Processing Systems Datasets and Benchmarks Track (Round 1) (2021). https://openreview.net/forum?id=XccDXrDNLek
44. Palmer, M., Gildea, D., Kingsbury, P.: The proposition bank: an annotated corpus of semantic roles. Comput. Linguist. **31**(1), 71–106 (2005). https://doi.org/10.1162/0891201053630264. https://aclanthology.org/J05-1004/
45. Pride, D., Knoth, P.: An authoritative approach to citation classification. In: Proceedings of the ACM/IEEE Joint Conference on Digital Libraries in 2020, JCDL 2020, pp. 337–340. Association for Computing Machinery, New York (2020). https://doi.org/10.1145/3383583.3398617
46. Pride, D., Knoth, P.: An authoritative approach to citation classification. JCDL 2020: The ACM/IEEE Joint Conference on Digital Libraries in 2020. ACM (2020). https://doi.org/10.1145/3383583.3398617
47. Qazvinian, V., Radev, D.R.: Scientific paper summarization using citation summary networks. In: Scott, D., Uszkoreit, H. (eds.) Proceedings of the 22nd International Conference on Computational Linguistics (Coling 2008), pp. 689–696. Coling 2008 Organizing Committee, Manchester, UK (2008). https://aclanthology.org/C08-1087/
48. Qwen: Qwen2.5 technical report (2025). https://arxiv.org/abs/2412.15115
49. Riabi, A., Mouilleron, V., Mahamdi, M., Antoun, W., Seddah, D.: Beyond dataset creation: critical view of annotation variation and bias probing of a dataset for online radical content detection. In: Rambow, O., Wanner, L., Apidianaki, M., Al-Khalifa, H., Eugenio, B.D., Schockaert, S. (eds.) Proceedings of the 31st International Conference on Computational Linguistics, pp. 8640–8663. Association for Computational Linguistics, Abu Dhabi, UAE (2025). https://aclanthology.org/2025.coling-main.578/
50. Roman, M., Shahid, A., Khan, S., Koubaa, A., Yu, L.: Citation intent classification using word embedding. IEEE Access **9**, 9982–9995 (2021). https://doi.org/10.1109/access.2021.3050547
51. Rücker, S., Akbik, A.: CleanCoNLL: a nearly noise-free named entity recognition dataset. In: Bouamor, H., Pino, J., Bali, K. (eds.) Proceedings of the 2023 Conference on Empirical Methods in Natural Language Processing, pp. 8628–8645. Association for Computational Linguistics, Singapore (2023). https://doi.org/10.18653/v1/2023.emnlp-main.533. https://aclanthology.org/2023.emnlp-main.533/
52. Shotton, D.: CiTO, the citation typing ontology. J. Biomed. Semant. **1**(Suppl. 1), S6 (2010). https://doi.org/10.1186/2041-1480-1-s1-s6
53. Shui, Z., et al.: Fine-tuning language models on multiple datasets for citation intention classification. In: Al-Onaizan, Y., Bansal, M., Chen, Y.N. (eds.) Findings of the Association for Computational Linguistics: EMNLP 2024, pp. 16718–16732. Association for Computational Linguistics, Miami, Florida, USA (2024). https://doi.org/10.18653/v1/2024.findings-emnlp.974. https://aclanthology.org/2024.findings-emnlp.974/

54. Singh, S., Yadav, A., Jain, J., Shi, H., Johnson, J., Desai, K.: Benchmarking object detectors with coco: a new path forward. In: Leonardis, A., Ricci, E., Roth, S., Russakovsky, O., Sattler, T., Varol, G. (eds.) ECCV 2024, pp. 279–295. Springer, Cham (2025). https://doi.org/10.1007/978-3-031-72784-9_16
55. Spiegel-Rosing, I.: Science studies: bibliometric and content analysis. Soc. Stud. Sci. **7**(1), 97–113 (2 1977). https://doi.org/10.1177/030631277700700111
56. Tan, Z., et al.: Large language models for data annotation and synthesis: a survey. In: Al-Onaizan, Y., Bansal, M., Chen, Y.N. (eds.) Proceedings of the 2024 Conference on Empirical Methods in Natural Language Processing, pp. 930–957. Association for Computational Linguistics, Miami, Florida, USA (2024). https://doi.org/10.18653/v1/2024.emnlp-main.54. https://aclanthology.org/2024.emnlp-main.54/
57. Team, G.: Gemma 3 technical report (2025). https://arxiv.org/abs/2503.19786
58. Team, L.: The llama 3 herd of models (2024). https://arxiv.org/abs/2407.21783
59. Teufel, S.: Argumentative zoning: information extraction from scientific text (1999). https://www.cl.cam.ac.uk/~sht25/thesis/t1.pdf
60. Teufel, S., Siddharthan, A., Tidhar, D.: Automatic classification of citation function. In: Jurafsky, D., Gaussier, E. (eds.) Proceedings of the 2006 Conference on Empirical Methods in Natural Language Processing, pp. 103–110. Association for Computational Linguistics, Sydney, Australia (2006). https://aclanthology.org/W06-1613/
61. Tjong Kim Sang, E.F., De Meulder, F.: Introduction to the CoNLL-2003 shared task: language-independent named entity recognition. In: Proceedings of the Seventh Conference on Natural Language Learning at HLT-NAACL 2003, pp. 142–147 (2003). https://aclanthology.org/W03-0419/
62. Tkachenko, U., Thyagarajan, A., Mueller, J.: Objectlab: automated diagnosis of mislabeled images in object detection data (2023). https://doi.org/10.48550/ARXIV.2309.00832. https://arxiv.org/abs/2309.00832
63. Valenzuela, M., Ha, V., Etzioni, O.: Identifying meaningful citations. In: AAAI Workshop: Scholarly Big Data, vol. 15, p. 13 (2015)
64. Yu, H., Liu, J., Zhang, X., Wu, J., Cui, P.: A survey on evaluation of out-of-distribution generalization (2024). https://arxiv.org/abs/2403.01874
65. Zha, D., et al.: Data-centric artificial intelligence: a survey. ACM Comput. Surv. **57**(5) (2025). https://doi.org/10.1145/3711118
66. Zheng, Y., Zhang, R., Zhang, J., Ye, Y., Luo, Z.: LlamaFactory: unified efficient fine-tuning of 100+ language models. In: Cao, Y., Feng, Y., Xiong, D. (eds.) Proceedings of the 62nd Annual Meeting of the Association for Computational Linguistics (Volume 3: System Demonstrations), pp. 400–410. Association for Computational Linguistics, Bangkok, Thailand (2024). https://doi.org/10.18653/v1/2024.acl-demos.38. https://aclanthology.org/2024.acl-demos.38/
67. Zimmermann, E., Szeto, J., Pasquero, J., Ratle, F.: Benchmarking a benchmark: how reliable is MS-coco? (2023). https://arxiv.org/abs/2311.02709

Can LLMs Predict Citation Intent? An Experimental Analysis of In-Context Learning and Fine-Tuning on Open LLMs

Paris Koloveas[1,2(✉)], Serafeim Chatzopoulos[1], Thanasis Vergoulis[1], and Christos Tryfonopoulos[2]

[1] IMSI, Athena RC, Athens, Greece
{pkoloveas,schatz,vergoulis}@athenarc.gr
[2] University of the Peloponnese, Tripolis, Greece
{pkoloveas,trifon}@uop.gr

Abstract. This work investigates the ability of open Large Language Models (LLMs) to predict citation intent through in-context learning and fine-tuning. Unlike traditional approaches relying on domain-specific pre-trained models like SciBERT, we demonstrate that general-purpose LLMs can be adapted to this task with minimal task-specific data. We evaluate twelve model variations across five prominent open LLM families using zero-, one-, few-, and many-shot prompting. Our experimental study identifies the top-performing model and prompting parameters through extensive in-context learning experiments. We then demonstrate the significant impact of task-specific adaptation by fine-tuning this model, achieving a relative F1-score improvement of 8% on the SciCite dataset and 4.3% on the ACL-ARC dataset compared to the instruction-tuned baseline. These findings provide valuable insights for model selection and prompt engineering. Additionally, we make our end-to-end evaluation framework and models openly available for future use.

1 Introduction

Citations are references of research articles to external sources of information included to support claims, provide context, criticize, or acknowledge prior work. Although their primary function is to inform and redirect the reader, citations are also frequently used for other purposes, such as serving as proxies of scientific impact in various types of analysis [18]. In such cases, understanding the exact intent of a citation is crucial, as not all types of citations should be considered. For instance, while measuring the impact of an article, citations that criticize the work should generally not be considered as contributing to its impact.

Predicting citation intent based on its context (i.e., the sentences in the manuscript that accompany the citation) and other related information, has become an important classification problem to support the aforementioned use cases. Existing approaches have traditionally relied on linguistic features [17], machine learning methods [32], and, recently, on domain-specific pre-trained language models (PLMs), such as SciBERT [3], that require large scientific datasets

W.-T. Balke et al. (Eds.): TPDL 2025, LNCS 16097, pp. 207–224, 2026.
https://doi.org/10.1007/978-3-032-05409-8_13

such as [21] and task-specific architectures[1]. In contrast, this work is the first to explore the potential of open, general-purpose Large Language Models (LLMs) – which, despite potentially encountering scientific text during their broad pre-training, are not specifically optimized for the scientific domain like SciBERT – to accurately identify citation intent, evaluating their effectiveness through in-context learning and fine-tuning on minimal task-specific data.

Large Language Models are advanced natural language processing systems trained on extensive text corpora to perform a wide range of language tasks. Unlike traditional pre-trained language models, LLMs are general-purpose models capable of adapting to new tasks with minimal additional training. Their ability to process and generate coherent text across diverse contexts makes them particularly suitable for tasks like citation intent classification, where understanding nuanced language patterns is essential.

In-context learning is a paradigm that allows LLMs to learn tasks given only a few examples in the form of demonstration [4,8]. In-context learning is particularly suited to citation intent classification, as it allows the models to leverage their contextual understanding of language to make accurate predictions.

In our study, we conduct an extensive experimental analysis of 12 general-purpose Instruction-tuned LLMs from 5 model families, on two widely used datasets for this task. In this context, we analyze the impact of multiple parameters on model performance and identify the optimal configurations and best-performing models for our problem. These experiments address the following research questions:

- *RQ1:* How well can pre-trained LLMs perform on citation intent classification without task-specific training?
- *RQ2:* What are the differences in performance between open LLMs of varying parameter counts?
- *RQ3:* How do different prompting-related parameters affect model performance?

Furthermore, we take the analysis a step further by selecting the top-performing cases from the aforementioned experiments for Supervised Fine-Tuning (SFT) on our datasets, allowing us to evaluate their optimal performance. This essentially addresses an additional research question:

- *RQ4:* How much does supervised fine-tuning with task-specific training affect the performance of the instruction-tuned models?

[1] In this paper, when referring to traditional PLMs in this context, we primarily mean models based on the encoder-only Transformer architecture, such as BERT and its derivatives (e.g., SciBERT), which were commonly fine-tuned for specific classification tasks. This distinguishes them from the general-purpose Large Language Models (LLMs) evaluated in this work, which typically utilize decoder-only or encoder-decoder Transformer architectures and are often leveraged for their generative and in-context learning capabilities.

Our experiments aim to contribute to the broader research community by guiding prompt engineering and model selection strategies for similar tasks. To further assist researchers, we openly[2] provide our complete testing suite and evaluation results, allowing seamless integration of Hugging Face models and easy configuration adjustments. We also publish the weights and checkpoints of the fine-tuned models[3] presented in Sect. 4.

2 Methodology

In this section, we elaborate on the evaluation methodology followed in our experimental study. We first provide an overview of the used models (Sect. 2.1), datasets (Sect. 2.2), and configuration parameters (Sect. 2.3). Finally, in Sect. 2.4, we present the technical specifications of the system we used for the experimentation.

2.1 Models

For our experiments, we selected the Instruction-tuned versions of five prominent open-weight model families: *LLaMA* [11], *Mistral* [15], *Phi* [1], *Gemma* [10], and *Qwen* [2,26]. A key challenge was performing the experiments on commodity hardware, both due to computational limitations and to demonstrate that citation intent classification can be executed efficiently with limited resources. This influenced the selection of models, which range in size from small (1B parameters) to medium-sized (27B parameters).

Since in-context learning inherently increases the number of tokens to each prompt (particularly in the many-shot scenario), we opted for a lower cutoff of 8,192 tokens in the context length. This ensures that all selected models could process the longest prompts in our experiments without truncation.

To reduce the memory footprint and computational requirements of our evaluation, we utilize the 8-bit (Q8) quantized versions of the models. This approach significantly reduces memory usage without compromising performance. *Quantization* involves converting model parameters from higher numerical precisions (e.g. 16-bit floating-point) to formats of lower numerical precision (e.g. 8-bit integers). This process enables more efficient computation and reduced memory usage while largely preserving model performance and expressive power [16].

The model variations used for our evaluation were the following:

- Llama 3 & 3.1 (8B), Llama 3.2 (1B, 3B)
- Mistral Nemo (12B)
- Phi 3 Medium (14B), Phi 3.5 Mini (3.8B)
- Gemma 2 (2B, 9B, 27B)
- Qwen 2 (7B), Qwen 2.5 (14B)

---

[2] https://github.com/athenarc/CitationIntentOpenLLM.

[3] https://huggingface.co/collections/sknow-lab/citationintentllm-67b72f1d5ca6113f960dba04.

2.2 Datasets

For our experiments, we used two datasets:

- *SciCite* [5] consists of 11,021 citation strings annotated with three classes: `Background Information`, `Method`, and `Results Comparison`.
- *ACL-ARC* [17] contains 1,941 citation strings split into six categories: `Background`, `Motivation`, `Uses`, `Extends`, `Compares or Contrasts`, and `Future`.

These two datasets are widely used in citation intent classification research. The SciCite dataset is larger and more diverse, with broad coverage across multiple scientific fields, namely, Computer Science, Medicine, Neuroscience, and Biochemistry, while the ACL-ARC dataset offers a more granular classification scheme, focused on Computational Linguistics. Accross our evaluation, we used the original splits of the datasets, which include training, validation, and test sets (75% - 8% - 17% for SciCite, and 87% - 7% - 6% for ACL-ARC).

2.3 Configuration Parameters

In this section, we describe the configuration parameters of the examined models, including in-context learning methods, system prompts, query templates, example methods, and temperature settings.

In-Context Learning Methods (ILM). To evaluate model performance, we applied four prompting methods[4] by following the In-Context Learning paradigm [4]: *Zero-shot* (no examples), *One-shot* (a single example per class), *Few-shot* (5 examples per class), and *Many-shot* (10 examples per class).

These prompting methods were selected to evaluate whether model performance improves as the number of examples increases, and to identify any saturation point where additional examples yield diminishing or negative returns. This aligns with prior literature on in-context learning methods, where these specific configurations have been extensively studied [8]. Incorporating examples directly into the prompts allows models to better understand the task and the expected output format, which is especially important for citation intent classification, where the citation context is key to determining the correct label.

System Prompts (SP). System prompts (SP) are foundational to our experimental design, establishing the context and expected behavior for the models in the citation intent classification task. They provide task-specific instructions, class definitions, and output guidelines. We developed and evaluated three distinct system prompt variations, shown in Fig. 1.

[4] Throughout the paper, we use "In-context Learning Methods" and "Prompting Methods" interchangibly.

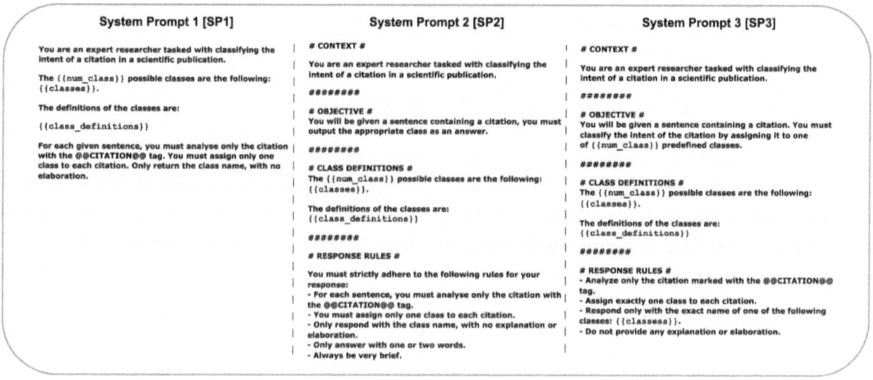

Fig. 1. Our System Prompts.

- **SP1:** This initial prompt offered a straightforward, intuitive instruction for the classification task.
- **SP2:** This prompt introduced more structure, drawing inspiration from the CO-STAR framework [31]. We adapted relevant CO-STAR components by definint the task *Context*, the *Objective* of the model, and detailed *Response Rules*. Given that our task requires a single, specific class label output, the stylistic components of CO-STAR (*Style*, *Tone*, and *Audience*) were not incorporated.
- **SP3:** Building upon SP2, this prompt further refined wording of the *Objective* and *Response Rules*. It also explicitly reiterated the expected labels in the *Response Rules* section, aiming to improve task clarity and consistency in the model's outputs.

Query Templates (QT). Query templates (QT) define the specific format used to present citation sentences to the model, whether as part of an in-context learning example or as the actual query requiring classification. We evaluated two template structures:

- **Simple Query:** Initially, we used a basic format where the citation sentence was followed by "Class:". For examples, the correct class was appended; for queries, this was left for the model to predict.
- **Multiple-choice Query:** We observed that some models struggled to adhere to the strict class-label-only output expected with the Simple Query, resulting in inconsistent performance. To mitigate this, we introduced a more structured template. Here, after the citation sentence, the model is explicitly prompted to choose the most appropriate citation intent from a presented list of all possible class labels.

Although the Multiple-choice template increases the token count per instance, it yielded significant performance improvements (detailed in Sect. 3.2) by providing clearer guidance to the models.

Example Presentation Formats (EPF). In our experiments, we explored two formats for presenting in-context examples to the models: *Inline* and *Conversational.*

- **Inline:** Example citation sentences and their corresponding classes (structured according to the defined query templates) are embedded directly and sequentially within the main prompt, immediately preceding the actual query sentence that the model needs to classify.
- **Conversational:** Examples are structured to simulate a dialogue. Each example consists of a "user" turn providing a citation sentence and an "assistant" turn providing the correct class. This series of example turns is provided before the final "user" query, which presents the new citation sentence for the model to classify. This format is also commonly referred to as a conversational or turn-taking format.

Temperature (T). Temperature is a hyperparameter that controls the randomness or creativity of a language model's outputs by adjusting the probability distribution of possible next tokens [16]. Lower temperatures (i.e., close to 0) correspond to greedy decoding, where the model deterministically selects the most probable token at each step, while higher temperatures (closer to 1) introduce greater variability by allowing the model to sample from a broader range of options.

For classification tasks, we aim for the model to output the most probable class label. Therefore, we use a temperature of 0 as the baseline, ensuring fully deterministic predictions. To explore how controlled randomness affects classification performance, we also evaluate higher temperatures, such as 0.2, 0.5, and 1.0. A temperature of 0.2 introduces a small degree of randomness but still heavily favors the most probable answer, while 0.5 strikes a balance between randomness and determinism. At 1.0, randomness is maximized, allowing us to assess whether excessive stochasticity degrades performance.

2.4 Technical Specifications

We conducted our experiments on an M1 Max Mac Studio with 64GB of memory, chosen to demonstrate the feasibility of running inference for Citation Intent Classification on commodity hardware.

For model hosting, we used LM Studio[5] which offers an intuitive interface for testing and interacting with models hosted on HuggingFace or locally. It also supports a local server mode compatible with the OpenAI API, allowing interaction through an API accessible in multiple programming languages. A command-line interface (CLI) tool[6] is also available for managing the server without using the UI.

[5] https://lmstudio.ai/.
[6] https://github.com/lmstudio-ai/lms.

Table 1. Highest Performance by Model.

SciCite			ACL-ARC		
Rank	Model	F1-Score	Rank	Model	F1-Score
1	Qwen 2.5 – 14B	78.33	1	Qwen 2.5 – 14B	63.68
2	Gemma 2 – 27B	77.86	2	Gemma 2 – 27B	58.95
3	Mistral Nemo – 12B	77.39	3	Gemma 2 – 9B	57.19
4	Gemma 2 – 9B	75.12	4	Qwen 2 – 7B	51.26
5	Phi 3 Medium – 14B	74.67	5	LLaMA 3.1 – 8B	48.45
6	LLaMA 3 – 8B	74.39	6	Mistral Nemo – 12B	48.11
7	Qwen 2 – 7B	72.89	7	Phi 3.5 Mini – 3.8B	43.74
8	LLaMA 3.1 – 8B	72.46	8	Phi 3 Medium - 14B	43.46
9	Gemma 2 - 2B	68.79	9	Gemma 2 - 2B	40.96
10	Phi 3.5 Mini – 3.8B	68.25	10	LLaMA 3.2 - 3B	40.07
11	LLaMA 3.2 - 3B	67.99	11	LLaMA 3 - 8B	38.06
12	LLaMA 3.2 - 1B	45.44	12	LLaMA 3.2 - 1B	24.60

3 Experimental Results and Analysis

This section presents the results of our experiments, focusing on model performance across various configurations and parameter settings. An initial overview of the peak F1-score achieved by each of the twelve models on both the SciCite and ACL-ARC datasets is summarized in Table 1. The subsections that follow provide a detailed analysis of top-performing model configurations, evaluate overall model rankings, and explore the influence of specific parameters.

3.1 Model Performance over Configurations

Our first evaluation focuses on identifying the top-performing models across the configurations described in Sect. 2. We employed two complementary approaches: (i) the Best Performer Evaluation identifies the single best model, and (ii) the Ranked Evaluation considers the relative performance of all models across configurations.

Best-Performer Evaluation. To identify the most effective models across configurations, we initially conducted a Best-Performer Evaluation. In particular, for each configuration, we examined a metrics table containing precision, recall, F1-score, and accuracy for all models. The model with the highest F1-score[7] in each configuration was selected as the best-performing model – in case of a tie, we used Accuracy as the deciding factor.

[7] All F1-scores reported in this paper are macro-averaged F1-scores (macro-F1).

Table 2. Model Ranking based on Best-Performing Count.

Dataset	Rank	Model	Overall	Zero-Shot	One-Shot	Few-Shot	Many-Shot
SciCite	1	Qwen 2.5 – 14B	125	24	42	28	31
	2	Mistral Nemo – 12B	25	0	0	14	11
	4	Gemma 2 – 27B	10	0	0	4	6
	4	Gemma 2 – 9B	8	0	6	2	0
ACL-ARC	1	Qwen 2.5 – 14B	129	19	22	40	28
	2	Gemma 2 – 27B	28	0	21	7	0
	3	Gemma 2 – 9B	11	5	5	1	0

Table 3. RRF-based Model Ranking.

SciCite			ACL-ARC		
Rank	Model	RankScore	Rank	Model	RankScore
1	Qwen 2.5 – 14B	144.163	1	Qwen 2.5 – 14B	146.496
2	Mistral Nemo – 12B	68.479	2	Gemma 2 – 27B	62.973
3	Gemma 2 – 27B	63.369	3	Gemma 2 – 9B	55.318
4	Gemma 2 – 9B	59.760	4	Qwen 2 – 7B	41.496
5	Qwen 2 – 7B	38.617	5	LLaMA 3.1 – 8B	40.844
6	LLaMA 3.1 – 8B	27.624	6	Phi 3.5 Mini – 3.8B	30.470
7	LLaMA 3 – 8B	26.159	7	Mistral Nemo – 12B	30.285
8	Phi 3.5 Mini – 3.8B	22.088	8	LLaMA 3.2 - 3B	23.984
9	Phi 3 Medium – 14B	19.370	9	Phi 3 Medium - 14B	21.269
10	Gemma 2 - 2B	19.253	10	LLaMA 3.2 - 1B	16.796
11	LLaMA 3.2 - 3B	18.286	11	Gemma 2 - 2B	16.534
12	LLaMA 3.2 - 1B	14.136	12	LLaMA 3 - 8B	16.359

The aggregated results of our evaluation are presented in Table 2. It is evident that Qwen 2.5 14B was the most dominant model on both datasets, significantly outperforming others across all prompting methods.

Ranked Evaluation. While the Best-Performer Evaluation provided insights into the most dominant models across configurations, it lacked the ability to capture nuances among high-performing models. For instance, a model that consistently ranked second in multiple configurations would not be reflected in that approach. To address this limitation, we adopted a ranking methodology inspired by Reciprocal Rank Fusion (RRF) [6]. This approach allowed us to evaluate all 12 models considering their relative performance across different configurations.

For each experimental configuration $c \in C$, models $M = \{m_1, m_2, \ldots, m_{12}\}$ were ranked based on their F1-scores – in case of a tie, Accuracy was used to determine the rank. Each model was then assigned a score based on its rank, where the score $S(m_k, c)$ for the k-th ranked model in configuration c was defined as $S(m_k, c) = \frac{1}{k}$. This score is inversely proportional to the rank, meaning that higher-ranked models (lower-k) receive higher scores, while lower-ranked models (higher-k) receive lower scores. To calculate the overall ranking score for each model m, we aggregated its scores across all configurations $c \in C$:

$$RankingScore(m) = \sum_{c \in C} S(m_k, c) \tag{1}$$

Table 3 presents the results of this ranked evaluation. The ranked evaluation aligns with the Best-Performer Evaluation in identifying Qwen 2.5 14B as the most dominant model. This view also allows us to gain insights into the relative performance of other the models, highlighting distinctions among high performers, as well as the performance of lower-ranked models.

Table 4. Parameter Performance Analysis of Top 5% Configurations.

Parameter	Setting	SciCite		ACL-ARC	
		Count	Percent	Count	Percent
In-context Learning Method	Few-shot	47	46.53%	55	61.11%
	Many-shot	38	35.64%	21	23.33%
	One-shot	14	13.86%	14	15.55%
	Zero-shot	4	3.96%	-	-
Temperature	0.0	31	30.69%	23	25.55%
	0.2	30	29.70%	22	24.44%
	0.5	20	19.80%	22	24.44%
	1.0	20	19.80%	23	25.55%
System Prompt	SP3	45	44.55%	38	42.22%
	SP2	28	27.72%	24	26.66%
	SP1	28	27.72%	28	31.11%
Query Template	Multiple-Choice	80	79.21%	58	64.44%
	Simple	21	20.79%	32	35.55%
Example Presentation	Conversational	53	54.64%	59	65.55%
	Inline	44	45.36%	31	34.44%

3.2 Parameter Performance Analysis

In this section, we examine how different parameter configurations drive model performance. Identifying the most impactful parameters was challenging due to the extensive search space (168 configurations per dataset, totaling 3,841 experiments for all models). To address this, we conducted a Quantile-Based Analysis focusing on the top 5% of configurations based on F1-scores. Examining parameter distributions within this high-performing subset (Table 4) reveals trends for optimal configurations across both datasets.

For the *In-context Learning Method*, Few-shot prompting was most prevalent in top SciCite configurations (46.53%), with Many-shot also prominent (35.64%). This Few-shot preference was stronger on ACL-ARC (61.11%), where Many-shot (23.33%) and One-shot (15.55%) were less frequent, and Zero-shot was absent from the top 5%. These results suggest moderate example counts (Few-shot) are broadly effective, though Many-shot also performs well on SciCite.

The optimal *Temperature* settings showed divergence between the datasets. SciCite favored lower values, with $T = 0.0$ (30.69%) and $T = 0.2$ (29.70%) being most frequent, indicating a preference for deterministic outputs, while higher temperatures ($T = 0.5$, $T = 1.0$, both 19.80%) were less common. In contrast, ACL-ARC displayed a more balanced distribution, where $T = 0.0$ and $T = 1.0$ (both 25.55%) were slightly ahead of $T = 0.2$ and $T = 0.5$ (both 24.44%), suggesting that varied levels of randomness can yield top results.

A shared preference for *System Prompt* SP3 emerged across both datasets, found in 44.55% of top SciCite and 42.22% of top ACL-ARC configurations. Secondary preferences, however, varied. SciCite showed equal representation for SP1 and SP2 (both 27.72%), whereas ACL-ARC favored SP1 (31.11%) over SP2 (26.66%). This indicates an advantage for the structured SP3, though simpler prompts also achieved high performance.

The *Query Template* parameter revealed a decisive trend, as the Multiple-Choice template was overwhelmingly favored on both SciCite (79.21%) and ACL-ARC (64.44%) when compared to the Simple template (SciCite: 20.79%; ACL-ARC: 35.55%). This highlights the significant effectiveness of explicit multiple-choice options.

Finally, considering the *Example Presentation Format*, the Conversational style was more frequent in top configurations for SciCite (54.64%) and especially ACL-ARC (65.55%), over the Inline format (SciCite: 45.36%; ACL-ARC: 34.44%). This suggests structuring examples conversationally generally yields better results.

These findings offer valuable insights into the parameter settings that consistently enhance performance across the two datasets.

Chi-Square Statistical Test (χ^2). To complement our parameter performance analysis, we also conducted a *Chi-Square Test of Independence* [12] to evaluate the relationship between parameter settings and F1-scores. This approach allowed us to determine whether specific parameter settings were significantly associated with performance outcomes and validate the results of our primary analysis. The results of the test (summarized in Table 5) largely reinforces the findings from our quantile-based analysis regarding the influence of different parameter settings.

Table 5. Chi-Square Test of Independence results for parameter settings and F1-Scores. *(Significance levels: ***p < 0.001, **p < 0.01, *p < 0.05)*

Parameter	SciCite		ACL-ARC	
	χ^2	p-value	χ^2	p-value
In-context Learning Method	29.857	1.48e-06 ***	49.025	1.29e-10 ***
Temperature	4.617	0.202	0.047	0.9973
System Prompt	6.024	0.0491 *	3.647	0.1615
Query Template	35.063	3.19e-09 ***	7.305	0.0068 **
Example Presentation	0.699	0.4031	8.604	0.0033 **

The *In-context Learning Method* showed a highly significant association with F1-scores for both SciCite ($p < 0.001$) and ACL-ARC ($p < 0.001$). This statistically underscores the importance of the number of examples provided, aligning with our earlier observation that Few-shot and Many-shot configurations were prevalent among the top performers.

Similarly, the *Query Template* was found to be highly significant for SciCite ($p < 0.001$) and also significant for ACL-ARC ($p < 0.01$). This supports the strong dominance of the Multiple-Choice template in the top 5% configurations, highlighting its critical role in guiding model output effectively.

Other parameters presented more nuanced relationships. The *System Prompt* was statistically significant for SciCite ($p < 0.05$), corroborating the advantage seen for SP3 in its quantile analysis. However, for ACL-ARC, while SP3 was also frequent in top configurations, the choice of system prompt did not emerge as a statistically significant factor overall.

Conversely, the *Example Presentation Format* was not statistically significant for SciCite, which aligns with the relatively balanced distribution (Conversational at 54.64%, Inline at 45.36%) observed in its top configurations. For ACL-ARC, however, this parameter was significant ($p < 0.01$), providing statistical backing for the clearer preference (65.55%) for the Conversational method seen in its quantile analysis.

Finally, the *Temperature* parameter did not show a statistically significant relationship with F1-scores on either dataset. This finding is consistent with the quantile analysis where, for SciCite, multiple temperature settings were present in top configurations (though lower ones were more frequent), and for ACL-ARC, the distribution was particularly balanced, suggesting that temperature, within the tested ranges, was not as decisive a factor as other parameters.

4 Fine-Tuning

In this section, we investigate the impact of fine-tuning in the performance of the instruction-tuned Qwen 2.5 14B model on citation intent classification.

4.1 Training Configuration

For this experiment, we used the SciCite and ACL-ARC datasets, which were converted into the Alpaca format [30]. This format includes a system prompt, an instruction, the citing sentence, and the true label. The use of Supervised Fine-Tuning (SFT) was motivated by its ability to adapt pre-trained models to specific tasks using minimal labeled data, making it an effective approach for citation intent classification. To perform the fine-tuning, we used the original training set of each dataset (8,243 examples for SciCite and 1,688 for ACL-ARC). For testing, we used the original test sets as seen in the previous experiments.

To fine-tune the Qwen 2.5 14B Instruct model, we used LLaMA-Factory [33] on an AWS g6e.12xlarge EC2 instance equipped with 4 NVIDIA L40S GPUs, providing a combined GPU memory of 192GB. The training process was conducted using fp16 mixed precision to optimize memory usage and speed. To prevent memory issues during fine-tuning, we employed DeepSpeed ZeRO Stage 3 Offload [27], which enabled efficient memory management by offloading optimizer states and gradients to the CPU. The training parameters included a learning rate of 5e-5, a batch size of 16, and 10 epochs. The model was optimized using AdamW, with a cutoff length of 512 tokens for input sequences.

To optimize the fine-tuning process, we employed Low-Rank Adaptation (LoRA), a widely used parameter-efficient fine-tuning (PEFT) method [13,14]. LoRA enables efficient adaptation of large language models by freezing the pre-trained model weights and introducing trainable low-rank matrices into the Transformer layers, significantly reducing the number of trainable parameters while maintaining performance. For this experiment, we configured LoRA with a rank of 8, alpha of 16, and a dropout of 0.1, which allowed us to fine-tune the model effectively without exceeding memory constraints. The outlined training parameters are also summarized in Table 6.

Table 6. Training Parameters for Fine-Tuning Qwen 2.5 14B.

Parameter	Value	Explanation
Learning Rate	5e-5	Controls step size for updating model weights during training
Epochs	10	Number of complete passes through the entire training dataset
Batch Size	16	Number of training examples processed in one iteration
Cutoff Length	512	Maximum sequence length (in tokens) for model inputs
Optimizer	AdamW	Algorithm used to adjust model weights to minimize loss
Compute Type	fp16	Numerical precision used for computations
Warmup Steps	500	Number of initial steps where learning rate gradually increases
DeepSpeed Offload	Enabled	Moves optimizer states/grads to RAM to save GPU memory
DeepSpeed Stage	3	Level of DeepSpeed ZeRO optimization
LoRA Rank	8	Dimension of the trainable low-rank matrices added by LoRA
LoRA Alpha	16	Scaling factor for the LoRA updates relative to the rank
LoRA Dropout	0.1	Dropout probability applied to LoRA layers for regularization

4.2 Results

After fine-tuning, we evaluated the new models using the same prompting methods as in Sect. 2.3 (i.e., zero-shot, one-shot, few-shot, and many-shot) to draw comparisons with the instruction-tuned Qwen 2.5 14B baseline. While our initial extensive experiments with in-context learning focused on 8-bit quantized models (Q8), for this fine-tuning evaluation, we also assessed the 16-bit floating-point (FP16) versions, to examine the impact of numerical precision on performance.

The overall results, presented in Table 7, clearly show that supervised fine-tuning significantly improved performance on both the SciCite and ACL-ARC datasets. On SciCite, the fine-tuned FP16 model achieved a peak F1-score of 86.84. Compared to the instruction-tuned FP16 baseline (F1-score of 80.41), this represents an 8.0% relative improvement. On ACL-ARC, the fine-tuned Q8 model obtained the highest F1-score of 68.48. This constitutes a relative improvement of nearly 4.3% over the instruction-tuned FP16 baseline (F1-score of 65.64). Overall, the highest F1-score achieved after fine-tuning was 86.84 on SciCite and 68.48 on ACL-ARC.

Examining the impact of numerical precision, the fine-tuned FP16 and Q8 models showed minor performance differences. FP16 models generally outperformed Q8 on SciCite, while the fine-tuned Q8 model slightly outperformed its FP16 counterpart on ACL-ARC. This suggests that while FP16 precision can offer a slight advantage, Q8 remains highly competitive and may offer robustness, particularly for tasks with more granular classification schemes like ACL-ARC's 6-class setup.

Table 8 highlights the impact of fine-tuning across the different prompting methods. On SciCite, fine-tuning led to consistent F1-score improvements across all prompting scenarios. These gains were particularly substantial in zero-shot and one-shot settings; for instance, the fine-tuned Q8 model improved upon the instruction-tuned FP16 baseline by over 12.5% in zero-shot (84.84 vs 75.38) and by nearly 10.7% in one-shot (85.46 vs 77.22). In few-shot and many-shot for SciCite, performance with the fine-tuned FP16 model approached saturation, achieving the highest F1-scores of 86.84 and 85.79, respectively.

Similar trends were observed on the ACL-ARC dataset. The fine-tuned models generally outperformed their instruction-tuned counterparts across prompting methods, with the fine-tuned Q8 model achieving the highest F1-scores in one-shot (68.48) and few-shot (67.58) setups. In contrast, the fine-tuned FP16 model yielded stronger results in zero-shot (60.29) and many-shot (67.62).

These results demonstrate that supervised fine-tuning not only boosts overall performance but also particularly enhances generalization in low-context (zero-shot and one-shot) scenarios, while still effectively leveraging the additional context provided in few-shot and many-shot settings.

4.3 Discussion

The primary goal of this work was to investigate the capability of large language models to perform citation intent classification, rather than to compete directly

Table 7. F1-Score Performance of Qwen 2.5 – 14B Instruct and Fine-tuned variants.

Model	SciCite	ACL-ARC
Qwen 2.5 – 14B Instruct Q8	78.33	63.68
Qwen 2.5 – 14B Instruct FP16	80.41	65.64
Qwen 2.5 – 14B Fine-tuned Q8	86.47	**68.48**
Qwen 2.5 – 14B Fine-tuned FP16	**86.84**	67.73

Table 8. F1-Score Performance of Qwen 2.5 âĂŞ 14B Instruct and Fine-tuned variants, divided by prompting method.

Dataset	Model	Zero-Shot	One-Shot	Few-Shot	Many-Shot
SciCite	Instruct Q8	75.74	76.32	78.33	78.23
	Instruct FP16	75.38	77.22	80.41	78.94
	Fine-tuned Q8	**84.84**	**85.46**	86.47	85.62
	Fine-tuned FP16	84.49	85.38	**86.84**	**85.79**
ACL-ARC	Instruct Q8	52.29	60.02	62.86	63.68
	Instruct FP16	52.47	61.73	65.64	64.39
	Fine-tuned Q8	59.92	**68.48**	**67.58**	67.19
	Fine-tuned FP16	**60.29**	67.73	66.94	**67.62**

with state-of-the-art methods. Nonetheless, it is worth noting that the fine-tuned model achieved performance on SciCite within less than a 3% margin of the best-reported results in the literature, surpassing most of the existing approaches (see Table 9 - Sect. 5). This demonstrates that LLMs can approach the performance of specialized models, even without task-specific architectures or optimization.

We consider a key advantage of LLMs to be their ease of use and deployment. Tools such as LM Studio and Ollama[8] allow models like those outlined in this paper to be deployed locally with zero technical expertise, making them accessible to users without a computer science background. In addition to their accessibility, LLMs offer significant adaptability. Unlike traditional methods, which often require complex pretraining or domain-specific tuning, LLMs can be fine-tuned for a wide range of scientometric tasks, such as citation recommendation, paper summarization, or trend analysis, without the need for bespoke architectures. Furthermore, LLMs can scale effectively to new scientific domains or datasets, requiring only small amounts of task-specific data to adapt to underexplored scientific fields; our fine-tuned models required only the several thousand citing sentences provided by our task-specific datasets for adaptation. This contrasts sharply with models like SciBERT, whose effectiveness stems from deliberate pre-training exclusively on a large corpus of scientific papers (millions of articles), optimizing it for scientific language understanding. While the general-

[8] https://ollama.com/.

purpose LLMs used in our study were likely exposed to scientific text within their vast, diverse pre-training data drawn from the web, this exposure is *incidental* rather than *targeted*. They were not specifically pre-trained or architected with the primary goal of processing scientific literature, unlike SciBERT. Our results demonstrate that even without such specialized scientific pre-training, general-purpose LLMs can achieve competitive performance through efficient fine-tuning on minimal task-specific data.

The promising results observed in this study suggest that the performance of LLMs in citation intent classification can be further improved with techniques such as chain-of-thought prompting and reasoning-focused models. These methods could enhance the models' ability to better distinguish subtle differences in intents, refining their predictions and improving overall classification accuracy.

5 Related Work

The theoretical beginnings of citation analysis can be traced back to foundational works such as [9] identification of reasons for citation [23] studies on citation function. Early annotation schemes, such as those by [29], were later adapted by [32] for supervised machine learning approaches to citation classification.

[17] introduced the ACL-ARC dataset, which contains nearly 2,000 citations from papers in the NLP field, annotated with a classification scheme of six classes. [25] extended this classification scheme by refining the comparison class to capture similarities, differences, and disagreement. Around the same time, [5] proposed a multitask model incorporating structural information from scientific papers. They also introduced the SciCite dataset, which is significantly larger and spans multiple scientific domains, with three intent classes.

[3] introduced SciBERT, a BERT-based [7] encoder language model pre-trained specifically on scientific text, which has since become the backbone of many citation intent classification methods. SciBERT has been widely adopted due to its ability to generalize across scientific domains. For example, [22] introduced ImpactCite, an XLNet-based method for citation impact analysis, which was later used by [24] to achieve state-of-the-art results on the SciCite dataset. Paolini et al. demonstrated the effectiveness of ensemble classifiers combining fine-tuned SciBERT and XLNet models.

Recent research has continued to explore PLM-based methods for citation intent classification. [20] used a prompt-based learning approach on SciBERT to identify citation intent, while [28] achieved state-of-the-art performance on the ACL-ARC dataset by proposing a multi-task learning framework that jointly fine-tunes SciBERT on a dataset of primary interest together with multiple auxiliary datasets to take advantage of additional supervision signals. [19] explored various prompting and tuning strategies on SciBERT, including fixed and dynamic context prompts, and found that parameter updating with prompts improved performance. They also briefly experiment on LLMs by evaluating the zero-shot performance of GPT-3.5, which performed well on their recently introduced ACT2 dataset but poorly on the ACL-ARC dataset. However, GPT-3.5

was not evaluated on SciCite. In contrast, our work is the first to focus entirely on evaluating and fine-tuning numerous open-weight, general-purpose LLMs without using models pre-trained explicitly and exclusively for the scientific domain.

Table 9 summarizes the F1-scores of notable works, highlighting the progression of methods and datasets. SciBERT-based methods dominate, while our work is the first to examine LLMs on this task without any reliance on SciBERT.

Table 9. Reported F1-Scores of notable works from the literature, sorted chronologically.

Method	SciCite	ACL-ARC
Feature-rich Random Forest [17]	–	53.00
Structural Scaffolds [5]	84.00	67.90
SciBERT [3]	85.22	–
ImpactCite [22]	88.93	–
CitePrompt [20]	86.33	68.39
EnsIntWS [24]	89.46	–
EnsIntWoS [24]	88.48	–
MTL Finetuning (Search) [28]	85.25	64.56
MTL Finetuning (TRL) [28]	85.35	75.57

6 Conclusions

This study investigated open Large Language Models (LLMs) for citation intent classification, demonstrating their viability with in-context learning, particularly when guided by optimized prompting strategies. We found that supervised fine-tuning with minimal data significantly boosts performance; notably, our fine-tuned Qwen 2.5 14B model achieved relative F1-score improvements of approximately 8% on SciCite and 4.3% on ACL-ARC over strong instruction-tuned baselines, reaching performance levels competitive with specialized systems. The detailed insights from our prompting parameter experiments, combined with our openly available evaluation framework and models, aim to facilitate further research and application of LLMs in scientometrics.

Acknowledgments. This work has received funding from the EU's Horizon Europe framework programme as part of the SciLake (GA: 101058573) and GraspOS (GA: 101095129) projects. Part of this work utilized Amazon's cloud computing services, which were made available via GRNET under the OCRE Cloud framework.

References

1. Abdin, M., et al.: Phi-3 technical report: a highly capable language model locally on your phone (2024). https://arxiv.org/abs/2404.14219
2. Bai, J., et al.: Qwen technical report (2023). https://arxiv.org/abs/2309.16609
3. Beltagy, I., Lo, K., Cohan, A.: Scibert: a pretrained language model for scientific text. arXiv preprint arXiv:1903.10676 (2019)
4. Brown, T.B., et al.: Language models are few-shot learners (2020). https://arxiv.org/abs/2005.14165
5. Cohan, A., Ammar, W., van Zuylen, M., Cady, F.: Structural scaffolds for citation intent classification in scientific publications. In: Proceedings of the 2019 Conference of the North American Chapter of the Association for Computational Linguistics: Human Language Technologies, Volume 1 (Long and Short Papers), pp. 3586–3596. Association for Computational Linguistics, Minneapolis, Minnesota (2019). https://doi.org/10.18653/v1/N19-1361. https://www.aclweb.org/anthology/N19-1361
6. Cormack, G.V., Clarke, C.L., Buettcher, S.: Reciprocal rank fusion outperforms condorcet and individual rank learning methods. In: Proceedings of the 32nd International ACM SIGIR Conference on Research and Development in Information Retrieval, pp. 758–759 (2009)
7. Devlin, J., Chang, M.W., Lee, K., Toutanova, K.: Bert: pre-training of deep bidirectional transformers for language understanding (2019). https://arxiv.org/abs/1810.04805
8. Dong, Q., et al.: A survey on in-context learning (2024). https://arxiv.org/abs/2301.00234
9. Garfield, E., et al.: Can citation indexing be automated. In: Statistical Association Methods for Mechanized Documentation, Symposium Proceedings, vol. 269, pp. 189–192. Washington (1965)
10. Gemma Team, et al.: Gemma 2: improving open language models at a practical size (2024). https://arxiv.org/abs/2408.00118
11. Grattafiori, A., et al.: The llama 3 herd of models (2024). https://arxiv.org/abs/2407.21783
12. Greenwood, P.E., Nikulin, M.S.: A Guide to Chi-Squared Testing. Wiley (1996)
13. Han, Z., Gao, C., Liu, J., Zhang, J., Zhang, S.Q.: Parameter-efficient fine-tuning for large models: a comprehensive survey (2024). https://arxiv.org/abs/2403.14608
14. Hu, E.J., et al.: Lora: low-rank adaptation of large language models (2021). https://arxiv.org/abs/2106.09685
15. Jiang, A.Q., et al.: Mistral 7B (2023). https://arxiv.org/abs/2310.06825
16. Jurafsky, D., Martin, J.H.: Speech and Language Processing: An Introduction to Natural Language Processing, Computational Linguistics, and Speech Recognition with Language Models, 3rd edn (2025). https://web.stanford.edu/~jurafsky/slp3/. Accessed 12 Jan 2025
17. Jurgens, D., Kumar, S., Hoover, R., McFarland, D., Jurafsky, D.: Measuring the evolution of a scientific field through citation frames. Trans. Assoc. Comput. Linguist. **6**, 391–406 (2018)
18. Kanellos, I., Vergoulis, T., Sacharidis, D., Dalamagas, T., Vassiliou, Y.: Impact based ranking of scientific publications: a survey and experimental evaluation. IEEE Trans. Knowl. Data Eng. **33**(4), 1567–1584 (2021). https://doi.org/10.1109/TKDE.2019.2941206

19. Kunnath, S.N., Pride, D., Knoth, P.: Prompting strategies for citation classification. In: Proceedings of the 32nd ACM International Conference on Information and Knowledge Management, CIKM 2023, pp. 1127–1137. Association for Computing Machinery, New York (2023). https://doi.org/10.1145/3583780.3615018
20. Lahiri, A., Sanyal, D.K., Mukherjee, I.: Citeprompt: using prompts to identify citation intent in scientific papers. In: 2023 ACM/IEEE Joint Conference on Digital Libraries (JCDL), pp. 51–55 (2023). https://doi.org/10.1109/JCDL57899.2023.00017
21. Lo, K., Wang, L.L., Neumann, M., Kinney, R., Weld, D.: S2ORC: the semantic scholar open research corpus. In: Jurafsky, D., Chai, J., Schluter, N., Tetreault, J. (eds.) Proceedings of the 58th Annual Meeting of the Association for Computational Linguistics, pp. 4969–4983. Association for Computational Linguistics, Online (2020). https://doi.org/10.18653/v1/2020.acl-main.447. https://aclanthology.org/2020.acl-main.447/
22. Mercier, D., Rizvi, S.T.R., Rajashekar, V., Dengel, A., Ahmed, S.: Impactcite: an xlnet-based solution enabling qualitative citation impact analysis utilizing sentiment and intent. In: Proceedings of the 13th International Conference on Agents and Artificial Intelligence - Volume 2: ICAART, pp. 159–168. INSTICC, SciTePress (2021). https://doi.org/10.5220/0010235201590168
23. Moravcsik, M.J., Murugesan, P.: Some results on the function and quality of citations. Soc. Stud. Sci. **5**(1), 86–92 (1975). https://doi.org/10.1177/030631277500500106
24. Paolini, L., Vahdati, S., Di Iorio, A., Wardenga, R., Heibi, I., Peroni, S.: "why do you cite?" an investigation on citation intents and decision-making classification processes (2024). https://doi.org/10.5281/ZENODO.11841798. https://zenodo.org/doi/10.5281/zenodo.11841798
25. Pride, D., Knoth, P.: An authoritative approach to citation classification. In: Proceedings of the ACM/IEEE Joint Conference on Digital Libraries in 2020, JCDL 2020, pp. 337–340. Association for Computing Machinery, New York (2020). https://doi.org/10.1145/3383583.3398617
26. Qwen, et al.: Qwen2.5 technical report (2025). https://arxiv.org/abs/2412.15115
27. Ren, J., et al.: Zero-offload: democratizing billion-scale model training (2021). https://arxiv.org/abs/2101.06840
28. Shui, Z., et al.: Fine-tuning language models on multiple datasets for citation intention classification (2024). https://arxiv.org/abs/2410.13332
29. Spiegel-Rosing, I.: Science studies: bibliometric and content analysis. Soc. Stud. Sci. **7**(1), 97–113 (1977)
30. Taori, R., et al.: Stanford alpaca: an instruction-following llama model (2023). https://github.com/tatsu-lab/stanford_alpaca
31. Teo, S.: How i won Singapore's GPT-4 prompt engineering competition (2023). https://towardsdatascience.com/how-i-won-singapores-gpt-4-prompt-engineering-competition-34c195a93d41
32. Teufel, S., Siddharthan, A., Tidhar, D.: Automatic classification of citation function. In: Proceedings of the 2006 Conference on Empirical Methods in Natural Language Processing, EMNLP 2006, pp. 103–110. Association for Computational Linguistics, USA (2006)
33. Zheng, Y., et al.: Llamafactory: unified efficient fine-tuning of 100+ language models. In: Proceedings of the 62nd Annual Meeting of the Association for Computational Linguistics (Volume 3: System Demonstrations). Association for Computational Linguistics, Bangkok, Thailand (2024). http://arxiv.org/abs/2403.13372

Citation Impact and Research Persistence: The Power of Positive Reinforcement

Jeppe Nicolaisen(✉)

University of Copenhagen, Copenhagen, Denmark
jep.nic@hum.ku.dk

Abstract. Inspired by the behavioral principle of reinforcement, this study explores the influence of citation impact on research persistence. Spanning 20 scientific topics and nearly 100,000 authors, citation impact is measured by the total number of citations an author's initial publication receives. Research persistence is defined as publishing at least one additional article on the same topic within the subsequent three-year period. Authors are classified into four citation quartiles. The percentage of persistent authors is compared across quartiles, and paired t-tests test the significance of differences between citation quartiles and persistence. A significant positive correlation is found between citation impact and research persistence. Authors in higher citation quartiles (Q3 and Q4) are more likely to continue publishing. For instance, authors in Q1 show a persistence rate of 26.2%, compared to 45.4% in Q4. This trend holds across most topics, with some topic-specific variations. The results support the idea that citation impact serves as positive reinforcement, motivating researchers to continue their work. The study highlights the need for more holistic academic evaluation criteria to reduce disparities between well-cited and less-cited researchers.

Keywords: Citation impact · Research persistence · The principle of reinforcement

1 Introduction

Identifying the factors that influence research productivity is central for optimizing the research process, fostering a healthy research culture, and ensuring that the scientific community continues to make meaningful contributions to knowledge. Research persistence and related concepts (e.g., research continuity, commitment and recurrence) are therefore important topics in fields like bibliometrics and science studies. However, only a few older studies have explored the extent to which citation impact affects research persistence. In a study by Lightfield [1] involving a sample of 83 sociology PhD graduates, it was found that later productivity was significantly influenced by the citation of earlier work. Cole and Cole [2] reported similar findings in two separate samples comprising 50 and 120 physicists, respectively. Reskin [3] sampled 238 chemists and discovered that early citations had a significant influence on later productivity for those working outside academia, but only a negligible influence on later productivity for those working within. While these studies are mono-disciplinary and small-scale, Fox [4] notes that they "lend support to the reinforcement principle".

W.-T. Balke et al. (Eds.): TPDL 2025, LNCS 16097, pp. 225–241, 2026.
https://doi.org/10.1007/978-3-032-05409-8_14

The principle of reinforcement is a key element in behavioral psychology originally formulated by B.F. Skinner [5], the renowned American psychologist who played a pivotal role in the development of behaviorism [6]. A reinforcement is a consequence that increases or decreases the frequency of the action that preceded the consequence. If the outcomes of an action are favorable, the likelihood of the action being repeated increases. Conversely, if the outcomes are unfavorable, the likelihood of the action being repeated decreases. Thus, a reinforcement can be positive or negative.

It may seem that the principle of reinforcement and the cumulative advantage feedback known from the Matthew effect [7] is more or less the same, but in fact, they are theoretically different. As explained by Fox [4]:

> "Literature on scientific productivity has often lumped reinforcement theory together with accumulation of advantage, and hence failed to distinguish between the two perspectives. Reinforcement, however, deals with why scientists continue to produce, and cumulative advantage deals, on the other hand, with how scientists are able to obtain the resources which facilitate research and publication".

Thus, the Matthew effect describes the long-term accumulation of advantages over time. The principle of reinforcement deals with the immediate consequences that influence the repetition of specific actions. While both principles involve the idea that past outcomes influence future outcomes, the Matthew effect is more macroscopic and societal, while the principle of reinforcement is microscopic and individual.

The purpose of the present study is to update and expand on how positive reinforcement in terms of citation impact influences research persistence. To make it the first large-scale study, it covers 20 scientific topics from a variety of fields and almost 100,000 authors. Simultaneously, to make it a proper study of the principle of reinforcement, the investigation is limited to a relatively short timeframe (2020–2023). In each topic, the persistence of authors is measured within a fixed publication window, and the citation impact of their earliest publication in this window is measured comparably. This allows for testing whether citation impact covaries with research persistence - specifically, to what extent citation impact predicts continued research on a given topic.

The remainder of the article is structured as follows: Sect. 2 elaborates on how research persistence is measured, followed by a detailed explanation of the data and methods in Sect. 3. Section 4 presents the empirical results, and Sect. 5 offers a comprehensive discussion, including an in-depth examination of the study's limitations and the particular challenges involved in assigning causal inference in studies of this kind.

2 Measuring Research Persistence

Although only three studies have dealt with the possible connection between citation impact and research persistence, research persistence has been a theme in several other studies. The phenomenon is of course measured over time. Yet, the length of time varies from study to study. Extremes are one-year out and uninterrupted, continuous presence. Thus, some studies have measured the research persistence of graduated PhDs by surveying just one year after graduation (e.g., [8; 9]). Others have taken quite a different approach when operationalizing the concept. Ioannidis, Boyack and Klavans [10] obtained data from the entire Scopus database until 2012 and identified how many authors had published at least one item each year in the previous 16-year period (1996–2011). Consequently, such uninterrupted, continuous presence over 16 years was their definition and operationalization of research persistence.

As illustrated by these extremes, different measures also vary in terms of recurrence. Thus, some require that a persistent researcher must be present at, before and after a specific point in time to count as such. By other measures, a persistent researcher only needs to be present at a given point in time and either before or after.

The seminal work by Price and Gürsey [11] laid the ground. By focusing on recurrence, they were able to split authors into groups of either continuants, newcomers, terminators or transients. Later, Braun, Glänzel and Schubert [12] employed the same classification in a study of the author flow in a selection of neuroscience journals. Even later, Moed [13] changed one of the author labels and added fixed publication windows. Authors who published in year Y and had at least one paper in the four years preceding Y, as well as at least one paper in the four years following Y, were categorized as continuants in year Y. Newcomers in year Y were defined as authors with no papers in the preceding four years but with at least one paper in the subsequent four years. Movers were identified as authors with publications in the four years preceding Y but no publications during the four subsequent years. Lastly, transients were characterized as those who, in year Y, exclusively published papers in that specific year, with no publications in the four years preceding or subsequent. Moed, Aisati and Plume [14] operated with the same labels and publication windows in their study of scientific migration in the Scopus database.

Inspired by this work, Nicolaisen and Frandsen [15] applied similar measures in a study of recurring authors. However, as recommended by Leydesdorff, Wouters and Bornmann [16], they operated with three-year publication windows where applicable. Author labels were also changed somewhat. Their synchronous measure is similar to the measure of movers, but reduced to a three-year publication window before Y. Their diachronous measure is similar to the measure of newcomers, but reduced to a three-year publication window after Y. Their immediate measure is similar to the extreme one-year out measure. Their continuant measure is similar to the original continuant measure, but limited to a three-year publication window before and after Y. Applying these four measures on a selection of general science journals, general medical journals and specialized medical journals, Nicolaisen and Frandsen [15] found that the specialized medical journals had higher percentages of recurring authors. Moreover, they found that the four different measures produced results that only differed slightly.

Most studies of research persistence and related concepts have employed binary measures and have therefore only counted whether an author published within an observed publication window or not. For instance, Moldwin and Morrow [17] measured the research persistence for solar and space physics PhDs using a three-year publication window after graduation. Consequently, like the diachronous measure [15], graduates needed only one publication in the subsequent three-year window to count as research persistent.

3 Method

To identify potential research topics for the analysis, a literature search was conducted to find recent source studies that had formulated search strings for topic searches. Three criteria were applied during the selection process. Firstly, it was determined to include exactly 20 topics. Therefore, the first 20 studies that met the remaining criteria were selected. Secondly, the topic search of each identified study should yield at least 200 retrieved documents (articles, reviews, or notes) for the year 2020. Thirdly, scientific topics should represent a multitude of fields. The selected source studies are listed in the bibliography [18–37].

All searches were conducted using the Scopus database. The search string from each selected source study served as the basis but was, in some cases, modified to adhere to the Scopus syntax and/or assigned appropriate field codes. All searches were limited to document types (articles, reviews, or notes), source type (journal) and publication years (2020–2023).

From the results of each topic search, the following data were extracted: The number of documents in the year 2020, the number of citations received by each 2020-document until the day of retrieval, Scopus Author IDs for each 2020-document, the number of publications in the years 2021–2023, and Scopus Author IDs for all documents from the years 2021–2023.

The Scopus Author ID is a unique identifier assigned to individual authors in the Scopus database, facilitating the distinction between authors with similar or identical names. It enables more accurate tracking of an author's publications and citations. It is important to note that some authors may change their Scopus Author ID, such as when merging existing IDs. Additionally, some publications lack information on author IDs. Consequently, in a few cases, the Scopus Author ID could not be determined, leading to the omission of those publications from the study.

In total, the sample consists of 17,725 documents published in 2020, comprising 99,106 authors, and 64,351 documents published from 2021 to 2023, comprising 392,485 authors. Detailed sample sizes for each scientific topic are presented in Table 1.

Citation impact was operationalized as the total number of citations received by an author's publication in the year 2020, measured at the point of data retrieval (February 11, 2024). This approach was chosen to ensure comparability across all topics within a fixed time window, and because a citation window of three years has been found to be a pragmatic compromise between a short and a long publication [16]. While it is acknowledged that citation practices vary across disciplines, using total citation counts within a uniform timeframe allows for consistent measurement across diverse fields.

Citation quartiles for each scientific topic were calculated individually based on the citation data retrieved for the 2020 documents. For a comprehensive overview of the specific citation quartiles for each scientific topic, please refer to the appendix. As an illustration, the first citation quartile for documents on the topic of acoustic neuroma includes those cited 0–1 times, the second quartile 2–4 times, the third quartile 5–9 times, and the fourth quartile 10–159 times.

Subsequently, the 2020 authors were sorted according to their respective citation quartiles. For example, if an author had published a document on acoustic neuroma, cited once at the time of retrieval, the author would be classified as a Q1-author. An author

Table 1. Sample data (A: Number of publications, 2020; B: Number of authors, 2020; C: Number of publications, 2021–2023; D: Number of authors, 2021–2023).

Topic	A	B	C	D
Acoustic neuroma	543	3,287	1,923	12,879
Aviation safety	440	1,742	1,749	7,568
Bioactive glass	557	3,326	2,072	12,727
Craniosynostosis	561	3,634	2,133	14,926
Discourse studies	1,134	2,091	4,101	8,186
Early childhood caries	245	1,253	686	3,978
Gender discourses in entrepreneurship	379	1,036	1,648	4,792
Gender-affirming surgery	279	1,321	1,247	7,209
Meningioma	1,480	9,866	5,342	38,347
Multi-criteria decision aid methods	1,755	6,214	6,585	24,264
Neurologic and neurosurgical research on COVID-19	1,083	8,567	4,819	46,183
Obsessive-compulsive disorder	1,655	11,095	5,648	38,506
Oral cancer	1,475	9,670	5,172	35,895
Periodontology	1,404	7,689	4,969	28,109
Psoriatic arthritis	1,303	9,256	4,735	38,399
Shoulder instability	593	3,177	2,071	12,301
Sickle cell disease	1,020	6,958	3,288	23,462
Takayasu arteritis	255	1,635	825	6,122
Trachoma	674	4,693	2,384	19,262
Workplace learning	890	2,596	2,954	9,370
Total	17,725	99,106	64,351	392,485

who had published a document on the same topic, cited 4 times, would be categorized as a Q2-author, and so forth.

It is important to note that citation practices differ across disciplines. To mitigate potential biases arising from this variability, citation quartiles were calculated individually for each topic, ensuring that comparisons are made relative to the norms within each specific research area. This approach reduces the influence of field-specific citation practices on the overall findings.

Research persistence was defined as the presence of at least one additional publication by an author within a three-year period following their initial publication in 2020. This operationalization is based on the diachronous measure described by Nicolaisen and Frandsen [15], which was chosen for its applicability across various disciplines and its ability to capture research continuity over a moderate time frame. Persistent authors were identified by comparing Scopus Author IDs from 2020 publications to those found in subsequent publications (2021–2023) on a topic-by-topic basis.

Subsequently, the percentage of persistent authors was calculated for each citation quartile (topic-by-topic), and the differences between quartiles for the entire selection of topics were tested using paired t-tests with a confidence interval of 0.05. Given the multiple pairwise comparisons conducted (six in total), Bonferroni correction was applied to adjust for the increased risk of Type I error. Consequently, the adjusted significance level was set at $\alpha = 0.05/6 = 0.0083$.

4 Results

The distribution of authors (2020) on citation quartiles is presented in Table 2.

Table 2. Number of authors (2020) within citation quartiles of each scientific topic.

Topic	Q1	Q2	Q3	Q4
Acoustic neuroma	702	816	724	1,045
Aviation safety	340	388	396	618
Bioactive glass	771	836	880	839
Craniosynostosis	962	472	1,025	1,175
Discourse studies	497	536	468	590
Early childhood caries	278	307	296	372
Gender discourses in entrepreneurship	247	272	260	257
Gender-affirming surgery	359	192	363	407
Meningioma	1,951	2,232	2,745	2,938
Multi-criteria decision aid methods	1,549	1,461	1,563	1,641
Neurologic and neurosurgical research on COVID-19	1,502	1,743	2,544	2,778
Obsessive-compulsive disorder	1,682	2,703	3,026	3,684
Oral cancer	1,829	2,696	2,531	2,614
Periodontology	1,723	1,969	1,981	2,016
Psoriatic arthritis	1,948	2,282	2,118	2,908
Shoulder instability	754	757	798	868
Sickle cell disease	1,680	1,480	1,783	2,015
Takayasu arteritis	449	188	392	606
Trachoma	1,069	1,043	1,219	1,362
Workplace learning	703	527	601	765

The number of authors gradually increases from Q1 to Q4. Figure 1 illustrates the tendency for the number of authors to be skewed toward Q4. This effect was anticipated, as numerous studies have demonstrated that documents with more authors also tend to receive more citations. For a recent overview, consult [38].

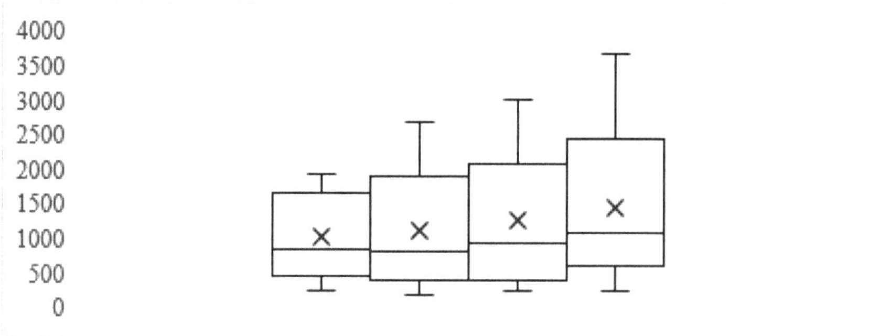

Fig. 1. Boxplots of authors (2020) in Q1-Q4 (left to right).

The number of persistent authors is also skewed toward Q4 (see Table 3). This skewness is partly attributed to the increasing number of authors in Q4. To account for this effect, the percentage of persistent authors in each quartile was calculated using the scores from Tables 2 and 3. The percentage scores are presented in parentheses in Table 3.

Table 3. Number and percentage of persistent authors within citation quartiles.

Topic	Q1	Q2	Q3	Q4
Acoustic neuroma	194 (27.6%)	272 (33.3%)	300 (41.4%)	516 (49.4%)
Aviation safety	62 (18.2%)	97 (25.0%)	108 (27.3%)	203 (32.8%)
Bioactive glass	280 (36.3%)	406 (48.6%)	453 (51.5%)	475 (56.6%)
Craniosynostosis	287 (29.8%)	185 (39.2%)	347 (33.9%)	435 (37.0%)
Discourse studies	52 (10.5%)	79 (14.7%)	82 (17.5%)	110 (18.6%)
Early childhood caries	63 (22.7%)	105 (34.2%)	137 (46.3%)	185 (49.7%)
Gender discourses in entrepreneurship	25 (10.1%)	51 (18.8%)	52 (20.0%)	78 (30.4%)
Gender-affirming surgery	124 (34.5%)	80 (41.7%)	152 (41.9%)	200 (49.1%)
Meningioma	506 (25.9%)	924 (41.4%)	1,085 (39.5%)	1,216 (41.4%)

(*continued*)

Table 3. (*continued*)

Topic	Q1	Q2	Q3	Q4
Multi-criteria decision aid methods	353 (22.8%)	530 (36.3%)	635 (40.6%)	910 (55.5%)
Neurologic and neurosurgical research on COVID-19	354 (23.6%)	473 (27.1%)	703 (27.6%)	968 (34.8%)
Obsessive-compulsive disorder	593 (35.3%)	1,066 (39.4%)	1,508 (49.8%)	1,924 (52.2%)
Oral cancer	749 (41.0%)	1,263 (46.8%)	1,265 (50.0%)	1,318 (50.4%)
Periodontology	593 (34.4%)	849 (43.1%)	1,023 (51.6%)	1,128 (56.0%)
Psoriatic arthritis	883 (45.3%)	1,144 (50.1%)	1,227 (57.9%)	1,685 (57.9%)
Shoulder instability	241 (32.0%)	282 (37.3%)	449 (56.3%)	462 (53.2%)
Sickle cell disease	425 (25.3%)	637 (43.0%)	893 (50.1%)	1,160 (57.6%)
Takayasu arteritis	74 (16.5%)	52 (27.7%)	158 (40.3%)	363 (59.9%)
Trachoma	253 (23.7%)	433 (41.5%)	537 (44.1%)	600 (44.1%)
Workplace learning	67 (9.5%)	91 (17.3%)	80 (13.3%)	158 (20.7%)
Total means	308.9 (26.2%)	451.0 (35.3%)	559.7 (40.0%)	704.7 (45.4%)

Taking the scientific topic of acoustic neuroma as an example: An author in Q1 had a 27.6% chance of being a persistent author, Q2: 33.3%, Q3: 41.4%, and Q4: 49.4%. This suggests that the citation impact of an author's 2020 document tends to predict the author's research persistence on this topic. A similar growing tendency is observed across scientific topics, with a few exceptions. In one topic (workplace learning), the percentage score for Q2 is higher than Q3 In one topic (meningioma), the percentage score for Q2 is slightly higher than that for Q3 and the same as Q4. In two topics (psoriatic arthritis and trachoma), the Q3 and Q4 scores are identical. In one topic (shoulder instability), the Q3 score is slightly higher than that for Q4. Nevertheless, the total percentage averages indicate an approximately nine percent growth from Q1 to Q2, and approximately five percent growth between Q2-Q3 and Q3-Q4. This trend is also illustrated by the boxplots in Fig. 2.

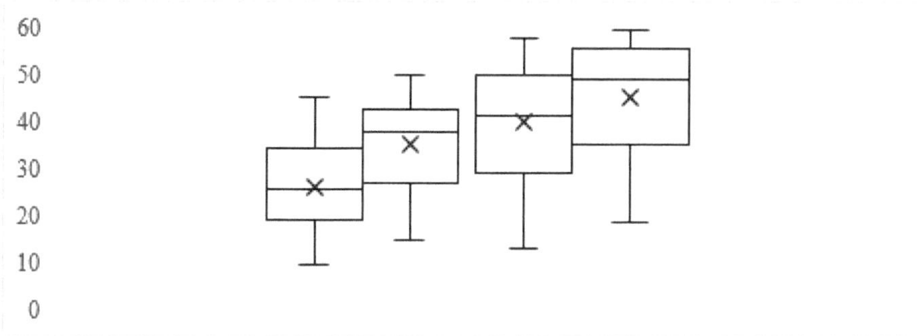

Fig. 2. Boxplots of the percentage of persistent authors in Q1-Q4 (left to right).

Paired t-tests were conducted to assess the growth. The mean percentage growth significantly increased from Q1 (M: 26.2 ± SD: 10.09) to Q4 (M: 45.4 ± SD: 12.45), resulting in a t-value of −9.28 with 19 degrees of freedom (df), and $p < 0.001$. Additionally, the gradual growth between Q1-Q2, Q2-Q3, and Q3-Q4 was found to be highly significant (see Table 4).

Table 4. Paired t-test results.

Topic	M ± SD	M ± SD	t-value	df	p-value
Q1-Q2	26.2 ± 10.09	35.3 ± 10.42	−9.13	19	< 0.001
Q1-Q3	26.2 ± 10.09	40.0 ± 12.94	−8.76	19	< 0.001
Q1-Q4	26.2 ± 10.09	45.4 ± 12.45	9.28	19	< 0.001
Q2-Q3	35.3 ± 10.42	40.0 ± 12.94	−3.51	19	0.002
Q2-Q4	35.3 ± 10.42	45.4 ± 12.45	−5,72	19	< 0.001
Q3-Q4	40.0 ± 12.94	45.4 ± 12.45	−4.46	19	< 0.001

5 Discussion

The results of the study indicate a significant relationship between citation impact and research persistence. Authors that produced a highly cited paper (Q4) are almost twice as likely to publish at least one additional paper in a subsequent three-year period compared to authors that produced a poorly cited paper (Q1). Moreover, the tendency of a higher rate of research persistence follows the rise in citation impact. Thus, authors that produced an intermediately cited paper (Q2) are approximately nine percent more likely to publish again during the observed period compared to authors that produced a poorly cited paper (Q1). Authors that produced a moderately cited paper (Q3) are about five percent more likely to publish again compared to authors that produced an intermediately cited paper (Q2). Authors that produced a highly cited paper (Q4) are about five percent more likely to publish again compared to authors that produced a moderately cited paper (Q3).

Consequently, this large-scale study of 20 different topics supports the findings from previous studies with a more limited scope [1–3]. It highlights the power of positive reinforcement, and how it seemingly serves as a motivational factor. When individuals receive positive consequences for their actions, they are more likely to feel motivated, engaged, and satisfied. This motivation likely contributes to a positive and productive environment, promoting a willingness to continue learning, working, and participating in ongoing research activities.

These findings have several broader implications for academic ecosystems. First, the demonstrated relationship between citation impact and research persistence suggests that current incentive structures, which often prioritize high-impact outputs, may inadvertently reinforce disparities between well-cited and less-cited researchers. This could lead to a concentration of resources and opportunities among already advantaged groups, potentially stifling diversity and innovation in underrepresented fields.

Second, the emphasis on citation impact as a measure of success highlights the need for institutions to adopt more holistic evaluation criteria that account for contributions beyond citation counts, such as teaching, mentorship, and societal impact.

Third, the observed patterns of research persistence call for a re-examination of resource allocation strategies, ensuring that early-career researchers and those in emerging or less-cited fields receive adequate support to sustain their contributions.

To address these challenges, institutions could implement policies that diversify funding criteria, promote cross-disciplinary collaboration, and provide targeted support for underrepresented researchers. Such measures could help balance the reinforcement dynamics observed in this study and foster a more equitable and innovative academic landscape.

It is important to address several potential limitations before drawing definitive conclusions on these matters. These pertain to the sample, the searching and matching procedures, publication and citation windows, and the question of causal inference. Additionally, objections to the principle of reinforcement itself need also be addressed.

The sample: Although the sample comprises almost 100,000 authors and 20 different topics, it is strictly speaking not a random sample. Based, as it is, on a selection of topics that have been researched in recent source studies, it is skewed toward these recent interests. Thus, a lean toward medical topics is noticeable. Consequently, it lacks the randomness necessary for true generalization to a broader population. This bias may skew the findings toward disciplines or topics with higher recent research activity, particularly in medical and life sciences. As a result, the generalizability of the conclusions to underrepresented fields may be limited.

The search procedures: The use of citation data from Scopus, while comprehensive, may exclude relevant publications due to database limitations, potentially influencing the accuracy of the results. Basing the search strings for the 20 topic searches on previous source studies involves a variety of search strategies. Some studies prioritize precision over recall, using just a few highly specific search terms. In contrast, others prioritize recall over precision, employing a range of search terms and synonyms. The retrieval effectivity of the 20 searches therefore varies from topic to topic. Consequently, the number of publications and authors retrieved in each topic is dependent on the implemented search strategy. Comparisons of topics on size alone is therefore not possible. However, comparisons within a topic are not affected similarly by the implemented search strategy. In each topic search, the recall and precision levels are the same for the initial and later sets of documents and authors.

The matching procedure: The study was conducted using Scopus Author ID for matching authors in the initial and later sets. Scopus assigns these unique identifiers using an algorithm, supplemented by manual feedback for validation [39]. It should be noted that not all Scopus Author IDs are attributed correctly, potentially introducing bias into the data. However, Schotten et al. [40] reported relatively high precision (98%) and recall (93.5%) rates for the author profiles in Scopus. Additionally, there is no reason to believe that the matching effectiveness varies significantly. Thus, for each topic, the recall and precision rates are likely the same or similar for authors in all four citation quartiles.

Publication and citation windows: Fields may have longer or shorter research cycles. Authors writing on some topics may therefore produce and be cited more rapidly compared to authors writing on other topics. As a result, citation impact and research persistence are relative to the specific topic. To address this variability, one approach is to use variable publication and citation windows that consider the temporal differences between fields. Alternatively, researchers may choose a compromise and utilize fixed publication and citation windows for all fields and topics. In this study, the latter approach was adopted. It is consequently important to acknowledge that both crude citation counts and the crude number of persistent authors are topic-relative. Caution should therefore be exercised when directly comparing different topics. This study only compares research persistence within topics, and as a result, is not as significantly challenged by issues related to publication and citation windows.

Causal inference: Establishing causality involves three essential operations: demonstrating covariance, eliminating spurious relations, and establishing the time order of occurrences (e.g., [41]). In this study of citation impact versus research persistence, the first operation has already been carried out successfully. Thus, covariance between citation impact and research persistence has been demonstrated.

Next is the question regarding possible spurious relations, i.e., whether the observed relationship between citation impact and research persistence may be explained by a third factor. This is no easy task. Social systems are complex, and numerous factors can influence observed relationships. It may therefore be difficult to identify and measure all relevant variables, making it challenging to account for every possible confounding factor.

One alternative explanation for the observed co-variance was proposed by Cole and Cole [2] in their small-scale studies on how citation impact affects research persistence. They named their alternative the sacred spark theory and explained that supporters of this theory might contend that scientists engage in scientific endeavors not solely for external rewards but due to an inherent drive or compulsion. Consequently, adherents of the sacred spark theory might argue that scientists who receive rewards and remain productive would continue to be productive even without external incentives. Separating the variance attributed to the principle of reinforcement from that attributed to the sacred spark theory proves to be challenging if not impossible. Once a scientist has received recognition or rewards, determining whether their continued productivity is solely influenced by these rewards becomes a complex task. “How can we say whether [the scientist] would have continued to be productive if [the scientist] had not been rewarded?” [2].

The relative short time order of occurrences makes it even more difficult to establish causality in the case of citation impact versus research persistence. As previously explained, the principle of reinforcement deals with the immediate consequences that influence the repetition of specific actions. This is why the study needs to operate with partly overlapping publication and citation windows. However, this overlap somewhat contests the requirement of cause before effect. For instance, in the present study, an author producing a paper in 2020 and another one in 2021 counts as research persistent. Yet all or most of the citation impact of the initial 2020-paper might first materialize or accumulate in the end of the citation window, i.e., after the second paper. Thus, in this case, effect comes before cause and not vice versa. At first, this appears to be a serious threat to the whole idea of citation impact influencing research persistence. However, it has been established that in most fields, early citation impact is correlated with later citation impact [42; 43]. Adams [44] even found that at the aggregate level, citation statistics based on a short citation window (years 1–2) correlate strongly with citation statistics based on longer citation windows (years 3–10). There is consequently reason to believe that typically, a research persistent author will have a good indication of the citation impact of the initial paper at the time of the second paper. Thus, the sheer size of the study provides some control for this time order issue.

Objections to the principle of reinforcement: The main critique of the principle of reinforcement has been that it oversimplifies human behavior by focusing solely on external stimuli and observable responses, neglecting internal cognitive processes, emotions, and individual differences. Noam Chomsky’s famous attack on B.F. Skinner’s ‘Verbal Behavior’ [45] centered on exactly that. Chomsky [46] argued that humans are not just passive responders to external stimuli, but are also actively processing information, engaging in complex cognitive activities, and influenced by internal mental states. He called the principle of reinforcement “perfectly useless”, and emphasized the importance of considering cognitive factors, such as thoughts, beliefs, and perceptions, in understanding human behavior.

Cognitive psychologists consider Chomsky’s critique “the most important refutation of behaviorism” [47] and “absolutely devastating” [48]. Advocates of behaviorism, on the other hand, have pointed out many factual errors in Chomsky’s critique [49], and accused him of “painting an absurd caricature” [50].

Behaviorists do not deny the influence of internal states, but contend that these internal states are themselves shaped by past interactions with the environment. Thus, environment-behavior relations are highly sensitive to history, making it difficult to control each and every variable [50]. This does not make the principle of reinforcement useless. On the contrary, it allows for a more nuanced understanding of behavior by considering the influence of environmental factors and social context.

Consequently, finding that citation impact tends to predict research persistence does not exclude the possibility that additional factors may also play a role. In this study, about a quarter of the poorly cited authors are found to be research persistent, and about half of the highly cited authors are found not to be. Obviously, we are dealing with a complex phenomenon where other factors than mere citation impact are involved. Some of them might be readily observable and studied from a behaviorist perspective. Others might be beneath the threshold of observability and consequently not readily accessible from that angle. The sacred spark theory is an example of the latter. Although a sacred spark is not directly observable, it does not follow that it is irrelevant. In fact, Cole and Cole [2] argued that "both theories might be correct", i.e., both the principle of reinforcement and the sacred spark theory may be needed to help explain the observed behavior. This aligns with the more recent Self-determination theory (SDT) that distinguishes between different types of motivation - intrinsic and extrinsic - when explaining human behavior [51; 52]. SDT posits that individuals are driven by a combination of external incentives (e.g., rewards, recognition) and internal desires (e.g., curiosity, passion for discovery). In the context of research persistence, highly cited authors who continue to publish may be motivated by extrinsic factors such as professional reputation or institutional pressures. Conversely, poorly cited authors who persist might be driven more by intrinsic motivation - a personal interest in their field or the internal satisfaction derived from research, regardless of external recognition.

Furthermore, SDT highlights the importance of three basic psychological needs - autonomy, competence, and relatedness - in fostering intrinsic motivation. Applying this framework to the phenomenon of research persistence suggests that authors may continue their work not merely because of external validation but because they find the research process inherently fulfilling or because it helps them maintain a sense of identity, belonging, or mastery in their academic community.

Thus, combining the reinforcement principle with intrinsic motivators rooted in the sacred spark theory offers a more nuanced explanation of research persistence. While citation impact provides one observable measure of reinforcement, intrinsic factors such as passion for the subject, intellectual curiosity, and personal values may serve as less visible but equally critical motivators. Future studies could benefit from examining how these intrinsic and extrinsic factors interact in shaping long-term scholarly engagement.

6 Conclusion

This large-scale study provides evidence for the significant role of citation impact as a predictor of research persistence, aligning with the behavioral principle of positive reinforcement. Authors who produce highly cited works are significantly more likely to continue publishing on the same topic within the next few years, demonstrating the reinforcing effect of citation recognition. While this study emphasizes short-term effects and immediate behavioral responses, it opens the door for further investigation into long-term dynamics, such as the cumulative advantages described by the Matthew effect.

The results also highlight the potential for existing academic incentive structures to inadvertently reinforce disparities, concentrating resources and opportunities among highly cited researchers. To mitigate these effects, it is crucial for institutions to consider more holistic evaluation criteria that extend beyond citation counts and recognize the broader contributions of researchers, including teaching, mentorship, and societal impact. In practical terms, institutions and funding bodies should recognize that citation impact may reinforce existing inequalities in academic careers. To counteract this, evaluative frameworks could be diversified to include contributions such as teaching, mentorship, and societal engagement. Additionally, targeted support for early-career researchers and those in less-cited fields could help ensure that motivation and persistence are not solely shaped by citation-based feedback. Such measures would foster a more equitable and resilient research ecosystem.

The study's correlational nature limits the ability to draw definitive causal conclusions. Future research, potentially incorporating experimental or quasi-experimental designs, could provide a deeper understanding of how citation impact and research persistence interact, further clarifying the mechanisms that drive scholarly engagement. Establishing causation would require controlling for confounding variables, such as career stage, funding availability, institutional support, co-authorship patterns, and other external factors that were beyond the scope of this analysis. Additionally, expanding the study's scope to include a wider range of academic environments and diverse research topics could help assess the broader applicability of these findings across disciplines.

Disclosure of Interests.. The author has no competing interests to declare that are relevant to the content of this article.

Appendix. Citation Quartiles (2020-Documents).

Topic	Q1	Q2	Q3	Q4
Acoustic neuroma	1	4	9	159
Aviation safety	2	5	11	151
Bioactive glass	6	13	23	187
Craniosynostosis	2	4	8	309
Discourse studies	0	2	6	118
Early childhood caries	1	5	11	286
Gender discourses in entrepreneurship	3	9	17	197
Gender-affirming surgery	3	6	13	138
Meningioma	1	4	11	1,025
Multi-criteria decision aid methods	5	13	30	463
Neurologic and neurosurgical research on COVID-19	6	18	46	4,727
Obsessive-compulsive disorder	2	7	16	1,966
Oral cancer	2	8	16	199
Periodontology	2	7	15	577
Psoriatic arthritis	3	8	17	1,021
Shoulder instability	1	4	10	100
Sickle cell disease	2	5	11	217
Takayasu arteritis	1	3	11	615

(continued)

(*continued*)

Topic	Q1	Q2	Q3	Q4
Trachoma	2	6	12	163
Workplace learning	2	5	11	137

References

1. Lightfield, T.E.: Output and recognition of sociologists. Am. Soc. **6**, 128–133 (1971). https://www.jstor.org/stable/27701738
2. Cole, J.R., Cole, S.: Social stratification in science. The University of Chicago Press, Chicago, IL (1973)
3. Reskin, B.F.: Scientific productivity and the reward structure of science. Am. Sociol. Rev. **42**(3), 491–504 (1977). https://doi.org/10.2307/2094753
4. Fox, M.F.: Publication productivity among scientists: a critical review. Soc. Stud. Sci. **13**(2), 285–305 (1983). https://doi.org/10.1177/030631283013002005
5. Skinner, B.F.: The Behavior of Organisms: An Experimental Analysis. B.F. Skinner Foundation, Cambridge; MA (1938)
6. Mackintosh, N.J.: B. F. Skinner (1904–1990). Nature **347**(6291), 332 (1990). https://doi.org/10.1038/347332b0
7. Merton, R.K.: The Matthew effect in science. Science **159**(3810), 56–63 (1968). https://doi.org/10.1126/science.159.3810.56
8. Anderson, G., Mulvey, P.: Physics doctorates one year later. https://files.eric.ed.gov/fulltext/ED534177.pdf (2012)
9. Keelor, B., Martinez, C., Kaleuati, K.: Earth & space science PhDs, class of 2003. https://web.archive.org/web/20240626053844/https://www.americangeosciences.org/sites/default/files/phdsurvey03_0.pdf (2005)
10. Ioannidis, J.P.A., Boyack, K.W., Klavans, R.: Estimates of the continuously publishing core in the scientific workforce. PLoS ONE **9**(7), e101698 (2014). https://doi.org/10.1371/journal.pone.0101698
11. Price, D.J.D., Gürsey, S.: Studies in scientometrics, Part I: transience and continuance in scientific authorship. Int. Forum Info. Docum. **1**(2), 17–24 (1976)
12. Braun, T., Glänzel, W., Schubert, A.: Publication and cooperation patterns of the authors of neuroscience journals. Scientometrics **51**(3), 499–510 (2001). https://doi.org/10.1023/A:1019643002560
13. Moed, H.F.: Citation Analysis in Research Evaluation. Springer, Dordrecht, The Netherlands (2005). https://doi.org/10.1007/1-4020-3714-7
14. Moed, H.F., Aisati, M., Plume, A.: Studying scientific migration in Scopus. Scientometrics **94**(3), 929–942 (2013). https://doi.org/10.1007/s11192-012-0783-9
15. Nicolaisen, J., Frandsen, T.F.: Epistemic community formation: a bibliometric study of recurring authors in medical journals. Scientometrics **127**(7), 4167–4189 (2022). https://doi.org/10.1007/s11192-022-04409-3
16. Leydesdorff, L., Wouters, P., Bornmann, L.: Professional and citizen bibliometrics: complementarities and ambivalences in the development and use of indicators - a state-of-the-art report. Scientometrics **109**(3), 2129–2150 (2016). https://doi.org/10.1007/s11192-016-2150-8
17. Moldwin, M.B., Morrow, C.: Research career persistence for solar and space physics PhD. Space Weather **14**(6), 384–390 (2016). https://doi.org/10.1002/2016SW001382

18. Alfaifi, A., AlMutairi, O., Allhaidan, M., Alsaleh, S., Ajlan, A.: The top 50 most-cited articles on acoustic neuroma. World Neurosurg. **111**, e454–e464 (2018). https://doi.org/10.1016/j.wneu.2017.12.090
19. Okine, E.A., Zarei, E., Roggow, B.J.: Exploring the intellectual insights in aviation safety research: a systematic literature and bibliometric review. Saf. Sci. **170**, 106354 (2024). https://doi.org/10.1016/j.ssci.2023.106354
20. Sujon, M.K., Noor, S.N.F.M., Zabidi, M.A.B., Shariff, K.A., Alam, M.K.: Bibliometric profiles of top 50 most cited articles on bioactive glass. Biomedical Glasses **6**(1), 70–84 (2020). https://doi.org/10.1515/bglass-2020-0007
21. Elarjani, T., et al.: Bibliometric analysis of the top 100 most cited articles on craniosynostosis. Child's Nervous System **37**(2), 587–597 (2021). https://doi.org/10.1007/s00381-020-04858-2
22. Raitskaya, L., Tikhonova, E.: The top 100 cited discourse studies: An update. Journal of Language and Education **5**(1), 4–15 (2019). https://doi.org/10.17323/2411-7390-2019-5-1-4-15
23. Patil, S.S., et al.: A bibliometric analysis of the 100 most cited articles on early childhood caries. Int. J. Pediatr. Dent. **30**(5), 527–535 (2020). https://doi.org/10.1111/ipd.12641
24. Ghosh, M.: Exploring gender discourses in entrepreneurship: a bibliometric analysis. Cogent Social Sciences **10**(1), 2299140 (2024). https://doi.org/10.1080/23311886.2023.2299140
25. Oleru, O.O., Rohde, C.H.: The most-cited publications in gender-affirming surgery: a cross-sectional bibliometric analysis. Plastic Surgery **32**(1), 54–63 (2024). https://doi.org/10.1177/22925503221088845
26. Almutairi, O., Albakr, A., Al-Habib, A., Ajlan, A.: The top-100 most-cited articles on meningioma. World Neurosurg. **107**, 1025–1032 (2017). https://doi.org/10.1016/j.wneu.2017.08.021
27. Basílio, M.P., Pereira, V., Costa, H.G., Santos, M., Ghosh, A.: A systematic review of the applications of multi-criteria decision aid methods (1977–2022). Electronics **11**(11), 1720 (2022). https://doi.org/10.3390/electronics11111720
28. Chan, K.I.P., Ignacio, K.H.D., Omar, A.T., Khu, K.J.O.: Top 100 most cited neurologic and neurosurgical articles on COVID-19: a bibliometric analysis. World Neurosurg. **157**, e137–e147 (2022). https://doi.org/10.1016/j.wneu.2021.09.118
29. Grover, S., Gupta, B.M., Ahmed, K.K.M., Kappi, M.: A scientometric research of high-cited publications in obsessive-compulsive disorders during 2012–2021. Iberoam. J. Sci. Measur. Commun. **2**(3), 1–14 (2022). https://doi.org/10.47909/ijsmc.171
30. Pena-Cristóbal, M., Diniz-Freitas, M., Monteiro, L., Diz Dios, P., Warnakulasuriya, S.: The 100 most cited articles on oral cancer. J. Oral Pathol. Med. **47**(4), 333–344 (2018). https://doi.org/10.1111/jop.12686
31. Corbella, S., Francetti, L., Taschieri, S., Weinstein, R., Del Fabbro, M.: Analysis of the 100 most-cited articles in periodontology. J. Investig. Clin. Dent. **8**(3), e12222 (2017). https://doi.org/10.1111/jicd.12222
32. Berlinberg, A., Bilal, J., Riaz, I.B., Kurtzman, D.J.B.: The 100 top-cited publications in psoriatic arthritis: a bibliometric analysis. Int. J. Dermatol. **58**(9), 1023–1034 (2019). https://doi.org/10.1111/ijd.14261
33. Allahabadi, S., Eftekhari, A., Feeley, S.E., Feeley, B.T., Lansdown, D.A.: Influential and highest cited shoulder instability articles: a bibliometric analysis. Orthop. J. Sports Med. **9**(3), 2325967121992577 (2021). https://doi.org/10.1177/2325967121992577
34. Okoroiwu, H.U., López-Muñoz, F., Povedano-Montero, F.J.: Bibliometric analysis of global sickle cell disease research from 1997 to 2017. Hematol. Transfus. Cell Ther. **44**(2), 186–196 (2022). https://doi.org/10.1016/j.htct.2020.09.156
35. Misra, D.P., Agarwal, V., Gasparyan, A.Y., Zimba, O., Sharma, A.: Highly cited papers in Takayasu arteritis on web of science and scopus: cross-sectional analysis. Clin. Rheumatol. **41**(1), 129–135 (2022). https://doi.org/10.1007/s10067-021-05901-6

36. Aquino-Canchari, C.R., Chavez-Bustamante, S.G.: The 100 most cited articles on trachoma: a bibliometric analysis. Int. Ophthalmol. **43**(11), 4235–4246 (2023). https://doi.org/10.1007/s10792-023-02834-8
37. Moosa, V., Shareefa, M.: Science mapping the most-cited publications on workplace learning. J. Workplace Learn. **32**(4), 259–272 (2020). https://doi.org/10.1108/JWL-10-2019-0119
38. Kousha, K., Thelwall, M.: Factors associating with or predicting more cited or higher quality journal articles: an annual review of information science and technology (ARIST) paper. J. Am. Soc. Inf. Sci. **75**(3), 215–244 (2024). https://doi.org/10.1002/asi.24810
39. Baas, J., Schotten, M., Plume, A., Côté, G., Karimi, R.: Scopus as a curated, high-quality bibliometric data source for academic research in quantitative science studies. Quant. Sci. Stud. **1**(1), 377–386 (2020). https://doi.org/10.1162/qss_a_00019
40. Schotten, M., Aisati, M., Meester, W.J.N., Steiginga, S., Ross, C.A.: A brief history of Scopus: the world's largest abstract and citation database of scientific literature. In: Research Analytics: Boosting University Productivity and Competitiveness through Scientometrics, pp. 31–58. CRC Press, Boca Raton, FL. (2017) https://doi.org/10.1201/9781315155890
41. Frankfort-Nachmias, C., Nachmias, D.: Research Methods in the Social Sciences (5. Edition). Arnold, London, UK (1997)
42. Abramo, G., Cicero, T., D'Angelo, C.A.: Assessing the varying level of impact measurement accuracy as a function of the citation window length. J. Informet. **5**(4), 659–667 (2011). https://doi.org/10.1016/j.joi.2011.06.004
43. Clermont, M., Krolak, J., Tunger, D.: Does the citation period have any effect on the informative value of selected citation indicators in research evaluations? Scientometrics **126**(2), 1019–1047 (2021). https://doi.org/10.1007/s11192-020-03782-1
44. Adams, J.: Early citation counts correlate with accumulated impact. Scientometrics **63**(3), 567–581 (2005). https://doi.org/10.1007/s11192-005-0228-9
45. Skinner, B.F.: Verbal behavior. Copley Publishing Group, Acton, MA (1957)
46. Chomsky, N.A.: A review of skinner's verbal behavior. Language **35**(1), 26–58 (1959)
47. Newmeyer, F.J.: The politics of linguistics. University of Chicago Press, Chicago, IL (1986)
48. Harris, R.A.: The Linguistics Wars. Oxford University Press, Oxford, UK (1993). https://doi.org/10.1093/oso/9780195072563.003.0002
49. MacCorquodale, K.: On Chomsky's review of skinner's verbal behavior. J. Exp. Anal. Behav. **13**, 83–99 (1970). https://doi.org/10.1901/jeab.1970.13-83
50. Palmer, D.C.: On Chomsky's appraisal of skinner's verbal behavior: a half century of misunderstanding. Behav. Analyst **29**(2), 253–267 (2006). https://doi.org/10.1007/BF03392134
51. Deci, E.L., Ryan, R.M.: Intrinsic Motivation and Self-Determination in Human Behavior. Plenum, New York, NY (1985). https://doi.org/10.1007/978-1-4899-2271-7
52. Ryan, R.M., Deci, E.L.: Self determination theory and the facilitation of intrinsic motivation, social development, and well-being. Am. Psychol. **55**(1), 68–78 (2000). https://doi.org/10.1037/0003-066X.55.1.68

Digital Archives

HistoryCLIP: Adaptive Multi-modal Retrieval of Imbalanced Long-Tailed Archival Data

Farid Alijani(✉), Elina Late, and Sanna Kumpulainen

Tampere University, Tampere, Finland
{farid.alijani,elina.late,sanna.kumpulainen}@tuni.fi

Abstract. We present **HistoryCLIP**, an adaptive multi-modal retrieval system, to address challenges of imbalanced and long-tailed historical archives with a comprehensive study on the utility of adapting vision-language models to such systems characterized by long-tailed sample distribution. We investigate three distinct fine-tuning techniques: full parameter fine-tuning, LoRA, and progressive layer unfreezing and benchmarked our results against the baseline in a diverse collection of historical archival data while created via stratified random sampling. Our extensive experiments with quantitative evaluation and qualitative analysis on both image-to-text and text-to-image retrieval tasks demonstrate that tailored fine-tuning substantially improves retrieval performance, offering critical insights into the adaptation of language-vision models for complex, domain-specific tasks. The proposed framework not only advances retrieval quality in the context of historical archives but also contributes to the broader understanding of fine-tuning methods for imbalanced multi-modal datasets.

Keywords: Multi-modal Retrieval Systems · Vision Language Models · Contrastive Learning · Imbalanced Long-tailed Distribution

1 Introduction

Historical image archives contain unique challenges for information retrieval systems due to contextual complexities, heterogeneous content, diverse metadata quality and severe imbalance nature for long-tailed label distributions [10]. Traditional text-based retrieval systems struggle with historical photograph archives due to evolving terminology and incomplete metadata [23]. Meanwhile, image-only approaches often fail to capture the crucial contextual information embedded in accompanying descriptions [22–24]. It embodies the need for robust multi-modal approaches capable of leveraging both visual and textual modalities across domains [13,49].

Such concerns practically complicate the development of effective multi-modal retrieval systems to accurately and efficiently access and interpret archival data. Although recent advancements in Vision-Language models (VLMs), *e.g.*,

W.-T. Balke et al. (Eds.): TPDL 2025, LNCS 16097, pp. 245–262, 2026.
https://doi.org/10.1007/978-3-032-05409-8_15

Contrastive Language-Image Pre-training (CLIP) [33], facilitated integration of visual and textual modalities, applying such methods to real-world historical datasets and contemporarily test collections reveal significant challenges and limitations which are barely visible in contemporary datasets. Such challenges vary from image quality to highly skewed distributions of content categories which practically leads into inconsistent searching for relevant documents [3]. Our approach centers on applying CLIP to a curated dataset containing long-tailed label distributions.

The core problem addressed in this paper is the difficulty to obtain reliable retrieval performance when confronted with highly imbalanced and long-tailed archival data, where a minority of labels dominates the dataset, and many labels are underrepresented. Such imbalance not only skews the learning process of standard retrieval algorithms but also introduces considerable noise and bias, undermining the utility of the retrieved information.

Our contributions are threefold. First, we present an extensively curated multi-modal dataset collected from various public historical archives, to address the real-world long-tailed sample distribution. Second, we systematically evaluate pre-trained CLIP architectures, enhanced by advanced fine-tuning methods, thus offering a robust comparative analysis of retrieval methods across severely imbalanced data conditions. Finally, our findings reveal actionable methods for adapting retrieval systems to the embodied challenges of historical archival data, by providing comparative analysis of the underlying performance variations.

2 Related Work

The rise of large-scale digital archives and multi-modal contents have initiated significant advancements in multi-modal retrieval systems. The fundamental objective of developing effective multi-modal retrieval systems is to close the semantic gap between visual and textual modalities by jointly learning their representations in a shared space which facilitates multi-modal retrieval tasks [13,49].

Early approaches relied primarily on handcrafted features and shallow learning methods, but recent years have witnessed remarkable progress in VLMs that learn joint embeddings for images and text [2]. Early influential models, including ViLBERT [29], LXMERT [4,39] and VisualBERT [25,26] employed transformer architectures, often pre-trained on large datasets of image-caption pairs for masked language or region modeling and image-text matching. A significant breakthrough was achieved with CLIP [33] which utilizes a simpler yet highly effective contrastive learning objective. It contains training separate image and text encoders utilizing architectures such as ResNet [35] or ViT [7] for images and transformers for text. It maximizes the similarity of the embeddings for related (image, text) pairs, while minimizing it for unrelated pairs. MS-CLIP [45] presents a framework to foster knowledge sharing and align semantic concepts more closely across modalities within a unified embedding space. It reduces the number of parameters by sharing transformer layers and incorporating lightweight modality-specific modules.

Although large-scale pre-trained VLMs offer robust generalization, transfer learning plays a substantial role to improve the downstream performance in domain adaptation such as historical archives [6,12]. The conventional method of full fine-tuning can be computationally demanding and prone to severe memory loss, as it updates all model parameters simultaneously using task-specific data [20]. Parameter-efficient transfer learning strategies have emerged to address the computational and data efficiency challenges in fine-tuning large-scale pre-trained VLMs. Hu *et al.* [17] proposed Low-Rank Adaptation (LoRA) which applies trainable rank-decomposed matrices into existing weights to enable efficient adaptation with minimal additional parameters. Although it was originally proposed for Large Language Models (LLMs), it demonstrated impressive performance on vision-language tasks with limited data [1,18,27], making it particularly suitable for adapting CLIP to historical domains while maintaining robust multi-modal alignment capabilities. Howard and Ruder [16] proposed gradual unfreezing as an alternative fine-tuning strategy in which most of the parameters are initially frozen except only the top layers then gradually unfreezing deeper layers over successive training stages. The rationale is to first adapt the task-specific higher-level representations while preserving the robust, general features learned in the lower layers during pre-training, potentially leading to more stable training and better adaptation. Li *et al.* [34] proposed scheduled unfreezing to enhance cross-lingual transfer capabilities in VLMs, to initiate the fine-tuning process by focusing on the topmost layers of the vision-language encoder. Subsequently, as training progresses, the strategy gradually unfreezes the model's layers in a top-down manner. This allows the model to first adapt its higher-level semantic representations to the new task and language, before fine-tuning the lower-level feature extractors. By strategically controlling which layers are trainable at different stages, it aims to improve the transfer of knowledge across languages in VLMs, potentially mitigating issues such as catastrophic forgetting and enabling more effective adaptation.

Real-world datasets, such as historical archives frequently contain imbalanced long-tailed label distributions, where a few Head labels contain abundant samples, while the remaining Tail labels are represented by significantly limited quantity of samples [11,47]. This creates a major obstacle for standard machine learning models to bias towards the majority labels and results in poor performance on the under-represented tail labels [15]. Common mitigation techniques, including data re-sampling, *e.g.*, SMOTE variants [44], loss re-weighting (*e.g.*, Class-Balanced Loss [5] or Focal Loss [28]), decoupled training [19] and logit adjustment [31] have been proposed to address long-tailed distributions, but mainly for classification settings. However, their application within the contrastive learning framework of CLIP for retrieval tasks is less explored. While acknowledging these methods, our work primarily concerns with assessing how different standard and efficient fine-tuning methods cope with the severe imbalance and long-tail distributions in historical datasets, without incorporating explicit long-tail mitigation algorithms. Analyzing the performance differences between these methods under such data conditions is our core investigation.

3 Dataset

3.1 Data Collection

We curated image-text pairs from four public digital archives— the U.S. National Archives Catalog [40], Europeana [8], World War Photos [42], and SMU Libraries Digital Collections [37]. These archives vary significantly in content: the U.S. National Archives Catalog and SMU collections generally offer richer metadata, while Europeana provides multilingual content, and the WWII Photos archive has sparser descriptions reflecting its specific focus. Image-text pairs are made by a standardized set of query phrases focused on the World War period, including World War photographs across different archives to ensure thematic consistency. Categorical labels were derived from this metadata and query phrases to construct the ground-truths.

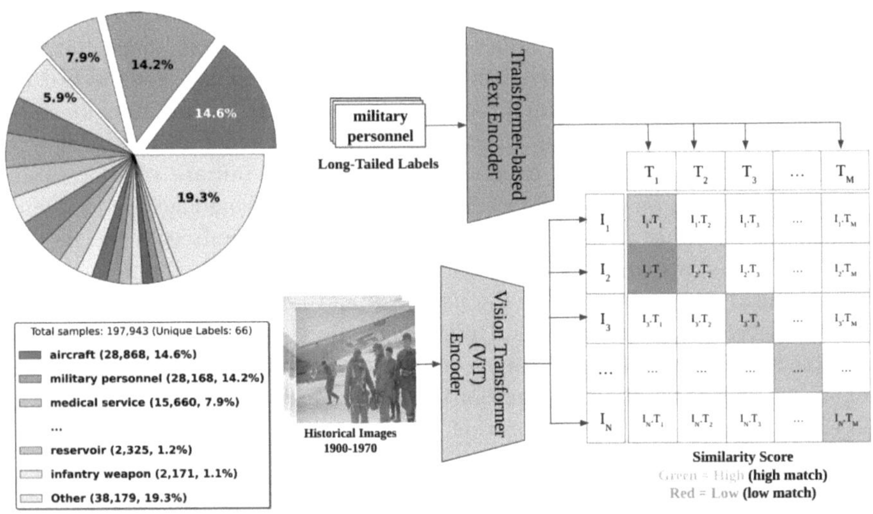

Fig. 1. HistoryCLIP multi-modal retrieval model. Textual and visual data from historical archives are encoded, and their similarity is computed as a sparse matrix (I, T) for image-to-text(I2T) and text-to-image(T2I) retrieval tasks, Transformer (e.g., CLIP Text Encoder), vision encoder (e.g., $ViT - B/32$).

We merged these collections to create a large-scale historical dataset with unified and comprehensive corpus, noted as HISTORY-X4. It contains the associated metadata for each retrieved content for retrieval evaluations. We utilize stratified random sampling for data splitting, based on the curated labels to ensure that inherent label imbalance and long-tailed distributions are present in the source archives as they are proportionally distributed in both splits which enables reliable performance evaluation under these challenging conditions. It reflects the real-world archival challenges for retrieval tasks and serves as the basis for our CLIP experiments. Figure 1 depicts a conceptual overview of the system architecture, which embeds historical images and textual labels into a shared space for retrieval.

3.2 Data Preprocessing

Table 1 indicates the size difference and unique label counts of each dataset. Prior to splitting, labels represented by only a single sample within their respective source dataset were eliminated to ensure robust stratification for analysis. To ensure compatibility with ViT image encoders, standard image preprocessing was applied: images were resized to 224 × 224 pixels (or 336 × 336 for $ViT-L/14@336px$) using bicubic interpolation, center-cropped, converted to RGB format, and tensorized. Crucially, images were normalized using the channel-wise mean (μ) and standard deviation (σ) calculated for each dataset.

Table 1. Summary of Historical Datasets. N: total samples, L: unique labels. Channel-wise mean (μ) and standard deviation (σ) used for image normalization.

Dataset	Period	Training ($N \times L$)	Validation ($N \times L$)	μ	σ
National Archive [40]	1900–1970	91,076 × 66	49,042 × 66	[0.682, 0.665, 0.635]	[0.264, 0.259, 0.254]
Europeana [8]	1900–1970	18,682 × 62	10,060 × 62	[0.509, 0.501, 0.478]	[0.277, 0.274, 0.271]
WWII [42]	1939–1945	16,267 × 10	8,760 × 10	[0.548, 0.552, 0.558]	[0.286, 0.286, 0.287]
SMU [37]	1900–1970	1,324 × 27	713 × 27	[0.454, 0.453, 0.456]	[0.267, 0.267, 0.267]
HISTORY-X4	1900–1970	127,357 × 66	68,578 × 66	[0.678, 0.662, 0.632]	[0.265, 0.259, 0.255]

3.3 Data Distributions and Characteristics

Label distributions across datasets exhibit a pronounced long-tailed pattern as depicted in Fig. 2. This long-tailed characteristic of label frequencies is consistent across the source archives and indicates the dominant contribution of National Archive with the majority of labels, broader spread of Europeana, concentration on specific war terms in WWII, and smaller overall contribution of SMU. This severe imbalance necessitates models capable of learning effectively from both high-frequency and rare categories.

4 Methods

4.1 Baseline Pre-trained CLIP

We adopt CLIP models as our baseline for multi-modal I2T and T2I retrieval tasks on historical datasets. CLIP was trained on 400 million image-text pairs

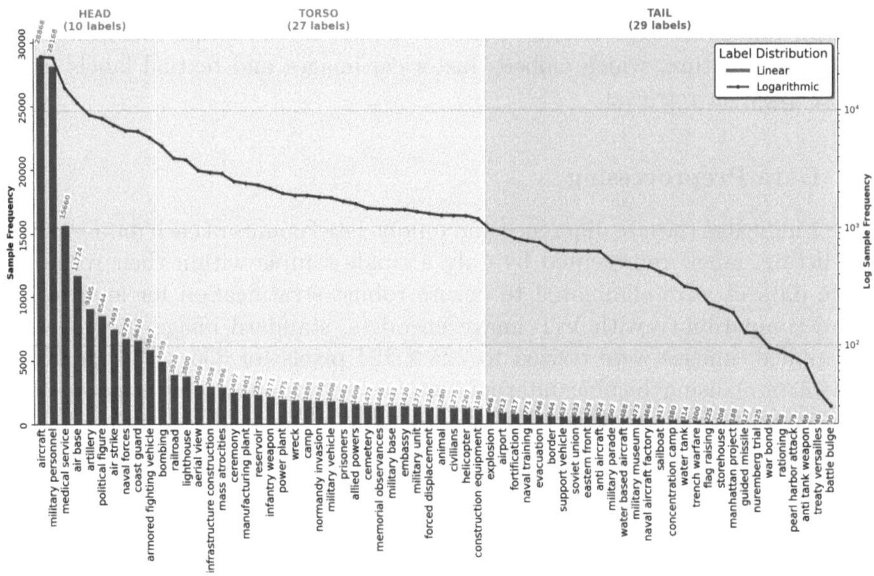

Fig. 2. `HISTORY-X4` long-tailed sample distribution with imbalance ratio of *962.3*. Sampling segmentation: Head $\geq$ 5000 samples, 1000 $<$ Torso $<$ 5000 samples and Tail $\leq$ 1000 samples.

from the web and demonstrates powerful zero-shot transfer capabilities across various tasks without the need for task-specific training data [33]. We leverage its ability to map images and arbitrary text descriptions into a shared semantic space as an ideal foundation for multi-modal retrieval tasks.

We evaluate four pre-trained CLIP variants with ViT-based image encoders ($ViT-B/16$, $ViT-B/32$, $ViT-L/14$, $ViT-L/14@336px$) as starting point for our fine-tuning methods. Our implementations leverages the transformed-based text encoder as described in [41] paired with ViT image encoder. These variants differ in model size and input resolution(Table 2), allowing us to assess the trade-off between computational efficiency and performance.

Although pre-trained CLIP models demonstrate strong capabilities, they encounter generalization challenges when applied to imbalanced historical archives, particularly with low-frequency Tail labels. This provides a strong incentive for fine-tuning approaches to improve retrieval performance.

4.2 Fine-Tuning Methods

Full Parameter Fine-Tuning. Comprehensive parameter updates enhance the model adaptability by learning specific dataset features [21]. We initialize pre-trained CLIP weights and update all the parameters of both text ($\sim 63M-123M$ parameters) and vision encoders ($\sim 88M - 304M$ parameters). Our fine-tuning is driven by symmetric contrastive loss function [33]. Given N image-text pairs, this loss operates on the matrix of cosine similarities (S_{ij}) between image ($I_i \in$

Table 2. CLIP architectural summary with ViT-based image encoder and transformer-based text encoder.

Specifications(ViT-)	B/32	B/16	L/14	L/14@336px
Patch Size	32×32	16×16	14×14	14×14
Input Resolution	224×224	224×224	224×224	336×336
Total Patches	50	197	257	577
Transformer Configuration				
Hidden Size (D)	768	768	1024	1024
Blocks	12	12	24	24
Attention Heads	12	12	16	16
Parameters ($\times 10^6$)				
Image Encoder	88.0	86.4	303.9	304.4
Text Encoder	63.2	63.2	123.6	123.6
Total	151.2	149.6	427.6	427.9

$\{I_1, \ldots, I_N\}$) and text ($T_j \in \{T_1, \ldots, T_N\}$) embeddings. Scaled by a learnable temperature τ, $\mathcal{L}_c(i,j)$ maximizes the similarity for positive pairs (S_{ii}) while minimizing it for negative pairs (S_{ij}, $i \neq j$):

$$\mathcal{L}_c(i,j) = -\frac{1}{2N}\sum_{i=1}^{N}\left(\log\frac{\exp(S_{ii}/\tau)}{\sum_{j=1}^{N}\exp(S_{ij}/\tau)} + \log\frac{\exp(S_{ii}/\tau)}{\sum_{j=1}^{N}\exp(S_{ji}/\tau)}\right). \quad (1)$$

To address the label imbalance common in real-world datasets, we incorporate a weighting mechanism [43], to address label imbalance and ensure rare labels contribute meaningfully to learning. The weighted loss for each positive pair (I_i, T_i) is scaled by a factor w_i inversely proportional to its class frequency. This prevents the model from being biased towards majority classes and improves performance on rare labels. Although powerful, it is computationally expensive for large model architectures of $ViT - L/14$ and $ViT - L/14@336px$ on extensive datasets, including `HISTORY-X4`. Additionally it risks overfitting, on small datasets, such as SMU, potentially compromising generalization performance.

LoRA. We employ LoRA as a parameter-efficient fine-tuning technique which significantly reduces computational and memory requirements while maintaining performance comparable to full fine-tuning [17]. The key insight is that weight updates during adaptation have intrinsically low rank. For a pre-trained weight matrix $\mathbf{W}_0 \in \mathbb{R}^{d \times k}$, (where d and k are input and output dimensions), LoRA parametrizes its update as $\mathbf{W} = \mathbf{W}_0 + \mathbf{BA}$ where $\mathbf{B} \in \mathbb{R}^{d \times r}$ and $\mathbf{A} \in \mathbb{R}^{r \times k}$ are trainable low-rank matrices with rank $r \ll \min(d,k)$. The original weights $\mathbf{W}_0$ remain frozen. We apply LoRA to three critical components in our CLIP implementation: 1) text encoder transformer blocks 2) vision encoder transformer blocks and 3) multi-modal projection layers for aligning text and vision embeddings into a shared space. Forward propagation is then computed using $y = \mathbf{W}_0\mathbf{x} + \frac{\alpha}{r}\mathbf{BAx}$ where α is a scaling factor. We set $r = 64$ and $\alpha = 2r$ based on empirical findings as a robust trade-off between performance and computational cost for large-scale vision-language models. We also follow [17,18] to initialize $\mathbf{A}$ with a normal distribution ($\sigma = \frac{1}{r}$) and $\mathbf{B}$ with zeros to ensure no initial impact. This approach reduces the trainable parameters by $\sim 95\%$ while maintaining general vision-language alignment capabilities of CLIP and mitigating catastrophic forgetting through constrained updates. Dropout is disabled in the base model to prevent stochasticity in the frozen backbone, but included in the LoRA implementation for regularization with a fixed value of 0.05. After fine-tuning, LoRA matrices can be merged with the original weights for inference without the risk of computational overhead [14].

Progressive Layer Unfreezing. We adopt progressive layer unfreezing as a hierarchical technique to gradually transit pre-trained layers from frozen to trainable states [16]. We divide the CLIP architecture into five distinct layer groups: 1) visual frontend for processing raw image inputs into initial embeddings, 2) visual transformer blocks to employ self-attention mechanisms and extract and refine visual features, 3) text frontend for processing tokenized text into initial embeddings, 4) text transformer blocks which utilize self-attention mechanisms to extract and contextualize textual features, and 5) projection layers which transform modality-specific embeddings into a shared multi-modal space.

The unfreezing schedule proceeds in P phases, starting with projection layers unfrozen and gradually incorporating deeper transformer blocks from both modalities:

$$\mathcal{L}_p = \begin{cases} \mathcal{P} & \text{if } p = 0 \\ \mathcal{P} \cup \mathcal{V}N_v - \lfloor \alpha_p \cdot N_v \rfloor \cup \mathcal{T}_{N_t - \lfloor \alpha_p \cdot N_t \rfloor} & \text{if } 0 < p < P-1 \\ \mathcal{P} \cup \mathcal{V} \cup \mathcal{T} \cup \mathcal{VF} \cup \mathcal{TF} & \text{if } p = P-1 \end{cases} \tag{2}$$

where $\mathcal{L}_p$ is the unfreezing schedule and represents the set of trainable layers in phase p, $\mathcal{P}$ denotes projection layers, $\mathcal{V}$ and $\mathcal{T}$ represent visual and text transformer blocks, $\mathcal{VF}$ and $\mathcal{TF}$ are visual and text frontend layers, N_v and N_t are the total number of visual and text transformer blocks, and $\alpha_p = p/(P-1)$ is the phase progression coefficient.

The phase transition in this approach is not predetermined by epoch count but rather guided by empirical convergence indicators [32,48]. We track several key metrics within a sliding window of size w to detect plateaus in the current phase. These metrics include the coefficient of variation of the loss to detect instability, the trend of the loss curve to identify worsening performance, the average epoch-to-epoch improvement to determine if it has fallen below a certain threshold, and the proximity to the current best loss value to determine if saturation has been reached. In our implementation, we adjust the learning rate and regularization, (weight decay), parameters dynamically across phases. Following [36,46], we compute new hyperparameters during transitions. Given a phase transition $p \to p+1$, the new learning rate and new weight decay are computed as follows:

$$\eta_{p+1} = \eta_0 \cdot \phi_p \cdot \gamma_{loss} \cdot \gamma_w \tag{3}$$

$$\lambda_{p+1} = \lambda_0 + \alpha_{p+1} \cdot \Delta\lambda_{max} \tag{4}$$

where η_0 and λ_0 are the initial learning rate and initial regularization respectively. ϕ_p is a phase-specific decay factor to gradually reduces the learning rate as we progress through phases. γ_w is scaling factor for learning rate based on the observation window size to ensure appropriate step magnitudes. γ_{loss} adjusts learning based on current optimization stability and increases the learning rate when the loss improves. And $\alpha_{p+1} \cdot \Delta\lambda_{max}$ progressively increases regularization throughout the fine-tuning which counterbalances the growing number of trainable parameters to prevent overfitting as more layers are unfrozen. This data-driven transition mechanism ensures that each layer group receives sufficient optimization before incorporating additional parameters [34]. By making informed decisions based on empirical evidence, we can adapt the optimization process to the specific needs of the model, ultimately leading to improved performance and efficiency in multi-modal retrieval tasks [38].

4.3 Evaluation Metrics

We employ standard information retrieval metrics to assess the performance of our multi-modal retrieval system across both I2T and T2I directions [9]. Given the single-labeled nature of our historical image dataset, we adapt these metrics to accurately reflect retrieval performance in this specific context.

Let $\mathcal{Q}$ represent the set of all queries, where each query q is an image (for I2T) or a text descriptor (for T2I). For query q, we define $\mathcal{R}_q$ as the set of relevant items and $\mathcal{S}_q^K$ as the top K items in the retrieved ranking. In our single-labeled dataset, for I2T retrieval, $|\mathcal{R}_q| = 1$ over all queries, q, whereas for T2I retrieval, we define $|\mathcal{R}_q|$ as the frequency of the label q in the dataset.

Precision at K ($P@K$) measures the proportion of relevant items among the top K retrieved results and mean Precision at K ($mP@K$) is computed by averaging it across all queries:

$$mP@K = \frac{1}{|\mathcal{Q}|} \sum_{q \in \mathcal{Q}} \frac{|\mathcal{S}_q^K \cap \mathcal{R}_q|}{K} \tag{5}$$

where for I2T retrieval with single labels, the maximum achievable $P@K$ is $\frac{1}{K}$ when the true label appears in the top K results [30].

Average Precision at K ($AP@K$) accounts for the ranking positions of relevant items within the top K results:

$$AP@K(q) = \frac{\sum_{j=1}^{|\mathcal{S}_q^K \cap \mathcal{R}_q|} \frac{j}{p_j + 1}}{\min(|\mathcal{R}_q|, K)} \tag{6}$$

where p_j is the position of the j-th relevant item in the ranking (using 0-based indexing). For I2T retrieval with a single relevant label at position r, this simplifies to $\frac{1}{r+1}$ if $r < K$ and 0 otherwise. The mean Average Precision at K ($mAP@K$) averages $AP@K$ across all queries and is computed as:

$$mAP@K = \frac{1}{|\mathcal{Q}|} \sum_{q \in \mathcal{Q}} AP@K(q). \tag{7}$$

Recall at K measures the proportion of relevant items successfully retrieved in the top K results and is calculated as:

$$Recall@K = \frac{1}{|\mathcal{Q}|} \sum_{q \in \mathcal{Q}} \frac{|\mathcal{S}_q^K \cap \mathcal{R}_q|}{|\mathcal{R}_q|} \tag{8}$$

where it is a binary value in I2T retrieval: 1 if the relevant label appears in the top K, and 0 otherwise [9]. In our implementation, we address the directional asymmetry of retrieval tasks in which for I2T, there exactly exist one relevant label per query ($|\mathcal{R}_q| = 1$), whereas for T2I, multiple relevant images may exist, calculated through frequency counting. For comprehensive evaluation, we report metrics at $K \in \{1, 5, 10, 15, 20\}$, allowing assessment across different retrieval depths. Lower K values highlight precision in immediately identifying relevant matches, while higher values demonstrate comprehensive retrieval capacity.

5 Results

5.1 Retrieval Performance

We evaluated the retrieval performance of the pre-trained CLIP models and the three fine-tuned methods (full parameter, LoRA, progressive unfreezing) on the `HISTORY-X4` validation set. Standard retrieval metrics, including $mP@K$, $mAP@K$, and $Recall@K$, are computed for both I2T and T2I retrieval tasks. The zero-shot performance of pre-trained CLIP models indicates basic retrieval capability,($e.g.$, $Recall@1 = 0.1$ for $ViT-L/14@336px$) and serves as a relatively low baseline on this specialized historical dataset (Table 3, dashed lines in Fig. 3). All three fine-tuning techniques demonstrated notable improvements across all metrics and tasks, highlighting the vital need for historical domain adaptation.

Figure 3 depicts significant performance enhancement for the representative CLIP $ViT-L/14@336px$ model and also demonstrates improvement percentage over the baseline for all retrieval metrics. The annotated improvement percentages quantify the relative gain calculated as $\frac{1}{metrics_{Baseline}} \times (metrics_{Fine-tuned} - metrics_{Baseline}) \times 100$, where metrics above 100% indicate that fine-tuning more than doubled the performance relative to the baseline.

Comparing fine-tuned methods for $ViT - L/14@336px$ (Fig. 3), progressive unfreezing consistently achieved the best performance across I2T and T2I tasks, establishing a clear advantage over the other methods, especially in $mAP@K$ and $Recall@K$. Full parameter fine-tuning and LoRA method showed remarkably similar performance levels, both significantly outperforming the baseline but generally falling slightly short of progressive unfreezing. This relative ranking among the fine-tuning methods (progressive > full $\simeq$ LoRA $\gg$ baseline) was observed consistently across all ViT backbones, as summarized by the key metrics in Table 3. The table further indicates that larger ViT architectures tend to provide higher absolute performance, both at baseline and after fine-tuning. While absolute baseline scores and improvement magnitudes varied slightly between I2T and T2I tasks, the overall effectiveness and relative ranking of the fine-tuning methods remained consistent. Performance gains for fine-tuned models tended to saturate at higher K values (e.g., $K = 10 \rightarrow K = 20$), particularly for $Recall@K$ and $mAP@K$.

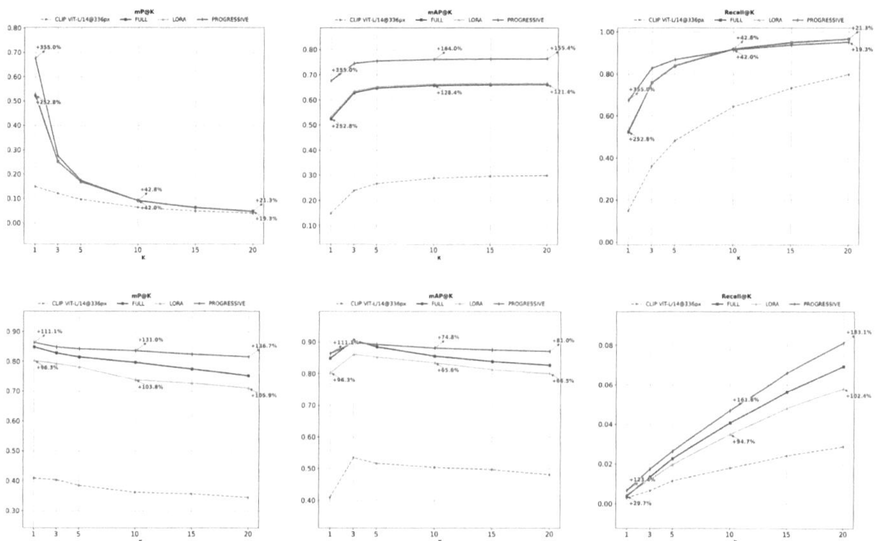

Fig. 3. Retrieval performance of CLIP $ViT-L/14@336px$ on `HISTORY-X4` validation set, comparing baseline against full parameter, LoRA, and progressive fine-tuning methods across I2T(top) and T2I(bottom) retrieval tasks.

Overall, the results strongly demonstrate that fine-tuning is crucial for effectively applying CLIP to imbalanced long-tailed historical archives. Amid the explored methods, progressive layer unfreezing consistently emerged as the most effective approach for maximizing retrieval performance on the `HISTORY-X4` dataset.

Table 3. HISTORY-X4 retrieval performance: baseline vs. best Fine-tuned method (progressive). baseline → progressive.

CLIP	I2T			T2I		
	R@1	R@10	mAP@20	R@1	R@10	mAP@20
$ViT-B/32$	0.12 → 0.43	0.50 → 0.85	0.23 → 0.56	0.00 → 0.00	0.01 → 0.02	0.36 → 0.81
$ViT-B/16$	0.13 → 0.45	0.55 → 0.86	0.25 → 0.60	0.00 → 0.00	0.01 → 0.03	0.38 → 0.82
$ViT-L/14$	0.14 → 0.63	0.62 → 0.90	0.29 → 0.72	0.00 → 0.00	0.02 → 0.05	0.43 → 0.87
$ViT-L/14@336px$	0.15 → 0.68	0.64 → 0.93	0.30 → 0.76	0.01 → 0.01	0.02 → 0.04	0.48 → 0.87

5.2 Retrieval Examples

To complement the retrieval performance of the model and gain a more comprehensive insight on historical archives, we present three I2T retrieval examples. Figure 4 compares the Top-3 predicted labels for baseline against the fine-tuned methods for representative images of Head, Torso, and Tail segments taken from HISTORY-X4.

Figure 4a depicts retrieval results for the Head class *naval forces*. The baseline predicts the related label *naval training* as Top-1 with probability of 0.52 and identifies the correct *naval forces* label with low probability (0.13) at rank 2. All fine-tuned models outperform the baseline, ranking *naval forces* as the Top-1 result with high probability (full: 0.64, LoRA: 0.59, progressive: 1.00), reinforcing that fine-tuning enhances retrieval precision for high-frequency labels. For the Torso label *power plant* (Fig. 4b), the baseline identifies the correct label relatively low, at rank 2 with low probability (0.36). Fine-tuning significantly improves this: full, LoRA, and progressive all correctly identify *power plant* as the Top-1 result with very high probability (≥ 0.96), highlighting fine-tuning effectiveness for mid-frequency labels. Figure 4c depicts retrieval results for the Tail label *fortification*. Baseline strongly predicts the correct label at rank 1 with probability of 0.72. All fine-tuned models not only predict *fortification* as Top-1, but they represented high confidence with higher probability (≥ 0.94) and outperform pre-trained baseline. The results of Fig. 4 reveal that fine-tuning not only boosts the retrieval performance when the baseline is relatively poor, *e.g.*, Head/Torso, but it also preserves and enhances performance even when the baseline is already good, *e.g.*, Tail.

We also analyze T2I retrieval performances of the fine-tuned models against the baseline, represented in Fig. 5. For the Head label, *medical service*, Fig. 5a represents the retrieved images for each strategy. The pre-trained baseline retrieves a mix of relevant and less relevant images within the Top-3. In contrast, fine-tuned models consistently retrieve highly relevant images, verified by their corresponding ground-truths as they demonstrate effective visual-text association for frequent labels after adaptation. Similarly, for Torso label, *ceremony*, Fig. 5b the baseline retrieves only one relevant image at rank 2. Fine-tuned models show clear improvement: full parameter and progressive fine-tuning retrieve three relevant *ceremony* images in the Top-3. LoRA retrieves two relevant images

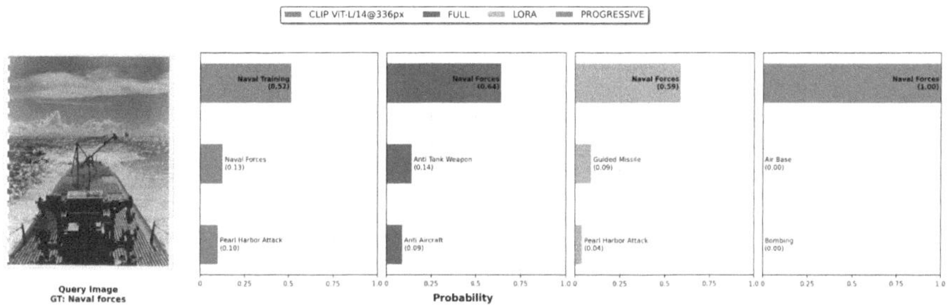

(a) Head sample: Ground-truth: *naval forces*

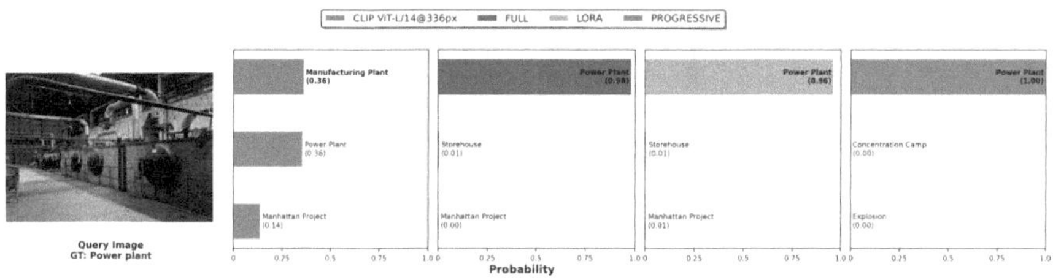

(b) Torso sample: Ground-truth: *power plant*

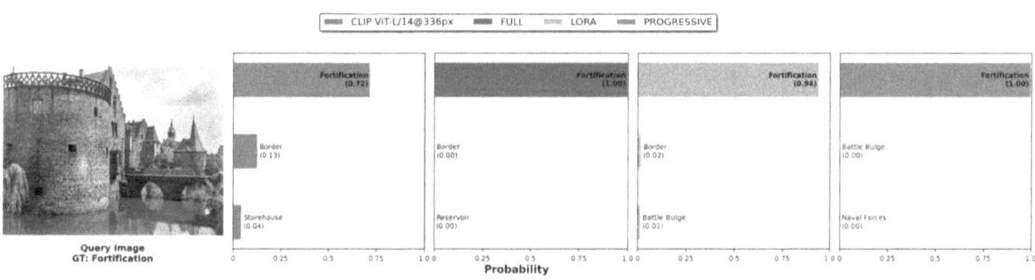

(c) Tail sample: Ground-truth: *fortification*

Fig. 4. I2T retrieval examples from HISTORY-X4), comparing Top-3 predicted labels for baseline vs. fine-tuned methods for images from different frequency segments.

but incorrectly ranks a *Normandy Invasion* image first, highlighting occasional variability between methods even for mid-frequency labels. Examining a Tail label, *trench warfare*, Fig. 5c shows that the pre-trained baseline retrieves a mix of irrelevant images, whereas fine-tuned models, effectively retrieve images clearly depicting trench warfare within Top-3, showcasing fine-tune capability to extend retrieval capability to lower-frequency labels. Full parameter and progressive fine-tuning show high precision in this example.

Figure 5d examines the Head label *political figure* as a case study to highlight the dataset complexity, driven by the nature of metadata. Although fine-tuned models generally improve T2I retrieval compared to the baseline, the progressive fine-tuning notably ranks a visually mismatched image (GT: *political figure*) as its Top-1 result. LoRA and full parameter fine-tuning achieve higher precision for this query. The model behavior in progressive fine-tuning suggests that its

(a) Head label: *medical service*

(b) Torso label: *ceremony*

(c) Tail label: *trench warfare*

(d) Biased sample: *political figure*

Fig. 5. HISTORY-X4 T2I retrieval examples. Each panel vertically stacks Top-3 results for baseline, full parameter, LoRA, and progressive fine-tuning for their corresponding query labels.

strong textual association learned during fine-tuning can override visual cues, particularly when relying on potentially ambiguous, metadata-derived ground truth field. This demonstrates a limitation of the current single-label, metadata-derived ground truth and motivates future work on visually grounded annotation refinement for historical archives.

6 Conclusion

This paper investigated multi-modal image-text retrieval for imbalanced, long-tailed historical archives using OpenAI CLIP. We presented `HISTORY-X4`, a curated historical image-text dataset reflecting such real-world challenges and comparatively analyzed pre-trained CLIP baselines against three fine-tuning methods: full parameter, LoRA, and progressive unfreezing.

Retrieval performance evaluation indicated that pre-trained CLIP has limited effectiveness in this specialized domain and uneven fields, while all fine-tuning methods outperformed the baseline across I2T and T2I retrieval tasks, validating the vital need for domain adaptation. Among the fine-tuning methods, progressive layer unfreezing consistently accomplished the highest retrieval metrics and LoRA performed comparably to full fine-tuning, offering a strong trade-off given its parameter-efficient implementation. Analyzing retrieval examples visually demonstrated improved retrieval of relevant results across Head, Torso, and Tail segments after fine-tuning. It also highlighted metadata limitations, such as single-label ground-truth where retrieval can occasionally be influenced more by textual embeddings than precise visual correspondence on diverse archival content.

The findings offer actionable insights to adapt state-of-the-art VLMs, *e.g.*, CLIP when coupled with effective fine-tuning, for more efficient exploration of historical archives. progressive unfreezing and LoRA demonstrated promising capabilities, with strong performance-efficiency trade-off. Although key limitations such as specific temporal range and simplified ground truths enable supervised learning, they may suffer capturing the full archival complexity.

Future work should concentrate on further improving the metadata quality of such historical archives by developing richer ground-truths through visually grounded annotation methods and investigating explicit long-tail learning techniques within the CLIP fine-tuning framework. It is also crucial to incorporate user perspectives through dedicated studies, in which we can acknowledge the user interpretation on original annotations for contextual understanding [23]. Such insights may lead to development of hybrid systems that leverage both automatic methods and human expertise, which can ultimately improve the retrieval performance and capabilities within digital humanities research.

Acknowledgments. This study was funded by the Research Council of Finland, grant number 351247. The authors wish to acknowledge CSC âĂŞ IT Center for Science, Finland, for generous computational resources.

References

1. Bai, Y., et al.: Advancing vision-language models with adapter ensemble strategies. In: Al-Onaizan, Y., Bansal, M., Chen, Y.N. (eds.) Findings of the Association for Computational Linguistics: EMNLP 2024, pp. 15702–15720. Association for Computational Linguistics, Miami, Florida, USA (2024)
2. Bayoudh, K.: A survey of multimodal hybrid deep learning for computer vision: architectures, applications, trends, and challenges. Inform. Fusion **105**, 102217 (2024)
3. Bayoudh, K., Knani, R., Hamdaoui, F., Mtibaa, A.: A survey on deep multimodal learning for computer vision: advances, trends, applications, and datasets. Vis. Comput. **38**(8), 2939–2970 (2022)
4. Cho, J., Lu, J., Schwenk, D., Hajishirzi, H., Kembhavi, A.: X-LXMERT: paint, Caption and Answer Questions with Multi-Modal Transformers. In: Webber, B., Cohn, T., He, Y., Liu, Y. (eds.) Proceedings of the 2020 Conference on Empirical Methods in Natural Language Processing (EMNLP), pp. 8785–8805. Association for Computational Linguistics, Online (2020)
5. Cui, Y., Jia, M., Lin, T.Y., Song, Y., Belongie, S.: Class-balanced loss based on effective number of samples . In: 2019 IEEE/CVF Conference on Computer Vision and Pattern Recognition (CVPR), pp. 9260–9269. IEEE Computer Society, Los Alamitos, CA, USA (2019)
6. Ding, N., et al.: Delta tuning: a comprehensive study of parameter efficient methods for pre-trained language models (2022)
7. Dosovitskiy, A., et al.: An image is worth 16x16 words: transformers for image recognition at scale. In: International Conference on Learning Representations (2021)
8. Europeana Foundation: Europeana (2024). https://www.europeana.eu/en
9. Faghri, F., Fleet, D.J., Kiros, J.R., Fidler, S.: Vse++: improving visual-semantic embeddings with hard negatives (2018)
10. Fiorucci, M., Khoroshiltseva, M., Pontil, M., Traviglia, A., Bue, A., James, S.: Machine learning for cultural heritage: a survey. Patt. Recogn. Lett. **133**, 102–108 (2020)
11. Fu, Y., et al.: Long-tailed visual recognition with deep models: a methodological survey and evaluation. Neurocomputing **509**, 290–309 (2022)
12. Han, Z., Gao, C., Liu, J., Zhang, J., Zhang, S.Q.: Parameter-efficient fine-tuning for large models: a comprehensive survey. Trans. Mach. Learn. Res. (2024)
13. Han, Z., Azman, A.B., Rina Binti Mustaffa, M., Binti Khalid, F.: Cross-modal retrieval: a review of methodologies, datasets, and future perspectives. IEEE Access **12**, 115716–115741 (2024)
14. Hao, T., et al.: Towards efficient vision-language tuning: more information density, more generalizability (2024)
15. He, H., Garcia, E.A.: Learning from imbalanced data. IEEE Trans. Knowl. Data Eng. **21**(9), 1263–1284 (2009)
16. Howard, J., Ruder, S.: Universal language model fine-tuning for text classification. In: Gurevych, I., Miyao, Y. (eds.) Proceedings of the 56th Annual Meeting of the Association for Computational Linguistics (Volume 1: Long Papers), pp. 328–339. Association for Computational Linguistics, Melbourne, Australia (2018)
17. Hu, E.J., et al.: LoRA: low-rank adaptation of large language models. In: International Conference on Learning Representations (2022)

18. Ji, Y., et al.: AdvloRA: adversarial low-rank adaptation of vision-language models (2024)
19. Kang, B., et al.: Decoupling representation and classifier for long-tailed recognition. In: International Conference on Learning Representations (2020)
20. Kirkpatrick, J., et al.: Overcoming catastrophic forgetting in neural networks. Proc. Natl. Acad. Sci. **114**(13), 3521–3526 (2017)
21. Kolesnikov, A., et al.: Big transfer (BiT): general visual representation learning. In: Vedaldi, A., Bischof, H., Brox, T., Frahm, J.-M. (eds.) ECCV 2020. LNCS, vol. 12350, pp. 491–507. Springer, Cham (2020). https://doi.org/10.1007/978-3-030-58558-7_29
22. Late, E., Ruotsalainen, H., Kumpulainen, S.: In a perfect world: exploring the desires and realities for digitized historical image archives. Proc. Assoc. Inform. Sci. Technol. **60**(1), 244–254 (2023)
23. Late, E., Ruotsalainen, H., Kumpulainen, S.: Image searching in an open photograph archive: search tactics and faced barriers in historical research. Int. J. Digit. Libr. **25**, 715–728 (2024)
24. Late, E., Ruotsalainen, H., Seker, M., Raitoharju, J., Männistö, A., Kumpulainen, S.: From textual to visual image searching: user experience of advanced image search tool. In: Linking Theory and Practice of Digital Libraries: 27th International Conference on Theory and Practice of Digital Libraries, TPDL 2023, Zadar, Croatia, September 26–29, 2023, Proceedings, pp. 277–283. Springer-Verlag, Berlin, Heidelberg (2023)
25. Li, L.H., Yatskar, M., Yin, D., Hsieh, C.J., Chang, K.W.: Visualbert: a simple and performant baseline for vision and language (2019)
26. Li, L.H., Yatskar, M., Yin, D., Hsieh, C.J., Chang, K.W.: What does BERT with vision look at? In: Jurafsky, D., Chai, J., Schluter, N., Tetreault, J. (eds.) Proceedings of the 58th Annual Meeting of the Association for Computational Linguistics, pp. 5265–5275. Association for Computational Linguistics, Online (2020)
27. Lialin, V., Deshpande, V., Yao, X., Rumshisky, A.: Scaling down to scale up: a guide to parameter-efficient fine-tuning (2024)
28. Lin, T.Y., Goyal, P., Girshick, R., He, K., Dollar, P.: Focal loss for dense object detection . In: 2017 IEEE International Conference on Computer Vision (ICCV), pp. 2999–3007. IEEE Computer Society, Los Alamitos, CA, USA (2017)
29. Lu, J., Batra, D., Parikh, D., Lee, S.: Vilbert: pretraining task-agnostic visiolinguistic representations for vision-and-language tasks. In: Wallach, H., Larochelle, H., Beygelzimer, A., d'Alché-Buc, F., Fox, E., Garnett, R. (eds.) Advances in Neural Information Processing Systems. vol. 32. Curran Associates, Inc. (2019)
30. Manning, C., Raghavan, P., Schütze, H.: Introduction to Information Retrieval. Cambridge University Press, An Introduction to Information Retrieval (2008)
31. Menon, A.K., Jayasumana, S., Rawat, A.S., Jain, H., Veit, A., Kumar, S.: Long-tail learning via logit adjustment. In: International Conference on Learning Representations (2021)
32. Prechelt, L.: Early stopping-but when? In: Neural Networks: Tricks of the Trade, This Book is an Outgrowth of a 1996 NIPS Workshop, pp. 55–69. Springer-Verlag, Berlin, Heidelberg (1998)
33. Radford, A., et al.: Learning transferable visual models from natural language supervision. In: Meila, M., Zhang, T. (eds.) Proceedings of the 38th International Conference on Machine Learning. Proceedings of Machine Learning Research, vol. 139, pp. 8748–8763. PMLR (2021)

34. Reinhardt, M., Geigle, G., Timofte, R., Glavaš, G.: Improving vision-language cross-lingual transfer with scheduled unfreezing. In: Gu, J., Fu, T.J.R., Hudson, D., Celikyilmaz, A., Wang, W. (eds.) Proceedings of the 3rd Workshop on Advances in Language and Vision Research (ALVR), pp. 155–166. Association for Computational Linguistics, Bangkok, Thailand (2024)
35. Saini, S.S., Rawat, P.: Deep residual network for image recognition. In: 2022 IEEE International Conference on Distributed Computing and Electrical Circuits and Electronics (ICDCECE), pp. 1–4 (2022)
36. Smith, L.N.: Cyclical learning rates for training neural networks. In: 2017 IEEE Winter Conference on Applications of Computer Vision (WACV), pp. 464–472 (2017)
37. Southern Methodist University Libraries: Degolyer library, smu (2024). https://www.smu.edu/libraries/digitalcollections
38. Sung, Y.L., Cho, J., Bansal, M.: Vl-adapter: parameter-efficient transfer learning for vision-and-language tasks. In: 2022 IEEE/CVF Conference on Computer Vision and Pattern Recognition (CVPR), pp. 5217–5227 (2022)
39. Tan, H., Bansal, M.: LXMERT: learning cross-modality encoder representations from transformers. In: Inui, K., Jiang, J., Ng, V., Wan, X. (eds.) Proceedings of the 2019 Conference on Empirical Methods in Natural Language Processing and the 9th International Joint Conference on Natural Language Processing (EMNLP-IJCNLP), pp. 5100–5111. Association for Computational Linguistics, Hong Kong, China (2019)
40. U.S. National Archives and Records Administration: National archives catalog (2024). https://catalog.archives.gov/
41. Vaswani, A., et al.: Attention is all you need. In: Guyon, I., et al., (eds.) Advances in Neural Information Processing Systems. vol. 30. Curran Associates, Inc. (2017)
42. World War Photos: World war photos - over 18,000 original photos from the second world war (2024). https://www.worldwarphotos.info/
43. Wu, C.Y., Manmatha, R., Smola, A.J., Krähenbühl, P.: Sampling matters in deep embedding learning. In: 2017 IEEE International Conference on Computer Vision (ICCV), pp. 2859–2867 (2017)
44. Xu, Z., Shen, D., Kou, Y., Nie, T.: A synthetic minority oversampling technique based on gaussian mixture model filtering for imbalanced data classification. IEEE Trans. Neural Netw. Learn. Syst. **35**(3), 3740–3753 (2024)
45. You, H., et al.: Learning visual representation from modality-shared contrastive language-image pre-training. In: Avidan, S., Brostow, G., Cissé, M., Farinella, G.M., Hassner, T. (eds.) Computer Vision - ECCV 2022, pp. 69–87. Springer Nature Switzerland, Cham (2022)
46. You, Y., et al.: Large batch optimization for deep learning: Training bert in 76 minutes. In: International Conference on Learning Representations (2020)
47. Zhang, Y., Kang, B., Hooi, B., Yan, S., Feng, J.: Deep long-tailed learning: a survey. IEEE Trans. Pattern Anal. Mach. Intell. **45**(9), 10795–10816 (2023)
48. Zhang, Y., Wei, Y., Yang, Q.: Learning to multitask. In: Bengio, S., Wallach, H., Larochelle, H., Grauman, K., Cesa-Bianchi, N., Garnett, R. (eds.) Advances in Neural Information Processing Systems. vol. 31. Curran Associates, Inc. (2018)
49. Zhou, K., Hassan, F.H., Hoon, G.K.: The state of the art for cross-modal retrieval: a survey. IEEE Access **11**, 138568–138589 (2023)

Studying Model Design Biases in LLMs for Multilingual Historical Newspaper Extraction; The Messina Earthquake Case Study

Sarah Oberbichler[1], Johanna Mauermann[2], The Trung Tran[3], and Carlos-Emiliano González-Gallardo[4](✉)

[1] Leibniz Institute of European History, Mainz, Germany
oberbichler@ieg-mainz.de
[2] University of Mainz, Mainz, Germany
jmauerma@students.uni-mainz.de
[3] University of Science and Technology of Hanoi, Hanoi, Vietnam
trungtt.bi12-452@st.usth.edu.vn
[4] Université de Tours, Tours, France
gonzalezgallardo@univ-tours.fr

Abstract. Large language models offer new opportunities for processing historical documents, yet their application raises questions of reliability. We present the first comprehensive and explainability-driven framework for evaluating model design bias in multilingual historical news article extraction, using newspaper coverage of the 1908 Messina earthquake as our test case across German, English, and French sources. Through systematic analysis of six state-of-the-art models, we uncover three critical bias patterns that, in addition to data quality, compromise extraction quality: contextual integration bias, overconfidence bias, and preference bias. Our evaluation reveals that these biases stem from alignment procedures rather than training data limitations, findings that establish methodological foundations for responsible AI deployment in digital humanities.

Keywords: article extraction · bias evaluation · historical newspapers

1 Introduction

Critical assessment of historical sources, datasets, and tools is essential, as neither data nor computational methods are neutral [2,13]. Bias can emerge at multiple stages—from archival curation to datafication and analytical tools—impacting representativity and quality [2,4,23]. These biases risk distorting interpretations, making systematic quality assessment crucial. As deep learning techniques of artificial intelligence (AI) become more integrated into historical research, evaluating both data and tools is necessary.

W.-T. Balke et al. (Eds.): TPDL 2025, LNCS 16097, pp. 263–286, 2026.
https://doi.org/10.1007/978-3-032-05409-8_16

This study investigates the application of instruct models powered by large language models (LLMs)[1] for multilingual historical newspaper article extraction (NAE), using newspaper coverage of the 1908 Messina earthquake as a case study. We focus on LLMs because of their accessibility to a broader range of researchers in digital history and humanities compared to traditional information retrieval methods. While we assess model performance in NAE, our primary objective extends beyond output evaluation. We aim to establish systematic methods for understanding LLMs' behavior in historical content processing, focusing on bias detection and analysis via explainability. Research on explainability seeks to clarify the function of alignment fine-tuning, investigate the reasons behind hallucinations, and measure the uncertainty associated with predictions made by language models [28].

With NAE, we developed a novel approach to historical document processing by enabling targeted, topic-specific extraction of articles from OCR-processed newspaper pages. Our method explores semantic-context-based extraction, bypassing traditional reliance on layout analysis and visual cues. The novelty of this strategy introduced distinct methodological challenges, as no pre-existing frameworks, benchmark datasets, or performance metrics existed for evaluation. To address this gap, we developed new datasets and designed evaluation and explainability frameworks that should help to understand the potential as well as the limitations and biases of this approach (Fig. 1). We made all our code and prompts accessible in a GitHub repository[2].

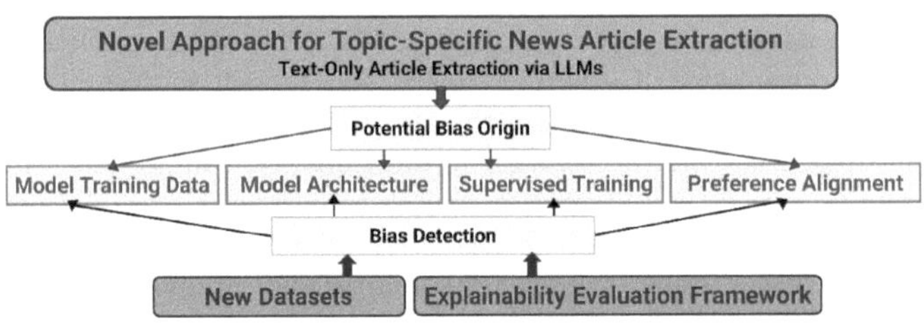

Fig. 1. Quality assessment and bias evaluation for a novel approach on NAE.

Drawing on [15], who defines bias as "a consistent pattern of error within a dataset, or within a method of data processing and analysis, that skews findings and interpretation," we examine three critical bias dimensions: (1) data selection bias, (2) model algorithmic bias, (3) and training/alignment bias [8,9].

While research on bias in AI predominantly focuses on social biases [5,7,9,10,17], our work addresses critical model design biases that can significantly distort outputs in historical document processing. Although social biases are inherent in historical sources, the successful extraction of original content

[1] All models used in this study are instruct models; however, we keep the acronym LLM in the text to facilitate the lecture.

[2] https://github.com/johannamauermann/LLM_Biases_Article_Extraction.

from multilingual cultural heritage data depends on three fundamental technical components: (1) comprehensive representation of diverse language and domain sources, (2) sophisticated semantic and contextual understanding capabilities, and (3) precise alignment optimized for extraction tasks. By applying rigorous source-critical approaches and systematic bias evaluation methods, researchers can identify limitations within these components and make informed decisions when deploying LLMs for historical document extraction. The reader is invited to consult our ethics statement in Appendix E.

2 Article Extraction and Classification Dataset

To conduct our study and analyze the behavior of different LLMs regarding biases, we first created a topic-specific evaluation dataset containing historical newspaper pages in German, English, and French, along with a manually curated ground truth covering the 1908 Messina earthquake in Italy.

2.1 The 1908 Messina Earthquake in Historical Newspapers

In the early hours of December 28, 1908, a massive earthquake struck Southern Italy, leaving widespread destruction in its wake. Messina, a city on the island of Sicily, was hit hardest by the earthquake, followed by a devastating tsunami and fires raging for days. Entire neighborhoods were leveled, and over half of the city's residents lost their lives. The devastation extended across the Strait of Messina to Reggio Calabria and nearby villages, with over 200,000 individuals killed, injured, or left without shelter [1,3,19,24].

This disaster, the deadliest earthquake ever recorded in Europe, captured global attention through extensive news reports. This extensive coverage makes the Messina earthquake an excellent case study for building a multilingual dataset, but it also presents significant challenges. Articles reporting on the Messina earthquake are often exceptionally long, and the event's complexity demands substantial contextual knowledge in order to identify relevant articles.

2.2 Dataset Description

We focused on data from three prominent newspapers of the time: *The Dresden Daily* (English), *Le Petit Parisien* (French), and *Norddeutsche Allgemeine Zeitung*(German). We collected the data using APIs from the German Digital Library (DDB)[3] and the French National Library (BNF)[4]. We utilized topic-specific keywords (*tremblement*, messine, séisme, earthquake*, messina, Erdbeben*, Messina*) to extract newspaper issues that potentially contain relevant articles, and we retained newspaper issues from the day of the earthquake until the end of 1909. While it is important to note that the list of keywords is not

[3] https://www.deutsche-digitale-bibliothek.de.
[4] https://www.bnf.fr.

exhaustive and that the dataset is not representative of the case study in rigorous historical terms, it should serve as a suitable foundation for evaluating the capabilities of LLMs in processing and understanding historical texts in different languages. We further manually created a ground truth (four eyes principle) as the benchmark for evaluation, which involved meticulously reviewing the newspaper issues and identifying and extracting relevant articles.

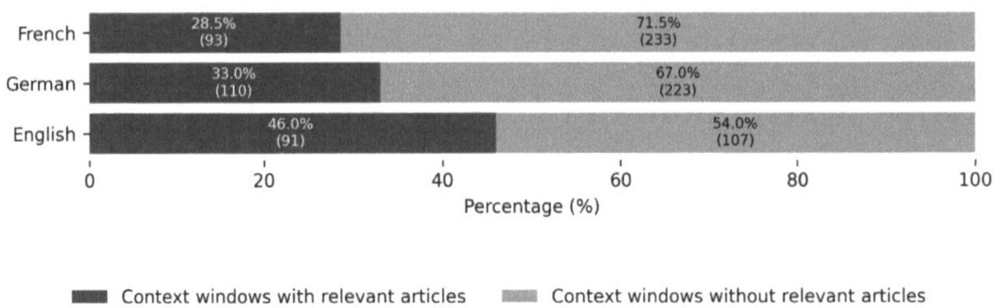

Fig. 2. Cumulative percentage and counts of context windows with relevant and irrelevant articles by language.

The final dataset comprises 875 entries containing context windows (1000 characters before topic-specific keywords and 2000 after) drawn from 528 distinct newspaper issues. Figure 2 illustrates the proportion of context windows with relevant articles related to the 1908 Messina earthquake. The final dataset also encompasses multiple layers of information, including detailed metadata and human-annotated ground truth extractions. It is designed to support a three-faceted evaluation of LLMs: (1) the capacity to classify content as relevant or not relevant to a specific topic (e.g., the 1908 Messina earthquake), (2) the accuracy in extracting complete relevant articles from the broader newspaper text, and (3) the ability to correctly delineate the beginning and end of an article, especially when several articles appear within the same newspaper issue.

By providing human-annotated ground truth in combination with prompts, including explainability and human-in-the-loop approaches, our dataset and evaluation framework allow for systematic assessment of how well LLMs can understand historical text, maintain contextual relevance, and perform precise information extraction. This framework helps to evaluate LLMs' effectiveness in handling real-world historical document processing tasks and how model design bias can affect the quality of the results. The dataset is publicly available in HuggingFace[5].

[5] https://huggingface.co/datasets/oberbics/Multilingual_Topic-Specific_Article-Extraction_and_Classification.

3 News Article Extraction (NAE) Approach and Evaluation Framework

Approaches to article separation in historical newspapers predominantly rely on layout information [14,26] or a combination of layout and semantic understanding [11,12,14,22]. While layout information is beneficial to delimit columns employing visual cues, it is also a bottleneck when facsimiles are unavailable or when they present poor quality. Our approach proposes a fundamentally different methodology leveraging purely textual content from OCR output, deliberately excluding layout information, to achieve efficient article extraction through prompt engineering. This text-centric methodology offers precise targeting of relevant content and enhanced processing efficiency by avoiding image analysis techniques. In addition, the flexibility of prompt-based article definition enables dynamic adaptation to varying scholarly requirements and historical contexts without necessitating modifications to the underlying extraction architecture. Given the novel nature of this semantic-only prompt-based approach to historical newspaper processing, no standardized evaluation frameworks exist.

Evaluation frameworks for layout-based article separation tasks traditionally rely on word counts or transcription metadata to compare model outputs with ground truth. However, when working with text-only sources, no positional metadata is available. Furthermore, traditional methods did not include explainability elements (as described in Sect. 3.1), which provide insights for identifying biases and risks. Consequently, we developed a comprehensive evaluation methodology to assess the efficacy of our text-based extraction paradigm, following a strategy grounded in explainability.

Explainability is fundamental when working with LLMs, given the need to understand the model's behavior in human-understandable terms [6]. This understanding enables the building of trust with the end user by clarifying the generation process in an understandable manner without the need for strong technical knowledge. Further, explainability is a critical tool for detecting and analyzing model design biases that might affect extraction quality and historical interpretation. Our explainability-based methodological strategy addresses a significant gap in historical document processing, establishing new protocols for evaluating prompt-based article extraction systems that can reveal both performance limitations and potential sources of bias.

3.1 Prompt Design and Parameters Settings

To systematically optimize our prompt engineering approach, we developed a controlled and resource-friendly test environment using a strategically sampled subset of the dataset described in Sect. 2. This subset comprised 15 newspaper pages from German, French, and English language sources, specifically curated to include boundary conditions such as articles with extreme length characteristics and structural discontinuities. Notably, we deliberately abstained from incorporating domain-specific knowledge about the 1908 Messina earthquake into the prompt design. This methodological choice allowed us to evaluate the model's autonomous contextual reasoning capabilities and historical event interpretation without explicit priming. Our iterative optimization process leveraged this sampled dataset to maximize development efficiency through (1) systematic performance analysis, where we conducted comprehensive testing of prompt variants against our sampled dataset, (2) failure mode analysis, where we performed detailed error analysis, and (3) iterative optimization of prompts until reaching convergence. This empirically driven approach ensured optimal prompt design while avoiding overfitting to the test corpus.

For our bias study, we selected instruction-based prompts as our simple prompting strategy and the chain-of-thought (CoT) [25] technique as our complex prompting strategy[6]. By prompting the model to articulate its reasoning, we aimed to better understand the stage at which potential biases emerged. This allowed us to trace reasoning patterns more effectively and gain insights into the model's behavior. We experimented with a simple user prompt in either English, French, and German (`Simple_{EN|FR|DE}`); and one complex user prompt (`Complex_{EN|FR|DE}`). For the German and French datasets, we applied the prompts in both the native language and English.

Concerning our baseline configuration, we set the temperature to $t = 0.0$ and seed to 42, to produce deterministic outputs by consistently choosing the highest probability token. We additionally implemented temperature $t = 0.2$ as a comparative condition to examine how introducing minimal randomness affects response quality and variability across all models. Although optimal parameter configuration typically varies between models, we deliberately applied identical settings across all systems to enable direct comparative analysis.

For the explainability component of our framework, we enhanced the prompts with three elements: (1) self-verification scoring mechanisms, (2) human verification notifications, and (3) model parameter adjustments to access underlying logits. An example of an LLM answer is shown in Example A.1 from Appendix A.

3.2 Article Comparison and Success Score

The article comparison employs a fuzzy string-matching algorithm designed to ensure that correct articles are accurately matched within a given context window when multiple articles are present. This process initiates with two primary inputs: ground truth articles and articles extracted using an LLM, both of which follow a preprocessing normalization stage to allow for consistent comparisons. The system applies character-level comparisons guided by a configurable similarity threshold, facilitating an effective bidirectional matching strategy that accommodates both one-to-many and many-to-one relationships between the ground truth and LLM outputs. This strategy also enables the identification of partial matches. During each comparison, the system utilizes sliding windows of n characters (with a default size of 50) to delineate matching boundaries between texts. This methodology assures a robust comparison, even when texts exhibit

[6] Both prompt strategies can be found in the GitHub repository.

minor discrepancies or contain OCR artifacts, thereby allowing for flexible and precise matching between the source materials and the extracted content.

We considered several key parameters to calculate a *success score (SSCr)* ranging from 0 to 1 to quantify the alignment quality. The description of each parameter can be consulted in Table 1 from Appendix D. The $SSCr$ is defined differently based on the alignment category:

- $SSCr = 0$ for **false positives** and **false negatives**, as these represent entirely incorrect alignments or missing matches;
- $SSCr = 1$ for **true negatives**, since these indicate correct non-matches;
- $SSCr = textsim_{g,a}$ for ground truth (g) and an extracted **aligned article** (a). The score is computed based on the degree of textual similarity between aligned segments, using the Eq. 1.

The textual similarity $SSCr = textsim_{g,a}$ for aligned articles is set to 1 and is reduced based on the normalized Levenshtein distance $d_{\text{lev}}^{g,a}$, the proportion of omitted characters $d_{\text{omit}}^{g,a}$, and the proportion of added characters $d_{\text{add}}^{g,a}$. Two penalties, α and β, weight omitted and added characters, respectively. A tolerance threshold τ is applied to $d_{\text{lev}}^{g,a}$ to account for minor OCR-related adjustments. Additionally, a formatting error penalty δ is considered. The final text similarity score is computed as

$$textsim_{g,a} = \max\left(0,\ 1 - (\max(0, d_{\text{lev}}^{g,a} - \tau) + \alpha \cdot d_{\text{omit}}^{g,a} + \beta \cdot d_{\text{add}}^{g,a}) - \delta\right), \quad (1)$$

where $\tau = 0.1$ and $\delta = 0.2$ if a formatting error is present (otherwise $\delta = 0$). α and β are set to 1.5 and 1 given that omitted characters are penalized more heavily, as even small omissions may significantly distort meaning.

This comprehensive scoring mechanism ensures that minor discrepancies do not result in disproportionate penalties, while more significant misalignments and omissions are accurately represented in the scoring. It allows for a nuanced evaluation that goes beyond a binary framework, facilitating the differentiation not only between correct and incorrect alignments but also among the aligned articles themselves, thereby highlighting cases where content was omitted, added, or otherwise inadequately extracted.

4 Model Performance Analysis for Bias Detection

Detecting and measuring bias in LLMs involves combining quantitative and qualitative analyses [20]. By following evaluation approaches that can reveal biases from different origins as outlined in Table 2 from Appendix D, we compare model evaluation metrics against close reading to get a deeper understanding of the limitations that skew model outputs. We distinguish between data quality issues (such as OCR errors) that represent external factors degrading performance across all models, and model bias that manifests as systematic patterns persisting independent of input quality—such as consistently exhibiting overconfidence.

We evaluate six models representing different paradigms: three open-weight models (Llama 3 70B from Meta, Nemotron 3.1 70B from Nvidia, and Qwen 2.5 72B from Alibaba Cloud) accessed via Together.ai[7], and three proprietary models (GPT-4o[8], Claude 3.5 Sonnet[9], and DeepSeek V3[10]) accessed through their respective APIs. The models were evaluated based on their ability to accurately identify content, align text correctly, and manage language-specific variations.

4.1 Temperature Response Performance

We established a default temperature of $t = 0.0$ for model evaluation. To assess the models' sensitivity to sampling parameters, we conducted supplementary experiments with the temperature adjusted to $t = 0.2$. Both temperature settings fall within the low range $[0, 0.3]$ to facilitate an in-depth examination of the stability of each model's internal representations and decision boundaries.

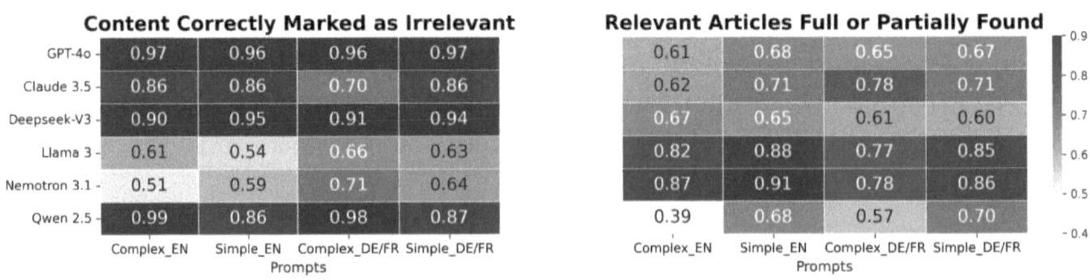

(a) $t = 0.0$

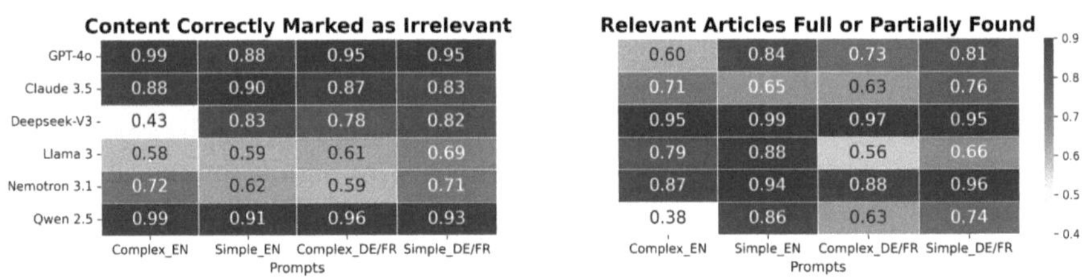

(b) $t = 0.2$

Fig. 3. Proportion of found relevant vs irrelevant articles with model temperature set to 0.0 and 0.2 aggregated across all languages.

As seen in Fig. 3, increasing the temperature parameter from 0.0 to 0.2 reveals significant alignment challenges across models, particularly in maintaining balanced performance between content correctly marked as irrelevant (precision) and relevant articles fully or partially found (recall). Deepseek V3 exhibits the

[7] https://api.together.ai.
[8] https://openai.com/api/.
[9] https://www.anthropic.com/api.
[10] https://api-docs.deepseek.com/api/deepseek-api.

most sensitivity, with its recall for relevant articles dramatically improving (from overall 0.63 to overall 0.96) while its precision in correctly identifying irrelevant content decreased to around 0.80 for most prompts (with an outlier for the complex English prompt). In contrast, Claude 3.5 gets overall slightly better results in correctly marking irrelevant articles with the temperature set to 0.2, and Nemotron 3.1 shows overall better results with the temperature set to 0.2. GPT-4o follows a similar pattern as Deepseek V3 towards better finding relevant articles with the higher temperature, however, just like Claude 3.5 and Qwen 2.5, it consistently prioritizes precision over recall across temperature settings. The different responses to temperature changes across models reveal fundamental differences in how these models handle uncertainty and make decisions.

Qualitative error pattern evaluation provides insights into the decision boundaries and the models' approach to uncertainty. With temperature $t = 0.0$, some models strongly focus on primary criteria: place (Messina), date (28 of December), and earthquake context, while ignoring locations related to the Messina earthquake but not Messina itself and disregarding aftershocks (despite explicit instructions in the prompts to include aftershock information). The too narrow focus also limited what qualified as an article (while we kept the definition broad on purpose). We show concrete examples in Examples A.2 and A.3 from Appendix A.

The error pattern analysis also showed that, despite demonstrating strong historical knowledge and geographic understanding in isolation, models can fail to synthesize these separate knowledge domains to reach accurate conclusions, especially when the temperature is set to $t = 0.0$. Nevertheless, setting a temperature $t \neq 0.0$ implies variability in the generated text, which limits reproducibility and makes evaluation difficult.

4.2 Language-Specific Performance

To analyze language-specific performance, we calculated total average success scores ($SSCr$) and conducted cross-lingual comparisons. Our evaluation, shown in Fig. 4, revealed notable variation across languages. French achieved the highest overall performance with an average accuracy of 0.78, followed by English (0.72) and German (0.70).

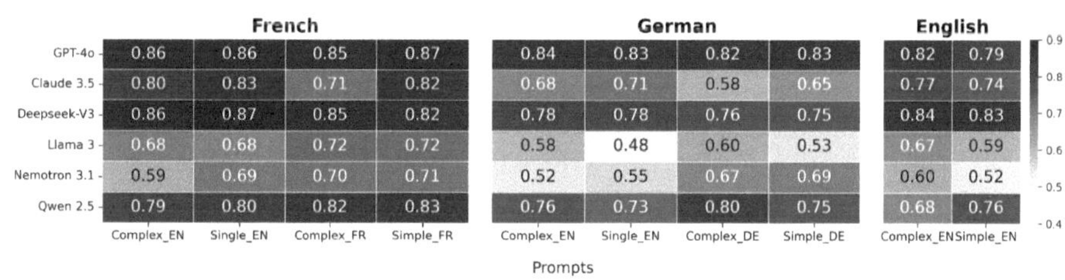

Fig. 4. Total average model accuracy (percentage of correct predictions) for the French, German, and English datasets.

However, these results do not necessarily indicate substantial superiority among source languages in the article extraction task. A more nuanced interpretation requires examining the composition of the dataset (Fig. 2), the differential performance of the models between correctly classifying irrelevant content versus correctly identifying relevant articles (Figs. 3a and 3b), and OCR impact (Fig. 13b). The apparently higher performance metrics in French can be attributed mainly to the distinct distribution of relevant versus irrelevant articles across these language corpora. All evaluated models with temperature $t = 0.0$ demonstrated stronger capabilities in correctly identifying irrelevant content than in detecting relevant articles. Consequently, languages with different proportions of irrelevant examples, as seen in the French and, to a lesser extent, in the German datasets, naturally yield different overall performance scores without necessarily reflecting superior language processing capacities. Additionally, the French dataset contained more OCR errors than other language datasets, negatively affecting model accuracy (see Sect. 5 and Appendix B).

Similarly, the language of the prompts had minimal impact on model performance. For example, for the French dataset, English prompts scored 0.75 versus 0.78 for native French prompts. On the German dataset, the difference between German and English prompts was only 0.03 as well.

4.3 Instruction Following Performance

Analysis of model output consistency further revealed variations in instruction adherence across the evaluated models. We evaluated how well the models maintain the requested output format (extracting original articles without summarizing or truncating), ensuring content completeness, and preserving original text. This analysis is a combination of quantitative and qualitative approaches. As a quantitative approach, we measured the article under-extraction frequency where models captured only portions of relevant content (Fig. 5), and structural parsing errors, where models failed to create separate XML tags for distinct articles within a context window (Fig. 6).

Our qualitative analysis of results with partial article extractions revealed distinct error patterns across models. Despite their differing capacities, both the

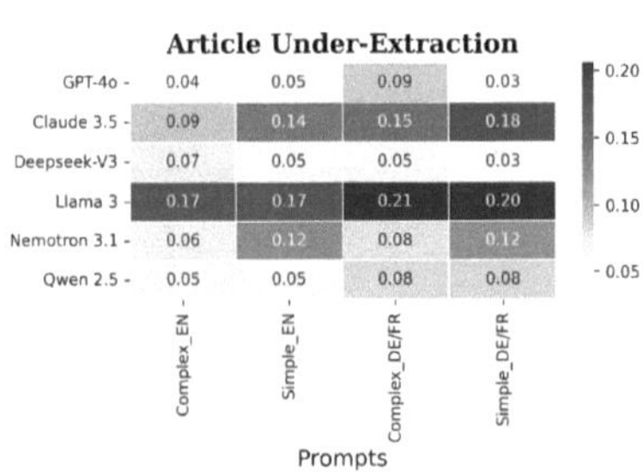

Fig. 5. Proportion of under-extracted articles across models and aggregated across all languages.

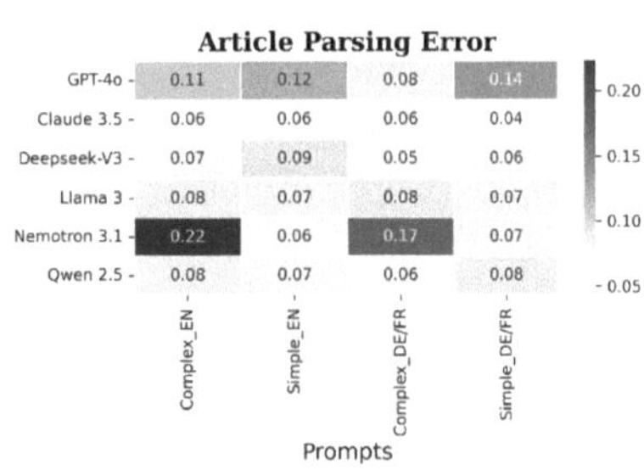

Fig. 6. Proportion of incorrectly parsed articles across models and aggregated across all languages.

mid-size Llama 3 and the substantially more capable Claude 3.5 frequently failed to process very long articles by either claiming they exceeded length limitations or simply appending phrases like "full content truncated for brevity" and truncating the content. These models disregarded explicit instructions against such behavior, which consequently lowered their performance on NAE.

Error patterns also varied in the article parsing. While Claude 3.5 demonstrated good parsing accuracy with minimal structural errors, GPT-4o exhibited considerable parsing difficulties when using simple prompts. Also noteworthy is Nemotron 3.1's systematic formatting deviation, not only in parsing articles, but also favoring markdown formatting conventions, mixing markdown and XML.

4.4 Confidence Elicitation and Logits Correlation

LLMs tend to be overconfident in their output and struggle to identify the factual knowledge boundary precisely [21]. For these reasons, it is relevant to quantify the confidence of the model during the generation process. Different techniques oriented to measure the fluctuations of the model's weights can be used in white-box environments in which access to the architecture and weights of the models is possible. However, when working in a black-box environment, model confidence must be assessed through alternative means: either by analyzing the model's prediction logits (when available) or through confidence elicitation techniques. Confidence elicitation is the process of extracting LLMs' uncertainty judgments through specific prompting strategies, without requiring model fine-tuning or accessing internal information [27]. We implement a dual approach where we analyze prediction logits to quantify statistical confidence while also employing elicitation by explicitly asking models to indicate when human verification is needed and requesting self-confidence scores for their responses.

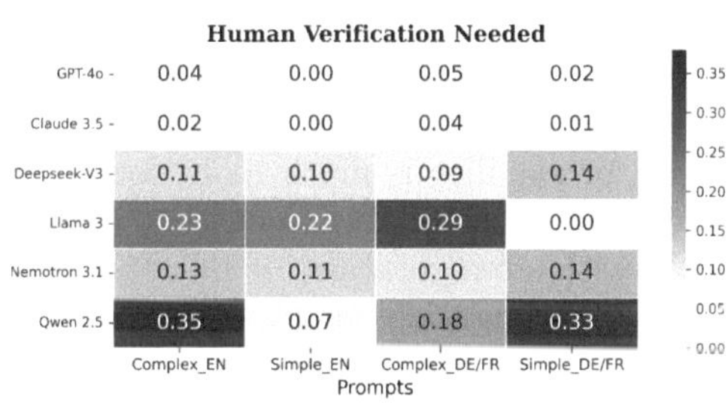

Fig. 7. Proportion of predictions where models requested human verification aggregated across all languages.

Analysis of human verification needed patterns, as shown in Fig. 7, reveals distinct behavioral characteristics across models and prompts. Among all models tested, GPT-4o and Claude 3.5 show the least frequency of requesting human verification, indicating model alignment with low uncertainty thresholds for decision-making. Llama 3 and Qwen 2.5 show opposite behavior, demonstrating an unnecessarily high tendency toward verification and uncertainty expression. Nemotron 3.1 and Deepseek V3 have shown the best balance in communicating uncertainty. Apart from analyzing responses using the <human_verification_needed> label, we also ask the model to rate its answers through a <confidence_score> ranging from 0 to 1. This score provides a more precise, quantitative measure of the model's confidence estimation, enabling deeper analysis of its certainty in various scenarios. Figures 8 and 9 illustrate the mean and standard deviation of the self-assessed confidence scores of each model for combined German, English, and French datasets. Claude 3.5 consistently demonstrates the highest self-confidence scores with a mean value of 0.93 ± 0.06. GPT-4o revealed a slightly lower but more stable mean confidence score of 0.86 ± 0.04. Llama 3 obtains a mean value of 0.73 ± 0.22, showing the lowest confidence score, while the most significant fluctuations. Figures 14a and 14b in Appendix B show the detailed values for each language.

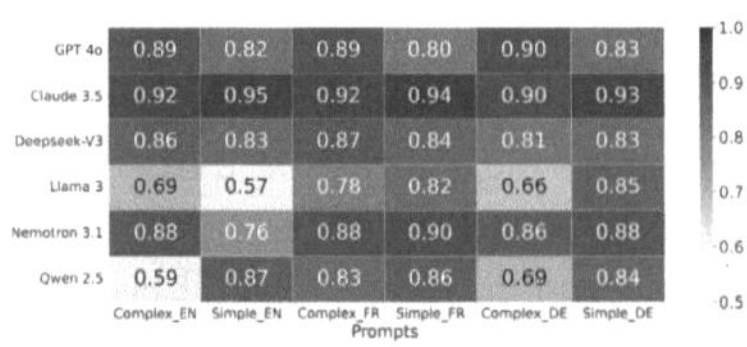

Fig. 8. Mean self-confidence scores across models.

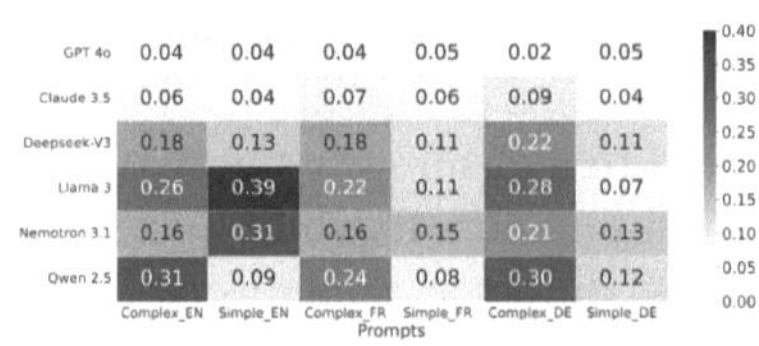

Fig. 9. Standard deviation of self-confidence scores.

Upon these analyses, we could also make a direct comparison between these scores and the logits from the last layer of the LLMs themselves to get more insights into the differences between the self-evaluated scores and the probability value for each token in the generated answer. Figures 10 and 11 show the mean value and standard deviation for the token probability of each model for the combined German, English, and French datasets. Claude 3.5 is excluded from this analysis, given that its API does not provide logits or full probabilities. Overall, the token probability is much more consistent compared to the confidence score, which is understandable given that it reflects the probability of each individual token with a temperature $t = 0.0$. Most tokens usually exhibit near-perfect probabilities, leading to lower variance in this metric. DeepSeek V3 stands out with a perfect mean token probability and no variability, which is possibly due to the use of a greedy decoding algorithm for the final layer of this model. Further experiments with temperature $t = 0.2$ reflected variations in the mean value token probability similar to GPT-4o, which shows the lowest and most variable token probability. This is opposite to what we have analyzed above on the confidence score and could be due to a more diverse and probabilistic token generation from GPT-4o. Other models show quite similar values, indicating a balanced behavior between confidence and variability. Figures 15a and 15b in Appendix B show the detailed values for each language.

To more effectively visualize the relationship between confidence scores and token probabilities, we computed their linear correlation. However, as our anal-

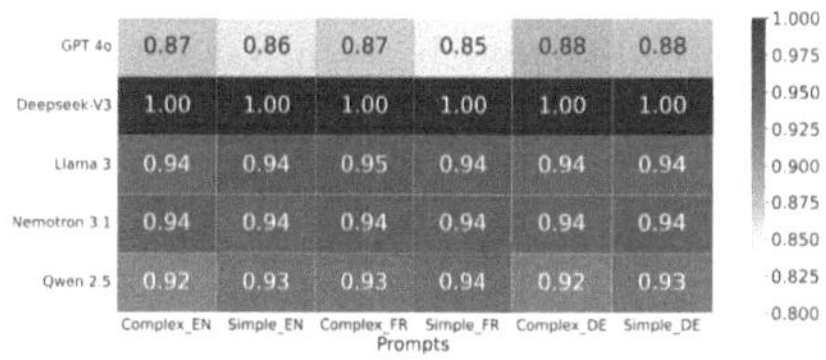

Fig. 10. Mean value of token probability with different setups.

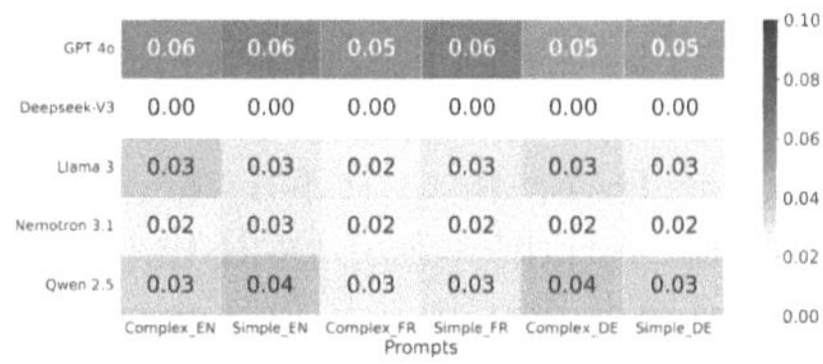

Fig. 11. Standard deviation value of token probability with different setups.

ysis suggests, using all tokens may not be ideal, as it often leads to redundant or uniform results. Therefore, we selected more distinctive tokens within each response that better reflect the model's confidence. Specifically, we utilized the token `True`/`False` from the `human_verification_needed` tag. When this token is `True`, indicating that the model lacks complete confidence and human verification may be required, we computed the adjusted probability as $1 - \mathit{probability}$, since a high token probability for `True` signifies uncertainty rather than confidence.

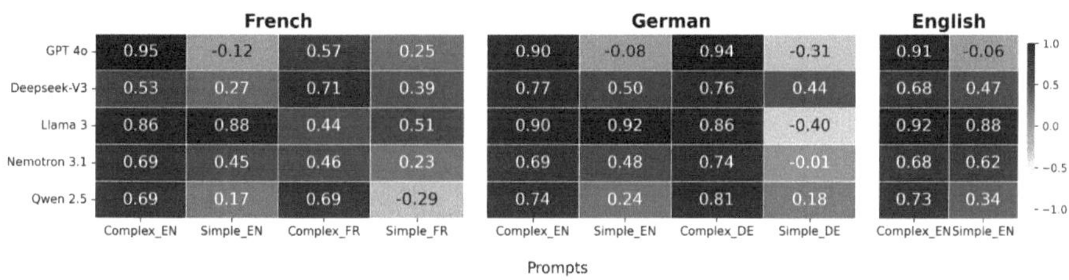

Fig. 12. Correlation between confidence score and Probability in human verification token across languages.

The resulting correlations are presented in Fig. 12. GPT-4o and Llama 3 both exhibit strong positive correlations under English complex prompts, suggesting that their confidence scores reliably reflect output quality in these contexts. In contrast, GPT-4o shows near-zero or even negative correlations for simple prompts. Similarly, Qwen 2.5 demonstrates positive correlations with complex prompts but weaker or negative correlations with simpler ones. Lastly, DeepSeek V3 and Nemotron 3.1 maintain moderately positive correlations across most scenarios. Overall, model confidence scores tend to be more reliable indicators of output quality under complex prompting conditions, while this reliability diminishes for simpler prompts.

5 Impact of OCR Errors

To systematically evaluate the impact of OCR transcription errors, we created a control ground truth sample comprising 88 manually corrected context transcripts (30 in French, 29 in German, and 29 in English) with a similar distribution of relevant and irrelevant content as the original dataset. Overall, the mean Character Error Rate (CER) across this control sample was 0.1388, indicating a substantial level of OCR-induced noise in the original data. However, the CER varied by language: French exhibited the highest CER (0.2008), followed by German (0.1377), while English had the lowest (0.0759).

(a) control sample with OCR errors

(b) corrected control sample

Fig. 13. Percentage of found relevant vs irrelevant articles on control sample aggregated across all languages.

Our quantitative analysis highlights the significant impact of OCR quality on LLM output. As illustrated in Fig. 13, the average model accuracy on the control sample notably improved following OCR correction. The results indicate a strong causal relationship, with all models exhibiting consistent performance trends across both the control sample and the full dataset. After OCR correction, models demonstrated markedly superior performance in identifying relevant articles. The open-weight models Llama 3, Nemotron 3.1, and Qwen 2.5 showed remarkable improvements, while their accuracy in marking articles as irrelevant remained consistent. GPT-4o and Claude 3.5, on the other hand, did not indicate significant OCR-related changes in performance. These findings underscore the importance of OCR postprocessing. Further details can be consulted in Figs. 16, 17 and 18 from Appendix C.

6 Overall Discussion and Conclusion

Temperature Variations Expose Contextual Integration Bias in LLMs. Our comparison between temperature settings reveals how models respond to parameter changes. With temperature set to $t = 0.0$, we observed some models exhibiting stronger contextual integration bias for articles lacking explicit identifying markers compared to temperature $t = 0.2$, resulting in failure to integrate related contextual information. This indicates that deterministic processing hampers models' ability to synthesize contextual relationships. This limitation further suggests that incorporating richer historical domain knowledge or knowledge graphs [18] might enable models to better synthesize temporal, cultural, and causal relationships into a cohesive narrative.

Overall Results show that all Models Deal Well with Multilingual Sources and Prompts. While it is often assumed that the higher representation of English in LLM training data would lead to superior performance, our findings did not reveal significant differences across the evaluated language datasets (English, German, and French), the models used, or the language of the prompt, despite observing different accuracy levels for each language dataset. Considering data composition, better results for precision, as well as the impact of OCR errors, these differences become statistically insignificant. This suggests that German and French are sufficiently well-represented in the training data.

Bias Through Format Sensitivity and Built-in Safety Constraints has a Notable Impact on the Quality of the Results. Our analysis indicates that some models exhibit a preference toward truncation, summarization, or rigid output formatting despite explicit prompting—likely as a result of built-in safety constraints or format-sensitive decoding mechanisms during the reinforcement learning with human feedback fine-tuning. While these features are designed to prevent the generation of inappropriate content and maintain stylistic consistency, they can inadvertently lead to the loss of critical contextual details. This behavior diminishes the models' capacity for information extraction, especially when creating historical research corpora.

Overconfidence Bias Limits Effective Human Oversight. Our evaluation revealed that overconfidence bias in certain LLMs significantly limits the opportunity for human intervention. When a model exhibits high confidence in its outputs—even in ambiguous cases—it is less likely to signal uncertainty or request human verification. This overconfidence hampers effective human involvement, as users receive outputs without the necessary prompts to critically review or correct errors. Our analysis of the correlation between token probability and self-verification further supports findings that over-confidence is mainly introduced by alignment procedures, rather than being an inherent feature of the pre-trained base model [16].

Disclosure of Interests. The authors have no competing interests to declare that are relevant to the content of this article.

A Model Output Examples

A.1 Example Model Output (Deepseek V3, Complex English Prompt, English Dataset, Temperature 0.0)

<think>
The first part of the text discusses Denmark's national security and defenses, which is irrelevant to the Messina earthquake. The second part reports shipping disasters in New Zealand and Brest, which are also irrelevant. The third part, "TERRIBLE WEATHER IN CALABRIA," mentions Reggio, a town affected by the Messina earthquake, and describes a violent storm and an earthquake shock. This is relevant as it discusses the consequences of the earthquake. The fourth part mentions an official decree regarding duty-free access for goods destined for earthquake sufferers, which is also relevant as it pertains to aid for the victims of the Messina earthquake. Both relevant parts are complete semantic units and are clearly distinguished from the preceding and following content. Confidence is high (0.9) because the relevant articles are clearly identifiable and complete. Human verification is not needed as the segmentation and relevance assessment are clear. **<think>**

<article> TERRIBLE WEATHER IN CALABRIA. Reggio, February 12. A violent storm accompanied by showers of hail and heavy rain swept the ruined town last night, while this morning an earthquake shock was felt. **<article>**

<article> Rome, February 12. An official decree announces that all consignments of goods from abroad destined for sufferers from the earthquake, including provisions, transportable houses, and materials for building, will be allowed access duty free until June 30th. **<article>**

<verification> Is the unit coherent? Yes. Is the subject present? Yes. Is the article complete? Yes. Have all articles been found? Yes. **<verification>**

<human_verification_needed> False **<human_verification_needed>**

<confidence> 0.9 **<confidence>**

<confidence_explanation> The relevant articles are clearly identifiable, complete, and directly related to the Messina earthquake and its consequences. **<confidence_explanation>**

A.2 Example 1: Uncertainty About Right Location

This example illustrates how the model exhibits uncertainty when classifying an earthquake event as relevant or not (e.g., mention of damage in Calabria as consequence of the Messina earthquake December 1908).

Ground Truth Article
EARTHQUAKE IN ITALY. Monte leone, December 28. Extensive damage was done here and at Mileto, Cantazaro, San Giorgio, and other Calabrian districts by a violent earthquake which occured at 5.50 o'clock this morning. [...]

Deepseek V3 Answer (complex-EN, temperature 0.0)
High confidence (1.0) that this article is not about the Messina earthquake, as the date and location are clearly different. No ambiguity exists in this case.
Deepseek V3 Answer (complex-EN, temperature 0.2)
The second section titled "EARTHQUAKE IN ITALY" explicitly reports on a December 28 earthquake affecting Calabrian districts (Monteleone, Mileto, Cantazaro, San Giorgio)[...]. It is a direct mention of Calabrian districts impacted by the 1908 Messina earthquake.
Nemotron 3.1 (complex-EN, temperature 0.0)
The confidence is relatively low because, although an article about an earthquake in Italy was found, it does not specifically mention the Messina earthquake of December 1908 or its consequences, which are the primary criteria for relevance. The article's relevance to the specified topic is partial at best, focusing on a different earthquake in Calabria.
Nemotron 3.1 (complex-EN, temperature 0.2)
The article about the earthquake in Italy is relevant, but it does not specifically mention the Messina earthquake of December 1908. However, since it is an earthquake in Italy and occurred in December, it might be related to the Messina earthquake. Further verification is not needed in this case.
Claude 3.5 Answer (simple-EN, temperature 0.0)
High confidence that this is not the 1908 Messina earthquake because: 1) Different locations are mentioned (none include Messina), 2) The scale of damage reported is much smaller than the catastrophic Messina earthquake, 3) While the month is December, no year is specified, but the context and reporting style suggest this is a different even
Claude 3.5 Answer (simple-EN, temperature 0.2)
While this article does discuss an earthquake in Italy in December 1908, it appears to be reporting on a different seismic event that occurred in Calabria [...]. The Messina earthquake affected Sicily and Calabria and was much more devastating, killing over 80,000 people.

A.3 Example 2: Classification Uncertainty

This example illustrates how the models exhibit uncertainty when determining whether a text qualifies as an article according to our criteria (own semantic unit).

Ground Truth Article

Lieutenant-Commander Reginald Belknap, American Naval Attache in Berlin, is temporarily on active duty in Italy. After accompanying a section of the American Fleet to Gibraltar, he was put in charge of the thousands of shelter-sheds erected in Italy for the protection of those rendered homeless by the late terrible earthquake at Messina.

Deepseek V3 Answer (complex-EN, Temperature 0.0)

The provided text does not contain any clearly distinguished semantic units with their own headlines. It appears to be a collection of unrelated snippets or news items without clear segmentation into articles.

Deepseek V3 Answer (complex-EN, Temperature 0.2)

The semantic unit is coherent and complete and there is a explicit mention of Messina earthquake consequences.

Claude 3.5 Answer (Complex-EN, Temperature 0.0)

The text appears to be a society/social news column from Berlin, with only a brief mention of Lieutenant-Commander Reginald Belknap's involvement in shelter construction after the Messina earthquake. This mention is too brief and incidental to constitute a relevant article about the Messina earthquake according to the given criteria.

Claude 3.5 Answer (simple-EN, Temperature 0.2)

I found one brief mention of the 1908 Messina earthquake within a larger article, but it's only a passing reference in the context of reporting on a naval officer's activities. Here is the relevant excerpt in XML format:

Nemotron 3.1 (complex-EN, Temperature 0.0)

High confidence due to the clear mention of the Messina earthquake and its consequences (homelessness and shelter-sheds), making the article's relevance unequivocal. The article's coherence and completeness are also evident, as it forms a self-contained unit within the provided text.

Nemotron 3.1 (complex-EN, Temperature 0.2)

The paragraph forms a coherent unit discussing Lieutenant-Commander Reginald Belknap's temporary duty in Italy, specifically in relation to the aftermath of the Messina earthquake.

B Confidence Score and Token Probability

(a) mean value

(b) standard deviation

Fig. 14. Mean and standard deviation confidence score across languages.

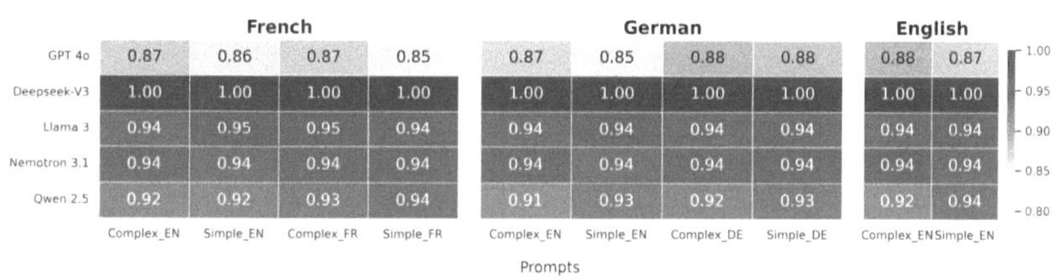

(a) mean value

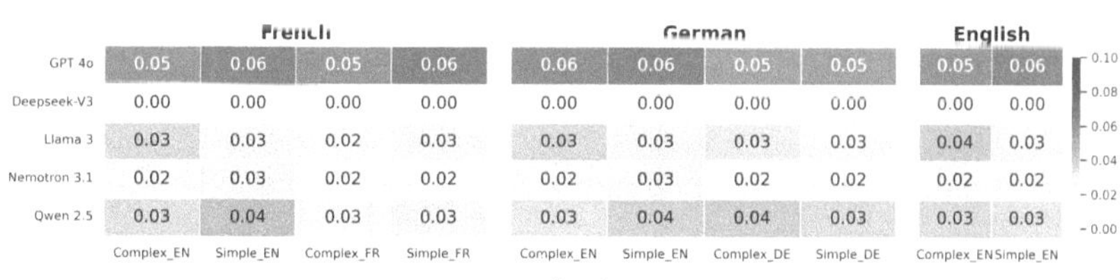

(b) standard deviation

Fig. 15. Mean and standard deviation of token probability across languages.

C OCR Impact

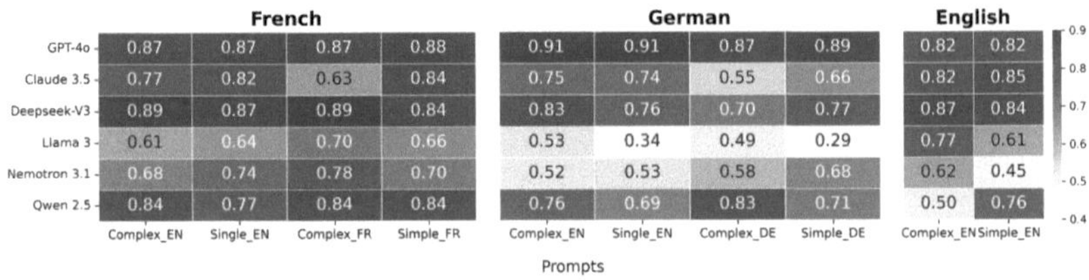

(a) control sample with OCR errors

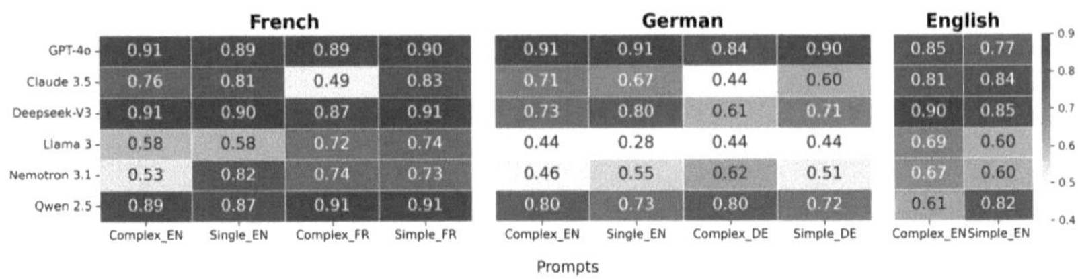

(b) corrected control sample

Fig. 16. Total average model accuracy (percentage of correct predictions) across French, German, and English control samples.

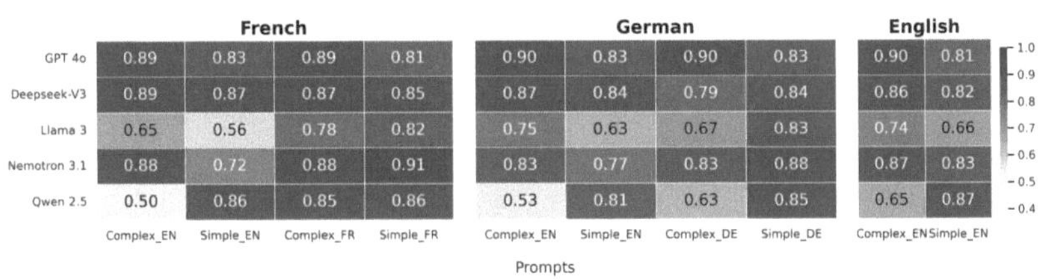

(a) control sample with OCR errors

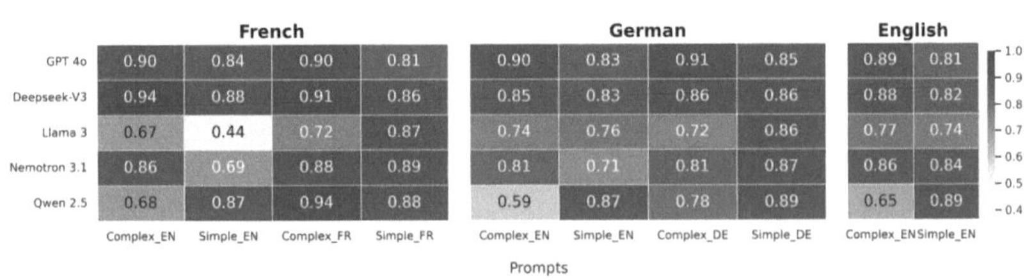

(b) corrected control sample

Fig. 17. Mean confidence score on control sample.

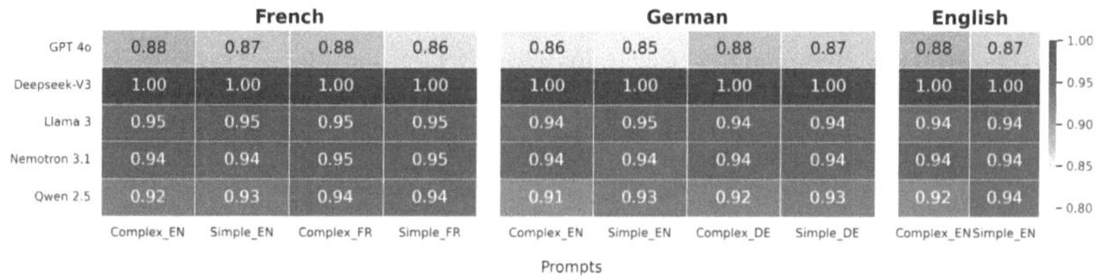

(a) control sample with OCR errors

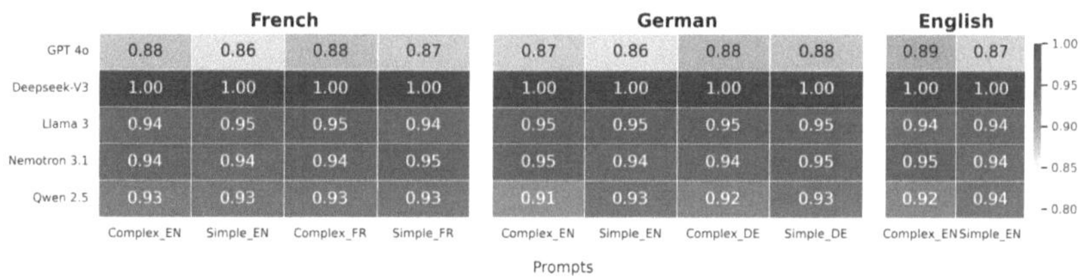

(b) corrected control sample

Fig. 18. Mean token probability on control sample.

D Parameter Setting, and Evaluation Approaches

Table 1. Parameters of the article boundary comparison and quality assessment framework, showing the key components used in the evaluation process.

Component	Parameter	Description
Article Boundary Comparison	Window Size	50 characters for start/end detection
	Similarity Threshold	65% minimum match requirement
	Fuzzy Matching	Character-level comparison for boundaries
	Bidirectional Search	Handles one-to-many and many-to-one matches
Quality Metrics	OCR Tolerance	0.1 threshold for character variations
	Omission Weight	1.5× penalty for missing characters
	Format Error	20% reduction in success score
	Levenshtein Distance	Normalized character-level differences
Error Thresholds	Over-Extraction	>4% added characters
	Under-Extraction	>4% omitted characters
	Content Mismatch	>20% Levenshtein distance
Classification	True Positive	No significant errors
	False Positive	Incorrect match detection
	False Negative	Missed match detection
	True Negative	Correct null detection

Table 2. Evaluation approaches for measuring LLM article extraction performance and associated biases.

Evaluation	Quantitative	Qualitative	Source of Potential Bias
Temperature response	Comparing extraction accuracy at temperature 0.0 vs 0.2	Error pattern analysis	Model architecture and preference alignment
Language performance	Cross-lingual accuracy comparison		Training data
Instruction following	Format adherence rates and instruction compliance metrics	Error pattern analysis	Supervised training
Confidence elicitation and human verification	Correlation between model prediction logits, self-expressed confidence, and actual performance	Analysis of confidence explanation	Preference alignment

E Ethics Statement

This study examines biases in LLMs applied to historical text processing, emphasizing the risks of misrepresentation, overconfidence, and contextual misalignment. While our findings highlight challenges in LLM reasoning, they also inform strategies for bias mitigation and responsible AI use in digital humanities. We ensure transparency by making our dataset and evaluation framework publicly available. No personally identifiable or sensitive data was used in this research (Tables 1 and 2).

References

1. Argnani, A., Alessandro Pino, N.: The 1908 messina straits earthquake: Cornerstones and the need to step forward. Seismol. Res. Lett. **94**(2A), 557–561 (2023). https://doi.org/10.1785/0220220355
2. Beelen, K., Lawrence, J., Wilson, D.C.S., Beavan, D.: Bias and representativeness in digitized newspaper collections: Introducing the environmental scan. Digital Scholarship Human. **38**(1), 1–22 (2022). https://doi.org/10.1093/llc/fqac037
3. Carcione, J., Kozák, J.: The messina-reggio earthquake of december 28, 1908. Stud. Geophys. Geod. **52**, 661–672 (2008). https://doi.org/10.1007/s11200-008-0043-x
4. Carter, R.G.S.: Of things said and unsaid: Power, archival silences, and power in silence. Archivaria **61**, 215–233 (2006). https://archivaria.ca/index.php/archivaria/article/view/12541
5. Dai, S., Xu, C., Xu, S., Pang, L., Dong, Z., Xu, J.: Bias and unfairness in information retrieval systems: New challenges in the llm era. In: Proceedings of the 30th ACM SIGKDD Conference on Knowledge Discovery and Data Mining, pp. 6437–6447. KDD '24, Association for Computing Machinery, New York, USA (2024). https://doi.org/10.1145/3637528.3671458

6. Doshi-Velez, F., Kim, B.: Towards a rigorous science of interpretable machine learning (2017). https://arxiv.org/abs/1702.08608
7. European Union Agency for Fundamental Rights: Bias in algorithms – Artificial intelligence and discrimination. Publications Office of the European Union (2022). https://doi.org/10.2811/25847
8. Ferrara, E.: Fairness and bias in artificial intelligence: A brief survey of sources, impacts, and mitigation strategies. Sci **6**(1) (2024). https://doi.org/10.3390/sci6010003
9. Ferrer, X., Nuenen, T.v., Such, J.M., Cote, M., Criado, N.: Bias and discrimination in AI: A cross-disciplinary perspective. IEEE Technol. Society Mag. **40**(2), 72–80 (2021). https://doi.org/10.1109/mts.2021.3056293
10. Gallegos, I.O., et al.: Bias and fairness in large language models: A survey. Comput. Linguist. **50**(3), 1097–1179 (2024). https://doi.org/10.1162/coli_a_00524
11. Girdhar, N., Coustaty, M., Doucet, A.: Benchmarking nas for article separation in historical newspapers. In: Leveraging Generative Intelligence in Digital Libraries: Towards Human-Machine Collaboration, pp. 76–88. Springer-Verlag, Berlin, Heidelberg (2023). https://doi.org/10.1007/978-981-99-8085-7_7
12. Gu, Z., et al.: Xylayoutlm: Towards layout-aware multimodal networks for visually-rich document understanding. In: IEEE/CVF Conference on Computer Vision and Pattern Recognition, CVPR 2022, New Orleans, LA, USA, June 18-24, 2022, pp. 4573–4582. IEEE (2022). https://doi.org/10.1109/CVPR52688.2022.00454
13. Herrmann, J.B., et al: Tool criticism in practice. on methods, tools and aims of computational literary studies. Digital Human. Quart. **17**(2) (2023)
14. Huang, Y., Lv, T., Cui, L., Lu, Y., Wei, F.: Layoutlmv3: pre-training for document AI with unified text and image masking. In: Proceedings of the 30th ACM International Conference on Multimedia, pp. 4083–4091. MM '22, Association for Computing Machinery, New York (2022). https://doi.org/10.1145/3503161.3548112
15. Kitchin, R.: Critical Data Studies: An A to Z Guide to Concepts and Methods. John Wiley & Sons (2024)
16. Leng, J., Huang, C., Zhu, B., Huang, J.: Taming overconfidence in LLMs: Reward calibration in RLHF (2025). https://arxiv.org/abs/2410.09724
17. Navigli, R., Conia, S., Ross, B.: Biases in large language models: Origins, inventory, and discussion. J. Data Inform. Qual. **15**(2) (Jun 2023). https://doi.org/10.1145/3597307
18. Pan, S., Luo, L., Wang, Y., Chen, C., Wang, J., Wu, X.: Unifying large language models and knowledge graphs: a roadmap. IEEE Trans. Knowl. Data Eng. **36**(7), 3580–3599 (Jul 2024). https://doi.org/10.1109/tkde.2024.3352100, http://dx.doi.org/10.1109/TKDE.2024.3352100
19. Parrinello, G.: Chapter 1. The 1908 Messina Earthquake. In: Earthquakes and Urbanism in Modern Italy, pp. 21–47. Berghahn Books, New York, Oxford (2015). https://doi.org/10.1515/9781782389514-005
20. Ranjan, R., Gupta, S., Singh, S.N.: A comprehensive survey of bias in LLMs: Current landscape and future directions (2024). https://arxiv.org/abs/2409.16430
21. Ren, R., et al.: Investigating the factual knowledge boundary of large language models with retrieval augmentation. In: Rambow, O., Wanner, L., Apidianaki, M., Al-Khalifa, H., Eugenio, B.D., Schockaert, S. (eds.) Proceedings of the 31st International Conference on Computational Linguistics, pp. 3697–3715. Association for Computational Linguistics, Abu Dhabi, UAE (Jan 2025). https://aclanthology.org/2025.coling-main.250/

22. Sun, W., Tran, H.T.H., González-Gallardo, C.E., Coustaty, M., Doucet, A.: LIAS: Layout Information-Based Article Separation in Historical Newspapers. In: Antonacopoulos, A., Hinze, A., Piwowarski, B., Coustaty, M., Di Nunzio, G.M., Gelati, F., Vanderschantz, N. (eds.) Linking Theory and Practice of Digital Libraries. Lecture Notes in Computer Science, vol. 15177, pp. 256–272. Springer (2024). https://doi.org/10.1007/978-3-031-72437-4_15
23. Traub, M.C.: Measuring Tool Bias & Improving Data Quality for Digital Humanities Research. Ph.D. thesis, Utrecht University (2020)
24. Vermiglio, C., Lombardi, R., Zarone, V.: The 1908 earthquake of messina: an accounting perspective on the city's reconstruction between faith and fascism. Account. Hist. **29**(1), 15–39 (2024). https://doi.org/10.1177/10323732221141412
25. Wei, J., et al.: Chain-of-thought prompting elicits reasoning in large language models. In: Proceedings of the 36th International Conference on Neural Information Processing Systems. NIPS '22, Curran Associates Inc., Red Hook, NY, USA (2022)
26. Weidemann, M., Michael, J., Laasch, B.: Citlabrostock/citlab-article-separation: Article separation (Oct 2019). https://doi.org/10.5281/zenodo.3520703
27. Xiong, M., et al.: Can LLMs express their uncertainty? an empirical evaluation of confidence elicitation in LLMs (Oct 2023). https://openreview.net/forum?id=gjeQKFxFpZ
28. Zhao, H., et al.: Explainability for large language models: a survey. ACM Trans. Intell. Syst. Technol. **15**(2), 1–38 (2024). https://doi.org/10.1145/3639372

Human-Centred Design for Digital Ecosystems: Actors, Roles and Responsibilities

Riitta Peltonen[1(✉)] and Marko Nieminen[2]

[1] The National Library of Finland, University of Helsinki, 00014 Helsinki, Finland
riitta.peltonen@helsinki.fi
[2] Aalto University, Espoo. 17, FIN-00076 Aalto, Finland

Abstract. Digital services, particularly public ones, are often developed within networks comprising multiple organisations with varying capacities. Effective management of such software ecosystems relies on a shared understanding of each party's responsibilities, an aspect not yet fully modelled or understood. Despite widespread recognition, human-centred design (HCD) in digital service development often falls short in this regard. Based on our research and experience, responsibilities for HCD typically lie with the organisation developing the digital service platform. Drawing from empirical data from an ecosystem consisting of libraries, archives, and museums (LAM), we identify the actor role types emerging from the data and examine how the distribution of work among actors influences HCD practices. We recognise the aspects of the platform's user experience (UX) and the UX of the information, and their implications for processes and responsibilities within the LAM ecosystem. We propose the use of HCD processes for orchestration and communication in ecosystems developing digital services. We complement Adner's "ecosystems as structure" approach by adding discrete HCD actions that enable the materialisation of a value proposition of the ecosystem.

Keywords: Digital ecosystem · digital platform · actors · human-centred design (HCD) · co-creation · Finna

1 Introduction

The development of digital products and services for both commercial and public use benefits from human-centred design principles [1–4] and user engagement in development [5, 6]. Public services are often produced in organisational networks, necessitating the coordination of work division among organisations [1, 2]. An 'organisational network' is a coalition of independent public organisations that collectively generate digital services. This can be referred to as a digital ecosystem.

However, guidance on sharing human-centred design (HCD) responsibilities across actors in digital ecosystems, and considerations for their application, is sparse. Kautonen and Nieminen [7] criticised the public sector for focusing on HCD during platform acquisition and procurement, neglecting the content creation phase. In an earlier paper, we have proposed a User Involvement Model for Meta-organisations, particularly in

W.-T. Balke et al. (Eds.): TPDL 2025, LNCS 16097, pp. 287–303, 2026.
https://doi.org/10.1007/978-3-032-05409-8_17

educational content service creation [8]. Yet, digital ecosystems still lack conceptual models for adapting standard HCD processes.

This paper examines Finna services, a shared interface for Finnish libraries, archives, and museums (LAM) as an ecosystem. Finna includes a national search service (Finna.fi) and an user interface (UI) platform service allowing LAM organisations to create their own search websites. Finna is an example of a project which has evolved into a national infrastructure and a considerable digital ecosystem. Finna Services has employed professional UI designers since its early years and has cultivated a small in-house UX team, systematically expanding its HCD methodology palette.

We analyse four digital service development projects within the Finna ecosystem, capturing project progression, HCD activities, and insights on adapting HCD processes. We analyse these development processes in contrast to standard HCD processes to identify unique features caused by the division of work across different actors.

To discuss the work division between different types of actors in the ecosystem, we need a robust actor framework. Existing frameworks for commercial software ecosystems do not capture all the nuances of ecosystems producing publicly funded services. Therefore, we also analyse existing service documentation to identify actors to supplement existing frameworks.

These aspects lead to our research questions: **RQ1. What actor roles can be identified and emerge from the data? RQ2. How do these roles influence HCD responsibilities and the project work?** Due to our empirical domain, our scope resides in public digital service creation.

2 Conceptual Background

2.1 HCD Processes

The necessity for co-creation and HCD in digital services is well acknowledged in standards [4], public services [1, 2], and Information System (IS) research [5]. IS literature also recognises that better performance is achieved when IT organisations facilitate interactions between involved parties to align the needs, goals, and interests of stakeholders [6].

HCD offers practical tools for this collaborative approach, with principles and processes outlined in the ISO-9241–210 [4] standard. The core methodologies of HCD have not changed significantly despite the evolution from traditional waterfall to agile software development methods, which have introduced new challenges for integrating HCD processes [9–12].

Numerous design processes fulfil the ISO-9241–210 [4], embodying the foundational principles of user-centred design as outlined by Gould & Lewis [13]. These models typically begin with user research and data analysis. All process models encompass a UI design phase that includes evaluating designs with end-users, followed by an implementation phase. While minor variations exist at the beginning and end of these processes, significant difference lies in whether the models start with a clearly defined point and scope or are aimed at innovating new opportunities [14–19].

Separately, similar HCD processes exist for content creation activities. Customising content for different users according to their needs is typical for content creation processes. Writing and structuring content consistently is also a crucial process requirement, as well as content assessment. Examples can be found in different fields, such as Blythe [20] in university online course content, Kwahk et al. [21] in health and medical information, and Kostur [22] and Carliner [23] in information design.

From these examples, Carliner [23] has proposed a more defined information design model that contains three levels: physical (ability to find information), cognitive (intellectual), and affective (emotional). Carliner's [23] framework includes information-specific research for business and user needs, setting requirements based on the findings, designing the information product according to those requirements, and testing the created product with the users. Applying ISO 9241–210 [4] purely to content creation would align with this.

For applying HCD methods in ecosystems, literature does not offer much guidance. In general, they recognise the need for HCD [1, 2, 6, 24] and need to learn to co-operate and to share responsibilities is recognised in multiple fields, for instance IS [25] and for meta-organisations [26]. HCD literature has presented guidance on how to apply HCD processes for decades, but their focus is typically internally within a single organisation or led by one entity that coordinates stakeholder participation and lacks the view how work is divided in the ecosystem.

Prior to this there have been some examples that have raised the same need. Kautonen and Nieminen [7] criticise Finnish public ICT procurement guidelines for only acknowledging usability requirements for the ICT contractor, omitting content providers. Kautonen [27] reports that, in the early years of Finna services, despite usability being one of the key development tracks in the Finna team developing the Finna platform, usability challenges remain that cannot be overcome by the design and development of the platform but require the involvement of the content-providing LAM organisations. We [8] have also suggested in our previous work, regarding the development of content service, a process model that incorporates HCD activities beyond the scope of the platform-creating organisation.

2.2 Software Ecosystem Actors

To analyse what to consider when applying HCD processes in an ecosystem, particularly who should be doing what, we need a robust framework to distinguish different types of actor organisations in the ecosystem. The Finna ecosystem could be characterised in more detail as a software ecosystem using the definition by Manikas and Hansen [28]. The Finna platform interconnects a set of actors, delivers a suite of collaboratively produced services, and each actor is driven by their own interests, while their interactions with others foster a symbiotic relationship.

The framework of a software ecosystem provides us with the concept of different types of actors as a tool to further analyse our problem. Manikas and Hansen [28] have done extensive literature research and identified a list of the commonly referenced software ecosystem actors in literature.

Their framework recognises five actor types: The Orchestrator is an entity responsible for the proper functioning of the ecosystem. The Niche Player is an entity that typically contributes by developing or adding components to the platform, producing functionality that customers require. The External Actor is an entity that utilises the possibilities of the ecosystem and, in doing so, provides indirect value to it. The Vendor is an entity that profits from selling the ecosystem's products to the end users. The Customer or End User is an entity that purchases or obtains the complete or partial product from the ecosystem or niche player. For our purpose, the roles in their list of actors appear sufficient.

The literature seems to focus on commercial software ecosystems, for instance, the Android platform with its applications or the Salesforce platform with consultation services [29]. The actors recognised from literature reflect that. The newer software ecosystem literature does not seem to offer much supplement to these. Since the Finna ecosystem is funded by the Ministry of Education and Culture, and its member organisations are non-commercial, the frameworks available in literature only offer a starting point. The actors identified in current literature may not capture all the nuances and dynamics associated with the Finna ecosystem.

Finna actors have been analysed previously in literature, not as software ecosystem actors, but stakeholders (even individual roles) who invest time or money into service design [30]. Kautonen's [30] analysis identifies eight types of stakeholders: designer, user, customer (organisation), peer, organisation, another internal unit, external partner, external financier, society. Her list is applicable to Finna, including roles that appear to be missing from other models. However, it overlooks the software ecosystem aspect.

For analysing the software ecosystem responsibilities, actor framework by Manikas and Hansen [28] is a better starting point. Some of the roles recognised by Kautonen [30] can complement it, but we assume that as part of the study, we will need to recognise the types of roles that would help to describe actors in the Finna ecosystem.

3 Research Questions, Context, Data and Methods

As the actor roles provided by the software ecosystem literature do not necessarily cover actors in Finna ecosystem, our first research question is "What actor roles can be identified and emerge from the data?". To reflect the ecosystem aspect, our second research question is "How do these roles influence HCD responsibilities and the project work?".

Our study focuses on the Finna service, a shared interface utilised by Finnish LAM organisations. This service encompasses the national search service Finna.fi and a platform that enables LAM organisations to develop their own search websites. While the creation of the platform is managed by the Finna team of the National Library of Finland, the content is produced by all the participating organisations.

Finna ecosystem is interesting as a case to study, since Finna Service is considered a success story, and since the start of the project Finna team has recognised the need to build HCD capabilities inside their development team. The Finna service has been operational for a decade. During this time, it has established itself as national LAM infrastructure. It presently engages with 450 libraries, archives, and museums that contribute content to the platform. Close to 100% Finnish university and public libraries have their metadata available in Finna.fi. End-user satisfaction of Finna is also high: the general NPS of Finna Services in 2023 was 61 [31].

To construct an initial overview of actors, we consulted publicly available documentation that describes the Finna services, its member organisations, and the prerequisites for joining the Finna network. We analysed data from 29 webpages from three different locations (Finna.fi, Finna's customer wiki, and Digime.fi). The pages selected had to 1) provide descriptions of the Finna service or 2) identify and describe the actors involved in Finna, or 3) outline the technical compatibility requirements, which could be perceived as dependencies on an actor. The content from these pages was copied into word documents, including text and images, and imported into Atlas.ti for analysis.

Our main empirical data originates from four Finna-affiliated projects (P1, P2, P3, P4), collected from two prior studies [8, 32]. These data comprised of interview transcripts, actor maps, timelines, and various artifacts. The re-analysis addresses the research questions of the current study and contents presented in this paper.

The data for P1, P2, and P3 were collected with comparatively similar research objectives, focusing on different types of technical development projects. These projects varied in duration, ranging from nine months to five years. Project P4 revolved around content presentation innovation, expanding the scope of the original dataset. P1 and P2, the longest of the four, were covered with semi-structured interviews, exploring several key topics: the trigger and progression of the project, the stakeholders involved, and the roles of experts engaged in the process. The interviews also sought insights on what aspects of the projects were successful and which were less effective, and why.

P1 involved interviews with three Finna team members and four representatives from content-providing organisations, while P2 interviews involved three Finna team members but only one from content provider organisation. P3 was the shortest and concluded around the time of the original study in 2018. Instead of individual interviews, a retrospective workshop was held with participating Finna team members. The workshop started with constructing timeline with post-it notes detailing all completed tasks. Following discussions focused on evaluating what elements of the project were successful, which were not i.e. areas identified for potential improvement.

P4 focused on the creation of the Finna Classroom pilot, specifically around the content creation pilot phase during 2019. This phase was meticulously documented, including recordings from the kick-off meeting with each of the seven participating organisations from the LAM organisations, email correspondences with these organisations, and the final interview transcripts from the involved teacher and six of the seven content providers. To augment this set of data, we incorporated additional artifacts such as a preliminary report detailing early user research findings, slides from innovation workshops, a comprehensive report of the workshop outcomes, and notes from a technical brainstorming session.

The data were analysed using Atlas.ti software following the five-step qualitative data analysis methodology described by Renner and Taylor-Powell [33] for analysing qualitative data. The steps are following: 1) familiarising oneself with the data by reading through it multiple times, 2) focusing the analysis, 3) categorising the information, recognising themes and patterns, and organising them into coherent categories which may be preset or emergent (ours were mostly emergent), 4) identifying patterns and connections within and between categories, and 5) interpreting the findings.

To address research question 1 (What actor roles can be identified and emerge from the data?), the focus was on identifying emergent roles. Each actor organisation was assigned roles that appeared suitable. To link with previous research, general software ecosystem roles by Manikas and Hansen [28] and those defined by Kautonen[30] were utilised where applicable. However, to capture the nuances of the Finna ecosystem, detailed descriptive tags derived from the data were additionally employed. Actors were then grouped based on the similarity of their role tag combinations. These groups were subsequently coded with descriptive tags, forming more abstract actor roles. These abstract roles were arranged in an onion map, illustrating the apparent level of participation of each actor role within the ecosystem (see Fig. 2).

To address research question 2 (How do these roles influence HCD responsibilities and the project work?), the data were examined from multiple perspectives. Each project had timeline documentation summarising roughly the activities and involved organisations over the duration of the projects, whether months or years.

These timelines have been abstracted according to the Double Diamond model of project phases. We adopted the Double- Diamond visualisation as it effectively embodies the principles of ISO 9241–210 [4], with the assumption that the starting point is not clear and requires research and innovation work. The Double Diamond process, depicted in Fig. 1, is structured into two diamond shaped phases, each comprising two sub-phases. The first diamond focusses on discovering the problem area through research, systematically outlining—via analysis, innovation, and prioritisation—the primary issue to be addressed. The second diamond revolves around solution generation, initially by developing potential solutions, followed by iterative refinement to select and implement a specific approach [34]. We regarded the solution development conducted on the platform side as the original solution phase and depicted modifications within integrated systems as supplementary solution phases. This representation visually conveys how developments in the platform, including UI tasks, are either delayed or even forked.

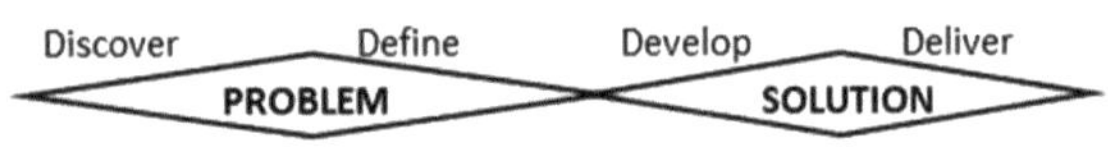

Fig. 1. The original Double Diamond visualisation of the Design Thinking process

The HCD activities and their respective actors were meticulously tagged within the dataset whenever identified. The collected data were then synthesised into a single table organised by the design phase in which they were noted (see Table 2). Similarly, additional desires expressed by informants regarding the adoption of HCD methods were systematically tagged upon mention. The materials were thoroughly reviewed multiple times and any phenomena associated with work conducted within the ecosystem were carefully identified and coded. These detailed phenomena were subsequently grouped into broader emergent themes, which were then classified according to their relevance to specific actors or user-centred design activities. Themes not aligned with these criteria were excluded.

4 Findings: Recognised Actor Roles and Related Findings

In this chapter we introduce the ten actor roles emerged from the data (Fig. 2), 12 findings and four sub-findings related to HCD and co-creation activities. In the Analysis and Discussion chapter we start to look what they bring to HCD processes.

4.1 Actor Roles

An active core group within the ecosystem, termed the 'Public Service Provider Tier', comprises seven actor roles: *main orchestrator, financier, power player, niche player type 1, niche player type 2* and *external contributor*. Like frameworks based on commercial software ecosystems, the service has *users*, which is perhaps the only actor role that does not require additional nuances.

The platform owner and developer, The National Library of Finland (NLF), emerged as *the main orchestrator*. This term is adopted as in one of the projects (P1), the orchestrator-like role was also on one of the power players.

The analysis of the data suggests **nuances among content provider organisations that tentatively merit more distinctive categorisation than merely labelling them all as niche players.** First, several specialised organisations exist, appointed by law, with national responsibilities and resources. These organisations have orchestrator-like duties within their respective fields, unlike ordinary LAM organisations that serve simpler purposes. We designate these as *power players*. In the Finna ecosystem, such organisations include The National Archives, The Finnish Heritage Agency, and the Library of Helsinki (the national development unit), with The National Library also playing a similar role in the library field but elevated to main orchestrator due to its ownership and development of the Finna platform. Second, ordinary LAM organisations are considered niche players. Those only wanting their content available through the national service finna.fi are termed niche player type 1, while those creating their own Finna-platform-based website for their organisation are called niche player type 2. Around the time of the original data gathering, some organisations from the latter group also developed their own backend systems.

The Ministry of Education and Culture **finances Finna Services and many of the content provider organisations**, thus having guidance power and emerging as the *financier* in the ecosystem.

Moreover, some **external public actors** sit on the Finna steering group, termed external contributors. Their role does not align with the external actor definition by Manikas and Hansen [28]; rather, they contribute as part of their responsibilities.

Additionally, **there appears to be a more detached contractor tier**, formed by two types of contractor actors: *public* and *commercial*. Public contractors, either corporations or unions owned by public/non-profit organisations, act as contractors for many of the core players, providing technical services. Commercial contractors are private companies. Public contractors seem to be in closer collaboration with the core of the ecosystem and active partners in project execution phases.

Relevant actors, yet practically external to the ecosystem, are communities developing open access software tools used either in Finna systems or integrated systems.

The division into service provider and contractor tiers is dictated by the level of active involvement within the ecosystem. Inspection of Finna's public event calendar reveals that all events are targeted at power and niche players. Even external contributors regularly attend Finna's steering group meetings, whereas contractors typically engage only when specific feature development necessitates their involvement.

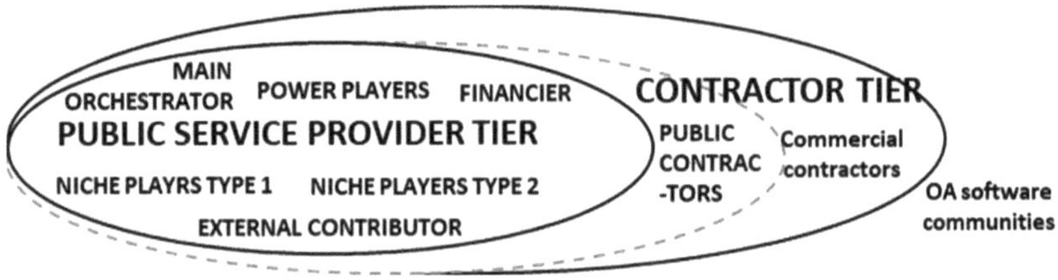

Fig. 2. Actors and roles in the Finna ecosystem

4.2 How the Division of Work Affects the Form of the Double Diamond

Finding F1. In the project focused on enhancing the UI of the platform, the process roughly followed a standard HCD approach with a brief research phase at the beginning, which can be described as the Double Diamond model, with the initial diamond being modest (refer to Fig. 3). P3 concentrated solely on Finna UI modifications without involving any backend system changes. With a clear starting point, the primary focus in P3 was updating the UI look and feel. While the first diamond was present in P3, its scale was limited as the project mainly utilised prior feedback and aspirations from organisations and customers, requiring only a summary and light analysis. Most of the effort was focused to iterating the design and its implementation.

Fig. 3. The process simplified to Double Diamond type of description in P3

Finding F2. In projects that involve platform development and the development of an integrated system, the integrated system must be developed first with its own develop and deliver phases independent of the platform develop and deliver phase. This results in the second diamond transforming into two slightly overlapping diamonds, with the additional diamond representing the necessary development in the integrated system. If multiple integrated systems require development, the progression of the diamonds may fork into two branches advancing at different speeds (see Fig. 4).

P1 involved integrating a new system into the Finna ecosystem and developing this system from scratch. In P1, the Solution Diamonds divided into two, each containing phases of Develop and Deliver. The first Solution Diamond addressed the design, development, and delivery of the integrated system, focusing on the needs of the organisation's admin users and spanning several years. The second Solution Diamond focused on designing, developing, and delivering the Finna platform, including considerations for end-users and aligning more closely with the original conception of the Solution Diamond. The development of the Finna platform could start only once the backend was prepared to transmit actual data via APIs. P2 was about the introduction of a new feature that required the integration of two new systems into the Finna ecosystem. The new feature required new development in those systems. The Solution Diamond split into two branches corresponding to each new system, and then again in both branches for development in the new system and for Finna work. Two-thirds of the niche players utilised backend system A. The responsible actor promptly undertook the necessary feature enhancements, with the development of the Finna platform solution promptly following upon the new APIs delivering the needed data. For the remaining third of the niche players, it was uncertain which backend systems would accommodate the new features and who would finance them. Reaching a consensus took months, and work related to integrated system B proceeded much later, causing the Solution Diamond to branch into two trajectories with different schedules. In the case of P2, the backend system developments were completed within months.

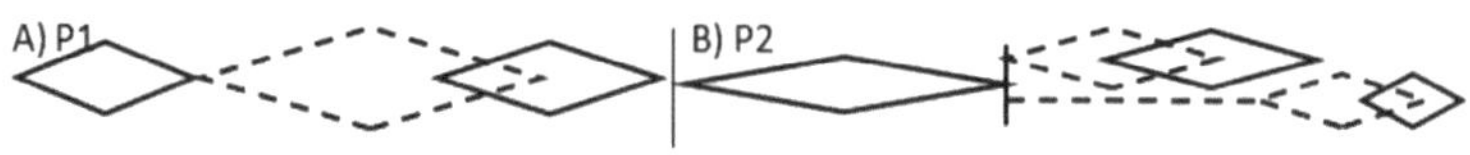

Fig. 4. The process simplified to Double Diamond type of description in A) P1, B)P2

Finding F3. When the solution phase diverges into multiple branches, the use of co-creation techniques must be considered independently of their prior application in the initially completed branch. In P2, within the first Solution branch, Finna collaborated with one active pilot organisation (a niche player), and this co-creation was considered effective. In the second branch, lacking a pilot organisation, informants from the project suggested that this phase would have benefitted from a pilot organisation representative of the entities, whose data in that solution differed somewhat from the data derived from organisations in the initial solution branch.

Finding F4. Content products necessitate their own user-centred design workflows within each organisation producing such products; each content product creation constitutes an independent mini Solution Diamond as presented in Fig. 5. P4 was about developing the content service Finna Classroom (concept and development of a minimum solution), requiring solely Finna UI-related development yet involving significant content creation activities from participating LAM organisations. In P4, both the concept creation and the platform development segment followed the Double Diamond model. The creation of the initial content products represented individual Solution Diamonds occurring parallel with platform development. The light user research and testing conducted for each content product made sense only within the context of the collections of the LAM organisation creating the content product, proving likely to be beneficial separately for each content product regardless of whether they were produced during the pilot or later. More details are available in our previous paper [8].

Finding F5. The creation of new types of content products creates UI work; hence, the initial content product creations and the final UI design and development of the platform must occur simultaneously. Finalising the platform prior to starting the creation of content products, intended for publication through it, would have been impractical. Therefore, maintaining a few pilot partners during the solution development proved to be good practice (Related practise F5.1). Details in our previous paper [8].

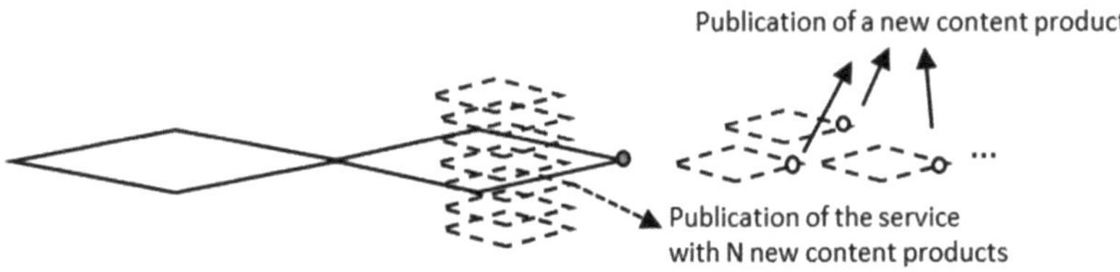

Fig. 5. The process simplified to Double Diamond type of description in P4

4.3 Power Roles Related Findings

Finding F6. The main orchestrator of the ecosystem is not always the orchestrator of significant cooperation projects. A substantial part of P1 involved developing an integrated system. The task of orchestrating cooperation within the ecosystem fell to one of the power players. In other projects, the orchestrating role remained with the main orchestrator.

Finding F7. When technical work starts to split or additionally fork, it is easy to overlook either niche players or end-users on some parts of the project. Legislation typically mandates power players to cater to other ecosystem organisations. However, when crafting digital services, considering end-to-end user scenarios is crucial, thus necessitating a focus on end-users. In the backend-system-focused project (P1), one of the power players, rather than the main orchestrator of the ecosystem, assumed the orchestrating role. It was only during the later stages of P1 that the end-user perspective was incorporated, coinciding with the development of the Finna platform and its user interface. Informants suggested delayed focus might have been because the project's early stages centred on establishing an entirely new backend system, primarily for employees of power and niche players. However, more than one informant, as an afterthought, suggested that considering end-users earlier would have been beneficial.

During the branching solution phase of P2, the main orchestrator initially engaged a pilot organisation in the first solution branch, while the second branch progressed without involving a pilot organisation or end-users. Retrospectively, an informant from the platform developer entity reflected that involving a pilot organisation in the second branch would have been beneficial. Nevertheless, throughout the project, the orchestrator ensured the involvement of niche players; they reviewed concepts materialised through wireframes and actively participated in co-creation during the first solution development phase. This approach suggests a systematic effort to ensure stakeholder involvement at each phase, though the necessity of extending co-creation methodologies to each distinct solution branch was perhaps underestimated.

Finding F8. The orchestrator plays a major role in the application of HCD methodologies. An overview of the usage of customer/human-centred design (see Table 1) reveals that the main orchestrator, or a project orchestrating organisation, generally facilitated or directly implemented these strategies. In P4, niche players undertook the user research and evaluations, yet even here, the main orchestrator facilitated access to end-users during the pilot. In P1, concept development involved co-creation with client organisations arranged by the orchestrator of the project.

Table 1. Summary of customer/user-centred design methods in projects

Phase	HCD-method	P1	P2	P3	P4
Concepting	Low level co-creation with ***customer organisations*** (arranged by the main orchestrator)		*x*		
	Deeper level co-creation with ***customer organisations*** (varied based on project, P1 arranged by the project orchestrator, P4 by the main orchestrator)	*x*			*x*
	Pilot ***organisation*** usage (arranged by the main orchestrator)		*x*		
	Usage of earlier learnings from **end-user** and customer organisation feedback (arranged by main orchestrator)	**x**		*x*	
	End-user research (arranged by the main orchestrator)				**x**
UI design	Professional UI design (arranged by the main orchestrator)	x	x	x	x
Design iteration	UI design review with **internal stakeholders** (arranged by the main orchestrator)			x	
	Low level UI design review with ***customer organisations*** (arranged by the main orchestrator)		*x*	*x*	
	Usability testing (arranged by the main orchestrator)	**x**		**x**	
Content creation	**User research** for content needs (enabled by the main orchestrator, done by niche players)				**x**
Content iteration	Content review with **internal stakeholders** (enabled by the main orchestrator, done by niche players)				x
	User evaluation of content (enabled by the main orchestrator, done by niche players)				**x**

Finding F9. In matters of conflict resolution in the ecosystem, the financier holds the decisive power, not the orchestrator. In two instances (P1, P2), conflicts related to project scope or backend system development responsibilities stalled progress, with resolutions only achieved through the financier's intervention.

4.4 Technical Expertise Related Findings

Finding F10. Communication and decision-making between the main orchestrator, power players, and niche players often occur without the inclusion of technical expertise. Several informants from P1 highlighted challenges in discussing technical matters with non-experts during the initial phases. To facilitate discussions, issues were often oversimplified, potentially leading to a 'lost-through-the-grapevine' phenomenon as information was relayed within or between organisations. Initial conceptual discussions prior to implementation decisions primarily involved the main orchestrator and the power player, excluding contractor tiers, and frequently took place at a higher, less technical level.

In P4, despite being a simpler undertaking, there were still mentions in the data about difficulties in addressing technical aspects. P2 and P3 began with clearer starting points and a more streamlined conceptual phase; only a few informants noted challenges in communication with niche players concerning development schedules and in distinguishing substantially small requests from deceptively complex ones. In both P1 and P2, contractor involvement began after implementation decisions.

Analysis of the data revealed two adaptive strategies that mitigated these challenges. Best practice utilising UI drafts and pilots facilitated more tangible discussions regarding end-to-end use cases (Related practice F10.1). In P1, the introduction of initial UI drafts simplified dialogue.

P2 and P4 implemented UI drafts in earlier stages to aid communication, and the engagement of one-on-one pilot partners in P2 and P4 proved beneficial (Related practice F10.2).

4.5 How General Division of Work Between Parties Seems to Affect the Project

Finding F11. Predicting schedules is challenging when work is distributed among various actors for multiple reasons. This insight emerged from comments by informants from projects P1, P2, and P3. For instance, the main orchestrator engages in platform development on a full-time basis, while representatives from different players manage ecosystem-related tasks alongside their other responsibilities.

In response to this issue, a practice has emerged: the orchestrator of the project, possessing the majority of development resources—both personnel and time—undertakes most of the work, involving others primarily for feedback, including in design aspects. (Related practice F11.1).

Finding F12. In extensive projects that require input from multiple actors, no single actor possesses the authority to compel action across organisations, and there is no representative equipped with the necessary time, resources, or expertise to oversee the entire end-to-end project across various entities. This was highlighted by a few informants from both P1 and P2 (technically demanding projects). Such issues notably affect tasks for which the organisations lack specific expertise, such as design activities.

5 Analysis and Discussion

In this chapter we combine individual findings into resolutions R1-R4 that contribute to the formulation of ecosystem-aware HCD (see Fig. 6).

R1. "Distributed Power Roles". Finna ecosystem has more power roles. Comparison with commercial software ecosystems reveals that the orchestrator's influence tends to be shared among the power actors.

R2. "Platform vs. Content UX". UX of the platform and UX of the information are addressed separately. Based on findings F1, F4, and F5, we draw conclusions about the distribution of basic HCD responsibilities, as shown on the right side of Fig. 6. If a development project allows the platform developer to innovate and implement solutions with minimal input from other actors, existing HCD processes are sufficient (F1).

For content service development projects, standard HCD processes are good for the platform development. However, content products require their own HCD workflows within each producing organisation. F5 and F5.1 indicate that the platform UI and the creation of initial content products should overlap in a joint pilot phase.

The clear division of responsibility from these findings is that the platform developer organisation should handle HCD activities related to the platform, while content provider organisations should manage HCD activities for content products.

A more nuanced conclusion is that the platform developer should be responsible for HCD activities that provide features benefiting most organisations using the platform, also common guidance for content production. Content provider organisations should focus on HCD activities that enhance the design of their own offerings. Based on the data used in this paper, content products fall into this category. In the broader Finna context, this could also include customising the platform for their own search services.

R3. "HCD for Orchestration". Findings F2, F3, F7, F8, F10 and F12 introduce a dimension related to HCD activities as means of communication and orchestration in ecosystems. These findings relate to what happens when the technical solution phase splits or forks due to development needs in both the platform and one or more integrated systems. A clear impact is that technical development, which must first be completed in the integrated systems, delays the platform development phase and, consequently, the UI development phase (F2).

This highlights how the ecosystem's nature subtly affects HCD processes. It may simply delay HCD activities or leave some activities out in one of the forks if not carefully managed, which is not ideal (F7, F10.1, F10.2, F3).

According to our findings (F10) communication about technical issues between platform developer and content provider organisations is hard. IS literature recognises similar issues [35]. HCD literature acknowledges that UI design produces artefacts (e.g., wireframes, initial UI prototypes etc.) that typically serve as boundary items, aiding collaboration [36]. Ofe and Sandberg [37] have recognised that not paying attention to boundary object to be used can cause delays for entire information system development. Also, our findings suggest that the use of HCD methods appears to facilitate communication (F10.1, F10.2) and understanding better what is natural boundary item in LAM system projects and how to time their usage feels relevant future research topic.

Finding F12 highlights that no single project manager can dictate activities across all organisations within a specific timeframe. We interpret this to mean that leading a major development project within an ecosystem also involves orchestration.

Our findings align with Adner's [38] structuralist approach to ecosystems. Adner [38] defines an ecosystem as "*the alignment structure of the multilateral set of partners that need to interact for a focal value proposition to materialise.*" He stresses the importance of analysing expectations regarding value creation and distribution among all parties involved in realising a new solution and the need for strategic planning of discrete actions to enable the materialisation of a value proposition.

We believe that our findings related to the HCD activities as means of communication in part also suggest that HCD and co-creation methods sometimes serve dual purposes, acting as both development tools and ecosystem management actions. Viewed through this lens, seemingly minor findings—such as the timing of UI drafts when the solution phase splits and the need to systematically involve both the organisation's customers and end-users throughout the project—could assume new significance. Oberländer et al. [25] build on Adner's thoughts, introducing three mechanism types in digital transformation: introduction, cooperation, and orchestration. HCD and co-creation methods could facilitate some of these.

Orchestration and communication should be considered aspects of HCD and co-creation activities. Based on finding F8, the orchestrator of the project can significantly impact what HCD activities are done and in which phase, and they just should ensure the timing is planned consciously.

R4. "The Strongest Should Orchestrate (by Using HCD)". Based on findings F6, F9, F11 we suggest that all power actors should be prepared to take occasional responsibility for orchestrating the ecosystem and have capabilities to utilise HCD methods. In Fig. 6, the box "Ecosystem communication and orchestration" responsibilities are not just the responsibility of the ecosystem's main orchestrator but may vary.

Some HCD activities, even though they are project work, may not be clearly related to one system or content and may be more orchestration by nature. Finding F6 highlighted that the project orchestrator is not always the main orchestrator of the ecosystem. In complex development projects, the role of the orchestrator should be consciously acknowledged. Finding F11 and related practice F11.1 are relevant here. The project orchestrator, engaging full-time, likely has the most resources for HCD and co-creation activities for orchestration purposes.

Not all HCD activities are initially planned as project work. In P4, the user research and co-creation workshop with organisations were conducted before the development received approval to proceed. Addo [39] introduces the concept of robust action—non-committal actions that help the platform orchestrator move in the desired direction without committing any party to a specific solution. Robust actions could provide an interesting context to reflect some HCD and co-creation activities in ecosystems.

When considering user research as input to innovation or a co-creation workshop with stakeholders prior to a commitment decision, as in P4, they appear to be robust actions on a smaller scale.

Based on our resolutions, the proposed framework in Fig. 6 presents elements and responsibilities for the participants in the ecosystem. Our aim in future work is to examine and deepen the presented aspects for increased clarity and applicability.

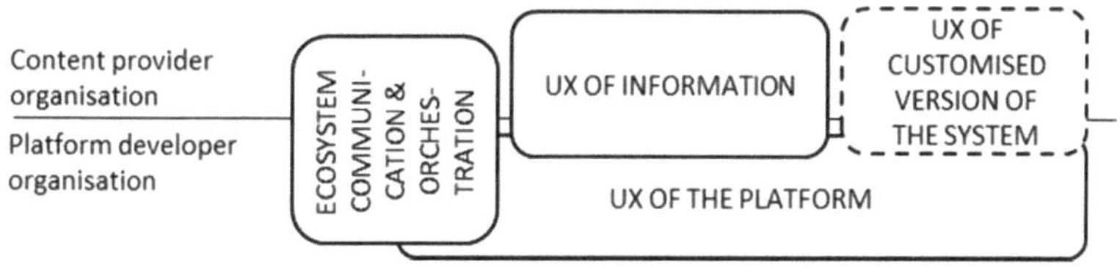

Fig. 6. The proposed elements and responsibilities for ecosystem-aware HCD process.

Reliability of the Study is Adequate, But it has Limitations. The project (P1, P2, P3, P4) covers different types of projects and work from a technical development and content production point of view. Since data is re-used, the data between the projects is not uniform. However, from each project, there are multiple information angles and sources, so we believe the data is reliable enough to capture the projects.

For LAM ecosystems, it would be important to capture also project work that involves the need for changes for LAM metadata practices or its transfer formats. The data from projects P1-P4 don't properly cover this type of work.

The findings could be relevant internationally for similar LAM ecosystems, domestically for less wide digital cultural ecosystems and, perhaps, transferable to other publicly funded digital ecosystems.

6 Conclusions

We have examined the Finna network as an example of a digital LAM ecosystem. Our analysis addressed research questions: 1) What actor roles can be identified and emerge from the data and 2) How do these roles influence HCD and co-creation responsibilities and the project work.

Our findings introduce a new dimension to consider in the application of HCD processes: the impact of the ecosystem. Our conceptualisation of the actor framework in the LAM ecosystem provides characteristics to consider when working with publicly funded digital ecosystems. Our findings suggest that HCD and co-creation methods can provide orchestrators concrete means to successfully guide the ecosystem forward.

We present four resolutions. *R1. Power roles are distributed in the ecosystem.* In addition to the orchestrator, we identified additional power roles: the financier and power players. *R2. UX needs to be considered in platform functions and content matters.* Both the HCD processes for UX of the platform and of content offered through the platform needs to be considered. *R3. HCD can be used in ecosystem orchestration.* Our findings also suggest that HCD activities may serve as discrete actions to study and align the value expectations and actions of the power and niche players and to communicate between organisations i.e. means to orchestrate the ecosystem. This framing may necessitate rethinking their usage and timing, especially in projects where development work is divided across multiple parties. *R4. The strongest actors, with their mandate and resources, should take the responsibility to orchestrate the ecosystem by using HCD.* The orchestration type of activities didn't only belong to just the ecosystem main orchestrator. All these resolutions are potentially relevant for digital libraries in the future. The public information systems for digital libraries are developed by multiple stakeholders (ecosystems) who have keen interest towards smooth functionality and clearly structured contents (user experience).

References

1. Stoker, G.: Public value management: a new narrative for networked governance?. Am. Rev. Pub. Adm. **36**(1), 41–57 (2006)
2. O' Flynn, J.: From new public management to public value: paradigmatic change and managerial implications. Aust. J. Pub. Adm. **66**(3), 353 (2007)
3. JUHTA: JHS 190 Design and development of public online service (In Finnish: JHS 190 Julkisen verkkopalvelun suunnittelu ja kehittäminen). (13 6 2014). Online, available: https://www.suomidigi.fi/sites/default/files/2020-07/JHS190_0.doc. [Accessed 31 Jan 2021]
4. ISO 9241–210: Ergonomics of human-system interaction – Part 210: human-centered design for interactive systems. In: International Standard Organisation. Geneve (2019)
5. Olphert, W., Damodaran, L.: Citizen participation and engagement in the design of e-government services: the missing link in effective ICT design and delivery. J. Assoc. Info. Syst. **8**(9) (2007)
6. Lempinen, H., Rajala, R.: Exploring multi-actor value creation in IT service processes. J. Info. Technol. **29**(2), 170–185 (2014)
7. Kautonen, H., Nieminen, M.: A critical look at the prerequisites of user-centred ICT procurements in the public sector (In Finnish: Julkisten ICT-hankintojen käyttäjäkeskeisyyden edellytysten kriittinen tarkastelu.). In: Hallinnon Tutkimus, vol. 38, no. 3, pp. 155–173. (2019)
8. Peltonen, R., Nieminen, M.: Creating digital LAM content for schools: modelling user involvement in multi-organisational context. In: Goh, D. H., Chen, SJ., Tuarob, S. (eds.) Leveraging Generative Intelligence in Digital Libraries: Towards Human-Machine Collaboration. ICADL 2023, vol. 14458, pp. 46–61. Springer Nature Singapore, Singapore (2023)
9. Barksdale, J., McCrickard, D.: Software product innovation in agile usability teams. an analytical framework of social capital, network governance, and usability knowledge management. Int. J. Agile Ext. Softw. Develop. **1**(1), 7–52 (2012)
10. Wale-Kolade, A.: Integrating usability work into a large inter-organisational agile development project: tactics developped by usability designers. J. Syst. Soft. **100**, 54–66 (2014)
11. Brehl, M., Meth, H., Maedche, A., Werder, K.: exploring principles of user-centered agile software development: a literature review. Info. Softw. Technol. **6**(11), 163–181 (2015)
12. Larusdottir, M., Gulliksen, J., Cajander, A.: A license to kill – improving UCSD in agile. J. Syst. Softw. **123**, 214–222 (2017)
13. Gould, J., Lewis, D.: Designing for usability: key principles and what designers think. Commun. ACM **28**(3), 300–311 (1985)
14. Mayhew, D.: The Usability Engineering Lifecycle: A Practitioner's Handbook for User Interface Design. Morgan Kaufmann Publishers, San Francisco (1999)
15. Holtzblatt, K., Beyer, H.: Contextual Design. Defining Customer-Centred Systems. Morgan Kaufmann Publishers, San Francisco (1998)
16. Holtzblatt, K., Beyer, H.: Contextual Design. Design for Life, Elsevier, Cambridge (2017)
17. Carroll, J., Rosson, M.: Usability engineering: scenario-based development of human computer interaction. Morgan Kaufmann Publishers Inc, San Francisco (2003)
18. Lauesen, D.: User Interface Design. A Software Engineering Perspective., Pearson Education Limited, Harlow (2005)

19. Cooper, A., Cronin, D., Noessel, C., Reimann, R.: About Face: The Essentials of Interaction Design. Wiley Publishing Inc, Indianapolis (2014)
20. Blythe, S.: Designing online courses: user-centered practices. Comput. Comp. **18**(4), 329–346 (2001)
21. Kwahk, J., Smith-Jackson T. L., and Williges, R. C.: From user-centered design to senior-centered design: designing internet health information portals. In: Proceedings of the Human Factors and Ergonomics Society Annual Meeting, vol. 45, no. 6, pp. 580–584 (2001)
22. Kostur, P.: Incorporating usability into content management. In: 2006 IEEE International Professional Communication Conference (2006)
23. Carliner, S.: Physical, cognitive, and affective: a three-part framework for information design. Techn. Commun. **47**(4), 561–576 (2000)
24. Fedorowicz, J., Sawyer, S., Tomasino, A.: Governance configurations for inter-organizational coordination: a study of public safety networks. J. Info. Technol. **33**(4), 326–344 (2018)
25. Oberländer, A. M., Karnebogen, P., Rövekamp, P., Röglinger, M., Leidner, D. E.: Understanding the influence of digital ecosystems on digital transformation: the OCO (orientation, cooperation, orchestration) theory. Info. Syst. J. **35**(1), 368–413 (2025)
26. Gulati, R., Puranam, P., Tushman, M.: Meta-organization design: rethinking design in interorganizational and community contexts. Strat. Manag. J. **33**(6), 571–586 (2012)
27. Kautonen, H.: Evaluating digital library's service concept and pre-launch implementation. In: Proceedings of the 5th International Conference of Applied Human Factors and Ergonomics AHFE 2014. Krakov, Poland (2014)
28. Manikas, K., Hansen, K. M.: Software ecosystems – a systematic literature review. J. Syst. Softw. **86**(5), 1294–1306 (2013)
29. Joshua, J. V., Alao, D. O., Okolie, S. O., Awodele, O.: Software ecosystem: features, benefits and challenges. Int. J. Adv. Comput. Sci. Appl. **4**(8) (2013)
30. Kautonen, H.: Conceptual model of stakeholders' investment-engagement in public services' design. Int. Des. Arch. **34**, 133–160 (2017)
31. Jacksen, S., Isotalo, J., Kirichenko, S.: User Survey of the Finna 2023 (In: Finnish: Finnan Käyttäjäkysely 2023). The National Library of Finland, Helsinki (2023)
32. Peltonen, R.: Asiakaskeskeisyys alustapalvelun kehittämisessä organisaatioverkostossa: Case: Kansalliskirjaston Finna-palvelu. Laurea University of Applied Sciences (2018)
33. Renner, M., Taylor-Powell, E.: Analyzing qualitative data. In: *Programme Development & Evaluation,* pp. 1–10. University of Wisconsin-Extension Cooperative Extension, Madison (2003)
34. Kochanowska, M., Gagliardi, W. R.: The double diamond model: in pursuit of simplicity and flexibility. In: Raposo, Neves, Silva (eds.) Perspectives on Design II. Springer Series in Design and Innovation, vol. 16. Springer Cham (2022)
35. Henttonen, K. M., Pulkkinen, M., Tyrvainen, P.: Health and orchestration of public-sector open-source software ecosystems roles, rules and tools. Scand. J. Info. Syst. **36**(2) (2025)
36. Zaitsev, A., Uri, G., Barney, T.: Boundary objects and change in agile projects. In: Proceedings of 25th Australasian Conference on Information Systems, Auckland, New Zealand, 8th-10th Dec. (2014)
37. Ofe, H., Sandberg, J.: The emergence of digital ecosystem governance: an investigation of responses to disrupted resource control in the Swedish public transport sector. Info. Syst. J. **33**(2), 350–384 (2023)
38. Adner, R.: Ecosystem as structure: an actionable construct for strategy. J. Manag . **43**(1), 39–58 (2017)
39. Addo, A.: Orchestrating a digital platform ecosystem to address societal challenges: a robust action perspective. J. Info. Technol. **37**(4), 359–386 (2022)

Real-Time Prediction of Wikipedia Articles' Quality

Pedro Miguel Moás[1] and Carla Teixeira Lopes[2(✉)]

[1] Faculdade de Engenharia, Universidade do Porto, R. Dr. Roberto Frias, 4200-465 Porto, Portugal
pmmoas@fe.up.pt

[2] INESC TEC, Faculdade de Engenharia, Universidade do Porto, R. Dr. Roberto Frias, 4200-465 Porto, Portugal
ctl@fe.up.pt

Abstract. Wikipedia is the largest and most globally well-known online encyclopedia, but its collaborative nature leads to a significant disparity in article quality. In this work, we explore real-time and automatic quality assessment within Wikipedia through machine-learning. We first constructed a dataset of 36,000 English articles and 145 features, then compared the performance of multiple classification and regression algorithms and studied how the number of classes and features affects the model's performance. The six-class experiments achieved a classifier accuracy of 64% and a mean absolute error of 0.09 in regression methods, which matches or beats most state-of-the-art approaches. Our model produces similar results on some non-English Wikipedias, but the error is slightly higher on other versions. We have also determined that the features measuring the article's content and revision history bring the largest performance boost.

Keywords: Wikipedia · Quality Assessment · Machine Learning

1 Introduction

Wikipedia is the world's largest and most well-known online encyclopedia and has kept its growing pace for years. As of June 2025, it contains over 7 million English articles [29], with versions across a list of 342 active languages [25]. Additionally, from June 2024 to May 2025, Wikipedia totalized close to 300 billion page views across 2 billion unique devices [22], suggesting that many people worldwide consider Wikipedia a viable source of information.

Wikipedia relies on human volunteers to add and maintain its content, averaging a rate of 8.8 edits per second from June 2024 to May 2025 [22]. However, since there is no centralized authority over the article editors, ensuring quality throughout the website is a challenging task.

Another central issue is the substantial discrepancy between the quality of English and non-English articles. For starters, non-English Wikipedias cover a much smaller number of articles [25]. Furthermore, they are often much more incomplete as well, as demonstrated by Roy et al. [17]. For instance, they determined that German articles are, on average, 30% shorter than English ones, and

W.-T. Balke et al. (Eds.): TPDL 2025, LNCS 16097, pp. 304–320, 2026.
https://doi.org/10.1007/978-3-032-05409-8_18

for Spanish articles, that value increases to 47%. Considering that around 57% of total Wikipedia traffic goes to non-English articles [22], this indicates a significant problem for international readers. These points show that Wikipedia's quality may vary significantly across different articles and languages. However, readers have no easy methods for quickly assessing quality, so they must rely on their judgment to determine a Wikipedia page's value.

Envisioning the construction of a Machine Learning (ML) model that automatically predicts the quality of Wikipedia articles, we conducted a thorough experimentation guided by the following research questions:

RQ1. Which ML algorithm yields the best performance in predicting the quality of Wikipedia articles?
RQ2. How does model performance vary with the number of output classes?
RQ3. Which subset of features produces the best performance?
RQ4. How effective is our model at predicting the quality of non-English articles?

In summary, in this article, we make 2 main contributions. First, we identify 145 features that can be automatically computed to predict the quality of Wikipedia articles. These features are grouped into five categories: content (33 features), style (72 features), readability (10 features), history (22 features), and network (8 features). We computed all the features for a set of 36,000 English articles and some features for four smaller groups of articles used in the multi-language evaluation: English (11,096 articles), French (11,195 articles), Portuguese (10,525 articles), and Russian (10,341 articles). These datasets are publicly available in a research data repository and can be used in future research [16]. Second, we design a machine-learning solution that effectively predicts Wikipedia article quality into six classes (FA, GA, B, C, Start, and Stub), outperforming most state-of-the-art approaches. The source code for the development and testing of the model is publicly available.

2 Background and Related Work

This section discusses different meanings of "quality" and analyzes the existing literature relating to the subject of this paper.

2.1 Information Quality

Information Quality (IQ) is an extraordinarily researched topic, and numerous ways exist to measure it. Lee et al. [13] systematize that process by representing quality as 15 different properties, such as *Accessibility*, *Believability*, and *Interpretability*. We do not plan to assess properties relating to the integrity of the information, as that would be more suitable for manual approaches. Regardless, there might be some correlation between some quality properties and others. Due to Wikipedia's collaborative aspect, contributors will, in theory, cooperate to improve the article continuously, so it is reasonable to assume that well-written articles will be trustworthy more often than not.

Some may say there is no truly objective way to quantify quality. However, there are undoubtedly measurable characteristics that people often relate to outstanding quality, and we plan to determine those and their correlation with excellence in written documents.

2.2 Wikipedia's Quality Scale

To monitor and maintain content quality, Wikipedia developed a nine-grade scale that rates articles from incomplete entries documents(Stubs and Starts) to comprehensive, well-written ones (Featured Articles) [27]. Among the six intermediate levels, this work focuses on three: Good Articles (GA), B-class, and C-class, listed in descending order of quality. Notably, most English Wikipedia consists of lower-quality articles, with Starts and Stubs accounting for more than 80% of its content, while the share of Featured and Good Articles is around 0.6% [27]. These values are only meant for internal use by Wikipedia's contributors and are not to be taken as official ratings. Besides, not every English article is rated, and the other versions of Wikipedia that assess their content will have distinct quality scales, evaluated with different criteria.

2.3 State of the Art

A systematic literature review was conducted to explore current methods for automatically assessing Wikipedia article quality [15]. The review included 149 papers, 71 of which employed machine learning techniques. While most studies focus on English Wikipedia, 35 examined non-English versions, and 7 addressed multilingual quality assessment.

We collected 321 unique features, all of which consider either the text of an article, its revision history, or how it relates to other articles within Wikipedia or the internet. The textual features, which factor in the content of the Wikipedia article, are the most recurring of the ones we collected, forming almost 90% of the set. Some studies also proposed IQ metrics—formula-based approaches that can function independently or support machine-learning models.

Both deep learning and classical algorithms have shown promising results. Deep learning achieved 68–76% accuracy in 6-class setups, though these methods are less suited for real-time applications so we are better off comparing ourselves with the classical learning accuracies, which range between 62% and 73% in the top 3. In simpler 2-class scenarios with balanced datasets, multiple studies reported accuracy above 95%.

In summary, the study of the automatic quality assessment of Wikipedia has become more prevalent over the years. Feature-based machine learning models appear to have been a solid option throughout the entire period, though. We will use these findings as a basis for our work, conducting further experimentation to develop better quality predictors.

3 Methodology

This section explains in detail all the steps involved in developing our solution. We opted for using a machine-learning approach, so we needed to define a dataset, automate the calculation of features, and then compare the performance of different algorithms, maximizing the model's accuracy. The datasets we constructed are entirely available in a research data repository [16], and the source code is fully accessible from a GitHub repository[1].

3.1 English Dataset Definition

Using MediaWiki's API, we first obtained a list of all the titles of each quality class. Wikipedia provides a category page for each quality class, listing the pages assessed as such, so we used the API to fetch the elements of each category.

Owning all the Wikipedia titles and the quality of their respective pages allowed us to create a randomized dataset more effortlessly. We decided not to include the FL and A-class items in our experiments for distinct reasons. First, the goal of Featured Lists is to thoroughly list other items, and often do not contain much more content. Regarding the A-class tier, they correspond to a tiny portion of Wikipedia [27] and do not follow the linear quality path, as being a GA (Good Article) is not a requirement for being A-class.

Collecting the articles was a straightforward process. We selected 6,000 random titles for each class and used MediaWiki's API to obtain their contents. We arrived at that number because we wanted to keep the dataset balanced, and the relatively low supply of FA's does not allow us to expand it further.

Network Graph Generation. We can view Wikipedia as an "interconnected network of articles", where each entry can link to other Wikipedia articles. For that reason, we can consider a collection of hyperlinked pages as a directed graph, where the nodes represent the articles and edges indicate the existence of a link between them [1]. Certain features require knowing some properties of the article's graph, such as the in-degree and out-degree. Therefore, before feeding the page contents to the feature calculator, we construct a network graph of each article we assess.

The Laboratory for Web Algorithms provides datasets of several networks [6], including Wikipedia. We used the `enwiki-2022` dataset, which contains over 6 million nodes and 159 million arcs, then processed them with the WebGraph framework I, a library that eases the manipulation of large Web graphs [5].

The `enwiki-2022` dataset was produced in the same week we ran the experiments described in this document, so the values are up-to-date. However, when we randomly select the 36,000 articles to include in our dataset, we sometimes encounter titles that are not present in `enwiki-2022`. Those occurrences are rare, so we skip the missing items and do not include them in the dataset.

[1] GitHub Repository URL: https://github.com/MOAAS/WikiQuality.

Training and Testing Datasets. After calculating each article's entire set of features, our final step was to partition our data into a training set and a testing set. We decided on a 70/30 split, 70% for training and 30% for testing data, as previously done by multiple authors [14,20]. Table 1 shows the final distribution of articles in our dataset. We initially picked 6,000 titles from each level of quality, but we did not compensate for missing items during the generation of network graphs. Fortunately, that step showed an insignificant number of missing results, so we consider our dataset practically balanced.

Table 1. Article quality distribution within the dataset

	FA	GA	B	C	Start	Stub	Total
Training	4,200	4,200	4,197	4,199	4,196	4,198	25,190
Testing	1,800	1,800	1,798	1,799	1,797	1,798	10,792
Total	6,000	6,000	5,995	5,998	5,993	5,996	35,982

3.2 Feature Set

This section describes our feature list and the processes involved in calculating it, which account for over 80% of the dataset's build time. Each feature belongs to one of five different categories: Content, Style, Readability, History, and Network, and every feature has an assigned identifier that always starts with the first letter of its category. We provide an exhaustive detailing of all the used features and their identifiers at our source code repository[2].

Content Features (33 Features). Content features analyze the length and structure of the article (e.g., Character Count, Citation Count, Number of Images). All of them can be directly obtained from the plain text and original wikitext, so they are the fastest to compute.

Style Features (72 Features). Style features evaluate how contributors write their sentences, measuring the used word classes and sentence types (e.g., Question Count, Verb Count). They can all be derived from the article's plain text. These features are also relatively fast to compute. However, the NLP process with the NLTK tool sometimes takes a while (up to a couple of seconds for very long articles, which potentially amounts to hours with 36,000 articles).

Readability Features (10 Features). Readability features assess how easy a text is to read, using carefully designed formulas that combine word, syllable, and character count. This includes metrics like Automated Readability Index [18], Coleman-Liau [7], and Flesh-Kincaid [11].

[2] https://github.com/MOAAS/WikiQuality/blob/main/ml/datasets/README.md.

Applying the formulas was a swift and straightforward process, considering they only require values we had previously determined with the assistance of NLP tools (e.g., number of syllables and number of sentences). Calculating the number of complex words was an exception, though, for we had also to collect the list of easy words[3] initially proposed by Dale and Chall [9].

History Features (22 Features). History features measure an article's revision history and analyze its authors and contributions (e.g., Number of Revisions, Number of contributors). Stable articles with trustworthy authors tend to be better than controversial articles with frequent edits. The features within this category aim to measure articles based on this principle.

Measuring history features takes significant time because we must first obtain the entire revision history of its respective article through MediaWiki's API. Pages with more contributions will take longer to acquire. For example, the United States article[4] has the second-largest history between English Wikipedia articles, reaching 52,329 revisions (June 2025) [28]. During experimentation, fetching all its contributions took around 60 s. However, analyzing our dataset, most articles rarely have that many edits. For instance, considering only the Stubs, Starts, and C-class articles, which comprise the majority of Wikipedia, 92.8% of them have under 500 revisions.

Network Features (8 Features). Network features consider Wikipedia as a graph, where its nodes represent articles and the edges are the citations between them. Some examples include the in-degree and out-degree of an article. We can derive nearly all the features from the article's network graph, except for NT (Number of Translations), which we obtain from the MediaWiki API. However, graph generation is a highly time-consuming step, so this category is likely the least appropriate for real-time quality assessment.

Feature Computation. Some features required us to isolate the text of the article from all the wikitext tags and templates. Therefore, we clean the article's wikitext before extracting its features, obtaining the filtered plain text. We remove some irrelevant sections during the cleaning process, such as references and footnotes. However, since we need those to compute certain features, we still preserve the original wikitext. We also remove many non-textual templates, like `{chess diagram}` and `{location map}`, and ignore formatting tags, such as `<small>` and `<center>`, only keeping the text inside them. Wikitext has a complex syntax and countless tags, so it is difficult to determine all the edge cases. However, even if our wikitext cleaner is not flawless, empirical findings show almost perfect results.

Several feature categories demand a specialized analysis of the plain text we extract from the wikitext (i.e., Natural Language Processing, NLP). We used

[3] http://countwordsworth.com/download/DaleChallEasyWordList.txt.
[4] Wikipedia article is available at: https://en.wikipedia.org/wiki/United_States.

NLTK (Natural Language Toolkit) [3,4], a library that allows Python programs to process natural language data. It provides tokenization for isolating sentences and words, and POS (part-of-speech) tagging for identifying word classes. We also relied on the `syllables` python package[5] to estimate the number of syllables in each word. Although these tools are powerful, they are mainly designed to work for English texts. Using them for a few other Western languages is possible, but they will not perform as accurately, so we must take that issue into account during experimentation.

3.3 Experimentation

This phase of our study was extensive, as it was essential for developing an accurate machine-learning model. This section details the experiments we conducted to answer the research questions we defined. Each experiment and respective model will have an assigned identifier with the following format:

`<CATEGORIES><CLASSES>/<ALGORITHM>_<TASK>`

We also explain this naming convention in Table 2. By default, our model will train with the six classes and all the described features (i.e., `CSRHN6/*`).

Table 2. Training Experiments: Naming Convention

Element	Description	Example
`<CATEGORIES>`	Feature categories included in the dataset. Each category is represented by its initial letter. Possible categories: Content, Style, Readability, History, Network.	CSRHN
`<CLASSES>`	Number of output classes considered for training the model. If it is less than 6, multiple levels of quality may have the same class (more information on Tables 5 and 6).	6
`<ALGORITHM>`	Algorithm used to train the model.	tree
`<TASK>`	Whether the chosen algorithm solves classification (c) or regression (r) tasks.	c

Algorithm Comparison. We used 16 machine-learning algorithms—eight for classification and eight for regression—and conducted extensive experiments to identify the most effective models and hyperparameters, as algorithm choice greatly influences performance.

We trained the models using *scikit-learn* [12]. Table 3 lists the different algorithms we experimented with, along with the hyper-parameters we found to be most suitable (unmentioned parameters were left to *scikit-learn*'s default values). We determined them using a combination of manual and grid search, which do

[5] The `syllables` package is available at: https://pypi.org/project/syllables/.

not necessarily give the optimal values but are still widely used in the current state-of-the-art [2].

Furthermore, many of these algorithms require the normalization of the input data to achieve maximum performance [10], so we invariably applied z-score scaling before training, which normalizes the features to have a mean value of 0 and a standard deviation of 1 [19].

Table 3. Used Machine Learning Algorithms and Hyper-Parameters

Algorithm Name	ID	Parameter Name	Parameter value for Classification	Regression
Decision Tree	tree	criterion	entropy	squared_error
		max_depth	15	15
Random Forest	forest	n_estimators	150	150
		criterion	entropy	squared_error
		max_depth	15	15
Ada Boost	ada	n_estimators	150	150
		learning_rate	0.1	0.1
		base_estimator	tree_c	tree_r
Gradient Boost	gboost	n_estimators	150	150
		learning_rate	0.01	0.01
Support Vector Machine	svc/svr	kernel	rbf	rbf
		C	2	2
Multi-Layer Perceptron	mlp	hidden_layer_sizes	(100)	(100)
		alpha	0.1	0.1
		max_iter	10,000	10,000
K-Nearest Neighbors	knn	n_neighbors	10	-
Gaussian Naive-Bayes	gnb	-	-	-
Logistic Regression	logreg	max_iter	10,000	-
Linear Regression	linreg	-	-	-

Quality Classes Mapping. Since most regression algorithms struggle with categorical labels, we converted quality labels to numerical values. Following Teblunthuis [21], who notes Wikipedia's quality levels aren't evenly spaced, we used a non-linear scale based on his ordinal regression model. This mapping, shown in Table 4), does not affect classification experiments because those algorithms do not consider the values of each label.

Table 4. Regression Experimentation Class Mapping vs. Linear Class Mapping

Class	FA	GA	B	C	Start	Stub
Default	1.0	0.9	0.7	0.6	0.4	0.0
Linear	1.0	0.8	0.6	0.4	0.2	0.0

Although the dataset distinguishes between six distinct classes of quality, we also decided to study the model performance on a smaller number of classes. We thus conducted four different experiments for every algorithm, varying the number of classes in each one, but keeping all the features. Table 5 shows how we aggregated quality classes for each regression experiment. For example, in 5-class experiments, the classes B and C are merged in one. It is also worth noting that the 5-class and 2-class mappings lead to an unbalanced dataset, as we merge the examples into the same classes. Therefore, in those cases, we randomly removed excess rows from every label until the classes were distributed evenly.

Table 5. Quality-to-class Mapping in Regression

# Classes	FA	GA	B	C	Start	Stub
6	1.0	0.9	0.7	0.6	0.4	0.0
5	1.0	0.9	0.6	0.6	0.4	0.0
3	1.0	1.0	0.6	0.6	0.0	0.0
2	1.0	1.0	0.0	0.0	0.0	0.0

Table 6. Quality-to-class Mapping in Classification

# Classes	FA	GA	B	C	Start	Stub
6	C_1	C_2	C_3	C_4	C_5	C_6
5	C_1	C_2	C_3		C_4	C_5
3	C_1	C_1	C_2		C_3	
2	C_1		C_2			

Although classification experiments do not look at the value numbers, they will be based on the regression mapping, meaning quality levels with equal value will be considered the same class. Table 6 clarifies which classes we merged together for the classification experiments.

Feature Subset Optimisation. We trained 14 extra models for each previously listed algorithm, in each run varying the feature set and keeping all six classes. Table 7 lists those experiments, showing the different combinations of feature categories we tested. The combination IDs follow the naming convention previously defined in Table 2.

Table 7. Model Experimentation: Feature Subset Combinations (Transposed)

Feat	CSRHN	SRHN	CRHN	CSHN	CSRN	CSRH	C	S	R	H	N	CSR	CSH	CRH	CH
C	×		×	×	×	×	×			×		×	×	×	×
S	×	×		×	×	×		×				×	×		
R	×	×	×		×	×			×			×		×	
H		×	×	×		×				×			×	×	×
N	×	×	×	×	×						×				
#	145	112	73	135	123	137	33	72	10	22	8	115	127	65	55

Multi-language Performance. We constructed four new datasets, each respective to a different language. They all distinguish six different levels of quality, but each Wikipedia version has a different naming convention for its quality levels. To avoid confusion, we normalized the classes into letter grades, ranging from A+ to F. Table 8 displays the mapping between the classes and their respective letters.

Table 8. Model Experimentation: Quality Levels per Language

Standard	A+	A	B	C	D	F
English [27]	FA	GA	B	C	Start	Stub
French [26]	AdQ	BA	A	B	BD	Ébauche
Portuguese [23]	6	5	4	3	2	1
Russian [24]	ИС	ХС	I	II	III	IV

We did not find any Wikipedia version that provides a list of articles for every quality level, aside from the English one. We instead used MediaWiki's API to obtain random articles, determining their quality from the discussion page. Although that approach produces an unbalanced dataset, it summarizes the quality distribution within each Wikipedia. We discarded some titles while collecting the articles, as some items had no quality assigned. Therefore, the dataset sizes slightly differ between them, with English having 11,096 articles, French 11,195, Portuguese 10,525, and Russian 10,341.

Besides considering diverse languages, we experimented with three different feature sets for each one: **CSRH**, **CRH**, and **CH**. We always excluded network features because we do not have access to WebGraph datasets for other Wikipedia versions. We also tested the model without style and readability features because those are mostly inaccurate outside the English domain, especially the readability ones [8]. We selected the *forest_r* models for these experiments as that algorithm performed best on the standard dataset.

4 Results

This section discusses the main findings of our machine-learning experiments. Apart from the ones listed in Sect. 4.4, where we analyze the performance of three top-performing regression models (*CSRH6/forest_r*, *CRH6/forest_r*, and *CH6/forest_r*) on a multi-language scenario, all the results relate to experiments on the English Wikipedia using the 36,000 articles dataset. Since our result data is extensive, we summarize the essential information using tables and graphs, but all the collected results are available in a research data repository [16].

4.1 Algorithm Performances

We collected multiple performance metrics from our experimentations. Figure 1 shows the best-performing model was the Support Vector Classifier, achieving 64% accuracy. Most of the other algorithms reached similar values, ranging from

60% to 62%. When applied to the training set, these models often achieved 95 to 100% accuracy. These high accuracies suggest our approach is vulnerable to overfitting, so we will only consider results from the testing set for the rest of this section.

Then, we decided to analyze algorithm performance per class, because we suspected the models were performing worse on certain quality levels. Figure 2 suggests all algorithms have more difficulty predicting the quality of mid-tier articles than the extreme ones, likely because B and C levels are very similar quality-wise.

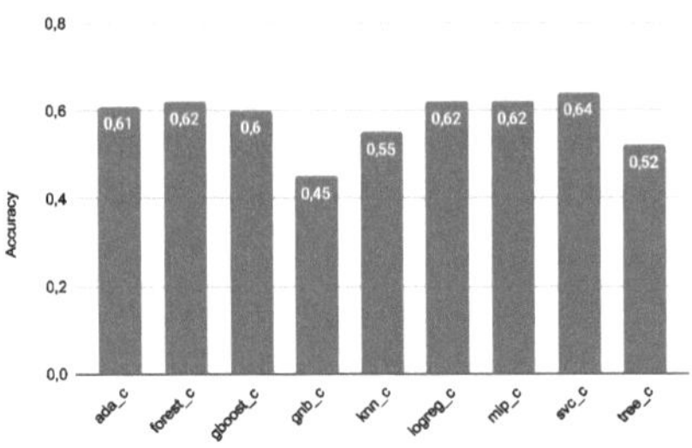

Fig. 1. Accuracy of classification models trained with all features and classes

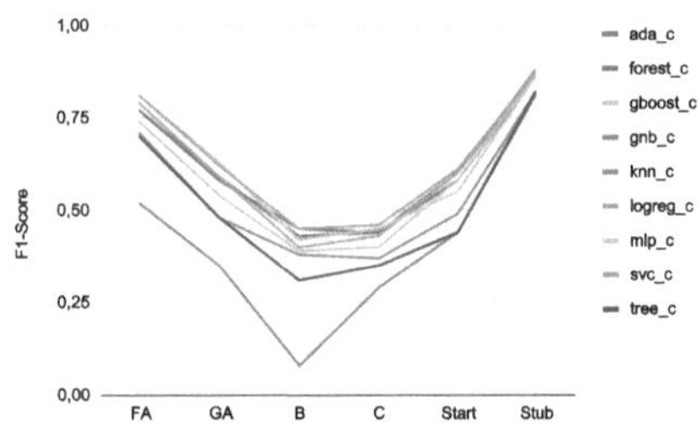

Fig. 2. F1-score of classification models trained with all features and classes, per article quality

We have also compared the performance of the multiple regression algorithms. We show the Mean Absolute Error (MAE) of the predictions in Fig. 3, as it is considered an appropriate indicator of the average error [30]. In this case, Random Forest has shown the best results (0.09), but almost all others display MAE values around 0.1. We also performed a per-class analysis of the regression results, showing the comparison in Fig. 4 and the following findings:

- Gradient Boosting shows a unique pattern compared to the other algorithms, achieving the lowest error rate for mid-tier articles.
- Most algorithms peak the MAE on the Start articles, probably because its quality value (0.4) is more distant from its adjacent levels (Stub - 0.0, C - 0.6). Conversely, the error bottoms at featured articles because its only adjacent level (GA) is only 0.1 points lower.
- Otherwise, the error rates usually do not vary significantly throughout the multiple classes.

4.2 Analysis of Number of Classes

It is expected that model accuracy increases as the number of classes decreases, but we decided to assess which algorithms would perform better with each number of classes.

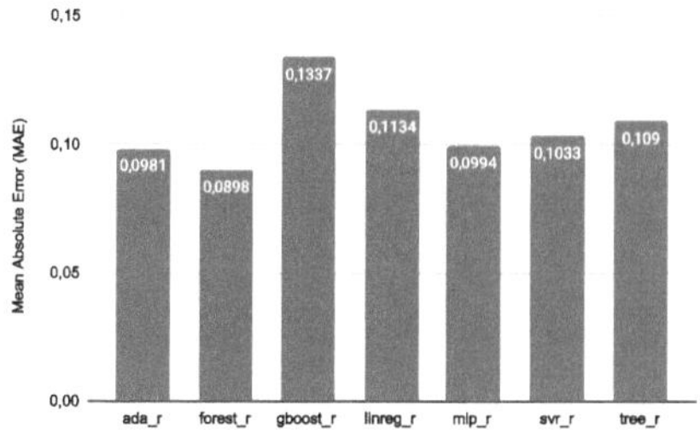

Fig. 3. MAE of regression models trained with all features and classes

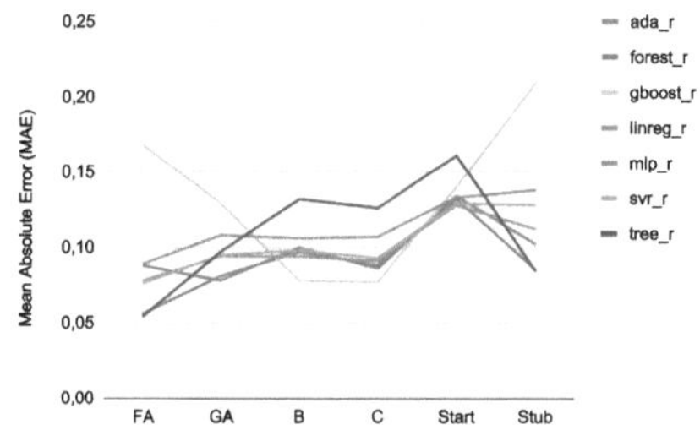

Fig. 4. MAE of regression models trained with all features and classes, per article quality

Comparing classification results is straightforward, as we can directly compare the obtained accuracies. However, for the regression algorithms, directly comparing the mean error does not give great insight into performance improvement, as fewer classes lead to more spaced-out levels of quality and may lead to a larger error. For that reason, we compared the values of $Avg_{Dist} = \frac{MAE}{Avg_{Spacing}}$, where $Avg_{Spacing} = \frac{1}{NumClasses-1}$. In other words, $Avg_{Spacing}$ is the average distance between two levels of quality, and Avg_{Dist} represents how many classes away will the model prediction be from the correct one.

Table 9 summarizes these results for both classification and regression algorithms, listing the most effective algorithms for each number of quality levels, and shows how well performance improves when the number of labels decreases. We can determine that Support Vector Classifiers (*svc_c*) and Random Forest Regressors (*forest_r*) are consistently good-performing models, independently of the used classes.

Table 9. Number of Classes: Most effective algorithms for each experiment

# Classes	Best Models	Accuracy	MAE	Avg_{Dist}
6	*svc_c*	64%	-	-
	forest_r	-	0.0898	0.4490
5	*svc_c*	73%	-	-
	forest_r	-	0.0878	0.3512
3	*ada_c*, *forest_c*, *svc_c*	81%	-	-
	forest_r	-	0.1333	0.2666
2	*forest_c*, *mlp_c*, *svc_c*	91%	-	-
	forest_r	-	0.1479	0.1479

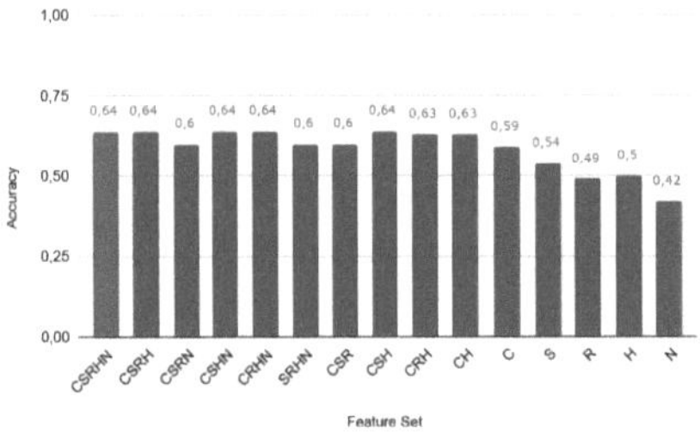

Fig. 5. Support Vector Classifier: Model accuracy

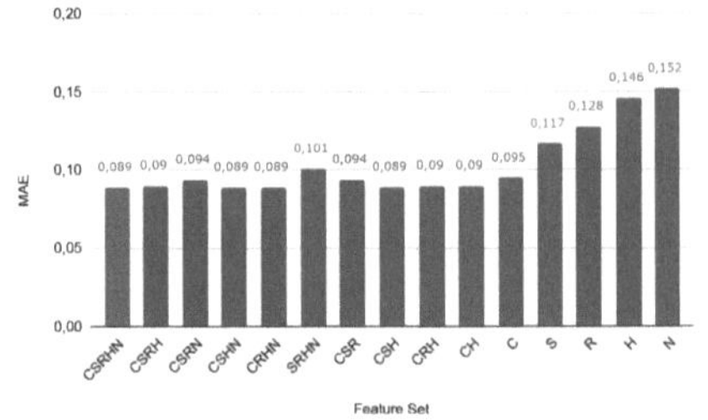

Fig. 6. Random Forest Regressor: Model MAE

4.3 Feature Category Importance

We observed that if a particular algorithm performs worse with a specific feature set, other algorithms will follow suit. As a result, we decided to focus this analysis solely on the *svc_ c* and *forest_ r* models, which are the best-performing classifier and regressor in every feature set.

Figures 5 and 6 show how the model performs when trained with different feature sets. It is unsurprising that using all features does not worsen performance, but we can quickly notice that not all categories are equally important. We can observe that content features have the best impact on the results, but keeping history features out also negatively affects performance. The charts also indicate that network features are not too crucial for accurately predicting an article's quality, which is fortunate considering their long computation times.

4.4 Multi-language Model Performance

As mentioned before, we constructed four new datasets, each respective to a different language. We then assessed the performances of three regression models: *CSRH6/forest_ r*, *CRH6/forest_ r*, and *CH6/forest_ r*. This experiment aims to simulate a real-time scenario, hence the usage of imbalanced datasets and regression models, which are better suited for predicting continuous values. Figure 7 shows that we can maintain the prediction error at an acceptable rate, even in other languages. We do not assess the MAE because these datasets are not balanced, so we want to give more weight to larger errors.

Additionally, we noticed that, on average, the model fares better against Portuguese articles. The relatively lower abundance of mid-tier Portuguese articles may explain that phenomenon, as it is more trivial to distinguish between articles that are much more distinct quality-wise. We can also observe that using fewer features significantly decreases model performance on non-English articles, which is surprising, considering that style and readability features are supposedly more accurate for English texts.

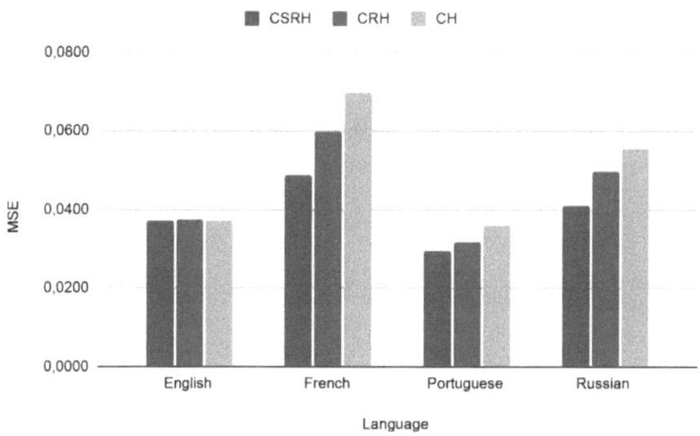

Fig. 7. Comparison between Mean Squared Error (MSE) of model predictions across different dataset languages

5 Discussion and Implications of Results

Wikipedia is a vast encyclopedia with a significant quality disparity between the millions of its articles, so it is difficult for users to determine the quality of the article they are reading efficiently. Envisioning the construction of a model that automatically predicts the quality of Wikipedia articles, we compared several algorithms with different sets of features in English articles and also in a multi-language scenario with English, French, Portuguese, and Russian articles.

We found that the best-performing algorithms for classification and regression were Support Vector Machines (SVM) and Random Forest, respectively (RQ1). The first achieved an accuracy of 64% and the second a Mean Absolute Error of 0.09. Our best-performing algorithms match or beat most state-of-the-art approaches, comparing our results with those we collected during the literature review.

As expected, decreasing the number of classes improved the model's accuracy (RQ2), but we considered the 5-class experiments to produce the most significant relative improvement, with an accuracy of 73%. Regardless, there does not seem to be an actual benefit to using less than six classes, as prediction misses only tend to occur on adjacent quality levels.

Regarding feature importance (RQ3), we found content features to be much more effective than the rest, but mixing them with the other categories led to a significant performance boost, especially history features. Additionally, we have shown that keeping the style and readability features improves performance for predicting non-English articles. We found that history features increase prediction time but considering them in a real-time scenario may still be justified by the performance gains. On the other hand, determining network features requires substantial computational effort for the benefit it generates, making them less suitable for real-time usage.

We also tested our model in randomly generated datasets of non-English Wikipedia articles (RQ4). All datasets showed promising results, though, on average, we can expect this solution to perform slightly worse in non-English Wikipedias. We have deposited the datasets used in the experiments and our results in a public repository. Finally, we provide this project's source code in a GitHub repository.

6 Conclusions

Wikipedia is a vast and evolving encyclopedia maintained by volunteers. We have successfully trained well-performing models for automatically predicting Wikipedia quality, designing a solution as good or better than state-of-the-art approaches.

Although this work has various benefits, it also comes with a few limitations. The main one, which is a common issue in many similar approaches, is that article features are simply not enough to measure quality. Downscaling entire articles into a few numbers guarantees the loss of critical information: The article's context, the integrity of the text, and the dimension of its theme are elements crucial to determining the quality and are virtually impossible to summarize for an approach like ours. It may be for this reason that these approaches never appear to reach perfect accuracy, seeming to peak around the 60%'s.

Moreover, even if we could make a perfect model of Wikipedia's quality scale, nothing guarantees that it would actually be a *good* measure of quality. That scale is maintained by many different editors across the most distinct WikiProjects, so it is heavily subject to human error. Editors are likely to unintentionally apply their biases to the evaluations, effectively leading to varying standards for the same level of quality. Additionally, we assume that the quality assessments are up-to-date with the latest changes to the article, which is not guaranteed.

We consider this study has potential for future research on a few paths. The set of features could be further tuned by assessing their importance individually instead of grouping them in categories. For instance, some style features are probably much more relevant than others, so upon further experiment, that category could see a severe reduction without significantly affecting model performance. Such an analysis could also help mitigate the model overfit we encountered. Authors may also wish to experiment with additional features or algorithms (e.g., deep learning), to try to further improve our results.

Acknowledgments. This work is funded by national funds through FCT – Fundação para a Ciência e a Tecnologia, I.P., under the support UID/50014/2023 (https://doi.org/10.54499/UID/50014/2023).

References

1. Bellomi, F., Bonato, R.: Network analysis for wikipedia. In: Proceedings of Wikimania 2005. Frankfurt, Germany (2005)

2. Bergstra, J., Bengio, Y.: Random search for hyper-parameter optimization. J. Mach. Learn. Res. **13**, 281–305 (2012). https://www.jmlr.org/papers/volume13/bergstra12a/bergstra12a.pdf
3. Bird, S., Klein, E., Loper, E.: Natural Language Processing with Python, 1st edn. O'Reilly Media, Inc. (2009)
4. Bird, S., Klein, E., Loper, E.: NLTK: Natural Language Toolkit (2025). https://www.nltk.org/. Accessed 26 June 2025
5. Boldi, P., Vigna, S.: The webgraph framework i: compression techniques. In: The 2004 World Wide Web Conference (WWW 2004), p. 602. Association for Computing Machinery (ACM), New York (2004). https://doi.org/10.1145/988672.988752
6. Boldi, P., Vigna, S.: Laboratory for Web Algorithmics - Datasets (2023). https://law.di.unimi.it/datasets.php. Accessed 12 Dec 2023
7. Coleman, M., Liau, T.L.: A computer readability formula designed for machine scoring. J. Appl. Psychol. **60**, 283 (1975). https://doi.org/10.1037/H0076540
8. Contreras, A., García-Alonso, R., Echenique, M., Daye-Contreras, F.: The SOL formulas for converting SMOG readability scores between health education materials written in Spanish, English, and French. J. Health Commun. **4**, 21–29 (2010). https://doi.org/10.1080/108107399127066
9. Dale, E., Chall, J.S.: A formula for predicting readability: instructions. Educ. Res. Bull. **27**, 37–54 (1948)
10. Jo, J.M.: Effectiveness of normalization pre-processing of big data to the machine learning performance. J. KIECS **14**, 547–552 (2019). https://doi.org/10.13067/JKIECS.2019.14.3.547
11. Kincaid, J.P., Fishburne, R.P., Rogers, R.L., Chissom, B.S.: Derivation of New Readability Formulas (Automated Readability Index, Fog Count and Flesch Reading Ease Formula) for Navy Enlisted Personnel. Technical report, Institute for Simulation and Training, University of Central Florida (1975)
12. scikit learn: Scikit-Learn: Machine Learning in Python (2025). https://scikit-learn.org/stable/. Accessed 26 June 2025
13. Lee, Y.W., Strong, D.M., Kahn, B.K., Wang, R.Y.: AIMQ: a methodology for information quality assessment. Inf. Manag. **40**, 133–146 (2002). https://www.sciencedirect.com/science/article/abs/pii/S0378720602000435
14. Medar, R., Rajpurohit, V.S., Rashmi, B.: Impact of training and testing data splits on accuracy of time series forecasting in machine learning. In: 2017 International Conference on Computing, Communication, Control and Automation, ICCUBEA 2017, pp. 1–6. Institute of Electrical and Electronics Engineers Inc., Pune, India (2018). https://doi.org/10.1109/ICCUBEA.2017.8463779
15. Moás, P.M., Lopes, C.T.: Automatic quality assessment of wikipedia articles — a systematic literature review. ACM Comput. Surv. **56**(4) (2023). https://doi.org/10.1145/3625286
16. Moás, P.M., Lopes, C.T.: Data of real-time prediction of Wikipedia articles' quality [dataset]. INESC TEC (2022). https://doi.org/10.25747/2rdd-rc08
17. Roy, D., Bhatia, S., Jain, P.: Information asymmetry in Wikipedia across different languages: a statistical analysis. J. Assoc. Inf. Sci. Technol. **73**, 347–361 (2022). https://doi.org/10.1002/ASI.24553
18. Senter, R., Smith, E.A.: Automated readability index. Technical report, Cincinnati Univ OH (1967)
19. Shalabi, L.A., Shaaban, Z., Kasasbeh, B.: Data mining: a preprocessing engine. J. Comput. Sci. **2**, 735–739 (2006). https://doi.org/10.3844/JCSSP.2006.735.739

20. Singh, V., Pencina, M., Einstein, A.J., Liang, J.X., Berman, D.S., Slomka, P.: Impact of train/test sample regimen on performance estimate stability of machine learning in cardiovascular imaging. Sci. Rep. **11**, 1–8 (2021). https://doi.org/10.1038/s41598-021-93651-5
21. Teblunthuis, N.: Measuring wikipedia article quality in one dimension by extending ores with ordinal regression. In: OpenSym 2021: 17th International Symposium on Open Collaboration, pp. 1–10. Association for Computing Machinery (ACM), Online, Spain (2021). https://doi.org/10.1145/3479986.3479991
22. Wikimedia: Wikistats - statistics for wikimedia projects (2025). https://stats.wikimedia.org. Accessed 26 June 2025
23. Wikipedia: Wikipédia:versão 1.0/avaliação (2018). https://pt.wikipedia.org/wiki/Wikip%C3%A9dia:Vers%C3%A3o_1.0/Avalia%C3%A7%C3%A3o. Accessed 26 June 2025
24. Wikipedia: Rossija/ocenki - vikipedija (2024). https://ru.wikipedia.org/wiki/%D0%92%D0%B8%D0%BA%D0%B8%D0%BF%D0%B5%D0%B4%D0%B8%D1%8F:%D0%A1%D0%BE%D0%B2%D0%B5%D1%82_%D0%B2%D0%B8%D0%BA%D0%B8-%D0%BF%D1%80%D0%BE%D0%B5%D0%BA%D1%82%D0%BE%D0%B2/%D0%A7%D0%B0%D0%92%D0%9E_%D0%BF%D0%BE_%D0%BE%D1%86%D0%B5%D0%BD%D0%BA%D0%B5_%D1%81%D1%82%D0%B0%D1%82%D0%B5%D0%B9. Accessed 26 June 2025
25. Wikipedia: List of wikipedias (2025). https://meta.wikimedia.org/wiki/List_of_Wikipedias. Accessed 26 June 2025
26. Wikipedia: Projet:Évaluation (2025). https://fr.wikipedia.org/wiki/Projet:%C3%89valuation. Accessed 26 June 2025
27. Wikipedia: Wikipedia: Content assessment (2025). https://en.wikipedia.org/wiki/Wikipedia:Content_assessment. Accessed 26 June 2025
28. Wikipedia: Wikipedia: Pages with the most revisions (2025). https://en.wikipedia.org/wiki/Wikipedia:Database_reports/Pages_with_the_most_revisions. Accessed 26 June 2025
29. Wikipedia: Wikipedia: Size of wikipedia (2025). https://en.wikipedia.org/wiki/Wikipedia:Size_of_Wikipedia. Accessed 26 June 2025
30. Willmott, C.J., Matsuura, K.: Advantages of the mean absolute error (MAE) over the root mean square error (RMSE) in assessing average model performance. Climate Res. **30**, 79–82 (2005). https://doi.org/10.2307/24869236

What Makes a User Click on a News Item? Understanding News Values of Visual Content in News Recommendation

Bruno N. Sotic and Jaap Kamps(✉)

ILLC, University of Amsterdam, Amsterdam, The Netherlands
{nadalic.sotic,kamps}@uva.nl

Abstract. It is common knowledge on the web and in digital libraries that results with an image result in far more engagement than those without. In contrast to textual features, our understanding of the visual cues is fragmented at best, and visual information is typically ignored in search, recommendation, and engagement analysis. We extend the most used news recommendation dataset (MIND) with the lead image of the news items, annotate each image using News Value Theory factors, and experiment with different LLM modalities to detect these factors. Our research provides a practical way to use currently ignored visual features as additional handles for search and recommendation in mixed media collections.

Keywords: Search and Recommendation · Visual Content Analysis · Visual Indicators · News Values Theory

1 Introduction

Multimedia access is central to digital libraries, which emerged to provide access to information regardless of media type [18,19]. While we have achieved high levels of effectiveness in textual search and recommendation, non-textual content is typically only accessed indirectly through textual context and metadata. Given the importance of visual information in selection decisions, visual aspects have great potential to improve content-based recommendations. This is important as indirect retrieval based on context has limitations. And alternatives like collaborative recommender systems are very effective in the context of high-volume engagement data, which is rarely available for digital library collections.

In recent years, research on news recommendation and user modelling has advanced rapidly, propelled by the digitization of media consumption and the increasing availability of large-scale behavioral datasets. Platforms structured around scroll-based feeds and headline scanning behaviors have further intensified interest in predicting attention and interaction [32]. Datasets such as Microsoft News Dataset (MIND), which offers millions of click logs, user profiles, and associated news content, have become benchmarks for training and evaluating engagement prediction models [1,30]. This makes further extensions of this data attractive, for example, machine translated versions for multilingual news recommendation exist [12].

However, while these advances have optimized the features predicting engagement - i.e., what types of content garner clicks - they often lack insight into the "why" behind

W.-T. Balke et al. (Eds.): TPDL 2025, LNCS 16097, pp. 321–339, 2026.
https://doi.org/10.1007/978-3-032-05409-8_19

these patterns. Media and communication scholars increasingly argue that theoretical and interpretive frameworks are needed to ground these models in social and discursive logics [5,23]. Such approaches aim not only to improve transparency and explainability but also to connect algorithmic prediction with culturally meaningful content structures.

(a) MIND data [30]

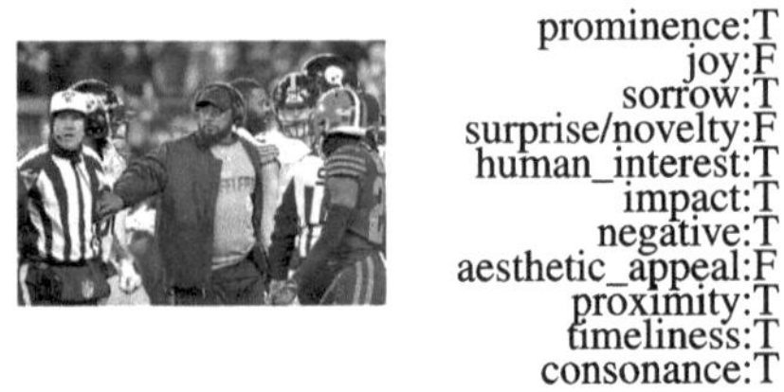

(b) MIND-NVT images and News Values

Fig. 1. MIND-NVT: News value of visual content in news recommendation.

In the news domain, there is a long-standing research tradition into *news values and news value theory (NVT)* [10,29]. Traditionally used to study journalistic gatekeeping and editorial routines, NVT has more recently been applied to model audience behavior, offering a bridge between normative communication theory and empirical user analysis [3]. Despite its promise, the operationalization of NVT in computational research faces two major limitations. First, while many studies use deductive codebooks to annotate content for news value factors, these annotated datasets are rarely released, hindering replication and resource sharing. Second, most applications of NVT are restricted to textual elements, overlooking the visual components of news (e.g., images and thumbnails) that significantly shape audience perceptions and emotional responses. As images increasingly serve as entry points to digital news stories, the visual encoding of news values demands systematic investigation.

This paper directly confronts these limitations by introducing MIND-NVT, the first large-scale, publicly available empirical dataset of human-annotated visual news values (see Fig. 1). Grounded in a deductively designed codebook derived from established NVT literature, we extend the theory's applicability to the visual domain. Our contributions are threefold: (1) We adapt News Value Theory for visual media by developing and applying the first NVT codebook for images to a substantial set of news thumbnails from the Microsoft MIND dataset, offering a structured vocabulary for analyzing visual discursive cues. (2) We provide a rigorously validated resource, detailing inter-annotator agreement for 11 news value factors across over 1,054 annotated news images, confirming the reliability and interpretability of our codebook dimensions. (3) To facilitate scalable analysis, we conduct experiments with automated content analysis methods, including supervised approaches, commercial Vision APIs, and Large-Language Models (LLMs), to assess the feasibility of automatically detecting these visually encoded news values, releasing all annotated data and modeling code publicly.

To the best of our knowledge, this work presents the first publicly accessible dataset that systematically annotates and validates visual news value factors within a large-scale corpus. It offers a novel resource for media scholars, computational social scientists, and digital humanities researchers seeking to connect theory-driven frameworks with machine-readable content analysis. This dataset and our accompanying analyses lay the groundwork for future advancements in explainable engagement prediction, studies of news framing, and multimodal content analysis rooted in robust social theory.

The rest of this paper is structured in the following way. Next, Sect. 2 discusses background and related work on visual indicators of news value and news recommendation. Section 3 introduces both the original MIND data and our extension with images and visual features. Section 4 details the annotation of the images with the factors of news value theory and an analysis of the resulting visual factors. Section 5 presents our experiments with automatically detecting visual news factors. In Sect. 6, we discuss our results and draw conclusions.

2 Background and Related Work

This section discusses background and related work on visual indicators of news value and recommendation.

News Value Theory (NVT) offers a foundational framework in media and communication research for understanding the principles that govern journalistic selection- why some events are reported as news while others are disregarded. First introduced by Galtung and Ruge [10] NVT outlines a set of criteria (called 'news factors') that contribute to an event's perceived 'newsworthiness,' such as impact (the scale of an event), conflict or negativity, prominence or eliteness (involvement of powerful and well-recognized figures), proximity (geographical or cultural closeness of an event), timeliness, and novelty or unexpectedness. These values are not arbitrary; instead, they align with cognitive and psychological tendencies in human information processing, like heightened attention to danger, deviance, or familiarity [9,27]. NVT posits that the more strongly an event embodies these characteristics, the more likely it is to be selected for coverage. These news values operate as both cognitive and institutional filters, shaping journalistic practices and audience perceptions across media systems [26,27]. Building on these theoretical foundations, researchers have extensively applied NVT in empirical studies by developing coding schemes to analyze textual news content systematically. This is typically done through manual or (semi-) automated content analysis, using codebooks derived from established definitions of news values. Such approaches have been used to investigate editorial decision-making [20,28], cross national media comparisons [8,9,26], and patterns of audience engagement [3,7,11,15,24,27].

For example, cross-national studies have employed NVT to investigate how cultural and political contexts influence the weighting of particular news value- such as how democratic systems might place greater emphasis on proximity or public interest [6]. Likewise, researchers have applied NVT to assess the dominance of values like negativity, personalization, or elite focus within specific media outlets or issue areas, often to test hypotheses regarding media bias or agenda-setting [4,11]. More recently, user engagement studies have linked the presence of particular news values—negativity, prominence, celebrity, impact/scale—to behavioral outcomes like click-through rates, shares, and comments [15,21,24,27], reinforcing the real-world impact of value-laden news content.

Despite this rich body of work, most applications of NVT remain focused on textual analysis. The role of visual content - especially photographs - has been relatively underexplored, even though images are known to significantly predict audience engagement, emotional responses, and perceptions of newsworthiness [7, 13, 17]. Given the highly visual nature of contemporary news consumption, where images often accompany or even precede the reading of text (e.g., on news apps, social media, or mobile platforms), this represents a notable gap in the empirical application of NVT. Relying solely on textual indicators of news value may obscure important semiotic cues embedded in visuals-particularly when studying outcomes like user attention or interaction. This motivates our approach, which systematically examines the visual encoding of news values in large-scale news datasets.

One notable effort to address this limitation is by Caple and Bednarek [7] who developed a discursive and multimodal approach to newsworthiness. In this view, news values are not inherent properties of events but are constructed through language, imagery, and layout. Visual semiotic resources - composition, camera angle, salience, framing, and subject matter - play a key role in signaling meaning. For instance, a close-up of a tearful face might signal "Emotionality" or "Human Interest," while a wide-angle image of destruction may indicate "Impact" or "Negativity." Caple and Bednarek [7] propose a taxonomy of visual news values that captures these nuanced indicators, illustrated in Table 1.

The present work builds directly on their framework by adopting their typology (Table 1) as a systematic coding scheme. The goal is twofold: first, to assess the empirical observability and consistency of these values in actual news images; and second, to evaluate the feasibility of automated classification using multimodal models. To our knowledge, no other studies have attempted this kind of systematic annotation and evaluation of visual NVT indicators at scale. Given NVT's relevance to audience engagement studies and the relative neglect of visual elements in prior work, we posit that incorporating visual news-value features may offer valuable signals for predicting the 'clickworthiness' of news content, and be used in future hypothesis testing or news recommender systems.

3 Data

This section introduces the original MIND data and our extension with the associated images and salient visual features.

3.1 Source Dataset: MIND

We selected the *MIcrosoft News Dataset* [MIND, 30] as our foundation because it uniquely combines large-scale behavioral logs with rich article metadata and direct links to lead images. MIND comprises approximately 1 million anonymized users, 160,000 English-language news articles, and 15 million impression records. Each impression entry records which news items were shown to a user and which were clicked (or ignored), and includes the user's recent click history. Article metadata provides titles, abstracts, categories, and linked entity tags—all indexed by hashed user and news IDs

Table 1. Visual Indicators of News Values in Images (Caple & Bednarek, 2015)

News Value	Key Devices in Image
Negativity	*Negative aspects of an event or issue*
Content	Aftermath of accidents or disasters, injured/wounded people, damage to property, arrests or court scenes, people showing negative emotions.
Camera technique	High camera angles (e.g., with minors or offenders), blurred or shaky footage suggesting instability or danger.
Timeliness	*Relevance in terms of time: recent, ongoing, seasonal*
Content	Seasonal or environmental cues (e.g., flora, Christmas trees), verbal text showing time (e.g., signage).
Proximity	*Geographical or cultural nearness)*
Content	Iconic landmarks (e.g., Tower Bridge, Uluru), cultural symbols (e.g., flags, uniforms), verbal text showing location or cultural ties.
Camera technique	Wide or telephoto lenses, dramatic angles, blurred or mobile camera indicating danger.
Eliteness	*High-status individuals or institutions*
Content	Recognisable figures (leaders, celebrities), people in uniform or media presence, flanked by military or bodyguards, elite settings (labs, police stations).
Camera technique	Low angles to show power or status.
Impact	*Significance of effects or consequences*
Content	Destruction aftermath, emotional reactions, sequential images showing cause and effect.
Novelty	*Unexpected or unusual aspects*
Content	Shocked or surprised people, unusual or norm-defying events, stark contrasts or juxtapositions.
Personalisation	*Human face of event or issue*
Content	Ordinary individuals, emotionally expressive or representative people.
Camera technique	Unequal positioning (foreground/background), close-ups highlighting emotion.
Consonance	*Stereotypical or expected representations*
Content	Familiar imagery fitting stereotypes (e.g., beer and breasts at Oktoberfest).
Aesthetic Appeal	*Visually pleasing aspects*
Content	Culturally beautiful people, places, or objects.
Camera technique	Dynamic/asymmetric composition, artistic lighting, color, or shutter speed.

for privacy. Critically, MIND's article URLs allow straightforward scraping of the corresponding lead images, enabling us to merge each thumbnail with its full engagement trace and metadata. We do not repeat MIND's full technical specification since that was extensively covered elsewhere [30].

However, several limitations are worth noting [25]. First, MIND captures only a short temporal window on a single English-language platform and excludes users with fewer than five total clicks, which may bias engagement patterns. Second, full article bodies are omitted due to licensing, constraining richer text–image analyses. Third, the dataset's ubiquity has led to potential overfitting and benchmark saturation. Despite these limitations, MIND's combination of behavioral logs and easily accessible article URLs makes it a practical starting point. By attaching visual NVT annotations to an established dataset, we enable other researchers to replicate and extend on previous work on audience-centric news values, without rebuilding user–engagement infrastructure from scratch.

3.2 Image Collection

To get the visual impressions, the approach was inspired by Xun et al. [32]. Cover images were crawled using the provided URLs for each news item, and a snapshot of the cover image was taken after it was located. We only focused on the image, since the codebook assumes that NV in images are visually constructed, hence independent from the discursive construction in the text and title. After the snapshot was taken, the images were resized to a recommended form of 200×170 pixels.

The image collection was restricted to news items that generated impressions within the MIND dataset, meaning they were actually displayed to a user on the news page, regardless of whether they were clicked. This design choice ensures alignment with future work aiming to model or assess the extent to which visual NV factors help explain engagement outcomes such as click-through rates, as demonstrated in prior studies [15]. A total of 15,080 images were successfully retrieved and systematically matched to their corresponding News IDs for consistent identification. This number represents the subset of news articles that had impressions in the MIND dataset (i.e., were shown to users) and for which images could be functionally retrieved via the provided URLs.

3.3 Image-to-Text Feature Extraction (Google Vision API)

To enrich the dataset and support downstream automated analysis, we drew inspiration from [2]'s framework for large-scale visual content analysis in communications and media. We use the Google Vision API to convert each news thumbnail image into a structured, textual representation. For all 15,080 images, the API returns:

Labels Object and scene tags with confidence scores
Objects Localized object detections with confidence scores
Safe Search Flags for violent, explicit, or medical content
Web Entities Concepts and entities matched against Google's Knowledge Graph
Logos, Landmarks, OCR Named entities and text (if present)
Facial Data Count of faces and facial emotion likelihoods
Color Features Mean RGB values

We follow earlier work [2, 14] in how we process the data. All outputs were saved as JSON files keyed by the original MIND news ID. To reduce noise, we discarded any tag or detection with confidence < 0.50. This preprocessing yields a concise "textual fingerprint" for each image—essentially a bag of tags—that can be used with traditional NLP pipelines (e.g., TF–IDF, topic models) or machine-learning classifiers (e.g., logistic regression, LightGBM, fine-tuned LLMs).

Although Vision API annotations are highly interpretable, they rely on proprietary, opaque models. Prior work has documented occasional semantic errors (e.g., mislabeling "Christmas tree" as generic "Tree") and a lack of insight into the API's internal categorization criteria [22]. Such noise can propagate into downstream analyses and should be considered when interpreting results.

4 Data Annotation and Reliability

This section details the annotation of the images with the factors of news value theory and an analysis of the resulting visual factors.

Table 2. Prevalence of Annotations per Label and Coder (Count and Proportion of Positive Cases) N = 200

Label	Coder 1		Coder 2		Coder 3	
	#True	%True	#True	%True	#True	%True
Prominence	97	48.5%	106	53.0%	97	48.5%
Joy	25	12.5%	39	19.5%	32	16.0%
Sorrow	4	2.0%	3	1.5%	3	1.5%
Surprise/Novelty	7	3.5%	9	4.5%	9	4.5%
Human Interest	35	17.5%	44	22.0%	34	17.0%
Impact	32	16.0%	37	18.5%	28	14.0%
Negative	16	8.0%	19	9.5%	18	9.0%
Aesthetic Appeal	27	13.5%	42	21.0%	27	13.5%
Proximity	24	12.0%	24	12.0%	25	12.5%
Timeliness	13	6.5%	24	12.0%	14	7.0%
Consonance	61	30.5%	126	63.0%	59	29.5%

4.1 Annotation with News Values

This study involved three coders, who collaboratively labeled the collected images based on the presence or absence of 11 news value factors, using the Caple and Bednarek [7] typology, as introduced in Sect. 2. Recognizing that certain news values, such as Human Interest, emphasize emotional expression, we sought to gain a more nuanced understanding of the emotional content depicted in the images. Therefore, we expanded our codebook to include two additional categories: Joy and Sorrow, both referring to emotions expressed by individuals within the images.

All coders were enrolled in a research MSc in Communication Science, and familiar with qualitative analysis and NVT. They were provided with the original theoretical literature and a detailed coding manual. To ensure consistency, three pilot rounds of coding (50 images per round) were conducted, followed by discussions to clarify discrepancies and refine the guidelines. After training, the coders jointly annotated a shared set of

200 images to assess inter-annotator agreement. As sufficient agreement was reached, the team independently annotated the remaining images, resulting in a total dataset of 1,054 annotated images. These 1,054 images were drawn by stratified random sampling across three click-through rate categories (low, medium, high). Disagreements during the shared annotation phase were resolved via a majority vote, as discussed in further detail later in this section.

The prevalence of each label per coder is presented in Table 2. Prominence, Consonance, and Human Interest were annotated most frequently, with prevalence rates ranging between 0.17 and 0.63. In contrast, Sorrow was rarely annotated, with the most prevalent value being 0.02. Low-prevalence categories proved particularly difficult to assess reliably and were manually sought out post-hoc. Despite the efforts, those frames occurred too rarely in the whole dataset to yield reliable coder agreement. Given this pattern, their presence is assumed to be negligible in the remainder of the dataset.

The annotation patterns also indicate variation across coders. Coder 2 (C2) consistently produced higher prevalence rates than C1 and C3 across several labels, most notably Consonance (C2: 0.63 vs. C1: 0.305; C3: 0.295) and Aesthetic Appeal (C2: 0.210 vs. C1 and C3: 0.135). This suggests C2 may have adopted a more liberal coding approach, particularly for more subjective variables. By contrast, C1 and C3 tended to converge more frequently in their label counts, reflecting a comparatively stricter annotation.

4.2 Interrater Agreement

Table 3. Cohen's κ Scores per Label and Coder Pair (N = 200)

Label	c1-c2 κ	c1-c3 κ	c2-c3 κ
Prominence	0.770	0.720	0.790
Joy	0.742	0.694	0.812
Sorrow	0.564	0.855	0.662
Surprise/Novelty	0.870	0.740	0.767
Human Interest	0.796	0.807	0.778
Impact	0.808	0.765	0.689
Negative	0.718	0.743	0.792
Aesthetic Appeal	0.705	0.786	0.705
Proximity	0.716	0.744	0.744
Timeliness	0.675	0.801	0.596
Consonance	0.319	0.262	0.268

Cohen's κ was calculated for all label combinations across coder pairs (C1–C2, C1–C3, and C2–C3), and the results are displayed in Table 3. Agreement strength was interpreted using standard thresholds [16].

The average agreement was substantial to almost perfect for most labels. Prominence, Joy, Human Interest, Impact, Negative, Aesthetic Appeal, and Proximity all achieved κ scores above 0.70 across coder pairs. Notably, Surprise/Novelty achieved particularly high κ scores (C1–C2: 0.870; C1–C3: 0.740; C2–C3: 0.767), which was unexpected given that this frame has previously been identified as difficult to operationalize [3].

Moderate to fair agreement was found for Sorrow (κ range: 0.564–0.855), and Consonance yielded poor reliability (κ range: 0.262–0.319), despite its high prevalence. This indicates that although coders often marked the presence of this frame, their judgments about its boundaries and applicability varied.

Since overall agreement can be influenced by a high number of 'absent' decisions (particularly in cases with low prevalence), Cohen's κ may overestimate reliability. To mitigate this, we calculate the proportion of positive and negative agreement—where both coder pairs agree on a frame being present or absent—using only the images in which at least one coder made a decision. Additionally, we report the Holsti index to provide a straightforward measure of overall agreement between coders

As shown in Table 4, most of the observed agreement was driven by the consistent absence of labels rather than their presence. Negative agreement scores were consistently high (often 1.000) for nearly all coder pairs and labels, indicating shared coder understanding of when a frame is not applicable. In contrast, positive agreement rates—indicating shared labeling of present instances—varied more widely. For instance, Consonance showed positive agreement as low as 0.319 between C1 and C3. This supports the conclusion that its poor κ score stems from uncertainty in positively identifying the frame, not from random variation or label sparsity alone. The only exceptions to this pattern were: Prominence, Human Interest, and Joy, which had relatively high prevalence and balanced positive and negative agreement. Impact, Aesthetic Appeal, and Nega-

Table 4. Holsti index for Inter Annotator (Positive and Negative) Agreement

Label	Holsti			Positive			Negative		
	c1-c2	c1-c3	c2-c3	c1-c2	c1-c3	c2-c3	c1-c2	c1-c3	c2-c3
Impact	0.945	0.940	0.915	0.725	0.667	0.585	1.000	1.000	1.000
Aesthetic Appeal	0.915	0.950	0.915	0.605	0.688	0.605	1.000	1.000	1.000
Consonance	0.625	0.690	0.595	0.427	0.319	0.391	1.000	1.000	1.000
Human Interest	0.935	0.945	0.930	0.717	0.725	0.696	1.000	1.000	1.000
Joy	0.930	0.925	0.945	0.641	0.583	0.732	1.000	1.000	1.000
Negative	0.955	0.960	0.965	0.591	0.619	0.682	1.000	1.000	1.000
Prominence	0.885	0.860	0.895	0.796	0.748	0.812	1.000	1.000	1.000
Proximity	0.940	0.945	0.945	0.600	0.633	0.633	1.000	1.000	1.000
Sorrow	0.985	0.995	0.990	0.400	0.750	0.500	1.000	1.000	1.000
Surprise/Novelty	0.990	0.980	0.980	0.778	0.600	0.636	1.000	1.000	1.000
Timeliness	0.945	0.975	0.930	0.542	0.688	0.462	1.000	1.000	1.000

tive showed relatively stable positive agreement, whereas Sorrow and Surprise/Novelty exhibited more variability in positive agreement scores across coder pairs.

Table 5. Per-Annotator Consistency with Majority Vote (Per Label)

Label	Coder 1	Coder 2	Coder 3
Impact	0.985	0.960	0.955
Aesthetic Appeal	0.975	0.940	0.975
Consonance	0.860	0.765	0.830
Human Interest	0.975	0.960	0.970
Joy	0.955	0.975	0.970
Negative	0.975	0.980	0.985
Prominence	0.925	0.960	0.935
Proximity	0.970	0.970	0.975
Sorrow	0.995	0.990	1.000
Surprise/Novelty	0.995	0.995	0.985
Timeliness	0.995	0.950	0.980

Moreover, Table 5 shows that each coder individually matched the majority vote over 95% of the time on all frames except Consonance (C1 86%, C2 76%, C3 83%), underscoring that our coders largely shared consistent thresholds—again with Consonance as a notable exception.

4.3 Subjectivity of Visual Aspects

Visual aspects can be more subjective and interpretative than textual features, so they are often ignored despite their significant role as a determinant of engagement. While the average agreement is high, individual cases have some degree of variation due to the task's inherent complexity for human annotators. The inter-coder reliability (ICR) analysis revealed a mixed landscape regarding the clarity and consistency of news value operationalizations. We find it important to detail this to help interpret experimental results based on this dataset.

Reliable Variables. Several variables showed strong reliability and conceptual clarity. "Human Interest," "Surprise/Novelty," "Prominence," "Impact," "Negative," and "Joy" exhibited high operationalization and consistency. Labels including "Proximity," "Aesthetic Appeal," "Sorrow," and "Timeliness" showed slightly lower but still good agreement, indicating moderate to substantial consistency.

Challenging or Inconsistently Applied Variables. Other variables presented significant challenges due to differences in interpretation. The label "Consonance" was poorly operationalized. Consonance showed the lowest agreement (κ ranging from 0.26 to

0.32). Coders struggled to identify whether an image aligned with stereotypical expectations consistently. For instance, one coder considered standard sports footage inherently consonant, while others reserved the label for more overt visual clichés. This ambiguity suggests the need for a more precise definition of what constitutes "expectedness" in imagery. Joy and Sorrow initially sparked disagreements over whether to rely on facial expressions or general image mood (e.g., bright lighting = joy). Through discussion, the team agreed to code these emotions only when they were explicitly visible in human expressions. Impact and Negativity were sometimes conflated due to overlapping definitions. Clarification was reached: Impact should denote visible consequences of an event, while Negativity refers to the overall emotional tone. Timeliness posed issues due to inconsistent or indirect visual cues. Coders differed in their use of indicators like seasonal flora or timestamps (sometimes unreadable), leading to occasional disagreement.

Low-Prevalence Variables. "Sorrow" and "Surprise/Novelty" appeared infrequently in the dataset. Despite having moderate κ scores, their rarity limits both the analytical power and interpretability of the results. Efforts were made to impute or augment the dataset with additional instances of these labels, but they could not be identified.

Readers should exercise caution when interpreting the variable Consonance, where subjectivity and coder disagreement were particularly high. Similarly, emotion-based labels (e.g., Joy, Sorrow) and indirect constructs (e.g., Timeliness, Surprise/Novelty) may be undercoded due to visibility issues or divergent interpretations. Low-prevalence variables should not be overinterpreted without further validation.

5 Experiments

This section details our experiments with automatically detecting visual news factors, and presents the main results and analysis.

5.1 Methodology

To explore the feasibility of automatically detecting the proposed news value (NV) dimensions in images, we treated each of our eleven core labels as a separate binary classification task and compared two complementary approaches. The first approach establishes a logistic-regression baseline using off-the-shelf Google Vision API tags, while the second harnesses the few-shot capabilities of OpenAI's GPT 4.1 using the same annotation codebook employed during human labeling as system prompt, as proposed by [31]. The objective is not to produce a production-grade classifier but to (a) calibrate which news-value dimensions are learnable from minimal, readily available features, and (b) scale annotation coverage across a larger corpus when supervised training data are sparse.

The first experiment began by partitioning our 1,054-image dataset into a 70/30 split (Table 6), yielding 721 images for model training and 333 held out for validation. This split was stratified to preserve each label's overall prevalence across both sets, ensuring that even low-frequency dimensions remained represented in training

Table 6. Distribution of Binary Variables in TEST and TRAIN Sets

Variable	TEST Set		TRAIN Set		N = 1,054
	False	True	False	True	
prominence	163	170	378	343	1,054
joy	280	53	622	99	1,054
sorrow	327	6	707	14	1,054
surprise_novelty	311	22	681	40	1,054
human_interest	273	60	612	109	1,054
impact	277	56	627	94	1,054
negative	316	17	675	46	1,054
aesthetic_appeal	282	51	596	125	1,054
proximity	317	16	651	70	1,054
timeliness	308	25	664	57	1,054
consonance	208	125	353	368	1,054

and validation. Nevertheless, several dimensions (i.e., Sorrow, Surprise/Novelty, Aesthetic Appeal) occur in fewer than 10% of images, presenting an inherent challenge for supervised learning.

We extracted a one-hot vocabulary of the top 200 Google Vision labels/objects/web entities/logos (min DF = 2), appended numerical face/emotion counts and SafeSearch scores, and trained a balanced one-vs-rest logistic-regression model. Performance was evaluated on the 333-image validation set using precision, recall, and F_1 metrics. This setup reveals which NV categories carry enough visual signal to be detected, and which dimensions remain effectively undetectable with simple Vision API tags.

In the second experiment, driven by the low prevalence of several labels, we explored the few-shot annotation capabilities of GPT-4.1 as a scalability tool. We applied three few-shot configurations: (1) using only the structured Vision API features (GPT-4 (Text)), (2) operating directly on the image itself (GPT-4 (image)), and (3) a combined mode integrating both inputs (Gpt-4(fusion))—to the full set of 1,054 images. Each variant was first benchmarked against the same 333-image (reported in experiment 1) validation set, using identical calculations for direct comparison to the logistic baseline. We then used the three GPT4.1 modalities to annotate the remaining images, effectively bootstrapping near-human-quality labels for all eleven dimensions without additional manual coding.

5.2 Results and Analysis

Table 7 compares a Vision-API-tag–based logistic regression against three few-shot GPT-4 variants (Image, Vision API text, fusion) on our 333-image held-out test. Across all 11 news-value categories, GPT-4's multimodal fusion model delivers the strongest balance of precision and recall, achieving a macro-F_1 of 0.420—more than double the

Table 7. Per-variable Performance (F_1, Precision, Recall) for All Models (N = 333)

Variable	Log. Reg.			GPT-4 Fusion			GPT-4 Image			GPT-4 Text		
	F_1	Prec	Rec	F_1	Prec	Rec	F_1	Prec	Rec	F_1	Prec	Rec
prominence	0.814	0.862	0.771	**0.902**	0.882	**0.924**	0.785	**0.958**	0.665	0.671	0.869	0.547
joy	0.581	0.531	**0.642**	**0.705**	0.886	0.585	0.660	0.680	**0.642**	0.600	**0.889**	0.453
sorrow	0.000	0.000	0.000	0.250	0.500	0.167	**0.571**	**0.500**	**0.667**	0.000	0.000	0.000
surprise_novelty	0.000	0.000	0.000	**0.359**	**0.412**	0.318	0.381	0.400	**0.364**	0.080	0.333	0.045
human_interest	**0.662**	**0.543**	0.850	0.639	0.495	0.900	0.579	0.416	**0.950**	0.497	0.376	0.733
impact_damage	0.000	0.000	0.000	0.215	0.778	0.125	**0.265**	0.750	**0.161**	0.069	**1.000**	0.036
negative	0.161	0.111	0.294	**0.509**	0.368	**0.824**	0.418	0.280	**0.824**	0.240	**0.375**	0.176
aesthetic_appeal	0.000	0.000	0.000	0.553	0.395	**0.922**	**0.581**	0.433	0.882	0.483	**0.583**	0.412
proximity	0.240	0.153	0.562	0.304	0.190	0.750	**0.329**	**0.206**	**0.812**	0.281	0.188	0.562
timeliness	0.333	0.245	0.520	0.419	0.275	**0.880**	0.400	0.259	**0.880**	**0.462**	**0.444**	0.480
consonance	0.000	0.000	0.000	0.581	0.417	0.960	0.607	0.440	**0.976**	**0.635**	**0.554**	0.744
Macro F_1		0.199			0.420			**0.430**			0.287	
Macro AUPRC		0.321			0.351			**0.356**			0.262	
Micro F_1		**0.872**			0.867			0.861			0.870	

GPT-text: input based on Vision API textual features only.
GPT-image: input based on the raw image alone.
GPT-fusion: combined Vision API features and image.

logistic baseline (0.199)—and a macro-AUPRC of 0.351 (versus 0.321). The image-only GPT-4 narrowly outpaces fusion on macro-F_1 (0.430) and macro-AUPRC (0.356), underscoring that visual cues alone encode much of the news-value signal. Meanwhile, the text-only variant lags (macro-F_1 = 0.287), highlighting the limits of raw tag data without image context. Micro-F_1 remains high (0.861–0.872) for all models, reflecting the ease of identifying *absences* (negative cases), but it masks the true gains GPT-4 achieves on *positive* detections.

High-visibility frames—Prominence, Joy, Human Interest, Negative sentiment, Aesthetic Appeal, and Consonance—see the largest improvements over the logistic baseline. For example, Prominence F_1 jumps from 0.814 (logistic) to 0.902 (fusion), Joy from 0.581 to 0.705, and Consonance from 0.000 (logistic fails to flag any positive instances) to 0.581 (fusion) or 0.607 (image-only). This demonstrates that our codebook's visually grounded categories are reliably captured by GPT-4's reasoning, especially when both image and text signals are combined.

However, abstract or low-salience frames remain challenging. Logistic regression detects virtually none of Sorrow, Surprise/Novelty, Impact, Aesthetic Appeal, or Consonance (all F_1 = 0.000). The fused GPT-4 recovers these to varying degrees—Sorrow F_1 = 0.250, Surprise/Novelty = 0.359, Impact = 0.215, Aesthetic Appeal = 0.553, Consonance = 0.581—yet recall-precision trade-offs are stark (e.g. Aesthetic Appeal recall = 0.922 vs. precision = 0.395). The image-only and text-only variants exhibit uneven strengths: image-only excels on visually overt categories (Consonance recall = 0.976,

Impact recall = 0.750), while text-only occasionally achieves perfect precision on sparse labels (Impact precision = 1.000) but sacrifices recall.

These findings underscore both the utility and limitations of the NV categories. Visually salient and emotional frames are highly detectable: GPT-4 fusion reliably flags positives without an unacceptable flood of false alarms, making them suitable targets for large-scale automatic annotation. In contrast, abstract or infrequent categories still suffer from low F_1 scores under few-shot conditions, suggesting that our codebook may need richer exemplars or that targeted fine-tuning is required to capture nuanced semantic layers. Finally, the high micro-F_1 scores across all methods confirm that *absences* of labels are trivially recognized, whereas true progress lies in boosting *positive* detection rates—a challenge that GPT-4 substantially outperforms simple tag-based classifiers on, but that remains an open frontier for the rarest NV frames.

5.3 Experiments on All Labeled Data

Table 8. Precision, Recall, and F_1-score per Variable for GPT-4.1 Models with Image, Text, and Combined Inputs (N = 1054)

Variable	GPT-4 Fusion			GPT-4 Image			GPT-4 Text		
	Prec.	Rec.	F_1	Prec.	Rec.	F_1	Prec.	Rec.	F_1
prominence	0.852	**0.920**	**0.885**	**0.924**	0.637	0.754	0.855	0.563	0.679
joy	**0.870**	0.618	**0.723**	0.718	**0.704**	0.711	0.859	0.441	0.583
sorrow	0.750	0.150	0.250	0.455	**0.500**	**0.476**	**1.000**	0.050	0.095
surprise_novelty	**0.509**	0.468	**0.487**	0.462	**0.484**	0.472	0.500	0.065	0.114
human_interest	**0.452**	0.888	**0.599**	0.379	**0.941**	0.540	0.359	0.710	0.477
impact	0.822	0.247	0.379	0.786	**0.293**	**0.427**	**1.000**	0.073	0.137
negative	0.433	**0.873**	**0.579**	0.369	**0.873**	0.519	**0.552**	0.254	0.348
aesthetic_appeal	0.430	**0.932**	0.589	0.468	0.881	**0.611**	**0.529**	0.415	0.465
proximity	**0.335**	**0.733**	**0.460**	0.313	0.651	0.423	0.277	0.500	0.357
timeliness	0.301	**0.841**	0.444	0.315	0.817	**0.454**	**0.352**	0.390	0.370
consonance	0.516	**0.963**	0.672	**0.538**	0.913	**0.677**	0.618	0.698	0.655
Macro F_1	**0.481**			0.465			0.309		
Macro AUPRC	**0.386**			0.357			0.262		
Micro F_1	**0.645**			0.613			0.513		

As our models were not fine-tuned on all the training data, we also report results on all the labeled data in Table 8. On the full 1,054-image dataset, all three GPT-4 variants maintain strong detection of *positive* news-value cases while naturally struggling more with the overwhelmingly negative majority. The GPT-4 Fusion (image + text) model achieves a macro-F_1 of 0.481 and micro-F_1 of 0.645, demonstrating that it correctly balances rare and common frames even as negatives dominate. Its recall remains exceptionally high for visually salient categories—Consonance (0.963), Aesthetic Appeal

(0.932), Human Interest (0.888), and Timeliness (0.841)—ensuring that few true positives are missed, while its precision (e.g. 0.852 on Prominence, 0.870 on Joy) keeps false alarms in check. The image-only model follows closely (macro-F_1 = 0.465, micro-F_1 = 0.613), indicating that raw visual cues suffice for many frames. In contrast, the text-only variant lags (macro-F_1 = 0.309, micro-F_1 = 0.513), underscoring that textual tags alone cannot capture the richness of image-based NV categories.

From a utility standpoint, these results affirm that our eleven NV categories—particularly those grounded in visual salience (Prominence, Aesthetic Appeal, Consonance) and basic emotional content (Joy, Negative)—are reliably predictable by a few-shot GPT-4 pipeline at scale. High recall on positives means the model can serve as a low-miss system for flagging news-worthy images. At the same time, respectable precision suggests it would not overwhelm downstream workflows with false positives. However, more abstract or infrequent labels (Sorrow F_1 = 0.250; Impact F_1 = 0.379; Surprise/Novelty F_1 = 0.487) remain under-detected, signaling that specific semantic nuances resist purely few-shot approaches and may require targeted fine-tuning or richer context to improve.

Comparing small vs. full-corpus performance (GPT-4 fusion), we see that scaling up benefits mid-frequency frames most: Joy's F_1 rises from 0.705 → 0.723, Negative from 0.509 → 0.579, Consonance from 0.581 → 0.672, and Aesthetic Appeal from 0.553 → 0.589. These gains suggest that broader exposure helps GPT-4 refine its concept of what counts as a "positive" example. In contrast, Prominence dips modestly (0.902 → 0.885) and Human Interest declines (0.639 → 0.599), likely due to annotation noise in the larger set introducing borderline cases. The micro-F_1 drop (from ≈ 0.867 → 0.645) merely reflects the heavier negative skew at scale—not worse per-label behavior—while the macro-F_1 gains confirm improved sensitivity to positives overall.

6 Discussion and Conclusions

This paper has presented a new multimodal resource for empirically validating photo-news values, grounding our work in Caple's typology of photographic news factors and the broader news-value theory literature. We scraped 15,080 news images from the Microsoft MIND dataset, enriched each with Vision API–derived textual tags, and then engaged human coders to annotate eleven binary news-value categories. Our inter-coder reliability analysis (Cohen's κ mostly above 0.70, Holsti indices above 0.90) confirmed that visually concrete and emotional frames—Prominence, Joy, Human Interest, Negative sentiment, Proximity, and Timeliness—are consistently identifiable by humans. In contrast, more subjective or abstract factors like Consonance and Sorrow exhibit lower agreement and will require refined definitions or additional training examples. Notably, these labels were also very infrequent in our 200-image sample (e.g., Sorrow in only 1–2%, Consonance varying between 30% and 63%), and that low prevalence further destabilized the reliability metrics.

Building on our manual annotations of 1,054 images (with a 333-image held-out test), we explored automated content analysis in two complementary ways: a logistic-regression baseline using only Vision API tags, and three few-shot GPT-4 variants (image-only, text-only, and image + text fusion). The logistic model achieved high micro-F_1 scores by trivially labeling most negatives, but it failed to detect virtually any positives for abstract frames (F_1 = 0.000 for Sorrow, Surprise/Novelty, Impact, Aesthetic Appeal, Consonance). In contrast, GPT-4 fusion more than doubled macro-F_1 (0.420 vs. 0.199) on the small test and rose further to 0.481 when scaled to the full 1,054 images, demonstrating that many common and moderately rare news-value labels can be automatically retrieved with high recall (e.g. Consonance recall = 0.963, Aesthetic Appeal recall = 0.932) and respectable precision (e.g. Prominence = 0.852, Joy = 0.870). Purely image-based GPT-4 performs nearly as well on visually grounded frames, while text-only cues lag behind, underscoring the utility of multimodal integration.

Despite these advances, automated methods still struggle with extremely rare or highly abstract categories. Rare frames like Sorrow ($F_1 \approx 0.250$) and Impact ($F_1 \approx 0.379$) see only modest gains from added data, suggesting a ceiling effect without targeted fine-tuning or more granular exemplars. Part of this limitation stems from the Vision API's own tag vocabulary—its generic labels cannot fully capture nuanced photo-journalistic constructs, and subjective categories like Consonance suffer from both low human agreement and mismatches between how the API describes imagery and how annotators interpret it.

Our study not only documents which news-value categories are reliably detectable—both by humans and by today's automated tools—but also highlights the conceptual and technical gaps that remain. For visually concrete and emotional frames, few-shot multimodal GPT-4 approaches approach human-level sensitivity; for abstract, subjective, or infrequent categories, richer codebooks, or domain-specific fine-tuning might be necessary to close the remaining performance gaps.

This resource paper lays the groundwork for a variety of future studies. Few-shot GPT-4 offers a turnkey annotation approach for the full dataset, while our human annotations serve as a robust baseline for evaluating model drift and reliability. Moreover, for the explainable-AI community, the Vision API tags provide interpretable features that can be used to understand classification output better.

Researchers can use our 15,080-image corpus—complete with Vision API features and human-annotated subsets—to test classic news-value hypotheses (e.g., whether the news value factors explain click-through rates) at scale. We have extracted all engagement data from the original MIND for the subset of 15,080 news items in MIND-NVT. An analysis of this is beyond the scope of the current paper. Initial results indicate both the complexity of predicting highly skewed and long-tailed click data, as well as some modest but statistically significant correlations with explicit news engagement factors. As expected, no single news factor is a global predictor, but news value factors influence click-through behavior in conjunction with other aspects on a micro-scale.

Despite its contributions, this study has several limitations. First, the annotated dataset (while substantial) is drawn exclusively from the Microsoft MIND corpus, which reflects a narrow temporal snapshot and a single English-language platform, potentially limiting generalizability. Second, several news value (NV) categories remain sparsely represented or could not be validated (Sorrow, Surprise/Novelty, Consonance), making them difficult to model reliably and inflating performance variance. Third, while Vision API annotations offer interpretable inputs, they may introduce noise or misclassifications. Finally, our use of few-shot GPT-4.1 bypasses fine-tuning, which, although efficient, may underperform on subtle or context-dependent frames.

Acknowledgments. The data annotation was supported by the University of Amsterdam (Digital Communication Methods Lab https://digicomlab.github.io/, and an HPC Board grant for Cloud Computing). Bruno N. Sotic and Jaap Kamps are partly funded by the Netherlands Organization for Scientific Research (NWO NWA # 1518.22.105). Jaap Kamps is further supported by (NWO CI # CISC.CC.016), the University of Amsterdam (AI4FinTech program), and ICAI (AI for Open Government Lab). Views expressed in this paper are not necessarily shared or endorsed by those funding the research.

Disclosure of Interests. The authors have no competing interests to declare that are relevant to the content of this article.

A Appendix

Our new resource is an extension of the popular *MIcrosoft News Dataset* (MIND), which can be downloaded from https://msnews.github.io/. Our MIND-NVT extension includes the crawled images, the News Value Theory (NVT) labels provided by our human annotators, Google Vision API extracts, and the full model specifications, setup, prompts, data, and files necessary to reproduce the experiments. All the extended data and documentation are available at the following repository: https://anonymous.4open.science/r/what-makes-users-click-D42F/README.md.

References

1. An, M., Wu, F., Wu, C., Zhang, K., Liu, Z., Xie, X.: Neural news recommendation with long- and short-term user representations. In: Korhonen, A., Traum, D., Màrquez, L. (eds.) Proceedings of the 57th Annual Meeting of the Association for Computational Linguistics, pp. 336–345, Association for Computational Linguistics (2019). https://doi.org/10.18653/v1/P19-1033. https://aclanthology.org/P19-1033/
2. Araujo, T., Lock, I., van de Velde, B.: Automated visual content analysis (AVCA) in communication research: a protocol for large scale image classification with pre-trained computer vision models. Commun. Methods Measures **14** (2020). https://doi.org/10.1080/19312458.2020.1810648. https://dare.uva.nl/search?identifier=a654a8f4-f002-42cd-93fe-09f1254590c0
3. Araujo, T., Van Der Meer, T.G.: News values on social media: exploring what drives peaks in user activity about organizations on twitter. Journalism **21**(5), 633–651 (2020). ISSN 1464-8849, 1741-3001. https://doi.org/10.1177/1464884918809299. https://journals.sagepub.com/doi/10.1177/1464884918809299
4. Bednarek, M., Caple, H.: Language and news values. In: Bednarek, M., Caple, H. (eds.) The Discourse of News Values: How News Organizations Create Newsworthiness. Oxford University Press (2017). ISBN 978-0-19-065393-4. https://doi.org/10.1093/acprof:oso/9780190653934.003.0004
5. Boatwright, B.C.: Embracing computational approaches to social media research: implications for theory and praxis in sport communication. Commun. Sport **13**(1), 6–32 (2025). ISSN 2167-4795. https://doi.org/10.1177/21674795231196429

6. Boukes, M., Vliegenthart, R.: News consumption and its unpleasant side effect: studying the effect of hard and soft news exposure on mental well-being over time. J. Media Psychol. **29**(3), 137–147 (2017). ISSN 1864-1105, 2151-2388. https://doi.org/10.1027/1864-1105/a000224. https://econtent.hogrefe.com/doi/10.1027/1864-1105/a000224
7. Caple, H., Bednarek, M.: Rethinking news values: what a discursive approach can tell us about the construction of news discourse and news photography. Journalism (2015). https://doi.org/10.1177/1464884914568078. https://journals.sagepub.com/doi/abs/10.1177/1464884914568078
8. Clausen, L.: Localizing the global: 'domestication' processes in international news production. Media Cult. Soc. (2004). https://doi.org/10.1177/0163443704038203. https://journals.sagepub.com/doi/abs/10.1177/0163443704038203
9. Eilders, C.: News factors and news decisions. Theoretical and methodological advances in Germany. Communications **31**(1), 5–24 (2006). https://doi.org/10.1515/COMMUN.2006.002
10. Galtung, J., Ruge, M.H.: The structure of foreign news. J. Peace Res. **2**(1), 64–91 (1965). ISSN 0022-3433. https://www.jstor.org/stable/423011
11. Harcup, T., O'Neill, D.: What is news?: news values revisited (again). Journal. Stud. **18**(12), 1470–1488 (2017). ISSN 1461-670X. https://doi.org/10.1080/1461670X.2016.1150193
12. Iana, A., Glavaš, G., Paulheim, H.: MIND your language: a multilingual dataset for cross-lingual news recommendation. In: Proceedings of the 47th International ACM SIGIR Conference on Research and Development in Information Retrieval, SIGIR 2024, pp. 553–563, Association for Computing Machinery (2024). ISBN 979-8-4007-0431-4. https://doi.org/10.1145/3626772.3657867. https://dl.acm.org/doi/10.1145/3626772.3657867
13. Keib, K., Espina, C., Lee, Y.I., Wojdynski, B.W., Choi, D., Bang, H.: Picture this: the influence of emotionally valenced images, on attention, selection, and sharing of social media news. Media Psychol. **21**(2), 202–221 (2018). ISSN 1521-3269. https://doi.org/10.1080/15213269.2017.1378108
14. Kim, M., Bas, O.: Seeing the black lives matter movement through computer vision? An automated visual analysis of news media images on Facebook. Soc. Media Soc. **9**(3), 20563051231195582 (2023). https://doi.org/10.1177/20563051231195582
15. Lagerwerf, L., Govaert, C.: Raising clickworthiness: effects of foregrounding news values in online newspaper headlines, pp. 95–119. Palgrave Macmillan (2021). ISBN 9783030450458. https://doi.org/10.1007/978-3-030-45046-5_6
16. Landis, J.R., Koch, G.G.: The measurement of observer agreement for categorical data. Biometrics **33**(1), 159–174 (1977). ISSN 0006-341X
17. Leckner, S.: Presentation factors affecting reading behaviour in readers of newspaper media: an eye-tracking perspective. Vis. Commun. **11**(2), 163–184 (2012). ISSN 1470-3572. https://doi.org/10.1177/1470357211434029
18. Lesk, M.: Experiments on access to digital libraries: how can images and text be used together. In: Bocca, J.B., Jarke, M., Zaniolo, C. (eds.) VLDB 1994, Proceedings of 20th International Conference on Very Large Data Bases, 12–15 September 1994, Santiago de Chile, Chile, pp. 655–667, Morgan Kaufmann (1994). http://www.vldb.org/conf/1994/P655.PDF
19. Lesk, M.: Understanding Digital Libraries, Second Edition (The Morgan Kaufmann Series in Multimedia and Information Systems). Morgan Kaufmann Publishers Inc., San Francisco (2004). ISBN 1558609245
20. Marques, F.P.J., Mont'Alverne, C.: What are newspaper editorials interested in? Understanding the idea of criteria of editorial-worthiness. Journalism **22**(7), 1812–1830 (2021). ISSN 1464-8849. https://doi.org/10.1177/1464884919828503

21. Park, C.S., Kaye, B.K.: Applying news values theory to liking, commenting and sharing mainstream news articles on Facebook. Journalism (2021). https://doi.org/10.1177/14648849211019895. https://journals.sagepub.com/doi/full/10.1177/14648849211019895
22. Peng, Y., Irina, L., Ali Salah, A.: Automated visual analysis for the study of social media effects: opportunities, approaches, and challenges. Commun. Methods Measures **18**(2), 163–185 (2024). ISSN 1931-2458. https://doi.org/10.1080/19312458.2023.2277956
23. Pouwels, J.L., Araujo, T., Atteveldt, W.V., Bachl, M., Valkenburg, P.M.: Integrating communication science and computational methods to study content-based social media effects. Commun. Methods Measures (2024). ISSN 1931-2458. https://www.tandfonline.com/doi/abs/10.1080/19312458.2023.2285766
24. Trilling, D., Tolochko, P., Burscher, B.: From newsworthiness to shareworthiness: how to predict news sharing based on article characteristics. Journal. Mass Commun. Q. **94**(1), 38–60 (2017). ISSN 1077-6990. https://doi.org/10.1177/1077699016654682
25. Vrijenhoek, S.: Do you MIND? Reflections on the MIND dataset for research on diversity in news recommendations. In: Boratto, L., Faralli, S., Marras, M., Stilo, G. (eds.) Advances in Bias and Fairness in Information Retrieval, pp. 147–154, Springer (2023). ISBN 978-3-031-37249-0. https://doi.org/10.1007/978-3-031-37249-0_12
26. Waheed, M., Schuck, A.R.T., Neijens, P.C., Vreese, C.H.D.: Values in the news. Journal. Stud. (2013). ISSN 1461-670X. https://www.tandfonline.com/doi/abs/10.1080/1461670X.2012.701910
27. Weber, P.: Discussions in the comments section: factors influencing participation and interactivity in online newspapers' reader comments. New Media Soc. **16**(6), 941–957 (2014). ISSN 1461-4448. https://doi.org/10.1177/1461444813495165
28. Welbers, K., Opgenhaffen, M.: Social media gatekeeping: an analysis of the gatekeeping influence of newspapers' public Facebook pages. New Media Soc. **20**(12), 4728–4747 (2018). ISSN 1461-4448. https://doi.org/10.1177/1461444818784302
29. Wikipedia: News values — Wikipedia, the free encyclopedia (2025). https://en.wikipedia.org/wiki/News_values. Accessed 10 May 2025
30. Wu, F., et al.: MIND: a large-scale dataset for news recommendation. In: Jurafsky, D., Chai, J., Schluter, N., Tetreault, J. (eds.) Proceedings of the 58th Annual Meeting of the Association for Computational Linguistics, pp. 3597–3606, Association for Computational Linguistics, Online (2020). https://doi.org/10.18653/v1/2020.acl-main.331. https://aclanthology.org/2020.acl-main.331/
31. Xiao, Z., Yuan, X., Liao, Q.V., Abdelghani, R., Oudeyer, P.Y.: Supporting qualitative analysis with large language models: combining codebook with GPT-3 for deductive coding. In: Companion Proceedings of the 28th International Conference on Intelligent User Interfaces, pp. 75–78, IUI 2023 Companion. Association for Computing Machinery (2023). ISBN 979-8-4007-0107-8. https://doi.org/10.1145/3581754.3584136
32. Xun, J., et al.: Why do we click: visual impression-aware news recommendation. In: Proceedings of the 29th ACM International Conference on Multimedia, pp. 3881–3890. ACM (2021). ISBN 978-1-4503-8651-7. https://doi.org/10.1145/3474085.3475514

Digital Humanities and Cultural Heritage

Blowin' in the Wind: The Challenges of Archiving Social Media for Digital Humanities Research

George Buchanan(✉) and Dana McKay

RMIT University, Melbourne, VIC, Australia
{george.buchanan,dana.mckay}@rmit.edu.au

Abstract. Social media is a fundamental source of information on human behaviour; it has been used to study everything from health information behaviour to the functions of democracy. Using this data for research, though, is challenging, particularly given requirements to retain research data post publication. Social media posts are often ephemeral, and notoriously difficult to re-find; a problem exacerbated by shifting social media company policies and algorithms. Nonetheless, research standards require retention of data. While at-scale digital libraries and archives of social media material have been studied, day to day collection practices of digital humanists are less well understood. We present a qualitative examination of the collection practices of 14 digital humanists, with a view to understanding how to support them in creating these important personal digital archives.

Keywords: Social media · digital humanities · digital archives

1 Introduction

Social media is a key data source for digital humanists, allowing them to study health behaviours [1, 2], social connections [3, 4], and even democracy itself [5, 6]. Social media posts, though, are often ephemeral—posters may delete them or deletion may be built into the structure of the social network, as with snapchat. They are also notoriously difficult to re-find [7], and are often not only text based—they may include or comprise images or video as well. Given these challenges, digital humanists often build personal research archives of social media content. These archives are necessary not only to conduct the research, but are also often required for good research practice, where data are retained for a fixed period after publication [8, 9].

Arguably, these archives created by digital humanists are at a nexus between being a data repository and a personal digital library. Like a personal digital library, the materials they contain are collected for use by one person, with the specific intention to organise and curate materials for later re-finding and reuse. In contrast to most personal digital libraries, though, the material they contain is not created by the owner, but rather by a plethora of other people. They also contrast with more traditional digital libraries in that

W.-T. Balke et al. (Eds.): TPDL 2025, LNCS 16097, pp. 343–359, 2026.
https://doi.org/10.1007/978-3-032-05409-8_20

their content is only rarely hierarchically organised long form text. Instead, it comprises a mixture short form text, images and video with networked relationships between items, and their creators.

The technical and social affordances of gathering social media data are complex. Social media companies have intermittently offered support for data gathering in the form of APIs, but these may be withdrawn with little notice [10], and they require technical knowledge to use. Social media companies may limit what can be gathered with their terms of use [11], and there are ethical considerations around respecting the users of social media services, even where the material is publicly available [9, 12]. Taken with the ephemerality and multimedia nature of social media data, gathering and organising this data can be challenging.

The field of digital libraries has concerned itself in the past with the management of research data, how digital humanists conduct their work, and the technical and human centric elements of personal digital libraries [13, 14]. Digital humanists collecting social media data sits at the nexus of all three. Digital humanities researchers are gathering social media data (created by other people) as resources for themselves to analyse and review as part of their research. These personal archives of online social media content are central the academic work of those analysing social media online data.

However, the body of literature on personal digital libraries is relatively scant [15], the structures involved are markedly different, and there is even less material on the individual practices, needs and requirements for those involved in gathering social media archives for their own purposes [16]. The fractured and thinly spread existing literature on this topic provides very little substance on which to build specific personal digital archive tools for social media content [17]. As a result, a field where the organisational, preservational, retrieval and analytical features of digital libraries could do so much, is severely under-developed.

In this paper, we add foundation for future work in understanding what personally managed social media archives need operationally and technically. We report a series of interviews with fourteen (14) digital humanities researchers who use social media as a source of research data. We present a series of new or strongly refined technical and user requirements for effective digital tools for personally managed social media archives. We further highlight barriers that are likely to remain prevalent, and opportunities that are under-exploited. This provides a foundation for both further empirical research into the needs of digital humanities scholars who gather social media data, and for the development of digital humanities tools that support their work.

The rest of this paper is structured as follows: we commence with a review of the current literature on personally managed digital archives in general, and of social media archives in particular. Next, we describe the qualitative interview methodology we used to elicit current practices, tools and working methods of digital humanities scholars gathering social media research data. We then report our findings, highlighting new factors and issues highlighted in our study. The paper concludes with a discussion to set out the need for future work, clarify the contribution made by this work, and the lessons it provides for digital tools to support personally managed social media archives for the digital humanities.

2 Literature Review

The use of social media for research purposes is a relatively new phenomenon, in part due to the novelty of social media itself, but also due to the frequent difficulties of obtaining social media at scale, and the lack of established practice in analysis and publication. Practices also vary between disciplines, due both to differences in the technical knowledge typical of contrasting research domains, and differences in the research methods that dominate in particular research areas. The withdrawal of APIs for major social media such as Twitter/X have led to a drop in the utility and practicality of automated methods that would traditionally have held sway in, say, computing, where there is an emphasis on quantitative methods and large-scale data.

This section examines the existing literature on digital humanities uses of social media data, research on personal digital libraries, and the existing empirical data on personal social media archives and their management, before arriving at our research aims.

2.1 Social Media and Digital Humanities

The digital humanities was an early adopter of social media to disseminate its research outputs and activities [18]. Research has started to emerge on how social media content is harvested and managed by digital humanities researchers [19, 20]. However, there has been an emphasis on larger-scale work, and this has given importance to national institutions and, in turn, policies and practices that match the concerns of such bodies [21]. For instance, there has been a concern about interchange and preservations standards [19], compliance concerns such as copyright and metadata formats [19, 20], and policies to address privacy [21].

Much of this research has stemmed from library and information science (e.g. [20]), and as is often found in that domain, there has been an emphasis on the use of surveys, in order to see how specific issues play out at scale [19, 20]. However, this presumes that social media archiving and digital humanities research are synonymous. This is often not in fact the case, and the project that supported this current paper was the result of discovering significant gaps between the research literature and the practical needs of practicing researchers.

2.2 Personal Digital Libraries

The field of digital libraries has been interested in the activities involved with personal archiving. Personal archiving occurs where a person gathers data or documents for work or leisure reasons with the aim of holding that material for later or ongoing use [22, 23]. The work of personal archiving has followed two tracks within digital library work: first, creating technologies to support personal collections, e.g. [15, 24]; and second, examining the practices and needs of digital libraries [21, 25]. There is also a wider field of interest in personal information management, which naturally includes the task of archiving [26, 27]. Much of the technical digital library work focuses on long-form documents (e.g. [24]), and predates the emergence of social media. Therefore, its translation into the contemporary challenge of personally archiving social media is indirect.

Furthermore, there is a potential confusion between archives of personal social media content (i.e. archiving one's own social media activity), and as an individual archiving founds social media content from other people or organisations. Cathy Marshall has already shown there to be very distinct expectations from social media users on one side, and institutions on the other regarding the principles and practices of personal archiving in social media [21, 28, 29]. In that context, for example, Marshall points out that concepts of privacy and expectations of agency are disjoint: people's expectations of what happens or could happen to their own social media are very different to the policies and practices of archiving institutions. When we move into a context where an individual researcher is gathering the social media content of others, this already complex picture gets even more elaborate, especially over time [25].

In addition, Marshall [21, 29], Jones [26] and others (e.g. [7]) have noted that personal archiving of any form tends to be ad-hoc, loosely planned and distributed over time, place and technology. What is not clear is how closely academic's individual practices with research material mirror that of the general public's personal archiving practices, or in contrast model the ideals of reference libraries. Previous research suggests that academics' behaviours here may be more ad-hoc than formal [30, 31], but the existing literature there is again on long-form material, and in the main is also nearly two decades old.

2.3 Foundations for Personally Managed Social Media Archives

The literature on social media archiving is not limited to the domain of digital libraries. Researchers in library and information science have produced guidance on how individuals can gather social media material of their own or produced by others [22]. However, that work is primarily aimed at the features of specific platforms, e.g. Facebook, to extract and download material, or use cross-platform tools such as If This Then That (ifttt.com) for the same purposes. That work does not give guidance as to how to manage collections of downloaded material, nor does it investigate what scholars or others with long-term interests in social media do to conserve it for future use.

Others have looked more specifically at the needs of particular groups that archive other people's social media, such as journalists [32]. Yet again, the primary approach is to examine existing library- and archive- institutional practice, and make surmises about how to adjust these for individual purposes. The needs of journalists are hypothesised without direct empirical data, but rather educated estimations of what practices might be needed. Nonetheless, such work is useful as it challenges the assumption that personal archives are synonymous with information about the self. The motivating research provides ample examples of the contexts in which journalists need to create their own collections of social media, However, it lacks clarity about what work they subsequently do with it, or the life-cycle of the social media materials that they gather.

A third strand of research examines personally managed social media archives as part of a research repertoire (e.g. [16]), very often considering the role and utility of this sort of archive as a store of content for qualitative analysis. That work has often built on the body of research on web archiving as a method in qualitative research [33]. That body of work distinguishes micro-archiving—by an individual—from macro-archiving—by an institution. This distinction is critical in helping distinguish a gap that runs through the literature in this section. While there has been an extensive literature on macro-archiving which is informed by the scholarly policies of university libraries and other institutions, the existing literature on micro-archiving has focused on the private material of the individual. Some works have contrasted the diverging expectations of the institutional and the personal perspectives, but there is consistent lack of work on the micro-archiving practices of scholars and researchers.

It is this gap that this work aims to close, drawing on the methodological approach that Cathy Marshall [21, 34] has demonstrated is powerful in understanding private micro-archiving: interrogating the personal practices of individuals, their over-arching aims, and the ways in which the current state of technology assists, hinders and subverts those aims in practice.

2.4 Summary

The field of social media is generally complex, as are the particulars of how to conduct research using social media data. Social media content is increasingly important as a resource for research, but how scholars navigate the complexities of long-term retention and storage is not clear. The previous evidence of social media archiving by the general population points to many problems, including transience and storage. However, it is not clear to what degree social media researchers face these barriers, and how effective their working strategies are to overcome them. To this end, it is vital to gather empirical evidence of how humanities researchers handle and retain social media data over time.

3 Method

With the lack of existing information on the archiving and management practices being used to manage personal research archives of social media content, we needed a method that would best elicit information in a domain where little was known. While a survey would more readily cover a wider number of participants, this method is known to be a poor fit for domains where there is insufficient knowledge to design a good survey instrument [35]. While previous research has used surveys, this was in order to understand predetermined issues directly related to a targeted research questions, such as whether a privacy policy existed or not [20]. As those researchers themselves pointed out, this was appropriate for their specific research goals, but they did not aim to find out how things were done, or why. These are the sorts of questions interviews are much better at teasing out [36].

This research was part of a larger project to build a digital infrastructure for supporting large-scale social media research. In the interviews reported here, the aim was to understand what current social media gathering practices were in the humanities in particular. Our scope was broad, aiming to capture the wider context within which our future system would be used. The issues we sought information on varied from understanding the technical infrastructures and resources scholars had and used, through to their overarching research method. With the previous research giving little idea of what factors may be at play, our design was semi-structured, focusing on a series of broad areas, with the more detailed questions being refined in light of insights from earlier interviews. The key questions we were examining included:

- The researcher's current social media project, its aim and scope
- Their research method and approach for that project
- Technical resources available to capture social media data
- Which platforms data was captured from
- What strategy they used to select the data to captured, and its time-span, storage space, and other content characteristics
- What format any gathered data was initially taken in
- How gathered data was structured and organised for use across the research project
- What analysis method(s) were used in the scope of the project
- How any of the above factors reflected their previous experience and skills in handling social media

Three pilot interviews were undertaken to identify and scope down some more detailed questions, and to assess the time taken for an interview. With these and the main interviews, the time was within 50 to 75 min. This is on the longer scale of interviews that is desirable, and typically there was a single break of five minutes to allow the interviewees a period of rest, following good standard practice [36].

Our target interviewees were active researchers in the broad field of digital humanities who had completed at least one previous social media research project, and had at least one current project underway. All were required to be at PhD student level or above. All the participants were working at an Australian university at the time of the interview, and all but two interviews were undertaken remotely. Notes were taken by the lead author across each interview, and a transcript was gathered automatically, along with an audio recording. These were examined and cross-referenced following the interview to arrive at the finalised notes and extracts from the interview.

Participants were recruited through mailing lists known to be used by digital humanities researchers in Australia, and through recommendations from the steering committee of the overall research project. No remuneration was given for participation. In total, fourteen interviews were taken, excluding the three pilot interviews. Participants ranged from PhD students to senior professors with over a decade of social media research, and worked at a variety of universities, from teaching-focussed institutions to high-profile research-intensive organisations. The whole of Australia was covered, except for the Northern Territories, the least populous of the country's states and territories.

For analysis, we used the general inductive method of Thomas [37] which includes inductive coding that can be informed by previous research, and also allows for a systematic analysis based on the number of occurrences of individual codes. The approach is frequently used in a mixed-methods context to support a combination of inductive discernment of patterns and a numerical characterisation of the relative frequency of ideas, concepts or contextual factors. As such, it is ideally suited to research that aims to provide foundations for requirements gathering and systematic analysis for later quantitative experimentation.

4 Findings

We now present the findings of our research. This section will begin by providing context to the results, including the platforms where data was gathered from and the technical resources available to the interviewees. We will then move to the archiving practices followed by our participants, highlighting how their research project, the available technology and the platform being studied interact. Thirdly, we will examine the impact of personal skills and experience on the methods adopted. We conclude with a summary of the themes that connect across these three complementary aspects of our findings.

Table 1. Participant Profiles

Participant Number	Social Media Experience	Research Method
P1	10 years +, 10 projects +	Qualitative
P2	10 years +, c. 7 projects	Qualitative
P3	3 years, 2 projects	Mixed methods, SNA
P4	5 years, 4 projects	Qualitative, Mixed methods
P5	7 years, 4 projects	Qualitative, SNA 'with help'
P6	4 years, 2 projects	Mixed Methods, Qualitative
P7	10 years +, 10 projects +	Quantitative, Mixed methods, SNA
P8	2 years, 2 projects	Qualitative
P9	7 years, 2 projects	SNA
P10	4 years, 3 projects	Qualitative, Mixed Methods
P11	10 years +, 6 projects	Mixed Methods
P12	7 years, 9 projects	Qualitative
P13	8 years, 5 projects	Mixed methods, qualitative, SNA
P14	3 years, 4 projects	Quantitative, SNA

Our fourteen participants are summarised in Table 1, giving their relative experience and a high-level summary of the research methods they have used in the context of their social media-related work. For brevity, social network analysis is shortened to SNA. As can be seen, there is a strong thread of purely qualitative research (10 participants), with half using mixed methods, a little over a third (5) using SNA, and two using other quantitative approaches. Only three respondents exclusively used quantitative methods. One of those who used SNA (P5) did so in the context of a collaborative team, and while capable of using some existing tools, relied on their colleagues to be sure that they had correctly set up and interpreted the results. The other methods were reported as ones that the participants used and were sufficiently confident with and they were able to execute them fully independently. While not tabulated, two of the participants were PhD students (both in the second half of their candidature), four were postdoctoral researchers, and the remaining eight were teaching and research faculty, of whom two were professors, three associate professors, and the remaining three were lecturers (assistant professors). There was a variety of intensity of social media work, with some like P1 primarily undertaking social media work, while for others (e.g. P9) social media research was part of a wider range of research.

The research was mostly conducted before the closure of the Twitter public API in February 2023, with only the last four interviews occurring after that point. However, as will be seen, there were concerns about the long-term availability of services even in the earliest interviews. Having set the broad context of the participant's social media work, we will now report the current work contexts that they were engaged in.

4.1 Social Media Platforms and Technical Resources

Our participants used a wide range of social media platforms, with the more frequently mentioned ones for their current project including Facebook (11 respondents), Twitter/X (8 respondents), Instagram (6 respondents) and TikTok (5 respondents). Facebook and Twitter were also frequently used previous projects, whether or not they were within the scope of the participants' current project. For those with longer-term engagement in social media (e.g. P1,2,7,11) had multiple experiences of most of the platforms they used, and had established methods for data gathering from those chosen sources.

We quickly discovered a range of specific operational constraints. The clear majority (9) of the participants reported a significant impact on their research of the computers they had access to. P2 explained "none of our [university] laptops are really adequate – the hard drives are too small for this sort of work."; P7 lifted a set of external hard drives saying "Because there's so much data I end up having to store stuff on these". There was a consistently reported lack of institutional support for the storage of the social media data, with only P14 saying "I personally have access to a large amount of uni storage, but that's only due to my [institutional] role…none of my colleagues would get that". All but two of the participants reported that their university computers were themselves inadequate, e.g. P3 said "there's just not enough space for anything like this". As a result, as with P7's gesture, storage was almost universally on external hard drives, pen drives or personal cloud storage (e.g. DropBox).

Four of the participants had some system for identifying which drive had what content, e.g. P7 had a Post-It note on their drives, while P4 had three different drives, each containing the data for one or two projects. Some (five) had a second copy of some of the data, but most (9) had only a single copy of each dataset. Thus, overall, the backup and storage strategies were rudimentary, and the failure or loss of a drive would mean the entire loss of the gathered data for most.

This technological constraint also applied to the available processing power. Again, P14 had access to extensive computer power, and a range of technical computing skills that enabled them to undertake SNA and other forms of quantitative analysis. However, this was not typical. While P3, 5, 9 had access to large-scale computing facilities through associates, and P13 had a 'home brew' resource, the remainder had only their personal work computer to do any analysis on. This proved problematic even for those not seeking to use computationally intensive methods, e.g. as P6 said "I'm not a geek and I don't know how to geek, but even I know our uni laptops don't have enough power…anything multimedia they struggle with, even using Zoom [for online meetings]". There was a consistent problem with consumer-level computer power, including on-machine storage as above, but also supporting multiple apps while undertaking analysis, access to sufficiently many computer screens and other problems. As P8 reported, "I do just take notes [on paper] as I look at stuff and compile it after", which "drags out" doing any analytical work.

A mixture of software systems were used for analysis, and reflected the most common systems used by the different approaches (e.g. R for SNA and quantitative work, NVivo for qualitative work), plus a consistent adoption of routine general-purpose software such as Excel, which was used for tabulating qualitative codes and doing simple quantitative analysis. None of our interviews revealed any particular influence from the choice of software. However, there was widespread use of specific discrete software or extensions for social media purposes. e.g. five participants used Instamancer, a tool for extracting content from Instagram. All but three participants had done some programming with APIs to extract information, though this varied in scope from downloading individual posts or accounts to large-scale extraction, as we will see below.

All our participants reported that archiving social media content was important to their research. There were a variety of reasons, and these interacted with their research approach. For those doing long-term research, this was in inherent need. E.g. P1 reported "...doing longitudinal research...there's changing [of APIs, formats] over time; lots of data needing lots of space; and you're going back to it at a later date."; similarly P4 noted "to see changes in behaviour, you need to look back not a week, but a year, two years, more". They both needed to "capture now data from right now, and last year" but also "I go back to what I gathered before and look at it again". As P8 noted "it's easy to get right-now data, but even with the APIs it's hard to get at the old stuff sometimes". Even in their short career they said "I have learned to gather now, stash it away for later, because that's easier than struggling with the barriers to older posts".

Where APIs allowed for extraction, even capable researchers combined retrospective searches to gather old material with gathering content for later use. P7 explained "part of the point is the most interesting...more controversial posts...can be deleted; accounts disappear or go offline; the API changes; the terms of service change; you can't rely on something you see today being something you can get tomorrow". There were also technical barriers: e.g. P1 noted that while Instagram could be mined back "as far as the data goes"..."I don't have access to the computing power to do that". This led to a variety of strategies for hoarding data for later use, including screen snapshots, "printing" to PDF, and collating data into bespoke databases to hold historic material.

Nine participants, e.g. P6, also noted that this is necessary "if you want to either work with others to let them re-analyse what you have". However, even this proved complex, e.g. as P11 noted with Twitter, there were intellectual property and terms-of-use issues that influenced their practices: "so you have that whole hydrate/de-hydrate thing, and the problem is that the identifiers and content I have today can point to nothing tomorrow... but I'm not supposed to hand on the actual content if it's not available". As a result, they always "take a copy of the source just in case..." so that it could be shared "unofficially" afterwards if needed. Again, this links back to the need for storage, and the scope and scale of data required to meet the need for future use increases.

4.2 Practices

Social media data was evaluated and used in very different ways, but there were stark differences between those using qualitative methods versus quantitative approaches.

For those using qualitative approaches, individual posts needed to be captured in context: e.g. if gathering posts on a subject, or person, they would seek to record not only the matching post, but also responses, and the context within which it was set (e.g. other recent posts from the same user). A lot of the selection of material to capture was done manually, often influenced by emerging research questions or themes where more material was seen as necessary. For example, P2 said "I don't want just the bare bones, the atoms, I need the context of the post – what came before or after it [on the screen], who responded"; similarly P8 reported "when I find something useful I'll screen-capture or PDF it – get the whole thread" and "I'll also gather other things around it, what else is going on at the time". Once gathered, data was stored in a personal folder for the project. Some initial analysis might be done immediately: e.g. P8 "I'll take a few notes straightaway before I forget… otherwise it's [the social media content] useless" but more often the strategy of P1 is typical "gathering stuff together and going over it later… usually within a week or so".

In contrast, those using quantitative methods relied more on (semi-)automated gathering tools, picking individual posts or whole threads as a policy, but not capturing much context. P13 was particularly clear on this approach "there's what's in and what's out – and for the scales we need, you can't, you shouldn't be distracted by hunting around". All those using quantitative approaches acknowledge the potential risk of misinterpretation, but as P7 explained "Of course context matters, but at the scale you need … you just can't; no one…can practically find that [amount of] time". Data in this case was often both downloaded in raw form and then organised afterwards for ingest or processing into standard tools (e.g. for Social Network Analysis), typically using limited manual processing to correct errors that emerged.

As can be gleaned from Table 1, half of our researchers used mixed methods in their current project, often alongside either purely (more often) qualitative or quantitative work. The scholars were adapting different strategies based on their intended approach to analysis, and (for example) some qualitative work was frequently used as a precursor to mixed-methods work (P4, 5, 6, 10, 13).

These differences in approaches interacted with the different technological limitations seen above. Those who created hand-picked content for their research projects also reported a more manual approach for organising, storing and retrieving that content across the project and the long-term. P6 explained their approach "I put stuff in the project folder over time. From time-to-time I then go over it again, particularly as I analyse it: finding gaps and getting more, changing file names so I know what's what". This fitted the central theme of our qualitative researchers: a gradual aggregation over time, with periodic organisation. P2 was a contrast "I put everything in careful order at the start… storing each account's data separately so I don't mix them up". They kept a written notebook to track what had been gathered, and each project had its own notebook. All the qualitative researchers would periodically move a project's materials onto an external drive when it was no longer an active piece of work, or as P8 explained "when I run out of space again, which is painfully often". Tracking material over the longer term thus became a task in itself, with P6 going on to say "I sometimes realise I've moved stuff off…and take hours finding where it is"…in their case due to a particularly small hard drive capacity.

In quantitative work, note-taking on individual posts or other content was usually short-term; e.g. P7 explained "mostly, in our team, we'll take notes when we check over data before we analyse it; then we might note data that needs a second look…if there are questions about completeness, or if it is actually in scope". More extensive notes were taken about entire datasets, outlining content that needed special handling, or might be reused. Longer term note-taking on individual items or sub-collections was typically material found to be of particular interest after analysis, e.g. P14 reported noting Twitter accounts that would be a good starting point for a second wave of analysis.

In contrast, most of the quantitative researchers had larger storage capacities, but also different strategies: P7 had a "decent" laptop, but said they "DropBoxed the hell" out of long-term storage, "cleaning out" files from their local machine when necessary, and relying on their database system to "keep everything in order". There was no attention to individual datapoints within a set once gathered: "there's too much data for me to look at individual posts…I just put everything in a database, and move that around when I need to". However, like the qualitative researchers, the total volume of material remained a problem: as P14 explained "I've got the project computer which is as good as we have, but we need more space all the time. We've got a big external drive, and even that isn't enough: now we have video and so many images…space is a big problem". Nonetheless, P14 reported that most of their colleagues had to "to work with what they've got" as their university had few openly available institutional resources, even if P14 had privileged access that they could personally call on.

There were consequences that emerged from their different approaches. The dynamic nature of social media raised conceptual, practical and ethical considerations. Posts might be deleted on the live platform, and there were varying approaches to reflecting this. Many used P2's approach of taking a "snapshot in time" and not revisiting data to see if it changed, or was removed. This implicitly applied to, e.g. some of the work that P7 was doing with live API data in their current project. However, when sharing data, or archiving it for later use, change could be more of a concern: P11 raised some of these concerns above, and for them, P7 and P14, there were cases where honouring terms-of-use meant that analyses were hard to reproduce, due to the deletion of accounts, individual posts, or the unavailability of previously available APIs or other access. As a result, there was some informal retention of original data by them, at last, as P7 said "so we can check if we got it right if we have to back to check".

Where the same data was being studied, be it quantitatively, qualitatively, or both, over extended spans of time to discern and analyse change, the volume of data naturally increased. Six interviewees were currently doing investigations that did some of this. P1's work returned regularly to accounts to interest to see change in behaviour, while P7 and P14 both used bespoke scripts and scheduled gathering of data within projects to look at quantitative changes in individual and group behaviour over time. This led to additional challenges, In contrast, P12 was scrutinising changes in the behaviour of individual accounts qualitatively to see adjustments in tone or content type.

The reuse of data by other research groups, or even within the same research team (especially if not co-located) was naturally influenced by this sort of instability. P4 reflected on a dilemma for them "there's nothing except, perhaps, my copy, to prove what I capture – it could all be gone tomorrow, and if someone disagrees…disbelieves me, it's hard to prove I'm not lying." They reported a case of seeing a particularly striking post that they included in a paper and when trying to show it to a colleague who was interested, found that "whoosh it had gone", though they were able to track down their own original copy which "proved I hadn't imagined it". As P7 noted, the "dilemma here is should I keep it to prove it was there? And if so, what happens, what should I do, if it is taken down?". P7 also had experience of taking just the post identifiers for a (very large) set of Twitter data, and sharing those "dehydrated" identifiers with another group just to find "so much had gone…they couldn't use it".

As hinted at with P4's example, a recurring challenge was refinding collected data, particularly for qualitative and mixed-methods researchers who were hand-selecting focused data. While the quantitative researchers tended to have large datasets, there was much less concern with individual data items (e.g. posts or responses). All the qualitative researchers bar P2 reported this as a challenge, in some form or other, and as P12 put it "between what bits of it you half-remember… the vicissitudes of time, where did you think you put it…it can be hard". Even tracking down specific quoted material could be frustrating if "it's not plugged in and if you use [system] search…it isn't that easy to use…and I think it often overlooks stuff".

An emerging change in practice was seen from our first interview: P1 and all but two of the interviewees reported the rising importance of short-form video such as TikTok. Only five scholars had completed a project with TikTok, and P2 had "briefly flirted" with a precursor, Vine. However, P2 and four others were already planning future projects that would include that material. P1, who had recent experience reported the impact of this on her research saying "The visual turn in internet research (and life) has created huge challenges" and noted there "Is not a lot in this area; perhaps because it is so data intensive"… and P5 reported "my training wheels are on even now…but I think it's where we're all going", reflecting on the increasing popularity of that form of content in new platforms. P5 explained that "I blew through my biggest hard drive in a flash"…and had to go out and get "a couple more just for that project".

4.3 Skills and Tools

Our participants routinely connected their preferred methods with their research approach, experience and research skills. A naïve expectation might be that quantitative researchers are more computationally oriented, and that their coding and programmatic skills may be stronger. While this is in a degree true, those who primarily or exclusively used qualitative methods demonstrated a strong degree of technical sophistication.

Both qualitative and quantitative researchers both used APIs to extract data from, example, Twitter, before it became more restricted. As an example, P1 exclusively undertakes qualitative research but across time used Twitter, Facebook and Instagram APIs, ran their own GitHub while explaining "I'm very self-taught. I've no formal training" [in programming].

The qualitative researchers often exploited their chosen analysis tools, e.g. NVivo, to help manage the coordination of their archives. P1 commented on their preference for it as "It has a strong filing system for diverse sources: it will all sit in one project", and P11, a mixed methods researcher, leaned on the same features by "not just coding for the content; also coding to help me keep it organised". While managing many archives was still a problem, NVivo or its close competitor NUDIST, did help scholars "keep things together in my head" (P12). This strategy was itself imperfect: e.g. P11 said the "sometimes get myself confused" about what was content coding versus an aid to managing the archive. Similarly, P9, an SNA expert, reported "knocking up a bit of a database" to help them remember where everything was kept, what cleaning of data had been done, and what software was used to analyse the content: "Otherwise there's too much to remember: how you did it, for what project, with what data...".

A number of participants, reflecting on their own acquisition of computational knowledge and skills, noted the ways in which the available tools built in biases. P12 reported that "I was lucky enough to have a sabbatical where I worked with more technical people that got me started" and that "many of my colleagues have never had that time". P1 reported "A lot of people are put off by the learning curve" and P9 explained that "I sort of got into SNA by accident. I used to be a numbers person, but I hadn't for years, then when I started [with social media content], the other postdoc dropped out and it was just me...so I had to". While in this case, the time was made available because of the needs of a project, the time available to acquire skill constrained what people could do individually, but also who got to develop those skills. As P8 explained that "having to do stuff by hand" reduces who can undertake research and that "that means ....that controls who gets to do it". The general lack of "easy to use" tools (P13) has a "big impact on what work can be done and by who". P1 followed this theme further, saying that the status quo "privileges certain kinds of analysis and interpretation over others...particularly over gender...as most computational stuff is white men...and they become the ones telling the stories of marginalised communities".

5 Discussion

Social media are an increasingly important focus of research. Our participants are only a sample of the many researchers who are now active in this research area. The long-term preservation of social media content is, naturally, a concern for institutions who want to conserve that material for later research. However, contemporary researchers need to create their own collections of social media material, and to organise and maintain those collections for use by themselves and, occasionally, others. This set of fourteen interviews of social media researchers in Australia is the first to examine the archival resources, needs and requirements for scholars who are creating independent archives of this type.

Our interviews revealed recurring themes, cross-cut by consistent factors such as resource limitations, personal practices and personal factors. If digital libraries as a field is to successfully supply effective tools for researchers on social media, we need to provide solutions that reflect these factors and meet the requirements of the scholars. Having presented our findings we now synthesise them to provide that under-framing.

One key lesson is that there is a significant need for off-device storage. While the storage capacity of PCs and laptops was on an upward curve for many years, the move to solid state devices curbed to reversed that growth, and our scholars used a combination of cloud and external device storage to sustain their long-term needs. However, this typically resulted in a fragmented set of separate archives.

That set of archives itself required oversight and administration, and while P2 was highly rigorous in their organising of their research material, they were an exception. Immediate ease of storage and informal management strategies were adequate in many ways, but added to the scholars' workloads when returning to materials. Even where cloud storage was used, this wasn't readily used to locate material, as either the on-computer search feature (e.g. on MacOS) or cloud-based search (e.g. DropBox) either hadn't indexed the content (e.g. as it was off-device), or, it searched across an entire device or service, rather than within the social-media archives themselves. These individual problems were confounded by content being archived across different devices and/or services. The present fragmentation of archives on one side, and the lack of separation between different archives or archives from other content on the other, both served to make managing data more complex.

An invidious reality about much of the external-device storage was that it was not backed up: there was in effect a single working copy. This is obviously a risky strategy in terms of data retention and availability in the long term. While this may seem baldly naïve, this was in part a product of a lack of institutional support, and in part a reflection of the costs of personally purchasing enough devices to store the data. The limited storage on the (typically) limited laptop devices researchers had: e.g. most had 256Gb or, in a couple of cases, fewer, was an underlying root of the problem. A second root cause was the often substantial size of the collections, especially where scholars were working with a lot of short-content video or extensive volumes of images.

Overall, considerable work was being undertake to capture information, but the lack of duplicates, fragmented storage and difficulty of discovery and re-discovery all point to the role a discrete online solution with integrated organisation, finding and backup services could potentially play: something akin to a personal online library. That resource would enable the separation of social media archives from other content, and should support multiple archives per user.

Annotation of various forms was used to help with the long-term use of archival content, be it for an entire archive or a single item. Most simply, filenames and folder structure were used, particularly in qualitative research, to answer this need. The use of systematic notetaking by P2 was the most developed, but all respondents who were doing qualitative work used widespread notetaking, at least in the short term, to plan future data gathering, possible analysis, or to capture context from the time the data was gathered. This was, as with P2's notebooks, normally separate from the data itself, which leaves an inherent risk of later separation between notes and content.

In principle archives that follow a library-like design could provide support for reuse and sharing, where there are not barriers such as terms-of-service or copyright. One issue that emerged across our entire set of interviewees was the issue of data that subsequently changed. More easily in the context of automatically gathered (and periodically re-gathered) material, version information about changes or removal could be kept alongside the original content from the time of gathering. This would aid traceability, but also enable analysis that sought to study changes over time. Our participants were normally capturing sequences of the same data, with comparisons being found with a mixture of manual and automatic methods. Again, a library-like system can potentially provide automated services that both help analysis as well as simply retain data.

The generally dynamic nature of the research was clearly producing significant demands of skill on the scholars: only three were conventionally trained computer scientists (P4,7,9) and yet most were writing scripts to control or assist data gathering, and all were having to deploy a range of techniques to manage the direct gathering of data over time. Much still needs to be investigated to better understand technical and other needs in detail.

We did not examine the coding practices in any significant detail. The changes in the type of date being gathered, the rules that applied to the data, and even its availability changed markedly in the working history of our participants. We did not closely consider if the research domains or tools influenced practices, and we had no more than three people working in related areas or topics. There are quite likely specifics we therefore did not capture, or had insufficient data to be confident of. The study of existing tools and practices in actual use would no doubt assist in the design of interactions and interfaces to support any purpose-built digital archive infrastructure.

The work of analysing social media content is known to be complex. We show here that there is similar complexity to the underlying mechanics, and an area where the domain of digital libraries can make a range of helpful interventions, up to and including the development of working systems. However, that time is necessarily some time in the future, and we hope this first outline serves to provide a platform for future research and development.

6 Conclusions and Future Work

Digital libraries have become the cornerstone of holding large-scale collections of long-form textual, audio and multimedia content. In contrast, digital archives in particular, and to a degree digital humanities, are less mature fields. In the context of contemporary humanities research, personally curated collections of social media content are vital resources. However, there is a dearth of material on the needs, requirements, contexts of use and practices of these collections. In this paper, we have drawn on the existing research on digital humanities, personal informatics and digital libraries to provide a foundation for developing a systemic understanding of prior work.

Acknowledgments. We would like to thank our participants for the donation of their time. We gratefully acknowledge the support of this research by Australian Research Data Commons.

References

1. De Choudhury, M., Morris, M.R., White, R.W.: Seeking and sharing health information online: comparing search engines and social media. In: Proceedings of the SIGCHI Conference on Human Factors in Computing Systems, pp. 1365–1376. ACM (2014)

2. Bender, J.L., Jimenez-Marroquin, M.-C., Jadad, A.R.: Seeking support on Facebook: a content analysis of breast cancer groups. J. Med. Internet Res. **13**, e16 (2011)
3. DeVito, M.A., Birnholtz, J., Hancock, J.T.: Platforms, people, and perception: using affordances to understand self-presentation on social media. In: Proceedings of the 2017 ACM Conference on Computer Supported Cooperative Work and Social Computing, pp. 740–754. Association for Computing Machinery, Portland, Oregon, USA (2017)
4. Ledbetter, A.M.: Friendship and social media. the psychology of friendship, pp. 93–108 (2016)
5. Meier, F., Elsweiler, D.: Studying politicians' information sharing on social media. In: Proceedings of the 2019 Conference on Human Information Interaction and Retrieval, pp. 237–241. Association for Computing Machinery, Glasgow, Scotland UK (2019)
6. Shoemark, P., Sur, D., Shrimpton, L., Murray, I., Goldwater, S.: Aye or naw, whit dae ye hink? Scottish independence and linguistic identity on social media. In: 15th Conference of the European Chapter of the Association for Computational Linguistics, pp. 1239–1248. Association for Computational Linguistics (2017)
7. Lindley, S.E., Marshall, C.C., Banks, R., Sellen, A., Regan, T.: Rethinking the web as a personal archive. In: Proceedings of the 22nd international conference on World Wide Web, pp. 749–760. Association for Computing Machinery, Rio de Janeiro, Brazil (2013)
8. Bender, J.L., Cyr, A.B., Arbuckle, L., Ferris, L.E.: Ethics and privacy implications of using the internet and social media to recruit participants for health research: a privacy-by-design framework for online recruitment. J. Med. Internet Res. **19**, e104 (2017)
9. Weinhardt, M.: Ethical issues in the use of big data for social research. Hist. Soc. Res./Historische Sozialforschung **45**, 342–368 (2020)
10. Cannelli, B., Musso, M.: Social media as part of personal digital archives: exploring users' practices and service providers' policies regarding the preservation of digital memories. Archiv. Sci. (2022)
11. Fiesler, C., Beard, N., Keegan, B.C.: No robots, spiders, or scrapers: legal and ethical regulation of data collection methods in social media terms of service. Inte. AAAI Conf. Web Soc. Med. **14**, 187–196 (2020)
12. Proferes, N., Jones, N., Gilbert, S., Fiesler, C., Zimmer, M.: Studying reddit: a systematic overview of disciplines, approaches, methods, and ethics. Soc. Med. + Soc. **7**, (2021)
13. Borgman, C., Wallis, J.C., Enyedy, N.: Building digital libraries for scientific data: an exploratory study of data practices in habitat ecology. In: International Conference on Theory and Practice of Digital Libraries, pp. 170–183. Springer (2006)
14. Borgman, C.L.: Scholarship in the digital age: Information, infrastructure, and the Internet. MIT Press (2010)
15. Al-Anazi, M., Hinze, A., Vanderschantz, N., Timpany, C., Cunningham, S.J.: Personal Digital Libraries: Keeping Track of Academic Reading Material. In: Tuamsuk, K., Jatowt, A., Rasmussen, E. (eds.) The Emergence of Digital Libraries – Research and Practices, pp. 39–47. Springer International Publishing, Cham (2014)
16. Lomborg, S.: Researching communicative practice: web archiving in qualitative social media research. J. Technol. Hum. Serv. **30**, 219–231 (2012)
17. Wong, A.K.-k., Chiu, D.K.W.: Digital curation practices on web and social media archiving in libraries and archives. J. Librarianship Info. Sci. 09610006241252661 (2024)
18. Ross, C., Terras, M., Warwick, C., Welsh, A.: Enabled backchannel: conference Twitter use by digital humanists. J. Docum. **67**, 214–237 (2011)
19. Vlassenroot, E., et al.: Web-archiving and social media: an exploratory analysis. Int. J. Digital Hum. **2**, 107–128 (2021)
20. Hemphill, L., Hedstrom, M.L., Leonard, S.H.: Saving social media data: Understanding data management practices among social media researchers and their implications for archives. J. Am. Soc. Inf. Sci. **72**, 97–109 (2021)

21. Marshall, C.C., Shipman, F.M.: On the institutional archiving of social media. In: Proceedings of the 12th ACM/IEEE-CS joint conference on Digital Libraries, pp. 1–10. Association for Computing Machinery, Washington, DC, USA (2012)
22. Condron, M.: Archiving social media. In: Marshall, B.H. (ed.) The complete guide to personal digital archiving, pp. 19–32 (2018)
23. Marshall, C.C.: How People Manage Information over a Lifetime. In: William, P.J., Jaime, T. (eds.) Personal Information Management, pp. 57–75. University of Washington Press, Seattle, WA (2011)
24. Jaballah, I., Cunningham, S.J., Witten, I.H.: Managing personal documents with a digital library. In: International Conference on Theory and Practice of Digital Libraries, pp. 195–206. Springer (2005)
25. Marshall, C.C.: Biography, ephemera, and the future of social media archiving. In: 18th ACM/IEEE on Joint Conference on Digital Libraries, pp. 253–262. Association for Computing Machinery, Fort Worth, Texas, USA (2018)
26. Jones, W.: Keeping found things found: The study and practice of personal information management. Morgan Kaufmann (2010)
27. Pikas, C.K.: Personal information management strategies and tactics used by senior engineers. Proc. Am. Soc. Info. Sci. Technol. **44**, 1–21 (2007)
28. Marshall, C.C., Bly, S.: Sharing encountered information: digital libraries get a social life. In: Fourth ACM/IEEE-CS joint conference on Digital libraries, pp. 218–227. Association for Computing Machinery, Tuscon, AZ, USA (2004)
29. Marshall, C.C., Shipman, F.M.: Social media ownership: using twitter as a window onto current attitudes and beliefs. In: Proceedings of the SIGCHI Conference on Human Factors in Computing Systems, pp. 1081–1090. ACM, Vancouver, BC, Canada (2011)
30. Buchanan, G., Cunningham, S.J., Blandford, A., Rimmer, J., Warwick, C.: Information seeking by humanities scholars. In: Ninth European Conference on Research and Advanced Technology for Digital Libraries, pp. 218–229. Springer, Vienna, Austria (2005)
31. Buchanan, G., Rimmer, J., Warwick, C., Blandford, A.: Exploring the digital library use of humanities academics In: ACM Users in the Wild Workshop, p. 6. ACM, Denver, Colorado (2005)
32. King, R.: Personal digital archiving for journalists: a "private" solution to a public problem. Library Hi Tech **36**, 573–582 (2018)
33. Brügger, N.: Web Archiving – between Past, Present, and Future. The Handbook of Internet Studies, pp. 24–42 (2011)
34. Marshall, C.C., Shipman, F.M.: The ownership and control of online photos and game data: Patterns, trends, and keeping pace with evolving circumstances. In: ACM/IEEE Joint Conference on Digital Libraries (JCDL), pp. 87–96. IEEE (2019)
35. Sharp, H., Preece, J., Rogers, Y.: Interaction Design. Wiley (2019)
36. Cairns, P., Cox, A.L.: Research methods for human-computer interaction. Cambridge University Press (2008)
37. Thomas, D.R.: A general inductive approach for analyzing qualitative evaluation data. Am. J. Eval. **27**, 237–246 (2006)

Exploring Semantic and Motion-Based Documentation for Intangible Cultural Heritage Integration

Makram Mestiri(✉), Khadhar Meriem, Jedidi Khalil, Ali S. Kheyrabadi, Zhivar Sedaghat, and Arnaud Huftier

Polytechnic University of Hauts-de-France, Valenciennes, France
makram.mestiri@uphf.fr

Abstract. Documenting intangible cultural heritage (ICH), given its dynamic and embodied nature, presents inherent challenges for preservation. This paper proposes a comprehensive approach combining motion-capture (MoCap) technology with heritage ontologies to capture and semantically document intangible industrial craft gestures. A MoCap database is developed, based on the CIDOC Conceptual Reference Model (CIDOC-CRM) and mapped to the Europeana Data Model (EDM) to ensure interoperability and data exchange. The focus is on technical implementation, covering ontology mapping of MoCap data and metadata, serialization to RDF, deployment in a triplestore, and transformation of legacy metadata into this semantic framework. A case study on traditional industrial craft gestures from the AnDyDataset and new MoCap from Hauts-de-France industrial heritage videos demonstrates the approach, focusing on textile weaving and metalworking. Craftspersons' gestures were recorded and represented as linked data, forming a knowledge graph connecting performance events, tools, and practitioners. Results show that using CIDOC-CRM and EDM allows for rich description of ICH events and MoCap recordings in a machine-readable, shareable form. This work contributes a model for safeguarding ICH via digital curation, discussing challenges in aligning motion data with heritage ontologies. Future work involves scaling the database and enhancing semantic alignment to preserve living heritage.

Keywords: Intangible Heritage · Motion Capture · Semantic Web · CIDOC-CRM · Europeana Data Model · Digital Preservation

1 Introduction

Intangible cultural heritage (ICH) is broadly defined by UNESCO as the living expressions, skills, and knowledge that communities and groups transmit from generation to generation [1]. Unlike tangible artifacts, intangible heritage, such as oral traditions, performing arts, rituals, or craftsmanship techniques, "is alive and in constant evolution", embodying a wealth of know-how rather than a static object. The importance of safeguarding intangible heritage lies not in any single material output, but in preserving the "wealth of knowledge and skills" that it represents. However, documenting these living

W.-T. Balke et al. (Eds.): TPDL 2025, LNCS 16097, pp. 360–377, 2026.
https://doi.org/10.1007/978-3-032-05409-8_21

practices poses significant challenges: they are ephemeral, context-dependent, and often reside solely in the bodies and memories of skilled practitioners and memories. In the face of globalization and industrialization, many traditional craft gestures and techniques risk being lost if not properly recorded and passed on [1, 2]. A key strategy for preserving intangible heritage is digitally documenting performance and skill. Recent years have seen growing interest in capturing the movements of artisans and performers using advanced digital technologies. In particular, motion-capture (MoCap) has emerged as a valuable tool to record the precise bodily motions involved in dance, craftsmanship, and other physical heritage. MoCap technology records the positions or joint angles of the human body in three dimensions over time. Unlike standard video, MoCap abstracts away the visual appearance and environment, focusing purely on the motion itself, which enables detailed analysis of each gesture and posture. This technique has been widely used in fields like film, gaming, sports and medicine, but its use for cultural heritage preservation has been relatively limited until recently. Nevertheless, pioneering projects such as i-Treasures and Mingei [4, 5] have demonstrated that motion capture can effectively document the "subtle details of an expertly executed craft", capturing nuances that might be lost in written or photographic records. For example, in craft domains like traditional pottery or weaving, high-resolution capture of hand and finger movements provides an invaluable record of technique [12]. This digital recording of artisan skills supports not only preservation, but also learning and transmission, e.g., by enabling apprentices to study expert motions or even allowing comparative analysis via software (Fig. 1).

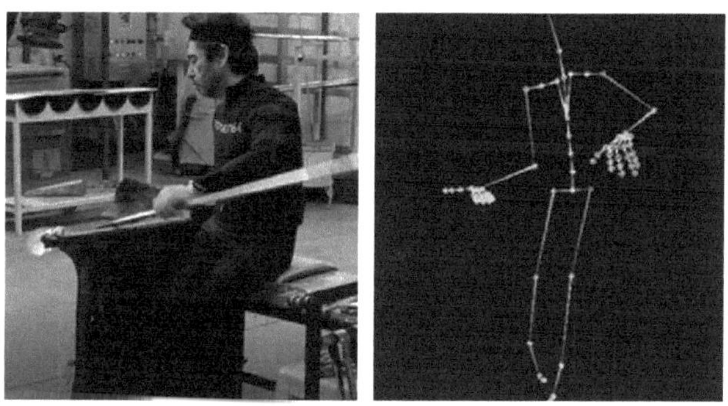

Fig. 1. Capturing the motions of a master glassblower using optical motion-capture system (left: artisan at work; right: real-time skeletal data). Project like Mingei demonstrate how expert craft gestures can be recorded as 3D motion data for preservation (source Mingei-project).

While motion capture yields rich data on how a craft is performed, making sense of this data in a cultural heritage context requires a structured approach to description and archiving. Raw motion datasets (often consisting of time-series of 3D coordinates or joint angles) on their own are not easily interpretable without contextual information: Who is the craftsperson? What heritage skill is being performed? When and where did this take place? Which tools or objects were involved? To ensure that captured performances of heritage crafts remain meaningful and accessible over the long term, we must integrate them with descriptive metadata and existing knowledge about the craft tradition. In the field of heritage informatics, this calls for adopting standardized ontologies and metadata models that can contextualize and interlink the data. By doing so, the intangible heritage records become part of a broader knowledge network, enabling search, retrieval, and reuse in ways traditional archives could not support. The development of a core ontology for multimedia resource discovery is a related effort that highlights the importance of structured data for digital resources [13]. This paper addresses the challenge of building a motion-capture database for intangible cultural heritage that is both richly descriptive and interoperable. We leverage two key semantic frameworks: the CIDOC Conceptual Reference Model (CIDOC-CRM), an ISO-standard ontology for cultural heritage information integration [10], and the Europeana Data Model (EDM), a widely used linked-data schema for sharing cultural heritage metadata across institutions [6]. Our approach uses CIDOC-CRM to model the complex relationships inherent in intangible heritage documentation (events, people, tools, digital files, etc.), and then maps the data to EDM so that it can be ingested by platforms like Europeana or other aggregators. In doing so, we ensure that our database of craft gestures is compatible with international heritage data ecosystems and can be cross-queried alongside other cultural heritage resources.

The case study guiding this work is focused on traditional industrial craft gestures from the Hauts-de-France region in northern France. This region, with its rich industrial history (textile mills, metalworking shops, coal mines, etc.), offers examples of craftsmanship at the intersection of artisanal skill and industrial processes. We specifically worked with local heritage experts to capture and document gestures from historic textile weaving and metal forge work, practices that are emblematic of the region's intangible industrial heritage. These include, for instance, the way an expert weaver at a Jacquard loom deftly ties broken threads or the posture and hammer swing technique of a blacksmith forging iron. Such "industrial craft" gestures encapsulate a blend of tacit knowledge and manual dexterity honed outside of modern automated processes. By preserving these via motion capture and semantic description, we create a lasting digital record that can aid in interpretation, education, and even revival of these crafts.

In the following sections, we first survey related work in documenting intangible cultural heritage with digital and semantic technologies (Sect. 2). We then detail the methodology (Sect. 3) for designing our ontology mapping and data model, explaining how CIDOC-CRM classes were specialized for intangible heritage events and how equivalences to EDM were established. The implementation (Sect. 4) describes how data from motion-capture sessions and existing metadata were transformed into RDF, stored in a triplestore, and enriched with links to external vocabularies. We then present the results (Sect. 5) of the case study, including example queries and observations on the expressiveness of the model. In the discussion (Sect. 6), we consider the implications of our approach: the advantages of semantic integration for digital curation of intangible heritage, challenges encountered (such as modeling time-based motion data and mapping nuances of CIDOC-CRM to EDM), and how this work fits into larger trends (e.g., initiatives like Europeana's efforts to incorporate intangible heritage). Finally, the conclusion summarizes our contributions and outlines future research directions, such as scaling up to a broader range of crafts and implementing advanced tools for analysis and user interaction with the MoCap heritage data. This work contributes a practical and reusable workflow for semantically documenting MoCap-based ICH recordings, providing a mapping between CIDOC-CRM and EDM, and publicly releasing tools and data for reuse across cultural institutions.

2 Related Work

Over the past two decades, intangible cultural heritage (ICH) has gained recognition as a critical area for preservation, with international frameworks like the 2003 UNESCO Convention urging member states to identify and safeguard living heritage practices [1]. Traditional methods of documentation, such as written descriptions, audio recordings of oral traditions, or video footage of performances, have served to capture some aspects of ICH. Museums and archives have expanded their scope to include not just objects, but also the "memory of the work" or *mémoire du travail*, i.e., the processes and know-how associated with traditional crafts and occupations [2]. However, digitizing ICH in a way that preserves its embodied and contextual nature remains an open challenge. Unlike a static artifact, a craft technique or dance exists only in performance and in the practitioners' competence. Carvalho [2] notes that museums increasingly see their role as not only preserving artifacts but also acting as spaces of knowledge and encounter that can transmit intangible heritage to the public. This shift has led to experiments in how to "archive the intangible", for instance, through interactive exhibits, demonstrations by living practitioners, or digital platforms.

2.1 Digital Preservation of Intangible Cultural Heritage

The rise of digital curation offers new tools to enhance ICH preservation. Researchers have explored building digital archives that aggregate various media and data about intangible practices. A key insight is that intangible heritage often has to be managed as dynamic documentation rather than static records. For example, the Europeana QueryLab platform takes a bottom-up approach to integrate databases on intangible heritage [8], noting that in many collections intangible elements are "managed as documents, rather than 'living assets'". To give "truly intangible" assets (like knowledge of local weaving patterns) a distinct identity in digital inventories, QueryLab introduced a specialized model (ICH-Light) and is developing a new ontology specifically for ICH data. Their evaluation against existing models like EDM has shown that certain extensions may be needed to adequately describe ICH within conventional cultural heritage schemas. This aligns with our approach in recognizing that a richer semantic model is required to handle the complexity of intangible heritage description.

Beyond institutional archives, academic projects have also driven innovation. The i-Treasures project (EU FP7, 2013–2017) was a seminal effort to apply advanced ICT for safeguarding ICH [4]. It targeted domains where human body motion is central, including dance, traditional crafts, and music, and employed a range of sensors to capture those performances in unprecedented detail. As part of building an "open and extendable platform providing access to ICH resources", i-Treasures combined multimodal data (video, audio, motion capture, even EEG for singers) to document rare know-how from

"Living Human Treasures" (master practitioners). For instance, in a pottery case study, they used motion capture specifically to record the detailed hand and finger movements during the creation process. The outcome was the i-Treasures ICH Dataset, comprising hundreds of recordings across various ICH forms (from contemporary dance to folk singing and craftsmanship) along with metadata for each. Grammalidis et al. present this dataset and discuss the metadata schema used to annotate it, which had to encompass both the technical sensor data and the cultural context of each performance. One of the lessons from i-Treasures is the importance of a robust metadata framework to accompany the raw sensor recordings; without it, the captured data cannot be effectively reused or understood outside the original project. Our work builds on this insight by introducing a domain ontology mapping for such data.

Another significant project is Mingei (2018–2022), which focused on the representation and safeguarding of craft [5]. Mingei explicitly aimed to capture both the tangible and intangible aspects of crafts, including traditional techniques of glass-blowing, silk weaving, and mastic gum harvesting. A core part of Mingei's approach was the use of motion capture and computer vision to digitize crafters' movements. As described by Papadopoulos et al. on the Mingei team, "the motion of the body is the most important tool of performing a craft", hence recording those motions is key to understanding expert craftsmanship. In practice, the Mingei team had to adapt MoCap techniques to non-laboratory settings: unlike typical controlled studio recordings, they captured artisans in their authentic workshops with minimal intrusion. This revealed some important considerations: (1) Recordings might need to be continuous over long durations to cover an entire craft process or segmented into logical units if a process involves distinct steps with different equipment; (2) Craft motions are highly variable and adaptive; an expert will subtly adjust each gesture to the material conditions. Intriguingly, Mingei observed that these small variations in motion are not noise, but rather carry information about the practitioner's expertise. This observation underscores the value of capturing motion data at a granular level and also hints at why purely manual documentation can miss critical details of mastery. To make such motion data useful, Mingei had to relate it back to the craft knowledge. Their published deliverables indicate the use of semantic descriptions for segmenting craft processes and linking them to narrative explanations, tool descriptions, and historical context. An important outcome of Mingei is that it validates a workflow consisting of capture, analysis, and semantic annotation of intangible craft heritage. Our work draws inspiration from Mingei, extending the idea by proposing a formal integration with CIDOC-CRM and EDM to maximize interoperability of the annotations.

Beyond craft, documenting other forms of embodied intangible heritage, such as traditional dance, presents similar challenges and opportunities for digital preservation. Research in this area explores capturing the nuances of movement and relating them to cultural context and knowledge systems [15].

2.2 Semantic Web Technologies in Heritage Data Management

The use of Semantic Web and Linked Data in cultural heritage has become mainstream in the past decade, aiming to improve data interoperability, enrichment, and longevity. In cultural heritage institutions, a variety of metadata standards have historically been used, each with their own structure. Ontologies like CIDOC-CRM were developed to serve as an interlingua or integrative framework that can connect these diverse datasets by providing a shared conceptualization. CIDOC-CRM in particular provides an event-centric model where every relevant aspect of heritage documentation can be represented as an entity with relationships. This high expressiveness makes CRM a natural choice for modeling complex scenarios, the choice of CIDOC-CRM is natural because of its great flexibility and capacity for extension to new cultural heritage information. Indeed, CRM has been extended with specialized modules to accommodate domain-specific needs. Intangible heritage, which often involves temporal events and conceptual objects, fits well into CRM's paradigm of events, actors, places, and things linked semantically. Modeling archaeological excavation activities using CIDOC CRM provides an analogous example of applying this framework to event-centric heritage data [14].

There have been efforts to model intangible heritage specifically using or extending ontologies. One example is the work by Hou and Wang [3], who developed an ontology for Chinese intangible cultural heritage and published an RDF dataset. Their approach was to first create a domain ontology capturing key concepts and relationships, then convert existing knowledge into RDF and link it to external reference points. This resulted in a local knowledge base that could be queried and visualized, demonstrating how semantic modeling supports the organization and sharing of ICH knowledge. Such localization underscores that while a base ontology provides the structure, it may need tailoring to fit the nuances of a particular ICH domain or cultural context. In our work, we remain within the standard CRM but introduce a mapping layer for the Europeana Data Model, which acts as a bridge to a broader, cross-cultural platform.

The Europeana Data Model (EDM) is a key standard in this context, as it is used by Europeana to aggregate data from thousands of institutions. EDM is a Linked Data compliant model that incorporates elements from Dublin Core, Dublin Core Terms, and OAI-ORE, among others. One of its design principles is to be extensible and to interoperate with existing domain ontologies, including CIDOC-CRM. For example, EDM does not reinvent classes for events or agents but can use existing ones; Europeana's guidelines explicitly allow providers to include event metadata using CRM or other event models. Over time, certain profiles of EDM have been proposed to handle specialized needs [6]. These show that EDM can be extended via community-defined classes. For instance, a collaboration led to an extension of EDM for better representing collections. In practice, aggregators like the Deutsche Digitale Bibliothek (DDB) found they needed to add terms to EDM to cover all their metadata [7]. DDB had initially used CIDOC-CRM internally, and when mapping to EDM, not all CRM details had a direct EDM equivalent, leading them to define additional extensions and mappings. This experience, reported by Neubert et al., reinforces the idea that ontology mapping between a detailed model (CRM) and a simpler exchange model (EDM) requires careful consideration and sometimes augmentation of the latter. For our purposes, EDM provides a target schema to ensure that our data (originally modeled in CRM) can be exported in a form that a platform like Europeana would accept. A notable advantage is that EDM supports linking to rich media types and web resources. Europeana accommodates content beyond images and text; it explicitly supports audio, video, and even 3D objects as digital resources. A MoCap recording can be treated as a digital representation of a cultural item in EDM, meaning our intangible heritage recordings can be ingested as first-class digital objects in the Europeana repository. The EDM framework, combined with CRM's detail, thus gives us a path to publish the craft gesture data as linked open data in alignment with best practices, enabling queries across datasets and integration with other heritage data. The potential of ontology-based thematic framing for cultural heritage content delivery is also highlighted in recent work [11].

In summary, the related work highlights: (1) the growing use of motion capture and multi-sensor setups to document intangible practices in high fidelity [4, 5]; (2) the necessity of semantic modeling and knowledge graphs to preserve the context and meaning of those practices beyond raw recordings [3, 10, 11, 14]; and (3) the practical considerations of mapping detailed heritage ontologies to broad sharing platforms like EDM [6–8]. Our work builds upon these foundations, bringing them together in an applied case study for a specific regional heritage scenario and contributing a concrete implementation blueprint for others to follow in creating semantically enriched ICH databases.

3 Methodology

Our methodology centers on designing a semantic data model that can represent motion-captured intangible heritage performances in a machine-readable, interoperable form. This involved two primary tasks: (1) defining how to use and, where necessary, extend CIDOC-CRM to model the entities and relationships in our craft gesture recordings; and (2) creating a mapping from the CRM-based model to the Europeana Data Model (EDM) to allow export and integration of the data into broader heritage data ecosystems. We also planned the technical pipeline for converting raw and legacy data into RDF and for hosting it in a triplestore for query and analysis. Below, we detail each aspect of the methodology.

3.1 Ontology Design and CIDOC-CRM Mapping

CIDOC-CRM was chosen as the core ontology for our database due to its expressiveness and its established use in cultural heritage integration. The CRM provides a high-level class hierarchy and properties that cover physical objects, events, actors, places, times, and information objects. Intangible cultural heritage, particularly craft performance, inherently involves several of these: it is an event carried out by actors at a place and time, potentially involving physical objects and producing intellectual products. We identified and how they map to CIDOC-CRM classes Fig. 2:

- **Heritage Craft Practice:** modeled as an instance of E55 Type or E28 Conceptual Object in CIDOC-CRM. We opted for E55 Type to represent the notion of a craft technique or style, using a custom namespace ich.
- **Performance Event:** corresponds to E7 Activity in CRM. We specialized it as ich:CraftPerformance, a subclass of E7 Activity. Each event has properties linking to the person (E21 Person), place (E53 Place), time (E52 Time-Span), technique (E55 Type), and objects (E19 Physical Object or E70 Thing).

- **Practitioner (Person):** modeled as E21 Person, linked to the event via P14 carried out by.
- **Digital MoCap Record:** treated as an E73 Information Object, with metadata and a link to the binary file. Linked from the event via P94 has created.
- **Associated Media:** also modeled as E38 Image or E73 Information Object, linked via P94.
- **Provenance and Curation:** modeled using relevant CRM classes or Dublin Core elements, such as E40 Legal Body and P104 is subject to rights statements.

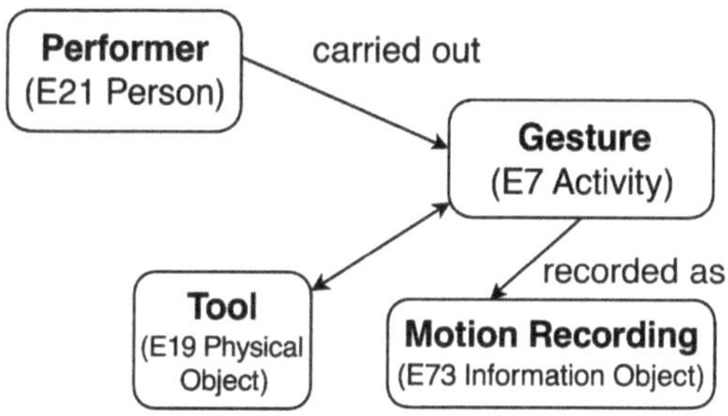

Fig. 2. Illustrates an example RDF structure representing a craft performance event, including the performer (E21 Person), the gesture (E7 Activity), the associated tool (E19 Physical Object), and the motion recording (E73 Information Object).

We largely stayed within the standard CIDOC-CRM (version 7.1) classes. One extension used was CRM Digital (CRMdig) for digital production details. Ontology mapping sessions with domain experts ensured the classes captured the real-world scenario. Custom sub-properties were added for clarity. The flexibility of CIDOC-CRM allowed incorporating intangible aspects without fundamental alteration.

3.2 Mapping to the Europeana Data Model (EDM)

Defining a mapping to EDM was the next step, enabling data sharing. EDM is object-centric, organizing metadata about a cultural heritage object (CHO) and linking it to digital resources and contextual entities.

- **edm:ProvidedCHO:** Each recorded performance was treated as a ProvidedCHO. Multiple performances of the same tradition were linked using dc:subject to a conceptual node for the intangible tradition. Mapped Dublin Core properties included dc:title, dc:description, dc:date, dc:creator/contributor, dc:coverage, dc:subject, and dc:type.
- **edm:Agent:** Created for the craftsperson, linked to the ProvidedCHO via dc:creator.
- **edm:Place and edm:TimeSpan:** Instantiated for the location and date, linked via dcterms:spatial and dcterms:temporal properties on the ProvidedCHO.
- **edm:PhysicalThing:** Included for significant tools or objects if they had a known identity, linked via edm:object or edm:isRelatedTo.

- **edm:WebResource:** Represents the digital file (MoCap data, video, image), connected via an ore:Aggregation. Edm:isShownBy and edm:hasView properties link to URLs. Each WebResource has metadata like dc:format and dc:rights.

Mapping from CRM to EDM involved:

- CRM Information Object (E73) corresponding to edm:WebResource [6, 10].
- CRM P94 has created relationship becoming edm:isShownBy or edm:hasView [6, 10].
- edm:Aggregation tying together the ProvidedCHO and WebResource(s).

Mapping was aided by existing guidelines and prior research Fig. 3. Some CRM detail was flattened into EDM fields, with references to context via linking.

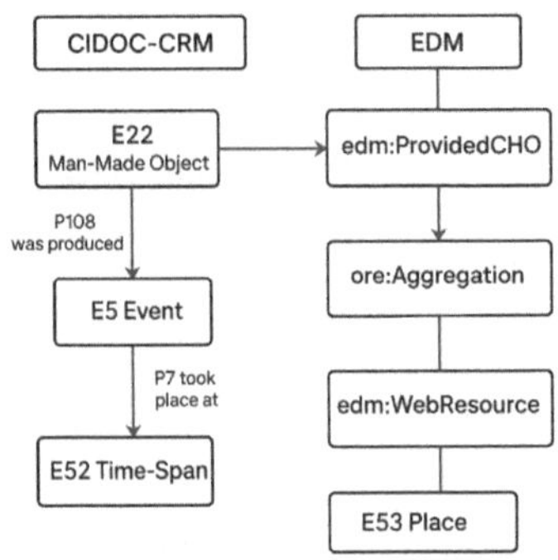

Fig. 3. Mapping of conceptual entities CIDOC-CRM/EDM

EDM's inability to fully capture event structure was a challenge, addressed by including human-readable statements in dc:description and using edm:isRelatedTo and dc:subject for semantic linking. A Python-based conversion script, together with SPARQL CONSTRUCT queries, was used to generate EDM-compliant RDF output from CIDOC-CRM instances. This alignment allows the semantic database to act as a standalone knowledge graph and a data provider to Europeana or any Linked Open Data consumer.

3.3 Data Acquisition and Metadata Transformation

The proposed workflow begins with on-site motion capture of craft performances while simultaneously collecting rich contextual metadata about practitioners, tools, place, and time; these raw sensor files and field notes are then semantically encoded by aligning each event, actor, object, and concept with appropriate CIDOC-CRM classes, producing an RDF graph that preserves provenance and relationships at a granular level like in Fig. 4. Next, the data are ingested into a triplestore, where they can be queried or validated, before an automated SPARQL CONSTRUCT transforms the CRM graph into Europeana Data Model (EDM) records, flattening essential fields (title, creator, date, place, subject) and linking MoCap files as edm:WebResource objects inside an ore:Aggregation. Finally, the EDM output, accompanied by derivative media for human preview, is packaged for export so the same dataset can circulate both as a high-fidelity internal knowledge graph and as a standards-compliant contribution to Europeana or any Linked-Open-Data ecosystem, ensuring long-term interoperability, discoverability, and scholarly reuse.

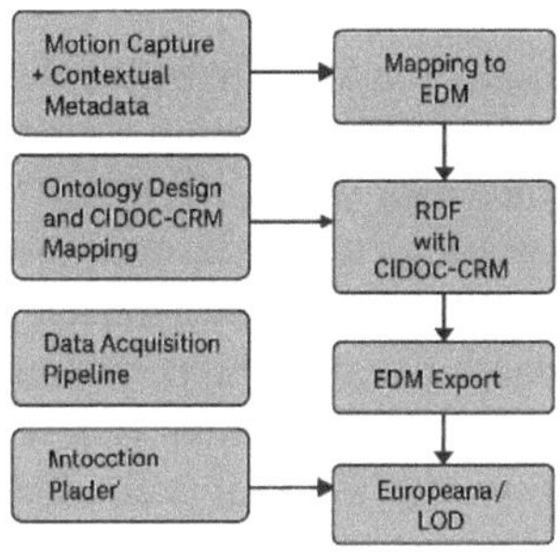

Fig. 4. End-to-End Semantic Pipeline: From Motion Capture to Linked-Open-Data

A pipeline for data acquisition and metadata transformation was established. For each session:

- **Motion Capture Session:** Recording sessions with practitioners were conducted using an optical MoCap system [5, 12]. Raw MoCap data files (C3D, TRC) and supplementary video were captured. Timelines of actions were noted.
- **Contextual Metadata Collection:** Interviews provided metadata on practitioner, technique significance, equipment details, date/time, and conditions. Recorded in a template, aligning with controlled vocabularies where possible.
- **Data Processing and Annotation:** Raw data was processed to derive skeletal motion (BVH, glTF). Actions were aligned with frame numbers, and key frames annotated. Annotations were stored internally. The process of tracing and analyzing hand gestures is an area of related research [12].
- **RDF Data Creation:** A Python script generated RDF triples based on the CRM model and ontology definitions. URIs were created, and triples output in Turtle syntax. Custom concepts were created for Hauts-de-France crafts, linked broadly to UNESCO domains.
- **Quality Check and Ingestion:** Generated RDF was validated and ingested into an Apache Jena Fuseki triplestore. The system backend includes Python scripts that convert motion capture metadata into CIDOC-CRM RDF. We used RDFLib for graph creation and SPARQLWrapper for endpoint testing. Each performance is ingested via a semiautomated pipeline, using predefined templates. The web interface is a minimal Flask-based application that renders performance metadata and links to visualizations of MoCap data. Ontology, extension, and concept scheme were loaded. Reasoning was optional. Turtle format was used for bulk loading.
- **Metadata Transformation to EDM:** SPARQL CONSTRUCT queries generated EDM triples from the CRM data. This output was serialized as RDF/XML.

This pipeline resulted in heritage craft performances captured as raw/processed motion data files, rich RDF graphs, and shareable EDM metadata records. Transformation steps were automated. The methodology harmonized high-tech data with high-level cultural heritage ontologies, involving both technologists and heritage professionals for data validity and cultural context preservation.

4 Implementation

We developed the plateform "Semantic MoCap: Semantic Motion-Capture Database for Intangible Heritage," for preserving and enhancing cultural heritage through the semantic integration of motion capture data with CIDOC-CRM and EDM ontologies. This system provides tools for researchers, cultural institutions, and heritage professionals to store, annotate, and retrieve motion capture data related to intangible cultural heritage practices, such as traditional dances, crafts, and performance arts. Key features include seamless integration with the CIDOC Conceptual Reference Model for structured heritage information, compatibility with the Europeana Data Model for interoperability with digital libraries, advanced tools for managing and querying motion capture data in a cultural context, and powerful SPARQL-based querying capabilities for exploring rich semantic relationships Fig. 5.

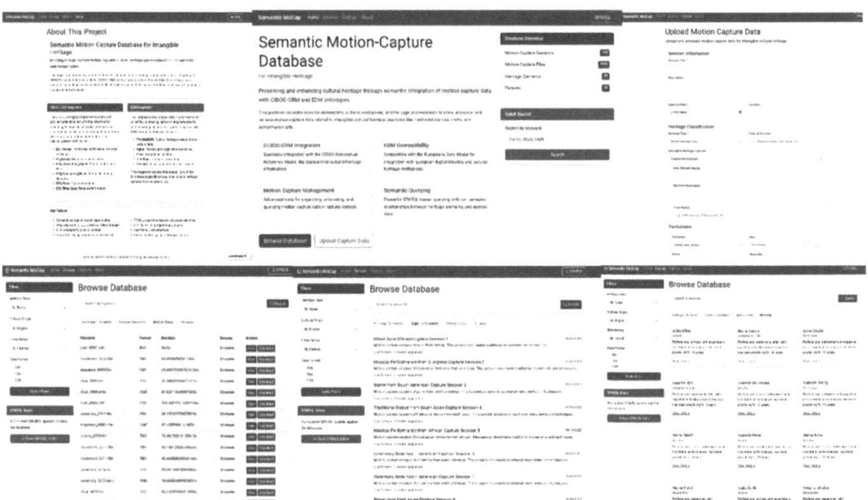

Fig. 5. Overview of the Semantic Motion-Capture Database for Intangible Heritage

The system was implemented iteratively, testing components with Hauts-de-France data and the AnDyDataset database.

4.1 Ontology and Triplestore Setup

CIDOC-CRM version 7.1.1 OWL was the base ontology. A small OWL file declared subclasses and subproperties. A SKOS concept scheme for HDF craft techniques was created, aligning with Wikidata where possible. Apache Jena Fuseki triplestore was deployed and configured. CRM, the extension, and concept scheme were loaded. Full text search was enabled. Reasoning was left off for performance. Turtle format was used for ingestion. Five performance events were documented:

- Jacquard Loom Weaving (Textile): captured at our laboratory based on old video. Focused on shuttle throwing and shed changing gestures. Captured upper body/arm motions. ~ 5 min, 18,000 frames. 3D skeleton animation derived. Metadata: performer, place (Wikidata linked), date, technique (Jacquard weaving concept), tool (historical loom linked to museum). Audio was also recorded.
- Hand Weaving on a Frame Loom (Textile): simpler loom, different gestures captured. Data model similar, classified as "Handloom weaving". Personal tool, not in a public catalog.
- Traditional Blacksmithing (Forge): at a heritage ironwork forge in Fournes-en-Weppes. Demonstrated forging a hook. Captured full-body motion, arm swings, and posture. Tools: hammer, anvil, tongs. Technique concept: "Forging (blacksmithing)". Marker occlusion addressed. Metadata: affiliation, place (protected historical site). Showcases industrial heritage.
- Woodworking (Cabinetmaking joinery): short capture of traditional joinery (chisel). Tested model generality. Added the concept "Traditional woodworking".
- Gesture Archive from Existing Video: retrospectively created from historical lace maker video. Manual annotation and computer vision used to synthesize pseudo-"MoCap". Data from non-MoCap sources integrated. The model treats it as an event and information object.

Total entries: ~ 1450 triples describing performances, plus concept, place, person definitions. Modest size, rich detail. Each linked to at least one motion file.

SPARQL queries were utilized to test data linking and retrieval, with examples including listing performances by technique, performer, and media, finding motion capture records for weaving, and retrieving full RDF descriptions. The data was accessible via a Fuseki SPARQL endpoint, and a simple web page listed performances, linking to motion data using SPARQL. Query responses were fast, and raw motion data points were not stored as triples to manage data size.

4.2 Integration with Europeana (Simulation)

Simulated publication to Europeana. EDM XML output validated with Europeana validator. Hypothetical ingestion into a test account showed items with metadata and thumbnails. Thumbnail URL needed for search results. Aligning with EDM ensures discoverability and shareability with other heritage items.

5 Results

Based on the implementation outcomes observed in the data, the project demonstrated the value of its semantic expressiveness, enabling detailed representation and complex queries. Critical insights derived from the specific case study further highlighted the practical benefits and capabilities achieved in a real-world context.

5.1 Data Outputs and Coverage

Five ICH performance events captured and semantically documented. Rich metadata records in triplestore link raw motion data with context. Knowledge base is a craft performance knowledge graph. Table 1 summarizes data:

Table 1. Data Output.

Event (Technique)	Triples	Key Entities (Person, Place, Tool)	Digital Files
Jacquard Loom Weaving (Textile)	~ 320	1 person, 1 museum place, 1 loom tool	1 BVH, 1 MP4, 1 image
Hand Frame Weaving (Textile)	~ 290	1 person, 1 workshop place, 1 frame-loom tool	1 BVH, 1 MP4
Forge Blacksmithing (Metalwork)	~ 330	1 person, 1 forge place, 2 tools (hammer, anvil)	1 BVH, 1 MP4, 1 image
Traditional Wood Joinery (Woodwork)	~ 300	1 person, 1 workshop place, 1 tool (chisel)	1 BVH, 1 MP4
Lacemaking (from video)	~ 210	1 person, 1 town place, (tool implicit: lace pillow)	1 MP4 (annotated)

Dataset: ~ 1450 triples on performances, plus definitions. Modest size, rich detail. Each linked to a digital motion file. Semantic richness is key, Relationships between entities (e.g., events, performers, tools) were verified using SPARQL queries to ensure RDF consistency and semantic coherence. Person entity reuse enabled queries like "show all events by Jane Doe". Successful EDM mapping ensured metadata population (Table 2 shows example).

This confirms meaningful information for portal ingestion, preserving context. Including visual media and raw data caters to different audiences.

5.2 Use of the System and Findings

The integrated dataset answers complex questions. Example: differences in weaving techniques on different looms based on motion. System gathers relevant data for comparative study. Experiment with hand speed in Jacquard vs. frame loom weaving utilized semantic data and annotations, finding slightly faster, broader motion in Jacquard weaving, matching anecdotal knowledge.

Approach captured context potentially lost in audiovisual archives (specific anvil, historic forge) as first-class facts. Linking to external sources enriches records. Confirmed CIDOC-CRM's capability for ICH events without fundamental issue, supporting ongoing work [9]. Implementation is a practical CRM profile for ICH crafts.

Table 2. Exemple Metadata.

Field	Value
Title	"Jacquard loom weaving demonstration, «Haut de france» (2021)"
Description	"Master weaver Jane Doe demonstrates traditional Jacquard loom weaving at La Manufacture, «Haut de france». Motion capture data recorded to preserve the technique."
Creator	"Doe, Jane (expert weaver)"
Type	"TEXTILE CRAFT PERFORMANCE (Intangible Cultural Heritage)"
Date	2021–07-05
Location	«Haut de france», France
Subject	Jacquard weaving; Traditional Craftsmanship; Hauts-de-France heritage
Relation (object)	Linked to "Jacquard loom (early 20th c.)" (the tool)
Media (isShownBy)	video URL of the motion visualization (MP4, 30s excerpt)
Media (hasView)	raw motion data file URL (BVH format)
Rights	"2021 ICH MoCap Project, CC BY-SA 4.0 license"

Limitations and challenges:

- **Time-series data:** CRM doesn't directly represent continuous time-series. Handled by external files, trading completeness for practicality. Alternatives like CRMsci or sub-action events could offer deeper analysis but increase triples.
- **Intangible vs. Tangible boundary:** Debate on "skill" as E55 Type or E21 Physical Thing. E55 Type used for classification.
- **Alignment with existing ICH ontologies:** Custom SKOS risks siloing. Mapping broad terms to existing ones (UNESCO, AAT) is ideal for merging.
- **Sustainability:** Long-term maintenance needs collaboration with institutions or archiving in repositories.
- **Privacy and Ethical Considerations:** Careful handling of living practitioner data, consent, anonymization options. Motion capture data as personal data requires secure storage. Aggregating by tradition for publication might be considered depending on privacy.

On Europeana mapping, some information loss to EDM noted. EDM's flat metadata doesn't fully capture specific roles or tools. Documented discrepancies suggest proposing EDM extensions. Despite losses, core elements survive for discoverability and shareability. Combining with other EDM datasets showed integration potential. Using standard ontologies prevents data silos. Performance: triplestore on modest resources without issues, fast queries. Scalable for reasonable records. Bottleneck is large media files (links). Qualitative feedback positive from specialists and practitioners, appreciating standards adherence and the concept of documenting intangible practice.

6 Discussion

Developing the MoCap-ICH database using CRM and EDM presents opportunities and challenges.

6.1 Significance for Heritage Informatics

Bridges technical data (MoCap) and cultural heritage documentation, enriching both. Cross-domain integration is central to heritage informatics. Ontology-driven design adds value via a self-descriptive semantic graph. Nodes and links carry processable meaning for software agents. Aligns with making cultural data FAIR. Reusability enhanced by linking to standard vocabularies. EDM integration addresses interoperability and dissemination. Example for structuring ICH content as aggregators embrace it. Limitations in EDM suggest potential schema evolution. Mapping indicates need for EDM extension or richer linked data submission.

For heritage professionals, a blueprint for documenting performance-based heritage. Ontology makes information queryable and linkable. Shifts documentation from unstructured to structured data while retaining richness. Adopting semantic heritage ontologies requires institutional capacity-building, which is best supported through concrete use case examples that others can emulate. User-friendly interfaces producing CRM-compliant RDF behind the scenes are envisioned. Step towards standardizing ICH documentation, it present Challenges and limitations:

- **Complexity vs. Usability:** CIDOC-CRM complexity requires expertise. Mitigated by templates/scripts, needing better tooling or simplified interface. Mapping to EDM non-trivial; two ontologies doubled effort. Ontology alignment frameworks could automate.
- **Data Volume and Granularity:** Not storing frame-level motion in RDF means no direct motion analysis in queries. Trade-off for practicality. CRMsci or sub-action events could add depth but increase triples.
- **Vocabulary Control:** Custom SKOS risks siloing. Aligning with global vocabularies (AAT) ideal for merging. Mapping to UNESCO domains ensures high-level sharing.
- **Sustainability:** Long-term maintenance needs institutional collaboration or repository archiving.
- **Privacy and Ethical Considerations:** Careful handling of living practitioner data, consent, anonymization. Motion capture as personal data requires secure storage. Aggregating by tradition for publication considered based on privacy.

6.2 Comparison with Other Approaches

Comparing semantic approach with traditional:

- Traditional (video + text PDF): captures content but not queryable/interoperable. RDF allows merging datasets for complex queries.
- Relational database: structure, but not easily shareable beyond API. RDF/ontologies adhere to open standards. Relational less flexible to schema changes; ontologies extensible.

- Relational/JSON for numeric computation: acknowledged limitation of our approach for direct motion analysis in SPARQL. Aim includes cultural context, lacking in those approaches.

Related projects:

- i-Treasures: multi-modal dataset, focus on AI for learning ICH, less emphasis on heritage standards integration.
- Mingei: close in spirit, mentions ontology use for narratives. Published details on semantic structure forthcoming. Our work emphasizes linking to EDM.
- QueryLab: ICH-Light model from examining inventories, need for new ontology aligns with our experience; fitting ICH into existing models tricky. We used CRM/EDM backbone/bridge; they custom lightweight schema. Trade-off: completeness vs. simplicity. Combined approach (CRM under the hood, simpler view) might be ideal.

6.3 Future Work and Extensions

Future directions:

- **Scaling to More Heritage Domains:** Testing on dance, music, rituals. Involves multiple performers, complex temporal structuring, integrating custom ontologies.
- **Incorporating Analysis Results:** Augmenting ontology with motion observations using CRMsci or other ontologies, adding layers of knowledge (e.g., proficiency indicators).
- **User Interfaces and Interaction:** Building interfaces for public/educator query without SPARQL. Portal showing visualizations/data via user-friendly web app with text/faceted search.
- **Collaboration and Crowdsourcing:** Multiple institutions/communities contributing to knowledge graph. Consistency and identifiers a challenge. Europeana could preserve links.
- **Evaluation of Preservation Impact:** Qualitative studies (e.g., apprentices learning from records) to assess capture of intangible practice essence. Smaller evaluations (expert recognition) feasible.

In summary, our approach integrates motion capture into heritage documentation via semantic standards. Overcame challenges, noting current models suffice with adaptations for ICH. Case study validated on small scale, showing promises (richer documentation, new queries, cross-collection linkages) and areas for further work (tool support, standard extensions, long-term maintenance).

7 Conclusion

This paper presented a framework for developing a MoCap database for ICH, demonstrating systematic preservation and sharing using semantic web. Leveraged CIDOC-CRM for context of craft performances and EDM for integration into aggregators/linked data. Case study on Hauts-de-France industrial craft gestures showed successful recording with MoCap and rich annotation in ontology-driven database.

Technical implementation contributions: Practical ontology mapping between CRM and EDM for ICH, bridging detailed internal records and simplified exchange formats [6, 7]. Implemented RDF serialization and triplestore deployment (Apache Jena Fuseki) to store/query heritage motion data, showing graph databases handle interlinked ICH info. Knowledge graph enables complex queries. Workflow for metadata transformation from raw data/observations to curated, semantic dataset, combining automation and expert input.

Case study results confirmed semantic database is detailed and interoperable. Recorded gesture contextualized in a web of meanings (people, places, objects, concepts). Using established ontologies/standards prevents data silos; records discovered/understood alongside other heritage resources. Aligning with Europeana schema paves way for dynamic records of artifact usage/skills, expanding digital heritage to intangible realm.

Broader insights/impact: Reinforces semantic web value for holistic heritage documentation/curation. Encoding craft knowledge in ontology facilitates preservation *in situ* in global network for transmission, comparison, enrichment. Contributes to standardizing ICH documentation. CIDOC-CRM (minimal extensions) capable of handling ICH content, augmented with domain vocabularies. Implementation a reference for CRM extensions/best-practice profiles for ICH. Interaction with EDM data provides feedback to aggregators [6, 8].

Future work: Scaling up needs streamlined tooling/automation. Integrating analytical features (motion analysis, ML classification) adds value [4, 5]. Integrating user feedback allows experts to augment records, moving to living repository.

Conclusion: Research showcases innovative marriage of MoCap and semantic knowledge representation to safeguard ICH. Methodology and case evidence: capturing "dance" of hands/tools feasible and documented in digital knowledge base. ICH importance for identity/diversity means such digital efforts are crucial. Ensure expertise of master craftsmen, "wealth of knowledge and skills" in gestures, passed on/studied by future generations. Step towards future where master's gestures valued/catalogued as artifacts, digital archives show how heritage moved/lived.

References

1. UNESCO: Convention for the Safeguarding of the Intangible Cultural Heritage. UNESCO, Paris (2003)
2. Carvalho, A.: "Intangible Heritage and Museums: New and Old Challenges?" *ICOM Documentation Centre Blog* (2017)
3. Hou, X., Wang, X.: "Modeling and representation of intangible cultural heritage knowledge using linked data and ontology. *Proc. Assoc. Info. Sci. Technol.* **56**(1), 409–412 (2019)
4. Grammalidis, N., et al.: "The i-treasures intangible cultural heritage dataset. In: *Proc. 3rd International Symposium on Movement and Computing (MOCO)*, Article 23. ACM (2016)
5. Papadopoulos, P., et al.: *Mingei Project Deliverable: The Mingei Knowledge Model.* (EU H2020 Mingei project on craft heritage)
6. Europeana Foundation. Europeana Data Model (EDM) Definition, v5.2.8 (2018)
7. Neubert, T., et al.: "Applying a linked data compliant model: the usage of the Europeana Data Model by the Deutsche Digitale Bibliothek." *Proc. Intl. Conf. on Dublin Core Metadata Appl.* (2014)

8. Europeana QueryLab. "QueryLab combines databases on intangible cultural heritage." *Europeana Pro Blog* (2024)
9. CIDOC CRM Special Interest Group. *Capturing Intangible Cultural Heritage (ICH) into data.* (Working group output) (2024)
10. Doerr, M.: "The CIDOC conceptual reference model: a new standard for knowledge sharing." *ERCIM News* (**54**) (2003)
11. Silvello, G.: Ontology-based Thematic Framing of Tangible and Intangible Cultural Heritage. IOS Press, Semantic Web Journal (2022)
12. Flanagan, P.: "Making tangible the intangible gestures of craft." In: *Contactless Human Activity Analysis,* (pp. 293–333). Springer (2021)
13. Doerr, M., Hunter, J., Lagoze, C.: Towards a core ontology for multimedia resource discovery. Int. J. Digit. Librar. **3**(3), 317–343 (2003)
14. Bindings, C., May, K., Tudhope, D.: Modelling archaeological excavation activities using CIDOC CRM. J. Comput. Cult. Herit. **3**(2), 1–21 (2010)
15. Van de Watering, J., Willems, S.: Capturing and representing traditional dance: challenges and opportunities. J. Folk. Res. **51**(3), 293–321 (2014)

The Text+ Registry: Federating Research Data Catalogues for the Digital Humanities

Tobias Gradl(✉), Leon Fruth, and Andreas Henrich

University of Bamberg, An der Weberei 5, 96049 Bamberg, Germany
{tobias.gradl,leon.fruth,andreas.henrich}@uni-bamberg.de
https://www.uni-bamberg.de

Abstract. The registry is a central component of the NFDI consortium Text+, designed to unify the cataloguing and discovery of text- and language-based research resources across diverse domains. Addressing the fragmentation and heterogeneity of existing catalogues, the registry employs a flexible, model-driven architecture that supports both automated metadata ingestion from external sources and manual curation by experts. Its sophisticated metamodelling concept accommodates the complexity of scholarly editions, collections, and lexical resources, balancing minimal entry requirements with the option for detailed enrichment. A key innovation is the provenance-aware metadata layering mechanism, which transparently documents the origin and evolution of each resource description, enabling both efficient reuse and expert-driven refinement. The hybrid approach allows the registry to consolidate complementary perspectives from multiple catalogues, resulting in richer and more sustainable metadata. To maximize findability and discoverability, the registry offers advanced search capabilities, including faceted and multilingual search, authority data integration, and persistent identifiers. These features, accessible via both web interfaces and APIs, facilitate cross-domain queries and integration with external infrastructures. By aligning with the FAIR principles and fostering interoperability, the Text+ Registry not only improves the visibility and accessibility of scholarly resources but also establishes a robust, extensible foundation for future semantic and knowledge graph-based research infrastructures.

Keywords: Hybrid data catalogue · Resource modelling · Resource findability

1 Introduction

Text+ is one of 26 interdisciplinary research data consortia coordinated under the German National Research Data Infrastructure (NFDI, Nationale Forschungsdateninfrastruktur) and of four consortia dedicated to the humanities.[1] Its mission is to enable the sustainable preparation, provision, and long-term preservation of text- and language-based research data, aiming to build a

[1] https://www.nfdi.de/consortia/?lang=en.

W.-T. Balke et al. (Eds.): TPDL 2025, LNCS 16097, pp. 378–394, 2026.
https://doi.org/10.1007/978-3-032-05409-8_22

flexible and scalable infrastructure tailored to the diverse needs of the scholarly community. Organised into three data domains–collections, lexical resources, and editions–Text+ collaborates closely with academic communities to develop and promote standards and best practices that are aligned with the FAIR principles (Findability, Accessibility, Interoperability, and Reuse) [21]. To this end, Text+ offers a comprehensive range of services, data, and consulting to institutions, projects, and individual researchers alike.

The current landscape of scholarly resource cataloguing in the humanities remains fragmented and heterogeneous, limiting both discoverability and sustainable research data management. Existing catalogues often focus on specific disciplines or resource types, providing detailed and relevant descriptions of resources, but lacking integration with external sources and broader reference systems. The Text+ Registry addresses these challenges by providing a unified, extensible infrastructure for the description, curation, and discovery of text- and language-based research resources. It consolidates information from existing catalogues and serves as a bridge to broader, interdisciplinary initiatives within and beyond the NFDI.

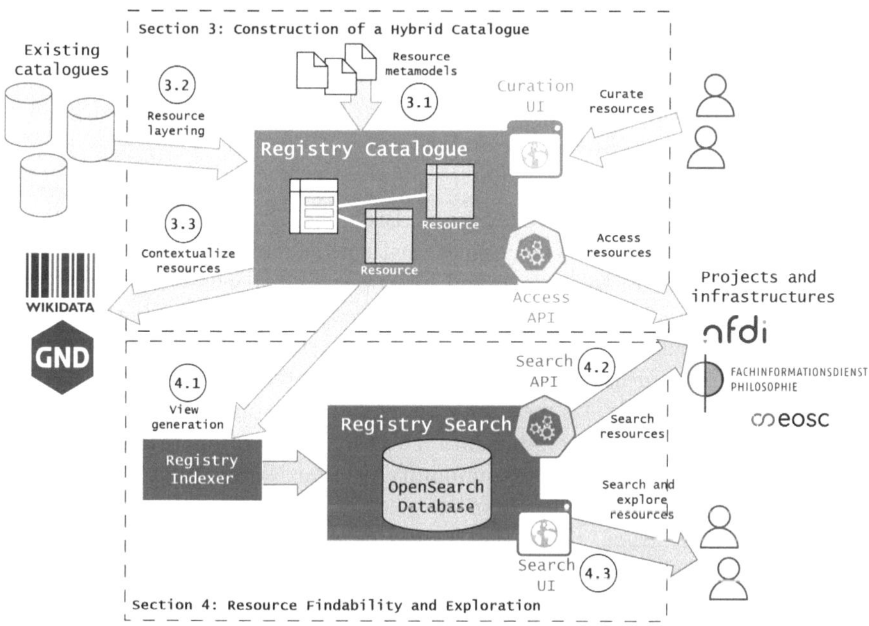

Fig. 1. High-level Text+ Registry Architecture.

This paper presents the design and implementation of the Text+ Registry, focusing on two foundational pillars (Fig. 1): its *hybrid curation and metadata layering*, and its advanced environment for *resource findability and exploration*. While the registry is developed in close collaboration with Digital Humanities

(DH) experts, we demonstrate the flexibility and configurability of these components, making them adaptable to use cases and domains beyond Text+. Section 2 motivates our approach by highlighting the need for sustainable, FAIR-aligned infrastructures that can adapt to evolving scholarly practices and data standards and bridge existing and upcoming domain-specific and broader initiatives. Section 3 details our hybrid catalogue approach, which employs a metamodelling strategy to support a variety of data models and enables flexible import, curation, and distribution of resource descriptions. Imported resource metadata are organized in composable, provenance-aware layers, supporting the consolidation of comprehensive resource descriptions and expert curation. Section 4 introduces the modular, multi-mode search component, which supports both cross-domain and domain-specific retrieval through a highly configurable Application Programming Interface (API) and a user friendly User Interface (UI). We conclude in Sect. 5 with a reflection on the current state of the registry, its applicability to other domains and planned future enhancements and directions.

2 Related Work

The landscape of catalogues and registries in the DH is shaped by two principal approaches: broad, general-purpose catalogues that prioritize coverage and interoperability, and specific, domain-focused catalogues that offer detailed, context-rich metadata. Both approaches serve distinct needs and are foundational to research infrastructures in the humanities.

Broad, General-Purpose Catalogues. Broad catalogues aim to aggregate a vast number of records across disciplines, institutions, and resource types. Their primary strength lies in their scale and interoperability, achieved by employing simple, generic metadata schemas. This facilitates the inclusion of heterogeneous resources but often at the cost of descriptive depth and domain specificity. WorldCat[2] is the world's largest bibliographic database, aggregating records from thousands of libraries globally. Its metadata integration is grounded in the use of the MARC 21[3] format for bibliographic data [15], with support for Resource Description and Access (RDA) and other community standards, making it invaluable for discovery but limited in offering domain-specific details. CrossRef[4] is a registry for scholarly publications, primarily focused on providing Persistent Identifiers (PIDs) and basic bibliographic metadata. Its simplicity ensures broad applicability but does not capture the nuanced characteristics of humanities resources. Metadata harmonization in CrossRef is based on the Metadata deposit schema [4], which follows the ISO/IEC 11179 metadata registry standard[5] and is intentionally generic to allow integration across a wide range of disciplines and publication types. The Common Language Resources and Technology Infrastructure

[2] https://search.worldcat.org.
[3] https://www.loc.gov/marc/bibliographic/.
[4] https://www.crossref.org.
[5] https://www.iso.org/standard/78914.html.

(CLARIN) Virtual Language Observatory (VLO)[6] aggregates metadata from over forty CLARIN centres and numerous external providers, offering a uniform search and discovery interface for language resources and tools. It uses the Component Metadata Infrastructure (CMDI) [19] to harmonize diverse metadata into a manageable set of fields, supporting faceted browsing and semantic annotation. The VLO supports a wide range of ingest formats including Dublin Core (DC, OLAC Metadata and CMDI profiles. Discovery capabilities in the VLO, such as search facets are based on the CMDI profile of DCMI Metadata Terms [5] and require ingested metadata to be (converted to) CMDI, allowing the utilization of ISOcat data categories for data processing [19]. While optimized for language resources, the core model for discovery (DCMI) is intentionally generic to support a wide array of resource types.

Broad catalogues excel at providing a "methodological commons" for the humanities, mediating between diverse research domains and enabling multidisciplinary discovery. However, their reliance on generic metadata often means that important contextual or technical details specific to certain resource types are omitted (e.g. WorldCat and CrossRef) or not immediately accessible for discovery (e.g. CLARIN VLO).

Specific, Domain-Focused Catalogues. In contrast, domain-specific catalogues are tailored to the needs and conventions of particular scholarly communities or resource types. They often employ rich, detailed metadata schemas that reflect the complexities and priorities of their respective domains, allowing for nuanced description, advanced search, and expert curation. The Catalog of Digital Scholarly Editions (CDSE)[7] focuses on digital scholarly editions. It uses TEI-XML[8] to capture essential bibliographic details, publication dates, material types, and links to academic reviews. Its data model is minimal yet structured to reflect specific aspects of digital editions. The Catalogue of Digital Editions (CDE) extends the CDSE approach with a more verbose schema, capturing technical, editorial, and institutional details, and offering machine-readable exports. The CDE is tailored to the digital editions community and provides information not typically available in broader catalogues. A European Gateway for the Academies of Sciences and Humanities (AGATE) is a project-oriented catalogue documenting research projects funded by the German Academies Programme. AGATE's metadata emphasizes project context, funding, methodologies, and team composition, rather than publication-level details [22]. These catalogues reflect the "clouds of knowing" within the humanities [13], providing deep contextualization and supporting specialized research needs. Their specificity, however, can introduce bias and limit interoperability across domains.

[6] https://vlo.clarin.eu.
[7] https://www.digitale-edition.de.
[8] https://git.uni-wuppertal.de/dhsfu/sde-catalog/-/blob/master/catalog_TEI.xml.

3 Construction of a Hybrid Catalogue

The increasing complexity and interdisciplinarity of DH research highlight limitations of both approaches described in Sect. 2. There is a pressing need for greater interoperability and the integration of diverse catalogues and databases to enhance findability, context, and provenance [9]. We propose the registry as an infrastructure component that combines the breadth of general-purpose catalogues with the depth of domain-specific ones, employing flexible data models and concepts such as provenance-aware metadata layering to support both comprehensive coverage and detailed description. In essence, the registry does not require the harmonization of heterogeneous data to a single schema upon data ingestion. Instead, it allows the specification of domain-specific integration models that preserve the specific details of the particular domains. To facilitate broad discovery and interoperability, these schemas are virtually integrated in subsequent phases of data processing to facilitate broad search scenarios, data exchange with aggregators and connection to knowledge graphs and other Linked Open Data (LOD)-based approaches.

3.1 Data Models as Functionality Drivers

The registry is designed as a generic catalogue, supporting diverse use cases for both users and connected systems. Its functionality is built upon data models that define the structure, behaviour, and interaction of metadata through declarative instructions. These data models serve as the foundation for dynamically generating UIs and APIs, ensuring adaptability to evolving community requirements and resource descriptions. For Text+, the registry accommodates the variability in resource descriptions (editions, collections and lexical resources[9]) by supporting specific data models for each type. While these models share common properties such as titles and licensing, they are tailored to the unique requirements of each domain. The registry adopts a *dynamic modeling principle*, enabling flexible definitions of data models that evolve over time. This approach ensures that APIs for data ingestion, export, and UIs are dynamically generated, rather than being rigidly tied to initial specifications.

Background. The concept of generating software components from formal models, such as Model-Driven Architecture (MDA), has been widely adopted in modern software development [17]. MDA emphasizes strict formalization of business logic, making it suitable for complex projects requiring independence from specific technologies. While humanities research often resists strict formalization due to its interpretive nature, the registry leverages a model-driven framework to balance formalization with flexibility. This enables the generation of forms and interfaces that adapt to the nuanced requirements of scholarly resources.

---

[9] https://gitlab.gwdg.de/textplus/registry/registry-models.

Resource Metamodel. The registry employs a *domain-specific metamodelling language* to formalize data models for resources. The design of the language has been influenced by JSON Schema[10] and XML Schema[11], the predominant schema languages for semi-structured data. For the model-driven approach of the registry, a fine-grained control of API and UI components is required. Early implementation prototypes have shown that established schema languages like JSON Schema and XML Schema could not adequately provide a necessary expressiveness. While they are well-suited for basic data validation and structural constraints, they lack the ability to specify advanced UI and API behaviours. For example, neither can they natively describe how fields should be rendered in multilingual contexts, nor can they express complex input logic such as conditional field visibility, dynamic field multiplicity, or custom validation workflows. Further examples of limited support include e.g. referencing and managing external controlled vocabularies or authority files, and explicit modelling of multilingual fields, including language-specific cardinality and validation. For this reason, a custom metamodelling language has been designed to address these limitations [8]. To support ingest use-cases based on these established languages, future versions of the registry will include an export mechanism for data models to JSON and XML schema. For the Text+ use case, the metamodelling language captures commonalities across domains while addressing specific features [8]. Listing 1 shows an excerpt from the rather complex editions data model, specified according to the metamodelling languge:

- *Main title* (line 7ff.): A multilingual field allowing *one entry per language* (`multilang: true && multiplicity: false`), with *mandatory* validation
- *Person* (line 15ff.): A *relation to a person*, supporting *controlled vocabularies* e.g. for role specifications within the relation, allowing *multiple entries* and *fallback options* for free-text entries (`strict: false`)
- *Source Medium* (line 22ff.): A mandatory field bound to a *controlled vocabulary*, allowing *multiple entries* and *free-text additions* (`strict: false`) when no match is found

The metamodelling language backs a sophisticated validation framework that ensures both schematic and semantic validity of resource descriptions.

Interface Generation. The registry dynamically transforms data models into representations required for various functionalities, including bulk ingestion, manual editing, and export of curated resource descriptions. REST-based APIs are central to the registry, facilitating client-server communication and integration with external systems. These APIs serialize and deserialize data based on specified models, ensuring compatibility with heterogeneous formats. Likewise, the user interface is rendered dynamically based on the metamodelling language and resource descriptions. For example:

[10] https://json-schema.org/.
[11] https://www.w3.org/XML/Schema.

```
entity: edition
primary: true
compositing: true
blocks:
  - name: basic_information
    properties:
    - field: main_title
      type: text
      mandatory: true
      multilang: true
      multiplicity: false
    ...
  - name: actors
    properties:
    - field: person
      relation: edition_person
      multiple: true
      strict: false
    ...
  - name: edenda
    properties:
    - field: medium
      type: vocabulary
      vocabulary: editions_quellenmedium
      multiple: true
      strict: false
      mandatory: true
    ...
```

Listing 1: Metamodelling example ("editions" data model)

- Multilingual text fields provide controls for adding and removing language-specific entries.
- Entity references use typeahead selectors to search for matching resources.
- Controlled vocabulary fields allow selection from predefined lists, with fallback options for free-text entries (if specified as non-strict).

This dynamic rendering ensures adaptability to evolving data models and user requirements, while maintaining consistency across interfaces. At present, individual resource descriptions remain bound to the data model version they have been specified in. Automatic migrations of resources following data model evolutions are among the upcoming tasks within the versioning concept of the registry.

3.2 Provenance-Aware Layering

Given the examples in the related work Sect. 2, the registry is designed to be able to bridge between existing cataloguing systems. Specific, domain-focused catalogues provide overlapping or complementary details about DH resources and the registry provides means to merge and enrich partial resource descriptions and redistribute them to broader aggregators and knowledge graphs. For this purpose, the registry implements a hybrid architecture that combines automated metadata aggregation from external sources with manual expert curation. This approach addresses the limitations of purely automated systems–often lacking domain-specific nuance–and purely manual systems that struggle with scalability. The design aligns with established paradigms–also from other areas of computer science, such as distributed file systems–that emphasize provenance-aware data integration and source-aware conflict resolution [1,10,12].

With respect to source integration and provenance-awareness the registry operates on three core principles:

- *Layer Isolation*: Each imported resource description is maintained as an isolated layer bound to its originating source (e.g. CDSE, CDE, AGATE), preserving provenance and update independence [1,14].
- *Dynamic Prioritization*: Layers are stacked according to customizable priorities (e.g. AGATE over CDE over CDSE), with field-level precedence rules determining which source provides specific metadata elements [14].
- *Curation Sovereignty*: A dedicated top-layer allows domain experts to override automated prioritization, modify or create new entries, preserving original source data while enabling contextual enrichment [20].

To ensure the connection of metadata to its originating source (*source provenance*), the registry persists source information with the imported metadata layer and includes a catalogue identifier (e.g. CDSE), the harvest timestamp and a version hash [1,14]. Curator accounts are based on connections to OAuth and Shibboleth based authentication providers (in Text+: GitHub, Open Researcher and Contributor ID (ORCID) and the German National Research and Education Network (DFN, Deutsches Forschungsnetz)-Authentication and Authorization Infrastructure (AAI)[12]). A version diff (*edit provenance*) is logged and contains the edit rationale to reflect e.g. textual changes to a title field, the manual change of field precedence in source layers or the contextualization of a person label to an authority file entry. A directed acyclic graph shows how composite fields are derived from source layers (*field-level lineage*) [1,3].

Currently, the composition algorithm distinguishes between aggregative and exclusive field configurations for simplicity. Aggregative fields (often in place for fields like language, topics or keywords) collect all values of imported layers and present them in an aggregative fashion for resource presentation. Exclusive fields (as e.g. for the title of a resource) only select the value of the topmost layer for presentation. While this behavior can be manually overriden by domain experts, a more sophisticated selection algorithm could respect aspects such as majority voting for categorical fields (e.g. language) or recency for temporal fields.

[12] https://www.aai.dfn.de/.

Use Case: Integrating Heterogeneous Edition Descriptions. Considering the Carl Maria von Weber Complete Edition (WeGA, Carl-Maria-von-Weber-Gesamtausgabe)[13] as an example, which collects the compositions, letters, diaries, and writings of Carl Maria von Weber. The project has resulted not only in a digital edition of Weber's works, documents, and correspondence, but the implementation of a sophisticated technological architecture that handles aspects of search, linked data integration, export formats and API. A review of the digital edition has distinguished the edition "as an example for a-state-of-the-art digital edition" [16]. Due to its realization and impact, references to the edition can be found in multiple catalogues, including the mentioned AGATE, CDE, and CDSE. The registry benefits from these complementary perspectives: While AGATE provides information on the project context, funding details and multilingual titles, CDE details technical aspects such as TEI/XML availability, and CDSE adds links to reviews and disciplinary classifications. The registry ingests the description of the Weber edition from each source in isolated layers, applies default prioritization as configured for the resource type of editions, generates a composite view including e.g. titles from AGATE (prioritized multilingual support), technical spec from CDE and reviews from CDSE, which are absent in higher layers. All source data is preserved for provenance queries and manual curation.

3.3 Contextualization Through Cross-Referencing and Authority Data

The Text+ Registry provides means to enhance the semantic richness of resource descriptions by systematically aligning metadata with authoritative external datasets. This contextualization strategy ensures interoperability while preserving disciplinary specificity, addressing a critical challenge in DH infrastructures. The registry currently implements two primary mechanisms for authority alignment: *entity resolution* and the use of *controlled vocabularies*. For the resolution of entities such as persons and institutions, Wikidata and the Gemeinsame Normdatei (GND) are used to disambiguate entities and to facilitate the persistent identification of entities across systems. The model-driven approach of the registry allows the declarative specification of existing interfaces of authority data providers. While this facilitates the connection to further sources for reference data such as the Research Software Directory (RSD) and the Social Sciences & Humanities (SSH) Open Marketplace, the registry also provides means to locally mirror controlled vocabularies that do not provide a machine-accessible interface, but provide means to download or copy vocabulary entries. Examples include the German Research Association (DFG, Deutsche Forschungsgemeinschaft) Classification of Scientific Disciplines[14], the base classification for disciplinary domains, and the System Package Data Exchange (SPDX) license list. In addition, the registry supports the creation and management of local vocabularies.

[13] https://weber-gesamtausgabe.de/en/Index.

[14] https://www.dfg.de/en/research-funding/proposal-funding-process/interdisciplinarity/subject-area-structure.

Automated vs. Manual Curation. While automated matching during ingestion attempts to resolve entity references [6], three factors necessitate expert intervention and curation:

- *Name ambiguity*: If source materials are not utilizing meaningful identifiers, but rely on names, a confident automatic disambiguation is often not possible.
- *Historical name variants*: pre-modern terminology often finds no corresponding entry in authority files.
- *Concept drift*: Terminologies such as disciplinary classification are evolving and might require manual reevaluation.

With its API-mediated architecture, the registry positions itself as a bridge between traditional catalogues and semantic infrastructures in terms of a three-layered architecture: in the *input layer*, heterogeneous metadata is harvested via OAI-PMH, Git, and custom connectors. The *alignment layer* performs statistical entity matching with fallback to manual reconciliation. Depending on the extent and precision of the information available for entity matching (e.g. identifiers, person name + affiliation, or person names only), automatic matching can be either sufficiently confident according to a configured threshold, can result in the generation of candidates that require manual selection or can terminate without any potential matches leaving the reconciliation task to domain experts. The *output layer* exports the resource and entity network in terms of semi-structured schemata that, at present, include representations aligned to specified domain models and an integrated variant that conforms to DataCite[15]. To further facilitate integration into knowledge graphs, exports as Resource Description Framework (RDF) and Data Catalog Vocabulary (DCAT) representations are planned as well as the addition of further authority files to mitigate national bias and broaden contextual coverage. Examples include ORCID for comprehensive researcher identification and contribution tracking, the British National Bibliography (BNB) for enriching British cultural/historical contexts and Virtual International Authority File (VIAF) for bridging international name authority variations.

4 Resource Findability and Exploration

To facilitate findability and exploration of the imported and curated resources, the registry offers both machine- and human-interoperable interfaces. The components relevant for the search and discovery (see Fig. 1) include both a REST-API for integrating registry data into external systems or workflows and a user interface to search and explore the resources. The data can be queried in a broad and general way, overarching all resource description types and in a specific and domain-focused fashion leveraging the data models of each resource type.

The following section provides an explanation on how the data is processed and indexed for retrieval-specific functionalities. The subsequent sections outline how the data is then utilized by a search API and user interface. Both can be dynamically configured for various use-cases and flexible data models.

[15] https://schema.datacite.org/.

4.1 View Generation

Layers (Sect. 3.2) are merged into a streamlined and flattened representation based on predefined or curated prioritizations. This approach simplifies the data while retaining all curated revisions, ensuring that enrichments, corrections, and updates are comprehensively integrated into final resource descriptions.

The *Registry Indexer*[16] processes and indexes the data to an OpenSearch instance[17]. To create a unified and searchable index to support sophisticated retrieval capabilities, the imported and curated resources from every resource type are processed into multiple indices and optimized for efficient search functionalities, outlined in the remainder of this paper. Each resource is stored in its original data model to leverage domain-specific queries in full depth. Additionally, a DataCite-mapped format is stored alongside the original schema, allowing the resources to be searched from a broad and cross-domain perspective, overarching multiple resource types. Furthermore, it ensures the interoperability of the data with other research projects. Initially seen simply as a key format for enabling interoperability, DataCite has proved effective in implementing comprehensive search capabilities across the heterogeneous domains of Text+ [18].

The registry's search components utilize advanced retrieval methods such as language specific processing of textual data. Metadata fields such as title and description are processed and stored in language-specific manner to improve the retrieval for various languages. Currently, four languages are supported - German, English, Spanish and French. For text fields lacking explicit language annotations, the language is automatically determined using the langdetect python library[18]. Each language's processing pipeline includes a custom set of stop-words and a stemmer to accurately derive word stems in the respective language. Further modifications are applied, such as decomposing German compound words (e.g., "Naturwissenschaft" is separated into "Natur" and "Wissenschaft"), which has shown to be beneficial for text retrieval, or removing elisions for French texts (e.g., "l'avion" is processed to "avion") [2].

After processing, data is indexed, with each resource category assigned to a separate index. Currently, this process is executed once every 24 h, where all resources are updated. Future plans include event-driven indexing of individual resources for real-time updates.

4.2 Search API

The indexed data is accessible through a REST-based API[19], which is based on preliminary work of the DH infrastructural contexts of DARIAH-DE and CLARIAH-DE [7]. The API is highly configurable through *search profiles*, allowing administrators to enable, disable, and fine-tune individual search features to address specific use-case requirements and to dynamically adapt to evolving data

16 https://gitlab.com/minfba/resinfra/registry-indexer.
17 https://opensearch.org/.
18 https://github.com/shuyo/language-detection.
19 https://gitlab.com/minfba/resinfra/generic-search/generic-search-api.

models. Search queries can be built by combining different query types, such as full-text queries that support Lucene's query parser syntax[20], as well as queries for (near) exact matches. Additionally, the API supports a range of configurable functionalities, including but not limited to:

- *Facet aggregations*, that return the count of occurrences of distinct categories within a specific field of the current result-set. This functionality is used for the faceted search within the user interface, giving an overview over the data and available filters to further refine the query.
- *Suggestions* assist users by proposing corrections for typographical errors in search terms, for instance suggesting "Goethe" when "Goehte" is queried. This is realized by using a n-gram language model.[21]
- *Fuzziness* accommodates minor typographical errors in user queries, ensuring that relevant results are still returned.
- *Highlighting* of matched text sections to increase the transparency of search results by clearly indicating the query-relevant content.

In Text+ there are currently four search profiles defined, one for each resource type (collections, editions, lexical resources) and one for the DataCite format for overarching queries over all resource types.

```
1 POST https://registry.text-plus.org/api/search/edition
2 {
3     "query": "brief",
4     "filter": {"properties.languages.@reference": ["lat"]},
5     "aggregations": true
6 }
```

Listing 2: Search request with query term "Brief" and filtering resources in latin.

Listing 2 shows an example request (line 1), searching with the query term "brief"[22] (line 2) and filtering the result set for resources in latin (line 3). The request furthermore enables aggregations, such as the before-mentioned *facet aggregations*. It utilizes the search profile "edition", considering only the editions resources, with its distinct data model and taking advantage of the domain-specific facets.

Use Case: Philfinder. An example demonstrating the interoperability of the registry is the access through the search REST-API by the PhilFinder[23], a discovery

[20] https://lucene.apache.org/core/2_9_4/queryparsersyntax.html.
[21] https://docs.opensearch.org/docs/latest/search-plugins/searching-data/did-you-mean/.
[22] German term for "letter".
[23] https://philportal.de/philfinder.

portal for philosophical research maintained by the Specialized Information Service (SIS, Fachinformationsdienst) Philosophy. The PhilFinder queries the search API to retrieve editions associated with specific individuals, such as Immanuel Kant, by leveraging authority file identifiers. It uses Wikidata as a LOD hub, leveraging its external links to other data and knowledge bases such as the GND, which is utilized as contextualization by the registry, as described in Sect. 3.3. The SIS manually started to enrich editions in the registry to retrieve data from the search API more reliably. Using the GND URI of Immanuel Kant[24] results, such as "Kant - Opus Postumum Online Edition"[25], can be retrieved and displayed in the PhilFinder. While this identifier-based search ensures high accuracy, it has rather low recall. Updating the underlying search profile to also include full-text queries, will increase the recall and give the user more options in the PhilFinder.

4.3 Search User Interface

The search user interface[26] is a website that queries the search API previously outlined. The UI is built to go beyond simple "known item" lookup searches and is developed as an exploratory search. According to [11] exploratory search involves dynamic, iterative tasks like continuously refining queries as users navigate and learn about the presented data. A number of advanced functionalities have been employed, to support this exploratory nature. The UI comprises three primary pages, a landing page, a faceted search interface and a resource view.

The landing page provides contextual information about the project and the registry and serves as an entry point. This gives new users a quick overview to see if the underlying data is relevant to their information needs. In addition, featured resources are displayed to highlight noteworthy content, which acts as good starting point for an exploration. In the future, displaying interesting facets on the landing page can provide more information about the available data and serve as a useful initial query. The search input, prominently placed in the middle of the interface, enables free-text queries, which opens the faceted search interface.

The faceted search interface allows users to search with free-text and filter resources using available facets and browse through the results. The facet view presents an overview of configured metadata facets–such as language, provenance, or scientific disciplines–each annotated with the count of matching resources in the current result set. These facets can be applied dynamically to filter and refine queries, guiding exploration more effectively than free-text search alone [23]. An interactive word-cloud on the faceted search page aggregates text from the current results, visually emphasising prominent terms, thereby helping users to find interesting queries. When clicking on a result the detailed metadata and information of the selected resource opens.

[24] http://d-nb.info/gnd/118559796.

[25] https://registry.text-plus.org/doc/registry_edition/4e1722d3-d85f-43ad-9afa-6ddda34087b4.

[26] https://gitlab.com/minfba/resinfra/generic-search/generic-search-frontend.

The resource view displays detailed metadata about a specific resource. The page also serves as an access point for the websites providing the resource's content, by presenting the relevant links. It furthermore shows connections to related resources in a graph visualization. This enables users to intuitively navigate the relationships between resources, facilitating the identification and navigation of related resources and contextualized entities.

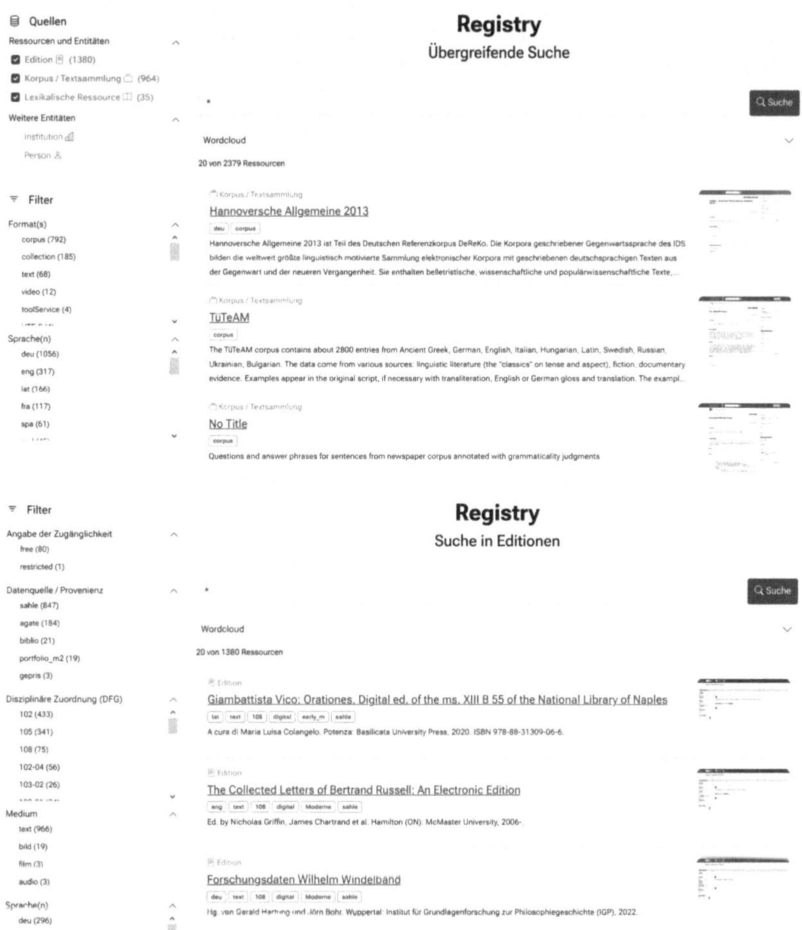

Fig. 2. The overarching search mode (top) allows users to execute a broad search over all resource types. The edition search mode (bottom) shows a high quantity of facets, utilizing the data model in-depth.

The search UI utilizes the API's ability to support multiple search profiles, thereby enabling both overarching searches across multiple data models and in-depth, model-specific searches. This is achieved by employing multiple *search modes*. Each mode is associated with a specific search profile and corresponding indices. In Text+ four search modes are configured, one for each of the three data domains and one overarching search mode utilizing the DataCite format. Depending on the selected search mode, certain features on the pages of the UI can be customized. The landing page, for instance, can be configured to show different information or featured resources. The faceted search page allows the configuration of available facets depending on the data model. The facets for the domain-specific modes are more in-depth, than the facets in the overarching search mode. Furthermore, each search mode can be visually distinguished by employing distinct colours or background images, thereby signifying to users that they are operating within a unique context and data model. Figure 2 shows the overarching search mode and the edition search mode, with visual and functional differences.

5 Future Work and Conclusion

The Text+ Registry demonstrates how a hybrid, provenance-aware infrastructure can unify the description, curation, and discovery of text- and language-based research resources across diverse domains. By combining automated metadata ingestion from authoritative external sources with flexible, expert-driven curation, the registry addresses both the need for comprehensive coverage and the demand for high-quality, domain-specific detail. Its metamodelling architecture supports adaptable data models, enabling the seamless integration of heterogeneous catalogues and the dynamic generation of user interfaces and APIs. The layered metadata approach ensures transparency, reusability, and sustainable maintenance, while advanced search and contextualization features significantly enhance the findability and accessibility of scholarly resources.

Looking ahead, future development will focus on expanding the integration of external authority data (such as of external authority and the BNB), further automating data linking and enrichment, and strengthening semantic interoperability with external knowledge graphs and research infrastructures. Continued emphasis will be placed on usability and community engagement, ensuring that the registry evolves as a sustainable, extensible, and widely adopted resource for the DH. By systematically aligning with the FAIR principles and responding to evolving scholarly needs, the Text+ Registry is well positioned to serve as a catalyst for connected, high-quality research data in the humanities and beyond.

Acknowledgments. This document was created in the context of the work of the association German National Research Data Infrastructure (NFDI) e.V. NFDI is financed by the Federal Republic of Germany and the 16 federal states, and the consortium Text+ is funded by the DFG - project number 460033370. The authors would like to thank for the funding and support. Furthermore, thanks also include all institutions and actors who are committed to the association and its goals.

References

1. Allen, M.D., Seligman, L., Blaustein, B.: Provenance Capture and Use: A Practical Guide. Technical report, The Mitre Corporation (2010)
2. Braschler, M., Ripplinger, B.: How effective is stemming and decompounding for German text retrieval? Inf. Retrieval **7**(3), 291–316 (2004). https://doi.org/10.1023/B:INRT.0000011208.60754.a1
3. Carata, L., et al.: A primer on provenance. Commun. ACM **57**(5), 52–60 (2014). https://doi.org/10.1145/2596628
4. CrossRef: Metadata deposit schema 5.4.0. Technical report, CrossRef (2025)
5. DCMI Usage Board: DCMI Metadata Terms. Technical report, DCMI (2020)
6. Fruth, L., Gradl, T., Henrich, A.: ADISS: Authority Data Integration Search System. P-361 (2025)
7. Gradl, T., Henrich, A.: Bibliothek Forschung und Praxis **40**(2), 222–228 (2016). https://doi.org/10.1515/bfp-2016-0027
8. Gradl, T., Kudella, C., Lordick, H., Schulz, D.: Towards a registry for digital resources - the text+ registry for editions. Datenbank-Spektrum **24**(2), 151–160 (2024). https://doi.org/10.1007/s13222-024-00479-0
9. Hedges, M., et al.: Digital Humanities Foresight - The future impact of digital methods, technologies and infrastructures. DARIAH-DE Working Papers (2019)
10. Herschel, M., Diestelkämper, R., Ben Lahmar, H.: A survey on provenance: what for? What form? What from? VLDB J. **26**(6), 881–906 (2017). https://doi.org/10.1007/s00778-017-0486-1
11. Marchionini, G.: Exploratory search: from finding to understanding. Commun. ACM **49**(4), 41–46 (2006). https://doi.org/10.1145/1121949.1121979
12. Massari, A., Peroni, S., Tomasi, F., Heibi, I.: Representing provenance and track changes of cultural heritage metadata in RDF: a survey of existing approaches, (2023). https://doi.org/10.48550/ARXIV.2305.08477
13. McCarty, W., Short, H.: Methodologies. Technical report, EADH (2002)
14. Muniswamy-Reddy, K.-K., et al.: Layering in provenance systems. In: Proceedings of the 2009 Conference on USENIX Annual Technical Conference. USENIX 2009, p. 10. USENIX Association, San Diego, California (2009)
15. OCLC: The WorldCat Metadata API – Functionality comparison. Technical report, OCLC (2024)
16. Roeder, T.: Die offene EditionswerkstattâĂŕ: Carl Maria von Webers Briefe in der digitalen WeGA (Rezension). (2020). https://doi.org/10.18716/RIDE.A.12.4
17. Sebastián, G., Gallud, J.A., Tesoriero, R.: Code generation using model driven architecture: a systematic mapping study. J. Comput. Lang. **56**, 100935 (2020). https://doi.org/10.1016/j.cola.2019.100935
18. Starr, J., Gastl, A.: isCitedBy: A metadata scheme for DataCite. D-Lib Magazine 17(1/2) (2011). https://doi.org/10.1045/january2011-starr
19. Uytvanck, D.V., Stehouwer, H., Lampen, L.: Semantic metadata mapping in practice: the virtual language observatory. In: Calzolari, N., et al. (eds.) Proceedings of the Eighth International Conference on Language Resources and Evaluation, LREC 2012, Istanbul, Turkey, 23–25 May 2012, pp. 1029–1034. European Language Resources Association (ELRA) (2012)
20. Wells, D.: Collaboration and Crowdsourcing with Data Cataloging. Technical report, Alation, Inc. (2020)
21. Wilkinson, M.D., et al.: The FAIR guiding principles for scientific data management and stewardship. Sci. Data **3**(1), 160018 (2016). https://doi.org/10.1038/sdata.2016.18

22. Wuttke, U., Ott, C., Adrian, D., Worthington, S.: Agate: Concept for a European Academies Internet Gateway for the Humanities and Social Sciences (2017). https://doi.org/10.5281/ZENODO.806179
23. Yee, K.-P., Swearingen, K., Li, K., Hearst, M.: Faceted metadata for image search and browsing. In: Proceedings of the SIGCHI Conference on Human Factors in Computing Systems. CHI 2003, pp. 401–408. Association for Computing Machinery, Ft. Lauderdale, Florida, USA (2003). https://doi.org/10.1145/642611.642681

A Comparative Analysis of Support Techniques for Assessing the Quality of Systematic Literature Reviews

Rand Alchokr[1(✉)], Athul Sunilkumar[1], Gunter Saake[1], Thomas Leich[2], and Jacob Krüger[3]

[1] Otto-von-Guericke University, Magdeburg, Germany
{rand.alchokr,Sunilkumar,saake}@ovgu.de
[2] Harz University & METOP GmbH, Wernigerode, Germany
tleich@hs-harz.de
[3] Eindhoven University of Technology, Eindhoven, The Netherlands
j.kruger@tue.nl

Abstract. The rapidly growing number of scientific publications poses numerous challenges for researchers engaged in literature analyses. Structured methodologies like systematic literature reviews are becoming increasingly expensive, considering their attempt to cover all relevant publications. Despite the increasing efforts needed, the importance of literature reviews also leads to an increasing growth in their number. While there are support techniques (e.g., guidelines, tools, checklists) for conducting literature analyses, a concise and clear overview of such techniques for assessing the quality of the analysis itself is missing. Such an overview can help researchers identify techniques for their work, understand ambiguities between them, support peer reviews, and guide future research by highlighting open gaps. In this paper, we address this lack of an overview by identifying existing techniques for assessing the quality of systematic literature reviews, comparing their properties, and discussing their pros and cons. For this purpose, we elicited 14 techniques through a systematic literature search covering 15 years (2007–2021). Overall, our contributions can help researchers identify feasible techniques for assessing the quality of literature analyses and can guide the development of new techniques, thereby facilitating the conduct and improving the quality of literature analyses.

Keywords: Systematic Literature Reviews · Quality Assessment · Computer Science · Software Engineering

1 Introduction

The increasing amount of scientific publications is one of the most complex challenges for researchers. Several factors, such as resource constraints, competition, and publication bias, contribute to increasing publications and complexity. An overwhelming amount of publications also leads to expensive and

W.-T. Balke et al. (Eds.): TPDL 2025, LNCS 16097, pp. 395–411, 2026.
https://doi.org/10.1007/978-3-032-05409-8_23

time-consuming processes during literature analyses. Researchers perform such analyses to identify the most relevant studies related to a research topic, understand the consequent knowledge, and stay up-to-date. A Systematic Literature Review (SLR) is a dedicated form of literature analysis that follows a systematically structured methodology to analyze, aggregate, and ideally summarize all findings on a particular topic [27,43]. Stemming from the medical domain, SLRs have become one of the most popular research methodologies in computer science and other domains to elicit existing evidence. Considering computer science and particularly software engineering, Kitchenham [26,27] was among the first to explore the idea of using SLRs as a means towards Evidence-Based Software Engineering (EBSE). EBSE envisions researchers collecting the current "best" evidence on a research topic and integrating it with practical experiences as well as human values into decision-making frameworks for developing and maintaining software. This idea underpins the value of SLRs in providing a systematic overview of a research topic that can guide other researchers and practitioners [11,40].

Unfortunately, conducting an SLR is resource-intensive, since it involves complex, multi-faceted, and time-consuming processes that necessitates substantial dedication and technical expertise to ensure reliability. Many researchers are developing semi-automatic techniques to facilitate different stages of a SLRs [3,9,12,14,19,31,32,42,44,45,55]. However, despite such advances, we are unaware of analyses or automation that ensure the quality of reporting (systematic) literature reviews. Due to the importance of SLRs as a research methodology for collecting evidence, there has been a surge in the number of publications reporting them in all scientific domains [4,17]. Even though this is a good sign for a move towards more evidence-based research, the quality of these reviews has been a controversial matter. Besides potential technical problems [28,47], serious pitfalls arise considering aspects like defining, reporting, and justifying the search strategy, search procedure, source selection, quality assessment criteria, or result synthesis [51].

Furthermore, the constant increase in publications has raised concerns regarding the reliability of SLRs in terms of comprehensively covering the literature, given the original intent of ensuring "thoroughness" and "completeness". Because SLRs build on a set of guidelines for framing research questions, sorting out studies, and analyzing the quality of primary studies, their credibility depends on the strength of such guidelines—and most reviews still make use of outdated guidelines or tools. For instance, the Database of Abstracts of Reviews of Effects (DARE) criteria are often used, even though they have severe limitations regarding completeness [4]. Additionally, the reporting quality of SLRs varies, limiting their readers' ability to assess their strengths and weaknesses [33]. To improve the quality of SLRs (particularly in computer science), it is important to constantly monitor existing guidelines, identify their limitations, and refine them if needed to improve credibility.

To address these problems, we employed an automated search on Scopus to identify techniques for SLRs in different domains, leading to a total of 14 publications in a period of 15 years (2007–2021). We explore these publications and extract from each one: the type of quality assurance (e.g., guideline, tool, checklist) it contributes (RQ_1), the scientific domain it stems from (RQ_2), as well as the pros and cons associated with the proposal (RQ_3). We argue that researchers, particularly those in computer science, software engineering, and digital libraries, benefit significantly from designing support infrastructures for a unified quality-assessment framework for SLRs.

2 Background and Related Work

Ideally, every scientific endeavor begins with a literature review, through which researchers can gain a comprehensive understanding of previous work in their area of interest. Thus, they obtain a solid foundation while avoiding unnecessary repetitions. There are established research methods, such as SLRs or systematic mapping studies, to consolidate the existing knowledge or evidence regarding a specific problem. Such methods emphasize a critical reflection of existing knowledge and may be used to identify open gaps. However, a literature review has limited scientific value if not conducted properly. For this reason, SLRs have arguably become the most established and widely used type of literature review in any scientific field (e.g., medicine, software engineering) [4,17,27,60], favored due to the systematic and replicable method of collecting literature. Over time, different scientific fields have proposed individual adaptations of the methodology, trying to improve its conduct while also accounting for specifics of their field (e.g., collecting techniques in software engineering instead of medical studies in medicine) [27,40,41,57].

An SLR comprises three main phases, each divided into sub-steps [27]: Planning, Conducting, and Reporting. Unfortunately, any systematic literature analysis is labor-intensive, error-prone, and time-consuming, which encouraged researchers to develop numerous techniques and tools to provide support for (semi-)automating parts of the process [6,9,12,15,16,19,31,32,42,44,45,55]. Some examples for such tools are SLuRp [6], StArt [13,16], or SLR-Tool [15]. Interestingly, while many other steps of the process are researched, assessing the quality of an SLR itself (in contrast to quality assessing the primary studies) is a controversial and less researched matter. In fact, there is a lack of consensus on how authors and reviewers of a literature review should assess a review's quality [10]. This is likely connected to the many steps involved, asking authors and reviewers to have a detailed understanding of searching, selecting, reading, comparing, classifying, and assessing publications. Moreover, a literature review must be judged based on its comprehensiveness, the depths of its analysis, and how broadly the existing literature is covered [5]. Since SLRs are intended to build on a standardized, replicable, and unbiased method following a stringent protocol, their associated risks are often unnoticed. For instance, some tertiary studies emphasize the importance of knowing potential threats to the initial search and its reporting in SLRs to ensure reliable evidence, but have found that important details in published literature reviews are missing [7,24,28]. Additionally, research questions should be established before conducting the review, but this may not always be possible. Specifically, plenty of literature reviews claim that the review itself serves as a foundation for formulating meaningful research questions. In such cases, only after obtaining a detailed understanding, the researchers can identify shortcomings in the current research, which enables the formulation of more relevant and meaningful research questions [5]. Also, training researchers to conduct SLRs remains a challenge, since the lack of guidelines and a consequent agreement on what constitutes high quality can lead to very different results. Lastly, many SLRs seem to build on outdated guidelines that lack critical updates [29], leading to potential quality issues in the review and its reporting. Reflecting on all challenges associated with SLRs, it is questionable to justify that these provide the best quality outcome [5,23]. An overview and synthesis of existing techniques for quality-assuring SLRs can help mitigate such problems.

3 Methodology

In this section, we describe the design of our SLR. To conduct our SLR, we followed the guidelines by Kitchenham et al. [27], which are the most established guidelines in software engineering [28].

3.1 Planning

Goal and Need. We aimed to identify publications that contribute techniques specifically designed for assessing the quality of SLRs. These contributions include tools, guidelines, checklists, and other evaluative techniques aimed at ensuring rigor and reliability in review processes.

Research Questions. To achieve our goal, we defined the following three Research Questions (RQs):

RQ_1 *What techniques for assessing the quality of a SLR exist?*
Our objective for this research question is to retrieve primary studies related to existing techniques for assessing the quality of an SLR.

RQ_2 *What fields of research do these techniques stem from?*
For context, it is important to identify the field a technique stems from.

RQ_3 *What are the pros and cons of the existing techniques?*
Finally, we aim to provide a detailed understanding of the individual techniques we identified, comparing their properties, pros, and cons.

Search Strategy. To identify relevant publications, we employed an automated search on Scopus. We chose Scopus because it is considered a high-quality database and covers various publishers and research fields, for instance, ACM, IEEE, Springer, and Elsevier. Scopus indexes only peer-reviewed publications, which is why we can assume a certain level of quality for the retrieved publications. Additionally, compared to other databases, Scopus provides search features that support researchers conducting an SLR, such as specific filtering and a query-building mechanism [46].

Search String. We constructed our search string by collecting keywords closely related to our research questions.

```
"('approach' OR 'measurement' OR 'appraisal' OR 'checklist' OR
'reporting') AND ('instrument*' OR 'tool*' OR 'guideline*' )
AND ('systematic literature review*' OR 'systematic review*' OR
'SLR') AND ('quality' OR 'evaluation' OR 'assessment')"
```

We argue that this search string is feasible to identify publications that are relevant to our research questions. Note that it is specific to Scopus and would require adaptations for other search engines. After we employed our automated keyword search, we followed up with a backwards snowballing [57,58] to complement and extend our search strategy—avoiding typical technical problems of automated searches and following established recommendations [28,47].

Selection Criteria. To answer our research questions, we defined Inclusion Criteria (IC) and Exclusion Criteria (EC) for filtering relevant primary studies. We defined the following four inclusion criteria:

IC_1 The publication is reviewed and published in a scientific journal, conference, or workshop.
IC_2 The publication is available in `pdf` format.
IC_3 The publication has been published between 2007 and 2021.
IC_4 The publication is concerned with quality assessing SLRs.

Furthermore, we defined four exclusion criteria:

EC_1 The publication is not written in English.
EC_2 The publication is a presentation or abstract only.
EC_3 The publication is a thesis, technical report, or similar work.
EC_4 The publication lacks publisher information or publication type.

Quality Assessment. We assessed the quality of each primary study to rate its importance and relevance for our research questions and to properly synthesize our findings. In detail, we answered the following six questions (Q) using the scoring of 1 for "Yes," 0.5 for "Partial," and 0 for "No" based on the recommendations by Kitchenham [22]:

Q_1 *Is there a clear statement about the goal of the reported research?*
Q_2 *Are the technique's design decisions justified?*
Q_3 *Is the procedure of how the research has been conducted thoroughly explained?*
Q_4 *Are the evaluation results thoroughly analyzed and reported?*
Q_5 *Does the evidence support the findings presented?*
Q_6 *Is the method used to obtain the results feasible?*

We remark that we employed these quality criteria on different types of publications (e.g., guidelines, tools). So, our ratings are subjective and can also vary depending on the type of research.

Data Extraction and Analysis. We extracted the publications from Scopus as a csv file and imported that file into a spreadsheet. To select publications, we first read each title and then the abstract to exclude those that do not fulfill our selection criteria. If we did not make an assessment, we read the respective publication completely. In case of any conflicts, we rechecked the corresponding publications and, in a few cases, we had to decide by majority vote. During snowballing, we added the newly identified publications to the spreadsheet. Afterwards, the second author extracted the relevant data (for consistency), while the others reviewed the results. This spreadsheet contains each publication's bibliographic data, the domain, name, and type (i.e., tool, guideline) of the technique, the phases that are targeted by the proposed method, and the pros and cons of each technique.

3.2 Conduct

We executed our literature search following the protocol we described in Sect. 3.1. We illustrate the steps of our conduct in Fig. 1. First, we executed our search string on Scopus, retrieving 13,674 publications as a csv file that we stored as a shared spreadsheet. Then, the first two authors inspected each publication independently to identify those relevant to answering our research questions based on the selection criteria we defined. Please note that if we had any doubts about a publication in Phase 2 or Phase 3, we included it rather than excluding it, as recommended by Okoli and Schabram [37]. We ended up with 14 publications. From the snowballing step, we identified six of these primary studies, which are P9âĂŞP14. Afterwards, the second author extracted all relevant data into the shared spreadsheet, which the first author fully validated to check for correctness and completeness. Finally, we performed a cross-validation of the selected publications, extracted data, and re-iterated the snowballing (including the newly found publications), which did not lead to new publications.

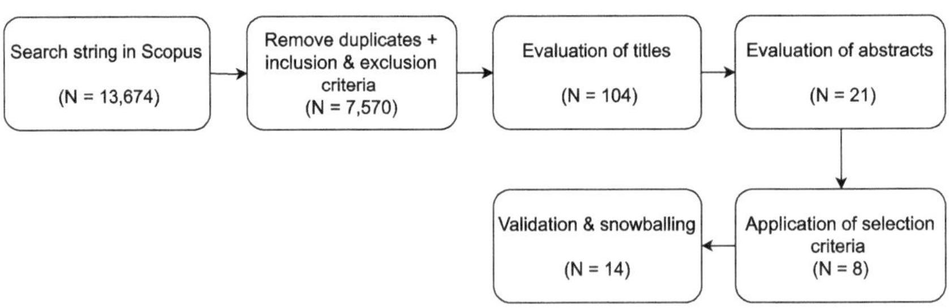

Fig. 1. Our process for identifying primary studies.

4 Results

Next, we present the results for each of our research questions.

Table 1. Summary of the retrieved publications on assessing the quality of SLRs.

Id	Ref	Year	Name	Domain	Specific Field	Target	Type	Access	Function
P1	[48]	2007	AMSTAR	Medical	Healthcare Randomized Trials	Plan, Conduct, Report	Checklist	Open	Manual
P2	[29]	2009	PRISMA	Medical	Healthcare Randomized Trials	Report	Checklist	Open	Manual
P3	[35]	2013	BPMN	General	General	Plan, Conduct, Report	Tool	Restricted	Automated
P4	[23]	2013	Kitchenham QA Reporting	Computer Science	Software Engineering	Report	Checklist	Open	Manual
P5	[56]	2014	Eco Evidence	General	Environmental Studies	Plan, Conduct, Report	Tool	Restricted	Semi-automated
P6	[5]	2015	Being Systematic in SLRs	General	General	Plan, Conduct, Report	Guideline	Open	Manual
P7	[50]	2016	Mixed Filter	Medical	Mixed Health Care Studies	Plan, Conduct, Report	Guideline	Open	Manual
P8	[49]	2017	AMSTAR-2	Medical	Health Randomized & Non-Randomized Trials	Plan, Conduct, Report	Checklist	Open	Manual
P9	[21]	2017	DARE by CDR	General	General	Report	Checklist	Open	Manual
P10	[18]	2018	MMAT	General	Mixed Studies	Plan, Conduct, Report	Checklist	Open	Manual
P11	[2]	2018	CASP (2018)	Medical	Healthcare Randomized Trials	Report	Checklist	Restricted	Manual
P12	[4]	2019	CATSER	Computer Science	Software Engineering	Report	Tool	Open	Manual
P13	[39]	2020	PRISMA (2020)	Medical	Healthcare Randomized Trials	Report	Checklist	Open	Manual
P14	[30]	2020	CASP (2020)	Medical	Healthcare Randomized Trials	Report	Checklist	Restricted	Manual

4.1 RQ_1: Existing Techniques

To address RQ_1, we examined each selected publication in detail. Through this process, we were able to gather valuable insights and summarize the key properties of each technique—which we specify in Table 1. Precisely, we provide an overview of all techniques, including the publication's reference, year of publication, name of the technique, the domain from which it stems, its specific field, its main assessment target, its type, its accessibility, and the degree of automation. In the following, we briefly introduce each of the techniques.

P1 – AMSTAR [48]. The *Assessment of Multiple SysTemAtic Reviews* was developed in 2007 based on formerly introduced studies to assess the quality and to appraise SLRs critically. More specifically, this technique concerns healthcare research, including SLRs of randomized trials for which the conducting researchers must assess the trials' reliability and validity. An expert group was formed using the nominal group technique to validate the checklist and finalize its features. Initially, AMSTAR included 37 items presented as a checklist or questionnaire. Through the nominal group technique, these items were reduced to 29, which measured 11 components. While these 11 components cover the entirety of an SLR, they only assess how it is reported. In particular, the formulated research questions, the search for relevant studies, the assessment of primary-study quality, the data extraction, and the reporting of the findings are checked.

P2 – PRISMA [29]**.** The *Preferred Reporting Items for Systematic reviews and Meta-Analyses* have the primary objective of improving the reporting of SLRs. Specifically, the goal is to define transparency standards, but not to propose quality criteria for the actual conduct. PRISMA is mainly useful when reviewing health-care interventions and helps readers to assess the trustworthiness and applicability of an SLR. This technique intends to improve the technique *QUality Of Reporting Of Meta-analyses* (QUOROM) [34], which is argued to possess poor reporting quality guidelines and to focus on meta-analyses of randomized controlled trials. In contrast, PRISMA was introduced to encompass both SLRs and meta-analyses. The technique follows Population Intervention Control Group Outcome and Study Design (PICOS) and encompasses a 27-item checklist and a 4-phase flow diagram.

P3 – BPMN [35]**.** The *Business Process Modeling Notation* is one of the few techniques that aims to fully automate a part of an SLR. So, its main objective is to reduce the time needed to conduct an SLR, contributing to the productivity and quality of conducting such reviews. Modeling the workflow of an SLR with the BPMN consists of three phases that map to the stages of the SLR itself: planning, conducting, and reporting.

P4 – Kitchenham Quality Assessment Reporting [23]**.** This technique aims to address quality issues within published studies that followed the guideline by Kitchenham and Charters [25]. For this purpose, 68 publications between 2005 and 2012 were identified, pertaining to the field of software engineering. The proposed 12-item quality assessment checklist was based on the guideline used [25]. A weighted scoring mechanism was used to derive a final quality checklist, resulting in an updated version of the guidelines [27]. These guidelines represent a standard quality assessment technique in software engineering SLRs.

P5 – Eco Evidence [56]**.** *Eco Evidence* aims to aid SLRs related to environmental science. This technique provides a structured standard report to ensure transparency and reproducibility. It is ideal for evaluating cause-effect relationships across diverse study types and for synthesizing results from both observational and experimental research. Eco Evidence combines a structured causal criteria approach, a weighted scoring system for evidence quality, and a database to store the published studies. It has an analyzer desktop tool that synthesizes the studies to test cause-effect hypotheses.

P6 – Being Systematic in SLRs [5]**.** This is a set of guidelines that mainly addresses the cons of conducting SLRs. Since many other publications focus on and support mitigating cons in this context, we concentrate on the claims in these guidelines that connect to the quality of an SLR. Particularly, it claims that objectivity and replicability are the main properties for assessing the quality of an SLR, which must be justified based on the transparency of the process.

P7 – Mixed Filter [50]**.** The *Mixed Filter* is intended to work for mixed empirical studies with different designs. It was applied to six journals from three fields: primary care, medical informatics, and public health/epidemiology. These fields were picked because they require addressing complex research questions with various research methods and designs of empirical studies. The performance of the Mixed Filter was analyzed using descriptive statistics drawn from the measurement of overall precision, sensitivity, and specificity across the six journals, which were the total relevant records that were drawn.

P8 – AMSTAR-2 [49]**.** This is an updated version of AMSTAR that was developed in 2017, almost 10 years after the introduction of its predecessor. It aims to extend the scope of AMSTAR to non-randomized trials in the healthcare domain. AMSTAR-2 includes 16 critical items. The main differences of this extension are the orientation of the research questions along the PICOS framework and improvements regarding the clarity of inclusion and exclusion criteria.

P9 – DARE by CDR [21]**.** The *Database of Abstracts of Reviews of Effects by the Centre for Reviews and Dissemination* provides a checklist that aims to evaluate the quality of SLRs related to multiple domains such as Software Process Improvement. Within the checklist, the planning and conduct phases are only considered based on their reporting. Overall, the checklist is based on four main questions with scores to assess the credibility, reliability, and quality of an SLR. Unlike more detailed techniques, DARE is accessible, easy to apply, and focused on methodological transparency [1].

P10 – MMAT [18]**.** The *Mixed Methods Appraisal Tool* was developed to appraise SLRs related to mixed studies, qualitatively and quantitatively. This tool considers five core methodological quality assessment design criteria: 1) Qualitative, 2) Randomized controlled trial, 3) Non-randomized, 4) Quantitative descriptive, and 5) Mixed methods studies. It includes five criteria for each of the above-mentioned main criteria. These are rated as "yes," "no," or "can't tell". The checklist of this tool helps a user fix the judging criteria. A table is provided for each category of study design that presents a detailed definition, designs, approaches, and explanation of the specific criterion. MMAT was developed based on already existing techniques, which were simplified.

P11 & P14 – CASP (2018/2020) [2,30]**.** The *Critical Appraisal Skills Programme* tool has two versions developed in 2018 and 2020, respectively. It is designed to be used as an educational or research-related tool. The first version was released as a requirement for conducting workshops, but without a scoring system. Moreover, it was designed exclusively for randomized trials. A group of reviewers was assigned to develop and control the items in this checklist and to associate these with a workshop format. For each of the 10 checklist questions, a response is classified as "yes," "no," or "can't tell." The resulting list with 10 items was found to be meaningful in several contexts [2]. Still, the main focus of CASP is data synthesis concerning techniques proposed in previous research [53], which involves three stages: line-by-line coding, development of descriptive themes, and generation of analytical themes.

P12 – CATSER [4]**.** The *Critical Appraisal Tool for Software Engineering Systematic Reviews* is based on AMSTAR-2 and is still under testing. CASTER aims to raise awareness regarding the criticality of quality assessing SLRs in software engineering. This is a community-collaborated method towards the development of a tool, which led to the insight that existing tools for such quality assessments mainly expand upon tools used in the healthcare domain. However, CASTER also raises the point that almost no effort has been made to improve these tools to keep pace with advances in the healthcare industry either.

P13 – PRISMA (2020) [39]**.** Considering the advancements in science and technology, and consequently in SLR methodologies, an update within the PRISMA guidelines was deemed necessary. After reviewing the methods employed in 220 publications and conducting a survey among 21 member teams, the new PRISMA (2020) was proposed. So, the updated PRISMA extensively relies on community experiences and feedback from co-authors of over 15 SLRs. There are several enhancements in this version, such as an updated checklist, justification of any possible alternative data-synthesis methodologies used, citation of all excluded studies, or addressing the source of data, code, and other materials used in SLRs. Finally, a revision of the flow diagram template to adapt it to the updated guidelines has been proposed.

On RQ_1**.** We identified 11 different techniques that have been proposed for assessing the quality of SLRs in the last 15 years. Please note that AMSTAR, CASP, and PRISMA exist in two versions each. All of the techniques are tools, guidelines, checklists, or a mixture of these, and are often applicable to a variety of literature analyses. The techniques mostly cover the reporting of an SLRs, with a few considering the conduct and reporting for assessing the quality. Positively, most techniques are publicly available.

4.2 $\mathbf{RQ_2}$: Fields of Research

SLRs in different domains (i.e., broader research areas) have, logically, varying sets of process steps. We provide an overview of all domains in Table 1. To identify these domains, we elicited which ones or which fields are explicitly mentioned in the respective publications. In some cases, we could clearly derive this information from the publication's context. For instance, we assigned the specific field of software engineering for the guideline by Kitchenham and Charters [25], which is within the broader domain of computer science. The same applies to the other techniques, for example, we assigned AMSTAR [48] to the specific field of healthcare randomized trials within the broader medical domain.

Table 2. Summary of the pros and cons of the retrieved techniques.

Id	Name	Pros	Cons
P1	AMSTAR [48]	• Ensures strong content validity through expert input and existing validated tools.. • Exploratory factor analysis refines and strengthens the tool by identifying essential items [38]. This ensures the extendability to non-randomized trials (healthcare).	• Requires more studies to confirm reproducibility and construct validity. • Quantifying bias remains difficult due to variability across study types and domains.
P2	PRISMA [29]	• Promotes clarity, transparency, and structured reporting in SLRs. • Adaptable to randomized and non-randomized studies. • Clearly outlines review protocols, information sources, and search strategies to support reproducibility. • Provides detailed insights into bias risks and helps readers in replication and updates of reviews.	• Is not recommended as a quality assessment tool, because it does not elaborate on the methodologies used in the SLR process. • The checklist itself was not developed through an SLR. • Evidence exists for some of the checklist items. • Inconsistent study quality, with some trials lacking clear reporting, and Small trials may be overestimated.
P3	BPMN [35]	• Based on an enhanced version of concrete guidelines proposed by [25] that contribute to quality. • It is automated, so it helps in reducing the time required to perform an overall SLR process. • It serves as a base for the development of further computational tools in the future.	• Its documentation cannot be considered top-notch, since it does not provide much information about practical scenarios. • Uncertainty about how the tool can adjust to the complexity of the studies. • It does not discuss important criteria like risks of bias.
P4	Kitchenham QA reporting [23]	• Addresses many major problems concerning the SLR reporting process. • Gives improvement scope for the future of quality evaluation of software engineering studies based on empirical methods.	• Poor agreement on the study content quality as the scoring mechanism was found to be error-prone, which makes the validation process somewhat stringent. • The use of an extractor checker for data extraction from broad lessons and surveys increases the risk of missing important issues or misinterpretation of the same.
P5	Eco Evidence [56]	• Offers a causal criteria-based summary and detailed reporting and uses a weighted rating mechanism to assess study strength [36]. • Applicable to theoretical and practical research contexts. • Features a reusable evidence bank in an open-access database, reducing workload and simplifying evidence extraction.	• Restricted to environmental studies. • Manual evidence scoring can be time-intensive. • Requires domain expertise. • It contributes a minimum regarding a quality assessment that aids the reporting phase.
P6	Being Systematic in SLR [5]	• Discusses in detail the key attributes that should be considered to enhance the SLR process and proposes a change in existing guidelines. • Considers a very wide variety of study domains. • Analytical, and consideration of the impacts of bias.	• Covers the entire SLR process and does not focus on the reporting phase.
P7	Mixed Filter [50]	• Gives high performance even though it varies by journal. • The filter exhibits a high sensitivity factor, which means it could retrieve almost all relevant studies. • Shows a high specificity and precision of over 60 %.	• Tested across limited journals, and thus could result in varied results across other journals.
P8	AMSTAR-2 [49]	• Extends AMSTAR for non-randomized trials. • Provides improved bias assessment and highly justified study design criteria. • Enhances clarity through defined critical domains. • With cautious use, it can support teaching and act as a checklist for SLRs. • Enables deeper performance quality assessment to identify flaws in poorly conducted reviews.	• Lacks explanation of systematic review methods; relies on the Cochrane Handbook for full guidance [20]. • Improper handling of bias may lead to inaccurate impact estimation. • There is no proper specification of risk of bias tools for non-randomized trials, leaving it to reviewers' discretion.
P9	DARE by CDR [21]	• Helps to minimize bias and ensure maximization of the overall validity of the review. • Provides a needed breakthrough in assessing SLRs related to Software Process Improvement. • Functions based on concrete guidelines provided by DARE checklist [1]. • Provides a scope of improvements and the possibility of extending the tool over other domains as well.	• Since the literature is weak, the testing of the technique could also come with limitations. With growing literature, better testing could be carried out to improve the current version. • High risks of bias exist that researchers could frequently extract wrong data. • Risk of missing some related keywords in search strings or over-constraints in the same could result in loss of publications.
P10	MMAT [18]	• Serves as a concrete technique for Mixed Studies Reviews (MSR) as it provides methodological quality assessment criteria across various study designs. • It focuses on a limited number of core criteria, and it is very time-efficient.	• Focuses more on methodological quality rather than the reporting quality; thus, it is difficult to judge the criteria needed. • It is difficult to ensure the trustworthiness of methodological quality. • A revision of this technique is necessary to ensure content validity and reliability.
P11,14	CASP (2018), (2020) [2,30]	• A large community assigned for ongoing evaluation and refinement. • Both versions (original and updated) remain relevant and improved, with added questions and responses [30]. • Higher-quality studies contribute to the technique. • The possibility of misinterpretation of the "tick box" checklist was addressed.	• The inferences of the technique were drawn based on a single case study, wherein it was made to appraise studies on semi-structured interview methodologies. • When covering various study types, the technique would yield different results. • Even though it is advised to use CASP over mixed datasets, it is still believed to be less feasible.
P12	CATSER [4]	• Developed collaboratively to tailor AMSTAR-2 for software engineering SLRs, retaining its strengths and all the advantages. • Addresses bias risk of SLR, reporting quality, and assessment using the latest guidelines available.	• A prototype that is under construction, and thus requires testing, refinements, and validation. • If not properly planned, all the cons of AMSTAR-2 could apply, too.
P13	PRISMA (2020) [39]	• Properly documented updates and refinement through collective reviewer feedback. • Includes an expanded checklist to reflect advances in SLRs. • Clearly describe and justify alternative data synthesis methods, and cite excluded studies with reasons.	• Limitations in the ability to collect feedback to a small extent. • Reporting guidelines addressing the presentation and synthesis of qualitative data should also be consulted [54]. • Possible risks in bias assessment.

On RQ_2**.** We can see that most techniques (7) relate to the medical domain, specifically healthcare randomized trials. The remaining seven publications cover four different domains, namely computer science (3), mixed studies (1), environmental studies (1), and all domains (2). For example, DARE by CDR is used mainly in healthcare and public policy research, but is adaptable to other domains like software engineering, education, and social sciences. The medical domain is more advanced regarding the use of SLRs, and its community is more accustomed to utilizing respective quality assurance techniques.

4.3 RQ_3: Pros and Cons

To answer this research question, we examined each publication, paying close attention to the weak points of each technique as well as its advantages. We searched whether the researchers explicitly mentioned this information. As some techniques have been extended, updated, or published in different versions (e.g., PRISMA, CASP), we investigated the most recent version and list its pros and cons in Table 2. Our objective was to elicit the techniques used in prominent SLR quality assessment techniques, and, finally, to note their strengths and weaknesses. In Table 2, we summarize our findings.

On RQ_3**.** The updated versions of AMSTAR, PRISMA, Kitchenham Guidelines, and CASP outperform their former versions. Thus, we consider the older versions to be infeasible for contemporary SLRs. One common weakness of most techniques is bias detection and handling. As this is considered a complicated issue that involves multiple social aspects, numerous studies are devoted to investigating this direction as an important quality assurance aspect. Furthermore, comparing the techniques adopted in the medical domain, we can observe that the updated versions of AMSTAR and PRISMA support a wider variety of healthcare trials than CASP. In contrast, CASP is best for assessing individual studies, not reviews. AMSTAR, Kitchenham QA, and Eco Evidence focus on quality and evidence strength, while PRISMA and DARE focus on reporting and inclusion criteria. The most promising and reliable techniques appear to be the updated versions of AMSTAR and PRISMA. Both stand out due to their wider applicability and adaptability and have been improved to support a broader range of healthcare trials, making them versatile for medical research. Moving to computer science, a promising prototype, CATSER, adopted the advantages of the latest version of AMSTAR and utilized it to benefit software engineering in the same sense.

5 Discussion

In Table 2, we list the advantages and disadvantages of each technique. As we can see, the disadvantages differ widely between individual techniques. However, we can conclude that none of them is perfect and we would consider none optimal for all use cases. For example, in the software engineering domain, the first set of guidelines for SLRs was proposed by Kitchenham and Charters [25]. Even though several improvements were made to these guidelines, these still do not properly handle SLR appraisal. The most widely used DARE criteria assess the quality of SLRs based on a checklist that relies on the same subset of questions [21,52,59] identified by Kitchenham back in 2004 [24]. Unfortunately, these fail to consider whether a review is synthesized and lack appropriate search strategies. A fundamental challenge identified was the low quality of data extraction forms, review protocols, and classification schemes. These could impose ambiguity and duplicate attributes. We must separate the techniques based on their coverage of design, reporting, and evaluation [8,33]. This is essential considering the emphasis on different stages of an SLR. Our emphasis is on the reporting. Here, the updated versions of AMSTAR, PRISMA, Kitchenham Guidelines, and CASP outperform their former versions and the other techniques.

Conducting an SLR is considered to be a highly manual, error-prone, and labor-intensive process, including tasks like data collection, extraction, and synthesis. It usually involves human judgment and decision-making. However, leveraging technologies like machine learning or natural language processing can facilitate the process. Researchers have recently developed tools to automate or semi-automate the steps or phases of the SLR process using different techniques. Previous work indicates positive results and a reduction of the effort and time required to conduct an SLR [44,45,47]. For instance, [9] identified several studies focused on the automation and corresponding challenges and solutions available. Similarly, automation could play a vital role in assessing the quality of SLRs efficiently and promptly. Based on the suggestions and recommendations referred to in the studies we summarize in Table 1, automation seems to be a promising direction because many steps have the potential to be automated or semi-automated.

Besides improving efficiency, automation could also enhance the quality of an assessment process by considering, for example, biases, discussions, disagreement settlements, or the synthesis process. Particularly steps in the conduct phase of an SLR are promising to automate, for instance, the search string formation, search process, and data extraction. In the reporting phase, a few steps could be automated. Since we found that most assessment techniques have pros, a valuable solution would be to modularize individual assessments to achieve a "plug and play" technique. Based on the field of research and type of review, individual modules could be configured and integrated to define the reviewing process and its assessment. For research groups, one researcher should serve as the moderator who oversees the process and ensures that the individual process steps and assessments are performed. In this context, automation would facilitate the process, assessment, and trustworthiness of an SLR by ensuring that established sets and guidelines are implemented.

6 Conclusion

In this paper, we performed a comparative analysis of prominent techniques used for quality assessing SLRs. We performed an SLR to identify these techniques.

This resulted in 14 publications covering a period of 15 years (2007–2021). We identified the techniques proposed and investigated, discussed, and summarized their properties. Additionally, we could identify their strengths and weaknesses and learned that most SLRs use outdated guidelines, leading to credibility issues considering their quality, a matter that needs to be critically addressed. We conclude that the medical domain is more advanced in literature analysis mechanisms overall, and bias detection is a major quality limitation that is still not covered in most of the studied techniques. In future work, we plan to expand our analysis by conducting an extended SLR involving other data sources, allowing us to obtain more in-depth insights and improve the validity of our work. Moreover, we plan to advance the proposed techniques regarding automation and to evaluate their validity. For this purpose, we envision to collect insights and steer discussions by conducting a workshop that invites interested parties to analyze our insights and improve them.

References

1. Centre for reviews and dissemination, about dare (2015). NHS Centre for Reviews and Dissemination (2015)
2. Critical appraisal skills programme (CASP) (2018), checklist (2018). www.casp-uk.net
3. Alchokr, R., Borkar, M., Thotadarya, S., Saake, G., Leich, T.: Supporting systematic literature reviews using deep-learning-based language models. In: International Workshop on Natural Language-Based Software Engineering, pp. 67–74 (2023)
4. Ali, N., Usman, M.: A critical appraisal tool for systematic literature reviews in software engineering. Inf. Softw. Technol. **112** (2019)
5. Boell, S., Cecez-Kecmanovic, D.: On being 'systematic' in literature reviews in is. J. Inf. Technol. **30** (2015)
6. Bowes, D., Hall, T., Beecham, S.: SLuRp - a tool to help large complex systematic literature reviews deliver calid and rigorous results. In: International Workshop of Evidential Assessment Software Technology (EAST), pp. 33–36 (2012)
7. Budgen, D., Brereton, P., Drummond, S., Williams, N.: Reporting systematic reviews: some lessons from a tertiary study. Inf. Softw. Technol. **95**, 62–74 (2018)
8. Chandler, J., Churchill, R., Higgins, J., Lasserson, T., Tovey, D., et al.: Methodological expectations of cochrane intervention reviews. SL Cochrane Collab. **3**(2), 1–14 (2016)
9. van Dinter, R., Tekinerdogan, B., Catal, C.: Automation of systematic literature reviews: a systematic literature review. Inf. Softw. Technol. **136** (2021)
10. Dixon-Woods, M., Agarwal, S., Jones, D., Young, B., Sutton, A.: Synthesising qualitative and quantitative evidence: a review of possible methods. J. Health Serv. Res. Policy **10**(1), 45–53 (2005)
11. Donnelly, C.A., et al.: Four principles to make evidence synthesis more useful for policy. Nature **558**, 361–364 (2018)
12. Durand, G.C., et al.: Exploring large scholarly networks with hermes. Extending Database Technology (2018)
13. Fabbri, S., Silva, C., Hernandes, E., Octaviano, F., Di Thommazo, A., Belgamo, A.: Improvements in the start tool to better support the systematic review process. In: International Conference on Evaluation and Assessment in Software Engineering (EASE), pp. 1–5 (2016)

14. Felizardo, K.R., Carver, J.C.: Automating systematic literature review. In: Contemporary Empirical Methods in Software Engineering, pp. 327–355 (2020)
15. Fernández-Sáez, A.M., Bocco, M.G., Romero, F.P.: SLR-tool a tool for performing systematic literature reviews. In: ICSOFT, pp. 157–166 (2010)
16. Hernandes, E., Zamboni, A., Fabbri, S., Di Thommazo, A.: Using GQM and TAM to evaluate StArt – a tool that supports systematic review. CLEI Electron. J. **15**(1) (2012)
17. Hoffmann, F., et al.: Nearly 80 systematic reviews were published each day: observational study on trends in epidemiology and reporting over the years 2000-2019. J. Clin. Epidemiol. **138** (2021)
18. Hong, Q.N., et al.: The mixed methods appraisal tool (MMAT) version 2018 for information professionals and researchers. Educ. Inf. **34**, 1–7 (2018)
19. Jonnalagadda, S.R., Goyal, P., Huffman, M.D.: Automating data extraction in systematic reviews: a systematic review. Syst. Rev. **4**(1), 1–16 (2015)
20. JPT, H., et al.: Cochrane handbook for systematic reviews of interventions version 6.5. John Wiley Sons (2024)
21. Khan, A.A., Keung, J., Niazi, M., Hussain, S., Zhang, H.: Systematic literature reviews of software process improvement: a tertiary study. In: Systems, Software and Services Process Improvement, pp. 177–190 (2017)
22. Kitchenham, B.: Procedures for performing systematic reviews. Keele UK Keele Univ. **33** (2004)
23. Kitchenham, B., Brereton, P.: A systematic review of systematic review process research in software engineering. Inf. Softw. Technol. **55**, 2049–2075 (2013)
24. Kitchenham, B., et al.: Systematic literature reviews in software engineering - a tertiary study. Inf. Softw. Technol. **52**(8), 792–805 (2010)
25. Kitchenham, B.A., Charters, S.: Guidelines for performing systematic literature reviews in software engineering. Technical report, Keele University and University of Durham (2007)
26. Kitchenham, B.A., Dyba, T., Jorgensen, M.: Evidence-based software engineering. In: International Conference on Software Engineering (ICSE), pp. 273–281 (2004)
27. Kitchenham, B.A., Budgen, D., Brereton, P.: Evidence-based software engineering and systematic reviews, vol. 4 (2015)
28. Krüger, J., Lausberger, C., von Nostitz-Wallwitz, I., Saake, G., Leich, T.: Search. review. repeat? an empirical study of threats to replicating SLR searches. Empirical Softw. Eng. **25**(1) (2020)
29. Liberati, A., et al.: The PRISMA statement for reporting systematic reviews and meta-analyses of studies that evaluate health care interventions: explanation and elaboration. J. Clin. Epidemiol. **62**(10), 1–34 (2009)
30. Long, H.A., French, D.P., Brooks, J.M.: Optimising the value of the critical appraisal skills programme (CASP) tool for quality appraisal in qualitative evidence synthesis. Res. Methods Med. Health Sci. **1**(1), 31–42 (2020)
31. Malheiros, V., Höhnr, E., Pinho, R., Mendonca, M., Maldonado, J.C.: A visual text mining approach for systematic reviews. In: International Symposium on Empirical Software Engineering and Measurement (ESEM), pp. 245–254 (2007)
32. Marshall, C., Brereton, P.: Tools to support systematic literature reviews in software engineering: a mapping study. In: International Conference on Evaluation and Assessment in Software Engineering (EASE) (2013)
33. Moher, D., Liberati, A., Tetzlaff, J., Altman, D.: Preferred reporting items for systematic reviews and meta-analyses: the PRISMA statement. PLoS Med. **8**, 336–341 (2009)

34. Moher, D., Cook, D., Eastwood, S., Olkin, I., Rennie, D., Stroup, D.: Improving the quality of reports of meta-analyses of randomised controlled trials: the quorom statement. Lancet **354**, 1896–900 (1999)
35. Molleri, J., Silva, L., Benitti, F.: Proposal of an automated approach to support the systematic review of literature process. In: International Conference on Software Engineering & Knowledge Engineering (SEKE), pp. 488–493 (2013)
36. Norris, R., Webb, J., Nichols, S., Stewardson, M., Harrison, E.: Analyzing cause and effect in environmental assessments: using weighted evidence from the literature. Freshw. Sci. **31**, 5–21 (2012)
37. Okoli, C., Schabram, K.: A guide to conducting a systematic literature review of information systems research. SSRN (2010)
38. Osborne, J.: What is rotating in exploratory factor analysis? Assessment **20**, 1–8 (2015)
39. Page, M.J., et al.: Updating guidance for reporting systematic reviews: development of the PRISMA 2020 statement. J. Clin. Epidemiol. **134**, 103–112 (2021)
40. Paré, G., Trudel, M.C., Jaana, M., Kitsiou, S.: Synthesizing information systems knowledge: a typology of literature reviews. Inf. Manag. **52**(2), 183–199 (2015)
41. Pejić-Bach, M., Cerpa, N.: Editorial: planning, conducting and communicating systematic literature reviews. J. Theor. Appl. Electron. Commer. Res. **14**(3), 190–192 (2019)
42. Ponsard, A., Escalona, F., Munzner, T.: Paperquest: a visualization tool to support literature review. In: Proceedings of the Conference Extended Abstracts on Human Factors in Computing Systems CHI, pp. 2264–2271 (2016)
43. Ralph, P., Baltes, S.: Paving the way for mature secondary research: the seven types of literature review. In: Proceedings of the Joint European Software Engineering Conference and Symposium on the Foundations of Software Engineering FSE, pp. 1632–1636 (2022)
44. Shakeel, Y., Alchokr, R., Krüger, J., Leich, T., Saake, G.: Incorporating altmetrics to support selection and assessment of publications during literature analyses. In: International Conference on Valuation and Assessment in Software Engineering (EASE), pp. 180–189 (2022)
45. Shakeel, Y., Krüger, J., Nostitz-Wallwitz, I.V., Saake, G., Leich, T.: Automated selection and quality assessment of primary studies: a systematic literature review. J. Data Inf. Qual. **12**(1) (2019)
46. Shakeel, Y., Krüger, J., Saake, G., Leich, T.: Indicating studies' quality based on open data in digital libraries. In: Business Information Systems Workshops, pp. 579–590 (2019)
47. Shakeel, Y., et al.: Automated literature analysis - threats and experiences. In: International Workshop on Software Engineering for Science (SE4Science), pp. 20–27 (2018)
48. Shea, B., et al.: Development of AMSTAR: a measurement tool to assess the methodological quality of systematic reviews. BMC Med. Res. Methodol. **7**(10), 1471–2288 (2007)
49. Shea, B.J., et al.: AMSTAR 2: a critical appraisal tool for systematic reviews that include randomised or non-randomised studies of healthcare interventions, or both. BMJ **358** (2017)
50. Sherif, R., Pluye, P., Gore, G., Granikov, V., Hong, Q.N.: Performance of a mixed filter to identify relevant studies for mixed studies reviews. J. Med. Libr. Assoc. **104**, 47–51 (2016)
51. Shreffler, J., Huecker, M.R.: Common pitfalls in the research process. Treasure Island (FL): StatPearls (1) (2022)

52. Silva, F., Santos, A., Soares, S., França, C., Monteiro, C., Maciel, F.: Six years of systematic literature reviews in software engineering: an updated tertiary study. Inf. Softw. Technol. **53**, 899–913 (2011)
53. Thomas, J., Harden, A.: Methods for the thematic synthesis of qualitative research in systematic reviews. BMC Med. Res. Methodol. **8**, 45 (2008)
54. Tong, A., Flemming, K., McInnes, E., Oliver, S., Craig, J.: Enhancing transparency in reporting the synthesis of qualitative research: Entreq. BMC Med. Res. Methodol. **12**(1), 1–8 (2012)
55. Tsafnat, G., Glasziou, P., Choong, M.K., Dunn, A., Galgani, F., Coiera, E.: Systematic review automation technologies. Syst. Rev. **3**, 1–15 (2014)
56. Webb, J., Miller, K., Stewardson, M., de Little, S., Nichols, S., Wealands, S.: An online database and desktop assessment software to simplify systematic reviews in environmental science. Environ. Model. Softw. **64**, 72–79 (2014)
57. Webster, J., Watson, R.T.: Analyzing the past to prepare for the future: writing a literature review. MIS Q. **26**(2) (2002)
58. Wohlin, C.: Guidelines for snowballing in systematic literature studies and a replication in software engineering. In: International Conference on Evaluation and Assessment in Software Engineering EASE, pp. 1–10 (2014)
59. Wohlin, C., Runeson, P., Hst, M., Ohlsson, M.C., Regnell, B., Wessln, A.: Experimentation in Software Engineering. Springer (2012)
60. Zhang, H., Babar, M.A.: Systematic reviews in software engineering: an empirical investigation. Inf. Softw. Technol. **55**(7), 1341–1354 (2013)

Knowledge Graphs

An End-to-End Pipeline for Knowledge Graph Population from 19th-Century Land Registry Digitised Tables

Solenn Tual[1(✉)], Nathalie Abadie[1], Joseph Chazalon[2], Bertrand Duménieu[3], and Julien Perret[2]

[1] LASTIG, Univ. Gustave Eiffel, IGN-ENSG, Champs-sur-Marne, France
{solenn.tual,nathalie-f.abadie}@ign.fr

[2] EPITA Research Laboratory (LRE), Le Kremlin-Bicêtre, France
joseph.chazalon@epita.fr, julien.perret@ign.fr

[3] CRH-EHESS, Paris, France
bertrand.dumenieu@ehess.fr

Abstract. Historical tables, such as administrative registers, represent vast and valuable sources of information for researchers. However, despite large-scale digitization efforts, extracting and structuring their content remains challenging. The French 19th-century Land Registry is a notable example: rich in detailed land use information, yet highly heterogeneous, and still largely underexploited. Although recent deep learning methods have improved information extraction (IE) from digitised documents, they often lack semantic structuring. Conversely, Semantic Table Interpretation (STI) techniques, mostly applied to natively digital tables, offer structuring and linking capabilities but are rarely used on historical sources. In this work, we propose a pipeline that combines deep learning-based IE with STI, guided by a domain ontology. The approach produces a knowledge graph that enables querying and exploration of historical records. We evaluate the resulting knowledge graph using several metrics, demonstrating the potential of our method for semantic enrichment of historical data.

Keywords: Information Extraction · Semantic Interpretation of Tables · Knowledge Graph · Historical Document Analysis

1 Introduction

Archives are filled with documents containing tables, such as administrative registers. These constitute vast corpora of semi-structured information of great interest to researchers in various fields such as history or geography. Although historical tables are increasingly being digitised on a large scale by GLAMs[1], information retrieval from them remains complex and requires handcrafted work.

[1] Galleries, Libraries, Archives, Museums.

W.-T. Balke et al. (Eds.): TPDL 2025, LNCS 16097, pp. 415–432, 2026.
https://doi.org/10.1007/978-3-032-05409-8_24

The French 19th-century Land Registry (also called the *Napoleonic Land Registry*) is a characteristic example of such historical archival corpora that would greatly benefit from large-scale extraction and dissemination. Established in the early 19th-century, it contains detailed information about land use and land cover changes at the plot scale across the entire country. Although the initial plot geometries are depicted on maps, detailed historical knowledge, including landmark's evolution, is described in registers whose structure and content vary between departments[2] and over time. It was used until the middle of the 20th-century (from 1930 to 1980 depending on the municipality). Some exploitation of these registers has been performed, but the spatial and temporal depth of these studies is often limited and always has required costly manual work [14,18,23].

Recent advances in deep learning have opened new possibilities for information extraction (IE) from such digitised historical sources [2,6], including text recognition and layout analysis. However, most processing pipelines rarely perform finer structuring steps or linking between automatically extracted entities. On the other hand, semantic table interpretation (STI) is a field of the Semantic Web mainly applied to annotate natively digital format tables (e.g., HTML, CSV) using generic knowledge graphs (e.g., Wikidata, DBpedia). It helps in structuring data and establishing meaningful links between different table values. STI is rarely applied to domain-specific tables [19] and even less so to historical tables. However, existing works [22] show that populating knowledge graphs using automatically extracted content from historical documents is possible and opens up new possibilities for research on them. Thus, by combining deep learning techniques with semantic technologies, it becomes possible to generate RDF resources, enabling the structuring, enrichment, and querying of the extracted information from historical tables such as the Napoleonic Land Registry.

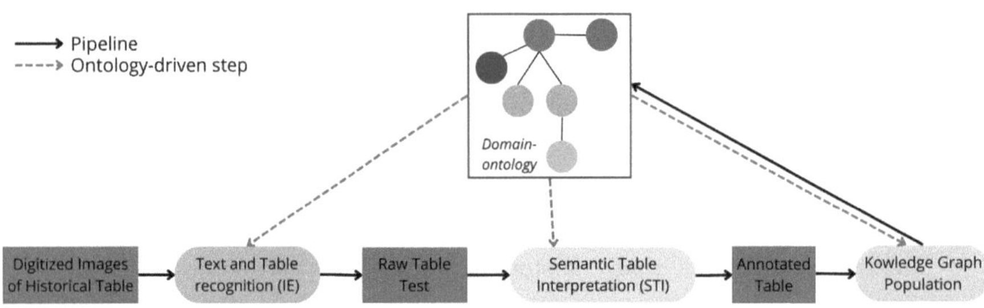

Fig. 1. Our end-to-end processing pipeline for knowledge graph population from digitised historical tables. The domain ontology guides information extractions steps, and is finally enriched by the KG population step.

After presenting the land registry tables (Sect. 2), we survey existing work on information extraction from historical tables, semantic table interpretation, and automated knowledge graph population from historical documents (Sect. 3).

[2] In France, the departments are the administrative units just above the municipalities.

Then, we present the complete processing pipeline (Sect. 4) whose goal is to populate a knowledge graph using tables from the 19th-century French Land Registry (as described in Fig. 1), including image annotation and semantic table interpretation methods that handle noisy text. Both steps are driven by a domain ontology dedicated to the description of landmarks and addresses evolution at the attribute scale. Finally, we present the implementation details of the pipeline applied to the Val-de-Marne land registry as well as the graph evaluation (Sect. 5).

Code, datasets and extra material are available at the following URL: https://github.com/solenn-tl/land_registry_tables_processing_TPDL_2025.

2 The 19th-Century French Land Registry: Description and Critical Analysis

The French land registry, known as the *Napoleonic Land Registry*, was established in 1809 under the First Empire to improve land tax assessment and distribution. By 1850, most French municipalities had such a registry, composed of maps and registers.

There are two map types: a municipal map (scale 1:10,000) showing section boundaries (identified by letters), and index maps (scale 1:1,000âĂŞ1:5,000) detailing plots within each section, each plot assigned a unique number. These maps were static and not updated, new plots from divisions or mergers retained existing numbers in registers, even if they no longer represented the same entity.

Two types of registers complement the maps. The initial register (*états de sections*) describes each plot at the time of mapping, grouped by section (as chapters), with a table listing the plots in ascending order. The mutation register (*matrice cadastrale*) tracks plot changes over time, grouping them by taxpayer. Each change generates a new row, with old ones crossed out. Changes in taxpayer property accounts can be traced using account numbers.

Produced and managed by departments, 19th-century land registry documents are now held by Departmental and sometimes Municipal Archives. These records form a large-scale source for studying land use, building history, and ownership evolution. Despite digitization, information retrieval is complex, involving manual navigation across document types, and large-scale extraction remains challenging [14,18,23]. A crowd-sourced transcription project has been initiated[3]. Existing automated approaches focus mainly on map vectorization [13,25], with no known work on automated knowledge extraction from the registers.

This work focuses on land registry documents digitized by the Val-de-Marne Departmental Archives[4], which covers 47 municipalities. The corpus originates from the former Seine and Seine-et-Oise departments, split and reorganized in 1968. In May 2025, 820 map images, 24,012 initial register images, and 158,677 mutation register images were digitized. This article focuses on initial registers,

[3] https://archives.vendee.fr/participer/reconstituez-les-paysages.
[4] https://archives.valdemarne.fr.

though the proposed method is designed to be generalized to mutation registers and other departments.

Initial registers describe municipal plots at a single point in time. Their structure, pre-printed by the department and manually filled, is divided into chapters by section. Tables often repeat information (e.g., taxpayers, addresses, land type), and resemble relational tables but include many manual exceptions (merged cells, brace-distributed values). Repeated data are sometimes replaced with variants of *idem* (e.g., "id", or column-wide vertical marks).

The Val-de-Marne digitized registers exhibit variations in pre-printed table formats—column order, titles, presence, and content (e.g., taxpayer details) differ between municipalities (see Fig. 2). The proposed pipeline aims to robustly extract and structure data across such layout differences.

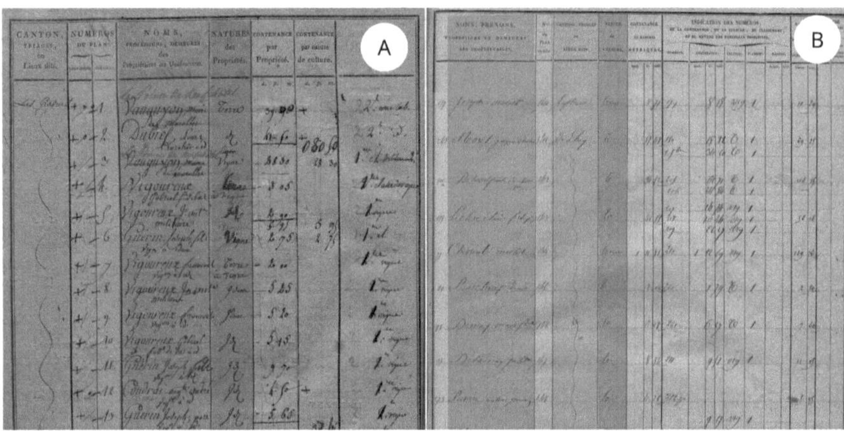

Fig. 2. Two different pre-printed tables extracted from the initial registers of Val-de-Marne Archives. (A) Municipality of Marolles-en-Brie (1810) and (B) Municipality of L'Hay (1842). Columns are colored by type of information: plot address (blue), plot number (green), taxpayer (red), nature (purple), taxpayer index number (yellow) which was added by writers in B but is absent in A. (Color figure online)

3 Related Works

In this section, we review three areas that are complementary to the goal of building a knowledge graph from historical tables: information extraction from historical tables, semantic table interpretation using knowledge graphs, and approaches to populating knowledge graphs from historical documents.

3.1 Information Extraction Applied to Historical Tables

Information extraction from digitised documents aims to locate, transcribe, and organise the text they contain into a structured computer-readable representation. There are two main types of information extraction system. Traditional approaches consist of a sequence of independent models chained together, and *end-to-end* approaches where the same model performs several steps at once. This field is making significant progress thanks to advances in deep learning. For these two types of approach, the regions containing the tables are generally isolated beforehand using a page classification or region detection system and might include a step of image preprocessing (segmentation of double-pages into pages, straightening).

Constum et al. [5] detect the table on the page, segment the rows and transcribe them using a HTR model [7]. A special character is used to implicitly materialise the separation of the row into cells. The nature of each cell is then deduced from its position in the row. This is possible because the order of the columns is known *a priori* by the authors and the structure of all the registers considered does not vary. *Petit-Pierre et al.* [24] propose to detect the columns and segments of text on the page and then group these segments into rows *a posteriori.* The text is transcribed using the HTR engine proposed by *Puigcerver* [26]. *Granell et al.* [15] deal with weather records recorded in navigation logs. The row segmentation task is performed by a pixel classification model [27]. Text transcription is performed at the row level using a *Convolutional Recurrent Neural Networks* (CRNN) model.

The main drawback of approaches involving prior segmentation of documents is that errors in dividing pages images into rows or columns are propagated to subsequent stages. Furthermore, once the segmentation has been carried out, the models can only rely on a reduced visual and textual context. Evaluation datasets must be produced for each stage (zone detection, text recognition).

Boilet et al. [2] propose a large-scale pipeline to process the 19th-century census registers of various French departments. The content of each page is transcribed in a structured way using the Document Attention Network (DAN) model [8], a convolutional encoder followed by a Transformer [32] decoder. This approach enables information of the same type to be retrieved without segmenting the image or materialising the exact position of rows and columns. The annotations are based on a 'key-value' model: for each area (row), the list of information to be extracted (corresponding to columns or named entities) is defined.

In parallel with approaches specialising in a particular type of document, some approaches such as DONUT [17] have aimed to offer models trained in a large number of tasks in order to be able to adapt quickly to new problems or document types. These approaches have been improved with the use of large language models (LLM) in the construction of vision-language models (VLLM), which then have superior reasoning capabilities, but so far show limited performance in the analysis of modern tables, as noted by *Scius-Bertrand et al.* [29].

3.2 Semantic Interpretation of Tables

Semantic Table Interpretation (STI) involves annotating table elements (rows, columns, cells, or entire tables) and their relationships using a knowledge graph (KG) to enhance semantic understanding. Applications include information retrieval, question answering, data enrichment, and KG population. Interest in STI has grown, especially through the SemTab competition[5], which introduced standardized tasks and evaluation protocols.

Research mainly targets CSV or HTML tables—native numerical formats—as reviewed by *Liu et al.* [19] and *Cremashi et al.* [9]. The former offers a taxonomy and benchmarks up to 2021; the latter extends them through 2024, incorporating LLM-based methods and refining STI subtasks. The main tasks include:

- **Column Type Annotation (CTA)**: assigns types (entity classes or datatypes) to columns [9].
- **Column Property Annotation (CPA)**: links column pairs through KG properties.
- **Cell Entity Annotation (CEA)**: maps the cell content to the KG entities.
- **Cell-New Entity Annotation (CNEA)**: detects mentions of entities absent from the KG [21].
- **Thematization**: associates the entire table with a KG concept.
- **Row-to-Instance Annotation**: assigns a KG entity to each row as its subject.

CEA resembles Entity Linking in NLP, while CTA and CPA align table structure with ontologies [9]. Typical pipelines include: data preparation (formatting, cleaning, normalization) [4,11], column classification [34], annotation of literal columns, subject column detection [3], and entity resolution (CEA and CNEA) using mention detection, candidate retrieval, and disambiguation (often with NER). Then, the entity types and intercolumn relations are predicted.

Approaches vary from heuristics (e.g. similarity measures, TF-IDF, voting), to feature engineering (traditional ML using lexical/statistical features), and deep learning (embedding-based models of table elements and KG entities).

Most of the STI works focus on simple relational tables. Complex formats, especially historical tables with nested or composite subjects, remain underexplored. General KGs such as Wikidata [33], DBpedia [20], and YAGO [30] are often used but lack coverage for domain-specific or historical data. Challenges include KG incompleteness, detection of NIL entities [9], and effective use of table metadata and context [19].

3.3 Knowledge Graph Population Using Data Extracted from Historical Documents

Currently, no studies jointly perform information extraction (IE) and semantic interpretation of historical tables. However, various approaches have been developed to extract information from historical documents and populate knowledge graphs (KGs) based on domain-specific ontologies. These methods target diverse sources, including trade directories [31], newspapers, scientific publications [22], notarial registers [12], and heterogeneous thematic corpora [10,16]. Few approaches offer a full pipeline from images to the KG population [31],

[5] https://www.cs.ox.ac.uk/isg/challenges/sem-tab/.

including segmentation and OCR transcription. Most focus on later stages — extracting structured knowledge from pretranscribed texts [10,16,22], whether transcribed manually or automatically. These methods apply a variety of NLP techniques such as keyphrase identification, Named Entity Recognition (NER) [22,31], Relation Extraction (RE), Entity Linking (EL), and coreference resolution to build triplets. For NER, both fine-tuned [22,31] and off-the-shelf models [10,16] are used to detect entity mentions in full texts or key sentences [22]. Dependency parsing helps identify relations between entities or attributes [22]. Often, entities and relations are aligned with domain ontologies [10,22,31]. In contrast, Open Information Extraction (OIE) approaches discover them without predefined schemas [16]. The knowledge extracted serves to initialize or enrich KGs. Generalist KGs (e.g., Wikidata, DBPedia) can complement domain-specific data but lack granularity. While Large Language Models (LLM) show promise for entity and relation extraction, their tendency to hallucinate can reduce output quality [10]. Fine-tuning pre-trained language models on domain-annotated corpora offers the best trade-off between accuracy and reliability.

4 End-to-End Pipeline for Historical Ontology Population

In this section, we present the pipeline developed to generate a knowledge graph from the 19th-century French Land Registry's initial registers. At the core of this pipeline is the PeGaZus ontology [1], designed to describe geographical features—represented as the `Landmark` class in the ontology—and their evolution over time at the attribute level. It defines concepts and properties related to land plots. The ontology is coupled with a geohistorical knowledge graph population algorithm that handles heterogeneous and fragmentary references to landmarks from diverse sources. The concepts of the PeGaZus ontology are applied throughout the pipeline, from image annotation to knowledge graph population.

4.1 Pre-processings

Registers Collection. The first step is to collect digitised documents from the target corpora along with their metadata. These metadata provide the context for the documents to be processed. They usually come from the inventory sheet. If these sheets are not structured (or not all in the same way), they need to be restructured to make them usable automatically [2]. It serves as a valuable source of knowledge for thematising the tables. For example, in the case of the land registry, we want to know the name of the municipality associated with each register, its type, its date of creation, and its period of validity. These metadata are leveraged in the step described in Sect. 4.3.

Images Classification. Once the digitised registers have been collected, an automated classification step is required to identify the images that contain the information to be extracted. In the case of the initial registers, we are targeting, on the one hand, the tables describing the plots and, on the other hand, the cover pages describing the sections containing the plots listed on the pages which follow. We consider five classes: cover pages, main tables, second page of main tables, intermediate summaries, and syntheses.

4.2 Information Extraction from Digitised Tables

Table and text structure recognition, performed using *end-to-end* approaches based on Transformer architectures such as DAN [8], enables the extraction of content from each page without prior image segmentation or text localization. We chose to fine-tune such type of model for several reasons: (1) page-level extraction prevents error propagation between chained information extraction (IE) tasks; (2) the model leverages the full-page context to transcribe each line, which is particularly useful for handling merged cells; and (3) it significantly reduces the time needed to produce training datasets, as no intermediate annotations (such as drawing boxes around words or rows) are required. Annotations are stored in structured text files (JSON).

Moreover, full-page recognition is highly compatible with the semantic table interpretation process, as annotated images can be treated as raw text-based numerical tables. Consequently, we propose an image annotation model guided by the concepts of the PeGaZus ontology. The columns to be extracted correspond to ontology concepts, allowing us to manually address some semantic table interpretation (STI) tasks early in the pipeline: Column-Type Annotation (CTA) and Column-Property Annotation (CPA). The type of entity associated to each row is also known (`Landmark` of type `Plot`). In the case of the initial registers, we extract columns containing plot addresses (`Landmark` as street or locality names), plot numbers, plot nature (`Nature` as house, mill, wine, garden, etc.), taxpayer information (`Taxpayer`), and, when available, the taxpayer index number from the taxpayers' summary (found either in the initial register or in the mutation register). The attention mechanism in architectures such as DAN enables the handling of variations in column labels, order, and presence across different versions of the initial registers, depending on the pre-printed table used. Finally, a post-processing step is required to replace the various forms of *idem* with the values they refer to.

4.3 Semantic Table Interpretation and KG Population

This step aims to enrich the raw transcription produced in the previous step. As Column-Type annotation (CTA) and Column-Property annotation (CPA) tasks of STI have already been solved previously, we focus on the table Context Retrieval and the Cell-Entity Annotation task (CEA) including to new entities discovery.

Context Retrieval. The initial land registry records are organized into chapters, each corresponding to a municipality section identified by a letter (A, B, etc.). To later link plots with other related landmarks (section, municipality etc.) and create plot identifiers, we have to retrieve the context of each extracted row (*which chapter of which register ?*). We therefore need to retrieve the identifier of the last previous page cover before the considered digitised image and the section letter written in it. The pages have been classified as described in Sect. 4.1. Information written on non-table pages are stored in the metadata.

CEA and CNEA. This task aims to link the raw text produced by the IE step to the KG existing resources or to create new entities and add them to the KG. These new entities can be used to annotate the table.

Case 1: Entity Linking with Existing Resources. For column types that already have entities in the ontology (e.g. the plot nature), we perform an entity linking (EL) process described in Fig. 3. In the case of the plot nature, 160 candidate SKOS concepts have been defined in the ontology, based on the most common natures observed in the old registers and from a list of natures in the current French land registry. They are represented as instances of the class `Nature`. They can have several alternative labels (including abbreviations) in the registers. The entity linking algorithm is as follows: first, the full cell text is compared with the candidate labels using a similarity measure. The mention is matched to the top 1 candidate. If there is no match and the mention consists in several words (potential enumeration), the similarity measure between the candidate labels and each word is computed. If there is still no match, the cell is associated with the NIL concept and should be handled by an expert. The Gestalt pattern matching approach [28] is used to compute a similarity measure between entities labels and mentions. We choose this measure because it is not too sensitive to noisy text. It could be replaced by others character string or text embeddings similarity measures.

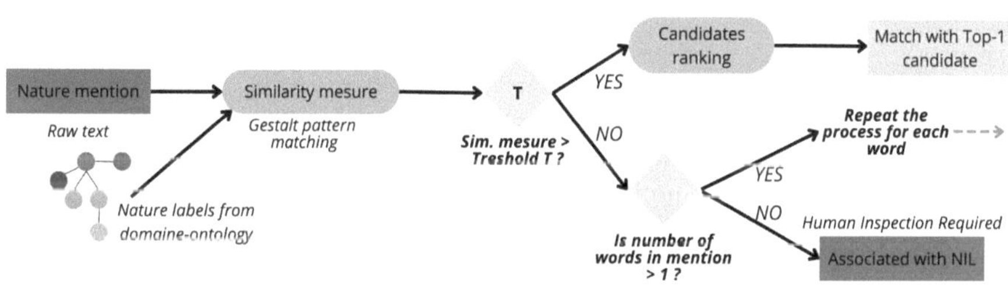

Fig. 3. Entity linking algorithm used to link instances of `Nature` with mentions of natures. The two steps help to deal with cells containing both single and enumarated nature mentions.

Case 2: New Entity Creation. For column types that do not already have associated entities in the ontology (e.g., taxpayers, plot addresses), new entities must be created and each cell must be linked to the corresponding resource. The specific algorithm used depends on the type of entities being created, with a focus on grouping similar mentions.

For plot addresses, we perform mention comparisons using a character string similarity measure (Normalized Levenshtein distance). Mentions that are similar within a specified threshold are grouped together, and an instance of `Landmark` is created for each group.

For taxpayers, the algorithm is more sophisticated (see Fig. 4). A fine-tuned named entity recognition (NER) model is employed to categorize the cell values into the following classes: name, firstnames, familystatus, title, activity, and address. Mentions with similar "name" values within a threshold T1 are grouped. Then, mentions within each group are further clustered according to similar "firstnames" using threshold T2. The groups are refined if there are more than two dissimilar "familystatus" values within a group, using threshold T3. Missing values for "firstnames" and "familystatus" are treated as empty strings. Finally, a post-processing step is applied to refine the groups. First, words of firstnames are compared word by word to ensure that they meet the similarity threshold before merging. Mentions are merged regardless of first name similarity if their index numbers match. When first names are similar, but index numbers differ, merging occurs only if the first names are highly similar. Once these steps are completed, an instance of `Taxpayer` is created for each group.

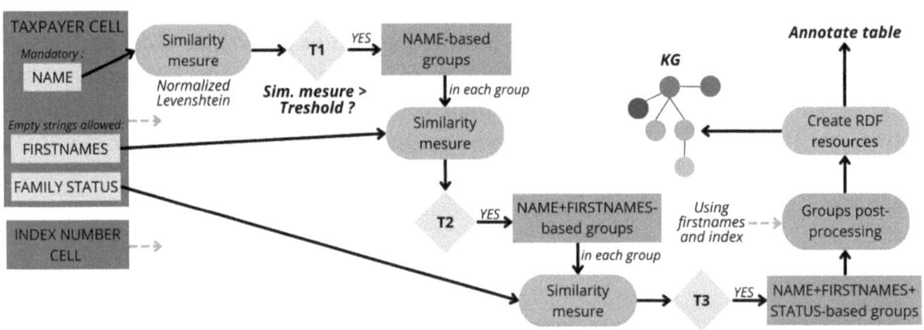

Fig. 4. Algorithm used to create instances of `Taxpayer` class. Each step aims to precise groups of mentions based on properties comparison.

Row-to-Instance Annotation. This last task aims to create an entity corresponding to a row. By definition, a row in an initial register describes an instance of `Landmark` of type `Plot`. The entity is created and associated with its identifier, whose value is equal to the concatenation of the section identifier and the plot number.

4.4 Knowledge Graph Population

Once the entities associated with each row have been identified, we can populate the knowledge graph according to the domain-ontology data scheme. This includes creating the relations between each plot and its attributes (e.g. the row and its entities). To keep track of the source of information used to create each KG instance, we also create instances describing rows, pages, and registers represented according to the RICO ontology. Then, we link them to the instance created from these pieces of documents. In further work, automatic processing of the mutation registers with this pipeline, in addition to the initial registers, would make us able to build a multidate knowledge graph using the PeGaZus algorithm by retrieving all the mentions of the same plot in the whole land registry corpus of a given area.

5 Implementation and Evaluation

In this section, we present the pipeline implementation to process the corpus of the initial registers of the land registry of the Val-de-Marne department. We also describe the datasets produced to train and evaluate the deep learning models and the gold standard graph used to evaluate the final output. The graph evaluation metrics are detailed, and the results are provided.

The following metrics are used to assess the various tasks in the pipeline and the end results. Their value is expressed as a percentage.

$$\text{Character Error Rate (CER)} = \frac{S + D + I}{N}$$

S, D and I are the number of substitutions, deletions, and insertions. $N$is the total number of characters in the reference.

$$\text{Precision} = \frac{|P \cap G|}{|P|} \quad \text{Recall (Agreement)} = \frac{|P \cap G|}{|G|} \quad \text{F1} = 2 \cdot \frac{precison \cdot recall}{(presion + recall)}$$

$$\text{False Discovery Rate (Surplus)} = \frac{|P \setminus G|}{|P|} \quad \text{False Negative Rate (Deficit)} = \frac{|G \setminus P|}{|G|}$$

P is the set of automatically predicted elements and G the set of elements in the gold standard. In the following evaluation, elements can be table rows and cells (information extraction) as well as instances, relations between instances, and datatype properties associated to each instance of the graphs.

5.1 Pre-processing

To ensure that all processed pages are simple pages, images with a width greater than their height are split into two parts. The page classification step is performed using a fine-tuned YOLOv11-CLS model[6], trained on the dataset

[6] https://docs.ultralytics.com/fr/tasks/classify/.

described in Table 1a. The images in the dataset are stratified by type and grouped by municipality. Training was carried out on a single NVIDIA A40 GPU with early stopping (detailed parameters in Table 1b). The best model was obtained at epoch 54. The accuracy reaches 100% on the validation set and 99.3% on the test set, with the remaining errors due to a single confusion between an intermediate summary page and the main table page.

Table 1. Page classification dataset and parameters

(a) Page classification subsets composition

	Train	**Val**	**Test**
Main table	413	57	86
Intermediate summary	198	38	30
2nd page of main table	89	22	27
Summary	30	3	4
Cover page	15	3	1

(b) YOLOv11 training parameters

Model	YOLOv11-CLS M
Epochs	200
Batch size	6
Seed	42

5.2 Information Extraction from Digitised Tables

To perform the text and table recognition step, we fine-tune the DAN model[7] (Document Attention Network) [8] following the strategy used on the census registers [2]. A dataset of 139 pages (2,650 rows) was created to train and evaluate the model. To select the pages, a stratified sampling was performed based on the three main types of pre-printed tables. Then, pages from each municipality are assigned to a subset. There are 97 pages in the training set, 22 in the validation set, and 28 in the test set. Special tokens are used to identify cells for each column. Additional tokens (see Fig. 5) are inserted into the text to capture text typography (crossed out, exponent) and layout characteristics (line breaks, *dito* marks, merged cells). These additions may provide a better understanding of the documents.

The model was fine-tuned over 2,000 epochs with a learning rate of 0.0001, optimized using AMSGrad, and a batch size of 2. Training was performed with two NVIDIA A40 GPUs. The results are encouraging, but largely improvable, with a Character Error Rate (CER) of 35.3% on the test set. Additional typography tokens are considered characters.

Several observations can be made regarding the metrics by cell types (see Table 2). They have been calculated using the Nerval library[8] with a threshold of 0 which means that only perfect matches are allowed. First, the cells in the columns related to "plot number" and "plot nature" from previous land registries

[7] https://pypi.org/project/atr-dan/.
[8] https://pypi.org/project/teklia-nerval/.

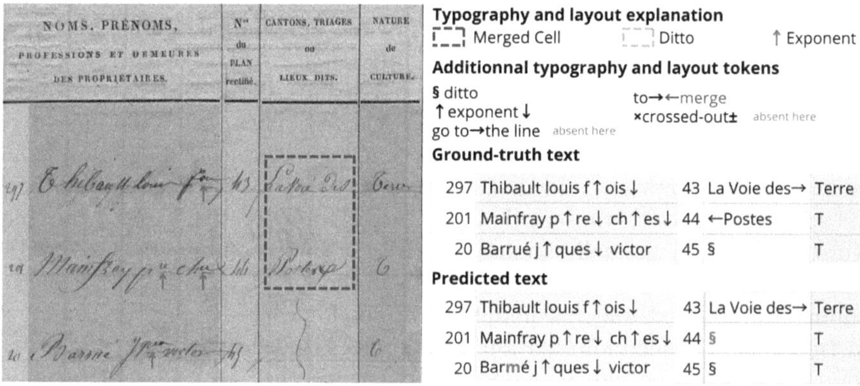

Fig. 5. Example transcription of three table rows. Typography tokens aim to help convey the writer's formatting and table completion behavior.

show lower F1-scores. This can be explained by the fact that these fields are present only in one of the three types of pre-printed tables in the dataset and are underrepresented in the training set. Second, the highest F1-scores are achieved for cells containing numeric values ("plot number" and "taxpayer index number"). The "plot nature" column also achieves a F1-score close to 70%, probably due to (1) the over-representations of certain values (as land, garden, house), and (2) the absence of special formatting like vertical or merged text for this particular element. The F1-score for "taxpayer" reaches 63% and 55% for "plot address" due to variable complexity.

Table 2. Performance on cell recognition per column type on the test set.

Cell type	Predicted	Matched	Precision	Recall	F1
Plot number	487	341	70.02	73.02	71.49
Plot nature	490	335	68.37	71.58	69.94
Taxpayer index number	384	251	65.36	74.04	69.43
Taxpayer	485	301	62.06	64.59	63.30
Plot address	328	178	54.27	57.42	55.80
Plot number(s) in prev. land registry	95	49	51.58	37.12	43.17
Plot nature(s) in prev. land registry	93	41	44.09	37.61	40.59
ALL	2362	1496	63.34	65.30	64.30

5.3 Semantic Table Interpretation and Graph Population

Evaluation Dataset. Semantic table interpretation results and the final population of the graphs are evaluated together because they are highly linked. We set up an evaluation process which includes the creation of a gold standard knowledge graph. First, the pages of the DAN test set are ranked using their CER. The municipality (L'Haÿ-les-Roses) whose pages have representative and diverse scores (ranked 1, 13 and 25 among 26) was selected. Then, using the fine-tuned DAN model, the table pages of a whole section (representing 26 pages) are transcribed. Missing rows are added, and erroneous rows are discarded. For both valid and missing rows, transcriptions are corrected or created. Cells in the "plot nature" column are manually annotated with the corresponding instances of the `Nature` class from the ontology. Similar cells in the "plot address" and "taxpayer" columns are grouped under a unique identifier for each instance of `Landmark` and `Taxpayer`. Detailed information for taxpayers is also structured (name, first names, etc.). Both graphs are populated following the ontology structure and matched to proceed to evaluation.

Knowledge Graph Evaluation. Before evaluating the KG himself, we compute some metrics on the table row detection produced by DAN, as they are relevant to explain several parts of the results regarding the final KG. 344 rows have been correctly predicted, 19 are missing, and 13 are erroneous (most of them are hallucinated rows). The precision, recall and false discovery rate are respectively equal to 96.4%, 94.8% and 3.6%.

The graph evaluation aims to assess the completeness and semantic precision of the knowledge graph (KG). We report agreement, surplus, and deficit rates in three elements: instances, object properties (relations between instances), and datatype properties.

Overall, agreement/surplus/deficit rates are 87.26%, 12.74%, 11.94% for instances, 78.5%, 21.5%, 19.9% for relations (object properties) and 87.35%, 12.65%, 16.66% for datatype properties attached to instances (values of datatype properties are not considered here). Table 3 presents a detailed analysis for class instances. A perfect agreement rate (100%) is achieved for instances derived from metadata (e.g., `Record` and `RecordSet`). The `Instantiation` class also exhibits a very high agreement rate, since every `Record` (page) and `RecordSet` (register) object in the gold standard has a corresponding instance in the `Instantiation` class. Discrepancies are mainly due to errors in table row recognition, which is the source of most of `Instantiation` objects. Regarding the creation of `Landmark` instances, two main factors influence the performances. The successful recognition of table rows directly implies high recall on `Plot`-type `Landmark` since each row corresponds to such type of object (and so on to the all `Landmark` instances as plots are the most represented type). The surplus and deficit in this class are attributed to hallucinated rows, which led to the creation of nonexistent plots, and to failure to correctly extract landmark mentions embedded in merged cells in the plot address column. These cells often contain special typographical tokens that are poorly detected by our IE model, preventing cell merging and causing segmentation errors in landmark labels. These same issues directly affect the `LandmarkRelation` class: when landmarks are not correctly instantiated, the spatial or semantic relations (e.g., between plots and addresses) are incorrectly represented in the KG. `Taxpayer` instances has also mixed results (60.53% of agreement). Transcription errors impact the creation of the groups of mentions either as the variation of the detail level associated to each mention to describe each taxpayer in the registers (i.e. name only or name and one or many first-names). Linking accuracy for plot nature mentions reaches 97%. A strict match on `?plot dcterms:identifier ?plotid` yields 92.54% recall, indicating that most plot identifiers present in the gold standard are correct in the generated graph. This result meets the good scores on "plot number" cell recognition with DAN.

Table 3. Instances by class evaluation

Type	Agreement	Deficit	Surplus	Actual	Predicted
addr:Event	100	0	0	1	1
rico:RecordSet	100	0	0	2	2
rico:Record	100	0	0	30	30
rico:Instantiation	95.44	4.56	3.33	395	390
addr:Attribute	95.20	4.80	3.43	1084	1050
addr:AttributeVersion	95.20	4.80	3.43	1084	1050
addr:Landmark	94.28	5.72	7.24	367	373
addr:Change	93.91	6.09	3.48	1446	1407
cad:Taxpayer	60.53	39.47	50.27	152	185
addr:LandmarkRelation	47.39	52.61	51.54	728	712

The pipeline's implementation on the Val-de-Marne historical land registry confirms its robustness, achieving 99.3% accuracy in page classification, 94.8% recall in row recognition, and around 80% agreement with the gold standard graph. Most residual errors are due to handwritten text recognition issues, particularly noisy outputs, and missed special tokens, which impact entity and relation extraction.

6 Conclusion

This article presents an end-to-end pipeline for the automated extraction and semantic structuring of information from digitised 19th-century French land registry tables. By combining deep learning-based information extraction with semantic table interpretation guided by the PeGaZus ontology, the approach enables the automated generation of a knowledge graph from complex handwritten historical documents. Applied and evaluated for a complete section of a municipality in the Val-de-Marne department, the pipeline demonstrates strong potential for large-scale analysis and dissemination of historical land registry data.

A key contribution of this work is the development of a complete processing chain for the RDF-based knowledge graph population from noisy and heterogeneous historical tables. The approach includes a semantic table interpretation method tailored to handwritten data using a domain ontology specifically designed to describe the evolution of landmarks and addresses over time. Future work will focus on extending the DAN training dataset to improve handwritten text and typography tokens recognition. Enhancing text recognition result would benefit to the automatic generation of `Taxpayer` and `Landmark` entities. Increasing the gold standard KG to produce an extended evaluation and adapting the pipeline to mutation registers to enable tracking of plot changes with the PeGaZus algorithm are relevant perspectives. We also plan to explore the potential of Vision-Language Large Models (VLLMs) to improve the IE process.

Acknowledgments. This work was funded by the Defense Innovation Agency of the French Armed forces Ministry.

References

1. Bernard, C., Tual, S., Abadie, N., Duménieu, B., Chazalon, J., Perret, J.: PeGazUs: a knowledge graph based approach to build urban perpetual gazetteers. In: Knowledge Engineering and Knowledge Management, pp. 364–381 (2025). https://doi.org/10.1007/978-3-031-77792-9_22
2. Boillet, M., Tarride, S., Schneider, Y., Abadie, B., Kesztenbaum, L., Kermorvant, C.: The socface project: large-scale collection, processing, and analysis of a century of French censuses. In: ICDAR, pp. 57–73 (2024). https://doi.org/10.1007/978-3-031-70543-4_4
3. Chabot, Y., Labbe, T., Liu, J., Troncy, R.: DAGoBAH: an end-to-end context-free tabular data semantic annotation system. In: SemTab@ISWC, pp. 41–48 (2019)
4. Chen, S., et al.: LinkingPark: an integrated approach for semantic table interpretation. In: SemTab@ISWC, pp. 65–74 (2020)
5. Constum, T., et al.: Recognition and information extraction in historical handwritten tables: toward understanding early 20th century Paris census. In: Document Analysis Systems, pp. 143–157 (2022). https://doi.org/10.1007/978-3-031-06555-2_10
6. Constum, T.: Extraction d'information dans des documents historiques à l'aide de grands modèles multimodaux. Phd thesis, Normandie Université, France (2024). https://theses.hal.science/tel-04913511
7. Coquenet, D., Chatelain, C., Paquet, T.: End-to-end handwritten paragraph text recognition using a vertical attention network. IEEE Trans. Pattern Anal. Mach. Intell. **45**(1), 508–524 (2022). https://doi.org/10.1109/TPAMI.2022.3144899
8. Coquenet, D., Chatelain, C., Paquet, T.: DAN: a segmentation-free document attention network for handwritten document recognition. IEEE Trans. Pattern Anal. Mach. Intell. **45**(7), 8227–8243 (2023). https://doi.org/10.1109/TPAMI.2023.3235826
9. Cremaschi, M., Spahiu, B., Palmonari, M., Jimenez-Ruiz, E.: Survey on Semantic Interpretation of Tabular Data: Challenges and Directions (2024). https://doi.org/10.48550/arXiv.2411.11891

10. Díaz, C., et al.: Automatic knowledge-graph creation from historical documents: the chilean dictatorship as a case study. In: Joint Proceedings of 2nd Workshop on KBC from PTLM (KBC-LM 2024) and 3rd Challenge on LM for KBC (LM-KBC 2024). CEUR Workshop Proceedings, vol. 3853 (2024). https://ceur-ws.org/Vol-3853/#paper8
11. Ell, B., et al.: Towards a large corpus of richly annotated web tables for knowledge base. Population (2017). https://doi.org/10.4119/UNIBI/2912802
12. Ellul, C., Azzopardi, J., Abela, C.: NotaryPedia: a knowledge graph of historical notarial manuscripts. In: On the Move to Meaningful Internet Systems: OTM 2019 Conferences, pp. 626–645 (2019). https://doi.org/10.1007/978-3-030-33246-4_39
13. Follin, J.M., Simonetto, E.: Vers une semi-automatisation du processus d'intégration de plan cadastral ancien dans une base de données multi-dates. In: Atelier Humanités Numériques Spatialisées (HumaNS'2018) (2018)
14. Franchomme, M., Schmitt, G.: Les zones humides dans le Nord vues à travers le cadastre napoléonienâĂŕ: les Systèmes d'Informations Géographiques comme outil d'analyse. Revue du Nord **396**(3), 661–680 (2012). https://doi.org/10.3917/rdn.396.0661
15. Granell, E., et al.: Processing a large collection of historical tabular images. Pattern Recognit. Lett. **170** (2023). https://doi.org/10.1016/j.patrec.2023.04.007
16. Jain, N., et al.: Generating domain-specific knowledge graphs: challenges with open information extraction. In: Proceedings of 1st International Workshop on Knowledge Graph Generation From (Text2KG 2022). CEUR Workshop Proceedings, vol. 3184, pp. 52–69 (2022)
17. Kim, G., et al.: OCR-free document understanding transformer. In: ECCV, pp. 498–517. https://arxiv.org/abs/2111.15664
18. Lenardo, I.D., Barman, R., Pardini, F., Kaplan, F.: Une approche computationnelle du cadastre napoléonien de Venise. Humanités numériques (3) (2021). https://doi.org/10.4000/revuehn.1786
19. Liu, J., Chabot, Y., Troncy, R., Huynh, V.P., Labbé, T., Monnin, P.: From tabular data to knowledge graphs: a survey of semantic table interpretation tasks and methods. J. Web Semant. **76**, 100761 (2023). https://doi.org/10.1016/j.websem.2022.100761
20. Mendes, P., Jakob, M., Bizer, C.: DBpedia: a multilingual cross-domain knowledge base. In: Proceedings of the Eighth International Conference on Language Resources and Evaluation (LREC 2012), pp. 1813–1817. European Language Resources Association (ELRA), Istanbul, Turkey (2012). https://aclanthology.org/L12-1323/
21. Möller, C.: Knowledge graph population with out-of-KG entities. In: The Semantic Web: ESWC 2022 Satellite Events, vol. 13384, pp. 199–214 (2022). https://doi.org/10.1007/978-3-031-11609-4_35
22. Nundloll, V., Smail, R., Stevens, C., Blair, G.: Automating the extraction of information from a historical text and building a linked data model for the domain of ecology and conservation science. Heliyon **8**(10), e10710 (2022). https://doi.org/10.1016/j.heliyon.2022.e10710
23. Olivier, S.: Le genêt textile (xviie-xixe siècle): Une dynamique agricole en Lodévois. Histoire Sociétés Rurales **23**(1), 137–168 (2005). https://doi.org/10.3917/hsr.023.0137
24. Petitpierre, R., Kramer, M., Rappo, L.: An end-to-end pipeline for historical censuses processing. IJDAR **26**(4), 419–432 (2023). https://doi.org/10.1007/s10032-023-00428-9

25. Petitpierre, R., Guhennec, P.: Effective annotation for the automatic vectorization of cadastral maps. Digit. Scholarsh. Humanit. (2023). https://doi.org/10.1093/llc/fqad006
26. Puigcerver, J.: Are multidimensional recurrent layers really necessary for handwritten text recognition? In: ICDAR, pp. 67–72 (2017). https://doi.org/10.1109/ICDAR.2017.20
27. Quirós, L.: P2pala: Page to page layout analysis tookit (2017). https://github.com/lquirosd/P2PaLA
28. Ratcliff, J.W., Metzener, D.E.: Pattern matching: the gestalt approach. Dr. Dobb's J. 46 (1988)
29. Scius-Bertrand, A., Fakhari, A., Vögtlin, L., Ribeiro Cabral, D., Fischer, A.: Are layout analysis and OCR still useful for document information extraction using foundation models? In: ICDAR, pp. 175–191 (2024)
30. Suchanek, F.M., Alam, M., Bonald, T., Chen, L., Paris, P.H., Soria, J.: YAGO 4.5: a large and clean knowledge base with a rich taxonomy. In: Proceedings of the 47th International ACM SIGIR Conference on Research and Development in Information Retrieval, pp. 131–140. ACM, Washington DC USA (2024). https://doi.org/10.1145/3626772.3657876
31. Tual, S., Abadie, N., Duménieu, B., Chazalon, J., Carlinet, E.: Création d'un graphe de connaissances géohistorique à partir d'annuaires du commerce parisien du 19 ème siècle: application aux métiers de la photographie. In: IC (2023). https://hal.science/hal-04121643
32. Vaswani, A., et al.: Attention Is All You Need. arXiv:1706.03762 (2017). http://arxiv.org/abs/1706.03762
33. Vrandečić, D., Krötzsch, M.: Wikidata: a free collaborative knowledgebase. Commun. ACM **57**(10), 78–85 (2014). https://doi.org/10.1145/2629489
34. Zhang, Z.: Effective and efficient semantic table interpretation using TableMiner+. Semantic Web **8**(6), 921–957 (2017). https://doi.org/10.3233/SW-160242

EUR-Lex-Triples: A Legal Relation Extraction Dataset from European Legislation

Nihed Bendahman[1,2(✉)], Karen Pinel-Sauvagnat[1], Gilles Hubert[1], and Mokhtar Boumedyen Billami[2]

[1] Université de Toulouse, IRIT, UMR 5505 CNRS, Toulouse, France
{nihed.bendahman,karen.sauvagnat,gilles.hubert}@irit.fr
[2] Berger-Levrault, 64 Rue Jean Rostand, 31670 Labège, France
{nihed.bendahman,mb.billami}@berger-levrault.com

Abstract. The field of Natural Language Processing (NLP) has witnessed exponential growth in recent years. With the rise of large language models, researchers have continuously expanded the scope of NLP tasks, pushing the boundaries of system capabilities. Nonetheless, some domains, such as the legal field, remain underexplored or progress at a slower pace. This is due to several challenges, including a highly specialized terminology, the substantial variability in legislative texts across countries which complicates generalization, and the limited availability of domain-specific resources and datasets. In this paper, we introduce EUR-Lex-Triples, a dataset annotated with triples formed by legislative references that are interconnected through relationships capturing the legal modifications they undergo. This dataset is built on the existing EUR-Lex-Sum corpus, which is composed of document-summary pairs collected from the European Union's legal platform EUR-Lex. Eur-Lex-Triples includes 9,193 unique triples (*subject, relation/predicate, object*). To the best of our knowledge, this is the first dataset of triples accessible for use in the legal domain. This resource aims to bridge existing gaps and foster progress in the legal NLP field. In particular, we explore potential applications, such as relation extraction and knowledge graph construction, which can be used in various NLP tasks, including fact-driven legal summarization or retrieval-augmented generation (RAG) systems.

Keywords: Legal domain · Relational Triples · Relation Extraction

1 Introduction

Relation extraction (RE) has been studied for years and remains an important task in NLP, as the extracted relations are then used in many downstream tasks such as Knowledge Base (KB) population and Information Retrieval (IR).

In specific domains, relation extraction can also be used by generic state-of-the-art models to adapt them to the peculiar vocabulary used. The legal

W.-T. Balke et al. (Eds.): TPDL 2025, LNCS 16097, pp. 433–451, 2026.
https://doi.org/10.1007/978-3-032-05409-8_25

domain is one of these specific domains that could benefit from dedicated relation extraction: legal documents such as legal acts, case laws, court judgements include a highly specialized terminology, and relation extraction can benefit to legal assistance tasks including case search, legal text summarization, or judgement prediction.

In this paper, we present EUR-Lex-Triples[1], a new annotated corpus of relational triples derived from the EUR-Lex-Sum corpus [2], itself collected from the European Law platform EUR-Lex [3]. As far as we know, this is the first dataset of annotated triples for the legal domain made publicly available. EUR-Lex is an important resource in the field of European law[2], providing several types of data annotated by experts, such as summaries of articles, topics, and keywords associated with documents. We propose here to enrich these resources by annotating paragraphs in triples (*subject, relation/predicate, object*), which convey the various links between legal texts. Figure 1 shows an excerpt from a EUR-Lex-Sum document, illustrating the profusion of triples in the corpus. In this example, the legal reference *Regulation 2018/1046* is a Subject Entity related to all the other references through the predicates *amending* and *repealing*.

A first possible use of EUR-Lex-Triples is the evaluation of relation extraction approaches. We therefore complete this paper with an evaluation of different state-of-the-art RE models in order to provide baselines on the dataset. Other usage scenarios can also be explored, that are detailed and discussed at the end of the paper. They include knowledge graph construction, classification or clustering, information retrieval, and abstractive summarization.

The rest of the paper is organized as follows. Existing datasets for RE as well as datasets for the legal domain are presented in Sect. 2. Section 3 details the construction process of EUR-Lex-Triples. Various use cases that can benefit from this dataset are then presented in Sect. 4, focusing on the evaluation of different state-of-the-art models for Relation Extraction. Section 5 discusses some limitations of our work and Sect. 6 concludes the paper.

2 Related Works

2.1 Existing Datasets for Relation Extraction

General-purpose relation extraction (RE) datasets have driven advances in information extraction, but they exhibit limitations in domain coverage. TACRED [1] and NYT [38], are large supervised corpora of sentence-level relation instances extracted from newspaper texts. Similarly, the SemEval-2010 Task 8 dataset [15] provides over 10,000 annotated sentences covering generic relations. While important, these resources focus on broad, open-domain relations (e.g., person-affiliation or cause-effect). More recent work [32] has introduced document-level RE benchmarks like DocRED, which contains relations from Wikipedia articles. However, none of these datasets target the legal domain or the unique relationship types found in legislative text - for example, one law repealing or amending

[1] https://github.com/NihedB/EUR-Lex-Triples.git.

[2] https://european-union.europa.eu/.

Text: Regulation 2018/1046 of the European Parliament and of the Council of 18 July 2018 on the financial rules applicable to the general budget of the Union, **amending Regulation 1296/2013**, **Regulation 1301/2013**, **Regulation 1303/2013**, **Regulation 1304/2013**, **Regulation 1309/2013**, **Regulation 1316/2013**, **Regulation 223/2014**, **Regulation 283/2014**, and **Decision 541/2014/eu** and **repealing Regulation 966/2012** (OJ L 193, 30.7.2018, p. 1).

Relational Triples: (Regulation 2018/1046, amending, Regulation 1296/2013), (Regulation 2018/1046, amending, Regulation 1301/2013), (Regulation 2018/1046, amending, Regulation 1303/2013), (Regulation 2018/1046, amending, Regulation 1304/2013), (Regulation 2018/1046, amending, Regulation 1309/2013), (Regulation 2018/1046, amending, Regulation 1316/2013), (Regulation 2018/1046, amending, Regulation 223/2014), (Regulation 2018/1046, amending, Regulation 283/2014), (Regulation 2018/1046, amending, Decision 541/2014/eu), (Regulation 2018/1046, repealing, Regulation 966/2012)

Fig. 1. Example of a EUR-Lex-Sum document. Law entities are highlighted in yellow while predicates are in green. Ten relational triples can be extracted from this text. (Color figure online)

another - which are prevalent in legal documents but absent from open-domain schemas. These limitations highlight the need for a specialized resource which focuses on legal texts. In the next section, we review the legal datasets that could serve as a base dataset for triples annotation.

2.2 Existing Datasets in Legal Domain

One of the key resources in the legal domain is the European Union's legal platform (EUR-Lex) [3] which brings together multiple data resources in various formats. Textual data can be accessed through the Europa portal[3], as well as the EuroVoc thesaurus[4], which is a multilingual and multidisciplinary thesaurus. More structured data are represented in the ELI Ontology[5] and the Cellar data repository[6], which offers a SPARQL endpoint to facilitate access to different concepts.

All these diverse resources have supported a wide range of applications across various NLP and Knowledge Engineering tasks, leading to the creation of multiple post-processed and derived datasets. One of the most prominent examples is the Europarl corpus [22], which comprises sentence-aligned translated texts derived from European Parliament proceedings. Its extensive size and broad linguistic coverage have made it a key resource for machine translation systems. More recently, the Multi-EUR-Lex [7] dataset has been presented as a

[3] https://eur-lex.europa.eu/legal-content/EN/TXT/?uri=CELEX%3A32019R0980.
[4] https://op.europa.eu/en/web/eu-vocabularies.
[5] https://interoperable-europe.ec.europa.eu/collection/eli-european-legislation-identifier/solution/eli-ontology.
[6] https://op.europa.eu/en/web/cellar.

multi-lingual and multi-label classification resource leveraging EuroVoc labels as well as EURLEX57K [6]. Meanwhile, the EUROPA [26] dataset is annotated with automatically generated keyphrases, and EUR-Lex-Sum [2] is a multilingual document-summary dataset.

Outside the EUR-Lex ecosystem, one can also cite Ledgar [30], LexGlue [9], ContractNLI [23], and CUAD [16], which are primarily centered on tasks like text classification, natural language understanding and question answering.

The closest work to that presented in this paper is the one in [4]. Authors discuss the building of knowledge graphs from Chinese legal documents, which inherently involves identifying and extracting relations between legal concepts. While this work indicates that relation extraction is a known and relevant challenge, there is no resulting dataset dedicated to RE.

In this work, we present EUR-Lex Triples, a dataset of triples based on EUR-Lex-Sum. Our dataset contributes to enrich the EUR-Lex ecosystem with the additional RE task. The specific use of EUR-Lex-Sum enables the annotation of summaries with triples, which opens up additional use cases for our dataset. All these use cases are discussed in more detail in Sect. 4.

3 EUR-Lex-Triples Construction

This section details the process to construct the EUR-Lex-Triples dataset from the English version of the EUR-Lex-Sum dataset, as well as some statistics and examples.

3.1 EUR-Lex-Sum

EUR-Lex-Triples is derived from the English part of the EUR-Lex-Sum dataset [2], a dataset that aligns documents (legal acts) with their summaries to allow text summarization tasks. Each legal document is associated to a unique CELEX identifier, which is an identifier that remains the same in every language available, as well as to a summary. Table 1 reports some statistics about the dataset.

Table 1. Total number of documents, summaries, and paragraphs in EUR-Lex-Sum, as well as the average number of tokens and paragraphs of each document.

Element	Number
Documents	1,504
Summaries	1,504
Paragraphs in Document	198,587
Median Paragraphs/Document	178
Median Paragraphs/Summary	51
Avg Tokens/Document	12,000
Avg Tokens/Summary	800

3.2 Methodology

Table 2. Number of occurrences of different entity and verb types across the dataset in documents (Docs) and summaries (Sums).

	Original Dataset		Selected Paragraphs		Annotated Triples	
	Docs	Sums	Docs	Sums	Docs	Sums
Entity						
Directive	37,563	5,841	11,898	2,448	6,720	2,501
Decision	23,940	4,469	3,786	885	1,329	854
Regulation	54,845	10,062	12,162	4,959	11,023	6,263
Resolution	5,535	333	275	30	18	12
Recommendation	3,548	446	248	5	40	4
Opinion	5,125	155	866	4	39	3
Verb						
To amend	2,631	1,514	1,996	1,056	5,032	2,366
To supplement	800	274	133	208	85	195
To repeal	2,517	1,204	2,397	1,036	4,021	1,872
To replace	307	225	106	105	152	213
To correct	84	10	11	4	5	4
To implement	10,826	1,652	1,394	698	281	158
To recast	38	61	2	6	5	5
To extend	464	112	74	15	2	0

The methodology we defined to annotate the EUR-Lex-Sum dataset follows five main steps:

1. **Extraction of entities and verbs.** Before implementing the text annotation process, we conducted a manual and empirical analysis of the documents to identify the relevant sets of entities and verbs to consider for annotation. To do so, we first parsed all the texts and extracted the different types of entities and verbs present using a set of rules and regular expressions. Next, we compared the extracted types with the legal references and changes defined in the European Legislation Identifier ontology of the EUR-Lex platform (ELI 1.4)[7]. The types of entities our parser identified match exactly with those defined in the ontology, namely *directive, decision, regulation, resolution, recommendation*, and *opinion*. Regarding the verbs, we kept the most present in the documents and summaries, removing verbs that are not representative of the legal context, such as *to have* or *to be*. The final list is the following: *to amend,*

[7] https://interoperable-europe.ec.europa.eu/collection/eli-european-legislation-identifier/solution/eli-ontology.

to supplement, to repeal, to replace, to correct, to recast, and *to extend*. These properties are also available in the SPARQL endpoint (e.g., URI for supplement: http://publications.europa.eu/resource/authority/fd_499/S). The initial distribution of the extracted entities and verbs in the dataset is given in Table 2, column *Original dataset*. Some examples of the selected entities and verbs are also given in Table 3.

2. **Paragraph segmentation.** The EUR-Lex-Sum documents and summaries are provided in their entirety without prior markup. Given their relatively long length (averaging 12k tokens), we decided to segment them before passing them to annotators. State-of-the-art approaches vary in the granularity of document segmentation, considering text at the sentence, paragraph, section, or entire document level. In this article, we chose to segment the texts at the paragraph level by using line breaks, as done in [1,14].
3. **Selection of the candidate paragraphs.** A triple consists of a subject (a legal reference/entity), a predicate (a legal change/verb), and an object (another legal entity). Therefore, a paragraph is selected for annotation only if it contains the necessary elements to form at least one valid triple, specifically two entities and one verb. This approach aims to prevent annotators from being overwhelmed by excessive text and to implement a preliminary filtering step. Table 2, Column *Selected paragraphs* gives some statistics regarding the candidate paragraphs.
4. **Automatic highlighting of entities and verbs.** Once candidate paragraphs selected, we tagged selected entities and verbs within the text to streamline the annotation process through automatic identification. This step aims to make annotation as easy and straightforward as possible. Subsequently, the annotator's role will be to construct triples from the elements already identified in the text.
5. **Manual annotation.** The final stage consists in the manual construction of triples by the annotators from the pre-selected paragraphs. More details on this step are given in the following section.

3.3 Annotation Process

To prepare the annotation process, we calculated the average time t required to annotate a single paragraph, being approximately *2 min*. Then, to ensure a fluid and accessible annotation process for annotators, we grouped the paragraphs of the dataset into packages, so that each contains roughly P paragraphs (P = 75), resulting on two hours and a half of annotation. Each package contains paragraphs of both documents and summaries.

By segmenting the dataset into packages of P = 75 paragraphs and ensuring that some packages are annotated by all annotators (see Sect. 3.4), we obtain N = 75 packages. Finally, each annotator received one or more packages, over a period that lasted 2 months.

Table 3. List of legal entities and verbs considered for triple annotation. Entities are legal references and verbs are legal changes made to references.

Entity	Example
Directive	Directive 64/224/EEC
Decision	Decision 2016/2338
Regulation	Regulation 1306/2013
Resolution	Resolution 1267/1999
Recommendation	Recommendation 1164/94/EEU
Opinion	Opinion 44/2014
Verb	Example
To amend	Regulation 2020/532, amended by Regulation 2020/2086.
To supplement	Commission Delegated Regulation 2020/760 of 17 December 2019 supplementing Regulation 1308/2013 of the European Parliament.
To repeal	regulation 2016/429 repeals regulation 576/2013 with effect from 21 April 2021.
To replace	regulation 652/2014, which was subsequently repealed and replaced by regulation 2021/690 establishing the single market programme (see summary).
To correct	Directive 2014/24/eu of the European Parliament and of the Council of 26 February 2014 on public procurement and correcting Directive 2004/18/ec
To implement	Regulation 1150/2000 implementing Decision 2007/436/EC
To recast	Regulation 765/2008 (see summary on Accreditation and market surveillance) recasts Directive 2004/42/EC and Regulation 305/2011
To extend	Directive 2004/42/EC extending directive 1999/13/EC

The texts were annotated by 10 different annotators, including the 4 authors of this article, along with PhD students and research engineers specializing in NLP or IR. 3 of the annotators have expertise in the legal domain. Each annotator received an individual training session, during which we explained the task and reviewed examples and counterexamples to ensure a clear understanding of the annotation task. Moreover, annotators received a document presenting several examples and further detailed guidelines to follow.

We developed an annotation tool in JavaScript and HTML in order to facilitate the sharing of the documents to annotate among different annotators and the automatic highlighting process. Its purpose is to display each document or summary to be annotated on a web page, with a set of functionalities such as: adding or deleting a triple, navigating through the different paragraphs of the same document, downloading the annotation document at the end, moving to the next document to be annotated, etc.

Figure 2 illustrates the welcome page of the annotation tool, which lists documents and summaries to be annotated in a given package. For each document/summary, the annotation tool then navigates across paragraphs to be annotated, as illustrated on Fig. 3. The main guidelines for annotating are recalled on each page. In a given paragraph, legal entities and legal verbs (legal changes) are highlighted to ease the annotation process.

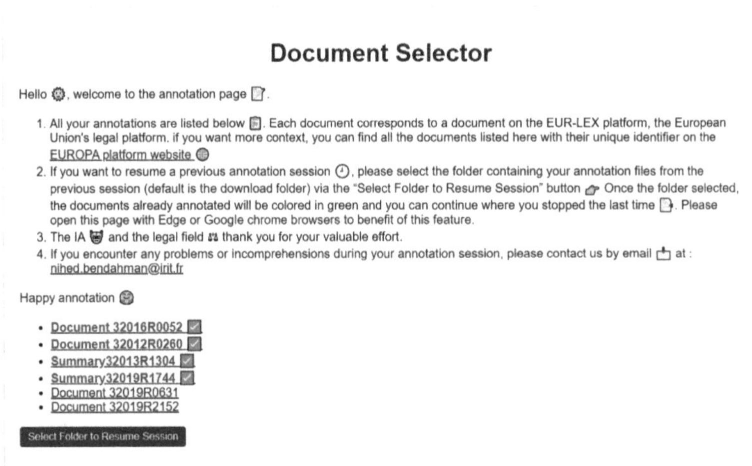

Fig. 2. Welcome web page. Documents and summaries to be annotated are listed (list cropped here for the example). Already annotated documents are marked in green. (Color figure online)

3.4 Inter-annotator Agreement

We selected 72 paragraphs to be annotated by all annotators, which represents 1% of total paragraphs. These paragraphs contains the same proportions of verb and entity types than in the full dataset. For example, the entity Directive is present in 34% of the corpus and in 34% of the 72 paragraphs. We measured inter-annotator agreement by computing Fleiss Kappa K [13]. The overall value of the agreement is K=0.78, showing a good agreement between the annotators. Given the corpus size and the time-intensive nature of annotation, each other paragraph was annotated by a single annotator.

3.5 Statistics and Distribution

Table 4 reports statistics on EUR-Lex-Triples at the end of the annotation process. The EUR-Lex-Triples dataset contains a total of 14,396 human-annotated triples, of which 9,193 are unique. This difference is explained by the fact that several paragraphs can contain the same triple.

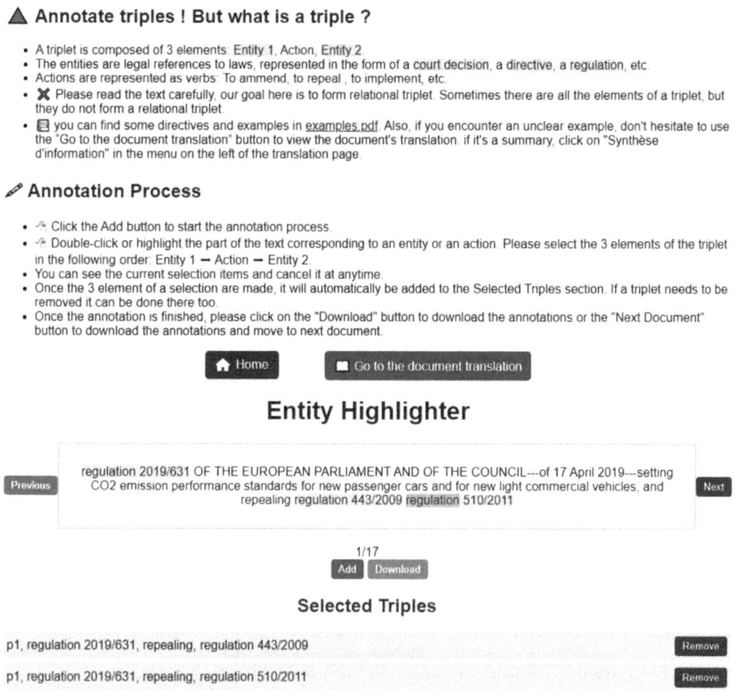

Fig. 3. Example of an annotation page for a given paragraph. Triples already selected by the annotator are at the bottom of the page.

Table 4. EUR-Lex-Triples statistics.

Element	Number
Annotated paragraphs	7,186
No_relation tag paragraphs	972
Triples	14,396
Unique triples	9,193

Detailed statistics regarding entities and verbs are given in Table 2, column *Annotated Triples*. It should be noted that the number of entities and verbs in the annotated triples is higher than in the selected paragraphs. This can be explained by the fact that an entity can belong to several triples, and that a verb occurrence can also lead to several triples. For instance, in the example of Fig. 1, *regulation 2018/1048* is the subject of 10 triples, and the only occurrence of the verb *amending* leads to 9 triples.

The following resources composing EUR-Lex-Triples are available on our Github[8]: (i) json files containing for each document, its text as well as its summary, the annotated paragraphs, and for each paragraph the triples derived from the annotation, (ii) the code used for the preprocessing of documents (regex used for entities and verbs extraction, and paragraph segmentation), (iii) the code used for the annotation tool we developed as well as the full guidelines.

3.6 Examples of Annotated Triples

Several situations were encountered during the annotation of paragraphs, leading to different levels of difficulty in identifying the triples to be constructed. In some cases, the way in which documents are written makes it difficult to identify the relations between entities. Table 5 shows examples of identified triples for various

Table 5. Examples of identified triples for various Eur-Lex-Sum paragraphs.

Paragraph	Relational triples	Comments
Delegated regulation 2020/2146 supplements regulation 2018/848 as regards exceptional production rules in organic production.	(regulation 2020/2146, supplements, regulation 2018/848)	
regulation 2019/5 of the European Parliament and of the Council of 11 December 2018 amending regulation 726/2004 laying down Community procedures for the authorisation and supervision of medicinal products for human and veterinary use and establishing a European Medicines Agency, regulation 1901/2006 on medicinal products for paediatric use and directive 2001/83/ec on the Community code relating to medicinal products for human use (OJ L 4, 7.1.2019, pp. 24-42)	(regulation 2019/5, amending, regulation 726/2004) (regulation 2019/5, amending, regulation 1901/2006) (regulation 2019/5, amending, directive 2001/83/ec)	
Council directive 89/107/eec of 21 December 1988 on the approximation of the laws of the Member States concerning food additives authorised for use in foodstuffs intended for human consumption (OJ L 40, 11.2.1989, p. 27). Directive as last amended by regulation 1882/2003.	(regulation 1882/2003, amended, directive 89/107/eec)	The verb to amend is in its passive form. The annotator must therefore built the triple in the reverse order.
directive 70/524/eec should be repealed. However labelling provisions applicable to compound feedingstuffs incorporating additives should be maintained until a revision of Council directive 79/373/eec of 2 April 1979 on the marketing of compound feedingstuffs (10) is completed.	No triple.	Although this paragraph contains all the elements to form a triple, the phrasing leads to no valid one.
Following Russia's invasion of Ukraine, the EU adopted several decisions amending decision 2014/145/cfsp: decision 2022/429, decision 2022/241, decision 2022/265, decision 2022/267, decision 2022/329, decision 2022/331, decision 2022/337, decision 2022/354, decision 2022/397.	No triple.	
Where emissions of a greenhouse gas from an installation are specified in Annex I to directive 2003/87/ec of the European Parliament and of the Council of 13 October 2003 establishing a scheme for greenhouse gas emission allowance trading within the Community and amending Council directive 96/61/ec (13) in relation to an activity carried out in that installation, the permit shall not include an emission limit value for direct emissions of that gas unless it is necessary to ensure that no significant local pollution is caused.	(directive 2003/87/ec, amending, directive 96/61/ec)	

[8] https://github.com/NihedB/EUR-Lex-Triples.git.

Eur-Lex-Sum paragraphs of different difficulty levels, from easy ones to more difficult and time consuming ones.

4 Possible Use Cases

In this section, we explore several use cases for EUR-Lex-Triples. First, we review various Relation Extraction models and evaluate a selection of them, discussing the adaptation of these models to the particular nature of triples in the dataset. Next, we illustrate how these triples can be integrated into knowledge graphs by proposing a Knowledge Graph model. Finally, we discuss additional applications, including information retrieval and triple-guided text generation.

4.1 Relation Extraction

We evaluated different state-of-the-art models of relation extraction on EUR-Lex-Triples in order to provide baselines on the dataset. The code used to run these models is also available on our Github.

Models. We considered 3 Pretrained Language Models (PLM): LEGAL-BERT which was specifically trained on legal data [8], BERT [11] and REBEL-Large [18], as well as 3 Large Langage Models (LLM): Mistral-7b [21], Zephyr-7b [31], Llama-2-13b [29], which differ in their hyper-parameter sizes and architectures.

Experimental Setup. All models were fine-tuned on the EUR-Lex-Triples dataset. For the PLMs, we kept the default configuration of hyperparameters and fine-tuned them for 6 epochs. For the LLMs, we applied the Low-Rank Adaptation (LoRA) method [17] and fine-tuned them for 3 epochs. We used the same train/test split as in EUR-Lex-Sum, namely 1,316 document–summary pairs for training and 188 document–summary pairs for testing. It is worth noting that we trained and tested all models using paragraph granularity. Among them, only the annotated paragraphs were used for training and testing. Additionally, we evaluated the LLMs using two other settings: Zero-shot semi-open RE prompting and In-Context learning. The used prompts are given in Table 6.

Metrics. Following state-of-the-art papers (e.g., [34,35] or [37]), we use the standard micro Precision, Recall, and F1 score to evaluate the results.

Results and Discussion. Results are presented in Table 7. Regarding the PLM results, a first observation is that LEGAL-BERT outperforms Bert. This is not surprising, since the model was trained on legal data. Moreover, also in an expected way, the best model remains REBEL-large, which is the only model among the evaluated ones to be dedicated to the relation extraction task.

Regarding now the results obtained by the LLMs, we can see that fine-tuning significantly increases the performance of in-context learning and even more of

Table 6. Zero-shot Semi-Open Relation Extraction and In-Context Learning prompts used to perform the Relation Extraction task.

Zero-Shot Semi-Open RE:

You're a relation triplet extraction system. Given a text, identify and list the relationships between entities within the text. Extract relationships both within a single sentence (intra-sentence) and across multiple sentences (inter-sentence).
Provide a list of triplets in the format ['ENTITY 1', 'RELATIONSHIP', 'ENTITY 2']. without any additional information. Do not explain how you extract them.
We consider *only* legal entities from this list: [regulation, decision, directive, resolution, recommendation, opinion].
The relationships from this set: [repeal, amend, supplement, implement, correct, replace, recast, extend].

In-Context Learning:

[Same prompt as for Zero-Shot Semi-Open RE]
Here are few examples:
[text]: Regulation (EU) 2019/980 of the European Parliament and of the Council of 21 June 2019 on the promotion of the use of SME growth markets (OJ L 193, 21.6.2019, pp. 1–10).
[response]:
[relational triplet: "None"]
[text]: Delegated Directive (EU) 334/109 supplementing Regulation (EU) 1566/874 on regulatory technical standards on key financial information in the summary of a prospectus, the publication and classification of prospectuses, advertisements for securities, supplements to a prospectus, and the notification portal.
[response]:
[relational triplet: [Directive (EU) 334/109, supplementing, Regulation (EU) 1566/874]]
[text]: Delegated Decision (EU) 2020/1273 amending and correcting Delegated Directive (EU) 2019/980.
[response]:
[relational triplet: [Decision (EU) 2020/1273, amending, Directive (EU) 2019/980] relational triplet: [Decision (EU) 2020/1273, correcting, Directive (EU) 2019/980]]
Now complete the following:

zero-shot prompting. LLM fine-tuning allows to obtain similar results to REBEL-large ones.

More generally, on all models, recall is worse than precision, showing the models' difficulty in identifying non-trivial triples. Regarding precision, one possible explanation concerns the difficulty of models to predict the cases where no valid triples can be extracted from the paragraph.

To conclude, we can see that the state-of-the-art models achieve relatively satisfactory results. However, there is still room for dedicated models to better adapt to the specificities of the legal domain.

4.2 Knowledge Graphs

A key motivation for extracting relational triples is to facilitate knowledge graph construction. In the legal domain, a knowledge graph of legislative acts and

Table 7. Results of baseline models for Relation Extraction.

Model		Precision	Recall	F1-Score
Legal-Bert		0.64	0.59	0.60
Bert		0.59	0.52	0.55
Rebel-Large		**0.88**	**0.75**	**0.80**
Mistral 7b	*Zero-shot*	0.38	0.29	0.32
	In-context	0.42	0.37	0.39
	Finetuning	0.84	<u>0.69</u>	<u>0.75</u>
Zephyr 7b	*Zero shot*	0.42	0.38	0.40
	In-context	0.52	0.44	0.48
	Finetuning	<u>0.85</u>	0.61	0.72
Llama 2 13b	*Zero-shot*	0.33	0.25	0.29
	In-context	0.33	0.31	0.33
	Finetuning	0.82	0.61	0.69

their inter-relations can greatly enhance legal information retrieval, consistency checking, and analytics. [10] explores representations of law as graphs, by implementing a legislative system as a property graph with nodes for laws (and their articles) and typed edges for the relations between laws. On the other hand, [20] built a knowledge graph from Indian legal corpora. Their pipeline includes data preprocessing, entity and relation extraction, and RDF triplet construction using the NyOn ontology [19]. Building such a legal knowledge graphs from text requires extracting the relevant entities and relations in a structured form.

In this section, to capture the intricate legal relationships embedded in European Union legislation, we illustrate a knowledge graph construction using EUR-Lex-Triples and EUR-Lex-Sum. We use the triples of our dataset along with additional information contained in documents (topic, keywords, named entities of documents such as Location, Organization and Person ones).

We model a Knowledge Graph containing the following nodes: Documents D, Named entities E (Organization, Location, Person), Legal entities E_j, Topics T of D, and Keywords K of D. The edges in the graph include: (i) the presence of a legal entity or a named entity in a document, (ii) legal changes between legal entities (triples of Eur-Lex-Triples), (iii) the topics of a document, (iv) the keywords of a document, and (v) the presence of a legal entity or a named entity in a document.

Figure 4 illustrates the graph model, showing the various nodes and edges. The Document node has one property, i.e., the *celex_id* of the document. Similarly, the Law Entity node has two properties: *type* (e.g., *Directive, Regulation*) and *code* (e.g., *2003/87/ec, 96/61/ec*).

Once the graph model had been established, we populated it with EUR-Lex-Triples (legal entities nodes and legal changes edges), as well as with extracted information from the text. Topics and keywords of the documents were retrieved

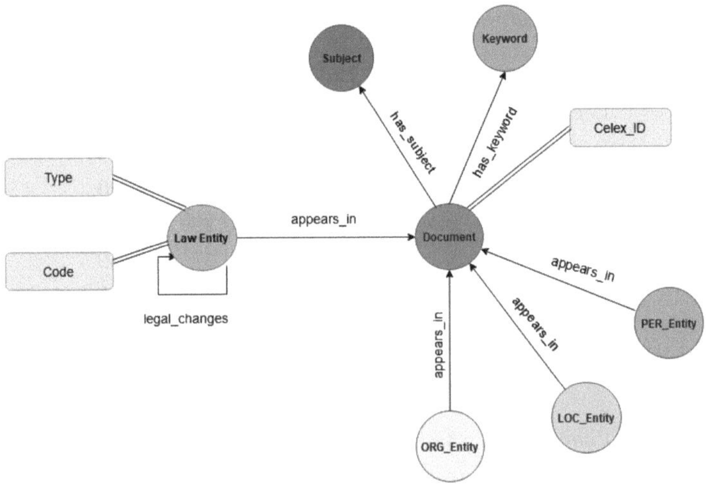

Fig. 4. The proposed knowledge graph model.

by web scrapping the EUR-Lex web pages of the documents. As for the named entities, they were extracted using a NER model fine-tuned on the Indian Court Judgements dataset[9]. Figure 5 shows an example of the constructed graph with three documents from the dataset. The documents are interconnected through the entities, triples, and shared topics they contain.

This representation supports multiple query types. For example, one can search for a specific legal reference to identify all legal changes affecting it or all legal changes it affects. It is also possible to retrieve the documents containing these references for direct consultation, or to extract the associated keywords and topics, thereby gaining insight into the relevant subjects. Obviously, other queries can be considered depending on the information need.

4.3 Other Possible Scenarios

Information Retrieval with Triples. Relational triples can serve as rich, structured resources for enhancing information retrieval (IR) and retrieval-augmented generation (RAG) systems, by providing a semantic interconnected backbone that improves query understanding, document ranking, and the quality of retrieved evidence [25]. For instance, the authors in [24] are interested in legal information retrieval and propose an approach based on a semantic description of legal provisions and a search strategy combining keywords and semantics.

On the other hand, Retrieval-Augmented Generation frameworks integrate relational triples from knowledge graphs directly into the generation process, providing a structured context. Recent works in RAG [25] show that fusing LLMs with KGs leads to more grounded reasoning and factual correctness. Triple-aware

[9] https://huggingface.co/opennyaiorg/en_legal_ner_trf. This NER model was the most effective one according to preliminary experiments.

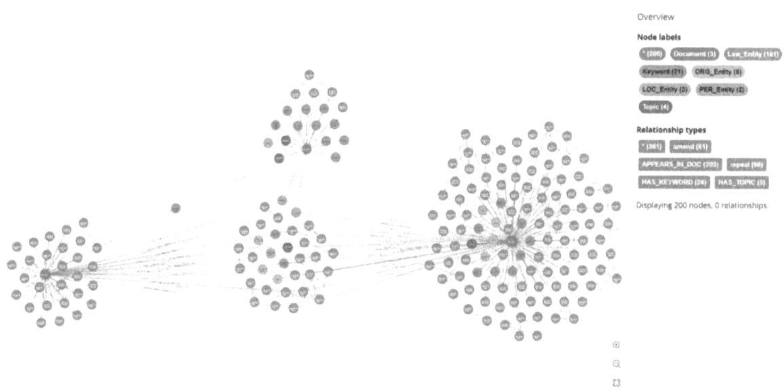

Fig. 5. Excerpt of 3 documents from the knowledge graph, implemented with Neo4j.

reasoning approaches [36] and hybrid models that combine language models with commonsense and domain-specific KG [27] ensure that generated content aligns with known relationships, mitigating hallucinations and logical inconsistencies.

Other possible applications involve question-answering, such as the approaches proposed in [28,33].

Fact-Driven Legal Summarization. Relational triples are also used in abstractive summarization. For example, the work in [5] uses triples retrieved from knowledge graphs to enrich the evaluation of the generated summaries factuality, in relation to the facts contained in the source documents. One can also cite the work of Feng et al. [12], which uses facts directly to train models in order to generate more enriched summaries. Our dataset could be used to adapt this kind of approaches to the legal field.

5 Limitations

The annotation process we followed has some limitations. Firstly, segmenting the text into paragraphs presents challenges, such as the presence of co-references between entities spanning multiple paragraphs. This occasionally resulted in ambiguous pointers to legal entities (e.g., "this directive [...]"), complicating the annotation task or making it impossible on some paragraphs. Secondly, the regular expressions implemented to identify entities may not be exhaustive, potentially leading to missed entities due to non-optimal data formatting. Finally, the proportion of paragraphs used to calculate inter-annotator agreement is restricted by the effort required of the annotators, and could be improved.

6 Conclusion

In this article, we presented EUR-Lex-Triples, a dataset of 9,193 relational triples for the legal domain. The dataset is built on the English version of the existing

EUR-Lex-Sum corpus, composed of document-summary pairs collected from the EU's legal platform EUR-Lex. This resource aims to bridge existing gaps and foster progress in the legal NLP field. We also proposed some usage scenarios for the dataset, such as the evaluation of Relation Extraction methods, Knowledge Graph construction or Information Retrieval and synthesis. To the best of our knowledge, this is the first triples dataset made publicly available for the legal domain.

Acknowledgements. This work was granted access to the HPC resources of IDRIS under the allocation 2024-AD011014740R1 made by GENCI.

References

1. Alt, C., Gabryszak, A., Hennig, L.: TACRED revisited: a thorough evaluation of the TACRED relation extraction task. In: Jurafsky, D., Chai, J., Schluter, N., Tetreault, J. (eds.) Proceedings of the 58th Annual Meeting of the Association for Computational Linguistics, pp. 1558–1569. Association for Computational Linguistics, Online (2020). https://doi.org/10.18653/v1/2020.acl-main.142, https://aclanthology.org/2020.acl-main.142
2. Aumiller, D., Chouhan, A., Gertz, M.: EUR-lex-sum: a multi- and cross-lingual dataset for long-form summarization in the legal domain. In: Goldberg, Y., Kozareva, Z., Zhang, Y. (eds.) Proceedings of the 2022 Conference on Empirical Methods in Natural Language Processing, pp. 7626–7639. Association for Computational Linguistics, Abu Dhabi, United Arab Emirates (2022). https://doi.org/10.18653/v1/2022.emnlp-main.519, https://aclanthology.org/2022.emnlp-main.519
3. Bernet, H., Berteloot, P.: Eur-lex: a multilingual on-line website for european union law. Int. Rev. Law Comput. Technol. **20**(3), 337–339 (2006). https://doi.org/10.1080/13600860600947109
4. Bi, S., Ali, Z., Wang, M., Wu, T., Qi, G.: Learning heterogeneous graph embedding for chinese legal document similarity. Knowl.-Based Syst. **250**, 109046 (2022). https://doi.org/10.1016/j.knosys.2022.109046, https://www.sciencedirect.com/science/article/pii/S0950705122005123
5. Cao, Z., Wei, F., Li, W., Li, S.: Faithful to the original: fact-aware neural abstractive summarization. In: Proceedings of the Thirty-Second AAAI Conference on Artificial Intelligence and Thirtieth Innovative Applications of Artificial Intelligence Conference and Eighth AAAI Symposium on Educational Advances in Artificial Intelligence. AAAI'18/IAAI'18/EAAI'18, AAAI Press (2018)
6. Chalkidis, I., Fergadiotis, E., Malakasiotis, P., Androutsopoulos, I.: Large-scale multi-label text classification on EU legislation. In: Korhonen, A., Traum, D., Màrquez, L. (eds.) Proceedings of the 57th Annual Meeting of the Association for Computational Linguistics, pp. 6314–6322. Association for Computational Linguistics, Florence, Italy (2019). https://doi.org/10.18653/v1/P19-1636, https://aclanthology.org/P19-1636
7. Chalkidis, I., Fergadiotis, M., Androutsopoulos, I.: MultiEURLEX - a multi-lingual and multi-label legal document classification dataset for zero-shot cross-lingual transfer. In: Moens, M.F., Huang, X., Specia, L., Yih, S.W.t. (eds.) Proceedings of the 2021 Conference on Empirical Methods in Natural Language Processing, pp. 6974–6996. Association for Computational Linguistics, Online and Punta

Cana, Dominican Republic (2021). https://doi.org/10.18653/v1/2021.emnlp-main.559, https://aclanthology.org/2021.emnlp-main.559
8. Chalkidis, I., Fergadiotis, M., Malakasiotis, P., Aletras, N., Androutsopoulos, I.: LEGAL-BERT: The muppets straight out of law school. In: Cohn, T., He, Y., Liu, Y. (eds.) Findings of the Association for Computational Linguistics: EMNLP 2020, pp. 2898–2904. Association for Computational Linguistics, Online (2020). https://doi.org/10.18653/v1/2020.findings-emnlp.261, https://aclanthology.org/2020.findings-emnlp.261/
9. Chalkidis, I., et al.: LexGLUE: a benchmark dataset for legal language understanding in English. In: Muresan, S., Nakov, P., Villavicencio, A. (eds.) Proceedings of the 60th Annual Meeting of the Association for Computational Linguistics (Volume 1: Long Papers), pp. 4310–4330. Association for Computational Linguistics, Dublin, Ireland (2022). https://doi.org/10.18653/v1/2022.acl-long.297, https://aclanthology.org/2022.acl-long.297
10. Colombo, A., Bernasconi, A., Ceri, S.: Modelling legislative systems into property graphs to enable advanced pattern detection (2024). https://arxiv.org/abs/2406.14935
11. Devlin, J., Chang, M.W., Lee, K., Toutanova, K.: BERT: pre-training of deep bidirectional transformers for language understanding. In: Burstein, J., Doran, C., Solorio, T. (eds.) Proceedings of the 2019 Conference of the North American Chapter of the Association for Computational Linguistics: Human Language Technologies, Volume 1 (Long and Short Papers), pp. 4171–4186. Association for Computational Linguistics, Minneapolis, Minnesota (2019). https://doi.org/10.18653/v1/N19-1423, https://aclanthology.org/N19-1423
12. Feng, S., Balachandran, V., Bai, Y., Tsvetkov, Y.: FactKB: generalizable factuality evaluation using language models enhanced with factual knowledge. In: Bouamor, H., Pino, J., Bali, K. (eds.) Proceedings of the 2023 Conference on Empirical Methods in Natural Language Processing, pp. 933–952. Association for Computational Linguistics, Singapore (2023). https://doi.org/10.18653/v1/2023.emnlp-main.59, https://aclanthology.org/2023.emnlp-main.59
13. Fleiss, J.L.: Measuring nominal scale agreement among many raters. Psychol. Bull. **76**(5), 378 (1971)
14. Han, X., et al.: FewRel: a large-scale supervised few-shot relation classification dataset with state-of-the-art evaluation. In: Riloff, E., Chiang, D., Hockenmaier, J., Tsujii, J. (eds.) Proceedings of the 2018 Conference on Empirical Methods in Natural Language Processing, pp. 4803–4809. Association for Computational Linguistics, Brussels, Belgium (2018). https://doi.org/10.18653/v1/D18-1514, https://aclanthology.org/D18-1514
15. Hendrickx, I., et al.: SemEval-2010 task 8: multi-way classification of semantic relations between pairs of nominals. In: Erk, K., Strapparava, C. (eds.) Proceedings of the 5th International Workshop on Semantic Evaluation, pp. 33–38. Association for Computational Linguistics, Uppsala, Sweden (2010). https://aclanthology.org/S10-1006
16. Hendrycks, D., Burns, C., Chen, A., Ball, S.: Cuad: an expert-annotated NLP dataset for legal contract review. In: Vanschoren, J., Yeung, S. (eds.) Proceedings of the Neural Information Processing Systems Track on Datasets and Benchmarks. vol. 1 (2021). https://datasets-benchmarks-proceedings.neurips.cc/paper_files/paper/2021/file/6ea9ab1baa0efb9e19094440c317e21b-Paper-round1.pdf
17. Hu, E.J., et al.: LoRA: low-Rank adaptation of large language models (2021). https://arxiv.org/abs/2106.09685

18. Huguet Cabot, P.L., Navigli, R.: REBEL: relation extraction by end-to-end language generation. In: Findings of the Association for Computational Linguistics: EMNLP 2021, pp. 2370–2381. Association for Computational Linguistics, Punta Cana, Dominican Republic (2021). https://aclanthology.org/2021.findings-emnlp.204
19. Jain, S., Harde, P., Mihindukulasooriya, N.: Nyon: a multilingual modular legal ontology for representing court judgements. In: Semantic Intelligence: Select Proceedings of ISIC 2022, pp. 175–183. Springer (2023)
20. Jain, S., et al.: Constructing a knowledge graph from Indian legal domain corpus. In: TEXT2KG/MK@ ESWC, pp. 80–93 (2022)
21. Jiang, A.Q., et al.: Mistral 7b (2023). https://arxiv.org/abs/2310.06825
22. Koehn, P.: Europarl: a parallel corpus for statistical machine translation. In: Proceedings of Machine Translation Summit X: Papers, pp. 79–86. Phuket, Thailand (Sep 13-15 2005). https://aclanthology.org/2005.mtsummit-papers.11
23. Koreeda, Y., Manning, C.: ContractNLI: a dataset for document-level natural language inference for contracts. In: Moens, M.F., Huang, X., Specia, L., Yih, S.W.t. (eds.) Findings of the Association for Computational Linguistics: EMNLP 2021, pp. 1907–1919. Association for Computational Linguistics, Punta Cana, Dominican Republic (2021). https://doi.org/10.18653/v1/2021.findings-emnlp.164, https://aclanthology.org/2021.findings-emnlp.164
24. Nazarenko, A., Wyner, A., Lévy, F., Zargayouna, H.: Semantic Search in Legislation. In: ECIR 2023 Workshop: Legal Information Retrieval, pp. 14–16 (2023). https://tmr.liacs.nl/legalIR/LegalIR2023_proceedings.pdf
25. Peng, B., et al.: Graph Retrieval-Augmented Generation: A Survey (2024). https://arxiv.org/abs/2408.08921
26. Salaün, O., Piedboeuf, F., Le Berre, G., Alfonso-Hermelo, D., Langlais, P.: EUROPA: a legal multilingual keyphrase generation dataset. In: Ku, L.W., Martins, A., Srikumar, V. (eds.) Proceedings of the 62nd Annual Meeting of the Association for Computational Linguistics (Volume 1: Long Papers), pp. 12718–12736. Association for Computational Linguistics, Bangkok, Thailand (2024). https://doi.org/10.18653/v1/2024.acl-long.687, https://aclanthology.org/2024.acl-long.687
27. Sanmartin, D.: KG-RAG: bridging the Gap Between Knowledge and Creativity (2024). https://arxiv.org/abs/2405.12035
28. Sun, Y., Shi, Q., Qi, L., Zhang, Y.: JointLK: joint reasoning with language models and knowledge graphs for commonsense question answering. In: Carpuat, M., de Marneffe, M.C., Meza Ruiz, I.V. (eds.) Proceedings of the 2022 Conference of the North American Chapter of the Association for Computational Linguistics: Human Language Technologies. pp. 5049–5060. Association for Computational Linguistics, Seattle, United States (2022). https://doi.org/10.18653/v1/2022.naacl-main.372, https://aclanthology.org/2022.naacl-main.372
29. Touvron, H., et al.: Llama 2: open Foundation and Fine-Tuned Chat Models (2023). https://arxiv.org/abs/2307.09288
30. Tuggener, D., von Däniken, P., Peetz, T., Cieliebak, M.: LEDGAR: a large-scale multi-label corpus for text classification of legal provisions in contracts. In: Calzolari, N., et al (eds.) Proceedings of the Twelfth Language Resources and Evaluation Conference, pp. 1235–1241. European Language Resources Association, Marseille, France (2020). https://aclanthology.org/2020.lrec-1.155
31. Tunstall, L., et al.: Zephyr: direct distillation of lm alignment (2023). https://arxiv.org/abs/2310.16944

32. Yao, Y., et al.: DocRED: a large-scale document-level relation extraction dataset. In: Korhonen, A., Traum, D., Màrquez, L. (eds.) Proceedings of the 57th Annual Meeting of the Association for Computational Linguistics, pp. 764–777. Association for Computational Linguistics, Florence, Italy (2019). https://doi.org/10.18653/v1/P19-1074, https://aclanthology.org/P19-1074
33. Yasunaga, M., Ren, H., Bosselut, A., Liang, P., Leskovec, J.: QA-GNN: reasoning with language models and knowledge graphs for question answering. In: Toutanova, K., et al (eds.) Proceedings of the 2021 Conference of the North American Chapter of the Association for Computational Linguistics: Human Language Technologies, pp. 535–546. Association for Computational Linguistics, Online (2021). https://doi.org/10.18653/v1/2021.naacl-main.45, https://aclanthology.org/2021.naacl-main.45
34. Ye, H., et al.: Contrastive triple extraction with generative transformer. In: Proceedings of the AAAI Conference on Artificial Intelligence **35**(16), 14257–14265 (2021) https://doi.org/10.1609/aaai.v35i16.17677, https://ojs.aaai.org/index.php/AAAI/article/view/17677
35. Zeng, X., Zeng, D., He, S., Liu, K., Zhao, J.: Extracting relational facts by an end-to-end neural model with copy mechanism. In: Proceedings of the 56th Annual Meeting of the Association for Computational Linguistics (Volume 1: Long Papers), pp. 506–514 (2018)
36. Zhang, H., Shafiq, M.O.: Triple-aware reasoning: a retrieval-augmented generation approach for enhancing question-answering tasks with knowledge graphs and large language models. In: Proceedings of the Canadian Conference on Artificial Intelligence (2024). https://caiac.pubpub.org/pub/bytcy6lo
37. Zheng, H., et al.: PRGC: Potential relation and global correspondence based joint relational triple extraction. In: Zong, C., Xia, F., Li, W., Navigli, R. (eds.) Proceedings of the 59th Annual Meeting of the Association for Computational Linguistics and the 11th International Joint Conference on Natural Language Processing (Volume 1: Long Papers), pp. 6225–6235. Association for Computational Linguistics, Online (2021). https://doi.org/10.18653/v1/2021.acl-long.486, https://aclanthology.org/2021.acl-long.486/
38. Zhu, T., et al.: Towards accurate and consistent evaluation: a dataset for distantly-supervised relation extraction. In: Scott, D., Bel, N., Zong, C. (eds.) Proceedings of the 28th International Conference on Computational Linguistics, pp. 6436–6447. International Committee on Computational Linguistics, Barcelona, Spain (Online) (2020). https://doi.org/10.18653/v1/2020.coling-main.566, https://aclanthology.org/2020.coling-main.566

Heterogeneous Graph Representation for Dataset Link Prediction on Dynamic and Sparse Scholarly Graphs

Ornella Irrera[1(✉)], Matteo Lissandrini[2], Daniele Dell'Aglio[3], and Gianmaria Silvello[1]

[1] Department of Information Engineering, University of Padova, Padova, Italy
{ornella.irrera,gianmaria.silvello}@unipd.it

[2] Department of Foreign Languages and Literatures, University of Verona, Verona, Italy
matteo.lissandrini@univr.it

[3] Department of Computer Science, Aalborg University, Aalborg, Denmark
dade@cs.aau.dk

Abstract. Scientific data are crucial for conducting and validating research, yet they are often undervalued and poorly integrated within the broader scientific ecosystem. This issue is reflected in the typically inadequate documentation of datasets and their weak connections to other research outputs in Scholarly Knowledge Graphs (SKGs).

Real-world SKGs present several challenges, including their large scale, heterogeneity (with nodes such as authors, venues, papers, and datasets), sparsity, and incompleteness (e.g., partial or missing descriptive nodes' metadata). SKGs are also dynamic, constantly evolving as new entities are introduced.

This paper presents a novel method for heterogeneous graph representation designed to improve publication-dataset link prediction – crucial for enhancing data discoverability and reuse. Our approach effectively addresses the challenges outlined, ensuring suitability for inductive settings. Extensive evaluations demonstrate that our method outperforms state-of-the-art techniques, showcasing its robustness and effectiveness in a wide range of scenarios. This makes it a viable solution for real-world applications, where it can contribute to improving search and access to scientific data within SKGs.

Keywords: Dataset link prediction · Scholarly knowledge graphs · Representation learning

1 Introduction

Sharing and reusing scientific data – encompassing observations, experimental results, and research-derived information – is now a key part of the scientific progress [4,26,36]. Scientific data allow for validating hypotheses, powering experiments, training AI algorithms, and accelerating research advancements. However, the historical absence of widely accepted practices for sharing,

W.-T. Balke et al. (Eds.): TPDL 2025, LNCS 16097, pp. 452–469, 2026.
https://doi.org/10.1007/978-3-032-05409-8_26

describing, and citing data has led to poorly documented datasets that are hard to find and only loosely connected to related research. As a result, many scientific datasets remain underappreciated and underutilized by the scientific community [5,6,26]. While proper data citation is crucial for giving credit to data curators, robust *publication-dataset linking* methods are essential for locating relevant datasets and connecting them to publications [9], enhancing the visibility of both datasets and their associated authors, improving reusability, and amplifying their overall impact on scientific research.

In this context, Scholarly Knowledge Graphs (SKGs), heterogeneous attributed graphs interconnecting research outcomes, are crucial for efficiently collecting, organizing, and exploring the vast amount of scholarly data – such as publications, authors, and keywords – and their interconnections. Several SKGs, such as the Microsoft Academic Knowledge Graph (MAKG) [32], Open Research Knowledge Graph (ORKG) [20], and the OpenAIRE Graph (OAG) [23], represent datasets along with other entities. These graphs are characterized by their *dynamic nature* (with new publications and datasets continually being added), *incompleteness* (with publications typically having rather complete metadata while datasets often lack adequate descriptions), and *sparsity* (loosely connected publications and datasets). Isolated or loosely connected datasets in SKGs, combined with incomplete and low-quality descriptive metadata, make these datasets difficult to discover and reuse effectively [18]. To address these issues, there is an urgent need for advanced automatic methods to infer missing links between publications and datasets, thereby enhancing SKG connectivity and dataset discoverability. These methods must be *robust* to manage heterogeneity, noise and sparsity, *adaptable* to leverage graph topology when text is lacking and *versatile* to eliminate the need for costly retraining whenever new data is added. Establishing links between publications and datasets is essential for building dense, interconnected research networks that support a variety of downstream tasks. No method has been developed explicitly for connecting publications with datasets. The most advanced approaches in the scholarly domain leverage Graph Representation Learning (GRL) [13,24,37], which transform graph elements into continuous vector spaces to capture structural and semantic properties. While not explicitly designed for publication-dataset link prediction, some GRL methods can be adapted for this purpose. These methods include both *homogeneous approaches* [16,21,30], which assume uniform node and edge types, and *heterogeneous approaches* [7,8,13,24,35,37], which are tailored for graphs with diverse type of nodes and relationships.

In this work, we propose the Scholarly Attention Network (SAN) method and evaluate its performance on dataset link prediction. SAN leverages heterogeneous graph representation and is designed to operate in real-world settings, accommodating heterogeneous, sparse, and noisy SKGs. Additionally, SAN works in both transductive and inductive scenarios – a capability tested for the first time here – and is effective whether full, or incomplete metadata are available. For evaluation, we rely on subsets of OAG, the backbone of the European Open Sci-

ence Cloud (EOSC, https://eosc.eu/), which is open-access, frequently updated, and comprizes scientific datasets.
We address three research questions:

RQ1 (Robustness). How well can dataset link prediction methods cope with the noise and sparsity commonly found in real-world SKGs?
RQ2 (Adaptability). Is it possible to strengthen the role of graph structure when textual metadata is limited?
RQ3 (Versatility). Can the models perform reliably in both transductive and inductive learning scenarios?

The main **contributions** of this work are as follows:

- Introduction of SAN, a novel heterogeneous graph representation method that demonstrates effectiveness and stability across transductive, inductive, and semi-inductive scenarios.
- A comprehensive evaluation across environments varying from metadata-rich to metadata-free, showing that SAN performs well in situations where text is scarce by effectively utilizing graph topology.
- A comparative analysis against existing graph-based baselines, revealing consistent improvements across all evaluated settings.

Outline. In Sect. 2 we describe current state-of-the-art GRL methods; in Sect. 3 we formalize the dataset link prediction task; in Sect. 4 we describe the SAN method; in Sects. 5 and 6 we describe the experimental setup and discuss the results. In Sect. 7, we report an ablation study. Finally, in Sect. 8, we draw some conclusions.

2 Related Works

2.1 Scholarly Knowledge Graphs (SKGs)

SKGs are structured representations of scientific outputs, interconnecting entities such as publications, authors, and datasets. Despite the growing recognition of the value of datasets, several scholarly graphs, like AMiner [27] and DBLP [22], primarily focus on mapping connections between publications.

In contrast, more recent SKGs have started incorporating datasets, such as the MAKG [32], which includes 200 million nodes and over 10 billion relationships; the ORKG [20], which contains about 5 million nodes and 50 million relationships; the DSKG [11], linking 2,000 datasets to 635,000 publications (and other Linked Data sources like MAKG, ORCID, and Wikidata); and the OAG [23], the largest with 227 million nodes and 15 billion relationships, offering open access to more than 60 million datasets. Recently, the MES graph [19], a subgraph of OAG, was published. It is semi-automatically curated and serves as a reliable ground truth dataset for testing graph-based machine learning algorithms.

On the other hand, we found that several state-of-the-art methods have been evaluated on resources that were excluded from our study due to various limitations – such as a high degree of homogeneity, task-specific design, reliance solely on metadata for prediction and recommendation, or a lack of representation of real-world SKGs. Specifically: (i) LinearSVM_Dataset is a bipartite graph with only 1,691 dataset titles (from DSKG [11]) and $88K$ abstracts from MAKG, offering limited structural and relational diversity; (ii) The DataFinder Dataset [31] is not a proper SKG, as it lacks critical node types such as authors, venues, and organizations, consisting solely of 17K textual queries paired with 7K relevant datasets; (iii) The Delve [1] subsets, include datasets linked to an average of two publications each – a connectivity level that does not reflect the higher sparsity observed in real-world SKGs, where most datasets are linked to only a single publication.

2.2 Publication-Dataset Link Prediction

To date, no existing method specifically addresses the problem of interlinking publications and datasets. A straightforward approach could involve generating separate embeddings for publications and datasets, and then combining them to assess their mutual relevance and establish meaningful connections between them. Several methods exist to generate the embeddings. Techniques like Node2Vec [15] and Metapath2Vec [10] capture structural features through graph exploration and generate node embeddings. Translational models like TransE [3] represent relationships as vector translations, making them effective for capturing semantic similarity between entities. ComplEx [28] extends this by handling asymmetric relations using complex-valued embeddings. Other methods instead rely on GRL.

Graph Representation Learning (GRL). Representation learning in graphs aims at converting nodes, edges, or entire graphs into continuous vector spaces in a way that the resulting representations effectively capture the graph's structural, semantic, and relational information. These representations are used to perform various tasks, including node classification, link prediction, and recommendation.

Some approaches are designed for homogeneous graphs. Graph Convolutional Networks (GCNs) [21] focuses on learning node embeddings by aggregating and transforming information from neighboring nodes with graph convolutions. GraphSAGE [16] samples a fixed set of representative neighbors from each node and aggregates neighbors' representations based on mean, LSTM or pooling techniques. GAT [30] employs a similar method and proved to be effective on inductive settings by learning nodes representations via attention mechanism.

Other GRL techniques focus on heterogeneous graphs [34], which is more challenging due to the multiple types of nodes and edges, and varying feature sets across nodes. HetGNN [37] addresses these challenges by sampling neighbors for each type from a node's neighborhood and aggregating them using a bi-LSTM. RGCN [8] builds on GCNs by incorporating edge and node types. Other methods use attention mechanisms: GATNE [7] handles multiplex graphs by integrating edge attributes, while HGT [17] employs a transformer-based and type-specific attention mechanism to manage diverse node and edge types. HAN [35] and MAGNN [13] leverage *metapaths*, sequences of node and edge types that define relational patterns, with HAN aggregating information from different metapaths and MAGNN performing both intra- and inter-metapath aggregation. HiNormer [24] uses two encoders, a local structure encoder and a heterogeneous relation encoder.

HAN, HGT, HetGNN, MAGNN, and HiNormer have been tested on various subsets of AMiner and DBLP, but they considered only heavily cleaned subgraphs without dataset nodes. HetGNN and HGT were evaluated for link prediction (HetGNN for author-author and HGT for paper-author links).

3 Task Definition and Challenges

This section provides a formal definition of SKG, heterogeneous GRL, and the publication-dataset link prediction task with its open challenges.

Definition 1. *A Scholarly Knowledge Graph (SKG) is a tuple*

$$\mathcal{G}:(\mathcal{V}, \mathcal{E}, \mathcal{A}, \mathcal{R}, \alpha, \beta)$$

where $\mathcal{V}, \mathcal{E}, \mathcal{A}, \mathcal{R}$ are the sets of nodes, edges, node types, edge types, respectively. Then, $\alpha:\mathcal{V}\rightarrow\mathcal{A}$ is a node type function that maps each node $v\in\mathcal{V}$ to one node type $a\in\mathcal{A}$, while $\beta:\mathcal{E}\rightarrow\mathcal{R}$ is an edge type function that maps each edge $e\in\mathcal{E}$ to an edge type $r\in\mathcal{R}$. An SKG is heterogeneous *if it has multiple node and edge types such that $|\mathcal{A}| + |\mathcal{R}| > 2$.*

An SKG typically combines structural information (edges) with semantic details (nodes and their types). Its heterogeneous nature introduces complexity but also enables the modeling of diverse relationships and attributes among different entities. The nodes' attributes are the *metadata* – data providing information about other data – which are represented as key–value pairs describing properties such as the title, DOI, and description of the research outcomes.

Definition 2. *We denote the* `publication` *as $\mathcal{V}_p$ and the* `dataset` *nodes as $\mathcal{V}_d$, where $\mathcal{V}_p \cap \mathcal{V}_d=\emptyset$. The goal of* publication-dataset link prediction *task is to estimate the likelihood of an edge existing between two nodes (u, v), where $u \in \mathcal{V}_p$ and $v\in\mathcal{V}_d$, such that $\psi : (\mathcal{V}_p\times\mathcal{V}_d)\rightarrow[0, 1]$.*

In this work, we do not take into account the semantics associated with the edges. Although various semantic types exist to describe different kinds of relations between entities, we do not consider them in our analysis.

The publication-dataset link prediction task presents significant challenges due to the sparse and incomplete nature of SKGs, which often contain multiple connected components, duplicated nodes, missing links, and heterogeneous,

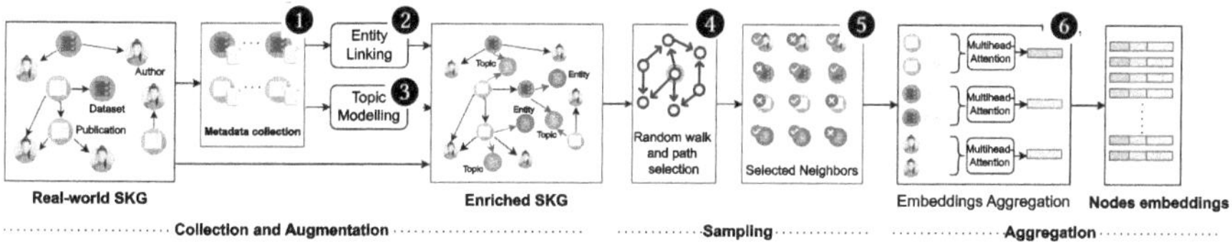

Fig. 1. The SAN Architecture comprising the collection and augmentation, neighbors sampling, and the aggregation phases.

incomplete metadata. Additionally, no existing methods are specifically designed to address link prediction in SKGs that exhibit these complexities. This challenge is further compunded by the absence of publicly available datasets tailored for this task. These factors underscore the problem's complexity and highlight the need for novel approaches to handle the structural intricacies and data gaps in SKGs.

We study the dataset link prediction task as a node-representation learning problem.

Definition 3. *Given an heterogeneous SKG $\mathcal{G}$, the objective of GRL is to learn a function $f\colon \mathcal{V} \rightarrow \mathbb{R}^d$ that maps each node $v \in \mathcal{V}$ to a d-dimensional embedding space, where $d \ll |\mathcal{V}|$. This embedding is designed such that for any two nodes $u \in \mathcal{V}_p$ and $v \in \mathcal{V}_d$, the dot-product of their corresponding vectors $\boldsymbol{u} \cdot \boldsymbol{v}$ approximates the scoring function ψ.*

GRL provides a way to map heterogeneous nodes into a shared embedding space, capturing their features and the graph's structure. This is crucial for the dataset link prediction task, where the relationship between query nodes (publications) and potential datasets must be effectively learned and represented in the embedding space.

4 Architecture

In this section, we present the SAN architecture, illustrated in Fig. 1. The pipeline consists of three phases: (1) collection and augmentation, (2) neighbor sampling, and (3) aggregation.

Collection and Augmentation. This phase is carried out offline to address the sparsity issue in SKGs. Given an SKG as input, SAN extracts the available textual metadata from the *publication* and *dataset* nodes (❶). Then, it performs entity linking (❷) [2] to identify and disambiguate entities within the textual content. Additionally, it applies topic modeling (❸) using BERTopic [14], which leverages transformer-based embeddings and c-TF-IDF to group similar documents based on shared topics.

The topics represent broader themes that act as central hubs within the SKG, connecting multiple disconnected components and improving the overall connectivity of the graph. On the other hand, entities are more specific and, when shared between nodes, suggest that those nodes are likely related by similar or closely related content. This distinction strengthens the graph's structure by using topics to boost general connectivity and entities to emphasize specific content overlaps between nodes. Entities and topics are subsequently integrated into the SKG as new nodes of type *entity* and *topic*. This phase results in an enhanced SKG. For each node, SAN extracts and concatenates two vectors: one based on graph topology using node2vec [15], and the other based on textual metadata using pre-trained models. In our case we employ the `all-MiniLM-L6-v2` sentence transformer[1] for longer textual metadata and `phrase-BERT` [33] for shorter text like topics. This phase aims to address the sparsity issue often affecting the SKGs, improving *robustness (RQ1)* by adding new nodes that enhance the graph's connectivity.

Sampling. Due to the small-world property of many graphs, multi-hop neighborhoods can include a substantial number of nodes. Therefore, given a target node v in the enriched SKG, this phase aims to explore the neighborhood of v and gather a representative set of neighbors of various types. A common neighbor sampling method, used in approaches such as GraphSAGE, is random sampling. However, this approach may produce an unrepresentative sample because SKGs are heterogeneous, with a highly imbalanced distribution of node types. In practice, the author nodes often lack disambiguation, leading to a large number of mostly isolated nodes in the SKG. In contrast, venue nodes are typically fewer and more interconnected.

Taking this issue into account, for a given target node v, we generate a set of random walks of length l originating from v (❹). We ignore edge directions in the SKG because for each edge we can assume there exists an edge in the opposite direction (e.g., for each `cites` edge we can assume a `cited by` exists in the opposite direction). Then, we select the k random walks with the highest similarity scores with the target node v, computed as follows:

$$\text{sim\_score}(v, \text{walk}_j) = \frac{1}{|\text{walk}_j|} \sum_{i \in \text{walk}_j} \frac{cos(\mathbf{v}_v, \mathbf{v}_i)}{d(v, i)}$$

where walk_j is one random walk, $m = |\text{walk}_j|$ is the number of publication and dataset nodes in the walk j, the node i is either a *publication* or a *dataset* ($i \in \{\mathcal{V}_\text{p} \cup \mathcal{V}_\text{d}\}$), $\mathbf{v}_v$ and $\mathbf{v}_i$ are the embeddings encoding the textual metadata of v and i respectively, $cos(\mathbf{v}_\text{v}, \mathbf{v}_i)$ is the cosine similarity, defined as $\frac{\mathbf{v}_\text{v} \cdot \mathbf{v}_i}{\|\mathbf{v}_\text{v}\| \|\mathbf{v}_i\|}$ and d is the distance – i.e., the number of nodes – between the target node v and the node i in the walk. In step (❺), SAN selects the top n publications and datasets with the highest cosine similarity to the target v from the k selected walks. For all other node types, it selects the n nodes closest to the target v within each type. In the sampling phase, the goal is to enhance *adaptability (RQ2)* by selecting a subset of representative neighbors instead of capturing the full neighborhood of

[1] https://huggingface.co/sentence-transformers/all-MiniLM-L6-v2.

a node. This strategy allows the model to adapt to dynamic graphs of varying sizes, without relying on global knowledge of the entire node set.

Aggregation. In the aggregation step (❻), SAN uses multihead attention [29] to combine neighbor vectors and derive the final embedding representation of the target node v. Multiple attention heads allow us to focus on different aspects of the input [29].

Formally, SAN combines three input matrices: Query ($\mathbf{Q}$), Key ($\mathbf{K}$), and Value ($\mathbf{V}$), of sizes (n_Q, d_{model}), (n_K, d_{model}), (n_V, d_{model}) where n_Q, n_K, n_V are the numbers of queries, keys, values embeddings respectively, and d_{model} their dimension. Queries, keys, and values are matrices constructed from node embeddings and used to compute attention scores. For each attention head $\vartheta_0, \ldots, \vartheta_\ell, \ldots, \vartheta_H$, these matrices are transformed as follows: $\mathbf{Q}_\ell{=}\mathbf{Q}\mathbf{W}_\ell^Q$, $\mathbf{K}_\ell{=}\mathbf{K}\mathbf{W}_\ell^K$, and $\mathbf{V}_\ell{=}\mathbf{V}\mathbf{W}_\ell^V$, where $\mathbf{W}_\ell^Q$, $\mathbf{W}_\ell^K$, and $\mathbf{W}_\ell^V$ are projection matrices of size (d_{model}, d_k) and $d_k{=}\frac{d_{model}}{H}$ is the dimensionality of the projection space for each head. For each head ϑ_ℓ, the attention scores are computed using the scaled dot-product attention mechanism:

$$\vartheta_\ell = \text{Attention}(\mathbf{Q}_\ell, \mathbf{K}_\ell, \mathbf{V}_\ell) = \text{softmax}\left(\frac{\mathbf{Q}_\ell \mathbf{K}_\ell^T}{\sqrt{d_k}}\right)\mathbf{V}_\ell.$$

The outputs from all heads are then concatenated and linearly projected to form the final output. The embeddings obtained are finally concatenated to obtain the final target node embedding representation.

We experimented with various embedding combination methods, including bi-LSTM, GRU, and mean pooling, both as replacements for multihead attention and for the final concatenation step. However, the combination of multihead attention and concatenation consistently outperformed these alternatives.

Multihead attention excels at capturing the intricate relationships between topological structures and textual metadata, allowing the model to understand how individual node features interact across different nodes and their descriptions. This capability is especially crucial in heterogeneous graphs, where different node and edge types may have varying levels of importance.

This phase enhances *versatility (RQ3)* by addressing the integration of multiple information sources, enabling the model to adjust to a range of real-world metadata scenarios.

Training. In this work, we used a mini-batch gradient descent training procedure. We optimized the model by minimizing the cross-entropy loss using negative sampling. Formally, the loss function is defined as:

$$\mathcal{L} = -\left(\sum_{(u,v)\in\mathcal{E}_{p,d}} \log\sigma\left(\mathbf{h}_u^\top \mathbf{h}_v\right) + \sum_{(u',v')\notin\mathcal{E}_{p,d}} \log\sigma\left(-\mathbf{h}_{u'}^\top \mathbf{h}_{v'}\right)\right),$$

where σ represents the sigmoid function, $\mathbf{h}_u$ and $\mathbf{h}_v$ are the embedding representations for publication u and dataset v, $\mathcal{E}_{\text{p,d}}$ denotes the set of positive edges

Table 1. Nodes and edges statistics of the used datasets.

	Nodes		Edge			
MES	Publication (P)	2,1K	P–P	450	P–A	9,8K
	Dataset (D)	3K	P–D	2,5K	D–A	10,2K
	Author (A)	9,5K	D–D	1,2K		
PubMed	Publication (P)	42,6K	P–P	18,3K	D–K	17K
	Dataset (D)	33,8K	P–D	29,5K	P–V	42,6K
	Author (A)	334K	D–D	8K	P–O	87,5K
	Keyword (K)	10,8K	P–A	180K	D–O	515
	Venue (V)	6,7K	D–A	94,6K		
	Organization (O)	14,8K	P–K	6,6K		

between publications and datasets. For each positive edge $(u, v) \in \mathcal{E}_{p,d}$, we sample uniformly at random a negative pair $(u', v') \notin \mathcal{E}_{p,d}$, of publications and datasets not directly connected in the ground-truth.

5 Evaluation

We evaluate SAN across three increasingly complex settings. In the first setting, referred to as **transductive**, the entire set of publications and datasets is accessible during training, and the SKG remains unchanged. This standard setup has also been adopted in previous works [13,24,37]. In the second setting, **semi-inductive**, new publications are introduced at test time, while all datasets are available during training. The task involves predicting links between these unseen publications and the known datasets, and is relevant in order to connect to new publications datasets which can be may be thematically related. It is worth noting that this semi-inductive scenario is sometimes labeled as simply "inductive" in prior work [37]. In contrast, we define a **fully inductive** setting as one where both new publications and new datasets appear during testing, closely reflecting the dynamics of real-world SKGs. The goal here is to predict links between the new, unseen publications and datasets. Further, we test the models' robustness in the absence of textual metadata under the following different metadata conditions for each setting. The **ideal metadata setup** represents the ideal scenario where all datasets are fully described by complete metadata – i.e., all the datasets have a title and a description. The **real metadata setup** represents intermediate scenarios where only 75%, 50%, or 25% of the datasets have complete metadata, with the datasets containing metadata randomly selected. This setting reflects real-world conditions, as in real SKGs, datasets may or may not have comprehensive and descriptive metadata. The implementation of SAN and the related datasets are available on GitHub[2].

Datasets and Measures. We use two SKGs extracted from the OAG [23]: MES [19] and PubMed[3]. MES is a curated scientific graph interconnecting pub-

[2] https://github.com/HeterogeneousGL-SAN/SAN.
[3] Datasets are available at https://doi.org/10.6084/m9.figshare.26661382.v1.

lications, datasets, and authors; it represents a reliable snapshot of the scientific activity of the European Marine Science (MES) community of OpenAIRE. PubMed is a larger subgraph of the OAG also interconnecting a set of publications and datasets, authors, venues, organizations and keywords. Differently from MES, PubMed is not curated. The statistics of the resulting SKG are described in Table 1. We divided the $P-D$ (publication-dataset) edges into five sets: training, validation, and three test sets (transductive, semi-inductive, and fully inductive). The $P-D$ edges in the three test sets were randomly extracted from the original MES and PubMed datasets. Publications and datasets included in the semi-inductive and fully inductive test sets were removed from the original MES and PubMed datasets. From the filtered MES and PubMed datasets, we extracted a set of $P-D$ edges for validation and left the remaining part to train the model. In MES, we used $2K$ edges for training, 155 for validation and 155 for each of the three test sets; in PubMed we used $26.8K$ for training, $1.8K$ for validation, and $1.8K$ for each of the three test sets. For evaluation, we use the Area Under the ROC Curve (AUC) curve and F1-score. AUC and F1-score have been extensively used to evaluate link prediction performances of several graph learning approaches [13,37]. The AUC is a performance metric that measures a model's ability to distinguish between classes. The F1-score, on the other hand, is the harmonic mean of precision and recall. It provides a balanced measure that accounts for both false positives and false negatives, making it particularly useful in scenarios with class imbalance.

Parameters of SAN. We initialized publication and dataset nodes with embeddings from the `all-MiniLM-L6-v2` pretrained sentence transformer, chosen for its effectiveness on short text. For keywords, entities, and topics – typically short phrases of one to five words – we used `phrase-BERT` to generate their embeddings. Additionally, topological embeddings for all nodes were computed using `node2vec` [15]. Entity extraction was performed on publication and dataset metadata using DBpedia Spotlight [25], with a confidence threshold of 0.75. Topics were identified via BERTopic [14], using a minimum cluster size of 2 documents.

SAN was trained for 100 epochs with early stopping to reduce training time, using a learning rate of 10^{-5} and a mini-batch size of 1024. For each target node, we sampled 5 neighbors from publication or dataset nodes, 5 from keyword, topic, or entity types, and 5 from venue, author, and organization types. The multi-head attention mechanism used 8 heads and produced embeddings of dimension 128. Hyperparameters – including number of epochs, learning rate, batch size, attention heads, and neighbor sampling counts – were tuned via grid-search.

Baselines. We compared SAN with five inductive graph-based baselines. For each baseline, we report the best results obtained through grid search. The node embeddings were initialized by concatenating the textual embeddings using `all-MiniLM-L6-v2` with those from `node2Vec`. GraphSAGE [16] (SAGE for brevity) and GAT [30] were trained for 200 epochs with a learning rate of 10^{-5}

and early stopping. The output dimension was set to 128. Similarly, HAN [35] and HGT [17] were trained for 200 epochs with a learning rate of 10^{-4}, also utilizing early stopping, with an output dimension of 128. HetGNN [37] (HGNN for brevity) was trained for 100 epochs with early stopping, a learning rate of 10^{-5}, and 10 neighbors per node type, as specified in the original paper. To implement the baselines we used PyTorch Geometric [12].

Certain baselines were excluded from this study. GATNE [7] was not considered because it requires multiple relation types within the same set of nodes. MAGNN [13] was excluded since it was designed for the node classification task, and was not designed for the inductive settings. HiNormer [24] was also not included, as it has not been designed for link prediction tasks.

6 Results

In this section, we report the experimental results for dataset link prediction on MES and PubMed for all the tested settings.

Table 2 present the results for the link prediction task on the MES and PubMed datasets in the three settings: transductive, semi-inductive, and fully inductive. On the MES dataset, SAN consistently outperforms all baselines in nearly all scenarios both in terms of AUC and F1 score, except when only 25% of the datasets have no metadata where SAGE and GAT perform better than SAN in terms of F1 score. All models perform best in the transductive setting with full metadata availability, the default and least realistic scenario in the current academic landscape. Notably, in this scenario, the performance of all examined models, including SAN, tends to decrease slightly in semi- and fully inductive settings. This is reasonable as the prediction is made for unseen nodes. SAN and SAGE are the only methods whose AUC and F1 exceed the 0.9 in transductive, semi-inductive and inductive settings. The exception is HAN, which performs significantly worse in the semi-inductive and inductive settings. When evaluating performance in more realistic conditions where some datasets lack metadata, we observe that as the percentage of datasets with metadata decreases (from 75% to 25%), the performance of all the tested models decreases. This decline underscores the importance of text-based features for baselines. Furthermore, as the percentage of datasets with metadata decreases, the ability of the baselines to generalize to new, unseen data diminishes. SAN is the only method that consistently maintains an AUC above 0.9 and an F1 score of at least 0.8, even when the 50% of the dataset nodes lack textual metadata. This suggests that the SAN approach, combining different node embeddings while incorporating topology-based features, effectively mitigates the impact of missing text-based features, significantly affecting the performance of other baselines. Interestingly, SAGE and GAT, designed for homogeneous graphs, emerge as the most resilient baselines. In the MES dataset, reducing metadata coverage to 25% leads to a significant performance drop across all methods. For instance, SAN's AUC falls by 0.1 when metadata availability decreases from 50% to 25%. This is due to the limited number of datasets with metadata – only 750 – insufficient for accurate prediction in the MES SKG. Notably, SAN is robust when applied to real-world, sparse, large, and not curated SKGs like PubMed. As in the previous case, the performance of all tested methods declines in semi-inductive and inductive settings, along with the decreasing availability of textual metadata. This is expected as the setting becomes increasingly challenging. SAN demonstrates the greatest resilience to the absence of textual metadata and inductive settings, remaining the only method maintaining an AUC above 0.9 and an F1 score above 0.8 across all settings with more than 25% available metadata and 0.8 and 0.7, respectively, at 25%. In this regard, none of the other tested methods surpass an AUC of 0.871 (SAGE) or an F1 score of 0.818 (GAT). Furthermore, performance drops substantially as the number of datasets with available metadata decreases. In the most challenging scenario, with only 25% of datasets containing available metadata and within an inductive setup, SAN surpasses the best baseline (GAT) by 43% in AUC and 25% in F1. We see that HAN and HGNN are the models with the lowest performance on the PubMed dataset, having the AUC and F1

Table 2. AUC and F1 score over the MES (left) and PUBMED (right) datasets in transductive (Tran), semi-inductive (Semi), and inductive (Ind) settings. 100% indicates that all the datasets have textual metadata. [75%, 50%, 25%] indicates the percentage of datasets having textual metadata.

			MES						PUBMED					
			SAGE	GAT	HGT	HAN	HGNN	SAN	SAGE	GAT	HGT	HAN	HGNN	SAN
100%	Tran	AUC	0.980	0.933	0.921	0.838	0.912	**0.986**	0.871	0.825	0.839	0.578	0.752	**0.967**
		F1	0.958	0.927	0.860	0.825	0.871	**0.959**	0.798	0.818	0.766	0.532	0.700	**0.878**
	Semi	AUC	0.973	0.904	0.883	0.593	0.899	**0.983**	0.860	0.821	0.793	0.470	0.743	**0.948**
		F1	**0.956**	0.890	0.827	0.653	0.862	0.945	0.790	0.812	0.654	0.433	0.709	**0.860**
	Ind	AUC	0.945	0.896	0.772	0.494	0.872	**0.948**	0.854	0.818	0.710	0.453	0.722	**0.943**
		F1	0.920	0.880	0.746	0.326	0.821	**0.944**	0.790	0.809	0.523	0.422	0.701	**0.858**
75%	Tran	AUC	0.933	0.889	0.856	0.834	0.830	**0.971**	0.727	0.731	0.771	0.572	0.691	**0.942**
		F1	0.920	0.858	0.785	0.823	0.778	**0.926**	0.731	0.747	0.679	0.529	0.617	**0.859**
	Semi	AUC	0.920	0.883	0.845	0.592	0.821	**0.969**	0.707	0.719	0.732	0.469	0.632	**0.940**
		F1	0.885	0.860	0.759	0.652	0.783	**0.894**	0.714	0.735	0.665	0.411	0.609	**0.847**
	Ind	AUC	0.907	0.840	0.734	0.515	0.812	**0.957**	0.703	0.710	0.643	0.459	0.652	**0.938**
		F1	0.872	0.814	0.709	0.369	0.775	**0.876**	0.712	0.734	0.462	0.389	0.573	**0.846**
50%	Tran	AUC	0.901	0.867	0.801	0.815	0.806	**0.951**	0.612	0.644	0.703	0.568	0.567	**0.932**
		F1	0.808	0.817	0.702	0.800	0.754	**0.843**	0.652	0.663	0.668	0.489	0.502	**0.803**
	Semi	AUC	0.851	0.833	0.787	0.582	0.789	**0.944**	0.603	0.630	0.701	0.483	0.564	**0.922**
		F1	0.797	0.788	0.714	0.642	0.735	**0.840**	0.634	0.644	0.576	0.435	0.488	**0.809**
	Ind	AUC	0.753	0.802	0.691	0.505	0.776	**0.943**	0.601	0.627	0.584	0.478	0.499	**0.921**
		F1	0.746	0.769	0.684	0.326	0.710	**0.795**	0.632	0.640	0.532	0.412	0.464	**0.797**
25%	Tran	AUC	0.831	0.826	0.780	0.784	0.802	**0.840**	0.547	0.585	0.688	0.559	0.451	**0.900**
		F1	0.717	**0.745**	0.689	0.690	0.705	0.700	0.566	0.582	0.668	0.478	0.456	**0.716**
	Semi	AUC	0.826	0.771	0.725	0.529	0.764	**0.835**	0.541	0.565	0.649	0.473	0.433	**0.896**
		F1	0.726	**0.732**	0.664	0.629	0.700	0.688	0.564	0.553	0.451	0.421	0.438	**0.707**
	Ind	AUC	0.735	0.748	0.650	0.444	0.732	**0.790**	0.531	0.559	0.512	0.448	0.411	**0.800**
		F1	**0.646**	0.612	0.624	0.284	0.617	0.628	0.556	0.551	0.371	0.398	0.401	**0.693**

Table 3. AUC and F1 scores over the MES dataset in transductive and 100% metadata available setting. The column "no augmentation" refers to the models run excluding topics and entities; "augmentation" reports the results on the enriched graph.

Method	Augmentation		No Augmentation	
	AUC	F1	AUC	F1
GAT	0.872	0.831	0.933	0.927
SAGE	0.901	0.882	**0.980**	**0.958**
HGT	0.932	0.868	0.921	0.860
HAN	0.863	0.844	0.838	0.825
HGNN	0.933	0.884	0.912	0.871
SAN	**0.986**	**0.959**	0.912	0.876

always lower than 0.58 and 0.76, respectively, showing their low effectiveness on real-world SKGs.

7 Ablation Study

Components Analysis. We first assess how the augmentation phase – specifically, the integration of entity and topic nodes – affects performances. In particular, we investigate whether the enriched graph structure enables more meaningful neighborhood interactions and improves the model's ability to capture relevant relationships. In Table 3 presents the performance of five systems with ("augmentation" column) and without ("no augmentation" column) this phase. For GAT and GraphSAGE, the inclusion of heterogeneous node types reduces model effectiveness. In SKGs, embeddings are generated differently depending on node type, and aggregating such diverse representations can hinder overall performance. In contrast, SAN and HGNN gain from the introduction of additional nodes, showing improved results on the enriched graph. This highlights that augmentation is especially advantageous for models designed to leverage structural properties and heterogeneity. For HAN and HGT, omitting the augmentation phase results in a slight performance decrease. In conclusion, augmentation benefits models like SAN and HGNN that leverage heterogeneity and graph structure, while it may have limited or negative effects on models not designed for diverse node types. To assess the effectiveness of different aggregation strategies within SAN, we compared multihead attention, bi-LSTM, GRU, and linear projection. The evaluation was based on AUC and F1 scores on the MES dataset across two settings: an ideal transductive scenario with 100% metadata availability, and a more realistic fully-inductive scenario with only 50% metadata available. Figure 2a shows that multihead attention demonstrates the highest robustness, with bi-LSTM and GRU following closely behind. In contrast, linear projection results in the lowest performance in the dataset link prediction task. These findings suggest that multihead attention is particularly well-suited, as it allows the model to focus on different parts of the embedding space, capturing diverse relational patterns and improving overall predictive performance. Moreover, in scenarios where textual metadata is limited, multihead attention can better leverage topological information, compensating for the lack of text-based features. Finally, we

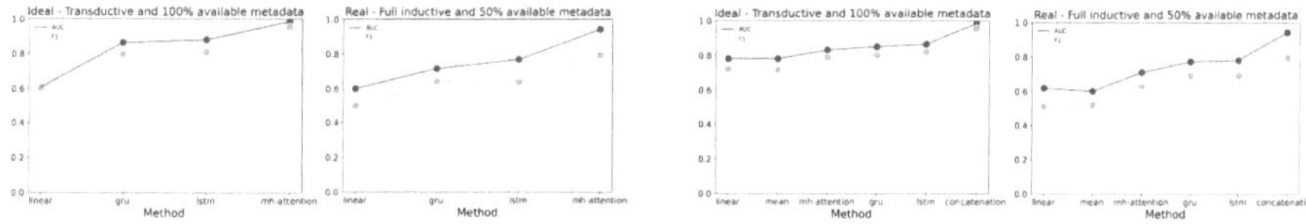

(a) Component-based analysis of the aggregation phase.

(b) Component-based analysis of the combination phase.

Fig. 2. Comparison of aggregation (on the left) and combination phases in the pipeline (on the right).

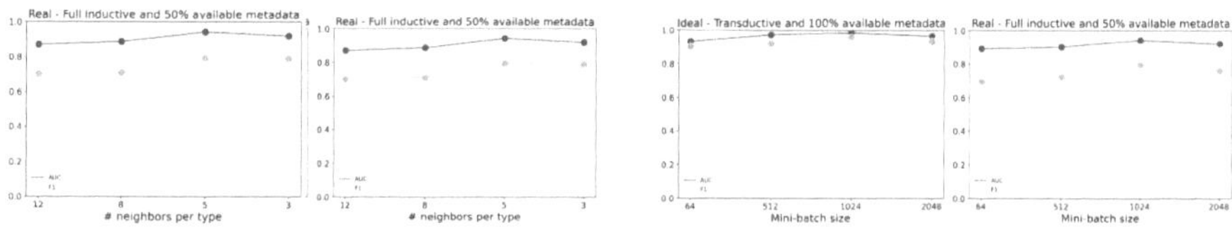

(a) Number of neighbors of a target node sampled for each node type.

(b) Mini-batch size analysis.

Fig. 3. Hyperparameter analysis: number of neighbors (on the left), and mini-batch size (on the right).

assessed the performance of SAN by experimenting with alternative embedding combination strategies in place of simple concatenation. While SAN originally relies on concatenation to merge embeddings, we evaluated several other methods, including bi-LSTM, GRU, multihead attention, linear projection, and mean pooling. Figure 2b presents the results on the MES dataset under both ideal and real-world conditions. Among the tested approaches, concatenation remains the most effective, whereas GRU and linear projection yield the weakest performance.

Hyperparameter Analysis. One key factor that affects efficiency, is the number of neighbors sampled for each node type when targeting a node v_t. SKGs tend to have an imbalanced distribution of node types, so selecting the most representative nodes is crucial to ensure a well-balanced set. Sampling too many nodes may introduce noise by including irrelevant or redundant information, while sampling too few could lead to an incomplete and unrepresentative set of neighbors. Another critical aspect influencing the overall efficiency of the model is the mini-batch size. Smaller batches enable faster training but increase the likelihood of overfitting. On the other hand, larger batches may reduce the risk of overfitting, yet they can lead to slower convergence and may require more computational resources. Figures 3a and 3b display our analysis on the MES dataset. We compared two scenarios: the ideal and the real-world setting. In both cases, performance shows slight variations with the number of neighbors considered, reaching a peak when selecting five neighbors per type. These small fluctuations suggest that multihead attention effectively mitigates the effects of additional or missing nodes, highlighting its adaptability and robustness in real-world SKGs. Regarding mini-batch size, we observe that batches smaller than 1024 lead to a higher risk of overfitting, while larger batches tend to result in slower convergence and increased computational requirements.

8 Conclusions

Scientific data is crucial for research progress, yet datasets are often poorly described and hard to find. While curated SKGs focus mostly on publications, those that include datasets tend to be large but uncurated, with incomplete metadata and weak interlinking. This results in SKGs that are noisy, sparse, and heterogeneous, making data discovery and citation difficult. In this context, link prediction becomes an essential task.

We propose SAN, a method for enriching SKGs and performing heterogeneous GRL. SAN adopts a three-phase approach: it enhances graph connectivity using text-derived nodes, selects relevant neighbors via random walks, and combines their representations with multihead attention. This architecture seamlessly integrates textual information with graph topology while not relying on complete metadata coverage. Additionally, we conduct extensive experiments across three settings (transductive, semi-inductive, fully inductive) and under two metadata conditions (ideal and real) using two benchmark datasets. Our evaluation emphasizes the often overlooked importance of generating predictions for newly added items without requiring model retraining. The results demonstrate SAN's effectiveness compared to five inductive baselines. We explored three research questions focused on **robustness**, **adaptability**, and **versatility**. Our findings show that SAN delivers strong publication-dataset link prediction performances even in inductive scenarios with little textual metadata available, thanks to its ability to extract and utilize topology-based features. Current methods struggle to effectively use high-quality textual metadata. As a consequence, future research should explore more advanced architectures to address this gap. Further experiments should use SAN for other link prediction tasks, like author-venue and publication-venue predictions, to encourage collaborations and suggest relevant venues.

Acknowledgments. This work is supported by the HEREDITARY Project, as part of the European Union's Horizon Europe research and innovation programme under Grant Agreement No GA 101137074.

References

1. Akujuobi, U., Zhang, X.: Delve: A dataset-driven scholarly search and analysis system. SIGKDD Explor. **19**(2), 36–46 (2017). https://doi.org/10.1145/3166054.3166059
2. Balog, K.: Entity-oriented search, The Information Retrieval Series, vol. 39. Springer (2018). https://doi.org/10.1007/978-3-319-93935-3
3. Bordes, A., Usunier, N., García-Durán, A., Weston, J., Yakhnenko, O.: Translating embeddings for modeling multi-relational data. In: Advances in Neural Information Processing Systems 26: 27th Annual Conference on Neural Information Processing Systems 2013. Proceedings of a meeting held December 5-8, 2013, Lake Tahoe, Nevada, United States, pp. 2787–2795 (2013), https://proceedings.neurips.cc/paper/2013/hash/1cecc7a77928ca8133fa24680a88d2f9-Abstract.html
4. Brickley, D., Burgess, M., Noy, N.: Google dataset search: building a search engine for datasets in an open web ecosystem. In: Proceedings of the ACM Web Conference 2019, WWW, pp. 1365–1375. ACM (2019). https://doi.org/10.1145/3308558.3313685, https://doi.org/10.1145/3308558.3313685
5. Buneman, P., et al.: Why data citation isn't working, and what to do about it. Database **2020** (2020)
6. Buneman, P., Dosso, D., Lissandrini, M., Silvello, G.: Data citation and the citation graph. Quant. Sci. Stud. **2**(4), 1399–1422 (2021). https://doi.org/10.1162/qss_a_00166
7. Cen, Y., Zou, X., Zhang, J., Yang, H., Zhou, J., Tang, J.: Representation learning for attributed multiplex heterogeneous network. In: Proceedings of the 25th ACM SIGKDD International Conference on Knowledge Discovery & Data Mining, KDD, pp. 1358–1368. ACM (2019). https://doi.org/10.1145/3292500.3330964
8. Chen, J., Hou, H., Gao, J., Ji, Y., Bai, T.: Rgcn: recurrent graph convolutional networks for target-dependent sentiment analysis. In: Knowledge Science, Engineering and Management - 12th International Conference, KSEM 2019, Proceedings, Part I. Lecture Notes in Computer Science, vol. 11775, pp. 667–675. Springer (2019). https://doi.org/10.1007/978-3-030-29551-6_59
9. Costello, M.J., Michener, W.K., Gahegan, M., Zhang, Z.Q., Bourne, P.E.: Biodiversity data should be published, cited, and peer reviewed. Trends Ecol. Evol. **28**(8), 454–461 (2013)
10. Dong, Y., Chawla, N.V., Swami, A.: metapath2vec: scalable representation learning for heterogeneous networks. In: Proceedings of the 23rd ACM SIGKDD International Conference on Knowledge Discovery and Data Mining, pp. 135–144. ACM, New York, NY, USA (2017). https://doi.org/10.1145/3097983.3098036
11. Färber, M., Lamprecht, D.: The data set knowledge graph: creating a linked open data source for data sets. Quant. Sci. Stud. **2**(4), 1324–1355 (2021)
12. Fey, M., Lenssen, J.E.: Fast graph representation learning with pytorch geometric. arXiv preprint arXiv:1903.02428 (2019)
13. Fu, X., Zhang, J., Meng, Z., King, I.: Magnn: Metapath aggregated graph neural network for heterogeneous graph embedding. In: Proceedings of the ACM Web Conference 2020, WWW, pp. 2331–2341. ACM, New York, NY, USA (2020). https://doi.org/10.1145/3366423.3380297
14. Grootendorst, M.: Bertopic: neural topic modeling with a class-based TF-IDF procedure. arXiv preprint arXiv:2203.05794 (2022)

15. Grover, A., Leskovec, J.: node2vec: scalable feature learning for networks. In: Proceedings of the 22nd ACM SIGKDD International Conference on Knowledge Discovery and Data Mining, pp. 855–864. ACM (2016). https://doi.org/10.1145/2939672.2939754
16. Hamilton, W., Ying, Z., Leskovec, J.: Inductive representation learning on large graphs. In: Advances in Neural Information Processing Systems 30: Annual Conference on Neural Information Processing Systems 2017, pp. 1024–1034. Curran Associates, Inc. (2017)
17. Hu, Z., Dong, Y., Wang, K., Sun, Y.: Heterogeneous graph transformer. In: Proceedings of the ACM Web Conference 2020, WWW, pp. 2704–2710. ACM (2020). https://doi.org/10.1145/3366423.3380027
18. Irrera, O., Lissandrini, M., Dell'Aglio, D., Silvello, G.: Reproducibility and analysis of scientific dataset recommendation methods. In: Proceedings of the 18th ACM Conference on Recommender Systems, RecSys 2024, Bari, Italy, October 14-18, 2024, pp. 570–579. ACM (2024). https://doi.org/10.1145/3640457.3688071
19. Irrera, O., Mannocci, A., Manghi, P., Silvello, G.: A novel curated scholarly graph connecting textual and data publications. J. Data Inform. Qual. **15**(3) (2023). https://doi.org/10.1145/3597310
20. Jaradeh, M.Y. et al.: Open research knowledge graph: Next generation infrastructure for semantic scholarly knowledge. In: Proceedings of the 10th International Conference on Knowledge Capture, K-CAP 2019, Marina Del Rey, CA, USA, November 19-21, 2019 pp. 243–246. ACM (2019). https://doi.org/10.1145/3360901.3364435
21. Kipf, T.N., Welling, M.: Semi-supervised classification with graph convolutional networks. arXiv preprint arXiv:1609.02907 (2016)
22. Lv, Q., et al.: Are we really making much progress? revisiting, benchmarking and refining heterogeneous graph neural networks. In: KDD '21: The 27th ACM SIGKDD Conference on Knowledge Discovery and Data Mining, pp. 1150–1160. ACM (2021). https://doi.org/10.1145/3447548.3467350
23. Manghi, P., et al.: Openaire research graph dump (Dec 2022). https://doi.org/10.5281/zenodo.7488618. A new version of this dataset is published every 6 months. The content available on the OpenAIRE EXPLORE and CONNECT portals might be more up-to- date with respect to the data you find here
24. Mao, Q., Liu, Z., Liu, C., Sun, J.: Hinormer: Representation learning on heterogeneous information networks with graph transformer. In: Proceedings of the ACM Web Conference 2023, WWW, pp. 599–610. ACM (2023). https://doi.org/10.1145/3543507.3583493
25. Mendes, P.N., Jakob, M., García-Silva, A., Bizer, C.: Dbpedia spotlight: shedding light on the web of documents. In: Proceedings the 7th International Conference on Semantic Systems, I-SEMANTICS, pp. 1–8 (2011)
26. Silvello, G.: Theory and practice of data citation. J. Am. Soc. Inf. Sci. **69**(1), 6–20 (2018)
27. Tang, J., Zhang, J., Yao, L., Li, J., Zhang, L., Su, Z.: Arnetminer: extraction and mining of academic social networks. In: Proceedings of the 14th ACM SIGKDD International Conference on Knowledge Discovery and Data Mining, pp. 990–998. ACM, New York, NY, USA (2008). https://doi.org/10.1145/1401890.1402008
28. Trouillon, T., Welbl, J., Riedel, S., Gaussier, E., Bouchard, G.: Complex embeddings for simple link prediction. In: Proceedings of the 33nd International Conference on Machine Learning, ICML 2016, New York City, NY, USA, June 19-24, 2016. JMLR Workshop and Conference Proceedings, vol. 48, pp. 2071–2080. JMLR.org (2016). http://proceedings.mlr.press/v48/trouillon16.html

29. Vaswani, A.: Attention is all you need. arXiv preprint arXiv:1706.03762 (2017)
30. Veličković, P., Cucurull, G., Casanova, A., Romero, A., Lio, P., Bengio, Y.: Graph attention networks. arXiv preprint arXiv:1710.10903 (2017)
31. Viswanathan, V., Gao, L., Wu, T., Liu, P., Neubig, G.: DataFinder: Scientific dataset recommendation from natural language descriptions. In: Proceedings of the 61st Annual Meeting of the Association for Computational Linguistics (Volume 1: Long Papers, pp. 10288–10303. ACL (2023). https://doi.org/10.18653/v1/2023.acl-long.573, https://aclanthology.org/2023.acl-long.573
32. Wang, K., Shen, Z., Huang, C., Wu, C., Dong, Y., Kanakia, A.: Microsoft academic graph: when experts are not enough. Quant. Sci. Stud. **1**(1), 396–413 (2020). https://doi.org/10.1162/qss_a_00021
33. Wang, S., Thompson, L., Iyyer, M.: Phrase-BERT: improved phrase embeddings from BERT with an application to corpus exploration. In: Proc. of the 2021 Conference on Empirical Methods in Natural Language Processing, pp. 10837–10851. ACL (2021)
34. Wang, X., Bo, D., Shi, C., Fan, S., Ye, Y., Philip, S.Y.: A survey on heterogeneous graph embedding: methods, techniques, applications and sources. IEEE Trans. Big Data **9**(2), 415–436 (2023). https://doi.org/10.1109/TBDATA.2022.3177455
35. Wang, X., et al.: Heterogeneous graph attention network. In: Proceedings of the ACM Web Conference 2019, WWW, pp. 2022–2032. ACM, New York, NY, USA (2019). https://doi.org/10.1145/3308558.3313562
36. Wilkinson, M.D., et al.: The fair guiding principles for scientific data management and stewardship. Sci. Data **3**(1), 160018 (Mar 2016). https://doi.org/10.1038/sdata.2016.18
37. Zhang, C., Song, D., Huang, C., Swami, A., Chawla, N.V.: Heterogeneous graph neural network. In: Proceedings of the 25th ACM SIGKDD International Conference on Knowledge Discovery and Data Mining, pp. 793–803. ACM (2019). https://doi.org/10.1145/3292500.3330961

ExtracTable: Human-in-the-Loop Transformation of Scientific Corpora into Structured Knowledge

Lena John[1](✉), Ahmed Malek Ghanmi[2], Tim Wittenborg[3,4], Sören Auer[1,3,4], and Oliver Karras[1]

[1] TIB - Leibniz Information Centre for Science and Technology, Hannover, Germany
{lena.john,soeren.auer,oliver.karras}@tib.eu

[2] Leibniz University Hannover, Hannover, Germany

[3] L3S Research Center, Leibniz University Hannover, Hannover, Germany
{tim.wittenborg,soeren.auer}@l3s.de

[4] Cluster of Excellence SE2A – Sustainable and Energy-Efficient Aviation, Technische Universität Braunschweig, Braunschweig, Germany

Abstract. As the volume of scientific literature grows, efficient knowledge organization becomes increasingly challenging. Traditional approaches to structuring scientific content are time-consuming and require significant domain expertise, highlighting the need for tool support. We present *ExtracTable*, a Human-in-the-Loop (HITL) workflow and framework that assists researchers in transforming unstructured publications into structured representations. The workflow combines large language models (LLMs) with user-defined schemas and is designed for downstream integration into knowledge graphs (KGs). Developed and evaluated in the context of the Open Research Knowledge Graph (ORKG), *ExtracTable* automates key steps such as document preprocessing and data extraction while ensuring user oversight through validation. In an evaluation with ORKG community participants following the Quality Improvement Paradigm (QIP), *ExtracTable* demonstrated high usability and practical value. Participants gave it an average System Usability Scale (SUS) score of 84.17 (A+, the highest rating). The time to progress from a research interest to literature-based insights was reduced from between 4 h and 2 weeks to an average of 24:40 min. By streamlining corpus creation and structured data extraction for knowledge graph integration, *ExtracTable* leverages LLMs and user models to accelerate literature reviews. However, human validation remains essential to ensure quality, and future work will address improving extraction accuracy and entity linking to existing knowledge resources.

Keywords: HITL · Knowledge Graph Integration · Literature Review · LLM · Modular framework · Knowledge Organization

W.-T. Balke et al. (Eds.): TPDL 2025, LNCS 16097, pp. 470–487, 2026.
https://doi.org/10.1007/978-3-032-05409-8_27

1 Introduction

Conducting literature reviews is indispensable for scientific research. This task is inherently challenging, as it requires a significant amount of time and effort to gain an overview of the existing research and knowledge on a specific topic, helping to support methodology, contextualize research, or identify gaps in knowledge [34]. With the rapid growth in scientific discovery and distribution of knowledge, it has become even more difficult to produce high-quality reviews [24]. Recent advancements in artificial intelligence (AI), particularly the rise of large language models (LLMs) and AI-based Literature Reviews [39], offer promising opportunities to streamline and automate repeatable and time-consuming processes [30]. However, despite their growing popularity, AI models face significant limitations, primarily the tendency to produce hallucinations, resulting in inconsistencies and confusion [29]. Combining AI capabilities with a consistent knowledge base, called neuro-symbolic AI, mitigates these risks by leveraging reliable knowledge representations to alleviate AI's unreliability [3]. The knowledge bases need to be Findable, Accessible, Interoperable, and Reusable (FAIR) [40] to address the requirements of the scholarly domain and AI technology [2]. Such solutions already exist, like the Open Research Knowledge Graph (ORKG)[1] and its neuro-symbolic service Ask [3], offering a novel approach by representing scientific information in a structured format, providing both human- and machine-readability. However, organizing knowledge at scale reintroduces the original challenge of requiring human oversight, leading to manual work and a circular dependency. To address this issue, an iterative, Human-in-the-Loop (HITL), AI-assisted knowledge organization approach is needed, constantly improving scholarly knowledge representation. Our contributions include 1) *ExtracTable*, a Human-in-the-Loop (HITL) approach comprising a workflow and modular implementation that combines large language model (LLM) support with Natural Language Processing (NLP) techniques to streamline, automate, and formalize literature review tasks. 2) The modular implementation of *ExtracTable* as a Jupyter-based framework to build scientific corpora and transform unstructured information into structured knowledge ready for knowledge graph integration. 3) An iterative evaluation with nine researchers over four months, demonstrating *ExtracTable*'s ability to improve efficiency while maintaining user oversight of automated processes. This work is structured as follows: In Sect. 2 we give an overview of the background and related work in the HITL context. Our approach is described in Sect. 3, followed by an outline of the implementation in Sect. 4. We evaluate the developed solution of *ExtracTable* in Sect. 5 and discuss the results in Sect. 6. We conclude our work in Sect. 7.

2 Background and Related Work

This section explores Knowledge Graphs (KGs), AI-driven automation, and HITL systems in scholarly knowledge organization, highlighting their roles in literature reviews and knowledge integration.

[1] https://orkg.org/.

Knowledge Organization. Knowledge Graphs (KGs) are designed to represent and interconnect information in a structured, machine-readable format [36], like the scientific knowledge graph (SKG) Semantic Scholar [38]. Manually preparing data for KGs, particularly SKGs, is time-consuming and lacks scalability, as it requires domain experts to search, interpret, and structure scientific literature [12]. Without domain experts, there is a higher risk of integrating incorrect, incomplete, or outdated information into the SKG, reducing its reliability and quality [15]. The quality of SKGs heavily depends on their construction method, with significantly different results between manual and automated methods [13]. The ORKG is a versatile scientific knowledge platform that uses crowdsourcing to organize and link scientific knowledge across various topics and domains [3]. Karras et al. [18–21] demonstrated how the ORKG can enhance and ensure FAIR [40] literature reviews, highlighting their importance in providing research with structured, long-term available data. The ORKG Assistant for Scientific Knowledge (Ask) [3] applies a neuro-symbolic approach using semantic search, LLMs, and KGs. It exemplifies a next-generation scholarly search and exploration system, combining semantic knowledge representation with AI.

Artificial Intelligence (AI). AI and NLP techniques can automate content generation and assignment [10], but these methods often lack transparency and accountability while struggling with semantic context [22]. Fully relying on AI-supported technologies poses significant risks, making human supervision and validation indispensable [31]. The study conducted by Danler et al. [9] demonstrates that, while AI-generated outputs can be of high quality, "*relying solely on AI-generated outputs for crafting a scientific paper is not advisable*" [9, p. 207]. Bacinger et al. [5] present Litre Assistant, a machine-learning-based solution to determining a corpus of scientific papers as the initial task of the Systematic Literature Review (SLR) process. Their work introduces a system that allows users to iteratively select desired papers as a set of training data for machine learning algorithms for an automated classification process. Ye et al. [43] propose a hybrid, "human-oriented", but AI-based workflow to support specific steps of an SLR. Their workflow screens full-text articles to extract relevant data and allows the user to perform inclusion and exclusion decisions, resulting in a spreadsheet of LLM-generated data. The work of Alshami et al. [1] introduces a method where humans review ChatGPT-generated data for literature setup, abstract screening, data extraction, and analysis. However, relying solely on ChatGPT restricts access to real-time data, limiting the research scope to the model's training data and reducing its applicability.

Human-in-the-Loop (HITL). Several previously mentioned works incorporate human oversight in selection, classification, processing, and representation to achieve more accurate results [1,3,5,43]. Consequently, research increasingly recognizes the value of HITL approaches [23]. Through providing iterative feedback, users validate outputs as well as refine and enhance the performance system over time to bridge the gap between efficiency and contextual relevance [8]. Schatz et al. [33] developed a workflow for curating a biomedical KG (DRKG) [14], that integrates HITL components. Their approach is particularly relevant as it addresses HITL usability aspects in the context of curating and enriching KGs. The work by Tsavena et al. [35] builds on the automated pipeline for curating SKGs introduced in SCICERO [11]. They propose a HITL validation module as a solution to incorporate human decision-making into the curation process. This module, one of two proposed validation mechanisms, establishes a hybrid approach that integrates human expertise to enhance the curation process. The authors report a significant improvement in the accuracy of automated KG generation, demonstrating an improvement in both precision and recall. SWARM-SLR by Wittenborg et al. [41] establishes a literature review workflow implemented by a modular framework that utilizes several AI-based tools to fulfill 65 requirements derived from SLR guidelines. While many requirements can be supported or even fulfilled by AI, the overall workflow still requires human expert intervention at several stages of the literature review, particularly for knowledge extraction and validation. Users remain crucial for guiding and validating tasks where automated approaches lack accuracy or contextual understanding [26].

Our work builds on the discussed approaches, emphasizing the role of HITL in the context of AI-assisted knowledge graph construction. In this spirit, we aim to develop a solution that transforms unstructured input into structured, human-validated outputs designed for downstream knowledge graph integration. Once integrated into knowledge graphs, these structured outputs can support the human- and machine-readable context needed by neuro-symbolic AI to sustainably advance scholarly knowledge organization.

3 Approach

We adopt the Quality Improvement Paradigm (QIP) [7] to guide the iterative development of *ExtracTable*, a Human-in-the-Loop (HITL) approach that includes a workflow and is realized as a modular framework for transforming scientific corpora into structured knowledge.

ExtracTable was developed in close collaboration with ORKG curators, researchers from diverse domains funded through grants to create structured comparisons, a key content type presenting tabular overviews of state-of-the-art research in the ORKG [27]. While their financial affiliation may introduce some bias, their interest in improving tools that support their contributions fosters practical, needs-driven feedback. An overview of the development process is shown in Fig. 1, with detailed tasks in Table 1. The *Project Learning* cycle focused on short-term usability improvements based on curator feedback, while the *Corporate Learning* cycle addressed long-term enhancements to ORKG infrastructure beyond the project.

3.1 Requirements

To define functional and non-functional requirements for *ExtracTable* (see Table 2), we drew inspiration from Wittenborg et al. [41], who specified requirements for the typical phases of an SLR. While our framework does not

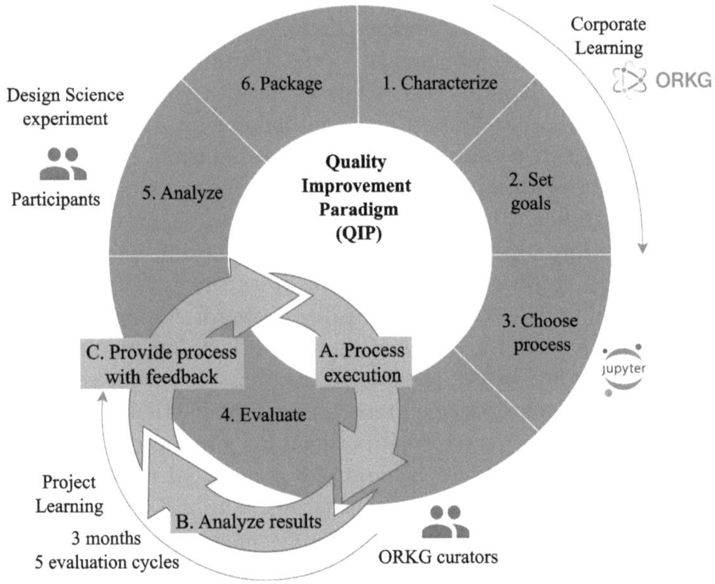

Fig. 1. Application of the Quality Improvement Paradigm (QIP) methodology to develop *ExtracTable*, together with ORKG curators. Derived from [28].

aim to replicate or enforce the rigor of a formal SLR, we adopt this process-oriented perspective to ensure relevance and alignment with real-world research workflows. In collaboration with the SWARM-SLR curators and domain experts, we adapted these ideas to guide the design of system requirements and support a more lightweight, customizable process for literature exploration. Our goal is to offer a modular framework for *ExtracTable* that enables generation and processing of a literature corpus without the complexity of a full SLR pipeline. To ensure modularity and usability, the workflow is divided into two stages, and users can start with the second if a relevant corpus already exists.

3.2 Workflow

We now describe how the *ExtracTable* approach, centered on its HITL workflow, meets the requirements outlined above. While not aiming to replicate the full SLR process, the two workflow stages draw inspiration from its typical phases and provide a practical structure for key tasks. Our workflow blends automation with human validation, enabling users to focus their expertise on interpreting and refining scientific content. To reduce manual effort, we automate time-consuming steps while preserving user control over key decisions. The workflow can start from any research interest without requiring pre-structured input, making it flexible and adaptable to diverse review scenarios.

Stage 1: Creating a scientific corpus of literature. This stage focuses on building a corpus of publications relevant to the user's research interest (see Fig. 2). After

Table 1. QIP step descriptions for the development of *ExtracTable*

Step	Description
1. Characterize	In the first phase, we examined research workflows, including topic selection, corpus retrieval, and structured overview creation. Collaborating with ORKG curators, we identified key content and technical requirements, resulting in a modular, adaptable framework for diverse SKG use cases.
2. Set goals	We defined functional and non-functional requirements to set the tool's scope, ensuring it addresses key pain points like time-consuming corpus creation and limited support for structured output (cf. Subsect. 3.1).
3. Choose process	We selected external ORKG curators as a focus group due to their research diversity and active involvement in literature-based knowledge graph curation. Using an iterative participatory design approach with bi-weekly meetings, we co-developed modular Jupyter Notebooks for *ExtracTable* tailored to flexible workflow stages (cf. Subsect. 3.2).
4. Execute	In this phase, we implemented and iteratively refined the framework with ongoing feedback. Over three months in five meetings, we made key design choices, including abstract-only publication support and splitting the workflow into two notebooks (cf. Sect. 4).
5. Analyze	We finalized the framework by incorporating feedback and evaluating its effectiveness through a design science experiment. This revealed usability issues, guided feature refinements, and validated alignment with real-world curation needs (cf. Sect. 5).
6. Package	Finally, we compiled reusable artifacts for *ExtracTable*, including framework components, evaluation metrics, and key insights, to support broader adoption. We also assessed ORKG's infrastructure to enable sustainable integration (cf. sections 5 and 6).

defining a research interest and optionally using the LLM to suggest keywords, users formulate a search query to retrieve publications from selected sources. Search parameters, such as output size or restricting to openly accessible full texts, are configurable to suit user preferences. Retrieved papers are reviewed and selected by the user, forming the input for Stage 2.

Stage 2: Knowledge extraction and validation. The second stage processes the knowledge within the corpus, as shown in Fig. 3. The user begins by defining the properties of the data model to be extracted from each paper. The LLM agent then parses and interprets the corpus, generating output based on the specified properties. If any information is not found, the LLM flags this to mitigate the risk of hallucination. The user can manually refine, revise, and modify the results to ensure accuracy, ultimately validating the output. The final results are formatted, and optionally, entity linking is performed to create output that is suitable for KG integration as a machine-readable file.

Table 2. Functional (FR) and non-functional (NR) requirements

Functional Requirements (FR)	Fulfillment
FR1: The framework should suggest relevant keywords based on a user-defined research interest.	Yes
FR2: The framework must allow a user to manually input and modify a search query to retrieve relevant literature.	Yes
FR3: The framework must support integration with external literature databases.	Yes
FR4: The framework must provide options to configure search parameters.	Yes
FR5: The framework should present retrieved search results in an interactive format.	Yes
FR6: The framework must enable a user to select and download relevant papers to create a literature corpus.	Yes
FR7: The framework must allow a user to use an existing corpus to proceed with knowledge extraction.	Yes
FR8: The framework must provide an interface to define a customizable data model, specifying the properties to extract from each publication.	Partial
FR9: The framework must extract information according to the user-defined data model from the provided literature corpus.	Yes
FR10: The framework should flag properties that cannot be extracted or are missing to alert users.	Yes
FR11: The framework must present the extracted data in an editable format to allow user refinement and approval.	Yes
FR12: The framework will support entity linking on the extracted and validated content for seamless KG-integration.	No
Non-Functional Requirements (NR)	**Fulfillment**
NR1: The framework must be implemented in a modular way, supporting the integration of new data sources or processing steps.	Yes
NR2: The framework should offer an interactive user interface.	Yes
NR3: The framework must unify data returned from various data sources into a consistent internal schema to support comparison.	Yes
NR4: The framework should be capable of handling literature corpora of varying sizes without significant loss in performance.	No
NR5: The framework should be well-documented, follow clean code principles, and be openly available to support long-term maintenance, reproducibility, and community contribution.	Yes

4 Implementation

We implement the described functions as a modular framework for *ExtracTable* in two Jupyter Notebooks using Python (NR5). These notebooks provide automated modules, visualizations, and browser-rendered interactive controls (NR2). To enhance usability, we leverage interactive HTML widgets from ipywidgets and the IPython toolkit for abstracting complex code interactions. Users can configure workflows via UI elements such as input fields and checkboxes, and extend functionality by adding query sources or modifying the UI and behavior as needed (NR1). The implementation is modular and flexible, designed to support integration with various knowledge graphs.

The **first stage** retrieves relevant papers based on a user-defined search query (FR2). To support query formulation, the framework can optionally sug-

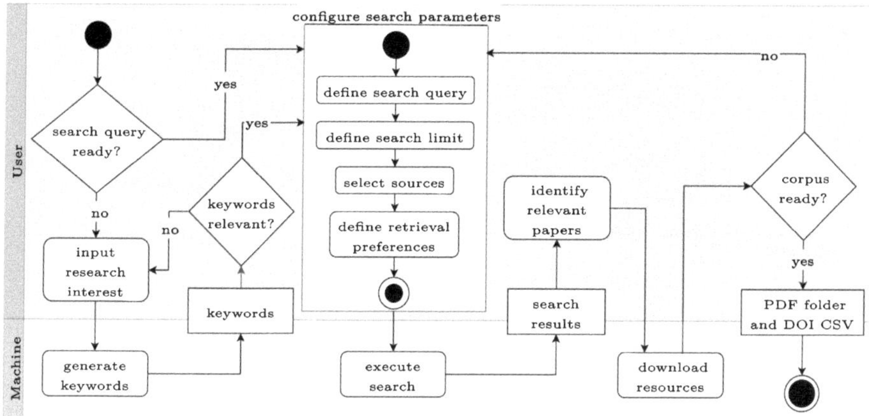

Fig. 2. Activity diagram for *Stage 1: Creating a scientific corpus of literature*, demonstrating user-machine interaction in the scientific literature corpus building process.

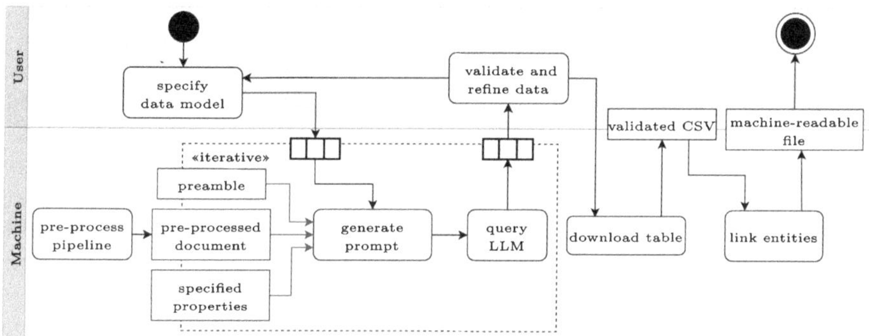

Fig. 3. Activity diagram for *Stage 2: Knowledge extraction and validation*, showing the tasks executed by both the user and machine to extract knowledge from the corpus.

gest keywords from the user's research interest (FR1). We integrate multiple APIs, including SemanticScholar, ArXiv, and the SerpApi wrapper, enabling real-time searches across diverse scholarly databases (FR3) based on user preferences (FR4). Returned JSON objects with varying schemas are unified for consistency (NR3). Key elements such as title, abstract, authors, publication date, and full-text links are presented within expandable accordions in the notebook (FR5), as shown in Fig. 4. Alternatively, users may work with an existing corpus, which can currently be imported from a Zotero collection (FR7).

Based on these suggestions, the user iteratively creates the corpus by selecting and downloading relevant papers (FR6). For reproducibility, the corresponding DOIs can be exported to a CSV file.

The **second stage** processes the corpus using an LLM. We use the Mistral-large-2 model, accessible via Mistral's API and currently free of charge.

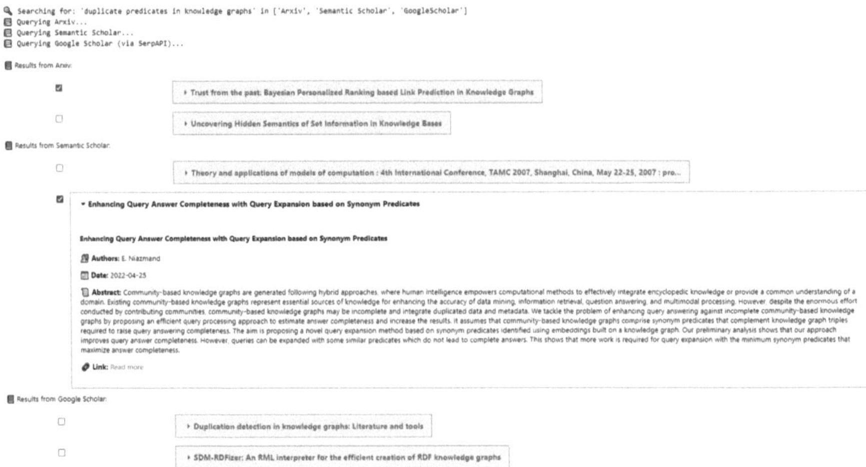

Fig. 4. Visualization of query results, where each paper is presented within an expandable accordion, providing access to detailed information relevant to the paper.

This model supports JSON-formatted outputs, enhancing structure and compatibility with downstream workflows. The tool prompts the LLM iteratively using user-defined properties (FR8) and pre-processed text extracted from each PDF. Pre-processing starts with raw text extraction via pdfminer. References and appendices are removed, and regex heuristics clean and reconstruct sentences and paragraphs to preserve context. Generated outputs (FR9) are displayed in a datagrid (FR11; see Fig. 5), allowing users to review, edit, and select entries for final CSV export. Users can also refine the data model and rerun extraction, though previous results may be overwritten. An example of prompt and output can be found in the repository.

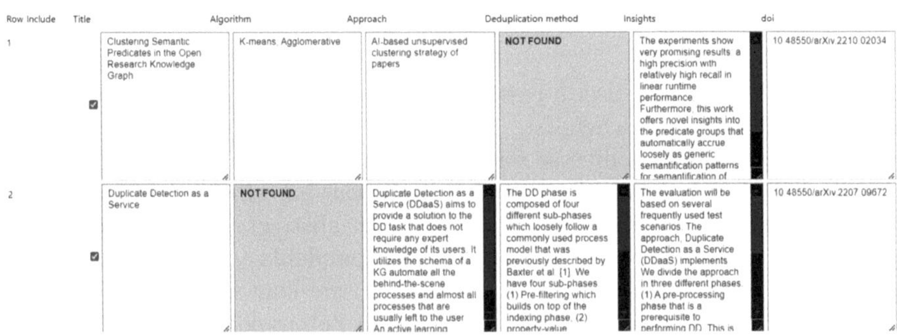

Fig. 5. Visualization of LLM-generated information. If a property is not found in the text, the tool renders a label "NOT FOUND" and displays it in red (FR10).

We have begun integrating entity linking (FR12) as a step toward semantic enrichment. At this stage, we use Falcon 2.0 [32] for entity extraction, identifying relevant concepts in free-text fields. Although Falcon already supports linking entities to knowledge graphs such as DBpedia [4] and Wikidata [37], we currently focus on extraction as a first step toward machine-actionability. This approach prepares the ground for entity linking and, ultimately, seamless integration with ORKG and other KGs in the future. Previous work [17] examined how knowledge representation evolves across formats and focused on semantically enriching tables by aligning entities and structuring content during KG import.

5 Evaluation

The framework *ExtracTable* is evaluated through a design science experiment involving prospective users to assess its practical usability and real-world applicability. To contextualize this evaluation, we consider the ORKG as a representative environment for scientific content creation. Following the goal definition template by Wohlin et al. [42], we define the experiment's objective as follows:

> *Research goal:* **Analyze** *ExtracTable* **with the purpose of** supporting systematic content creation for scientific KGs **in terms of** usability (effectiveness, efficiency, satisfaction) **from the perspective of** potential future users familiar with the ORKG **in the context of** the ORKG.

The goal leads to the research question:

> *Research question:* How does the developed tool *ExtracTable* impact the usability of systematic content creation for scientific knowledge graphs, from the perspective of potential future users familiar with the ORKG?

The experiment aims to assess the practical usability of the developed tool *ExtracTable* for creating scientific content for knowledge graphs. To this end, we collaborated with ORKG curators who have previously created comparisons as part of literature reviews. Each participant will first subjectively assess the time they spent on manually creating one of their existing comparisons, reflecting state-of-the-art research in a specific domain. They will then recreate the same comparison using *ExtracTable*, without reviewing the original version to avoid bias. We used a within-subject design to assess usability and enable meaningful self-comparison across diverse domain experts.

The developed framework *ExtracTable* is the independent variable, while effectiveness, efficiency, and satisfaction are the dependent variables for usability. Effectiveness is measured by participants' perception and objectively by the number of identified papers, along with the accuracy of extracted data compared to the established comparison. Efficiency is assessed through participants' perception and objectively by the time taken to create the comparison. Satisfaction is evaluated subjectively after each stage and overall using the System Usability Scale (SUS) [25] at the experiment's conclusion.

With particpants' consent, both screen and audio were recorded during the sessions to enable detailed post-analysis. The experiment is described in a document [16] provided to participants at the start, outlining the study context and presenting title and description of their most recent comparison. ExtracTable runs locally on a computer provided by the experimenter. Sessions are conducted either in person or remotely via TeamViewer, ensuring a consistent experience. A questionnaire collects demographic data, ORKG usage frequency, and consent. Participants rate their agreement with statements regarding the tools' usefulness and user experience using a Likert scale. The SUS is administered at the end of each session, alongside open-ended questions for additional qualitative feedback.

The target group consists of individuals familiar with the ORKG who have created at least one comparison. Participants were recruited through an open call and convenience sampling, with participation being voluntary. Each session lasts approximately 60 min and follows a structured procedure:

1. Introduction to the workflow, questionnaire, and experiment document.
2. 5–10 minutes for participants to read the provided document.
3. Completion of initial questionnaire pages, collecting demographic information and baseline data.
4. Participants proceed through the two stages of *ExtracTable*, responding to related questionnaire items.
5. Completion of the SUS and provision of general feedback.

Results. The raw data [16] is published on Zenodo. Nine participants took part, including external curators and internal ORKG team members not involved in the tool's development, mostly from Semantic Web or neuro-symbolic AI fields. Participants reported varied ORKG usage frequencies, ranging from weekly to monthly, with experience spanning from a few months to several years, reflecting different levels of expertise with the system. Figure 6 presents the participants' responses regarding subjective efficiency and effectiveness, showing strong agreement that the tool makes corpus creation and knowledge extraction 'faster' and 'easier', and a weaker agreement to its ability to render 'better results'.

Figure 7 represents the resulting SUS scores. We achieve an overall SUS score of 84.17 ($min = 75$, $max = 90$, $\sigma = 4.86$), regarded as A+ score – the highest usability rating [25]. Participants expressed general satisfaction with *ExtracTable*, with comments like *"The workflow should be integrated to ORKG as soon as possible. I will like to use it"* and *"Very helpful system!!!"*. Specific feedback highlighted features like the *"Keywords extraction option is an amazing idea"*. Suggestions for improvement included adding *"Properties should have descriptions (for more accurate extraction)"* and *"focus could be on extracting entities that align with the similar papers already available in the ORKG"*.

The reported durations for the participants' original comparison varied significantly, with the fastest comparison taking approximately 4 h to complete, while the longest required around 2 weeks. We acknowledge that these self-reported durations are prone to imprecision but still provide an indicative measure of the time involved. Completing the workflow with our framework – from defining a

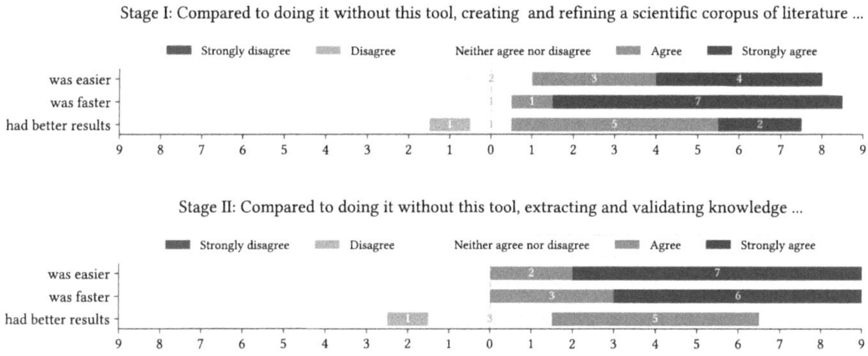

Fig. 6. Participants' agreement to statements for Stage 1 (above) and 2 (below).

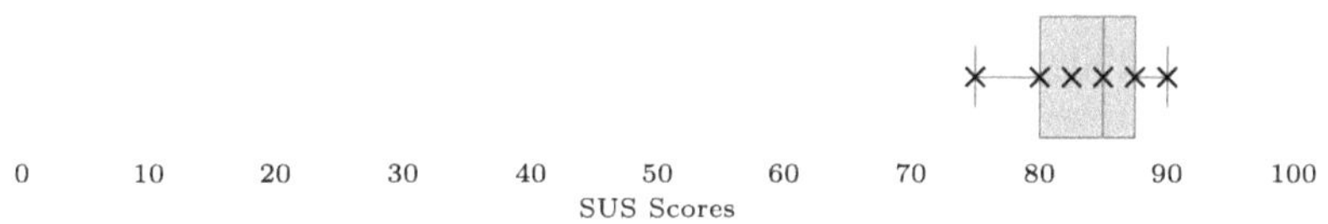

Fig. 7. SUS scores and boxplot distribution, scoring an average of 84.17 (A+ according to the Lewis and Sauro benchmarks [25]).

research interest based on their original comparison to successfully creating a new ORKG comparison – took an average of 1,480 s (24:40 min), with a minimum of 1,023 s (17:03 min) and a maximum of 1,996 s (33:16 min), as detailed in Fig. 8.

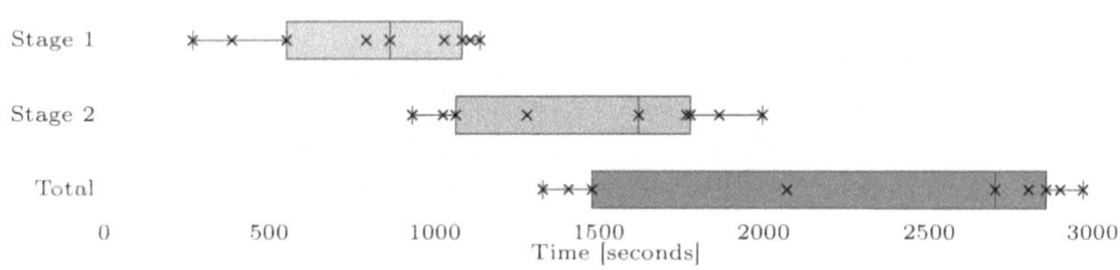

Fig. 8. Visualization of the time spent by participants across two workflow stages.

We also assess the tool's ability to replicate the original comparison by evaluating the number of publications it identifies against those included in the original set. The newly generated comparisons contained an average of 5 papers ($min = 1$, $max = 8$, $\sigma = 2.2$), whereas the original comparisons had an average of 11 papers. Overall, 98% of the newly created comparisons differed from the originals, with only 2% showing overlapping results. Since the majority of the retrieved papers did not match the original set, it was difficult to objectively assess the quality of the information generated by the tool.

QIP. The QIP methodology showed that curators are a valuable user group for guiding tool development. To improve CSV-based integration of literature tables, enhanced semantification is currently being developed to better align entities within the ORKG [17].

Threats to Validity. Based on Wohlin et al. [42], we identify potential threats to the validity of our experiment. *Conclusion Validity.* Participants may subconsciously replicate elements from their original ORKG comparison. To reduce this risk, we did not inform them that the task was based on their previous work. Participants came from diverse research fields but worked on their own prior content, minimizing the impact of disciplinary differences while supporting broader generalizability. *Internal Validity.* Participants may have been predisposed to emphasize the tool's benefits in comparison to doing it without the tool, particularly ease and speed. As part of the participants were ORKG curators, their financial affiliation could have introduced a bias toward favorable feedback, given the tool's relevance to their ongoing work. Additionally, self-reported durations for prior comparison creation, collected in unobserved settings, are prone to imprecision, adding uncertainty when comparing to the objectively timed tool-based workflow. *Construct Validity.* To capture genuine reactions and difficulties, we encouraged participants to comment on their experience during each task. This ensured feedback reflected their actual interactions with the tool. *External Validity.* With only nine participants, generalizability is limited. Nonetheless, the range of disciplinary backgrounds offers insight into the tool's broader applicability. Future evaluations should involve more diverse and numerous participants to strengthen external relevance.

6 Discussion and Future Work

Experiment. We interpret the mean SUS score using Bangor et al.'s [6] adjective scale, where *ExtracTable*'s score of 84.17 ranks at the upper boundary of "Good", and an A+ in the Lewis and Sauro's benchmarks [25], indicating a positive user experience. Participants described *ExtracTable* as intuitive, easy to navigate, and effective for task execution. *ExtracTable* significantly reduced the time needed to create content in the ORKG compared to participants' prior methods. While this shows strong potential for streamlining workflows, it does not automatically ensure higher-quality outputs. Participants appreciated the simplified corpus creation and extraction process but expressed concerns about accuracy and over-reliance on automated suggestions. Those who invested more time refining the corpus reported better outcomes, suggesting deeper engagement improves quality. Still, not all agreed the tool consistently produced better results, exposing a gap between automation and human expectations. This disparity points to a key challenge in HITL systems: balancing automation with human judgment to ensure both efficiency and high-quality, contextually relevant results. Addressing this requires enhancing the extraction process and incorporating iterative feedback loops to refine accuracy. Although the experiment aimed to replicate a prior comparison, measuring replication quality through the number of identified papers proved unfeasible as an indicator of replication quality, underscoring the challenge of replicating structured research output in a HITL system. Unlike automated systems, our approach relies on user insights and interpretations, making the process subjective and context-dependent.

Requirements. ExtracTable satisfies most core requirements defined for the HITL framework. It guides users from defining a research interest to extracting and editing data, with CSV export for seamless integration into scholarly KGs like the ORKG. The modular pipeline supports extensibility, adaptability, and long-term semantic preservation. However, key limitations remain. Entity linking (FR12) is not yet implemented, leaving extracted entities disconnected from existing KG resources. Incorporating entity alignment and exporting in formats like JSON-LD or RDF would improve semantic interoperability. Additionally, performance degrades with large datasets (NR4), as processing occurs sequentially per document. Future work should focus on performance optimization and parallelization strategies. Participants also requested more control over the data model (FR8). Allowing users to define domain-specific properties and extraction instructions would improve precision and adaptability across fields. This aligns with feedback on the need for more customizable and explainable outputs. Crucially, while automation accelerates literature processing, LLM-based extractions still require human validation (FR10, FR11). Without critical oversight, there's a risk of misinterpreting or blindly trusting generated results. This underscores the ethical implications of AI-assisted research, especially risking the loss of genuine understanding and knowledge internalization.

Future Work. Future development should allow storing and refining outputs with customizable data models, enabling users to iteratively improve extraction accuracy. Users can selectively re-run extractions on specific cells while preserving high-quality results, enhancing the HITL process. Semantic structuring, like linking content to knowledge graph entities and supporting interoperable formats, will strengthen the system's utility. Ongoing improvements in scalability and model configurability will stabilize and enrich the tool. Lastly, research should focus on user guidance for validating and interpreting extractions, e.g., by highlighting source passages in PDFs, ensuring human oversight in AI-driven workflows.

7 Conclusion

Our work contributes *ExtracTable*, a Human-in-the-Loop (HITL) approach for structuring scientific content, demonstrated in the context of the ORKG to showcase its suitability for downstream knowledge graph integration. Aligned with the Quality Improvement (QIP) paradigm, *ExtracTable* comprises a two-stage workflow—*Creating a scientific corpus of literature* and *Knowledge extraction and validation*—implemented as a modular framework in a Jupyter notebook environment. This framework assists researchers in identifying relevant publications, extracting key information, and structuring knowledge into reusable formats ready for integration into scientific knowledge graphs.

By automating repetitive tasks and enabling researchers to interactively refine outputs, *ExtracTable* reduces the manual effort typically involved in processing large volumes of literature. It moves toward making large-scale literature reviews more efficient and helps researchers keep pace with the rapidly expanding body of scientific knowledge. While evaluation results showed the tool is highly usable and accelerates the process, we identified areas for improvement. Additional support is needed to engage users in the knowledge extraction process, alongside feedback loops to further enhance the quality of extracted information.

Acknowledgements. The authors would like to thank the Federal Government and the Heads of Government of the Länder, as well as the Joint Science Conference (GWK), for their funding and support within the framework of the NFDI4Ing and NFDI4DataScience consortia. This work was partially funded by the German Research Foundation (DFG) - project number 442146713 and project number 460234259.

References

1. Alshami, A., Elsayed, M., Ali, E., et al.: Harnessing the Power of ChatGPT for Automating Systematic Review Process: Methodology, Case Study, Limitations, and Future Directions. Systems **11**(7), 351 (2023). https://doi.org/10.3390/systems11070351
2. Auer, S., et al.: The SciQA scientific question answering benchmark for scholarly knowledge. Sci. Rep. **13**(1), 7240 (2023)
3. Auer, S., et al.: Open research knowledge graph: a large-scale neuro-symbolic knowledge organization system. In: Handbook on Neurosymbolic AI and Knowledge Graphs. IOS Press (2025)
4. Auer, S., Bizer, C., Kobilarov, G., et al.: DBpedia: a nucleus for a web of open data. In: The Semantic Web. pp. 722–735. Springer, Berlin, Heidelberg (2007). https://doi.org/10.1007/978-3-540-76298-0_52
5. Bacinger, F., Boticki, I., Mlinaric, D.: System for semi-automated literature review based on machine learning. Electronics **11**(24), 4124 (2022). https://doi.org/10.3390/electronics11244124
6. Bangor, A., Kortum, P., Miller, J.: Determining what individual SUS scores mean: adding an adjective rating scale. J. Usability Stud. **4**(3), 114–123 (2009)
7. Basili, V.R., Caldiera, G., Rombach, H.D.: Experience Factory. In: Encyclopedia of Software Engineering. John Wiley & Sons, Ltd (2002). https://doi.org/10.1002/0471028959.sof110
8. Dalvi Mishra, B., Tafjord, O., Clark, P.: Towards teachable reasoning systems: using a dynamic memory of user feedback for continual system improvement. In: Proceedings of the 2022 Conference on Empirical Methods in Natural Language Processing, pp. 9465–9480. Association for Computational Linguistics, Abu Dhabi, United Arab Emirates (Dec 2022). https://doi.org/10.18653/v1/2022.emnlp-main.644
9. Danler, M., Hackl, W.O., Neururer, S.B., Pfeifer, B.: Quality and effectiveness of AI tools for students and researchers for scientific literature review and analysis. In: dHealth 2024, pp. 203–208. IOS Press (2024). https://doi.org/10.3233/SHTI240038, https://ebooks.iospress.nl/doi/10.3233/SHTI240038

10. Dessì, D., Osborne, F., Reforgiato Recupero, D., et al.: Generating knowledge graphs by employing natural language processing and machine learning techniques within the scholarly domain. Futur. Gener. Comput. Syst. **116**, 253–264 (2021). https://doi.org/10.1016/j.future.2020.10.026
11. Dessí, D., Osborne, F., Reforgiato Recupero, D., et al.: SCICERO: a deep learning and NLP approach for generating scientific knowledge graphs in the computer science domain. Knowl.-Based Syst. **258**, 109945 (2022). https://doi.org/10.1016/j.knosys.2022.109945
12. Hofer, M., Obraczka, D., Saeedi, A., et al.: Construction of knowledge graphs: current state and challenges. Information **15**(8), 509 (2024). https://doi.org/10.3390/info15080509
13. Huaman, E., Fensel, D.: Knowledge graph curation: a practical framework. In: Proceedings of the 10th International Joint Conference on Knowledge Graphs, pp. 166–171. IJCKG '21, Association for Computing Machinery, New York, NY, USA (Jan 2022). https://doi.org/10.1145/3502223.3502247
14. Ioannidis, V.N., Song, X., Manchanda, S., et al.: DRKG - Drug Repurposing Knowledge Graph for Covid-19 (2020). https://github.com/gnn4dr/DRKG/
15. Jain, N.: Domain-specific knowledge graph construction for semantic analysis. In: Harth, A., Presutti, V., Troncy, R., Acosta, M., Polleres, A., Fernández, J.D., Xavier Parreira, J., Hartig, O., Hose, K., Cochez, M. (eds.) ESWC 2020. LNCS, vol. 12124, pp. 250–260. Springer, Cham (2020). https://doi.org/10.1007/978-3-030-62327-2_40
16. John, L.: Human-in-the-loop workflow for neuro-symbolic scholarly knowledge organization - experiment material [data set]. Zenodo (2025). https://doi.org/10.5281/zenodo.15228337
17. John, L., Farfar, K.E., Auer, S., Karras, O.: SciMantify - a hybrid approach for the evolving semantification of scientific knowledge. In: 25th International Conference on Web Engineering (ICWE) 2025 (2025). https://doi.org/10.15488/19006, accepted at ICWE 2025. Proceedings to appear
18. Karras, O.: KG-EmpiRE: a community-maintainable knowledge graph for a sustainable literature review on the state and evolution of empirical research in requirements engineering. In: 2024 IEEE 32nd International Requirements Engineering Conference (RE), pp. 500–501 (2024). https://doi.org/10.1109/RE59067.2024.00063, iSSN: 2332-6441
19. Karras, O.: Research knowledge graphs for sustainable literature reviews in software engineering and beyond. In: Software Engineering 2025–Companion Proceedings, pp. 10–18420. Gesellschaft für Informatik, Bonn (2025)
20. Karras, O., et al.: Organizing scientific knowledge from engineering sciences using the open research knowledge graph: the tailored forming process chain use case. Data Sci. J. (2024). https://doi.org/10.5334/dsj-2024-052
21. Karras, O., Wernlein, F., Klünder, J., Auer, S.: Divide and conquer the empire: a community-maintainable knowledge graph of empirical research in requirements engineering. In: 2023 ACM/IEEE International Symposium on Empirical Software Engineering and Measurement (ESEM), pp. 1–12 (Oct 2023). https://doi.org/10.1109/ESEM56168.2023.10304795
22. Khalid, M., Khattak, H.A., Ahmad, A., et al.: Explainable prediction of medical codes through automated knowledge graph curation framework. In: 2022 19th International Bhurban Conference on Applied Sciences and Technology (IBCAST), pp. 331–336 (Aug 2022). https://doi.org/10.1109/IBCAST54850.2022.9990551, iSSN: 2151-1411

23. Kommineni, V.K., König-Ries, B., Samuel, S.: From human experts to machines: An LLM supported approach to ontology and knowledge graph construction (Mar 2024). https://doi.org/10.48550/arXiv.2403.08345, arXiv:2403.08345 [cs]
24. Larsen, K.R., Hovorka, D., Dennis, A., West, J.: Understanding the elephant: the discourse approach to boundary identification and corpus construction for theory review articles. J. Assoc. Inform. Syst. **20**(7) (Jul 2019). https://doi.org/10.17705/1jais.00556
25. Lewis, J.R., Sauro, J.: Item benchmarks for the system. J. Usability Stud. **13**(3) (2018)
26. Mosqueira-Rey, E., Hernández-Pereira, E., Alonso-Ríos, D., et al.: Human-in-the-loop machine learning: a state of the art. Artif. Intell. Rev. **56**(4), 3005–3054 (2023). https://doi.org/10.1007/s10462-022-10246-w
27. Oelen, A., Jaradeh, M.Y., Farfar, K.E., Stocker, M., Auer, S.: Comparing research contributions in a scholarly knowledge graph. In: International Conference on Knowledge Capture (2019). https://doi.org/10.15488/9388
28. Oliveira, K.M.d.: Software Quality Assurance by means of Methodologies, Measurements and Knowledge Management Issues. thesis, Université de Valenciennes et du Hainaut-Cambrésis (Jun 2014). https://hal.science/tel-01094776
29. Perković, G., Drobnjak, A., Botički, I.: Hallucinations in LLMs: understanding and addressing challenges. In: 2024 47th MIPRO ICT and Electronics Convention (MIPRO), pp. 2084–2088 (2024). https://doi.org/10.1109/MIPRO60963.2024.10569238
30. Rathi, H., Malik, A., Behera, D.C., Kamboj, G.: P21 a comparative analysis of large language models (LLM) utilised in systematic literature review. Value Health **26**(12), S6 (2023). https://doi.org/10.1016/j.jval.2023.09.030
31. Ren, M., Chen, N., Qiu, H.: Human-machine collaborative decision-making: an evolutionary roadmap based on cognitive intelligence. Int. J. Soc. Robot. **15**(7), 1101–1114 (2023). https://doi.org/10.1007/s12369-023-01020-1
32. Sakor, A., Singh, K., Patel, A., Vidal, M.E.: Falcon 2.0: an entity and relation linking tool over wikidata. In: Proceedings of the 29th ACM International Conference on Information & Knowledge Management, pp. 3141–3148. CIKM '20, Association for Computing Machinery, New York, NY, USA (Oct 2020). https://doi.org/10.1145/3340531.3412777
33. Schatz, K., Korn, D., Tropsha, A., Chirkova, R.: Workflow for domain- and task-sensitive curation of knowledge graphs, with use case of DRKG. In: 2022 IEEE International Conference on Big Data (Big Data), pp. 3692–3701 (Dec 2022). https://doi.org/10.1109/BigData55660.2022.10020536
34. Snyder, H.: Literature review as a research methodology: an overview and guidelines. J. Bus. Res. **104**, 333–339 (2019). https://doi.org/10.1016/j.jbusres.2019.07.039
35. Tsaneva, S., Dessì, D., Osborne, F., Sabou, M.: Enhancing Scientific Knowledge Graph Generation Pipelines with LLMs and Human-in-the-Loop. Baltimore (2024). https://ceur-ws.org/Vol-3780/paper1.pdf
36. Vahdati, S., Palma, G., Nath, R.J., Lange, C., Auer, S., Vidal, M.-E.: Unveiling scholarly communities over knowledge graphs. In: Méndez, E., Crestani, F., Ribeiro, C., David, G., Lopes, J.C. (eds.) TPDL 2018. LNCS, vol. 11057, pp. 103–115. Springer, Cham (2018). https://doi.org/10.1007/978-3-030-00066-0_9
37. Vrandečić, D., Krötzsch, M.: Wikidata: a free collaborative knowledgebase. Commun. ACM **57**(10), 78–85 (2014). https://doi.org/10.1145/2629489

38. Wade, A.D.: The semantic scholar academic graph (s2ag). Companion Proceedings of the Web Conference 2022 (2022). https://api.semanticscholar.org/CorpusID:251597885
39. Wagner, G., Lukyanenko, R., Paré, G.: Artificial intelligence and the conduct of literature reviews **37**(2), 209–226 (2022). https://doi.org/10.1177/02683962211048201
40. Wilkinson, M.D., Dumontier, M., Aalbersberg, I.J., et al.: The FAIR guiding principles for scientific data management and stewardship. Sci. Data **3**(1), 160018 (2016). https://doi.org/10.1038/sdata.2016.18
41. Wittenborg, T., Karras, O., Auer, S.: SWARM-SLR - streamlined workflow automation for machine-actionable systematic literature reviews. In: Linking Theory and Practice of Digital Libraries, pp. 20–40. Springer Nature Switzerland, Cham (2024). https://doi.org/10.1007/978-3-031-72437-4_2
42. Wohlin, C., Runeson, P., Höst, M., et al.: Experimentation in Software Engineering. Springer Publishing Company, Incorporated (May (2012)
43. Ye, A., Maiti, A., Schmidt, M., Pedersen, S.J.: A Hybrid semi-automated workflow for systematic and literature review processes with large language model analysis. Future Internet **16**(5), 167 (2024). https://doi.org/10.3390/fi16050167, number: 5 Publisher: Multidisciplinary Digital Publishing Institute

Author Index

W.-T. Balke et al. (Eds.): TPDL 2025, LNCS 16097, pp. 489–490, 2026.
https://doi.org/10.1007/978-3-032-05409-8

MIX
Papier aus verantwortungsvollen Quellen
Paper from responsible sources
FSC® C105338

If you have any concerns about our products,
you can contact us on
ProductSafety@springernature.com

In case Publisher is established outside the EU,
the EU authorized representative is:
Springer Nature Customer Service Center GmbH
Europaplatz 3, 69115 Heidelberg, Germany

Printed by Libri Plureos GmbH
in Hamburg, Germany